IRISH VERSE

With Illustrations from the National Gallery of Ireland

Appletree Press

Contents

from Patrick's Breastplate — Anon. (trans Kuno Meyer)
The Crucifixion — Evie Hone
6/7

The Old Woman — Joseph Campbell
The Fisherman's Mother — Helen Mabel Trevor
8/9

'Icham of Irlaunde' — Anon.
In Joyce's Country (detail) — Frederick Burton
10/11

The Lake Isle of Innisfree — W. B. Yeats
A Cottage Garden — Walter Osborne
12/13

On Stella's Birthday — Jonathan Swift
Esther Johnson — James Latham
14/15

'The Harp That Once Through Tara's Halls' — Thomas Moore
The Marriage of Strongbow and Aoife (detail) — Daniel MacLise
16/17

Dear Black Head — Anon. (trans Samuel Ferguson)
Molly MacRee — Thomas Jones
18/19

THE STARS STAND UP IN THE AIR — Anon. (trans Thomas MacDonagh)
Gap of Dunloe (detail) — Henry Brocas Snr
20/21

HE BIDS HIS BELOVED BE AT PEACE — W. B. Yeats
The Meeting on the Turret Stairs — Frederick Burton
22/23

ON HIS OWN DEAFNESS — Jonathan Swift
St Patrick's Close — Walter Osborne
24/25

I SEE HIS BLOOD UPON THE ROSE — Joseph Plunkett
A Convent Garden — William Leech
26/27

from THE WINDING BANKS OF ERNE — William Allingham
Children Dancing at a Crossroads (detail) — Trevor Fowler
28/29

''TIS THE LAST ROSE OF SUMMER' — Thomas Moore
cartoon for *The Sonnet* — William Mulready
30/31

JUNE — Francis Ledwidge
The Lilac Phlox (detail) — Mildred Butler
32/33

BEFORE THE WORLD WAS MADE — W. B. Yeats
The White Dress — Dermod O'Brien
34/35

REST ONLY IN THE GRAVE — James Clarence Mangan
The Last Circuit of Pilgrims at Clonmacnoise — George Petrie
36/37

from THE BALLAD OF READING GAOL — Oscar Wilde
A Courtroom Scene (detail) — Jack B. Yeats
38/39

EXILES — George Russell (AE)
A Spirit in a Landscape — George Russell
40/41

MY HOPE, MY LOVE — Anon. (trans Edward Walsh)
A Connemara Girl — Augustus Burke
42/43

THE BLACKBIRDS — Francis Ledwidge
Rooftops, Thomastown — Mildred Butler
44/45

THE LARK IN THE CLEAR AIR — Samuel Ferguson
Annie Callwell — Frederick Burton
46/47

THE MEETING OF THE WATERS — Thomas Moore
A View near Avoca (detail) — George Barrett
48/48

THE MOTHER — Padraig Pearse
In the Phoenix Park (detail) — Walter Osborne
50/51

ON AN ISLAND — J. M. Synge
A Four-Oared Currach — Jack B. Yeats
52/53

IS IT A MONTH — J. M. Synge
Looking at the Sea — William Orpen
54/55

AN IRISH AIRMAN FORSEES HIS DEATH — W. B. Yeats
A Connemara Landscape — Paul Henry
56/57

IRELAND — Francis Ledwidge
The Potato Diggers — Paul Henry
58/59

from Patrick's Breastplate

Christ with me, Christ before me, Christ behind me,
Christ in me, Christ beneath me, Christ above me,
Christ on my right, Christ on my left,
Christ when I lie down, Christ when I sit down,
    Christ when I arise,
Christ in the heart of every man who thinks of me,
Christ in the mouth of every one who speaks of me,
Christ in every eye that sees me,
Christ in every ear that hears me.

Anon. (trans Kuno Meyer)

The Old Woman

As a white candle
In a holy place,
So is the beauty
Of an aged face.

As the spent radiance
Of the winter sun,
So is a woman
With her travail done.

Her brood gone from her,
And her thoughts as still
As the waters
Under a ruined mill.

Joseph Campbell
(1879-1944)

'Icham of Irlaunde'

Icham of Irlaunde
Ant of the holy londe of irlonde
Gode sir pray ich ye
for of saynte charite,
come ant daunce wyt me,
in irlaunde.

Anon.

The Lake Isle of Innisfree

I will arise and go now, and go to Innisfree,
And a small cabin build there, of clay and wattles
made:
Nine bean-rows will I have there, a hive for the
honey-bee,
And live alone in the bee-loud glade.

And I shall have some peace there, for peace comes
dropping slow,
Dropping from the veils of the morning to where the
cricket sings;
There midnight's all a glimmer, and noon a purple
glow,
And evening full of the linnet's wings.

I will arise and go now, for always night and day
I hear lake water lapping with low sounds by the
shore;
While I stand on the roadway, or on the pavement
grey,
I hear it in the deep heart's core.

W. B. Yeats
(1865-1939)

On Stella's Birthday

Stella this day is thirty-four
(We shan't dispute a year or more),
However Stella, be not troubled,
Although thy size and years are doubled,
Since first I saw thee at sixteen
The brightest virgin on the green,
So little is thy form declin'd
Made up so largely in thy mind.
Oh, would it please the gods to split
Thy beauty, size, and years, and wit,
No age could furnish out a pair
Of nymphs so graceful, wise and fair
With half the lustre of your eyes,
With half your wit, your years and size:
And then before it grew too late,
How should I beg of gentle Fate
(That either nymph might have her swain)
To split my worship too in twain.

Jonathan Swift
(1667-1745)

'The Harp That Once Through Tara's Halls'

The harp that once through Tara's halls
The soul of music shed,
Now hangs as mute on Tara's walls
As if that soul were fled.
So sleeps the pride of former days,
So glory's thrill is o'er,
And hearts that once beat high for praise,
Now feel that pulse no more!

No more to chiefs and ladies bright
The harp of Tara swells;
The chord alone that breaks at night,
Its tale of ruin tells.
Thus Freedom now so seldom wakes,
The only throb she gives
Is when some heart indignant breaks,
To show that still she lives.

Thomas Moore
(1779-1852)

Dear Black Head

Put your head, darling, darling, darling,
Your darling black head my heart above;
Oh, mouth of honey, with the thyme for fragrance,
Who, with heart in breast, could deny you love?

Oh, many and many a young girl for me is pining,
Letting her locks of gold to the cold wind free,
For me, the foremost of our gay young fellows;
But I'd leave a hundred, pure love, for thee!

Then put your head, darling, darling, darling,
Your darling black head my heart above;
Oh, mouth of honey, with the thyme for fragrance,
Who, with heart in breast, could deny you love?

Anon. (trans Samuel Ferguson)

The Stars Stand up in the Air

The stars stand up in the air
The sun and the moon are gone,
The strand of its waters is bare,
And her sway is swept from the swan.

The cuckoo was calling all day,
Hid in the branches above,
How my stórín is fled away,
'Tis my grief that I gave her my love!

Three things through love I see –
Sorrow and sin and death –
And my mind reminding me
That this doom I breathe with my breath.

But sweeter than violin or lute
Is my love – and she left me behind.
I wish that all music were mute,
And I to all beauty were blind.

She's more shapely than swan by the strand,
She's more radiant than grass after dew,
She's more fair than the stars where they stand –
'Tis my grief that her ever I knew!

Anon. (trans Thomas MacDonagh)

He Bids his Beloved be at Peace

I hear the Shadowy Horses, their long manes a-shake,
Their hoofs heavy with tumult, their eyes glimmering
white;
The North unfolds above them clinging, creeping
night,
The East her hidden joy before the morning break,
The West weeps in pale dew and sighs passing away,
The South is pouring down roses of crimson fire:
O vanity of Sleep, Hope, Dream, endless Desire,
The Horses of Disaster plunge in the heavy clay:
Beloved, let your eyes half close, and your heart beat
Over my heart, and your hair fall over my breast,
Drowning love's lonely hour in deep twilight of rest,
And hiding their tossing manes and their tumultuous
feet.

W. B. Yeats
(1865-1939)

On His Own Deafness

Deaf, giddy, helpless, left alone,
To all my Friends a Burthen grown,
No more I hear my Chuch's Bell,
Than if it rang out for my Knell:
At Thunder now no more I start,
Than at the Rumbling of a Cart:
Nay, what's incredible, alack!
I hardly hear a Woman's Clack.

Jonathan Swift
(1667-1745)

I See his Blood upon the Rose

I see his blood upon the rose
And in the stars the glory of his eyes,
His body gleams amid eternal snows,
His tears fall from the skies.

I see his face in every flower;
The thunder and the singing of the birds
Are but his voice – and carven by his power
Rocks are his written words.

All pathways by his feet are worn,
His strong heart stirs the ever-beating sea,
His crown of thorns is twined with every thorn,
His cross is every tree.

Joseph Plunkett
(1887-1916)

from The Winding Banks of Erne

Adieu to evening dances, when merry neighbours
meet,
And the fiddle says to boys and girls, 'Get up and
shake your feet!'
To 'shanachus' and wise old talk of Erin's days gone
by–
Who trench'd the rath on such a hill, and where the
bones may lie
Of saint, or king, or warrier chief; with tales of fairy
power,
And tender ditties sweetly sung to pass the twilight
hour.
The mournful song of exile is now for me to learn–
Adieu, my dear companions on the winding banks
of Erne!

William Allingham
(1824-1889)

''Tis the Last Rose of Summer'

'Tis the last rose of summer
Left blooming alone;
All her lovely companions
Are faded and gone;
No flower of her kindred,
No rose-bud is nigh,
To reflect back her blushes,
To give sigh for sigh.

I'll not leave thee, thou lone one!
To pine on the stem;
Since the lovely are sleeping,
Go sleep thou with them.
Thus kindly I scatter
Thy leaves o'er the bed,
Where thy mates of the garden
Lie scentless and dead.

So soon may *I* follow
When friendships decay,
And from Love's shining circle
The gems drop away.
When true hearts lie wither'd
And fond ones are flown,
Oh! who would inhabit
This bleak world alone?

Thomas Moore
(1779-1852)

June

Broom out the floor now, lay the fender by,
And plant this bee-sucked bough of woodbine there,
And let the window down. The butterfly
Floats in upon the sunbeam, and the fair
Tanned face of June, the nomad gipsy, laughs
Above her widespread wares, the while she tells
The farmers' fortunes in the fields, and quaffs
The water from the spider-peopled wells.

The hedges are all drowned in green grass seas,
And bobbing poppies flare like Elmo's light,
While siren-like the pollen-stained bees
Drone in the clover depths. And up the height
The cuckoo's voice is hoarse and broke with joy.
And on the lowland crops the crows make raid,
Nor fear the clappers of the farmer's boy,
Who sleeps, like drunken Noah, in the shade.

And loop this red rose in that hazel ring
That snares your little ear, for June is short
And we must joy in it and dance and sing,
And from her bounty draw her rosy worth.
Ay! soon the swallows will be flying south,
The wind wheel north to gather in the snow,
Even the roses spilt on youth's red mouth
Will soon blow down the road all roses go.

Francis Ledwidge
(1891-1917)

Before the World was Made

If I make the lashes dark
And the eyes more bright
And the lips more scarlet,
Or ask if all be right
From mirror after mirror,
No vanity's displayed:
I'm looking for the face I had
Before the world was made.

What if I look upon a man
As though on my beloved,
And my blood be cold the while
And my heart unmoved?
Why should he think me cruel
Or that he is betrayed?
I'd have him love the thing that was
Before the world was made.

W. B. Yeats
(1865-1939)

Rest Only in the Grave

I rode till I reached the House of Wealth –
'Twas filled with riot and blighted health.

I rode till I reached the House of Love –
'Twas vocal with sighs beneath and above!

I rode till I reached the House of Sin –
There were shrieks and curses without and within.

I rode till I reached the House of Toil –
Its inmates had nothing to bake or boil.

I rode in search of the House of Content
But never could reach it, far as I went!

The House of Quiet, for strong and weak
And poor and rich, I have still to seek –

That House is narrow, and dark, and small
But the only Peaceful House of all.

James Clarence Mangan
(1803-1849)

from The Ballad of Reading Gaol

At last the dead man walked no more
Amongst the Trial Men,
And I knew that he was standing up
In the black dock's dreadful pen,
And that never would I see his face
For weal or woe again.

Like two doomed ships that pass in storm
We had crossed each other's way:
But we made no sign, we said no word,
We had no word to say;
For we did not meet in the holy night,
But in the shameful day.

A prison wall was round us both,
Two outcast men we were:
The world had thrust us from its heart,
And God from out His care:
And the iron gin that waits for Sin
Had caught us in its snare.

Oscar Wilde
(1854-1900)

Exiles

The gods have taken alien shapes upon them
Wild peasants driving swine
In a strange country. Through the swarthy faces
The starry faces shine.

Under grey tattered skies they strain and reel there:
Yet cannot all disguise
The majesty of fallen gods, the beauty,
The fire beneath their eyes.

They huddle at night within low clay-built cabins;
And, to themselves unknown,
They carry with them diadem and sceptre
And move from throne to throne.

George Russell (AE)
(1867-1935)

My Hope, My Love

My hope, my love, we will go
Into the woods, scattering the dews,
Where we will behold the salmon, and the ousel in its
    nest,
The deer and the roe-buck calling,
The sweetest bird on the branches warbling,
The cuckoo on the summit of the green hill;
And death shall never approach us
In the bosom of the fragrant wood!

Anon. (trans Edward Walsh)

The Blackbirds

I heard the Poor Old Woman say:
'At break of day the fowler came,
And took my blackbirds from their songs
Who loved me well thro' shame and blame.

No more from lovely distances
Their songs shall bless me mile by mile,
Nor to white Ashbourne call me down
To wear my crown another while.

With bended flowers the angels mark
For the skylark the place they lie,
From there its little family
Shall dip their wings first in the sky.

And when the first surprise of flight
Sweet songs excite, from the far dawn
Shall there come blackbirds loud with love,
Sweet echoes of the singers gone.

But in the lonely hush of eve
Weeping I grieve the silent bills.'
I heard the Poor Old Woman say
In Derry of the little hills.

Francis Ledwidge
(1891-1917)

The Lark in the Clear Air

Dear thoughts are in my mind
And my soul soars enchanted,
As I hear the sweet lark sing
In the clear air of the day.
For a tender beaming smile
To my hope has been granted,
And tomorrow she shall hear
All my fond heart would say.

I shall tell her all my love,
All my soul's adoration;
And I think she will hear me
And will not say me nay.
It is this that fills my soul
With its joyous elation,
As I hear the sweet lark sing
In the clear air of the day.

Samuel Ferguson
(1810-1886)

The Meeting of the Waters

There is not in the wide world a valley so sweet
As that vale in whose bosom the bright waters meet;
Oh! the last rays of feeling and life must depart,
Ere the bloom of that valley shall fade from my heart.

Yet it *was* not that nature had shed o'er the scene
Her purest of crystal and brightest of green;
'Twas *not* her soft magic of streamlet and hill,
Oh! no, – it was something more exquisite still.

'Twas that friends, the belov'd of my bosom, were
near,
Who made every dear scene of enchantment more
dear,
And who felt how the best charms of Nature improve,
When we see them reflected from looks that we love.

Sweet vale of Avoca! how calm could I rest
In thy bosom of shade, with the friends I love best,
Where the storms that we feel in this cold world
should cease,
And our hearts, like thy waters, be mingled in peace.

Thomas Moore
(1779-1852)

The Mother

I do not grudge them: Lord, I do not grudge
My two strong sons that I have seen go out
To break their strength and die, they and a few,
In bloody protest for a glorious thing,
They shall be spoken of among their people,
The generations shall remember them,
And call them blessed;
But I will speak their names to my own heart
In the long nights;
The little names that were familiar once
Round my dead hearth.
Lord, thou art hard on mothers:
We suffer in their coming and their going;
And tho' I grudge them not, I weary, weary
Of the long sorrow – And yet I have my joy:
My sons were faithful, and they fought.

Padraig Pearse
(1879-1916)

On an Island

You've plucked a curlew, drawn a hen,
Washed the shirts of seven men,
You've stuffed my pillow, stretched the sheet,
And filled the pan to wash your feet,
You've cooped the pullets, wound the clock,
And rinsed the young men's drinking crock;
And now we'll dance to jigs and reels,
Nailed boots chasing girls' naked heels,
Until your father'll start to snore,
And Jude, now you're married, will stretch on
the floor.

J. M. Synge
(1871-1909)

JACK B YEATS

Is it a Month

Is it a month since I and you
In the starlight of Glen Dubh
Stretched beneath a hazel bough
Kissed from ear and throat to brow,
Since your fingers, neck, and chin
Made the bars that fence me in,
Till Paradise seemed but a wreck
Near your bosom, brow, and neck
And stars grew wilder, growing wise,
In the splendour of your eyes!
Since the weasel wandered near
Whilst we kissed from ear to ear
And the wet and withered leaves
Blew about your cap and sleeves,
Till the moon sank tired through the ledge
Of the wet and windy hedge?
And we took the starry lane
Back to Dublin town again.

J. M. Synge
(1871-1909)

An Irish Airman Foresees his Death

I know that I shall meet my fate
Somewhere among the clouds above;
Those that I fight I do not hate,
Those that I guard I do not love;
My country is Kiltartan's Cross,
My countrymen Kiltartan's poor,
No likely end could bring them loss
Or leave them happier than before.

Nor law, nor duty bade me fight,
Nor public men, nor cheering crowds,
A lonely impulse of delight
Drove to this tumult in the clouds;
I balanced all, brought all to mind,
The years to come seemed waste of breath,
A waste of breath the years behind
In balance with this life, this death.

W. B. Yeats
(1865-1939)

Ireland

I called you by sweet names by wood and linn,
You answered not because my voice was new,
And you were listening for the hounds of Finn
And the long hosts of Lugh.

And so, I came unto a windy height
And cried my sorrow, but you heard no wind,
For you were listening to small ships in flight,
And the wail on hills behind.

And then I left you, wandering the war
Armed with will, from distant goal to goal,
To find you at the last free as of yore,
Or die to save your soul.

And then you called to us from far and near
To bring your crown from out the deeps of time,
It is my grief your voice I couldn't hear
In such a distant clime.

Francis Ledwidge
(1891-1917)

First published in 1991 by
Appletree Press Ltd
The Old Potato Station
14 Howard Street South
Belfast BT7 1AP
Tel: +44 (0) 28 90 243074
Fax: +44 (0) 28 90 246756
Web site: www.appletree.ie
Email: reception@appletree.ie

British Library Cataloguing-in-Publication Data
A little book of Irish verse
1. Ireland. English poetry
821.008

ISBN 0-86281-284-4

Acknowledgements are due to the following:
for all illustrations to the National Gallery of Ireland;
for 'The Old Woman' by Joseph Campbell to Simon Campbell.

9 8 7

System Theory

Inter-University Electronics Series

Books in Series

Vol. 1: *Jamieson et al.* Infrared Physics and Engineering, 1964
Vol. 2: *Bennett and Davey.* Data Transmission, 1965
Vol. 3: *Sutton.* Direct Energy Conversion, 1966
Vol. 4: *Schwartz, Bennett, and Stein.* Communications Systems and Techniques, 1966
Vol. 5: *Luxenberg and Kuehn.* Display Systems Engineering, 1968
Vol. 6: *Balakrishnan.* Communication Theory, 1968
Vol. 7: *Collin and Zucker.* Antenna Engineering, Part 1, 1969
Collin and Zucker. Antenna Engineering, Part 2, 1969
Vol. 8: *Zadeh and Polak.* System Theory, 1969
Vol. 9: *Schwan.* Biological Engineering, 1969
Vol. 10: *Clynes and Milsum.* Biomedical Engineering Systems, 1969

Inter-University Electronics Series, Vol. 8

System Theory

L. A. Zadeh and E. Polak

Department of Electrical Engineering and Computer Sciences
University of California, Berkeley

McGraw-Hill Book Company

New York
St. Louis
San Francisco
London
Sydney
Toronto
Mexico
Panama

System Theory

Library of Congress Catalog Card Number 68-9051

72747

1234567890 MAMM 7654321069

Inter-University Electronics Series

Series Purpose

The explosive rate at which knowledge in electronics has expanded in recent years has produced the need for unified state-of-the-art presentations that give authoritative pictures of individual fields of electronics.

The Inter-University Electronics Series is designed to meet this need by providing volumes that deal with particular areas of electronics where up-to-date reference material is either inadequate or is not conveniently organized. Each volume covers an individual area, or a series of related areas. Emphasis is upon providing timely and comprehensive coverage that stresses general principles, and integrates the newer developments into the overall picture. Each volume is edited by an authority in the field and is written by several coauthors, who are active participants in research or in educational programs dealing with the subject matter involved.

The volumes are written with a viewpoint and at a level that makes them suitable for reference use by research and development engineers and scientists in industry and by workers in governmental and university laboratories. They are also suitable for use as textbooks in specialized courses at graduate levels. The complete series of volumes will provide a reference library that should serve a wide spectrum of electronics engineers and scientists.

The organization and planning of the Series is being carried out with the aid of a Steering Committee, which operates with the counsel of an Advisory Committee. The Steering Committee concerns itself with the scope of the individual volumes and aids in the selection of editors for the different volumes. Each editor is in turn responsible for selecting his coauthors and deciding upon the detailed scope and content of his particular volume. Over all management of the Series is in the hands of the Consulting Editor.

Frederick Emmons Terman

Preface

What is system theory? To some, it is not much more than an assortment of various mathematical techniques for system analysis—an assortment drawn for the most part from the theory of difference and differential equations, control theory, circuit theory, automata theory, information theory, mathematical programming, dynamic programming, variational calculus, applied mechanics, theory of dynamical systems, functional analysis, theory of probability, game theory, and other fields.

To others—and, in particular, to those who call themselves system theorists or system scientists—system theory is more than a conglomerate of parts of various fields and disciplines. To them, system theory is a discipline in its own right—a discipline which aims at providing a common abstract basis and unified conceptual framework for studying the behavior of various types and forms of systems. Within this framework, then, system theory may be viewed as a collection of general methods as well as special techniques and algorithms for dealing with problems in system analysis, synthesis, identification, optimization and other areas within its domain.

Viewed in this perspective, a system theorist is a scientific generalist whose interests and expertise cut across many established fields of science. It does not matter to him whether a system is electrical, mechanical, economic, biological, chemical, or whatnot in nature. What matters is whether it is linear or nonlinear, discrete-time or continuous-time, lumped or distributed, deterministic or stochastic, continuous-state or discrete-state, passive or active, etc. In short, it is the mathematical structure of a system, and not its physical form or area of application, that is of interest to a system theorist.

As a discipline, system theory has two major parts. First, there is the foundation, which is mainly concerned with the assignment of precise meaning to such fundamental concepts as system, state, linearity, causality, passivity, determinateness, equivalence, stability, controllability, observability, etc., and with the exploration of the basic properties of these and related concepts. Second, there is the collection of various methods, techniques, and algorithms for studying the behavior of systems of special types such as differential systems, finite-state systems, modular systems, stochastic systems, learning systems, distributed systems, large-scale systems, etc.

The present volume has no pretense at being an exhaustive treatise on either the foundations or the methods of system theory. Rather, its much more limited objective is to provide the reader—who is assumed to have a fair degree of mathematical maturity—with a collection of self-contained and authoritatively written chapters dealing with a selected subset of basic topics in system theory. To be more specific, the concepts of system, state, and aggregate, which form an important part of the foundation of system theory, are treated in Chapter 1 by L. A. Zadeh. The theory of linear time-invariant systems, which concretizes some of the concepts introduced in Chapter 1, is presented by E. Polak in Chapter 6. The theory of finite-state systems and the theory of linear modular systems, both of which play important roles in digital information processing and coding, are treated by A. Gill in Chapters 2 and 5. The mathematically sophisticated state-space theory of linear time-varying systems, which is due to A. V. Balakrishnan, is described in Chapter 3. The theory of stochastic finite-state systems, to which J. W. Carlyle has made basic contributions, is dealt with in Chapter 10. The recently developed branch of system theory which is concerned with systems governed by nonlinear functional equations is surveyed by I. W. Sandberg in Chapter 8. An exposition of some basic results in classical stability theory is presented by a noted Soviet control theorist, A. Letov, in Chapter 9. Basic results relating to the decomposition of large-scale systems are described by P. P. Varaiya in Chapter 12. A different approach to the analysis of large-scale systems based on the work of G. Kron is described by B. K. Harrison in Chapter 7. Some network interpretations of systems problems are presented by T. E. Stern in Chapter 4. An approach to the theory of learning systems which makes extensive use of the stochastic approximation technique of H. Robbins is described by K. S. Fu in Chapter 11. And, finally, a sophisticated analysis of the conditions for optimality is presented by P. L. Falb and E. Polak in Chapter 13.

A few comments may help the reader to view the contents of this volume in a proper perspective. In the first place, the many advances made in system theory and related fields during the past few years have enlarged its scope to a point where it has become virtually impossible to present a reasonably complete treatment of all, or even most, of the basic topics in system theory within the compass of a single volume. Thus, because of the limitations on space, the editors were faced with many difficult decisions involving the selection of topics to be included in the present volume—decisions which were influenced in the main by answers to the following questions: (*a*) Is the topic under consideration of sufficient importance and broad interest to warrant its inclusion in the volume? (*b*) Can it be presented in a compact and self-contained fashion in a single chapter without requiring too much by way of mathematical background and prior familiarity with the subject? (*c*) Are self-contained and compact expositions of it available in the literature? (*d*) Can a highly qualified author be found to contribute a chapter on the subject in question?

Second, the editors have not attempted to impose upon the contributors to this volume a uniform notation and terminology, since such notation and terminology does not as yet exist in system theory. Indeed, the diversity of the points of view, notation, and terminology in this volume is a reflection of the fact that system theory is a discipline in a state of rapid growth and changing orientation—a discipline which has many strata since it cuts across a number of established fields and is strongly influenced by them. Will it develop into an important field of science and engineering? This volume would not have been written if its authors did not feel, or at least hope, that the answer to the question is in the affirmative.

L. A. Zadeh
E. Polak

Note to the Reader

The following system of numbering and cross-referencing is used in this book: At the top of each page in the outer margin appear chapter and section numbers in boldface italic type; for example, ***3.8*** at the top of a page means that the discussion on that page is part of Chapter *3*, Section *8*. In addition, each item (definition, theorem, example, comment, remark, etc.) is given a number that appears in the left-hand margin; such items are numbered consecutively within each section. Item numbers and all cross-references in the text are in italic type. Cross-references are of the form "by Definition *5.6.3*"; this means "by the definition which is item *3* of Section *6* in Chapter *5*." When we refer in a section to an item within the same section, only the item number is given; thus, "substituting in *7*" means "substituting in Eq. *7* of this section." Also, "*7 et seq.*" means "Eq. *7* and what follows Eq. *7*."

Contents

Foreword *v*
Preface *vii*
Note to the Reader *xi*

I. General System Theory

1 The concepts of system, aggregate, and state in system theory. L. A. ZADEH 3
2 Finite-state systems. A. GILL 43
3 State space theory of linear time-varying systems. A. V. BALAKRISHNAN 95
4 Some network interpretations of systems problems. T. E. STERN 127

II. Linear Systems

5 Linear modular systems. A. GILL 179
6 Linear time-invariant systems. E. POLAK 233
7 Large-scale linear systems. B. K. HARRISON 279

III. Nonlinear Systems

8 A survey of the theory of some systems governed by nonlinear functional equations. I. W. SANDBERG 315
9 Stability theory. A. LETOV 347

IV. Stochastic and Learning Systems

10 Stochastic finite-state system theory. J. W. CARLYLE 387
11 Learning system theory. K. S. FU 425

V. Optimal Systems

12 Decomposition of large-scale systems. P. P. VARAIYA 467
13 Conditions for optimality. P. L. FALB AND E. POLAK 489
Index 513

Part One

GENERAL SYSTEM THEORY

1

The concepts of system, aggregate, and state in system theory

L. A. Zadeh[1]
Department of Electrical Engineering and Computer Sciences
University of California, Berkeley

1 *Introduction*

What is a system? What is a state of a system? How can these notions be given precise and yet general meaning, and how can they be related to some of the other basic concepts in system theory? These are the central questions to which our introductory chapter is addressed.

A system, according to a dictionary definition, is a collection of objects united by some form of interaction or interdependence. In this sense, almost everything is a system of one kind or another. Indeed, in its broad interpretation, the notion of a system is one of the most pervasive ideas in the domain of human thought.[2]

Not quite so pervasive, but very basic nonetheless, is the notion of a state of a system. Roughly, a state of a system at any given time is the information needed to determine the behavior of the system from that time on. Thus, in kinematics, the state of a rigid body in rectilinear motion is its position and velocity. In electric circuits, the state of a network is a vector whose components are the capacitor voltages and inductor currents. In the case of a thermochemical catalytic process, the state may be the concentrations of the reagents, their temperatures, and their partial pressures.

[1] This research was supported in part by the National Aeronautics and Space Administration under Grant NsG 354-(s-5) and in part by the National Science Foundation under Grant GK-2277.

[2] Discussions of the concepts of system and state from modern points of view may be found in [1–9] and their references.

In what follows, we shall not attempt to present a survey or a critique of the many special ways in which the notions of system and state have been defined in various fields of science. Rather, our aim is to define these and related notions in a general and mathematically precise way, with a view to providing a firm foundation for the construction of a broad conceptual framework for system theory. Our point of departure will be the same as in [1–2], that is, the conception of a system as a set of input-output pairs.[1] However, our approach will be simpler and more direct. In order to make our exposition self-contained, we do not assume that the reader is familiar with the material presented in [1–2].[2]

As will be seen later, when one starts with the definition of a system as a set of input-output pairs, a state of the system can be defined very naturally as a tag attached to a subset of input-output pairs satisfying certain consistency conditions. Such a subset will be referred to as an *aggregate*. The concept of an aggregate will play an important role in our approach and, in particular, will serve to provide a very natural way for introducing the basic ideas of state equivalence, system equivalence, input-output-state relations, etc.

Notational preliminaries

For the convenience of the reader, we list first several commonly used abbreviations and conventions which will be employed without further explanation in this chapter.

1. Lowercase boldface letters denote vectors, for example, $\boldsymbol{\alpha}$, $\mathbf{u}$, $\mathbf{x}$.
2. Greek and italic letters denote scalar-valued variables, functions, and operators, for example, α, $u(t)$, L.
3. Braces denote a set or a family, for example, $\{x\}$ is a set with

[1] The definition of a system as a set of input-output pairs and, more particularly, as a *relation* rather than as a mapping or an operator (see *1.2.8*), constitutes one of the basic differences between the point of view introduced in [1] and the conventional definitions of a system which one finds in the literature of control theory and automata theory. In these theories, a system is usually defined through its state equations or as a mapping from the space of inputs to the space of outputs.

[2] The important work of K. Krohn and J. Rhodes [10–11] and subsequent contributions by P. Zeiger [12], R. Kalman [5], M. Arbib [26], T. Windeknecht [9], and others have shown that some of the concepts and techniques of abstract algebra can be useful in analyzing the behavior of certain types of systems, especially finite-state systems and linear discrete-time systems. Even in the case of the very general class of systems considered in this chapter, some of the definitions and results can be expressed more compactly through the use of algebraic notation and terminology. We do not use such notation herein in order not to make familiarity with modern algebra a prerequisite for the understanding of our exposition of the basic concepts of system theory.

generic element x. $\{x|P\}$ is a set of x's having property P, for example, $\{x|5 < x < 10\}$ is the open interval (5,10). When necessary, the notation $\{f(t,\alpha)\}_\alpha$ will be used to place in evidence the variable (α in this case) which generates the family. The terms *set, collection, family,* and *space* will be used interchangeably.

4. The symbol (a,b) is used in two different senses: (1) As an ordered pair of variables a and b, and (2) as the open interval $\{x|a < x < b\}$, when a and b take values on the real line $(-\infty,\infty)$. In the latter case, the symbol $[a,b]$ will be used, as usual, to denote the closed interval $\{x|a \le x \le b\}$.

5. $\triangleq$ stands for *equal by definition,* or *denotes.*

6. $\Rightarrow$ stands for *implies.* Thus, $A \Rightarrow B$ means "In order that B be true, it is sufficient that A be true."

7. $\Leftrightarrow$ denotes *implies and is implied by.*

8. $\forall$ is an abbreviation for *for all;* $\exists$ is an abbreviation for *there exists.*

9. $\in$ stands for *belongs to* or *is an element of.* $\notin$ stands for *does not belong to.*

10. R^n denotes the space of ordered n-tuples of real numbers. Thus, $R^1 \triangleq (-\infty,\infty)$ and $R^n \triangleq \{(x_1, \ldots ,x_n)\}$, with $x_i \in R^1$, $i = 1, \ldots, n$.

11. If $X = \{x\}$ and $Y = \{y\}$, then $X \times Y \triangleq \{(x,y)\}$.

We turn next to notations which are specific to system theory. The symbol t will stand, as usual, for time. The range of the variable t will be denoted by T, with the understanding that unless otherwise indicated T is the real line $(-\infty,\infty)$. In the case of so-called *discrete-time systems,* T will be assumed to be the set of integers $\ldots, -1, 0, 1, 2, \ldots$.

A time function $\mathbf{v}$ is understood to be a set of pairs $\{(t,\mathbf{v}(t))\}$, $t \in T$, where $\mathbf{v}(t)$ denotes the *value* of $\mathbf{v}$ at time t. The range of $\mathbf{v}(t)$ will be denoted by $R[\mathbf{v}(t)]$ and, unless stated to the contrary, will be assumed to be independent of t. Usually, for each t, $\mathbf{v}(t)$ will be an ordered n-tuple of real numbers, so that $R[\mathbf{v}(t)] = R^n$.

If $\mathbf{v}$ is a time function defined over $(-\infty,\infty)$, then the set of pairs $\{(t,\mathbf{v}(t))\}$, $t \in I$, where I is an interval, is called a *segment* of $\mathbf{v}$ *over the observation interval* I or, for short, a *segment.* Such a segment will be denoted by $\mathbf{v}_I$ or, more explicitly, by $\mathbf{v}_{[t_0,t_1]}$, if $I = [t_0,t_1]$. Correspondingly, we shall write $\mathbf{v}_{(t_0,t_1]}$ when I is the semiclosed interval $(t_0,t_1]$; and $\mathbf{v}_{(t_0,t_1)}$ when I is the open interval (t_0,t_1). When no confusion with the time function $\mathbf{v}$ can arise, its segment $\mathbf{v}_I$ will be abbreviated to $\mathbf{v}$. The length of $\mathbf{v}$ will be denoted by $l(\mathbf{v})$ and will be identified with the length of the interval $[t_0,t_1]$. Thus $l(\mathbf{v}) \triangleq t_1 - t_0$.

A segment of $\mathbf{v}$ which comprises a segment $\mathbf{v}^0$ followed by a segment $\mathbf{v}^1$ will be denoted by $\mathbf{v}^0\mathbf{v}^1$. More explicitly, if $\mathbf{v}^0 \triangleq \mathbf{v}_{[t_0,t_1]}$ and $\mathbf{v}^1 \triangleq \mathbf{v}_{[t_1,t_2]}$, then $\mathbf{v}^0\mathbf{v}^1 \triangleq \mathbf{v}_{[t_0,t_2]}$, with $\mathbf{v}^0$ and $\mathbf{v}^1$ being segments of $\mathbf{v}^0\mathbf{v}^1$. (See Fig. *1.1.1.*) Note that

$$l(\mathbf{v}^0\mathbf{v}^1) = l(\mathbf{v}^0) + l(\mathbf{v}^1)$$

In illustrating various concepts which will be introduced in later sections, it will frequently be convenient to deal with time functions

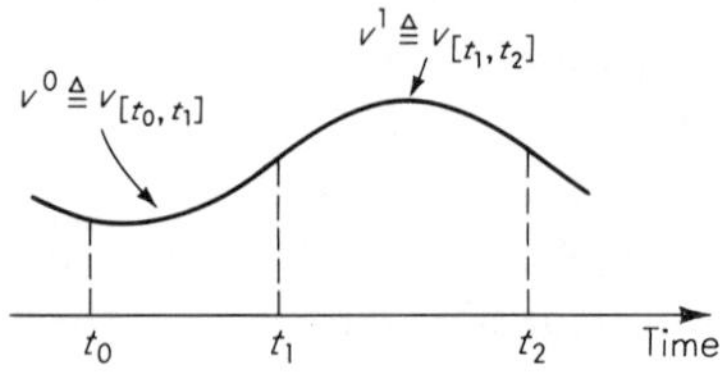

Fig. 1.1.1 Product notation for contiguous segments of a time function.

which are sequences of binary symbols, for example, 0, 1 or *a*, *b*. According to the convention stated earlier, such a time function should be written as, say, $v = \{(0,a),(1,b),(2,b),(3,a),(4,a), \ldots\}$, where the first element of each pair indicates the time of occurrence of the second element. To reduce the cumbersomeness of this notation, we shall write v in the usual form, $v = abbaa \cdots$, indicating separately, if needed, the time of occurrence of the first symbol.

This completes the notational preliminaries. We are now ready to turn to defining some of the basic concepts of system theory.

A word of warning: On first exposure, an uninitiated reader may find the definitions formulated in the following sections to be somewhat artificial and bearing little resemblance to his prior notions of the meaning of such terms as system, state, etc. In time, however, he will come to realize that these abstract-sounding definitions are entirely natural and that they merely serve to give precise meaning, couched in mathematical notation and terminology, to various ill-defined notions which occur in the traditional approaches to system analysis.

2 *Definition of an abstract object*

As a preliminary to defining a system, we shall introduce a closely related notion—the notion of an *abstract object*.

In order to avoid stating various definitions both for the case where t is continuous (that is, its range is an interval) and for the case where t is discrete ($t = \ldots, -1,0,1,2, \ldots$), we shall restrict our attention to the former case and assume that T, the range of t, is the real line. With minor modifications, the same definitions will usually apply when t is discrete or, more generally, when t ranges over a subset of the real line.

With this understanding, consider a physical object $\mathcal{P}$ which is associated with a set of measurable attributes, say, mass, height, width, color, velocity, etc. Let the values of these attributes at time t be denoted by $v_1(t), \ldots, v_n(t)$. Clearly, from the mathematical point of view, what matters about $\mathcal{P}$ is not the physical identity of the time functions $v_1, \ldots, v_n$ but the mathematical relations between them. In essence, it is these relations, stripped of their physical identity, that constitute an *abstract object.*

To transform this rather vague idea into a precisely defined concept, it will be helpful to first focus our attention on a consistency condition which will play an important role in subsequent definitions. The significance of this condition will become clearer later, after the notion of an abstract object is related to that of its state.

Closure under segmentation

For each t_0 and t_1 in $(-\infty, \infty)$, with $t_1 \geq t_0$, let $V \triangleq \{\mathbf{v}_{[t_0,t_1]}\}$ denote a family of segments, with the understanding that to each interval $[t_0,t_1]$ may correspond more than one segment $\mathbf{v}_{[t_0,t_1]}$.

Let $\tau \in [t_0,t_1]$ and let the segments $\mathbf{v}_{[t_0,t_1]}$, $\mathbf{v}_{[t_0,\tau]}$, and $\mathbf{v}_{[\tau,t_1]}$ be denoted by $\mathbf{v}$, $\mathbf{v}^0$, and $\mathbf{v}^1$, respectively. Then, in accordance with the notation for contiguous segments, we can write $\mathbf{v} = \mathbf{v}^0\mathbf{v}^1$.

The family of segments $V = \{\mathbf{v}^0\mathbf{v}^1\}$ will be said to be *closed under segmentation* or, for short, *satisfy the CUS condition* if and only if for each τ in $[t_0,t_1]$ both $\mathbf{v}^0$ and $\mathbf{v}^1$ belong to V. In symbols, the CUS condition may be expressed as

1 $$\mathbf{v}^0\mathbf{v}^1 \in V \Rightarrow \mathbf{v}^0 \in V \quad \text{and} \quad \mathbf{v}^1 \in V$$

for all t_0, t_1 in $(-\infty, \infty)$, all $\mathbf{v}$ in V, and all τ in $[t_0,t_1]$. Equivalently, the family V is closed under segmentation if and only if every segment of a segment which is a member of V is also a member of V.

Note that from $\mathbf{v}^0 \in V$ and $\mathbf{v}^1 \in V$ it does not necessarily follow that $\mathbf{v}^0\mathbf{v}^1 \in V$. If $\mathbf{v}^0 \in V$ and $\mathbf{v}^0\mathbf{v}^1 \in V$, then $\mathbf{v}^1$ will be said to be a *continuation* of $\mathbf{v}^0$ in V.

2 *Example* As a simple illustration, let $v_{[t_0,t_1]}$ be defined by the equation

$$v(t) = \alpha + \beta(t - t_0) \qquad t_0 \leq t \leq t_1$$

where t_0, t_1, α, and β range over $(-\infty, \infty)$. Clearly, the CUS condition is satisfied in this case. On the other hand, if $v(t)$ were defined by

$$v(t) = 1 + \beta(t - t_0)$$

then the CUS condition would not be satisfied.

The CUS condition can readily be extended to the case where v is an ordered n-tuple of segments (defined on the same interval) and V is a family of such n-tuples. For example, if $\mathbf{v}$ is an ordered pair, $\mathbf{v} = (\mathbf{u},\mathbf{y})$, where $\mathbf{u} \triangleq \mathbf{u}_{[t_0,t_1]}$ and $\mathbf{y} \triangleq \mathbf{y}_{[t_0,t_1]}$, then the CUS condition *1* becomes

3 $$(\mathbf{u}^0\mathbf{u}^1,\mathbf{y}^0\mathbf{y}^1) \in V \Rightarrow (\mathbf{u}^0,\mathbf{y}^0) \in V \quad \text{and} \quad (\mathbf{u}^1,\mathbf{y}^1) \in V$$

where $\mathbf{u}^0 \triangleq \mathbf{u}_{[t_0,\tau]}$, $\mathbf{u}^1 \triangleq \mathbf{u}_{[\tau,t_1]}$, $\mathbf{y}^0 \triangleq \mathbf{y}_{[t_0,\tau]}$, and $\mathbf{y}^1 \triangleq \mathbf{y}_{[\tau,t_1]}$. As before, a pair $(\mathbf{u}^1,\mathbf{y}^1)$ will be said to be a *continuation* of $(\mathbf{u}^0,\mathbf{y}^0)$ in V if $(\mathbf{u}^0\mathbf{u}^1,\mathbf{y}^0\mathbf{y}^1) \in V$.

Abstract objects

Earlier in this section, an abstract object was vaguely identified with a set of relations among the time functions which represent its attributes. Having formulated the CUS condition, we are now in a position to define the concept of an abstract object in concrete and yet very general terms.

4 **Definition** An abstract object $\mathcal{A}$ is a family of ordered pairs of time functions

$$\mathcal{A} = \{(\mathbf{u}_{[t_0,t_1]},\mathbf{y}_{[t_0,t_1]})\} \qquad t_0, t_1 \in (-\infty, \infty)$$

satisfying the CUS condition, that is, $(\mathbf{u}_{[t_0,t_1]},\mathbf{y}_{[t_0,t_1]})$ belongs to $\mathcal{A} \Rightarrow$ every segment of $(\mathbf{u}_{[t_0,t_1]},\mathbf{y}_{[t_0,t_1]})$ belongs to $\mathcal{A}$.

The segments $\mathbf{u} \triangleq \mathbf{u}_{[t_0,t_1]}$ and $\mathbf{y} \triangleq \mathbf{y}_{[t_0,t_1]}$ are termed, respectively, *input* and *output* of $\mathcal{A}$, and the pair $(\mathbf{u},\mathbf{y})$ is said to be an *input-output pair belonging to* $\mathcal{A}$. Thus, in essence, an abstract object $\mathcal{A}$ is a collection of input-output pairs,

5 $$\mathcal{A} = \{(\mathbf{u},\mathbf{y})\}$$

satisfying the CUS condition.

The families of time functions

6 $$\mathcal{D}(\mathcal{A}) \triangleq \{\mathbf{u} | (\mathbf{u},\mathbf{y}) \in \mathcal{A}\}$$

and

7 $$\mathcal{R}(\mathcal{A}) \triangleq \{\mathbf{y} | (\mathbf{u},\mathbf{y}) \in \mathcal{A}\}$$

constitute, respectively, the *domain* and *range* of $\mathcal{A}$. These families represent, respectively, the sets of all input and outputs that can be associated with $\mathcal{A}$. For a diagrammatic representation of an abstract object $\mathfrak{A}$ with input $\mathbf{u}$ and output $\mathbf{y}$, we shall employ the conventional block diagram form shown in Fig. *1.2.1*.

8 *Comment* The above definition of an abstract object is merely a formal expression of the fact that any interaction with a physical object involves varying some of the attributes of this object and observing the resulting variations in other attributes. The attributes that are varied play the role of inputs (causes) and the resulting variations are the outputs (effects). In taking the point of view that an abstract object is a collection of its input-output pairs, we are in effect asserting that so long as our interaction with an object takes

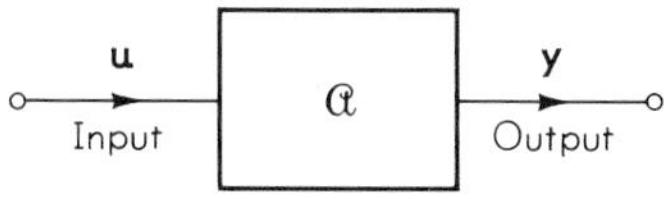

Fig. 1.2.1 Diagrammatic representation of a system $\mathfrak{A}$ with input $\mathbf{u}$ and output $\mathbf{y}$.

place through the observation of the variations in its attributes, it is logical to identify the object in question with the totality of possible observations of variations in its attributes. The totality of such observations, then, constitutes an abstract object.

It is important to observe that the definition of an abstract object does not imply that to each input $\mathbf{u}$ corresponds a unique output $\mathbf{y}$. On the contrary, to each input $\mathbf{u}$ will correspond in general a number of possible outputs, each of which constitutes a possible *response* of $\mathfrak{A}$ to $\mathbf{u}$. As will be seen later, the nonuniqueness of response to a given input reflects the dependence of the output not only on the input but also on the initial state of the object. In mathematical terminology, because of the nonuniqueness of the dependence of output on input, an abstract object is a *relation* rather than a function or an operator.

9 *Example* To illustrate the notion of an abstract object at this point, we shall consider just one simple example involving input-output pairs which are sequences of binary symbols. To distinguish between input and output symbols, the former are denoted by 0, 1 and the latter by a, b.

The input-output pairs of lengths 1, 2, and 3 for this object, call it $\mathfrak{A}$, are listed below, with the understanding that any sequence of 0s and 1s can be an input sequence.

Input-output pairs of length 1:

$$(0,a) \quad (0,b) \quad (1,a) \quad (1,b)$$

Input-output pairs of length 2:

(00,*ab*) (00,*ba*) (01,*ba*) (01,*ab*)
(10,*aa*) (10,*ba*) (11,*ab*) (11,*ba*) (11,*bb*)

Input-output pairs of length 3:

(000,*aba*) (010,*baa*) (100,*bab*) (111,*aba*) (000,*bab*) (001,*bab*)
(111,*bba*) (110,*bba*) (111,*bba*) (001,*aba*) (110,*baa*) (011,*abb*)
(100,*aab*) (101,*aab*) (010,*aba*) (101,*bab*) (110,*aba*) (011,*bab*)

We could expand this list indefinitely by listing input-output pairs of lengths 4, 5, etc. In this particular case, however, it is easy to show that the input-output pairs of length 3 determine all input-output pairs of longer length. An abstract object with this property (i.e., one in which input-output pairs of finite length k determine all input-output pairs of longer length) will be said to have *finite memory.* More concretely, a finite memory object will be said to have memory of length k if given any input-output pair $(\mathbf{u}^0_{[t_0,t_1]},\mathbf{y}^0_{[t_0,t_1]})$ of length k (i.e., one in which $t_1 - t_0 = k$) and given any continuation $\mathbf{u}^1_{[t_1,t_2]}$ of $\mathbf{u}^0_{[t_0,t_1]}$ in $\mathfrak{D}(\mathcal{A})$ [i.e., an input $\mathbf{u}^1$ such that $\mathbf{u}^0\mathbf{u}^1 \in \mathfrak{D}(\mathcal{A})$], there is just one continuation $\mathbf{y}^1$ of $\mathbf{y}^0$ in $\mathcal{R}(\mathcal{A})$. In other words, if $(\mathbf{u}^0\mathbf{u}^1,\mathbf{y}^0\mathbf{y}^1) \in \mathcal{A}$ and $(\mathbf{u}^0,\mathbf{y}^0)$ is of length k, then $\mathbf{y}^1$ is uniquely determined by $\mathbf{u}^0$, $\mathbf{y}^0$ and $\mathbf{u}^1$. Thus for a finite-memory system $\mathbf{y}^1$ can be expressed as a function of $\mathbf{u}^0$, $\mathbf{y}^0$ and $\mathbf{u}^1$

$$\mathbf{y}^1 = \mathbf{f}(\mathbf{u}^0,\mathbf{y}^0,\mathbf{u}^1)$$

and, more particularly, for $t = \ldots, -1, 0, 1, 2, \ldots$, $\mathbf{u}^1 = (t,\mathbf{u}_t)$ and $\mathbf{y}^1 = (t,\mathbf{y}_t)$, we can write

$$\mathbf{y}_t = f(\mathbf{u}_{t-k}, \ldots, \mathbf{u}_{t-1},\mathbf{y}_{t-k}, \ldots, \mathbf{y}_{t-1},\mathbf{u}_t,t)$$

where $\mathbf{u}_t$ and $\mathbf{y}_t$ denote the values of $\mathbf{u}$ and $\mathbf{y}$ at time t.

To show that the abstract object under consideration has finite memory, it is sufficient to invoke the CUS condition. Specifically, consider an input-output pair of length 3 such as (010,*aba*). From this sequence, we can deduce an input-output pair of length 4 of the form $(010u^1,abay^1)$ as follows. For the input sequence 0100, the output sequence can be either *abaa* or *abab*. Now, by the CUS condition, the last three symbols in this pair must be an input-output pair. In the list of input-output pairs, we find (100,*bab*) but not (100,*baa*). Consequently, (0100,*abab*) belongs to $\mathcal{A}$, while (0100,*abaa*) does not. In a similar way, all input-output pairs of length greater than 3 can be deduced from pairs of length 3.

In the foregoing, we have indicated how the CUS condition can be employed to deduce input-output pairs of length >3 from those of length 3. Clearly, all pairs of shorter length can also be deduced from those of length 3 by a trivial application of the CUS condition. It is easy to verify that all input-output pairs of length 1 and 2 in the given list are segments of input-output pairs of length 3.

Input-output relations

In general, it is not practicable to list all input-output pairs which define an abstract object $\mathcal{A}$ since such pairs are usually not finite in number. For this reason, it is customary to characterize $\mathcal{A}$ by an *input-output relation,* that is, by an equation or an algorithm which can be used to generate all input-output pairs belonging to $\mathcal{A}$.

The most common example of an input-output relation is a differential equation. Thus, when we say that $\mathcal{A}$ is characterized by the input-output relation

10 $$a_n(t)\frac{d^n y}{dt^n} + \cdots + a_0(t)y = b_n(t)\frac{d^n u}{dt^n} + \cdots + b_0(t)u$$

which is a linear differential equation in u and y, we mean that any ordered pair (u,y) which satisfies *10* is an input-output pair for $\mathcal{A}$, and conversely any $(u,y) \in \mathcal{A}$ satisfies *10*.†

To illustrate, suppose that the input-output relation for $\mathcal{A}$ is expressed by

11 $$\frac{dy}{dt} + y = u$$

The general solution of this equation yields an explicit expression for all input-output pairs which satisfy *11*. Specifically, such input-output pairs can be expressed as $(u(t),y(t))$, $t \geq t_0$, in which $y(t)$ is related to u by

12 $$y(t) = \alpha e^{-(t-t_0)} + \int_{t_0}^{t} e^{-(t-\xi)}u(\xi)\,d\xi$$

where α can be any real number. [Note that from setting $t = t_0$ in *12* it follows that $\alpha = y(t_0)$.] In this representation, to each value of α (which will subsequently be called a state of $\mathcal{A}$) corresponds a set of input-output pairs defined by *12*. We will make use of this observation in our later discussion of the notions of aggregate and state.

Another common example of an input-output relation is a difference equation relating input and output sequences. For example, the difference equation

13 $$y_{t+1} - cy_t = u_t \qquad t = \ldots, -1, 0, 1, \ldots$$

† Although we have not stated so explicitly, it is understood that $u(t)$ and $y(t)$ range over R^1 and that u and y are time functions on which the operations involved in *10* can be performed.

is an input-output relation in the sense that it defines all input-output pairs belonging to an object $\mathcal{A}$. More explicitly, such input-output pairs are expressed by (u_t, y_t), $t \geq t_0$, where y_t is related to u by the solution of *13*, namely

14 $$y_t = \alpha c^{t-t_0} + \sum_{\xi=t_0}^{t} c^{t-\xi-1} u_\xi \qquad t \geq t_0$$

in which α [$= y(t_0)$] ranges over R^1. As in *11*, to each value of α (which will subsequently be called a state of $\mathcal{A}$) corresponds a set of input-output pairs of $\mathcal{A}$ defined by *14*.

Still another way of defining sets of input-output sequences is provided by graphs such as shown in Fig. *1.2.2*. In this case, u_t and y_t

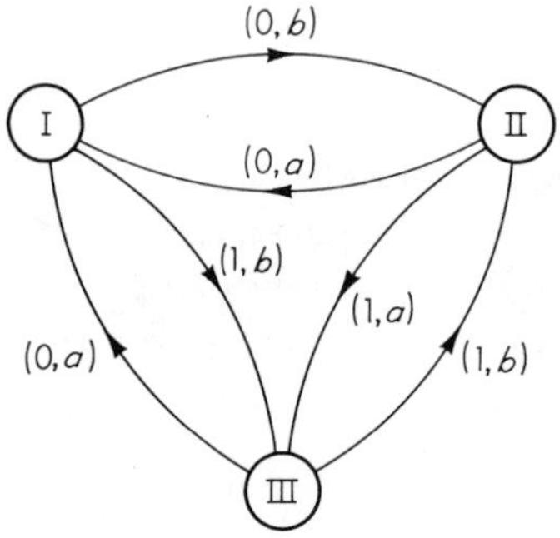

Fig. 1.2.2 State diagram for a finite-state system.

range over finite sets which for simplicity are taken to be {0,1} and {*a*,*b*}, respectively, and each transition from one node (represented by a circle) to another is associated with an input-output pair of length 1. For example, starting in node I and applying the input sequence 01101, one gets the output sequence *babab*. This generates the input-output pair (01101,*babab*). All other input-output pairs which belong to the object in question can be generated in a similar fashion.

Objects whose input-output relations can be characterized in this fashion are called *finite-state systems.* A graph such as shown in Fig. *1.2.2* is called a *state diagram* and, as will be seen later, the nodes of such a graph play the role of the states of the object which it defines.

It should be noted that most of the abstract objects which we used for illustrative purposes in this section fall into the category of time-invariant linear systems. Since the notions of time invariance and linearity play important roles in system theory, it will be helpful at this juncture to relate these notions to the conception of an abstract object as a collection of input-output pairs. However, since we are not concerned in this chapter with the properties of any particular class of systems, our discussion of time invariance and linearity will be very brief and limited essentially to definitions of these terms. More detailed discussions of the implications of time invariance and linearity may be found in [1] and other texts and papers dealing with linear and nonlinear system theory [13–26].

Time invariance

As a preliminary to defining time invariance, it is convenient to introduce a notation for translates of a segment. Specifically, let $\mathbf{v} = \mathbf{v}_{[t_0,t_1]}$

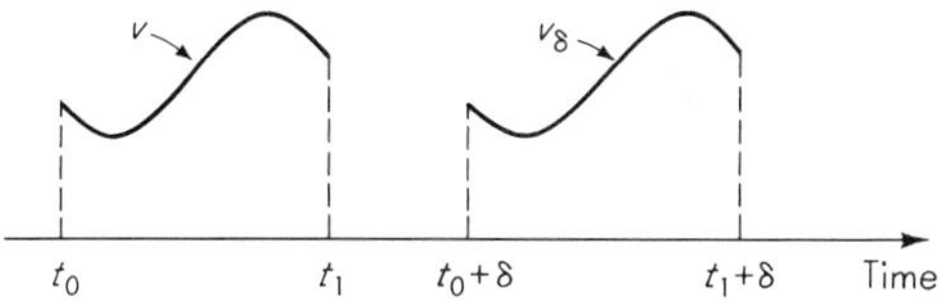

Fig. 1.2.3 Translate of a segment.

be a segment. Then, by a *translate of* $\mathbf{v}$ *by amount* δ is meant a segment $\mathbf{v}_\delta$ such that (see Fig. *1.2.3*)

15 $$\mathbf{v}_\delta(t) \triangleq \mathbf{v}(t - \delta) \qquad t_0 + \delta \leq t \leq t_1 + \delta$$

Roughly speaking, time invariance of an abstract object has to do with invariance of its input-output pairs under translations in time. More specifically, let $(\mathbf{u},\mathbf{y})$ be an input-output pair for an abstract object $\mathcal{A}$ and let $(\mathbf{u}_\delta,\mathbf{y}_\delta)$ denote a translate of $(\mathbf{u},\mathbf{y})$ by amount δ. Then $\mathcal{A}$ is a *time-invariant* abstract object if and only if the following holds true

16 $$(\mathbf{u},\mathbf{y}) \in \mathcal{A} \Rightarrow (\mathbf{u}_\delta,\mathbf{y}_\delta) \in \mathcal{A} \qquad \text{for all real } \delta$$

In other words, $\mathcal{A}$ is time-invariant if and only if the set $\mathcal{A} = \{(\mathbf{u},\mathbf{y})\}$ is closed under all translations in time.

It is easy to verify that the abstract objects defined by the input-output relations *11* and *13* are time-invariant. More generally, any input-output relation which has the form of a differential or difference equation with constant coefficients defines a time-invariant abstract object. It should be noted that the abstract object of Example *9* is tacitly assumed to be time-invariant because the times of occurrence of the first symbols in each input-output pair are not specified. This implies that not only the input-output pairs in Example *9* but also all their translates belong to the object under consideration.

Linearity

The importance of the notion of linearity stems from two facts: (1) Linearity, when it is present, greatly simplifies the analysis of system behavior; (2) many systems encountered in the real world are linear, at least to a first approximation.

Linearity can be defined quite simply in terms of the collection of input-output pairs which characterize an abstract object. Specifically, let $\mathcal{A} = \{(\mathbf{u},\mathbf{y})\}$, and let $(\mathbf{u}^0,\mathbf{y}^0)$ and $(\mathbf{u}^1,\mathbf{y}^1)$ be any pair of input-output pairs in $\mathcal{A}$. In terms of these input-output pairs, the definition of linearity can be worded as follows.

17 **Definition** An abstract object $\mathcal{A}$ is *linear* if and only if

18 $$(\mathbf{u}^0,\mathbf{y}^0) \in \mathcal{A} \quad \text{and} \quad (\mathbf{u}^1,\mathbf{y}^1) \in \mathcal{A} \Rightarrow (k_0\mathbf{u}^0 + k_1\mathbf{u}^1,\ k_0\mathbf{y}^0 + k_1\mathbf{y}^1) \in \mathcal{A}$$

for all real k_0 and k_1. In other words, $\mathcal{A}$ is linear if and only if any linear combination of any two input-output pairs in $\mathcal{A}$ is also an input-output pair in $\mathcal{A}$. Equivalently, $\mathcal{A}$ is linear if and only if $\mathcal{A}$ is a linear vector space.

Clearly, the input-output relations *11* and *13* define abstract objects which are linear in the sense defined above. Thus, in the case of *11*, we can write

19 $$\frac{dy^0}{dt} + y^0 = u^0$$

20 $$\frac{dy^1}{dt} + y^1 = u^1$$

and on forming a linear combination of *19* and *20*, we have

21 $$\frac{d}{dt}(k_0y^0 + k_1y^1) + k_0y^0 + k_1y^1 = k_0u^0 + k_1u^1$$

which satisfies *18* provided the domain and range of $\mathcal{A}$ are linear vector spaces, as they are tacitly assumed to be. The same applies to *13*.

3 *Some basic notions stemming from the concept of an abstract object*

This section is devoted to the discussion of several basic notions which stem from the concept of an abstract object as a collection of input-output pairs. The first of these notions is that of

1 **Containment** An object $\mathcal{A}$ will be said to be *contained* in object $\mathcal{B}$, written as $\mathcal{A} \subset \mathcal{B}$, if the set $\mathcal{A}$ is a subset of $\mathcal{B}$. In terms of input-output pairs, this means that every input-output pair belonging to $\mathcal{A}$ also belongs to $\mathcal{B}$.

2 *Example* Consider two objects $\mathcal{A}$ and $\mathcal{B}$ which are characterized by the state diagrams shown in Fig. *1.3.1*. It is easy to verify by inspection that every input-output pair which belongs to $\mathcal{A}$ also belongs to $\mathcal{B}$.

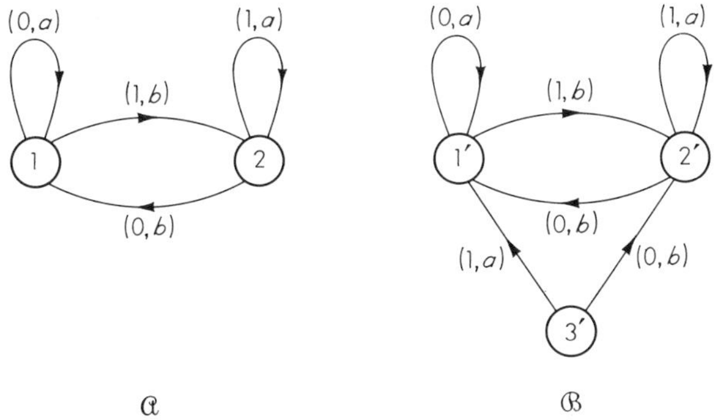

Fig. 1.3.1 State diagrams for $\mathcal{A}$ and $\mathcal{B}$, with $\mathcal{A} \subset \mathcal{B}$.

The converse, however, is not true, e.g., the input-output pair $(01,ba)$ belongs to $\mathcal{B}$ but not to $\mathcal{A}$.

3 *Example* Suppose that $\mathcal{A}$ and $\mathcal{B}$ are characterized, respectively, by the input-output relations

4 $\mathcal{A}$: $$\frac{dy}{at} = u$$

5 $\mathcal{B}$: $$\frac{d^2y}{dt^2} = \frac{du}{dt}$$

In this case, the input-output pairs for $\mathcal{A}$ and $\mathcal{B}$ may be expressed in the explicit form

6 $\mathcal{A}$: $$\left(u(t),\, \alpha + \int_{t_0}^{t} u(\xi)\, d\xi\right) \qquad t \geq t_0$$

7 $\mathcal{B}$: $$\left(u(t),\, \beta_0 + \beta_1(t - t_0) + \int_{t_0}^{t} u(\xi)\, d\xi\right) \qquad t \geq t_0$$

where α, β_0, and β_1 range over R^1. Clearly, every input-output pair belonging to $\mathcal{A}$ also belongs to $\mathcal{B}$. Hence, $\mathcal{A} \subset \mathcal{B}$.

The notion of containment leads to a very basic concept, namely, the concept of *equivalence*.[1]

[1] The concept of equivalence as defined here corresponds to that of weak equivalence in [1]. What is referred to therein as *equivalence* will be called *strong equivalence* in this chapter.

8 **Definition** $\mathcal{A}$ and $\mathcal{B}$ are equivalent, written as $\mathcal{A} = \mathcal{B}$, if $\mathcal{A}$ and $\mathcal{B}$ are equal as sets, that is, if $\mathcal{A} \subset \mathcal{B}$ and $\mathcal{B} \subset \mathcal{A}$. In words, this means that $\mathcal{A}$ and $\mathcal{B}$ are equivalent if every input-output pair which belongs to $\mathcal{A}$ also belongs to $\mathcal{B}$ and vice versa.

9 *Example* Let $\mathcal{A}$ be characterized by the system of differential equations

10 $$\mathcal{A}: \qquad \frac{dy}{dt} = v \qquad \frac{dv}{dt} = u$$

and let $\mathcal{B}$ be characterized by the differential equation

11 $$\mathcal{B}: \qquad \frac{d^2y}{dt^2} = u$$

It is easy to verify that the input-output pairs for $\mathcal{A}$ and $\mathcal{B}$ are expressed, respectively, by

12 $$\left(u(t),\ \alpha_0 + \alpha_1(t - t_0) + \int_{t_0}^{t} d\lambda \int_{t_0}^{\lambda} u(\xi)\, d\xi\right) \qquad t \geq t_0$$

where α_0 and α_1 range over R^1, and

13 $$\left(u(t),\ \beta_0 + \beta_1(t - t_0) + \int_{t_0}^{t} d\lambda \int_{t_0}^{\lambda} u(\xi)\, d\xi\right) \qquad t \geq t_0$$

where β_0 and β_1 range over R^1. Clearly, every input-output pair which belongs to $\mathcal{A}$ also belongs to $\mathcal{B}$ and vice versa. Hence, $\mathcal{A} = \mathcal{B}$.

14 *Example* Let $\mathcal{A}$ and $\mathcal{B}$ be the objects characterized by the state diagrams shown in Fig. *1.3.2*. It is easy to verify that every input-output pair which belongs to $\mathcal{A}$ also belongs to $\mathcal{B}$ and vice versa. Hence, $\mathcal{A} = \mathcal{B}$.

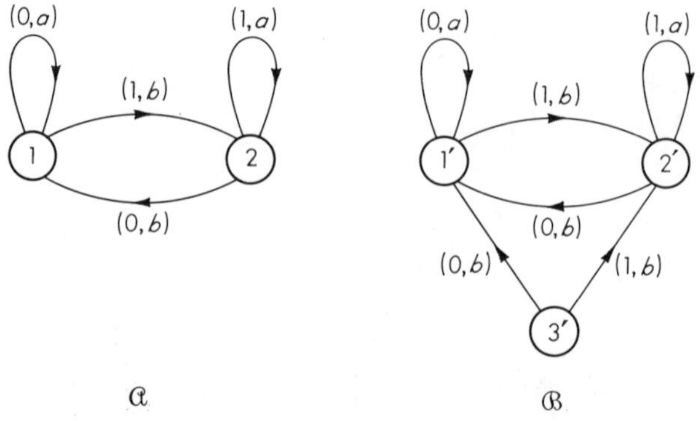

Fig. 1.3.2 Example of equivalent systems.

Equivalence and indistinguishability

Consider the following identification problem. Suppose that an experimenter is given a black box which is known to contain either $\mathcal{A}$ or $\mathcal{B}$, with the input-output relations of $\mathcal{A}$ and $\mathcal{B}$ known to the experimenter. The experimenter is free to apply to the black box any input $\mathbf{u}$ which is admissible for both $\mathcal{A}$ and $\mathcal{B}$ (i.e., a $\mathbf{u}$ such that $\mathbf{u} \in \mathfrak{D}(\mathcal{A}) \cap \mathfrak{D}(\mathcal{B})$ and observe the response $\mathbf{y}$. Then, based on the knowledge of the input-output pair $(\mathbf{u},\mathbf{y})$, the experimenter is supposed to decide whether the black box contains $\mathcal{A}$ or $\mathcal{B}$. If the experimenter can not determine this from $(\mathbf{u},\mathbf{y})$, no matter what $\mathbf{u}$ is chosen and what $\mathbf{y}$ is observed, then $\mathcal{A}$ and $\mathcal{B}$ are said to be *indistinguishable under a single experiment.*

From the definition of equivalence, it follows at once that equivalence implies and is implied by indistinguishability under a single experiment. However, it is possible that two objects are indistinguishable under a single experiment and yet are distinguishable under a multiple experiment, that is, an experiment in which the experimenter has at his disposal more than one copy of the black box. For example, the objects shown in Fig. *1.3.2* are equivalent and yet they are distinguishable under a multiple experiment in the sense that if the experimenter has two identical copies of the black box containing, say, $\mathcal{B}$, then starting in node $3'$ one copy would produce b in response to 0 while the other copy would produce b in response to 1. These responses could not be obtained if the same inputs were applied to two identical copies of $\mathcal{A}$. This implies that $\mathcal{A}$ and $\mathcal{B}$ are distinguishable by the multiple experiment in question even though they are indistinguishable under a single experiment.

As will be seen later, indistinguishability under a multiple experiment corresponds to what will be called *strong equivalence,* denoted by $\mathcal{A} \equiv \mathcal{B}$. Strong equivalence implies equivalence, but not vice versa.

4 *The notion of a system*

So far, our discussion has been concerned with a single abstract object $\mathcal{A}$ associated with input $\mathbf{u}$ and output $\mathbf{y}$. To be more general, we have to consider collections of abstract objects $\mathcal{A}_1, \ldots, \mathcal{A}_N$ in which some of the inputs or outputs associated with, say, $\mathcal{A}_i$, may be constrained to be equal (for all t) to some of the inputs or outputs of other objects in the collection. Such a combination of abstract objects will be called a *system.* It should be noted that, under this definition, every abstract object is a system and every system is an abstract object. For this reason, we shall henceforth use the term *system* to describe both an abstract object and a collection of abstract objects.

A simple example of a combination of abstract objects which form a system is shown in Fig. *1.4.1*. Here, the system $\mathcal{A}$ (represented by

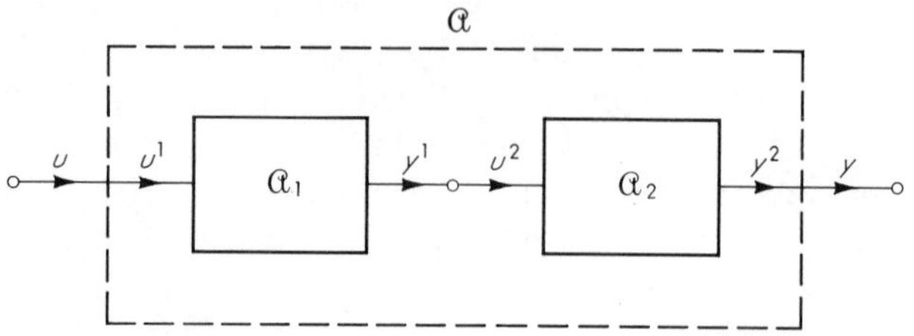

Fig. 1.4.1 Tandem combination of $\mathcal{A}_1$ and $\mathcal{A}_2$.

dotted block) with input u and output y comprises two objects, $\mathcal{A}_1$ and $\mathcal{A}_2$, connected as shown in the diagram. This connection represents the following constraint between the inputs and outputs of $\mathcal{A}_1$ and $\mathcal{A}_2$: $y^1 = u^2$, with the input and output of $\mathcal{A}$ related to those of $\mathcal{A}_1$ and $\mathcal{A}_2$ by $u = u^1$ and $y = y^2$.

A question which naturally arises when one deals with a combination of two or more systems is the following: Suppose that a system $\mathcal{A}$ is specified as a given combination of N component systems, $\mathcal{A}_1, \ldots, \mathcal{A}_N$, each of which is defined as a specified set of input-output pairs. How can one deduce from the knowledge of these sets of input-output pairs and the way in which the components of $\mathcal{A}$ (that is, $\mathcal{A}_1, \ldots, \mathcal{A}_N$) are combined the set of input-output pairs which constitutes $\mathcal{A}$? This question presents one of the central problems of system theory. We shall refer to it as the problem of *input-output analysis.*

There are two basic ways in which the problem of input-output analysis can be formulated. Essentially, the difference between these formulations lies in the way in which the sets of input-output pairs constituting the components of the given system are defined. Specifically, in the *explicit form,* these sets are defined by their respective characteristic functions, i.e., by functions which assign the value 1 to each input-output pair which belongs to a particular component system and 0 to those that do not. More concretely, if a generic input-output pair associated with a component system $\mathcal{A}_i$, $i = 1, \ldots, N$, is denoted by (u^i,y^i), then $\mathcal{A}_i$ is defined explicitly by the characteristic function $\mu_i(u^i,y^i)$:

1 $$\begin{aligned} \mu_i(u^i,y^i) &= 1 \quad \text{for } (u^i,y^i) \in \mathcal{A}_i \\ &= 0 \quad \text{for all ordered pairs of time functions which do not belong to } \mathcal{A}_i \end{aligned}$$

Thus, the knowledge of the characteristic function of $\mathcal{A}_i$ is equivalent to having a listing or explicit characterization of all input-output pairs which belong to $\mathcal{A}_i$.

In the *implicit form*, the component systems are defined by their respective input-output relations rather than by characteristic functions. In this case, in order to determine the input-output pairs belonging to, say, $\mathcal{A}_i$, it is necessary to "solve" the input-output relation defining $\mathcal{A}_i$. The problem of input-output analysis is labeled *implicit* in this case because the characterization of $\mathcal{A}_i$ by an input-output relation is implicit rather than explicit in nature.

It will be helpful at this juncture to summarize the two formulations of the problem of input-output analysis in parallel terms.

2 **Problem of input-output analysis in explicit form** Given a system $\mathcal{A}$ as a specified combination of component systems $\mathcal{A}_1, \ldots, \mathcal{A}_N$, with each $\mathcal{A}_i$, $i = 1, \ldots, N$, defined by a characteristic function $\mu_i(u^i,y^i)$. Determine the characteristic function of $\mathcal{A}$ from (1) the knowledge of the characteristic functions of $\mathcal{A}_1, \ldots, \mathcal{A}_N$, and (2) the constraints on the inputs and outputs of $\mathcal{A}_1, \ldots, \mathcal{A}_N$ imposed by the way in which they are combined.

3 **Problem of input-output analysis in implicit form** Given a system $\mathcal{A}$ as a specified combination of component systems $\mathcal{A}_1, \ldots, \mathcal{A}_N$, with each $\mathcal{A}_i$, $i = 1, \ldots, N$, defined by an input-output relation (e.g., a differential equation). Determine the corresponding input-output relation for $\mathcal{A}$ from (1) the knowledge of the input-output relations for $\mathcal{A}_1, \ldots, \mathcal{A}_N$, and (2) the constraints on the inputs and outputs of $\mathcal{A}_1, \ldots, \mathcal{A}_N$ imposed by the way in which they are combined.

As we shall see presently, on a purely formal—but not necessarily computational—level, problem *2* is much easier to solve than problem *3*. On an analytical level, problem *3* can be solved completely only for certain types of systems, e.g., systems defined by differential equations with constant coefficients.

To illustrate this point, consider a tandem combination $\mathcal{A}$ of two systems $\mathcal{A}_1$ and $\mathcal{A}_2$ (Fig. *1.4.1*), in which $\mathcal{A}_1$ and $\mathcal{A}_2$ are defined by their respective characteristic functions

4
$$\begin{aligned} \mu_1(u^1,y^1) &= 1 \qquad \text{if } (u^1,y^1) \in \mathcal{A}_1 \\ &= 0 \qquad \text{if } (u^1,y^1) \notin \mathcal{A}_1 \end{aligned}$$

5
$$\begin{aligned} \mu_2(u^2,y^2) &= 1 \qquad \text{if } (u^2,y^2) \in \mathcal{A}_2 \\ &= 0 \qquad \text{if } (u^2,y^2) \notin \mathcal{A}_2 \end{aligned}$$

Here the interconnection constraint is expressed by $u^2 = y^1$, with the input and output of $\mathcal{A}$ identified with u^1 and y^2, respectively.

The constraint $u^2 = y^1$ implies that (u^1,y^2) is an input-output pair for $\mathcal{A}$ if and only if there exists a time function y^1 such that (u^1,y^1) and (y^1,y^2) are input-output pairs for $\mathcal{A}_1$ and $\mathcal{A}_2$, respectively. To express this in a more compact form, we note that the statement "$(u^1,y^1) \in \mathcal{A}_1$ and $(y^1,y^2) \in \mathcal{A}_2$" is expressible as the equation[1]

6 $$\min [\mu_1(u^1,y^1),\mu_2(y^1,y^2)] = 1$$

where min $[a,b]$ denotes the smaller of the two numbers a, b, with the understanding that min $[a,a] = a$. Furthermore, the statement "There exists y^1 such that $(u^1,y^1) \in \mathcal{A}_1$ and $(y^1,y^2) \in \mathcal{A}_2$" can be expressed as

7 $$\max_{y^1} \min [\mu_1(u^1,y^1),\mu_2(y^1,y^2)] = 1$$

This implies that the characteristic function of $\mathcal{A}$ can be expressed in terms of those of $\mathcal{A}_1$ and $\mathcal{A}_2$ as follows

8 $$\mu(u^1,y^2) = \max_{y^1} \min [\mu_1(u^1,y^1),\mu_2(y^1,y^2)]$$

The above relation defines the set of input-output pairs of the tandem combination of $\mathcal{A}_1$ and $\mathcal{A}_2$ in terms of the sets of input-output pairs of $\mathcal{A}_1$ and $\mathcal{A}_2$. Thus, in principle, *8* provides a solution to the problem of input-output analysis for the case where $\mathcal{A}_1$ and $\mathcal{A}_2$ are connected in tandem and the sets of input-output pairs for $\mathcal{A}_1$, $\mathcal{A}_2$, and $\mathcal{A}$ are described by their respective characteristic functions.

The same approach to the problem of input-output analysis can be used in the more general case where a system $\mathcal{A}$ is an arbitrary combination of a finite number of objects $\mathcal{A}_1, \ldots, \mathcal{A}_N$. To illustrate, consider the system shown in Fig. *1.4.2*, which is composed of three interconnected objects $\mathcal{A}_1$, $\mathcal{A}_2$, and $\mathcal{A}_3$. In this case, the input u and output y of $\mathcal{A}$ are identified with u_2^1 and y^3, respectively, and the interconnection constraints read

$$y_1^1 = u_1^2 \qquad y_2^1 = u_1^3 \qquad y_1^3 = u_2^2 \qquad y_1^2 = u_1^1 \qquad y_2^2 = u_2^3$$

Now let $\mathcal{A}_1$, $\mathcal{A}_2$, and $\mathcal{A}_3$ be defined, respectively, by their characteristic functions $\mu_1(u_1^1,u_2^1;y_1^1,y_2^1)$, $\mu_2(u_1^2,u_2^2;y_1^2,y_2^2)$, $\mu_3(u_1^3,u_2^3;y_1^3)$.[2]

[1] Alternatively and more simply, we could write $\mu_1(u^1,y^1)\mu_2(y^1,y^2) = 1$. We use min rather than the product because the former has wider generality (e.g., is applicable when, as in the case of fuzzy systems (see [24]), the characteristic functions take values in the interval [0,1]). Note that for binary variables min $[a,b] = ab$ and max $[a,b] = a + b - ab$, where + denotes sum. More generally, one can employ the notation min $[a,b] = a \wedge b$ and max $[a,b] = a \vee b$ to simplify the writing of equations such as *8* and *9*.

[2] When a system has multiple inputs and/or outputs, it is helpful to use a semicolon in the characteristic function to separate the input variables from the output variables.

Then, by inspection, the characteristic function for $\mathcal{A}$ can be expressed in terms of μ_1, μ_2, and μ_3 as follows:

9 $$\mu(u_2^1,y_1^3) = \max_{y_1^1,\, y_2^1,\, y_1^2,\, y_2^2} \min\,[\mu_1(y_1^2,u_2^1;y_1^1,y_2^1),\mu_2(y_1^1,y_1^3;y_1^2,y_2^2),\mu_3(y_2^1,y_2^2;y_1^3)]$$

As was pointed out earlier, this equation is merely a compact expression for the statement "An input-output pair (u_2^1,y_1^3) belongs to $\mathcal{A}$ if and only if there exist y_1^1, y_2^1, y_1^2, and y_2^2 such that $(y_1^2,u_2^1;y_1^1,y_2^1)$, $(y_1^1,y_1^3;y_1^2,y_2^2)$, and $(y_2^1,y_2^2;y_1^3)$ are input-output pairs for $\mathcal{A}_1$, $\mathcal{A}_2$, and $\mathcal{A}_3$, respectively."

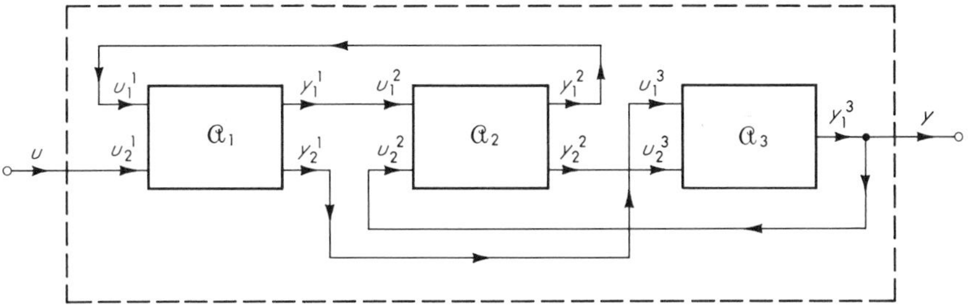

Fig. 1.4.2 Example of a system which is a combination of three component systems $\mathcal{A}_1$, $\mathcal{A}_2$, and $\mathcal{A}_3$.

In the foregoing examples, we assumed that the objects comprising a system are defined by their respective characteristic functions and that the problem is to express the characteristic function of the system in terms of the characteristic functions of its components. The examples show that, in general, the problem of input-output analysis in explicit form is easy to solve, at least on a purely formal level.

Next, let us turn our attention to the case where a system is composed of objects which are defined by their respective input-output relations and the problem is to find an expression for the input-output relation for the system in terms of those of its components. For concreteness, assume that $\mathcal{A}_1$ and $\mathcal{A}_2$ are connected in tandem as in Fig. *1.4.1* and that their respective input-output relations read

10 $\mathcal{A}_1$: $$(p^2 + 3p + 2)y^1 = u^1$$

11 $\mathcal{A}_2$: $$(p + 3)y^2 = pu^2$$

where p denotes the derivative operator d/dt. Then, as is shown in [1], the input-output relation for $\mathcal{A}$ is given by

$$(p + 3)(p^2 + 3p + 2)y^2 = pu^1$$

More generally, if the input-output relations for $\mathcal{A}_1$ and $\mathcal{A}_2$ are of the form

12 $\mathcal{A}_1$: $$L_1(p)y^1 = M_1(p)u^1$$

13 $\mathcal{A}_2$: $$L_2(p)y^2 = M_2(p)u^2$$

where L_1, M_1, L_2, and M_2 are differential operators such that L_1 and M_2 have no factors in common, then it can be proved [1] that the input-output relation for $\mathcal{A}$ is given by

14 $$L_1(p)L_2(p)y^2 = M_1(p)M_2(p)u^1$$

As will be shown in Chap. *5*, the problem of input-output analysis in implicit form can be solved completely when $\mathcal{A}_1, \ldots, \mathcal{A}_N$ are systems whose input-output relations are linear differential equations with constant coefficients. Unfortunately, this is just about the only case in which the problem of input-output analysis in implicit form can be solved analytically. In particular, no analytic procedure is available for the solution of this problem when the input-output relations of $\mathcal{A}_1, \ldots, \mathcal{A}_N$ are linear differential equations with time-varying coefficients. For example, in the case of the tandem combination of Fig. *1.4.1*, suppose that $\mathcal{A}_1$ and $\mathcal{A}_2$ are characterized by input-output relations of the form

15 $\mathcal{A}_1$: $$[a_n^1(t)p^n + \cdots + a_0^1(t)]y^1 = [b_n^1(t)p^n + \cdots + b_0^1(t)]u^1$$

16 $\mathcal{A}_2$: $$[a_n^2(t)p^n + \cdots + a_0^2(t)]y^2 = [b_n^2(t)p^n + \cdots + b_0^2(t)]u^2$$

where the $a_i^1(t)$, $a_i^2(t)$, $b_i^1(t)$, $b_i^2(t)$, $i = 1, \ldots, n$, are specified time-varying coefficients. In this case, there is no general analytic procedure for expressing the input-output relation for $\mathcal{A}$ in the form of a differential equation

17 $$L(p,t)y^2 = M(p,t)u^1$$

where $L(p,t)$ and $M(p,t)$ are polynomials in p with time-varying coefficients.

This concludes our brief discussion of the notion of a system and the problem of input-output analysis. We are now ready to proceed to the definition of the notions of aggregate and state.

5 *Aggregates and states*

Although the notion of state has a long history of use in many fields of science, especially in analytic dynamics, thermodynamics, and quantum mechanics, it is hard to find a definition of it in the scientific literature which does not suffer either from narrowness or imprecision. In what follows, we shall show how the concept of state can be given a precise and yet very general meaning by interpreting it as a tag attached to a subset of input-output pairs in $\mathcal{A}$. The reader must be warned, however, that the naturalness of this point of view will not be apparent in the initial stages of our discussion.

Let $\mathcal{A}$ be a system defined as a set of input-output pairs

$$\mathcal{A} = \{(u,y)\}$$

satisfying the CUS condition (see Sec. *2*). For each t_0, let $\mathcal{A}(t_0)$ denote the subset of $\mathcal{A}$ comprising all input-output pairs which start at t_0, that is,

1 $$\mathcal{A}(t_0) = \{(\mathbf{u}_{[t_0,t]}, \mathbf{y}_{[t_0,t]})\} \qquad t \geq t_0$$

It would be natural to attempt to group together those input-output pairs in $\mathcal{A}(t_0)$ which exhibit a particular characteristic or have some specified property in common. With this in view, let $\mathcal{A}_{\boldsymbol{\alpha}_0}(t_0)$ denote a specified subset of input-output pairs in $\mathcal{A}(t_0)$, with the index $\boldsymbol{\alpha}_0$ serving as an identifying label. For suggestiveness, such a subset will be referred to as a *bundle of input-output pairs* or, simply, a *bundle,* and $\boldsymbol{\alpha}_0$ will be called its *tag.*

To illustrate, consider a system $\mathcal{A}$ defined by the input-output relation

$$\frac{dy}{dt} + y = u$$

By solving this equation for y, we can express $\mathcal{A}(t_0)$ explicitly as

$$\mathcal{A}(t_0) = \{\mathcal{A}_{\alpha_0}(t_0)\}_{\alpha_0} \qquad \alpha_0 \in (-\infty, \infty)$$

where

2 $$\mathcal{A}_{\alpha_0}(t_0) = \left\{u(t),\ \alpha_0 e^{-(t-t_0)} + \int_{t_0}^{t} e^{-(t-\xi)} u(\xi)\, d\xi,\ t \geq t_0\right\}_u$$

and $u(t) \in (-\infty, \infty)$. In this case, for each α_0, *2* defines a bundle of input-output pairs in $\mathcal{A}(t_0)$, with u being the generating variable.

As in the above example, usually our concern will be not with a single bundle $\mathcal{A}_{\boldsymbol{\alpha}_0}(t_0)$, but with a family of bundles, $\{\mathcal{A}_{\boldsymbol{\alpha}_0}(t_0)\}$, for each t_0. Such a family would be generated by permitting $\boldsymbol{\alpha}_0$ to vary over some space Σ_{t_0}. The subscript t_0 in Σ_{t_0} serves to anticipate the possibility that the range of $\boldsymbol{\alpha}_0$ may be dependent on t_0. When Σ_{t_0} is independent of t_0, it will be denoted by Σ.[1]

[1] In terms of the notation described in Notational Preliminaries (Sec. *1*), $\{\mathcal{A}_{\boldsymbol{\alpha}_0}(t_0)\}$ should be interpreted as $\{\mathcal{A}_{\boldsymbol{\alpha}_0}(t_0)\}_{\boldsymbol{\alpha}_0}$, that is, a family of bundles of input-output pairs starting at t_0, with $\boldsymbol{\alpha}_0$ being the generating variable. When both t_0 and $\boldsymbol{\alpha}_0$ are varied, the resulting family of bundles will be denoted by $\{\mathcal{A}_{\boldsymbol{\alpha}_0}(t_0)\}_{\boldsymbol{\alpha}_0, t_0}$. A bundle in this family which comprises input-output pairs starting at, say, t_1, will be denoted by $\mathcal{A}_{\boldsymbol{\alpha}_1}(t_1)$, where $\boldsymbol{\alpha}_1$ is a tag for the bundle in question and $\boldsymbol{\alpha}_1 \in \Sigma_{t_1}$.

To recapitulate, for each t_0 in $(-\infty, \infty)$ we assume that in some as yet unspecified way the input-output pairs in $\mathcal{A}(t_0)$ are grouped (bundled) together on the basis of some property which they have in common. A generic bundle is denoted by $\mathcal{A}_{\boldsymbol{\alpha}_0}(t_0)$, with its identifying tag $\boldsymbol{\alpha}_0$ being an element of a specified space Σ_{t_0}. For each t_0, varying $\boldsymbol{\alpha}_0$ over Σ_{t_0} generates a family of bundles which we denote by $\{\mathcal{A}_{\boldsymbol{\alpha}_0}(t_0)\}$. The members of this family are subsets of input-output pairs in $\mathcal{A}(t_0)$. These subsets need not be disjoint.

So far we have not made any restrictive assumptions regarding the ways in which the input-output pairs in $\mathcal{A}(t_0)$ may be grouped together into bundles. Now, to pave the way for the introduction of the notion of state, we shall focus our attention on a special way of bundling the input-output pairs in $\mathcal{A}(t_0)$. The resulting bundles will be referred to as *aggregates of input-output pairs* or, simply, *aggregates,* and their tags will constitute the *states* of $\mathcal{A}$. As will become more apparent later, the concept of an aggregate is intrinsically more basic than that of state, mainly because a state is merely a tag for an aggregate and as such is less intrinsic in relation to $\mathcal{A}$.

In order to qualify to be called aggregates, the bundles in the family $\{\mathcal{A}_{\boldsymbol{\alpha}_0}(t_0)\}$, $\boldsymbol{\alpha}_0 \in \Sigma_{t_0}$, must satisfy four consistency conditions which are set forth below. The motivation for these conditions will become clear once we have defined the notion of state.

3 **Covering** This condition requires that, for each t_0, the family of bundles $\{\mathcal{A}_{\boldsymbol{\alpha}_0}(t_0)\}_{\boldsymbol{\alpha}_0,t_0}$ be a covering for $\mathcal{A}(t_0)$ in the sense that the subset of input-output pairs starting at t_0, $\mathcal{A}(t_0)$, be the union of the bundles $\{\mathcal{A}_{\boldsymbol{\alpha}_0}(t_0)\}$, $\boldsymbol{\alpha}_0 \in \Sigma_{t_0}$, that is,

4 $$\bigcup_{\boldsymbol{\alpha}_0} \mathcal{A}_{\boldsymbol{\alpha}_0}(t_0) = \mathcal{A}(t_0)$$

The purpose of this condition is to insure that every input-output pair in $\mathcal{A}(t_0)$ belongs to at least one bundle in the family $\{\mathcal{A}_{\boldsymbol{\alpha}_0}(t_0)\}$, $\boldsymbol{\alpha}_0 \in \Sigma_{t_0}$.

5 **Closure under truncation** Let $(\mathbf{u}^0\mathbf{u}^1,\mathbf{y}^0\mathbf{y}^1)$ be an arbitrary input-output pair in $\mathcal{A}(t_0)$, with $(\mathbf{u}^0,\mathbf{y}^0)$ representing a left truncate of $(\mathbf{u}^0\mathbf{u}^1,\mathbf{y}^0\mathbf{y}^1)$.† Then, the condition in question requires that if $(\mathbf{u}^0\mathbf{u}^1,\mathbf{y}^0\mathbf{y}^1)$ is in a bundle $\mathcal{A}_{\boldsymbol{\alpha}_0}(t_0)$, so must be every left truncate of this pair. In symbols

6 $$(\mathbf{u}^0\mathbf{u}^1,\mathbf{y}^0\mathbf{y}^1) \in \mathcal{A}_{\boldsymbol{\alpha}_0}(t_0) \Rightarrow (\mathbf{u}^0,\mathbf{y}^0) \in \mathcal{A}_{\boldsymbol{\alpha}_0}(t_0)$$

for all $(\mathbf{u}^0\mathbf{u}^1,\mathbf{y}^0\mathbf{y}^1) \in \mathcal{A}_{\boldsymbol{\alpha}_0}(t_0)$, all t_0, and all $\boldsymbol{\alpha}_0 \in \Sigma_{t_0}$.

† In accordance with the notation introduced in Sec. *1,* $(\mathbf{u}^0\mathbf{u}^1,\mathbf{y}^0\mathbf{y}^1)$ is an input-output pair comprising an input-output pair $(\mathbf{u}^0,\mathbf{y}^0)$ followed by an input-output pair $(\mathbf{u}^1,\mathbf{y}^1)$. The input-output pairs $(\mathbf{u}^0,\mathbf{y}^0)$ and $(\mathbf{u}^1,\mathbf{y}^1)$ are, respectively, left and right truncates of the input-output pair $(\mathbf{u}^0\mathbf{u}^1,\mathbf{y}^0\mathbf{y}^1)$.

7 **Uniqueness** By analogy with the domain and range of a system (see Sec. *2*), we can define the domain and range of a bundle of input-output pairs $\mathcal{A}_{\boldsymbol{\alpha}_0}(t_0)$ as the sets

8 $$\mathcal{D}(\mathcal{A}_{\boldsymbol{\alpha}_0}(t_0)) \triangleq \{\mathbf{u}|(\mathbf{u},\mathbf{y}) \in \mathcal{A}_{\boldsymbol{\alpha}_0}(t_0)\}$$

and

9 $$\mathcal{R}(\mathcal{A}_{\boldsymbol{\alpha}_0}(t_0)) \triangleq \{\mathbf{y}|(\mathbf{u},\mathbf{y}) \in \mathcal{A}_{\boldsymbol{\alpha}_0}(t_0)\}$$

The uniqueness condition requires that to each input $\mathbf{u}$ in $\mathcal{D}(\mathcal{A}_{\boldsymbol{\alpha}_0}(t_0))$ correspond a unique $\mathbf{y}$ in $\mathcal{R}(\mathcal{A}_{\boldsymbol{\alpha}_0}(t_0))$. Equivalently, this condition may be expressed compactly by the implication

10 $$\{(\mathbf{u},\mathbf{y}) \in \mathcal{A}_{\boldsymbol{\alpha}_0}(t_0) \text{ and } (\mathbf{u},\mathbf{y}') \in \mathcal{A}_{\boldsymbol{\alpha}_0}(t_0)\} \Rightarrow \mathbf{y} = \mathbf{y}'$$

If the uniqueness condition is satisfied, then $\mathbf{y}$ can be expressed as a function of the input $\mathbf{u}$ and $\boldsymbol{\alpha}_0$, with the latter identifying the bundle $\mathcal{A}_{\boldsymbol{\alpha}_0}(t_0)$ to which $(\mathbf{u},\mathbf{y})$ belongs. We shall express this by writing

11 $$\mathbf{y} = \bar{A}(\boldsymbol{\alpha}_0;\mathbf{u})$$

where $\bar{A}$ is a function from $\Sigma_{t_0} \times \mathcal{D}(\mathcal{A}_{\boldsymbol{\alpha}_0}(t_0))$ to $\mathcal{R}(\mathcal{A}_{\boldsymbol{\alpha}_0}(t_0))$. Later on, this equation will be referred to as an *input-output-state relation* for $\mathcal{A}$.

12 **Continuation** Let $(\mathbf{u}^0,\mathbf{y}^0)$ be an input-output pair in $\mathcal{A}_{\boldsymbol{\alpha}_0}(t_0)$ over an interval $[t_0,t_1]$, and let $(\mathbf{u}^1,\mathbf{y}^1)$ be an input-output pair in $\mathcal{A}(t_1)$ over an interval $[t_1,t]$. As in Sec. *2*, the input-output pair $(\mathbf{u}^1,\mathbf{y}^1)$ will be said to be a *continuation* of $(\mathbf{u}^0,\mathbf{y}^0)$ in $\mathcal{A}_{\boldsymbol{\alpha}_0}(t_0)$ if the input-output pair $(\mathbf{u}^0\mathbf{u}^1,\mathbf{y}^0\mathbf{y}^1)$ is in $\mathcal{A}_{\boldsymbol{\alpha}_0}(t_0)$. In effect, $(\mathbf{u}^1,\mathbf{y}^1)$ is merely a right truncate of an input-output pair in $\mathcal{A}_{\boldsymbol{\alpha}_0}(t_0)$.

The continuation condition requires that the set of all continuations of $(\mathbf{u}^0,\mathbf{y}^0)$ in $\mathcal{A}_{\boldsymbol{\alpha}_0}(t_0)$ be a bundle of input-output pairs in the family $\{\mathcal{A}_{\boldsymbol{\alpha}_0}(t_0)\}_{\boldsymbol{\alpha}_0,t_0}$. If the tag of this bundle is denoted by $\boldsymbol{\alpha}_1$ (with $\boldsymbol{\alpha}_1 \in \Sigma_{t_1}$), then the condition in question can be expressed as the equality

13 $$\{(\mathbf{u}^1,\mathbf{y}^1)|(\mathbf{u}^0\mathbf{u}^1,\mathbf{y}^0\mathbf{y}^1) \in \mathcal{A}_{\boldsymbol{\alpha}_0}(t_0)\} = \mathcal{A}_{\boldsymbol{\alpha}_1}(t_1)$$

which should hold for all t_0 in R^1, all $\boldsymbol{\alpha}_0$ in Σ_{t_0}, all $(\mathbf{u}^0,\mathbf{y}^0)$ in $\mathcal{A}_{\boldsymbol{\alpha}_0}(t_0)$, and all $t_1 \geq t_0$, $t \geq t_1$ (see Fig. *1.5.1*).

To illustrate the four consistency conditions stated above, consider the time-invariant finite-state system defined in Example *1.2.9*, and assume that for each t_0, $t_0 = \ldots, -1, 0, 1, \ldots$, the input-output pairs of length $l \leq 3$ are bundled together into three groups indexed by I, II and III, that is, $\Sigma_{t_0} = \{\text{I},\text{II},\text{III}\}$, independent of t_0. The members of the three bundles $\mathcal{A}_{\text{I}}$, $\mathcal{A}_{\text{II}}$, and $\mathcal{A}_{\text{III}}$ [with t_0 omitted as argument in $\mathcal{A}_{\text{I}}(t_0)$, $\mathcal{A}_{\text{II}}(t_0)$, and $\mathcal{A}_{\text{III}}(t_0)$ because the bundles are the same for all t_0] are tabulated in Table *1.5.1*.

It is easy to verify by exhaustive testing that this bundling of input-output pairs of length ≤ 3 satisfies the four consistency conditions. Specifically, for $l \leq 3$

1. The covering condition is satisfied because the union of $\mathcal{a}_{\mathrm{I}}$, $\mathcal{a}_{\mathrm{II}}$, and $\mathcal{a}_{\mathrm{III}}$ is $\mathcal{a}$.
2. The closure under truncation condition is satisfied because the left truncates of every input-output pair in each bundle are in the same bundle. For example, the left truncates of (000,*bab*), which belongs to $\mathcal{a}_{\mathrm{I}}$, are (0,*b*) and (00,*ba*), both of which belong to $\mathcal{a}_{\mathrm{I}}$.

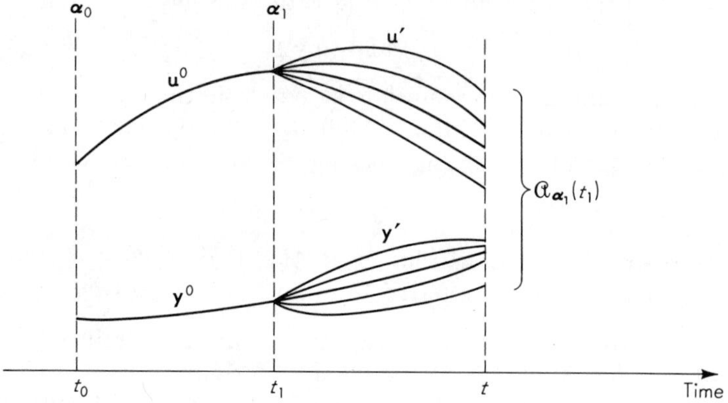

Fig. 1.5.1 Illustration of the continuation condition.

Table 1.5.1

I	II	III
(0,*b*)	(0,*a*)	(0,*a*)
(1,*b*)	(1,*a*)	(1,*b*)
(00,*ba*)	(00,*ab*)	(00,*ab*)
(01,*ba*)	(01,*ab*)	(01,*ab*)
(10,*ba*)	(10,*aa*)	(10,*ba*)
(11,*bb*)	(11,*ab*)	(11,*ba*)
(000,*bab*)	(000,*aba*)	(000,*aba*)
(001,*bab*)	(001,*aba*)	(001,*aba*)
(010,*baa*)	(010,*aba*)	(010,*aba*)
(011,*bab*)	(011,*abb*)	(011,*abb*)
(100,*bab*)	(100,*aab*)	(100,*bab*)
(101,*bab*)	(101,*aab*)	(101,*bab*)
(110,*bba*)	(110,*aba*)	(110,*baa*)
(111,*bba*)	(111,*aba*)	(111,*bab*)

3. The uniqueness condition is satisfied because, in each bundle, to every input sequence of length ≤ 3 corresponds a unique response. For example, for input-output pairs in $\mathcal{A}_{\mathrm{I}}$, to the input (000) corresponds a unique response *bab*. Likewise, for input-output pairs in $\mathcal{A}_{\mathrm{II}}$, to the input (000) corresponds a unique response (*aba*). The same is true for all input-output pairs in each bundle.

4. As an example of how the continuation condition is checked, consider an input-output pair such as $(0,b)$ in $\mathcal{A}_{\mathrm{I}}$. By inspection, the continuations (of length ≤ 2) of this input-output pair in $\mathcal{A}_{\mathrm{I}}$ are found to be:

14
$$\begin{array}{c}(0,a)\\(1,a)\\(00,ab)\\(01,ab)\\(10,aa)\\(11,ab)\end{array}$$

which are members of $\mathcal{A}_{\mathrm{II}}$. In a similar fashion, we can verify that the set of all continuations of $(0,b)$ in $\mathcal{A}_{\mathrm{I}}$ coincides with $\mathcal{A}_{\mathrm{II}}$.

An additional illustration of the four consistency conditions is provided by the following

15 *Example* Let $\mathcal{A}$ be a time-invariant system defined as a family, $\{\mathcal{A}_{\alpha_0}(t_0)\}$, of bundles of input-output pairs

16
$$\mathcal{A}_{\alpha_0}(t_0) = \{[u(t),y(t)],\ t \geq t_0\}$$

where

17
$$y(t) = \alpha_0 e^{-(t-t_0)} + \int_{t_0}^{t} e^{-(t-\xi)} u(\xi)\, d\xi$$

in which α_0 ranges over $(-\infty,\infty)$. Thus $\Sigma_{t_0} = (-\infty,\infty)$.

In this case, the covering, uniqueness, and closure under truncation conditions are satisfied by the definition of $\mathcal{A}$. To verify that the continuation condition is satisfied, let us pick an input-output pair in $\mathcal{A}_{\alpha_0}(t_0)$, say, $(u^0(t),y^0(t))$, $t_0 \leq t \leq t_1$, and demonstrate that the set of all of its continuations in $\mathcal{A}_{\alpha_0}(t_0)$ coincides with $\mathcal{A}_{\alpha_1}(t_1)$ for some α_1 in $(-\infty,\infty)$.

Specifically, let (u^1,y^1) be a continuation of (u^0,y^0) in $\mathcal{A}_{\alpha_0}(t_0)$. Then, since $(u^0u^1,y^0y^1) \in \mathcal{A}_{\alpha_0}(t_0)$, we must have

18
$$y^1(t) = \alpha_0 e^{-(t-t_0)} + \int_{t_0}^{t} e^{-(t-\xi)} u(\xi)\, d\xi \qquad t \geq t_1$$

Now, $y^1(t)$ as given by *18* can be rewritten successively as

19 $$y^1(t) = \alpha_0 e^{-(t-t_0)} + \int_{t_0}^{t_1} e^{-(t-\xi)} u^0(\xi)\, d\xi + \int_{t_1}^{t} e^{-(t-\xi)} u^1(\xi)\, d\xi \qquad t \geq t_1$$

$$= \alpha_0 e^{-(t-t_0)} + e^{-(t-t_1)} \int_{t_0}^{t_1} e^{-(t_1-\xi)} u^0(\xi)\, d\xi + \int_{t_1}^{t} e^{-(t-\xi)} u^1(\xi)\, d\xi \qquad t \geq t_1$$

20 $$= \alpha_1 e^{-(t-t_1)} + \int_{t_1}^{t} e^{-(t-\xi)} u^1(\xi)\, d\xi \qquad t \geq t_1$$

where

21 $$\alpha_1 = \alpha_0 e^{-(t-t_0)} + \int_{t_0}^{t_1} e^{-(t_1-\xi)} u^0(\xi)\, d\xi$$

From inspection of *20*, it follows at once that the set of all continuations of (u^0,y^0) in $\mathcal{A}_{\alpha_0}(t_0)$, that is,

22 $$\{(u^1(t),y^1(t)),\ t \geq t_1 | (u^0u^1,y^0y^1) \in \mathcal{A}_{\alpha_0}(t_0)\}$$

coincides with $\mathcal{A}_{\alpha_1}(t_1)$, and hence that the continuation condition is satisfied by the input-output pairs defined by *16*.

Aggregates and states

Our main purpose in introducing the notion of a bundle of input-output pairs and in formulating a set of consistency conditions which families of such bundles must satisfy was to set the stage for defining the aggregates and states of a system in terms of its input-output pairs. We are now in a position to do this concisely and in a way which adds considerable insight to the meaning of the concept of state and its basic properties.

23 **Definition** Let a system $\mathcal{A}$ be defined as a collection of input-output pairs

24 $$\mathcal{A} = \{(\mathbf{u},\mathbf{y})\}$$

satisfying the CUS condition (see Sec. *2*). Let $\{\mathcal{A}_{\alpha_0}(t_0)\}_{\boldsymbol{\alpha}_0,t_0}$ be a family of bundles of input-output pairs satisfying the covering *3*, closure under truncation *5*, uniqueness *7*, and continuation *12* conditions. Such a family will be said to be *consistent*, and a bundle $\mathcal{A}_{\boldsymbol{\alpha}_0}(t_0)$ in a consistent family will be said to be an *aggregate*.

25 **Definition** Let $\mathcal{A}_{\alpha_0}(t_0)$ be an aggregate in $\mathcal{A}$ at time t_0. The identifying tag $\boldsymbol{\alpha}_0$ of $\mathcal{A}_{\boldsymbol{\alpha}_0}(t_0)$ is a *state of* $\mathcal{A}$ *at time* t_0. The range of $\boldsymbol{\alpha}_0$, Σ_{t_0} is the *state space of* $\mathcal{A}$ *at time* t_0. When Σ_{t_0} is independent of t_0—as is usually the case—it is denoted by Σ and is referred to more simply as the *state space of* $\mathcal{A}$.

When necessary to place in evidence the dependence of state on time, we shall denote it as $\mathbf{x}(t)$ or $\mathbf{x}_t$, according as t ranges over $(-\infty,\infty)$

or the set of integers. Thus, it will be understood that, for each t_0, $\mathbf{x}(t_0)$ is a variable ranging over Σ_{t_0}, with $\boldsymbol{\alpha}_0$ representing a generic value of $\mathbf{x}(t_0)$. On occasion, $\boldsymbol{\alpha}_0$ or $\mathbf{x}(t_0)$ will be referred to as the *initial state* of $\mathcal{A}$ at time t_0 in order to differentiate it from a state of $\mathcal{A}$ at some subsequent time t.

26 *Comment* The definition of a state of a system $\mathcal{A}$ as a tag for an aggregate in $\mathcal{A}$ underscores the fact that the states of $\mathcal{A}$ do not have a unique identity and have much less intrinsic connection with $\mathcal{A}$ than the aggregates in $\mathcal{A}$. This, however, naturally raises the question: Are the aggregates in $\mathcal{A}$ uniquely determined by the four consistency conditions *3*, *5*, *7*, and *12*? It can be shown that this question can be answered affirmatively for certain classes of systems, e.g., systems whose input-output relations have the form of linear differential equations with constant coefficients (Theorem *3.9.1* in [1]). An example to the contrary is furnished by the two finite-state systems shown in Fig. *1.3.2*. In this case, $\mathcal{A}$ and $\mathcal{B}$ have the same set of input-output pairs but not the same family of aggregates. In the terminology of finite-state systems, $\mathcal{B}$ is not strongly connected, that is, it contains states (state *3′*) which are not reachable from other states (*1′* and *2′*). If the aggregates were required to be reachable from one another [in the sense that for each $\boldsymbol{\alpha}_0$ and each $\boldsymbol{\alpha}_1$ there exists $\mathbf{u}_{[t_0,t_1]}$ such that $\mathcal{A}_{\boldsymbol{\alpha}_1}(t_1)$ is the set of all continuations of $(\mathbf{u}_{[t_0,t_1]},\mathbf{y}_{[t_0,t_1]})$ in $\mathcal{A}_{\boldsymbol{\alpha}_0}(t_0)$], then the family of aggregates would be uniquely determined by the four consistency conditions.

Input-output-state relations

In consequence of the uniqueness condition, to each $\mathbf{u}$ in the domain of an aggregate $\mathcal{A}_{\boldsymbol{\alpha}_0}(t_0)$ corresponds a unique $\mathbf{y}$ in its range. Thus, for any input-output pair in $\mathcal{A}_{\boldsymbol{\alpha}_0}(t_0)$ we can write

27 $$\mathbf{y} = \bar{\mathbf{A}}(\boldsymbol{\alpha}_0;\mathbf{u})$$

or equivalently

28 $$\mathbf{y} = \bar{\mathbf{A}}(\mathbf{x}(t_0);\mathbf{u})$$

where $\bar{\mathbf{A}}$ is a function from $\Sigma_{t_0} \times \mathcal{D}(\mathcal{A}_{\boldsymbol{\alpha}_0}(t_0))$ to $\mathcal{R}(\mathcal{A}_{\boldsymbol{\alpha}_0}(t_0))$. In view of their form, these relations will be referred to as the *input-output-state relations* for $\mathcal{A}$.

It should be noted that an input-output-state relation expresses an output segment $\mathbf{y}$ as a function of initial state $\boldsymbol{\alpha}_0$ and an input segment $\mathbf{u}$. Since there is no convenient way of expressing a segment of a time function as a function of other time functions, the information provided by an input-output-state relation will usually be presented in the form of an equation

29 $$\mathbf{y}(t) = \mathbf{A}(\mathbf{x}(t_0);\mathbf{u})$$

in which $\mathbf{y}(t)$, rather than $\mathbf{y}$, is expressed as a function of $\mathbf{x}(t_0)$ and $\mathbf{u}$. Like *27* and *28*, this equation will be referred to as an input-output-state relation. It is important to observe that when $\mathcal{A}$ is defined by an input-output relation having the form of a differential or difference equation, *29* expresses the general solution of such an equation, with $\mathbf{x}(t_0)$ representing the initial conditions.

Having defined the states of $\mathcal{A}$, we are now in a position to see more clearly the motivation for the less obvious consistency conditions imposed on the bundles of input-output pairs of $\mathcal{A}$. Specifically, the uniqueness condition *7* serves to insure that if $\mathcal{A}$ is initially (at t_0) in some state $\boldsymbol{\alpha}_0$, then the response of $\mathcal{A}$ to any given input $\mathbf{u}$ in $\mathfrak{D}(\mathcal{A}_{\boldsymbol{\alpha}_0}(t_0))$ is uniquely determined by that input and $\boldsymbol{\alpha}_0$ through the input-output-state relation *27*. This, of course, expresses a key property of the notion of a state of a system, viz., that the knowledge of state at time t_0 is sufficient to determine the response of the system to any input starting at time t_0. In other words, the state of a system contains all the information about its past history that is relevant to the prediction of its future behavior.

The continuation condition has the following interpretation. Suppose that $\mathcal{A}$ is initially (at t_0) in some state $\boldsymbol{\alpha}_0$ and that an input $\mathbf{u}^0$, $\mathbf{u}^0 \triangleq \mathbf{u}_{[t_0,t_1]}$ is applied to $\mathcal{A}$. Then at time t_1, $\mathcal{A}$ will be in a state $\boldsymbol{\alpha}_1$ which defines uniquely an aggregate $\mathcal{A}_{\boldsymbol{\alpha}_1}(t_1)$. Thus, $\boldsymbol{\alpha}_1$ can be regarded as the initial state (at time t_1) for any input starting at t_1. We shall say that $\boldsymbol{\alpha}_0$ is *taken by* $\mathbf{u}^0$ into $\boldsymbol{\alpha}_1$.

The above interpretation contains an important conclusion, namely, that $\mathcal{A}_{\boldsymbol{\alpha}_1}(t_1)$ is uniquely determined by $\boldsymbol{\alpha}_0$ and $\mathbf{u}^0$. This does not imply that $\boldsymbol{\alpha}_1$ is uniquely determined by $\boldsymbol{\alpha}_0$ and $\mathbf{u}^0$ since each bundle may be tagged in a number of different ways. However, as will be seen in Sec. *6*, all such tags are equivalent to one another. Consequently, $\boldsymbol{\alpha}_1$ is uniquely determined, to within equivalent states (see *1.6.1*), by $\boldsymbol{\alpha}_0$ and $\mathbf{u}^0$. In a general form, this will be expressed by the equation

30 $$\mathbf{x}(t) = \mathbf{F}(\mathbf{x}(t_0);\mathbf{u}_{[t_0,t_1]})$$

which will be referred to as a *state equation* for $\mathcal{A}$. In this equation, $\mathbf{F}$ is a function from $\Sigma_{t_0} \times \mathfrak{D}(\mathcal{A}_{\boldsymbol{\alpha}_0}(t_0))$ to Σ_t which expresses the state at time t in terms of the state at time t_0 and the input segment over the interval $[t_0,t]$.

To illustrate the notions introduced in the foregoing discussion, it will be helpful to consider two examples which were employed previously, namely, Example *1.2.9* and Example *1.5.15*.

In Example *1.2.9*, it is easy to verify by inspection of $\mathcal{A}_{\mathrm{I}}$, $\mathcal{A}_{\mathrm{II}}$, and $\mathcal{A}_{\mathrm{III}}$ that these aggregates comprise, respectively, input-output pairs starting in nodes I, II, and III. For example, the input-output pair (010,*baa*) in $\mathcal{A}_{\mathrm{I}}$ results from applying 0 starting in node I—which yields *b* and leads to node II; then applying 1 starting in node II—which yields *a* and leads to node III; and then applying 0 starting in node III—which yields *a* and leads to node I. In short, the input-output pair (010,*baa*) results from applying the input sequence 010 starting in node I—which yields the output sequence *baa* and leads to node I.

Combining this observation with the fact that $\mathcal{A}_{\mathrm{I}}$, $\mathcal{A}_{\mathrm{II}}$, and $\mathcal{A}_{\mathrm{III}}$ have been verified to be aggregates of input-output pairs of $\mathcal{A}$, it follows that the tags I, II, and III, which represent the nodes of the graph defining $\mathcal{A}$ (Fig. *1.2.2*), constitute the states of $\mathcal{A}$. From the graph, it follows at once that if the state of $\mathcal{A}$ at time t is denoted by x_t, then we can write

31 $$x_{t+1} = f(x_t,u_t) \qquad t = \ldots, -1, 0, 1, \ldots$$

32 $$y_t = g(x_t,u_t)$$

where f and g are tabulated below

33

u_t \ x_t	I	II	III
0	II	I	I
1	III	III	II

34

u_t \ x_t	I	II	III
0	*b*	*a*	*a*
1	*b*	*a*	*b*

By iteration, *31* can be used to yield an expression for x_t, $t \geq t_0$, in terms of x_{t_0} and $u_{t_0}, \ldots, u_{t-1}$. Thus,

35 $$x_t = f(f(\ldots,f(f(x_{t_0},u_{t_0}),u_{t_0+1}), \ldots, u_{t-1}))$$

which is a state equation for $\mathcal{A}$ in the sense of *30*. Then, on substituting this expression into *32*, we have

36 $$y_t = g(f(\ldots,f(f(x_{t_0},u_{t_0}),u_{t_0+1}), \ldots, u_{t-1}),u_t)$$

which is an input-output-state relation for $\mathcal{A}$. Thus, in combination, equations of the form *31* and *32* completely define a finite-state system and place in evidence its states and aggregates.

It should be noted that, in the literature of finite-state systems, it is customary to define a time-invariant finite-state system as a triple of finite sets U (range of u_t), Y (range of y_t), and Σ (range of x_t), and the pair of functions f and g defined by *31* and *32*. Thus, what is the point of departure in the conventional approach is a terminal point in the approach used in this chapter.

Turning to Example *15*, we note that in this case the input-output state relation *29* reads

37 $$y(t) = x(t_0)e^{-(t-t_0)} + \int_{t_0}^{t} e^{-(t-\xi)}u(\xi)\,d\xi \qquad t \geq t_0$$

This equation is obtained from the definition of $\mathcal{A}_{\alpha_0}(t_0)$ (see *16*) merely by replacing α_0 with $x(t_0)$ in *17*.

From *21*, it follows that the state equation *30* can be expressed in the explicit form

38 $$x(t) = x(t_0)e^{-(t-t_0)} + \int_{t_0}^{t} e^{-(t-\xi)}u(\xi)\,d\xi \qquad t \geq t_0$$

Note that in the example under consideration $y(t) = x(t)$ for all t. More generally, the output at time t is a function of the input at time t and the state at time t, that is,

39 $$y(t) = g(x(t),u(t),t)$$

This equation results from *29* by letting $t_0 = t$ in the input-output-state relation. Conversely, the input-output-state relation can be obtained from *39* by combining *39* with the state equation *30*, that is, by substituting the right-hand member of *30* in place of $\mathbf{x}(t)$ in *39*, yielding

40 $$\mathbf{y}(t) = \mathbf{g}(\mathbf{F}(\mathbf{x}(t_0);\mathbf{u}_{[t_0,t]}),\mathbf{u}(t),t)$$

which expresses $\mathbf{y}(t)$ as a function of $\mathbf{x}(t_0)$ and $\mathbf{u}_{[t_0,t]}$.

6 *State and system equivalence*

The preceding sections were devoted in the main to the introduction of three basic concepts: System, aggregate, and state. In essence, we have defined a system as a collection of input-output pairs; we have defined an aggregate as a bundle of input-output pairs satisfying certain consistency conditions; and we have defined a state as a tag attached to an aggregate.

As was pointed out earlier, since a state is merely a tag or a name for an aggregate, it is not as intrinsic a concept as that of an aggregate, in the sense that the same aggregate can be described by a variety of different tags whereas to each tag will correspond but one aggregate. These considerations motivate the following definition of state equivalence.

1 **Definition** Let $\boldsymbol{\alpha}_0^1$ and $\boldsymbol{\alpha}_0^2$ denote two states in Σ_{t_0}. Then $\boldsymbol{\alpha}_0^1$ and $\boldsymbol{\alpha}_0^2$ will be said to be *equivalent at* t_0, written as $\boldsymbol{\alpha}_0^1 \simeq \boldsymbol{\alpha}_0^2$, if and only if they are tags for the same aggregate, that is,

2
$$\mathcal{A}_{\boldsymbol{\alpha}_0^1}(t_0) = \mathcal{A}_{\boldsymbol{\alpha}_0^2}(t_0)$$

The conventional definition of equivalent states (see Ref. 1, p. 71) is somewhat less general than the above definition; it corresponds to making the following simplifying assumptions concerning $\mathcal{A}$.

Let $\mathfrak{D}(\mathcal{A}_{\boldsymbol{\alpha}_0}(t_0))$ denote the domain of the relation $\mathcal{A}_{\boldsymbol{\alpha}_0}(t_0)$, that is,

3
$$\mathfrak{D}(\mathcal{A}_{\boldsymbol{\alpha}_0}(t_0)) \triangleq \{\mathbf{u} | (\mathbf{u},\mathbf{y}) \in \mathcal{A}_{\boldsymbol{\alpha}_0}(t_0)\}$$

If $\mathcal{A}$ is such that $\mathfrak{D}(\mathcal{A}_{\boldsymbol{\alpha}_0}(t_0))$ is independent of both $\boldsymbol{\alpha}_0$ and t_0,† then $\mathfrak{D}(\mathcal{A}_{\boldsymbol{\alpha}_0}(t_0))$ will be denoted more simply by $\mathfrak{U}$ and will be called the *input-function space* of $\mathcal{A}$. Thus,

4
$$\mathfrak{U} \triangleq \{\mathbf{u} | (\mathbf{u},\mathbf{y}) \in \mathcal{A}_{\boldsymbol{\alpha}_0}(t_0)\} \qquad \text{independent of } \boldsymbol{\alpha}_0 \text{ and } t_0$$

If $\mathcal{A}$ has an input-function space, then the definition of equivalent states *2* can be replaced by the simpler definition

5
$$\{\boldsymbol{\alpha}^1 \simeq \boldsymbol{\alpha}^2\} \Leftrightarrow \{\forall \mathbf{u}[\bar{A}(\boldsymbol{\alpha}^1;\mathbf{u}) = \bar{A}(\boldsymbol{\alpha}^2;\mathbf{u})]\} \qquad \mathbf{u} \in \mathfrak{U}$$

where $\bar{A}(\boldsymbol{\alpha};\mathbf{u})$ and $\bar{A}(\boldsymbol{\alpha}^2;\mathbf{u})$ denote, respectively, the responses of $\mathcal{A}$ to $\mathbf{u}$ starting in states $\boldsymbol{\alpha}^1$ and $\boldsymbol{\alpha}^2$. In words, *5* means that $\boldsymbol{\alpha}^1$ and $\boldsymbol{\alpha}^2$ are equivalent states of $\mathcal{A}$ if and only if for all inputs $\mathbf{u}$ in $\mathfrak{U}$ the response of $\mathcal{A}$ to $\mathbf{u}$ starting in state $\boldsymbol{\alpha}^2$ is identical with the response of $\mathcal{A}$ to $\mathbf{u}$ starting in state $\boldsymbol{\alpha}^1$.

The same concept of equivalence applies when we speak of a state $\boldsymbol{\alpha}$ of a system $\mathcal{A}$ as being equivalent to a state $\boldsymbol{\beta}$ of a system $\mathcal{B}$. In this case

6
$$\{\boldsymbol{\alpha} \simeq \boldsymbol{\beta}\} \Leftrightarrow \{\forall \mathbf{u}[\bar{\mathbf{A}}(\boldsymbol{\alpha};\mathbf{u}) = \bar{\mathbf{B}}(\boldsymbol{\beta};\mathbf{u})]\}$$

where $\bar{\mathbf{B}}[\boldsymbol{\beta};\mathbf{u}]$ denotes the response of $\mathcal{B}$ to $\mathbf{u}$ starting in state $\boldsymbol{\beta}$.

7 *Example* Consider the two systems of Example *1.3.3*, for which the respective input-output-state relations read

$$\mathcal{A}: \qquad y(t) = \alpha + \int_{t_0}^{t} u(\xi)\, d\xi$$

$$\mathcal{B}: \qquad y(t) = \beta_0 + \beta_1(t - t_0) + \int_{t_0}^{t} u(\xi)\, d\xi$$

† Note that $\mathfrak{D}(\mathcal{A}_{\boldsymbol{\alpha}_0}(t_0))$ is independent of t_0 if $\mathcal{A}$ is time-invariant. However, this is not a necessary condition.

In this case, the state $\alpha = 0$ of $\mathfrak{A}$ is equivalent to the state $\boldsymbol{\beta} = (0,0)$ $[\boldsymbol{\beta} \triangleq (\beta_0,\beta_1)]$ of $\mathfrak{B}$.

8 *Example* Consider the finite-state systems $\mathfrak{A}$ and $\mathfrak{B}$ shown in Fig. *1.3.1*. Here it is obvious by inspection that $1 \simeq 1'$ and $2 \simeq 2'$. On the other hand, the state $3'$ of $\mathfrak{B}$ has no equivalent in $\mathfrak{A}$.

9 **Strong equivalence** In Sec. *3* two systems $\mathfrak{A}$ and $\mathfrak{B}$ were defined to be equivalent, written as $\mathfrak{A} = \mathfrak{B}$, if $\mathfrak{A} = \mathfrak{B}$ in the set-theoretic sense, that is, if every input-output pair belonging to $\mathfrak{A}$ also belongs to $\mathfrak{B}$ and vice versa. As was pointed out, if $\mathfrak{A} = \mathfrak{B}$, then $\mathfrak{A}$ and $\mathfrak{B}$ are indistinguishable by a simple experiment.

There are many cases in which a stronger concept of equivalence, namely one in which $\mathfrak{A}$ and $\mathfrak{B}$ are indistinguishable by any multiple experiment, is more appropriate. A convenient way of expressing strong equivalence of $\mathfrak{A}$ and $\mathfrak{B}$ is contained in the following definition.

10 **Definition** $\mathfrak{A}$ and $\mathfrak{B}$ are *strongly equivalent*, written as $\mathfrak{A} \equiv \mathfrak{B}$, if and only if, for each t_0, to every state $\boldsymbol{\alpha}$ in the state space of $\mathfrak{A}$ there is an equivalent state $\boldsymbol{\beta}$ in the state space of $\mathfrak{B}$ and vice versa. In symbols, if the responses of $\mathfrak{A}$ and $\mathfrak{B}$ to an input $\mathbf{u}$ starting in states $\boldsymbol{\alpha}$ and $\boldsymbol{\beta}$ at time t_0 are denoted by $\bar{A}(\boldsymbol{\alpha};\mathbf{u})$ and $\bar{B}(\boldsymbol{\beta};\mathbf{u})$, respectively, then we can write compactly

11
$$\mathfrak{A} \equiv \mathfrak{B} \Leftrightarrow \forall\boldsymbol{\alpha}\exists\boldsymbol{\beta}\forall\mathbf{u}\forall t_0[\bar{A}(\boldsymbol{\alpha};\mathbf{u}) = \bar{B}(\boldsymbol{\beta};\mathbf{u})]$$
and
$$\forall\boldsymbol{\beta}\exists\boldsymbol{\alpha}\forall\mathbf{u}\forall t_0[\bar{A}(\boldsymbol{\alpha};\mathbf{u}) = \bar{B}(\boldsymbol{\beta};\mathbf{u})]$$

In similar symbols, the expression for the definition of equivalence becomes

12
$$\mathfrak{A} = \mathfrak{B} \Leftrightarrow \forall\boldsymbol{\alpha}\forall\mathbf{u}\forall t_0\exists\boldsymbol{\beta}[\bar{A}(\boldsymbol{\alpha};\mathbf{u}) = \bar{B}(\boldsymbol{\beta};\mathbf{u})]$$
and
$$\forall\boldsymbol{\beta}\forall\mathbf{u}\forall t_0\exists\boldsymbol{\alpha}[\bar{A}(\boldsymbol{\alpha};\mathbf{u}) = \bar{B}(\boldsymbol{\beta};\mathbf{u})]$$

Note that the only difference between *11* and *12* stems from the difference in the orders of quantifiers. Thus, in the case of equivalence, the state $\boldsymbol{\beta}$ in *12* depends on $\boldsymbol{\alpha}$, $\mathbf{u}$, and t_0, whereas in the case of strong equivalence, $\boldsymbol{\beta}$ in *11* depends only on $\boldsymbol{\alpha}$.

The notions of equivalence and strong equivalence are of central importance in system theory. A detailed discussion of the properties and consequences of these notions is presented in [1]. Here we shall restrict ourselves to a few comments centering on the role of the notion of state in system equivalence.

First, we observe that the notion of equivalence is independent of the notion of state whereas that of strong equivalence is not. This implies that the equivalence of $\mathcal{A}$ and $\mathcal{B}$ does not imply that $\mathcal{A}$ and $\mathcal{B}$ are strongly equivalent, although the reverse is clearly true, that is, $\mathcal{A} \equiv \mathcal{B} \Rightarrow \mathcal{A} = \mathcal{B}$. Essentially, this means that the indistinguishability of $\mathcal{A}$ and $\mathcal{B}$ under a single experiment does not imply their indistinguishability under a multiple experiment.

To illustrate, consider the finite-states system shown in Fig. *1.3.2*. It is easy to verify by inspection that every input-output pair of $\mathcal{A}$ is also an input-output pair for $\mathcal{B}$, and vice versa. On the other hand, the state $3'$ of $\mathcal{B}$ is clearly not equivalent to any state of $\mathcal{A}$. Hence, $\mathcal{A}$ and $\mathcal{B}$ are not strongly equivalent.

While it is not true in general that $\mathcal{A} = \mathcal{B} \Rightarrow \mathcal{A} \equiv \mathcal{B}$, there are types of systems for which equivalence implies strong equivalence. Among such systems [1] are strongly connected finite-state systems and differential systems of finite order. Note that the system $\mathcal{B}$ in Fig. *1.3.2* is not strongly connected, since state $3'$ in $\mathcal{B}$ is not reachable from other states.

7 *Association of states with a system*

In this section, we shall focus our attention on the following basic problem: Suppose that a system $\mathcal{A}$ is defined as a set of input-output pairs,

1 $$\mathcal{A} = \{(\mathbf{u},\mathbf{y})\}$$

possibly, but not necessarily, through an input-output relation. If we can find a family of bundles $\{\mathcal{A}_{\boldsymbol{\alpha}_0}(t_0)\}_{\boldsymbol{\alpha}_0,t_0}$ satisfying the conditions of covering, closure under left truncation, uniqueness, and continuation, then, as shown in Sec. *5*, the tags $\{\boldsymbol{\alpha}_0\}$ of aggregates $\{\mathcal{A}_{\boldsymbol{\alpha}_0}(t_0)\}$ are the states of $\mathcal{A}$ and the relation

2 $$\mathbf{y}(t) = \mathbf{A}(\boldsymbol{\alpha}_0;\mathbf{u}_{[t_0,t]})$$

is an input-output-state relation for $\mathcal{A}$. The problem is: How can one find a family of bundles satisfying these conditions, i.e., a family of aggregates of $\mathcal{A}$? Since the states of $\mathcal{A}$ are the tags of its aggregates, we shall refer to this problem as the problem of *associating states with a system*.

The association of states with a system $\mathcal{A}$ which is defined as a collection of input-output pairs results in a *system with a state structure*, or SSS, for short, which is characterized by the input-output-state relation *2* and which is equivalent to $\mathcal{A}$ in the sense of *1.3.8*. It is important to note, however, that if $\mathcal{A}_\sigma$ is an SSS which corresponds to a particular aggregation of input-output pairs in $\mathcal{A}$ and if $\mathcal{A}_\lambda$ is another such SSS which corresponds to a different mode of aggregation of input-output pairs in $\mathcal{A}$, then, in general, $\mathcal{A}_\sigma$ and $\mathcal{A}_\lambda$ will not be strongly equivalent in the sense of *1.6.10*. Clearly, if all the SSS which are equivalent to $\mathcal{A}$ are strongly equivalent to one another, then there is one and only one family of bundles which qualify as aggregates of $\mathcal{A}$.

As an aid in finding a family of aggregates of $\mathcal{A}$, it is very helpful to establish a basic property of input-output-state relations which, as will be seen below, is equivalent to the continuation condition. Specifically, from inspection of *1.2.13*, it is obvious that, since the input-output pair $(\mathbf{u}^1,\mathbf{y}^1)$ belongs to the bundle $\mathcal{A}_{\boldsymbol{\alpha}_1}(t_1)$, we can write

3 $$\mathbf{y}^1(t) = \mathbf{A}(\boldsymbol{\alpha}_1;\mathbf{u}^1_{[t_1,t]})$$

where $\boldsymbol{\alpha}_1$ is independent of $\mathbf{u}^1$ and is dependent solely on $\boldsymbol{\alpha}_0$ and $\mathbf{u}^0$, that is,

4 $$\boldsymbol{\alpha}_1 = \mathbf{F}(\boldsymbol{\alpha}_0;\mathbf{u}^0_{[t_0,t_1]})$$

Furthermore, it is also clear that the continuation condition is satisfied if *3* and *4* hold true.

This observation makes it possible to make the following assertion: Suppose that the bundling of input-output pairs of $\mathcal{A}$ is defined by the input-output-state relation

5 $$\mathbf{y}(t) = \mathbf{A}(\mathbf{x}(t_0);\mathbf{u}_{[t_0,t]})$$

through

6 $$\mathcal{A}_{\boldsymbol{\alpha}_0}(t_0) \triangleq \{(\mathbf{u}_{[t_0,t]},\bar{\mathbf{A}}(\mathbf{x}(t_0);\mathbf{u}_{[t_0,t]}))\}_{\mathbf{u}}$$

where $\boldsymbol{\alpha}_0 = \mathbf{x}(t_0) =$ initial state, $\mathbf{u} = \mathbf{u}_{[t_0,t]}$, and

7 $$\mathbf{y}_{[t_0,t]} = \bar{\mathbf{A}}(\mathbf{x}(t_0);\mathbf{u}_{[t_0,t]})$$

is an input-output-state relation (equivalent to *5*) which expresses the output segment [rather than $\mathbf{y}(t)$] as a function of the initial state $\mathbf{x}(t_0)$ and the input segment $\mathbf{u}_{[t_0,t]}$. Then the bundling in question satisfies the continuation condition if and only if the input-output-state relation *5* satisfies the identity

8 $$\mathbf{y}(t) = \mathbf{A}(\mathbf{x}(t_0);\mathbf{u}_{[t_0,t]}) = \mathbf{A}(\mathbf{x}(t_1);\mathbf{u}_{[t_1,t]})$$

where $\mathbf{x}(t_1)$ depends only on $\mathbf{x}(t_0)$ and $\mathbf{u}_{[t_0,t_1]}$, that is,

9 $$\mathbf{x}(t_1) = \mathbf{F}(\mathbf{x}(t_0);\mathbf{u}_{[t_0,t_1]})$$

This identity expresses the so-called *response separation property* of *5*. Thus, the continuation condition implies and is implied by the response separation property.

In effect, the response separation property of the input-output-state relation affords a convenient way of checking on whether or not the continuation condition is satisfied by the family of bundles which is generated by the input-output-state relation in question. Using this property, the association of states with a given system involves only two steps: (*a*) Finding a relation of the form *2*, with $\boldsymbol{\alpha}_0$ ranging over a space Σ_{t_0}, such that every input-output pair in $\mathcal{A}$ can be represented in this form and, conversely, for every t_0 and every $\boldsymbol{\alpha}_0$ in Σ_{t_0}, $(\mathbf{u},\bar{\mathbf{A}}(\mathbf{x}(t_0);\mathbf{u}))$ is an input-output pair in $\mathcal{A}$; and (*b*) verifying that *2* has the response separation property. If (*a*) and (*b*) are satisfied, then the $\boldsymbol{\alpha}_0$ qualify as the states of $\mathcal{A}$ at time t_0 and the relation

10 $$\mathbf{y}(t) = \mathbf{A}(\boldsymbol{\alpha}_0;\mathbf{u})$$

may be regarded as an input-output-state relation for $\mathcal{A}$.

As was pointed out earlier (Sec. *5*), when $\mathcal{A}$ is defined by an input-output relation which has the form of a differential or difference equation, a relation of the form *2* constitutes an expression for the general solution of the equation. In such cases, then, the association of states with a system involves merely a check on whether the general solution has the response separation property.

11 *Example* As a simple illustration of the above procedure, suppose that $\mathcal{A}$ is defined by the input-output relation

12 $$(p + 1)y = u$$

In this case, the general solution may be written as

13 $$y(t) = \alpha_0 e^{-(t-t_0)} + \int_{t_0}^{t} e^{-(t-\xi)}u(\xi)\,d\xi \qquad t \geq t_0$$

which is of the form $y(t) = A(\alpha_0;u_{[t_0,t]})$, with α_0 ranging over the real line $(-\infty,\infty)$.

To verify that *13* has the response separation property, we have to verify that there exists a real number α_1 independent of $u_{[t_1,t]}$ such that, for all α_0, t_0, t_1, t, and u, we have the identity

14 $$\alpha_0 e^{-(t-t_0)} + \int_{t_0}^{t} e^{-(t-\xi)}u(\xi)\,d\xi = \alpha_1 e^{-(t-t_1)} + \int_{t_1}^{t} e^{-(t-\xi)}u(\xi)\,d\xi$$

Clearly, *14* can be satisfied by relating α_1 to α_0 and $u_{[t_0,t_1]}$ by the equation

15 $$\alpha_1 = \alpha_0 e^{-(t_1-t_0)} + \int_{t_0}^{t_1} e^{-(t_1-\xi)}u(\xi)\,d\xi$$

This equation is a concrete form of *4* for the case under consideration. In effect, it is a state equation for $\mathcal{A}$ induced by the input-output-state relation *13*.

It is of interest to observe that *13* would not have the response separation property if the exponents of the two terms in the right-hand member of *13* were not identical. For example, if $y(t)$ were given, say, as

16 $$y(t) = \alpha_0 e^{-2(t-t_0)} + \int_{t_0}^{t} e^{-(t-\xi)} u(\xi)\, d\xi$$

then *16* would not have the response separation property. More generally, it is easy to verify that if the input-output-state relation is of the form

17 $$y(t) = \sum_{i=1}^{n} \alpha_i e^{-a_i(t-t_0)} + \int_{t_0}^{t} h(t-\xi) u(\xi)\, d\xi$$

where the α_i range over the real line, then the response separation property requires that the function $h(t)$ be a linear combination of the exponentials $e^{-a_i t}$, $i = 1, \ldots, n$.

State separation property

In the foregoing discussion, we assumed that the point of departure for associating states with a given system $\mathcal{A}$ is an input-output-state relation for $\mathcal{A}$ of the form

18 $$\mathbf{y}(t) = \mathbf{A}(\mathbf{x}(t_0);\mathbf{u}_{[t_0,t]}) \qquad t \geq t$$

where $\mathbf{x}(t_0)$, the state at time t_0, is a variable ranging over a state space Σ_{t_0}.

If *18* has the response separation property, then we can write

19 $$\mathbf{A}(\mathbf{x}(t_0);\mathbf{u}_{[t_0,t]}) = \mathbf{A}(\mathbf{x}(t_1);\mathbf{u}_{[t_1,t]})$$

where $\mathbf{x}(t_1)$ is related to $\mathbf{x}(t_0)$ and $\mathbf{u}_{[t_0,t]}$ by the state equation

20 $$\mathbf{x}(t_1) = \mathbf{F}(\mathbf{x}(t_0);\mathbf{u}_{[t_0,t_1]})$$

As shown in [1], an important consequence of the response separation property is the so-called *state separation property* (or the *semigroup property*) of the state equation *20*. When written in a form analogous to *19*, this property may be expressed as the identity

21 $$\mathbf{x}(t) = \mathbf{F}(\mathbf{x}(t_0);\mathbf{u}_{[t_0,t]}) = \mathbf{F}(\mathbf{x}(t_1);\mathbf{u}_{[t_1,t]})$$

where

22 $$\mathbf{x}(t_1) = \mathbf{F}(\mathbf{x}(t_0);\mathbf{u}_{[t_0,t_1]})$$

with the understanding that *21* holds for all t_0, t_1, t ($t_0 \leq t_1 \leq t$), $\mathbf{x}(t_0)$, and $\mathbf{u}_{[t_0,t]}$. In words, the state separation property means: If an input segment $\mathbf{u}_{[t_0,t]}$ is divided arbitrarily into two segments $\mathbf{u}_{[t_0,t_1]}$ and $\mathbf{u}_{[t_1,t]}$, and if an initial state $\mathbf{x}(t_0)$ is carried by $\mathbf{u}_{[t_0,t]}$ into $\mathbf{x}(t)$ and by $\mathbf{u}_{[t_0,t_1]}$ into $\mathbf{x}(t_1)$, then $\mathbf{x}(t_1)$ is carried by $\mathbf{u}_{[t_1,t]}$ into $\mathbf{x}(t)$.

In most cases of practical interest, the dependence of $\mathbf{y}(t)$ on $\mathbf{u}_{[t_0,t]}$

in the input-output-state relation *18* is such that, as $t_0 \to t$, *18* tends to a relation of the form

23
$$\mathbf{y}(t) = g(\mathbf{x}(t),\mathbf{u}(t),t)$$

which implies that the output at time t depends only on the state at time t, the input at time t, and t. Systems of this type will be said to be *proper*. An example of a proper system (see Ref. 1, chap. 4) is a system defined by an input-output relation of the form

24
$$(a_n p^n + \cdots + a_0)y = (b_m p^m + \cdots + b_0)u$$

in which $n \geq m$.

A proper system may be characterized by the equation

25
$$\mathbf{y}(t) = \mathbf{g}(\mathbf{x}(t),\mathbf{u}(t),t)$$

and the state equation

26
$$\mathbf{x}(t) = \mathbf{F}(\mathbf{x}(t_0);\mathbf{u}_{[t_0,t]})$$

In effect, these two equations define the system in question through the input-output-state relation

27
$$\mathbf{y}(t) = \mathbf{g}(\mathbf{F}(\mathbf{x}(t_0);\mathbf{u}_{[t_0,t]}),\mathbf{u}(t),t))$$

which results from substituting *26* into *25*.

An important property of proper systems may be expressed in the following form.

28 **Assertion** If the state equation *26* has the state separation property, then the input-output-state relation *27* will have the response separation property and, consequently, the $\mathbf{x}(t)$ in *26* will qualify as the states of the system defined by *25* and *26*.

The truth of this assertion follows at once from making use of *21* and *22* in *27*.

The above assertion provides a very convenient way of associating states with a *differential system*, that is, a system whose input-output relation has the form of a differential equation. Thus, suppose that the given differential equation (or equations) defining $\mathcal{A}$ can be shown to be equivalent to the equations

29
$$\mathbf{y}(t) = \mathbf{g}(\mathbf{x}(t),\mathbf{u}(t),t)$$

30
$$\dot{\mathbf{x}}(t) = \mathbf{f}(\mathbf{x}(t),\mathbf{u}(t),t)$$

in which $\mathbf{x}(t)$ ranges over a space Σ_t. Then, the following can be asserted (corollary 2.3.36 in Ref. 1):

31 **Assertion** If equation *30* has a unique solution for $\mathbf{x}(t)$ for every initial state $\mathbf{x}(t_0)$, then the solution, expressed as

32 $$\mathbf{x}(t) = \mathbf{F}(\mathbf{x}(t_0);\mathbf{u}_{[t_0,t]})$$

will have the state separation property. Coupled with Assertion *28*, this implies that if we can demonstrate that *29* and *30* are equivalent to the differential equation (or equations) defining $\mathcal{A}$ (in the sense of having the same set of solutions), then we can conclude that the $\mathbf{x}(t)$ in *29* and *30* qualify as the states of $\mathcal{A}$.

As a simple illustration, consider a system $\mathcal{A}$ defined by the input-output relation

33 $$(a_n p^n + \cdots + a_0)y = u$$

in which the a_i are real-valued coefficients and the input and output at time t are real-valued variables. On defining

34 $$\begin{aligned} x_1(t) &= y(t) \\ x_2(t) &= py(t) \\ &\cdots\cdots \\ x_n(t) &= p^{n-1}y(t) \end{aligned}$$

the differential equation *31* can be replaced by the single vector differential equation

35 $$\dot{\mathbf{x}}(t) = \mathbf{A}\mathbf{x}(t) + \mathbf{B}u(t)$$

together with the equation

36 $$y(t) = \mathbf{C}\mathbf{x}(t)$$

in which $\mathbf{x} = (x_1, \ldots, x_n)$ and the matrices $\mathbf{A}$, $\mathbf{B}$, and $\mathbf{C}$ are given by

37 $$\mathbf{A} = \begin{bmatrix} 0 & 1 & 0 & \cdots & 0 \\ 0 & 0 & 1 & \cdots & 0 \\ \cdots & \cdots & \cdots & \cdots & \cdots \\ -\dfrac{a_0}{a_n} & \cdot & \cdot & \cdots & -\dfrac{a_{n-1}}{a_n} \end{bmatrix} \qquad \mathbf{B} = \begin{bmatrix} 0 \\ \cdot \\ \cdot \\ \cdot \\ \dfrac{1}{a_n} \end{bmatrix}$$

$$\mathbf{C} = [1 \quad 0 \quad \cdots \quad 0]$$

Equation *35* has a unique solution which can be written as

38 $$\mathbf{x}(t) = \mathbf{\Phi}(t - t_0)\mathbf{x}(t_0) + \int_{t_0}^{t} \mathbf{\Phi}(t - \xi)\mathbf{B}u(\xi)\, d\xi$$

where $\mathbf{\Phi}(t)$ is the solution of the equation

39 $$\dot{\mathbf{\Phi}} = \mathbf{A}\mathbf{\Phi} \qquad \mathbf{\Phi}(0) = \mathbf{I} \qquad \text{identity matrix}$$

It follows from Assertion *30*—and can also be readily verified directly—that *38* has the state separation property. Consequently, from *28* we can conclude that $\mathbf{x}(t)$ as defined by *34* qualifies as a state vector for $\mathcal{A}$.

In more general cases, the association of states with a system can be carried out in a similar manner, with the response and state separation properties of the input-output-state relations and state equations serving as the bridge between the definition of a state as a tag for an aggregate and its expression in terms of the input and output of $\mathcal{A}$. Detailed expositions of the techniques for associating states with a system may be found in some of the references listed below, especially [1] and [25]. In addition, a number of methods relevant to this problem in the context of linear differential systems will be discussed in Chap. *5*.

REFERENCES

1 Zadeh, L. A., and C. A. Desoer: "Linear System Theory," McGraw-Hill, New York, 1963.

2 Zadeh, L. A.: The Concept of State in System Theory, pp. 39–50, in "Views on General Systems Theory," M. Mesarovic (ed.), Wiley, New York, 1964.

3 Mesarovic, M.: Foundations for a General Systems Theory, pp. 1–24, in "Views on General Systems Theory," M. Mesarovic (ed.), Wiley, New York, 1964.

4 Arbib, M.: Automata Theory and Control Theory—A Rapprochement, *Automatika*, vol. 3, pp. 161–189, 1966.

5 Kalman, R.: Algebraic Aspects of the Theory of Dynamical Systems, pp. 133–146, in *Proc. Intern. Symp. Differential Equations and Dynamical Systems,* J. Hale and J. LaSalle (eds.), Academic, New York, 1967.

6 Wymore, W.: "A Mathematical Theory of Systems Engineering," Wiley, New York, 1967.

7 Salovaara, S.: On Set Theoretical Foundations of System Theory—A Study of the State Concept, *Acta Polytech. Scand.*, no. 15, pp. 1–74, 1967.

8 Nerode, A.: Linear Automaton Transformations, *Proc. Am. Math. Soc.*, vol. 9, pp. 541–544, 1958.

9 Windeknecht, T.: Mathematical Systems Theory: Causality, *Math. Systems Theory,* vol. 1, no. 4, pp. 279–288, 1967.

10 Krohn, K., and J. Rhodes: Algebraic Theory of Machines, pp. 341–384, in *Proc. Symp. Math. Theory of Automata,* J. Fox (ed.), *Polytech. Inst. Brooklyn,* New York, 1962.

11 Krohn, K., and J. Rhodes: Algebraic Theory of Machines, *Trans. Am. Math. Soc.*, vol. 115, pp. 450–464, 1965.

12 Zeiger, P.: Cascade Decomposition of Automata Using Covers, in M. Arbib (ed.), "Algebraic Theory of Machines, Languages and Semigroups," pp. 55–80, Academic, New York, 1968.
13 Kalman, R. E.: On the General Theory of Control Systems, *Proc. First Intern. Congr. IFAC, Moscow*, 1960; also "Automatic and Remote Control," pp. 481–492, Butterworth, London, 1961.
14 Ogata, K.: "State Space Analysis of Control Systems," Prentice-Hall, Englewood Cliffs, N.J., 1966.
15 Newcomb, R. W.: "Linear Multiport Synthesis," McGraw-Hill, New York, 1966.
16 Kuh, E. S., and R. A. Rohrer: "Theory of Linear Active Networks," Holden-Day, San Francisco, 1967.
17 Fel'dbaum, A. A.: "Optimal Control Systems," Academic, New York, 1965.
18 Athans, M., and P. L. Falb: "Optimal Control," McGraw-Hill, New York, 1966.
19 Schwarz, R. J., and B. Friedland: "Linear Systems," McGraw-Hill, New York, 1965.
20 Tou, J. T.: "Modern Control Theory," McGraw-Hill, New York, 1964.
21 Timothy, L. K., and B. E. Bona: "State Space Analysis," McGraw-Hill, New York, 1968.
22 Peschon, J.: "Discipline and Techniques of System Synthesis," Blaisdell, Boston, 1965.
23 Leondes, C.: "Modern Control Systems Theory," McGraw-Hill, New York, 1965.
24 Zadeh, L. A.: "Fuzzy Sets and Systems," *Proc. Symp. System Theory, Polytech. Inst. Brooklyn*, April, 1965, pp. 29–37.
25 Ho, B. L., and R. Kalman: Effective Construction of State Variable Models from Input-output Relations, pp. 449–459, in *Proc. 3d Allerton Conf.*, 1965.
26 Arbib, M.: A Common Framework for Automata Theory and Control Theory, *SIAM J. Control*, vol. 3, no. 2, pp. 206–222, 1965.

2

Finite-state systems

A. Gill[1]
Department of Electrical Engineering and Computer Sciences
University of California, Berkeley

1 *Introduction*

A *finite-state system* (abbreviated FSS) is an idealized model for a large number of physical devices and phenomena encountered in many fields of science and technology. Ideas and techniques developed for FSS have been found useful in such diverse problems as the investigation of human nervous activity, the analysis of English syntax, and the design of digital computers, to cite only a few examples. Essentially, every system which operates at discrete instants of time and whose input, output, and internal structure can assume only a finite number of distinct configurations can be represented abstractly as an FSS. Due to this generality, the theory of FSS constitutes one of the most important building blocks in system theory.

This chapter presumes no specialized mathematical background, other than familiarity with common set-theoretical terms. Consequently, the material is presented in a rather informal fashion, with heavy reliance on the reader's intuition and power of visualization.

[1] The writing of this chapter was supported in part by the Air Force Office of Scientific Research, Office of Aerospace Research, United States Air Force, under AFOSR Grant AF-AFOSR-639-67 and by the United States Department of the Navy, Office of Naval Research, under Contract Nonr-222(53).

2 *FSS—definition*

A *complete, deterministic finite-state system* $\mathfrak{M}$ is defined by the following:

1 A finite, nonempty set $U = \{\alpha_1,\alpha_2, \ldots ,\alpha_p\}$, called the *input alphabet* of $\mathfrak{M}$. An element of U is called an *input symbol.*

2 A finite, nonempty set $Y = \{\beta_1,\beta_2, \ldots ,\beta_q\}$, called the *output alphabet* of $\mathfrak{M}$. An element of Y is called an *output symbol.*

3 A finite, nonempty set $S = \{\sigma_1,\sigma_2, \ldots ,\sigma_n\}$, called the *state set* of $\mathfrak{M}$. An element of S is called a *state.*

4 A *next-state function* f which maps the set of all ordered pairs (σ_i,α_j) into S.

5 An *output function* g which maps the set of all ordered pairs (σ_i,α_j) into Y.

$\mathfrak{M}$ will sometimes be written as $\langle U,Y,S,f,g\rangle$.

Physically, $\mathfrak{M}$ can be interpreted as a device (see Fig. *2.2.1*) whose

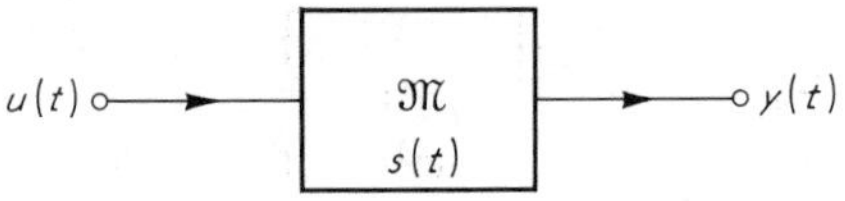

Fig. 2.2.1 Finite-state system.

input, output, and internal state at time t are denoted by $u(t)$, $y(t)$, and $s(t)$, respectively. These variables are defined for discrete—and for convenience, integral—values of t only, and assume values taken from U, Y, and S, respectively. Given the state and input of $\mathfrak{M}$ at time t, f specifies the state at time $t + 1$, and g the output at time t:

6 $$s(t + 1) = f(s(t),u(t))$$

7 $$y(t) = g(s(t),u(t))$$

The application of a sequence of l input symbols (or an *input sequence* of *length* l) to $\mathfrak{M}$ results in a sequence of states (a *state sequence*) and a sequence of output symbols (an *output sequence*) of the same length. Given an input sequence $\bar{u}$, the state of $\mathfrak{M}$ when $\bar{u}$ is applied (the *initial state* of $\mathfrak{M}$), and the functions f and g, the corresponding state sequence $\bar{s}$ and output sequence $\bar{y}$ can be computed recursively from *6* and *7*.

An *incomplete* FSS is one in which f and/or g are not defined for all (σ_i,α_j) pairs. A *nondeterministic* FSS is one in which f and/or g are not defined uniquely. Since such FSS will not be treated in this chapter, the adjectives *complete* and *deterministic* will be henceforth omitted.

3 *Transition tables and graphs*

The functions f and g defining the FSS $\mathfrak{M}$ are called the *characterizing functions* of $\mathfrak{M}$. They can be specified by means of a table, called a *transition table*, whose format is shown in Table *2.3.1*. The intersection of row σ_i and column α_j is $f(\sigma_i,\alpha_j)$ in the subtable labeled $s(t+1)$, and $g(\sigma_i,\alpha_j)$ in the subtable labeled $y(t)$.

Alternatively, these functions can be specified by means of an oriented graph, called a *transition graph*, which can be constructed as follows: The graph has n vertices, labeled as the n states of $\mathfrak{M}$; if $Y_{ij} = \{\alpha_{i1},\alpha_{i2}, \ldots ,\alpha_{ir}\}$ is the set of input symbols such that $f(\sigma_i,\alpha_{i\nu}) = \sigma_j$, and if $g(\sigma_i,\alpha_{i\nu}) = \beta_{i\nu}$, then a branch is drawn from vertex σ_i to vertex σ_j, pointing toward the latter and bearing the label α_{i1}/β_{i1}, α_{i2}/β_{i2}, . . . , α_{ir}/β_{ir} (if Y_{ij} is empty, the branch is deleted).

The advantage of the transition graph is both conceptual and computational. It enables one to visualize an FSS as a mechanism which traces paths along a given graph in accordance with the input sequence, with distinct paths corresponding to distinct modes of behavior. Given an initial state and an input sequence, it also enables one to determine the corresponding state and output sequences by inspection of the branch labels.

In subsequent discussions, the transition graph specifying an FSS $\mathfrak{M}$ will be referred to simply as the FSS $\mathfrak{M}$. Correspondingly, the vertex representing the state σ_i will be called simply state σ_i.

Table 2.3.1 General transition table

$s(t)$ \ $u(t)$	$s(t+1)$				$y(t)$			
	α_1	α_2	. . .	α_p	α_1	α_2	. . .	α_p
σ_1 σ_2 . . . σ_n			Entries from S				Entries from Y	

4 Examples of FSS

1 *Example* Consider the process whereby an English text composed of the 26 roman characters and spaces is scanned, and every word ending with ART is marked. This process can be represented by an

Table 2.4.1 Transition table for FSS of Example *2.4.1*

$s(t)$ \ $u(t)$	$s(t+1)$ A	R	T	π	λ	$y(t)$ A	R	T	π	λ
1	1	2	4	4	4	0	0	0	0	0
2	1	4	3	4	4	0	0	0	0	0
3	1	4	4	4	4	0	0	0	1	0
4	1	4	4	4	4	0	0	0	0	0

FSS in the following manner: The input alphabet consists of A, B, . . . , Z and space (for simplicity, space will be denoted by π, and all letters other than A, R, T by λ). The output alphabet consists of

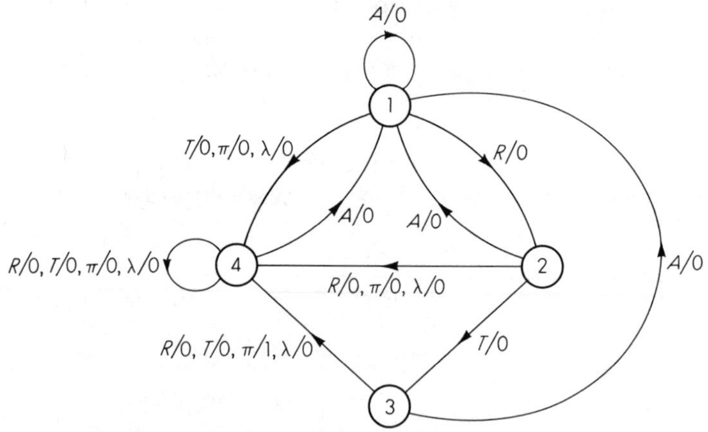

Fig. 2.4.1 FSS of Example *2.4.1*.

mark and *no mark* (denoted by 0 and 1, respectively). The state set represents the following four conditions: last letter scanned is A (state 1); last two letters scanned are AR (state 2); last three letters scanned are ART (state 3); none of the previous conditions (state 4). The f and g functions are specified tabularly in Table *2.4.1* and graphically in Fig. *2.4.1*.

2 *Example* Figure *2.4.2* represents a neural net. The fiber marked v_{in}

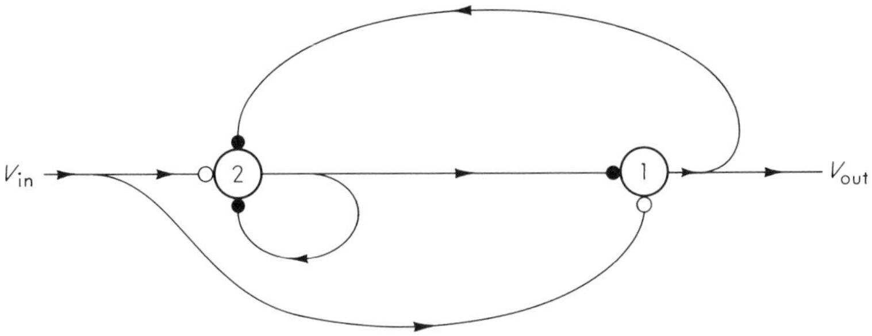

Fig. 2.4.2 A neural net for Example *2.4.2*.

is excited with stimuli of values 0 or 1 at times $t_0, t_1, t_2, \ldots$. A large circle represents a neuron whose output at $t_{\nu+1}$ is 1 if and only if the number of its stimulated excitatory inputs (indicated by heavy dots) minus the number of its stimulated inhibitory inputs (indicated by small circles) equals or exceeds the threshold (the integer labeling the neuron)

Table 2.4.2 Transition table for FSS of Example *2.4.2*

$s(t)$ \ $u(t)$	$s(t+1)$: 0	$s(t+1)$: 1	$y(t)$: 0	$y(t)$: 1
00	00	00	0	0
01	00	00	1	1
10	01	00	0	0
11	11	00	1	1

at time t_ν. The neural net can be modeled by an FSS whose input (v_{in}) and output (v_{out}) alphabets are both $\{0,1\}$. The state set consists of four states representing all four possible output configurations (00,01,10,11) of the two neurons (the first digit equals the output of the neuron labeled 2, and the second digit the output of the neuron labeled

1). The f and g functions are specified tabularly in Table *2.4.2* and graphically in Fig. *2.4.3*.

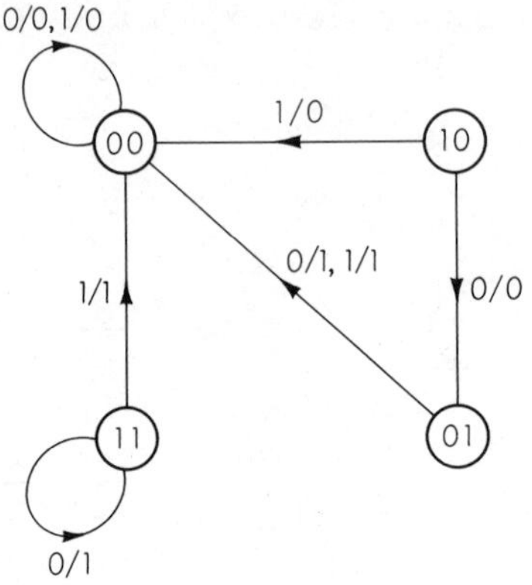

Fig. 2.4.3 FSS of Example *2.4.2*.

5 *Synthesis of FSS*

If the order of the input alphabet of an FSS $\mathfrak{M}$ is p, then every input symbol can be encoded into a sequence of $p' = [\log_2 p]$ binary digits,

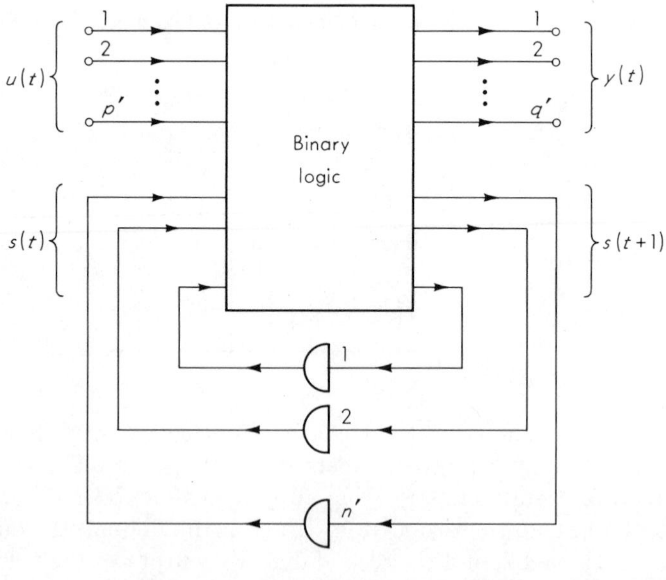

Fig. 2.5.1 General realization of FSS.

where $[\log_2 x]$ denotes the least integer which equals or exceeds $\log_2 x$. Similarly, if the order of the output alphabet is q, every output symbol can be encoded into a sequence of $q' = [\log_2 q]$ binary digits, and if the order of the state set is n, every state can be encoded into $n' = [\log_2 n]$ binary digits. With $u(t)$, $y(t)$, and $s(t)$ thus encoded, $\mathfrak{M}$ can be simulated by means of a binary switching network, the general form of which is shown in Fig. *2.5.1*. In this figure, the D-shaped elements are unit delays, and the binary logic box is a combinational network (AND gates, OR gates, and inverters, for example) which realizes the characterizing functions of $\mathfrak{M}$. The design of the logic box is beyond the scope of this chapter, and the reader is referred to any textbook on switching circuits for details.

1 *Example* The FSS of Example *2.4.2* can be simulated by the switching circuit shown in Fig. *2.5.2* (delays 1 and 2 represent the first and second

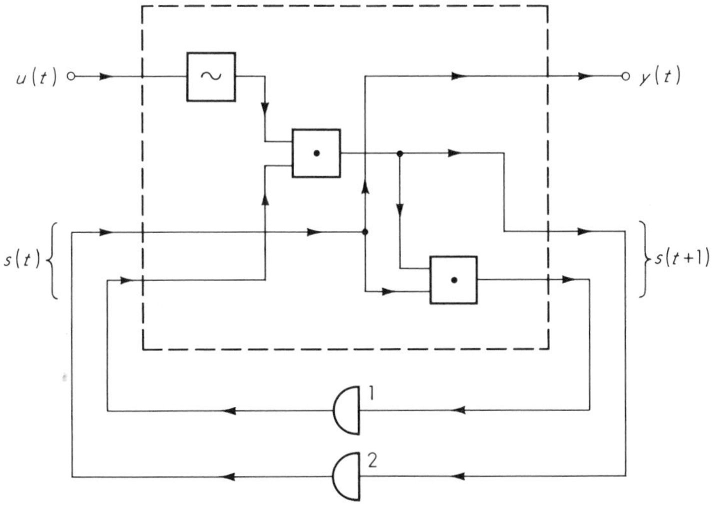

Fig. 2.5.2 Realization of FSS of Example *2.4.2*.

digits, respectively, in the binary code for the state; an element marked with $\sim$ is an inverter; an element marked with $\cdot$ is an AND gate).

6 *Isomorphism of FSS*

Two FSS are *compatible* if they have identical input alphabets.

Let $\mathfrak{M}_1$ be the FSS $\langle U_1, Y_1, S_1, f_1, g_1 \rangle$, and $\mathfrak{M}_2$ the FSS $\langle U_2, Y_2, S_2, f_2, g_2 \rangle$. $\mathfrak{M}_1$ and $\mathfrak{M}_2$ are said to be *isomorphic* to each other if they are compatible (that is, $U_1 = U_2$) and if a one-to-one correspondence can be established between the states of $\mathfrak{M}_1$ and $\mathfrak{M}_2$ in the following manner: If σ_1 in S_1 corresponds to σ_2 in S_2, then, for all α_i in U_1 (or U_2):

1 $$f_1(\sigma_1,\alpha_i) \text{ corresponds to } f_2(\sigma_2,\alpha_i)$$

2 $$g_1(\sigma_1,\alpha_i) = g_2(\sigma_2,\alpha_i)$$

Thus, the transition graphs of $\mathfrak{M}_1$ and $\mathfrak{M}_2$ are identical, except for possible variations in state labeling.

7 *Connected and strongly connected FSS*

An FSS $\mathfrak{M}$ is said to be *connected with respect* to σ_i if every state σ_j in $\mathfrak{M}$ is reachable from σ_i with an input sequence of a finite length (σ_i reaches itself with an input sequence of length 0). $\mathfrak{M}$ is *strongly connected* if it is connected with respect to every one of its states (in this case every state is reachable from every other state).

1 **Theorem** Let $\mathfrak{M}$ be an n-state FSS, where the state σ_j is reachable from σ_i. Then σ_j is reachable from σ_i by an input sequence of length $n - 1$ or less.

Proof In the transition graph of $\mathfrak{M}$, consider any path leading from σ_i to σ_j. By omitting all loops (if any) from this path, one obtains a path leading from σ_i to σ_j which does not touch any given state more than once. Since the number of states in $\mathfrak{M}$ is n, the number of branches in the latter path is at most $n - 1$.

Thus, the set of states reachable from σ_i in $n - 1$ steps or less is the set of all states reachable from σ_i in any number of steps. If this set includes all the states of $\mathfrak{M}$, then $\mathfrak{M}$ is connected with respect to σ_i.

8 *State equivalence*

Let $\bar{u}$ denote an input sequence applied to an FSS $\mathfrak{M}$ whose initial state is σ_i. The state of $\mathfrak{M}$ after the last symbol of $\bar{u}$ is applied (the final state of $\mathfrak{M}$) will be denoted by $F(\sigma_i,\bar{u})$, and the output of $\mathfrak{M}$ when the last symbol is applied will be denoted by $G(\sigma_i,\bar{u})$. F and G will be called the *extended characterizing functions* of $\mathfrak{M}$. The set of all input sequences of length k or less constructable from the input alphabet U will be denoted by U_k (U_∞ is the set of all finite input sequences).

Let $\mathfrak{M}_1$ be an FSS with the input alphabet U, the state set S_1 and the extended characterizing functions F_1 and G_1. Let $\mathfrak{M}_2$ be an FSS compatible with $\mathfrak{M}_1$ (possibly $\mathfrak{M}_1$ itself), with the state set S_2 and the extended characterizing functions F_2 and G_2. Then a state σ_1 of $\mathfrak{M}_1$ and σ_2 of $\mathfrak{M}_2$ are *k-equivalent* if, for all $\bar{u}$ in U_k,

1 $$G_1(\sigma_1,u) = G_2(\sigma_2,u)$$

Otherwise, σ_1 and σ_2 are said to be *k-distinguishable*. Assuming that $S_1 \cap S_2 = 0$ (which can always be enforced by renaming elements in S_1 or S_2), $S = S_1 \cup S_2$ can be partitioned into *k-equivalence classes* such that two states are in the same class if and only if they are k-equivalent. This partition is called the *k-equivalence partition* of S and denoted by π_k.

If *1* holds for all $\bar{u}$ in U_∞, σ_1 and σ_2 are simply called *equivalent* (written $\sigma_1 \approx \sigma_2$); otherwise they are called *distinguishable*. S is partitionable into *equivalence classes* such that two states are in the same class if and only if they are equivalent. This partition is the *equivalence partition* of S, denoted by π.

Thus σ_1 and σ_2 are equivalent if and only if there is no way of discovering by external observations whether the given FSS is $\mathfrak{M}_1$ in state σ_1 or $\mathfrak{M}_2$ in σ_2 (when these are the only alternatives).

9 *Equivalence partitioning of an FSS*

1 **Lemma** If $\pi_k \neq \pi$, then the number of classes in π_{k+1} exceeds the number of classes in π_k.

Proof Let σ_1 and σ_2 be k-equivalent but $(k+1)$-distinguishable states, and let $\bar{u}$ be the shortest input sequence, say of length l $(l > k)$, such that $G_1(\sigma_1,\bar{u}) \neq G_2(\sigma_2,\bar{u})$. Then there must exist an input sequence $\bar{v}$ of length $l - k - 1$, such that $F_1(\sigma_1,\bar{v}) = \sigma_1'$ and $F_2(\sigma_2,\bar{v}) = \sigma_2'$ are k-equivalent but $(k+1)$-distinguishable. Hence σ_1' and σ_2' are in the same class of π_k but distinct classes of π_{k+1}. On the other hand, any two states which are k-distinguishable must be $(k+1)$-distinguishable.

Thus, unless $\pi_k = \pi$, π_{k+1} is a proper refinement of π_k. Since the number of classes in any partition can never exceed the total number of states, we have:

2 **Theorem** If S has n states, then $\pi_{n-1} = \pi$.

The following recurrence procedure can now be formulated for finding π: Construct π_1 by assigning states to the same class if and only if they are 1-equivalent. Construct π_{k+1} from π_k in the following manner:

If σ_1 and σ_2 are in distinct classes of π_k, or if $F_1(\sigma_1,\alpha)$ and $F_2(\sigma_2,\alpha)$ are in distinct classes of π_k for some α in U, then σ_1 and σ_2 are assigned to distinct classes in π_{k+1}. Otherwise, they are assigned to the same class in π_{k+1}. If π_r is the first partition such that $\pi_{r-1} = \pi_r$, then $\pi_{r-1} = \pi$ (by *2*, $r \leq n$).

3 *Example* For the FSS of Fig. *2.9.1* (in this case $\mathfrak{M}_1$ and $\mathfrak{M}_2$ refer to the

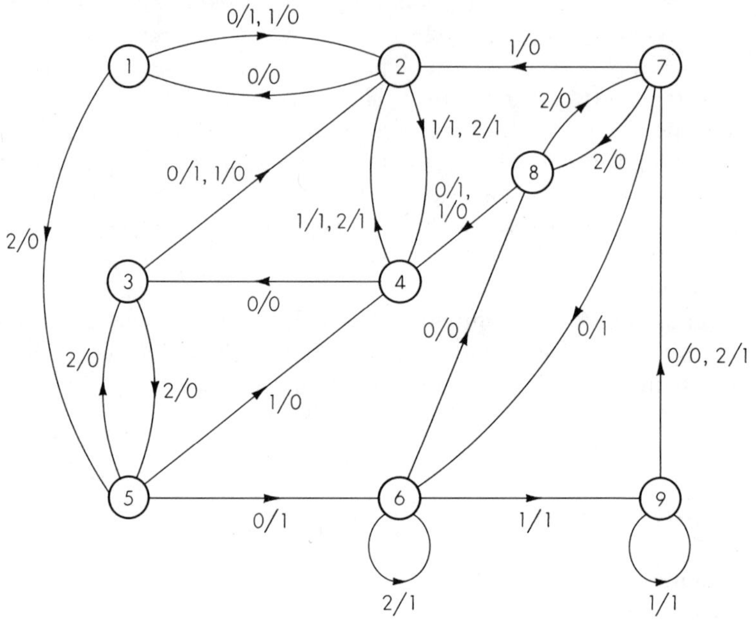

Fig. 2.9.1 FSS of Example *2.9.3*.

same FSS), we have:

4
$$\pi_1 = \{1,3,5,7,8\},\ \{2,4,6,9\}$$
$$\pi_2 = \{1,3,5,7,8\},\ \{2,4,6\},\ \{9\}$$
$$\pi_3 = \{1,3,5,7,8\},\ \{2,4\},\ \{6\},\ \{9\}$$
$$\pi_4 = \{1,3,8\},\ \{2,4\},\ \{5,7\},\ \{6\},\ \{9\} = \pi_5 = \pi$$

10 *FSS equivalence*

Two compatible FSS $\mathfrak{M}_1$ and $\mathfrak{M}_2$ are said to be *equivalent* (written $\mathfrak{M}_1 \approx \mathfrak{M}_2$) if to each state σ_1 of $\mathfrak{M}_1$ there corresponds at least one state of $\mathcal{M}_2$ which is equivalent to σ_1, and to each state σ_2 of $\mathcal{M}_2$ there corresponds at least one state of $\mathcal{M}_1$ which is equivalent to σ_2. Otherwise $\mathcal{M}_1$ and $\mathcal{M}_2$ are *distinguishable*. Thus $\mathcal{M}_1$ and $\mathcal{M}_2$ are equivalent if and only if there is no way of discovering by external observations whether the given FSS—regardless of its initial state—is $\mathcal{M}_1$ or $\mathcal{M}_2$ (when these are the only alternatives).

Let $\mathcal{M}_1$ and $\mathcal{M}_2$ be the FSS $\langle U,Y_1,S_1,f_1,g_1\rangle$ and $\langle U,Y_2,S_2,f_2,g_2\rangle$, respectively ($S_1 \cap S_2 = 0$). To establish whether or not $\mathcal{M}_1 \approx \mathcal{M}_2$, one can construct the equivalence partition π of $S = S_1 \cup S_2$: If every class in π contains elements from *both* S_1 and S_2, then $\mathcal{M}_1 \approx \mathcal{M}_2$; otherwise $\mathcal{M}_1 \not\approx \mathcal{M}_2$.

Clearly, if $\mathcal{M}_1$ and $\mathcal{M}_2$ are isomorphic they must also be equivalent.

11 *The minimal form*

Let $\mathcal{M}$ be the FSS $\langle U,Y,s,f,g\rangle$. Denote the equivalence classes of $\mathcal{M}$ by $C_1, C_2, \ldots, C_m$, and let σ_i be any element of C_i. Now, define a machine $\check{\mathcal{M}}$, described by $\langle U,Y,\check{S},\check{f},\check{g}\rangle$ where $\check{S} = \{\Sigma_1,\Sigma_2, \ldots ,\Sigma_m\}$ and where $\check{f}$ and $\check{g}$ are defined as follows:

1 If $f(\sigma_i,\alpha_j)$ is in class C_k, then $\check{f}(\Sigma_i,\alpha_j) = \Sigma_k$.

2 If $g(\sigma_i,\alpha_j) = \beta_k$, then $\check{g}(\Sigma_i,\alpha_j) = \beta_k$.

By definition of state equivalence, the construction implied by *1* is independent of the particular σ_i selected from C_i. $\check{\mathcal{M}}$, therefore, is uniquely constructible from $\mathcal{M}$.

3 **Theorem** (*a*) No two states in $\check{\mathcal{M}}$ are equivalent. (*b*) $\check{\mathcal{M}} \approx \mathcal{M}$. (*c*) There is no machine equivalent to $\mathcal{M}$ with fewer states than $\check{\mathcal{M}}$.
Proof Consider the m-class partition $C'_1, C'_2, \ldots, C'_m$ of $S \cup \check{S}$, where C'_i consists of all states in the class C_i of S plus the state Σ_i of $\check{S}$. From the construction rules *1* and *2* and the partitioning procedure in Sec. *9*, it follows that this partition is the equivalence partition of $S \cup \check{S}$. (*a*) and (*b*) then follow immediately. For (*c*), suppose $\mathcal{M}'$ has fewer states than $\check{\mathcal{M}}$, and $\mathcal{M}' \approx \mathcal{M}$. Hence $\mathcal{M}' \approx \check{\mathcal{M}}$, and every state in $\check{\mathcal{M}}$ is equivalent to at least one state in $\mathcal{M}'$. Consequently, there are at least two states in $\check{\mathcal{M}}$ which are equivalent to the same state in $\mathcal{M}'$—a contradiction of (*a*).

$\check{\mathcal{M}}$ is called the *minimal form* of $\mathcal{M}$, and is unique up to isomorphism (i.e., except for state labeling). If $\mathcal{M}$ and $\check{\mathcal{M}}$ have the same number of states, $\mathfrak{M}$ is said to be a *minimal* FSS. Insofar as the external behavior of an FSS is concerned, it can always be replaced with its minimal form, with obvious advantages in both analysis and synthesis.

4 *Example* Figure *2.11.1* shows the minimal form of the FSS of Example

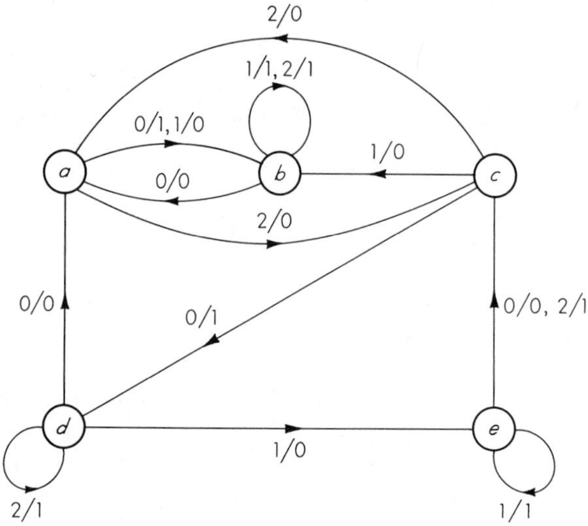

Fig. 2.11.1 Minimal form of FSS of Fig. *2.9.1*.

2.9.3. State *a* represents the equivalence class {1,3,8}, *b* the class {2,4}, *c* the class {5,7}, *d* the class {6}, and *e* the class {9}.

12 *Classification of experiments*

The process of applying input sequences to an FSS, observing corresponding output sequences, and drawing conclusions regarding the internal structure of the FSS is called an *experiment*.

An experiment may be a *preset* experiment, where the entire input is determined in advance, or an *adaptive* experiment of *iteration index* ρ, where the input consists of ρ subsequences—each subsequence (except the first) being determined on the basis of preceding observations. An experiment may be a *simple* experiment, where only a single FSS is employed, or a *multiple* experiment of *multiplicity* ξ, where ξ identical FSS are employed—all at the same initial state. The *length* of an experiment is the total number of input symbols required for its execution. An experiment is *realizable* if its length is finite. The length, iteration index, and multiplicity of an experiment may be regarded as rough measures of its cost and used as criteria for comparing various experimentation schemes.

In subsequent discussions, the *admissible set* of an FSS $\mathfrak{M}$ will refer to a set of states which are known to include the (unknown) initial state of $\mathfrak{M}$. Elements of this set will be called *admissible states.*

13 *Diagnosing experiments*

The *diagnosing problem* for an FSS $\mathfrak{M}$ is formulated as follows: $\mathfrak{M}$ is specified in its minimal form, and is known to have the admissible set $A = \{\sigma_{i1},\sigma_{i2}, \ldots ,\sigma_{im}\}$; find the initial state of $\mathfrak{M}$ (i.e., perform an experiment such that the true initial state can be deduced from the records of input and output sequences). An experiment which solves this problem is called a *diagnosing experiment* for $\mathfrak{M}$ and A. The input sequence employed in a simple, preset diagnosing experiment is called a *diagnosing sequence* for $\mathfrak{M}$ and A, of which the *minimal diagnosing sequence* is one whose length is smaller than or equal to the length of any other diagnosing sequence.

The diagnosing problem for an admissible set of order 1 is, of course, trivial. The diagnosing problem for an admissible set of order 2 is of special significance, and an experiment solving it will be called a *pairwise diagnosing experiment.*

14 *The pairwise diagnosing experiment*

1 **Theorem** The diagnosing problem for an n-state FSS $\mathfrak{M}$ with two admissible states is always solvable by a simple preset experiment of length $l \leq n - 1$.

Proof Since $\mathfrak{M}$ is minimal, its admissible states, say σ_1 and σ_2, are distinguishable, and there exists an input sequence $\bar{u}$ such that $G(\sigma_1,\bar{u}) \neq G(\sigma_2,\bar{u})$. By *2.9.2*, if σ_1 and σ_2 are distinguishable, they are $(n - 1)$-distinguishable, and hence the shortest such $\bar{u}$ is of length at most $n - 1$.

A minimal diagnosing sequence for the admissible set $\{\sigma_{i0},\sigma_{j0}\}$ will be denoted by $\mathcal{E}(\sigma_{i0},\sigma_{j0})$. To find $\mathcal{E}(\sigma_{i0},\sigma_{j0})$, the following procedure can be followed: Suppose l is the integer such that σ_{i0} and σ_{j0} are in distinct classes of π_l but the same class of π_{l-1}. Then σ_{i0} and σ_{j0} are l-distinguishable but $(l - 1)$-equivalent; they must have a pair of successors, say,

σ_{i1} and σ_{j1}, respectively, which are $(l-1)$-distinguishable but $(l-2)$-equivalent, reachable from σ_{i0} and σ_{j0} by applying the input symbol $\alpha_{(1)}$. Similarly σ_{i1} and σ_{j1} have a pair of successors σ_{i2} and σ_{j2}, respectively, which are $(l-2)$-distinguishable but $(l-3)$-equivalent, reachable from σ_{i1} and σ_{j1} by the input symbol $\alpha_{(2)}$. Continuing in this fashion a sequence $\alpha_{(1)}\alpha_{(2)} \cdots \alpha_{(l-1)}$ can be determined which takes σ_{i0} and σ_{j0} into a pair of 1-distinguishable states, which yield distinct output symbols when some input symbol, say $\alpha_{(l)}$, is applied. $\alpha_{(1)}\alpha_{(2)} \cdots \alpha_{(l)}$, therefore is the desired sequence $\mathcal{E}(\sigma_{i0},\sigma_{j0})$.

2 *Example* Figure *2.14.1* shows a minimal FSS whose k-equivalence partitions are given by:

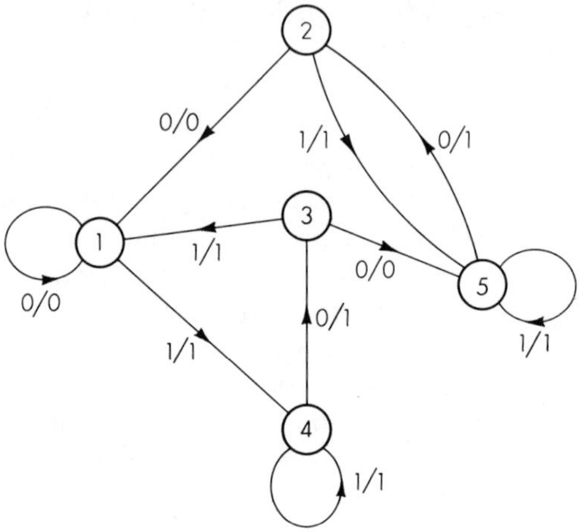

Fig. 2.14.1 FSS of Example *2.14.2*.

3
$$\begin{aligned}
\pi_1 &= \{1,2,3\},\ \{4,5\} \\
\pi_2 &= \{1,2\},\ \{3\},\ \{4,5\} \\
\pi_3 &= \{1,2\},\ \{3\},\ \{4\},\ \{5\} \\
\pi_4 &= \{1\},\ \{2\},\ \{3\},\ \{4\},\ \{5\} = \pi
\end{aligned}$$

States 4 and 5 are in distinct classes of π_3 but the same class of π_2. Hence 4 and 5 are 3-distinguishable but 2-equivalent ($l = 3$). Their successors which are 2-distinguishable but 1-equivalent are states 3 and 2, respectively (by inspection of π_1, π_2, and the graph), reachable from 4 and 5 with the input symbol 0. The successors of 3 and 2 which are 1-distinguishable are states 1 and 5, reachable from 3 and 2 with the input symbol 0 (or 1). States 1 and 5 yield the output symbols 0 and 1, respectively, when the input symbol 0 is applied. Hence $\mathcal{E}(4,5)$ is (000) [or (010)]: If the initial state is 4, (000) yields the output sequence (101), and if the initial state is 5, (000) yields the output sequence (100) [(010) yields (110) and (111), respectively].

15 *Simple diagnosing experiments*

In designing a simple preset diagnosing experiment for an FSS $\mathfrak{M}$ with the admissible set $A = \{\sigma_{i1},\sigma_{i2}, \ldots ,\sigma_{im}\}$, one searches for an input sequence which, when applied to $\mathfrak{M}$ at each one of these m states, yields m distinct output sequences. Such an input sequence, clearly, is a diagnosing sequence for A. Now, let $A^{(\nu)}$ denote the set of states (of order m or less) reachable from the admissible states by some input sequence $\bar{u}$ after ν steps. Since the total number of states in $\mathfrak{M}$ is n, there can be at most $\sum_{q=1}^{m} \binom{n}{q} = \eta$ different sets $A^{(\nu)}$; hence, after a number of steps not exceeding η, $\bar{u}$ must take A into some set $A^{(\nu)}$ which has been encountered previously. Thus, if the first η symbols of $\bar{u}$ do not constitute a diagnosing sequence, then $\bar{u}$—regardless of its length—cannot be such a sequence. The search for a diagnosing sequence, therefore, is a finite process and involves the examination of at most p^η sequences, where p is the order of the input alphabet of $\mathfrak{M}$. There are cases, however, where this search is futile, as demonstrated by the FSS of Fig. *2.15.1*, where the admissible set is $\{1,2,3,4\}$. Clearly, any minimal diagnosing sequence must initiate with 0; but the input sequence 00 destroys all chances of distinguishing between 1 and 2, and 01 all chances of distinguishing between 3 and 4. Hence no diagnosing sequence exists in this case.

Suppose, however, that 0 is applied and the output observed before any additional symbols are applied. If the output is 0, one can rule out 3 and 4 as initial states; if the output is 1, one can rule out 1 and 2. In the first case, 1 can be applied as a second symbol, to yield 0 if the initial state is 1 and 1 if the initial state is 2; in the second case, 0 can be applied as a second symbol, to yield 1 if the initial state is 3 and 0 if the initial state is 4. Thus, while no diagnosing sequence exists for $\{1,2,3,4\}$, the initial state can be identified by a simple adaptive experiment. Whether such an experiment exists in any given case, and the design of such an experiment if one exists, can be found by examining at most p^η input sequences (see [66]).

There are cases where the diagnosing problem cannot be solved by any simple experiment—preset or adaptive. For example, if the admissible set for the FSS of Fig. *2.15.1* is {5,6,7,8}, the application

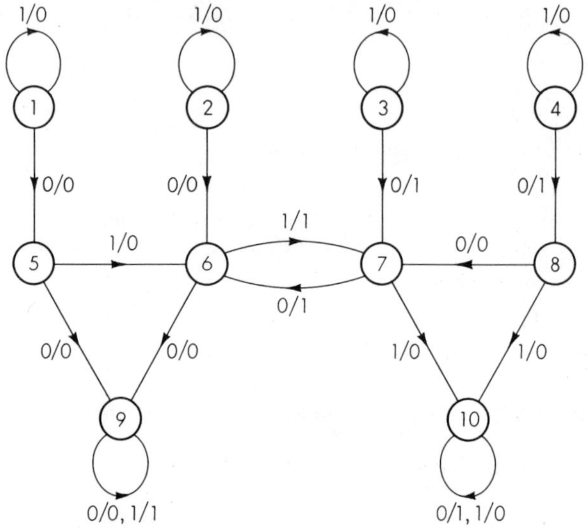

Fig. 2.15.1 FSS for examples in Sec. *15*.

of 0 destroys all chances of distinguishing between 5 and 6, and the application of 1 destroys all chances of distinguishing between 7 and 8. Thus, there exists no simple or adaptive experiment which can guarantee the identification of the initial state. (Note that, if the initial state happens to be 5, application of 11 will identify it; however, there is no a priori guarantee that such an experiment will terminate successfully.)

16 *Multiple diagnosing experiments*

The following result will be found useful in the ensuing discussion.

1 **Theorem** In an n-state minimal FSS, any set of r states $(2 \leq r \leq n)$ contains at least two states which are $(n - r + 1)$-distinguishable.
Proof By *2.9.1*, the number of classes in π_k is at least k, and hence the number of states in each class is at most $n - k$. In particular, the number of states in each class of π_{n-r+1} is at most

$$n - (n - r + 1) = r - 1$$

which implies the theorem.

Now, suppose ξ identical "copies" of an n-state FSS $\mathfrak{M}$ (all in the same initial state) are available for experimentation. If the admissible set A_1 of $\mathfrak{M}$ is of order m, then—by *1*—there must be an input sequence of length $n - m + 1$ or less which, when applied to $\mathfrak{M}$, yields an output sequence on the basis of which it is possible to rule out at least one state of A_1. A_1 can now be replaced with the admissible set A_2, whose order is at most $m - 1$. Again, by *1*, there must be an input sequence of length $n - m + 2$ or less which, when applied to a second copy of $\mathfrak{M}$, serves to eliminate at least one state of A_2 and to replace A_2 with A_3, whose order is at most $m - 2$. Continuing in this fashion, one finally attains an admissible set of order 1, whose single element is the true initial state of $\mathfrak{M}$. Such an experiment, clearly, requires at most $m - 1$ copies of $\mathfrak{M}$, and the application of at most

2 $$\sum_{r=2}^{m} (n - r + 1) = \tfrac{1}{2}(2n - m)(m - 1)$$

input symbols. We thus have:

3 **Theorem** The diagnosing problem for an n-state FSS with m admis-

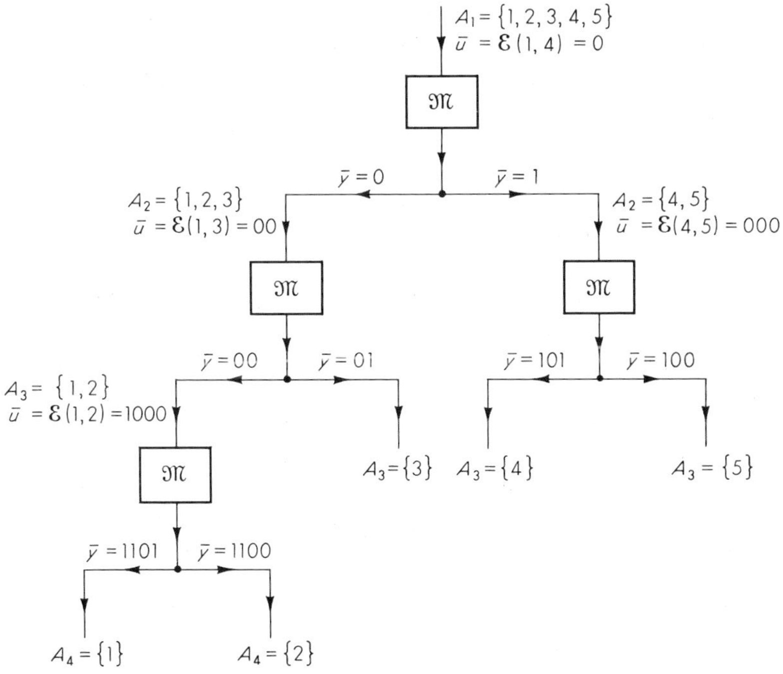

Fig. 2.16.1 Multiple-experimental tree for Example *2.16.4*.

sible states is always solvable by a multiple adaptive experiment of length $l \leq \frac{1}{2}(2n - m)(m - 1)$ and multiplicity $\xi \leq m - 1$.

4 *Example* It is easy to verify that no diagnosing sequence exists for the FSS of Fig. *2.14.1*, with the admissible set $\{1,2,3,4,5\}$ (try applying 0 or 1!). The diagnosing problem, therefore, can be solved only by a multiple experiment. The progress of such an experiment, under all possible conditions, is depicted by Fig. *2.16.1*. In the notation adopted above, $A_1 = \{1,2,3,4,5\}$, where 1 and 4 (as well as other pairs of states) are 1-distinguishable. Applying $\bar{u} = \mathcal{E}(1,4) = 0$ yields the output sequence $\bar{y} = 0$ if the true initial state is not 4, and 1 if the true initial state is not 1. The states of A_1 to which $\bar{y} = 0$ is attributable are 1, 2, and 3; those to which $\bar{y} = 1$ is attributable are 4 and 5. The admissible set for the second copy, therefore, is either $A_2 = \{1,2,3\}$ or $A_2 = \{4,5\}$, depending on the actual output observed. The remainder of the diagram can be similarly interpreted.

The tree exemplified by Fig. *2.16.1* is called a *multiple-experiment tree*. Its root is A_1, and each one of its paths terminates in an A_ν set consisting of one element only. In any particular case, only one of the paths is actually pursued—the one which terminates with the true initial state. The multiple experiment tree shows explicitly how a multiple *preset* diagnosing experiment can be conducted: If the tree contains ξ boxes, apply to ξ copies of $\mathfrak{M}$ the respective input sequences associated with these boxes (simultaneously, if so desired); the observed output sequences correspond to a tree path which terminates in the true initial state.

17 *Homing experiments*

The *homing problem* for an FSS $\mathfrak{M}$ is formulated as follows: $\mathfrak{M}$ is specified in its minimal form, and is known to have the admissible set $A = \{\sigma_{i1}, \sigma_{i2}, \ldots, \sigma_{im}\}$; take $\mathfrak{M}$ into a known final state (i.e., perform an experiment such that the state attained at the end of the experiment can be deduced from the records of input and output sequences). An experiment which solves this problem is called a *homing experiment* for $\mathfrak{M}$ and A. The input sequence employed in a simple preset homing experiment is called a *homing sequence* for $\mathfrak{M}$ and A, of which the *minimal homing sequence* is one whose length is smaller than or equal to the length of any other homing sequence.

In designing a simple preset homing experiment for $\mathfrak{M}$, one searches for an input sequence which, when applied to $\mathfrak{M}$ at each one of the admissible states, yields distinct output sequences whenever the final states are distinct. Such a sequence, clearly, is a homing sequence for A.

18 *Preset homing experiments*

In what follows, we shall construct a series of sets $A_1, A_2, \ldots, A_L$, where $A_i = \{A_{i1}, A_{i2}, \ldots, A_{ir_i}\}$, and where A_{ij} is a set of states of the n-state FSS $\mathfrak{M}$ under investigation. A_1 consists of a single set only—namely the admissible set $A = \{\sigma_{i1}, \sigma_{i2}, \ldots, \sigma_{im}\}$ of $\mathfrak{M}$. If each A_{ij} is a *singleton* (i.e., a set with one element only), A_i is taken as A_L—the last in the series. Otherwise, A_{i+1} can be constructed from A_i as follows: Let A_{id} be any of the sets in A_i which are not singletons; if ν_i is the order of A_{id}, there are two states in A_{id}, say, σ and σ', which are $(n - \nu_i + 1)$-distinguishable. Let the set of states into which the input sequence $\mathcal{E}(\sigma, \sigma') = \mathcal{E}_i$ takes A_{ij} be denoted by A'_{ij}. Partition each A_{ij} such that two states belong to the same class if and only if the output sequences they yield to $\mathcal{E}_i$ are identical. Partition A'_{ij} accordingly (i.e., if two states in A_{ij} are assigned to different classes, their successors in A'_{ij} must also be assigned to different classes). A_{i+1} is then taken as the set of all classes resulting from the partitioning of all A'_{ij}. Since A_{id} is surely partitionable into at least two classes, the number of sets in A_{i+1} always exceeds the number of sets in A_i. Hence, after at most m applications of the above procedure, one attains the final set A_L where all elements are singletons. By construction, the input sequence $\mathcal{E}_1\mathcal{E}_2 \cdots \mathcal{E}_{L-1}$ takes the admissible set A into the set A_L, such that each state of A_L is reached with a different output sequence. Thus, $\mathcal{E}_1\mathcal{E}_2 \cdots \mathcal{E}_{L-1}$ is a homing sequence for A. Since ν_i does not exceed m, the length of this sequence is at most $(n-1)(m-1)$. Thus, we have:

1 **Theorem** The homing problem for an n-state FSS with m admissible states is always solvable by a simple preset experiment of length $l \leq (n-1)(m-1)$. (If every pair of states in the FSS is h-distinguishable, $l \leq h(m-1)$.)

2 *Example* For the FSS of Fig. *2.14.1* and the admissible set $\{1,2,3,4,5\}$, we have:

3
$$\begin{aligned} A_1 &= \{\{1,2,3,4,5\}\} & \mathcal{E}_1 &= \mathcal{E}(1,4) = 0 \\ A_2 &= \{\{1,5\}, \{2,3\}\} & \mathcal{E}_2 &= \mathcal{E}(1,5) = 0 \\ A_3 &= \{\{1\}, \{2\}, \{1,5\}\} & \mathcal{E}_3 &= \mathcal{E}(1,5) = 0 \\ A_4 &= \{\{1\}, \{1\}, \{1\}, \{2\}\} \end{aligned}$$

Hence, the homing sequence for $\{1,2,3,4,5\}$ is 000.

19 Adaptive homing experiments

An adaptive homing experiment for the FSS $\mathfrak{M}$ and admissible set $A = \{\sigma_{i1},\sigma_{i2}, \ldots ,\sigma_{im}\}$ can be conducted as follows: A must contain two states, say, σ_{i1} and σ_{i2}, which are $(n - m + 1)$-distinguishable. Apply $\mathcal{E}(\sigma_{i1},\sigma_{i2})$ and observe the corresponding output sequence. On the basis of the observation, one can determine a set A' of final states whose order is at most $m - 1$. If A' is not a singleton, it is considered as a revised admissible set, and treated as A above. After at most m applications of this procedure, one attains an admissible set consisting of one element only, and hence a known final state. The length of this experiment is $\sum_{r=2}^{m} (n - r + 1)$, the closed form of which is given in *2.16.2*. We thus have:

1 **Theorem** The homing problem for an n-state FSS with m admissible states is always solvable by a simple adaptive experiment of length $l \leq \frac{1}{2}(2n - m)(m - 1)$ and iteration index $\rho \leq m - 1$.

2 *Example* For the FSS of Fig. *2.14.1* and the admissible set $\{1,2,3,4,5\}$ (when the true initial state is 4), we have:

3
$$\begin{aligned} A &= \{1,2,3,4,5\} \qquad & \mathcal{E}(1,4) &= 0;\ \text{output: } 1 \\ A' &= \{2,3\} & \mathcal{E}(2,3) &= 00;\ \text{output: } 01 \\ A'' &= \{2\} \end{aligned}$$

The known final state, then, is 2.

20 Identification of FSS

The *identification problem* for an FSS $\mathfrak{M}$ is formulated as follows: $\mathfrak{M}$ is known to belong to a specified finite class of compatible, distinguishable, and minimal FSS, denoted by $C = \{\mathfrak{M}_1,\mathfrak{M}_2, \ldots ,\mathfrak{M}_N\}$; find the minimal form of $\mathfrak{M}$ (up to isomorphism). An experiment which solves this problem is called an *identification experiment* for $\mathfrak{M}$ and C. Suppose some state σ_i in $\mathfrak{M}_i$ is equivalent to some state σ_j in $\mathfrak{M}_j$ $(j \neq i)$; then there is no a priori assurance that an identification experiment exists for $\mathfrak{M}$ and C (since $\mathfrak{M}$ may be $\mathfrak{M}_i$ in the initial state σ_i). A set C where no state in any $\mathfrak{M}_i$ is equivalent to any state in any $\mathfrak{M}_j$ $(j \neq i)$ is called an *exclusive* set of FSS.

1 **Theorem** If $\mathfrak{M}_1$ and $\mathfrak{M}_2$ are strongly connected and distinguishable FSS, then no state in $\mathfrak{M}_1$ is equivalent to any state in $\mathfrak{M}_2$.

Proof Suppose state σ' of $\mathfrak{M}_1$ is equivalent to σ'' of $\mathfrak{M}_2$. Since $\mathfrak{M}_1$ is strongly connected, there is an input sequence which takes σ' into every state of $\mathfrak{M}_1$. Since states reachable from σ' and σ'' with the same input sequence must be equivalent, it follows that every state of $\mathfrak{M}_1$ is equivalent to some state in $\mathfrak{M}_2$. Similarly one can show that every state in $\mathfrak{M}_2$ is equivalent to some state in $\mathfrak{M}_1$. By definition then, $\mathfrak{M}_1$ and $\mathfrak{M}_2$ are equivalent, which contradicts the assumption in the theorem.

2 **Corollary** A finite set of compatible, distinguishable, minimal, and strongly connected FSS must be exclusive.

21 *The sum of FSS*

Let $\mathfrak{M}_1$ and $\mathfrak{M}_2$ be compatible FSS described by $\langle U,Y_1,S_1,f_1,g_1\rangle$ and $\langle U,Y_2,S_2,f_2,g_2\rangle$, respectively, where no state in S_1 bears the same label as a state in S_2 (that is, $S_1 \cap S_2 = 0$). Then the *sum* of $\mathfrak{M}_1$ and $\mathfrak{M}_2$, denoted by $\mathfrak{M}_1 + \mathfrak{M}_2$, is an FSS described by $\langle U,\ Y_1 \cup Y_2,\ S_1 \cup S_2,\ f,\ g\rangle$, where f and g are constructed as follows: If σ_1 is any state in S_1 and σ_2 any state in S_2, then, for all α_i in U:

1 $$f(\sigma_1,\alpha_i) = f_1(\sigma_1,\alpha_i) \qquad f(\sigma_2,\alpha_i) = f_2(\sigma_2,\alpha_i)$$

2 $$g(\sigma_1,\alpha_i) = g_1(\sigma_1,\alpha_i) \qquad g(\sigma_2,\alpha_i) = g_2(\sigma_2,\alpha_i)$$

Thus, the transition graph (or table) of $\mathfrak{M}_1 + \mathfrak{M}_2$ is simply the union of the transition graphs (or tables) of $\mathfrak{M}_1$ and $\mathfrak{M}_2$. More generally, let $\mathfrak{M}_1, \mathfrak{M}_2, \ldots, \mathfrak{M}_N$ be compatible FSS, where S_i is the state set of $\mathfrak{M}_i$ and where $S_i \cap S_j = 0$ whenever $i \neq j$ (this can always be enforced by state relabeling). Then the *sum* of $\mathfrak{M}_1, \mathfrak{M}_2, \ldots, \mathfrak{M}_N$, denoted by $\sum_{\nu=1}^{N} \mathfrak{M}_\nu$, is an FSS whose transition graph (or table) is the union of the transition graphs (or tables) of $\mathfrak{M}_1, \mathfrak{M}_2, \ldots, \mathfrak{M}_N$. Clearly, insofar as diagnosing and homing experiments are concerned, the FSS $\sum_{\nu=1}^{N} \mathfrak{M}_\nu$ is indistinguishable from $\mathfrak{M}_1$, *or* $\mathfrak{M}_2$, *or* $\mathfrak{M}_3, \ldots,$ *or* $\mathfrak{M}_N$—depending on the initial state of $\sum_{\nu=1}^{N} \mathfrak{M}_\nu$ (if this state is taken from S_i, then $\sum_{\nu=1}^{N} \mathfrak{M}_\nu$ is indistinguishable from $\mathfrak{M}_i$).

A direct consequence of the above definition is the following:

3 **Theorem** If $C = \{\mathfrak{M}_1,\mathfrak{M}_2, \ldots ,\mathfrak{M}_N\}$ is an exclusive set of FSS, then $\sum_{\nu=1}^{N} \mathfrak{M}_\nu$ is a minimal FSS.

22 *Simple identification experiments*

Consider an FSS $\mathfrak{M}$, known to belong to the exclusive set

$$C = \{\mathfrak{M}_1, \mathfrak{M}_2, \ldots, \mathfrak{M}_N\}$$

where S_i is the state set of $\mathfrak{M}_i$ and $S_i \cap S_j = 0$ $(i \neq j)$. In view of the preceding discussion, the problem "$\mathfrak{M}$ is one of the $\mathfrak{M}_i$; find which one!" is seen to be equivalent to the following problem: "$\mathfrak{M}$ is $\sum_{\nu=1}^{N} \mathfrak{M}_i$; find to which S_i its initial state belongs." Now, if the initial state σ of $\sum_{\nu=1}^{N} \mathfrak{M}_i$ is in S_i, then any successor of σ must also be in S_i. Hence, the latter problem can be restated as follows: "$\mathfrak{M}$ is $\sum_{\nu=1}^{N} \mathfrak{M}_i$; take $\mathfrak{M}$ into a known final state." This problem is precisely the homing problem for $\sum_{\nu=1}^{N} \mathfrak{M}_i$ and $S_1 \cup S_2 \cup \cdots \cup S_N$. As shown in Secs. *18* and *19*, this problem can always be solved by a simple preset or a simple adaptive experiment. In summary, then, the identification experiment for $\mathfrak{M}$ and C is carried out by performing on $\mathfrak{M}$ a homing experiment, as if $\mathfrak{M}$ were the FSS $\sum_{\nu=1}^{N} \mathfrak{M}_i$ with the admissible set $S_1 \cup S_2 \cup \cdots \cup S_N$; if the final state is found to belong to S_i, then the minimal form of $\mathfrak{M}$ is given by $\mathfrak{M}_i$.

Suppose the order of any S_i is at most n. Since C is exclusive, $\mathfrak{M}_i + \mathfrak{M}_j$ is a minimal FSS for any i and $j \neq 1$; hence, by *2.14.1*, any two states in $\sum_{\nu=1}^{N} \mathfrak{M}_i$ are $(2n-1)$-distinguishable. Also, the order of the admissible set $S_1 \cup S_2 \cup \cdots \cup S_N$ is at most Nn. By *2.18.1*, then, we have:

1 **Theorem** The identification problem for an FSS $\mathfrak{M}$ and an exclusive set $C = \{\mathfrak{M}_1, \mathfrak{M}_2, \ldots, \mathfrak{M}_N\}$, where each $\mathfrak{M}_i$ has at most n states, is always solvable by a simple preset experiment of length

$$l \leq (2n-1)(Nn-1)$$

By *2.21.3* we have:

2 **Corollary** $\mathfrak{M}$ is known to be a strongly connected FSS; in addition, its input and output alphabets and the bound to the order of its state set are known. Then the minimal form of $\mathfrak{M}$ can always be determined (up to isomorphism) by a simple preset experiment.

23 *Finite-memory FSS*

An FSS $\mathfrak{M}$ is said to be a *finite-memory* FSS if the output of $\mathfrak{M}$ can be expressed in the form

1 $$y(t) = \tilde{g}(u(t),u(t-1), \ldots ,u(t-\mu),y(t-1),y(t-2), \ldots ,y(t-\mu))$$

for some finite μ. μ is called the *memory* of $\mathfrak{M}$ if, in addition to *1*,

2 $$y(t) \neq \tilde{g}(u(t),u(t-1), \ldots ,u(t-\mu+1),y(t-1),y(t-2), \ldots , y(t-\mu+1))$$

Thus, $\mathfrak{M}$ has the memory μ if the knowledge of present input and past μ inputs and outputs is sufficient to determine the present output, and if such a determination is impossible when μ is decreased by 1.

3 **Theorem** Let $\mathfrak{M}$ be a minimal FSS. Then the state of $\mathfrak{M}$ can be expressed in the form

4 $$s(t) = \tilde{f}(u(t-1),u(t-2), \ldots ,u(t-\mu),y(t-1),y(t-2), \ldots , y(t-\mu))$$

if and only if $\mathfrak{M}$ is a finite-memory FSS with the memory μ or less.

Proof Suppose that $\mathfrak{M}$ has memory μ or less and that *4* does not hold. Then the transition graph of $\mathfrak{M}$ has two paths of length μ which represent the same input sequence and same output sequence of length μ, and which terminate in two distinguishable states. This implies that, for some $\nu \geq 0$ the $(\mu + \nu)$th output cannot be uniquely determined from the knowledge of present input and past μ inputs and outputs—a contradiction. Now, if *4* holds and if g is the output function of $\mathfrak{M}$, we can write

5 $$\begin{aligned} y(t) &= g(s(t),u(t)) \\ &= g(\tilde{f}(u(t-1),u(t-2), \ldots ,u(t-\mu),y(t-1),y(t-2), \ldots , y(t-\mu)),u(t)) \\ &= \tilde{g}(u(t),u(t-1), \ldots ,u(t-\mu),y(t-1),y(t-2), \ldots ,y(t-\mu)) \end{aligned}$$

and hence $\mathfrak{M}$ is an FSS of memory μ or less.

The preceding proof implies:

6 **Corollary** Let $\mathfrak{M}$ be a finite-memory FSS with memory μ. Any two paths in the transition graph of $\mathfrak{M}$ which describe the same input sequence and same output sequence (these are called *matching paths*) must intersect at their νth state where $\nu \leq \mu$. There must be at least one pair of matching paths of length $\mu - 1$ which do not intersect at any state.

24 *Determination of FSS memory*

1 **Theorem** If $\mathfrak{M}$ is a finite memory FSS with n states and memory μ, then $\mu \leq n(n-1)/2$.

Proof The transition graph of $\mathfrak{M}$ must exhibit at least one pair of matching paths of length $\mu - 1$ which do not intersect. Call these paths π_1 and π_2; denote the ith state in π_1 and π_2 by σ_1 and σ_2, respectively, and the jth state by σ_1' and σ_2', respectively ($i < j \leq \mu$). If $\sigma_1 = \sigma_1'$ and $\sigma_2 = \sigma_2'$, the paths assume the form shown in Fig. *2.24.1a*.

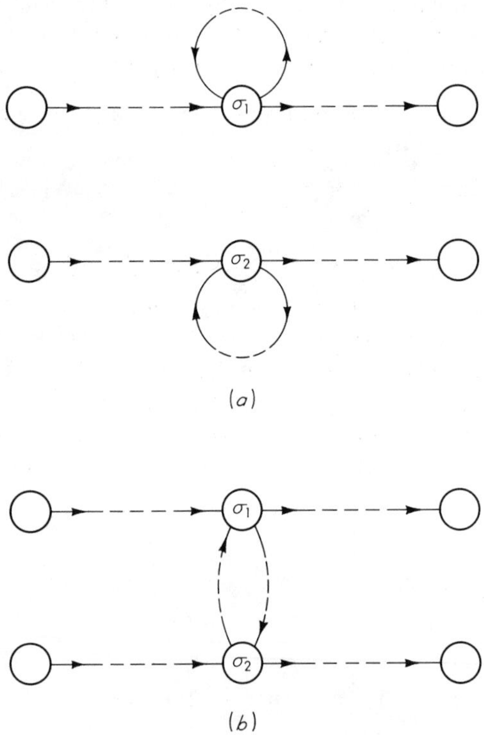

Fig. 2.24.1 Illustrating proof to Theorem *2.24.1*.

The two loops in this figure represent matching paths of infinite length —a contradiction of *2.23.6*. Hence $\sigma_1 = \sigma_1'$ and $\sigma_2 = \sigma_2'$ is an impossibility. Now, suppose $\sigma_1 = \sigma_2'$ and $\sigma_2 = \sigma_1'$. In this case the paths assume the form shown in Fig. *2.24.1b* where, again, there are two matching paths of infinite length (the loop initiating at σ_1 and the loop initiating at σ_2)—a contradiction of *2.23.6*. Thus the *unordered* pairs (σ_1,σ_2) and (σ_1',σ_2') cannot be identical. Since the number of distinct unordered pairs of states in $\mathfrak{M}$ is $\binom{n}{2} = n(n-1)/2$, the theorem follows.

A procedure for determining whether a given FSS $\mathfrak{M}$ is a finite-memory FSS can now be formulated: List all sets of matching paths of lengths 1, 2, 3, etc., appearing in the transition graph of $\mathfrak{M}$. μ is the least integer such that all matching paths intersect at their μth state or earlier. If no such μ is found for any value less than $n(n-1)/2$, then $\mathfrak{M}$ is not a finite-memory FSS.

Once the memory μ of a finite-memory FSS is established, the function $\tilde{g}$ (as defined by *2.23.1*) can be displayed in a tabular form by listing $y(t)$ for all possible combinations of arguments $u(t)$, $u(t-1)$, $\ldots$, $u(t-\mu)$, $y(t-1)$, $y(t-2)$, $\ldots$, $y(t-\mu)$.

2 *Example* Consider the FSS of Fig. *2.24.2*. In this case the matching

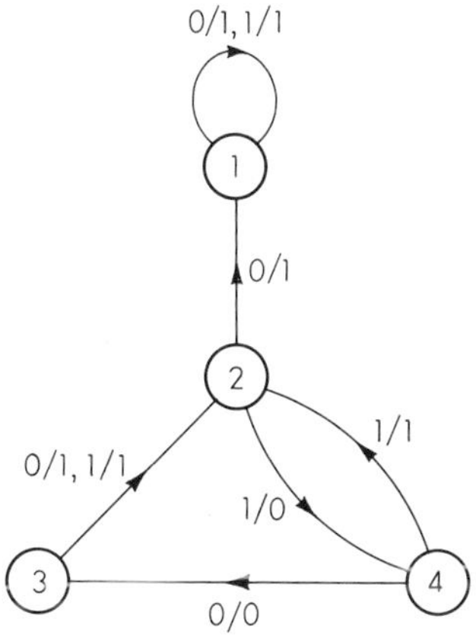

Fig. 2.24.2 FSS for Example *2.24.2*.

paths of length 1 are those describing 0/1 and 1/1, which do not satisfy the intersection requirement. However, the matching paths of length 2 —namely those describing (0/1)(1/1), (0/1)(0/1), (1/1)(0/1), and (1/1)(1/0)—do satisfy this condition. Hence the FSS has the memory 2. Table *2.24.1* tabulates the function $\tilde{g}$ for this FSS (impossible combinations of arguments are deleted). It can be noted that some of the arguments of $\tilde{g}$ are redundant: If columns $u(t-1)$ and $u(t-2)$ are omitted, identical combinations of $u(t)$, $y(t-1)$, and $y(t-2)$ yield

Table 2.24.1 $\tilde{g}$ **table for Example** *2.24.2*

$y(t-2)$	$y(t-1)$	$u(t-2)$	$u(t-1)$	$u(t)$	$y(t)$
0	0	1	0	0	1
0	0	1	0	1	1
0	1	0	0	0	1
0	1	0	0	1	0
0	1	0	1	0	1
0	1	0	1	1	0
0	1	1	1	0	1
0	1	1	1	1	0
1	0	0	1	0	0
1	0	0	1	1	1
1	0	1	1	0	0
1	0	1	1	1	1
1	1	0	0	0	1
1	1	0	0	1	1
1	1	0	1	0	1
1	1	0	1	1	1
1	1	1	0	0	1
1	1	1	0	1	1
1	1	1	1	0	1
1	1	1	1	1	1

Table 2.24.2 **Reduced** $\tilde{g}$ **table for Example** *2.24.2*

$y(t-2)$	$y(t-1)$	$u(t)$	$y(t)$
0	0	0	1
0	0	1	1
0	1	0	1
0	1	1	0
1	0	0	0
1	0	1	1
1	1	0	1
1	1	1	1

identical $y(t)$ values. The tabulation of $\tilde{g}$ with the redundant arguments omitted is shown in Table *2.24.2*.

25 *Synthesis of finite-memory FSS*

Figure *2.25.1* shows a general switching network which can be used for the realization of a finite-memory FSS with binary input and output alphabets and with memory μ. The delays are employed to obtain $u(t-1)$, $u(t-2)$, . . . , $u(t-\mu)$ and $y(t-1)$, $y(t-2)$, . . . , $y(t-\mu)$ from the $u(t)$ and $y(t)$ lines. The binary logic is a combinational switching network realizing the function $\tilde{g}$.

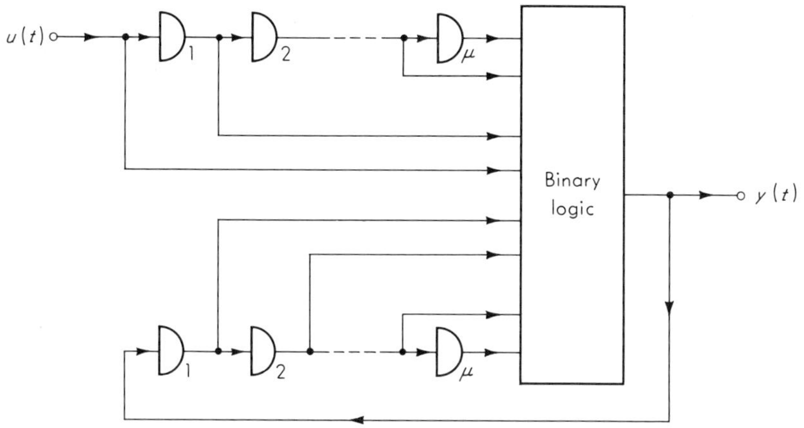

Fig. 2.25.1 General realization of finite-memory FSS.

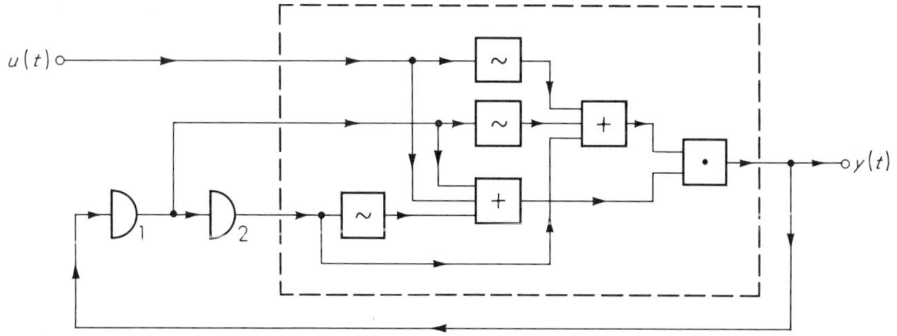

Fig. 2.25.2 Realization of FSS of Example *2.25.1*.

1 *Example* Figure *2.25.2* shows the realization of the FSS of Example *2.24.2*, whose (reduced) $\tilde{g}$ function is given in Table *2.24.2* (the elements in the diagram marked $+$, $\cdot$, and $\sim$ are OR gates, AND gates, and inverters, respectively).

26 *Successor partitions*

A *successor partition* divides the state set of an FSS $\mathfrak{M}$ into *successor classes* as follows: The states σ_1 and σ_2 are in the same class if and only if,

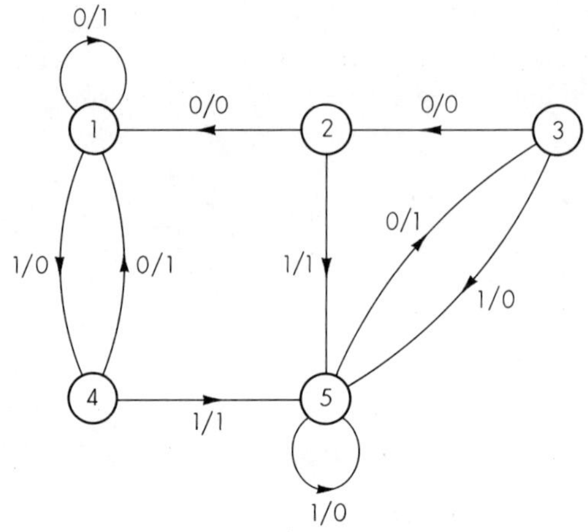

Fig. 2.26.1 FSS for Example *2.26.1*.

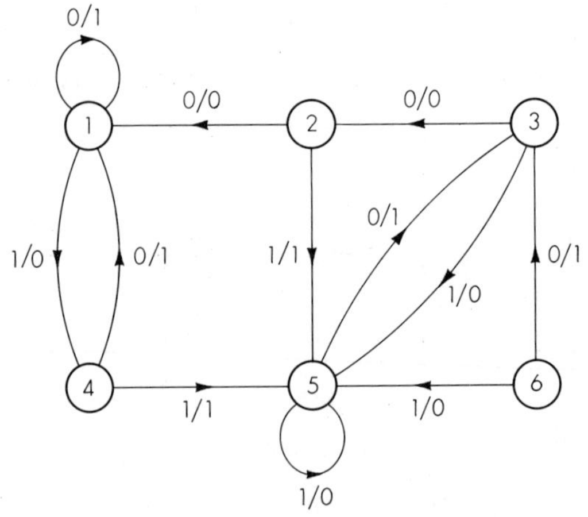

Fig. 2.26.2 FSS for Example *2.26.2*.

for every input symbol α, $f(\sigma_1,\alpha)$ and $f(\sigma_2,\alpha)$ are again in the same class. (Note that in contrast with the equivalence partition, the successor partition is independent of the output function.) If $\mathfrak{M}$ has n states, then the partitions consisting of n classes or a single class are both, trivially, successor partitions.

1 *Example* A successor partition for the minimal FSS shown in Fig. *2.26.1* consists of the classes $\{1,2,3\}$, $\{4,5\}$.

The order of any successor class can be increased arbitrarily by adding redundant states. More specifically, if $C_i = \{\sigma_{i1},\sigma_{i2}, \ldots ,\sigma_{ir}\}$ is a successor class of $\mathfrak{M}$, a state σ_{n+1} can be added to the state set of $\mathfrak{M}$ in the following manner: $f(\sigma_{n+1},\alpha) = f(\sigma_{i1},\alpha)$ and $g(\sigma_{n+1},\alpha) = g(\sigma_{i1},\alpha)$ for all input symbols α. Clearly, the revised FSS is equivalent to $\mathfrak{M}$; C_i now includes σ_{n+1} as well as the original r states. Thus, one can always force any successor partition to be *uniform*, i.e., to consist of equal-order classes.

2 *Example* For the FSS of Fig. *2.26.1*, the nonuniform partition $\{1,2,3\}$, $\{4,5\}$ can be rendered uniform by adding a state 6 which is equivalent to 5 (the revised FSS is shown in Fig. *2.26.2*). The new successor partition is $\{1,2,3\}$, $\{4,5,6\}$. Note that the uniformity has been achieved at the cost of destroying the minimality of the FSS.

27 *Cascade decomposition of FSS*

To simplify construction, installation and maintenance, it is desirable to realize FSS in the form of a string of subsystems where the ith subsystem ($i > 1$) accepts its input from the output of the ($i - 1$)st. Such a string is called a *cascade connection* of FSS. A cascade connection of two FSS is shown in Fig. *2.27.1*. Two FSS, say, $\mathfrak{M}_1$ and $\mathfrak{M}_2$, constitute

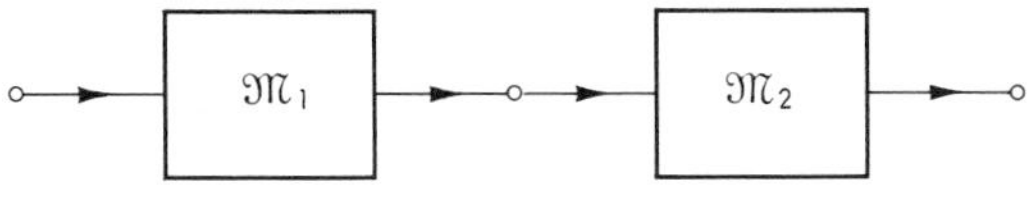

Fig. 2.27.1 A cascade connection of two FSS.

the *cascade decomposition* of an FSS $\mathfrak{M}$, if the FSS whose realization is the cascade connection of $\mathfrak{M}_1$ and $\mathfrak{M}_2$ is equivalent to $\mathfrak{M}$. If $\mathfrak{M}_2$ follows $\mathfrak{M}_1$, the overall FSS is denoted by $\mathfrak{M}_1\mathfrak{M}_2$.

Given an n-state FSS $\mathfrak{M}$, the cascade decomposition of $\mathfrak{M}$ can be found as follows: Let $C_1, C_2, \ldots, C_m$ denote the uniform successor partition of $\mathfrak{M}$, and let $C_i = \{\sigma_{i1},\sigma_{i2}, \ldots ,\sigma_{ir}\}$ for $i = 1, 2, \ldots, m$. $\mathfrak{M}_1$ is an FSS with the same input alphabet as $\mathfrak{M}_1$, say $\{\alpha_1,\alpha_2, \ldots ,\alpha_p\}$, an output alphabet consisting of the mp symbols $\gamma_{i\alpha_\nu}$ ($i = 1,2, \ldots ,m$; $\nu = 1,2, \ldots ,p$), and the state set $\{\Sigma_1,\Sigma_2, \ldots ,\Sigma_m\}$. $\mathfrak{M}_2$ is an FSS whose input alphabet is the output alphabet of $\mathfrak{M}_1$, whose output alphabet is the same as that of $\mathfrak{M}$, and whose state set is $\{\sigma_1,\sigma_2, \ldots ,\sigma_r\}$. If, in $\mathfrak{M}$, α_ν takes σ_{ij} into σ_{kl} with the output β, then in $\mathfrak{M}_1$, α_ν takes Σ_i into Σ_k with the output γ_{id_ν} and, in $\mathfrak{M}_2$, γ_{id_ν} takes σ_j into σ_k with the output β. By construction, then, $\mathfrak{M}_1\mathfrak{M}_2$ is an FSS whose input and output alphabets are the same as those of $\mathfrak{M}$ and whose state set consists of all $mr = n$ ordered pairs (Σ_i,σ_j). Moreover, α_ν takes (Σ_i,σ_j) into (Σ_k,σ_l) with the output β if and only if α_ν takes σ_{ij} into σ_{kl} with the same output β. Thus, (Σ_i,σ_j) and σ_{ij} are equivalent for all i, j, and hence $\mathfrak{M} \approx \mathfrak{M}_1\mathfrak{M}_2$.

1 *Example* For the FSS of Fig. *2.26.2*, $C_1 = \{1,2,3\}$ and $C_2 = \{4,5,6\}$. The transition graphs for $\mathfrak{M}_1$ and $\mathfrak{M}_2$ are shown in Fig. *2.27.2*.

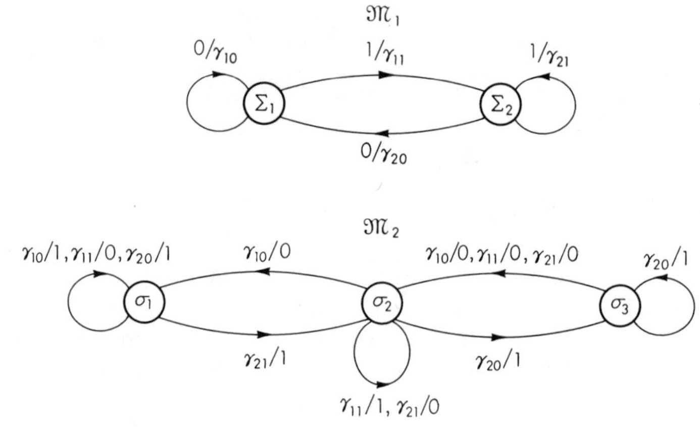

Fig. 2.27.2 Transition graphs for Example *2.26.1*.

28 *State-determined FSS*

An FSS is called a *state-determined* FSS if the argument $u(t)$ of its output function is redundant, i.e., if

1 $$y(t) = g(s(t))$$

Consider an arbitrary FSS $\mathfrak{M}$, defined by

2 $$s(t + 1) = f(s(t),u(t))$$

3 $$y(t) = g(s(t),u(t))$$

Define a variable s', such as $s'(t)$ is the ordered pair $(s(t),u(t))$. *3*, then, can be written as

4 $$y(t) = g'(s'(t))$$

Also, by *2* and the definition of s'

5 $$s'(t+1) = (s(t+1),u(t+1)) = (f(s(t),u(t)),u(t+1))$$

or

6 $$s'(t+1) = f'(s'(t),u(t+1))$$

Defining a variable u' such that $u'(t) = u(t+1)$, *6* becomes

7 $$s'(t+1) = f'(s'(t),u'(t))$$

4 and *7* define a state-determined FSS $\mathfrak{M}$. Apart from the fact that an input sequence applied to $\mathfrak{M}'$ at time t is to be applied to $\mathfrak{M}$ at time

Table 2.28.1 Transition table for FSS of Example *2.28.8*

	$s(t+1)$		$y(t)$	
$s(t)$ \ $u(t)$	0	1	0	1
1	1	3	0	0
2	3	1	0	1
3	2	2	1	0

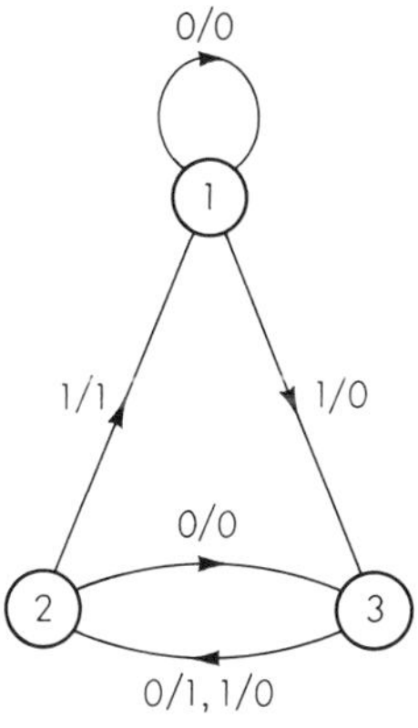

Fig. 2.28.1 FSS of Example *2.28.8*.

$t+1$, $\mathfrak{M}$ and $\mathfrak{M}'$ are indistinguishable. Hence, by an appropriate redefinition of the state variable, every FSS can be represented as a state-determined FSS. Although such a representation is usually achieved at the cost of a larger state set (the state set of $\mathfrak{M}'$ may be p times larger than that of $\mathfrak{M}$, where p is the order of the input alphabet of $\mathfrak{M}$), it is sometimes more amenable to theoretical treatment than the common representation.

8 *Example* Table *2.28.1* and Fig. *2.28.1* show an FSS which is not state-determined. Table *2.28.2* and Fig. *2.28.2* show the representation of this

Table 2.28.2 Transition table for FSS of Table *2.28.1*, represented as a state-determined FSS

$s(t)$ \ $u(t)$	$s(t+1)$: 0	$s(t+1)$: 1	$y(t)$
1_0	1_0	1_1	0
1_1	3_0	3_1	0
2_0	3_0	3_1	0
2_1	1_0	1_1	1
3_0	2_0	2_1	1
3_1	2_0	2_1	0

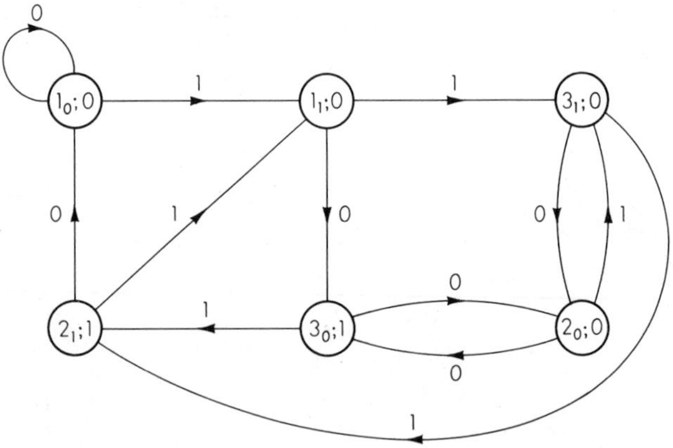

Fig. 2.28.2 FSS of Fig. *2.28.1*, represented as a state-determined FSS.

FSS as a state-determined FSS. In the latter, σ_α denotes a state which corresponds to the ordered pair (σ,α), where σ is a state in the original FSS and α an input symbol. In the transition graph of the state-determined representation, the output symbols are associated with the vertices instead of the branches [the label σ_α; β attached to a vertex indicates that the corresponding state is σ_α and that $g(\sigma_\alpha) = \beta$].

29 *Regular expressions*

Regular expressions are expressions for the description of certain binary sequences of special interest in the theory of finite-state systems. They are defined recursively as follows: given the symbols 0, 1, λ, and $\emptyset$, and the operations $+$, $\cdot$, and $*$, then:

1 0, 1, λ, or $\emptyset$ are regular expressions.
2 If E_1 and E_2 are regular expressions, so are $E_1 + E_2$, $E_1 \cdot E_2$, and E_1^*.
3 No expression is regular unless it is constructable via rules *1* and *2* in a finite number of steps.

Regular expressions are employed to describe specific sequences as well as sets of sequences. λ denotes the sequence of zero length (the *null sequence*) and $\emptyset$ the empty set. $E_1 + E_2$ denotes the union of E_1 and E_2. $E_1 \cdot E_2$ (or simply E_1E_2) is the set of all sequences e_1 followed by e_2 such that e_1 is in E_1 and e_2 in E_2 (this set is called the *concatenation* of E_1 and E_2). E_1^*, called the *iterate* of E_1, is defined by

4 $$E_1^* = \lambda + E_1 + E_1E_1 + E_1E_1E_1 + \cdots$$

The following identities are consequences of the preceding assumptions:

5 $E_1 + E_2 = E_2 + E_1$

6 $E_1 + (E_2 + E_3) = (E_1 + E_2) + E_3 \qquad E_1(E_2E_3) = (E_1E_2)E_3$

7 $(E_1 + E_2)E_3 = E_1E_3 + E_2E_3 \qquad E_1(E_2 + E_3) = E_1E_2 + E_1E_3$

8 $E_1 + \emptyset = \emptyset + E_1 = E_1 \qquad E_1\emptyset = \emptyset E_1 = \emptyset$

9 $E_1\lambda = \lambda E_1 = E_1$

10 $E_1 + E_1 = E_1$

11 $E_1^* = \lambda + E_1E_1^*$

12 $E_1E_1^* = E_1^*E_1$

13 $E_1^*E_1^* = E_1^*$

14 $\emptyset^* = \lambda \qquad \lambda^* = \lambda$

For simplicity, the set $0 + 1$ will be denoted by x. Thus, x^* denotes the class of all finite binary sequences (including the null sequence).

15 *Example* The set of all sequences which contain two consecutive zeros, or which contain an even number of 1s and do not end with 0, is given by $x^*00x^* + (0^*10^*1)^*$.

30 *Finite-recognition systems*

A finite-recognition system (abbreviated FRS), is an FSS satisfying the following requirements: (*a*) It is state-determined; (*b*) its output alphabet is $\{0,1\}$; (*c*) its admissible set consists of one state only, i.e., it has a fixed initial state to be denoted by σ_I. Our discussion will be restricted to *binary* FRS, where the following additional requirement is imposed: (*d*) The input alphabet is $\{0,1\}$.

Let G be the extended output function of the FRS $\mathfrak{M}$ (see Sec. *8*). The input sequence $\bar{u}$ is said to be *recognizable* by $\mathfrak{M}$ if $G(\sigma_I,\bar{u}) = 1$. The set of all sequences recognizable by $\mathfrak{M}$ is called the *recognizable set* of $\mathfrak{M}$, denoted by M. Thus, a sequence $\bar{u}$ is in M if and only if the application of $\bar{u}$ takes $\mathfrak{M}$ from the initial state σ_I to a final state σ associated with the output symbol 1.

31 *Determination of recognizable sets*

Consider an FRS $\mathfrak{M}$ with the state set $\{\sigma_1,\sigma_2, \ldots ,\sigma_n\}$ (where one of the σ_i is the initial state σ_I). The regular expressions $e_{ij}{}^k$ are defined recursively (for all i, j ranging from 1 through n and k ranging from 0 through n) as follows:

1 $$e_{ij}{}^0 = \text{set of input symbols taking } \sigma_i \text{ to } \sigma_j \text{ (may be 0, 1, } x\text{, or } \emptyset)$$

2 $$e_{ij}{}^k = e_{ij}^{k-1} + e_{ik}^{k-1}(e_{kk}^{k-1})^*e_{kj}^{k-1} \qquad k > 0$$

3 **Lemma** $e_{ij}{}^k$ is the set of all input sequences taking the state σ_i into the state σ_j without passing through any intermediate state σ_ν where $\nu > k$.

Proof (by induction on k) For $k = 0$, no intermediate state is permissible, and $e_{ij}{}^0$ is simply the set of all input sequences taking σ_i directly to σ_j—precisely as defined in *1*. Assuming that *3* holds for $k - 1$: e_{ij}^{k-1}, e_{ik}^{k-1}, e_{kk}^{k-1}, and e_{kj}^{k-1} are the sets of all sequences taking σ_i to σ_j, σ_i to σ_k, σ_k to σ_k, and σ_k to σ_j, respectively, without passing through any intermediate σ_ν where $\nu > k - 1$. *3* then follows.

4 **Theorem** Let $\mathfrak{M}$ be an FRS with the state set $\{\sigma_1,\sigma_2, \ldots ,\sigma_n\}$, where σ_i is the initial state σ_I and where $\sigma_{l_1}, \sigma_{l_2}, \ldots, \sigma_{l_r}$ are the states associ-

ated with the output symbol 1. Then the recognizable set of $\mathfrak{M}$ is given by

5 $$M = e_{il_1}^n + e_{il_2}^n + \cdots + e_{il_r}^n$$

Proof By *3*, $e_{il_h}^n$ is the set of input sequences taking the initial state σ_I into the state σ_{l_h} (whose output is 1) via *any* intermediate state. Thus, M as given in *5* is the set of all input sequences taking $\mathfrak{M}$ into states associated with 1, which implies that M is the recognizable set of $\mathfrak{M}$.

By construction, we proved the following:

6 **Corollary** The recognizable set of any FRS is given by a regular expression.

7 *Example* Figure *2.31.1* shows an FRS where $n = 2$, $\sigma_I = \sigma_1$, and where

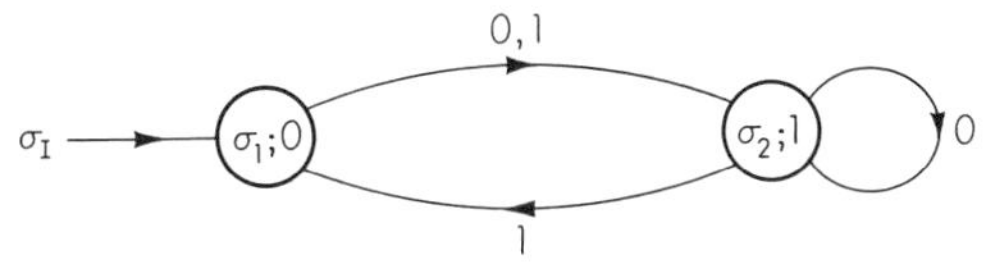

Fig. 2.31.1 FRS for Example *2.31.7*.

state σ_2 is the only one associated with the output symbol 1. In this case, by *5*, *2*, and *1*

8 $$M = e_{12}{}^2 = e_{12}{}^1 + e_{12}{}^1(e_{22}{}^1)^*e_{22}{}^1$$

9 $$e_{12}{}^1 = e_{12}{}^0 + e_{11}{}^0(e_{11}{}^0)^*e_{12}{}^0$$

10 $$e_{22}{}^1 = e_{22}{}^0 + e_{21}{}^0(e_{11}{}^0)^*e_{12}{}^0$$

11 $$e_{11}{}^0 = \emptyset \qquad e_{12}{}^0 = x \qquad e_{21}{}^0 = 1 \qquad e_{22}{}^0 = 0$$

Hence

12 $$e_{12}{}^1 = x + \emptyset(\emptyset)^*x = x \qquad e_{22}{}^1 = 0 + 1(\emptyset)^*x = 0 + 1x$$

13 $$M = x + x(0 + 1x)^*(0 + 1x)$$

For any given $\mathfrak{M}$, the form of M is not unique: It depends on the algorithm used for constructing M and on the way in which the states are labeled.

32 *Derivatives of regular expressions*

Given a regular expression E, the set of sequences which complete a fixed sequence e to form sequences in E is called the *derivative* of E with respect to e and denoted by $\partial_e[E]$. That is, $\partial_e[E]$ is a regular expression which contains e_1 if and only if E contains ee_1. The recursive determination of derivatives is facilitated by the following rules: If α_i is any symbol in the input alphabet then

1 $$\partial_{\alpha_1}[\alpha_1] = \lambda$$

2 $$\partial_{\alpha_1}[\alpha_i] = \emptyset \qquad \alpha_i \neq \alpha_1$$

3 $$\partial_{\alpha_1}[E_1 + E_2] = \partial_{\alpha_1}[E_1] + \partial_{\alpha_1}[E_2]$$

4 $$\partial_{\alpha_1}[E_1E_2] = \begin{cases} \partial_{\alpha_1}[E_1]E_2 & \text{if } E_1 \text{ does not include } \lambda \\ \partial_{\alpha_1}[E_1]E_2 + \partial_{\alpha_1}[E_2] & \text{if } E_1 \text{ includes } \lambda \end{cases}$$

5 $$\partial_{\alpha_1}[E^*] = \partial_{\alpha_1}[E]E^*$$

6 $$\partial_{\alpha_1\alpha_2\cdots\alpha_r}[E] = \partial_{\alpha_r}[\partial_{\alpha_1\alpha_2\cdots\alpha_{r-1}}[E]]$$

7 $$\partial_\lambda[E] = E$$

8 *Example* Consider the regular expression $E = x^*0 = (0 + 1)^*0$. By the preceding rules

9 $$\begin{aligned} \partial_{\alpha_1}[E] &= \partial_{\alpha_1}[(0 + 1)^*]0 + \partial_{\alpha_1}[0] \\ &= \partial_{\alpha_1}[0 + 1](0 + 1)^*0 + \partial_{\alpha_1}[0] \\ &= (\partial_{\alpha_1}[0] + \partial_{\alpha_1}[1])(0 + 1)^* + \partial_{\alpha_1}[0] \end{aligned}$$

Hence, the derivatives of E with respect to all sequences of length 1 and 2 are given by

10 $$\partial_0[E] = (\lambda + \emptyset)(0 + 1)^*0 + \lambda = (0 + 1)^*0 + \lambda = E + \lambda$$

11 $$\partial_1[E] = (\emptyset + \lambda)(0 + 1)^*0 + \emptyset = (0 + 1)^*0 = E$$

12 $$\begin{aligned} \partial_{00}[E] &= \partial_0[\partial_0[E]] = \partial_0[E + \lambda] = \partial_0[E] + \partial_0[\lambda] \\ &= E + \lambda + \emptyset = E + \lambda \end{aligned}$$

13 $$\begin{aligned} \partial_{01}[E] &= \partial_1[\partial_0[E]] = \partial_1[E + \lambda] = \partial_1[E] + \partial_1[\lambda] \\ &= E + \emptyset = E \end{aligned}$$

14 $$\partial_{10}[E] = \partial_0[\partial_1[E]] = \partial_0[E] = E + \lambda$$

15 $$\partial_{11}[E] = \partial_1[\partial_1[E]] = \partial_1[E] = E$$

Directly from the definition of a derivative, we have:

16 **Corollary** Let $\partial_e[E]$ be the derivative of the regular expression E with respect to the sequence e ($e \neq \lambda$). Then e is included in E if and only if λ is included in $\partial_e[E]$.

The following theorem will be presented without proof (for proof, [19]):

17 **Theorem** Every regular expression E has a finite number n of distinct

derivatives, each of which equals the derivative of E with respect to some sequence of length $n - 1$ or less.

33 *Determination of FRS from regular expression*

Given a regular expression E, a state-determined FSS, denoted by $\mathfrak{M}_E$, can be constructed recursively in accordance with the following rules: $\mathfrak{M}_E$ has n states, corresponding to the n distinct derivatives of E; the state corresponding to $\partial_e[E]$ will be denoted by $\sigma_{\partial_e[E]}$ (in particular, $\mathfrak{M}_E$ has the state $\sigma_{\partial_\lambda[E]} = \sigma_E$). When the input is 0, σ_E leads to $\sigma_{\partial_0[E]}$; when the input is 1, σ_E leads to $\sigma_{\partial_1[E]}$. In general, when the input is 0, $\sigma_{\partial_e[E]}$ leads to $\sigma_{\partial_0[\partial[E]]}$; when the input is 1, $\sigma_{\partial_e[E]}$ leads to $\sigma_{\partial_1[\partial_e[E]]}$. All states $\sigma_{\partial_e[E]}$ where $\sigma_e[E]$ includes λ are associated with the output 1, all other states are associated with the output 0.

By construction, the input sequences which take $\mathfrak{M}_E$ from σ_E to $\sigma_{\partial_e[E]}$ are those sequences in E which initiate with e. By *2.32.16*, on the other hand, e is in E if and only if $\sigma_{\partial_e[E]}$ is associated with the output 1. Hence, the set of all input sequences leading $\mathfrak{M}_E$ from σ_E to states associated with the output 1 is precisely E. $\mathfrak{M}_E$, therefore, is an FRS (with the initial state σ_E) whose recognizable set is E. In conclusion, we can state:

1 **Theorem** Every regular expression is the recognizable set of some FRS.

Let σ_{E_1} and σ_{E_2} be any distinct states in $\mathfrak{M}_E$. By construction, then, E_1 and E_2 are distinct, and hence there is at least one input sequence which yields the output $00 \cdots 01$ when applied to σ_{E_1} but not when applied to σ_{E_2} (or conversely). Thus, σ_{E_1} and σ_{E_2} are distinguishable and hence $\mathfrak{M}_E$ is a minimal FRS.

Note that, in constructing $\mathfrak{M}_E$, one has to establish whether any two derivatives of E are equal or not. Such establishment can often be achieved via the identities *2.29.5* to *2.29.14*. Neglecting to establish equality among derivatives results in the inclusion of redundant states and hence in a nonminimal representation of the FRS. One can show that the number of distinct forms assumed by a derivative of E such that one form cannot be obtained from another via identities *5*, *6*, *8*, *9*, and *10* in Sec. *29* is finite [19]. Thus, by a finite process, one can always determine a finite set of derivatives which contains, as a subset, all n distinct derivatives of E. This set can be used to construct a nonminimal FRS, whose minimization by standard means results in $\mathfrak{M}_E$.

2 *Example* To construct the FRS whose recognizable set is

$$E = (1 + 01^*0)^*01^*0$$

compute:

$\partial_\lambda[E] = E$ $\quad\partial_{00}[E] = E + \lambda$ $\quad\partial_{000}[E] = 1^*0E + 1^*0$

$\partial_0[E] = 1^*0E + 1^*0$ $\quad\partial_{01}[E] = 1^*0E + 1^*0$ $\quad\partial_{001}[E] = E$

$\partial_1[E] = E$ $\quad\partial_{10}[E] = 1^*0E + 1^*0$ $\quad\partial_{010}[E] = E + \lambda$

$\partial_{11}[E] = E$ $\quad\partial_{011}[E] = 1^*0E + 1^*0$

3 $\partial_{100}[E] = E + \lambda$

$\partial_{101}[E] = 1^*0E + 1^*0$

$\partial_{110}[E] = 1^*0E + 1^*0$

$\partial_{111}[E] = E$

Since derivatives with respect to sequences of length 3 do not constitute new expressions, no additional derivatives need to be evaluated. The states of $\mathfrak{M}_E$ are given by:

4 $$\sigma_1 = \sigma_E \qquad \sigma_2 = \sigma_{1^*0E+1^*0} \qquad \sigma_3 = \sigma_{E+\lambda}$$

Since $E + \lambda$ is the only derivative which includes λ, σ_3 is the only state associated with output 1. The transition graph of $\mathfrak{M}_E$ is shown in Fig. *2.33.1*.

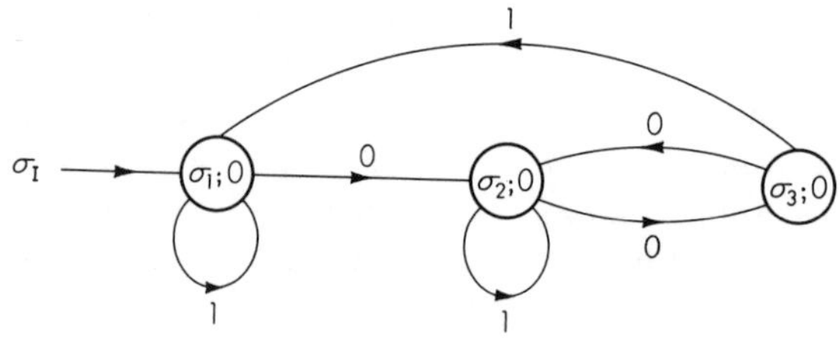

Fig. 2.33.1 FRS for Example *2.33.2*.

34 *Realization of FRS*

In this section we shall show how an FRS can be synthesized directly from the regular expression which describes its recognizable set. The realization is in the form of a switching network, where the basic elements are AND gates, OR gates, inverters, and unit delays (see

Fig. *2.34.1* for symbology). The basic elements form *subsystems*, each of which has an input terminal $u(t)$, output terminal $y(t)$ and a terminal labeled ST which serves as the input terminal for a starting signal. A

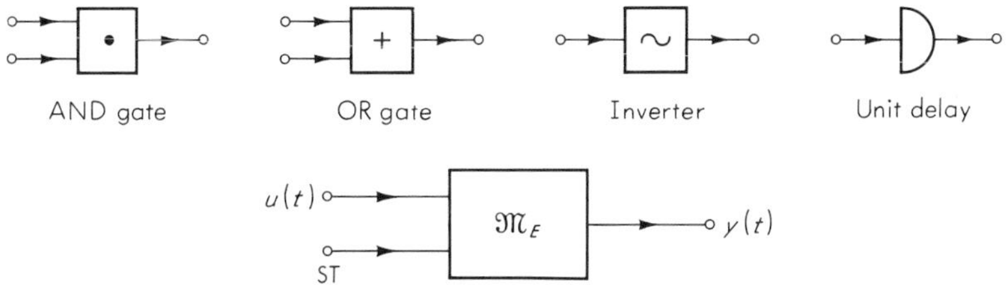

Fig. 2.34.1 Basic components and a subsystem realizing E.

subsystem is said to realize the regular expression E, and is denoted by $\mathfrak{M}_E$, if it satisfies the following condition: $y(t) = 1$ if and only if 1 has been applied to the ST terminal at time $t - d$ and the sequence $u(t - d + 1)u(t - d + 2) \cdots u(t)$ is an element of E.

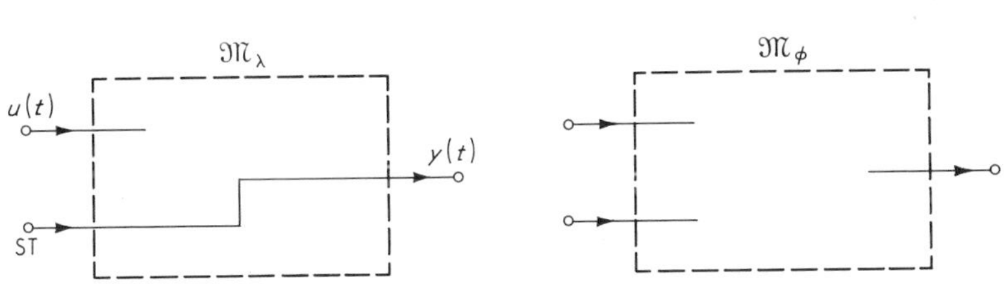

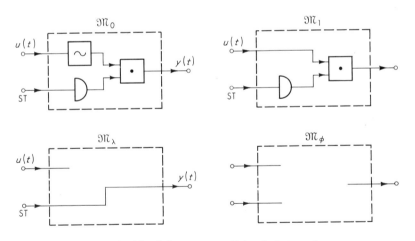

Fig. 2.34.2 Subsystems realizing 0, 1, λ, and ϕ.

Figure *2.34.2* shows the networks which realize 0, 1, λ, and $\emptyset$. Figure *2.34.3* shows the networks which realize $E_1 + E_2$, E_1E_2 (employing the realizations of E_1 and E_2) and E_1^* (employing the realization of E_1). Using these subsystems, the network which realizes any given regular expression can be constructed recursively.

1 *Example* Figure *2.34.3* shows the realization of the FRS whose recognized set is $(0 + 11^*0)^*$.

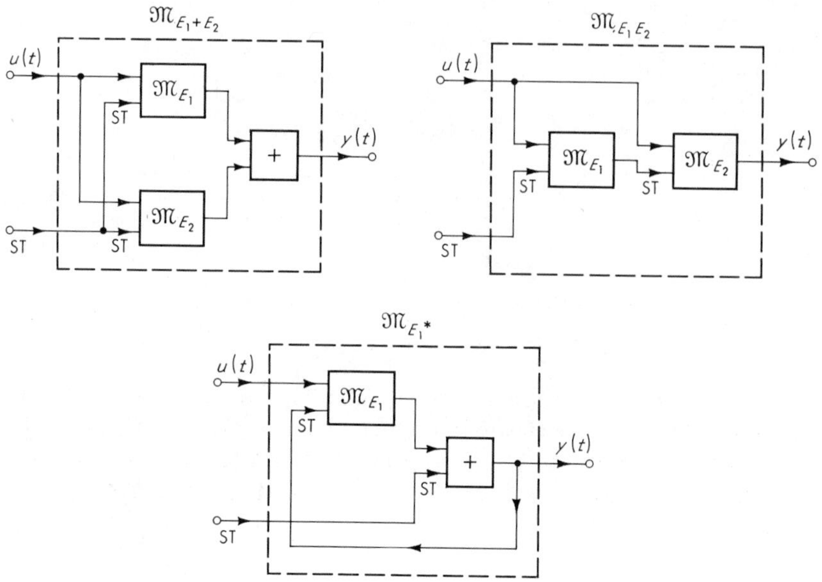

Fig. 2.34.3 Subsystems realizing $E_1 + E_2$, E_1E_2, and E_1^*.

35 *Extended regular expressions*

The regular expression language may be enriched by adding the operations $\cap$ and $'$: if E_1 and E_2 are regular expressions, then $E_1 \cap E_2$ is the intersection of E_1 and E_2, and E_1' is the set of all finite sequences not in E_1.

Given the transition graphs of the FRS $\mathfrak{M}_{E_1}$ and $\mathfrak{M}_{E_2}$, consider an FRS $\mathfrak{M}$ constructed as follows: Let the state sets of $\mathfrak{M}_{E_1}$ be $\{\sigma_1,\sigma_2, \ldots ,\sigma_{n_1}\}$ (with σ_I the initial state) and that of $\mathfrak{M}_{E_2}$ be $\{\sigma_1',\sigma_2', \ldots ,\sigma_{n_2}'\}$ (with σ_I' the initial state). The state set of $\mathfrak{M}$ consists of all ordered pairs (σ_i,σ_j') [with (σ_I,σ_I') the initial state]. If the input symbol α takes σ_i to σ_k and σ_j' to σ_l', then the same symbol takes the state (σ_i,σ_j') of $\mathfrak{M}$ into (σ_k,σ_l'). If σ_i and σ_j' are associated with the output symbols β and β', respectively, then (σ_i,σ_j') is associated with the Boolean product $\beta\beta'$. By construction, an input sequence takes $\mathfrak{M}$ from (σ_I,σ_I') to (σ_i,σ_j') if and only if it takes $\mathfrak{M}_{E_1}$ from σ_I to σ_i and $\mathfrak{M}_{E_2}$ from σ_I' to σ_j'; hence, this sequence is in the recognizable set of $\mathfrak{M}$ if and only if it is in the recog-

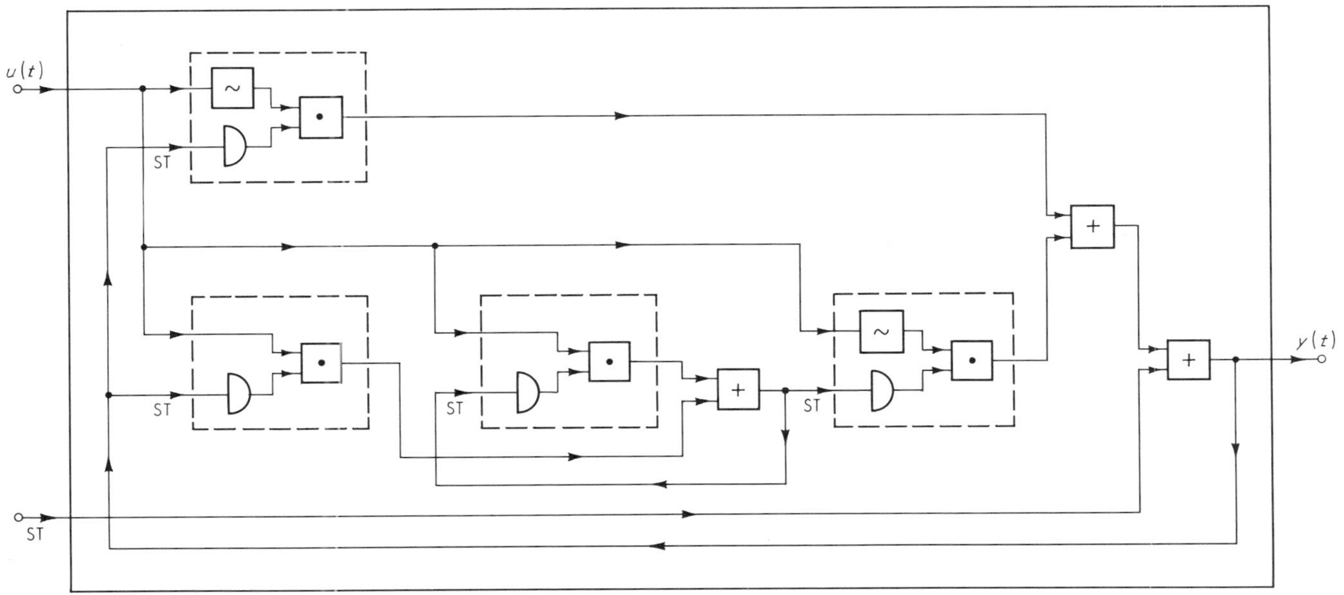

Fig. 2.34.4 Realization of FRS for Example *2.34.1*.

nizable sets of both $\mathfrak{M}_{E_1}$ and $\mathfrak{M}_{E_2}$. Thus $\mathfrak{M}$ is the FRS $\mathfrak{M}_{E_1 \cap E_2}$. [The FRS $\mathfrak{M}_{E_1+E_2}$ can be similarly constructed by associating (σ_i, σ_j') with the Boolean sum $\beta + \beta'$ instead of the product $\beta\beta'$.]

Given the transition graph of $\mathfrak{M}_{E_1}$, the graph of $\mathfrak{M}_{E_1'}$ can be obtained simply by replacing every output symbol 0 with 1 and conversely.

Subsystems accommodating the new operations in the synthesis of FRS are shown in Fig. *2.35.1*.

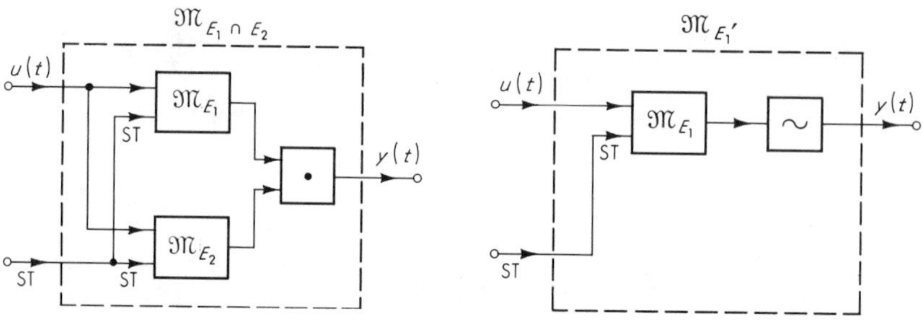

Fig. 2.35.1 Subsystems realizing $E_1 \cap E_2$, and E_1'.

REFERENCES

1 Aizerman, M. A., L. A. Gusev, L. I. Rozoner, I. M. Smirnova, and A. A. Tal': Finite automata, *Automation and Remote Control*, vol. 21, pp. 156–164 (1960).

2 Aizerman, M. A., L. A. Gusev, L. I. Rozoner, I. M. Smirnova, and A. A. Tal': On methods for realizing a finite automaton whose cyclical nature is determined by the variation of the input state, *Automation and Remote Control*, vol. 21, pp. 1576–1594 (1960).

3 Aizerman, M. A., L. A. Gusev, L. I. Rozoner, I. M. Smirnova, and A. A. Tal': Clock conversion in sequential machines and the synthesis of relay networks, *Automation and Remote Control*, vol. 23, pp. 1376–1398 (1963).

4 Arden, D.: Delayed logic and finite state machines, in "Theory of Computing Machine Design," University of Michigan Press, Ann Arbor, pp. 1–35 (1960).

5 Armstrong, D. B.: A programmed algorithm for assigning internal codes to sequential machines, *Trans. IRE*, vol. EC-11, pp. 466–472 (1962).

6 Armstrong, D. B.: On the efficient assignment of internal codes to sequential machines, *Trans. IRE*, vol. EC-11, pp. 611–622 (1962).

7 Aufenkamp, D. D.: Analysis of sequential machines, *Trans. IRE*, vol. EC-7, pp. 299–306 (1958).

8 Aufenkamp, D. D., and F. E. Hohn: Analysis of sequential machines, *Trans. IRE*, vol. EC-6, pp. 276–285 (1957).

9 Bavel, Z.: On the total length of an experiment, *Proc. 5th Ann. Symp. Switching Theory and Logical Design*, pp. 234–248 (1964).

10 Beatty, J., and R. E. Miller: Some theorems for incompletely specified sequential machines with applications to state minimization, *Proc. 3d Ann. Symp. Switching Theory and Logical Design*, pp. 123–136 (1962).

11 Bellman, R.: Sequential machines, ambiguity and dynamic programming, *J. Assoc. Comp. Mach.*, vol. 7, pp. 24–28 (1960).
12 Bellman, R.: "Adaptive Control Processes," Princeton University Press, Princeton, N.J., pp. 119–123 (1961).
13 Bennett, W. S.: Minimizing and mapping sequential circuits, *Trans. AIEE*, vol. 74, pt. 1, pp. 443–447 (1955).
14 Blokh, A. S.: Equivalent transformations of sequential machines, *Automation and Remote Control*, vol. 21, pp. 1057–1061 (1960).
15 Brown, F. M.: Code transformation in sequential machines, *Trans. IEEE*, vol. EC-14, pp. 822–829 (1965).
16 Brzozowski, J. A.: Properties of regular expressions and state diagrams, *Dep. Elec. Engineering Princeton Univ. Tech. Rept.* 15 (March, 1962).
17 Brzozowski, J. A.: A survey of regular expressions and their applications, *Trans. IRE*, vol. EC-11, pp. 324–335 (1962).
18 Brzozowski, J. A.: Canonical regular expressions and minimal state graphs for definite events, in "Mathematical Theory of Automata," Polytechnic Press, Brooklyn, pp. 529–561 (1963).
19 Brzozowski, J. A.: Derivatives of regular expressions, *J. Assoc. Comp. Mach.*, vol. 11, pp. 481–494 (1964).
20 Brzozowski, J. A.: Regular expressions from sequential circuits, *Trans. IEEE*, vol. EC-13, pp. 741–744 (1964).
21 Brzozowski, J. A.: Roots of star events, *Proc. 7th Ann. Symp. Switching and Automata Theory*, pp. 88–95 (1966).
22 Brzozowski, J. A.: On single-loop realizations of sequential machines, *Inform. and Control*, vol. 10, pp. 292–314 (1967).
23 Brzozowski, J. A., and E. J. McCluskey: Signal flow graph techniques for sequential circuit state diagrams, *Trans. IEEE*, vol. EC-12, pp. 67–75 (1963).
24 Brzozowski, J. A., and J. F. Poage: On the construction of sequential machines from regular expressions, *Trans. IEEE*, vol. EC-12, pp. 402–403 (1963).
25 Buchi, J. R.: Regular canonical systems and finite automata, *Univ. Mich. Res. Inst. Tech. Rept.* 2794-7-J (December, 1959).
26 Burks, A. W.: The logic of fixed and growing automata, *Ann. Computation Lab.*, Harvard University Press, Cambridge, Mass. vol. 29, pp. 147–188 (1959).
27 Burks, A. W., and H. Wang: The logic of automata, *J. Assoc. Comp. Mach.*, vol. 4, pp. 193–218, 279–297 (1957).
28 Burks, A. W., and J. B. Wright: Theory of logical nets, *Proc. IRE*, vol. 41, pp. 1357–1365 (1953).
29 Burks, A. W., and J. B. Wright: Sequence generators, graphs, and formal languages, *Inform. and Control*, vol. 5, pp. 204–212 (1962).
30 Cadden, W. J.: Equivalent sequential circuits, *Trans. IRE*, vol. CT-6, pp. 30–34 (1959).
31 Chaitin, G. J.: An improvement on a theorem of E. F. Moore, *Trans. IEEE*, vol. EC-14, pp. 466–467 (1965).
32 Copi, I. M., C. L. Elgot, and J. B. Wright: Realization of events by logical nets, *J. Assoc. Comp. Mach.*, vol. 5, pp. 181–196 (1958).
33 Curtis, H. A.: Multiple reduction of variable dependency of sequential machines, *J. Assoc. Comp. Mach.*, vol. 9, pp. 324–344 (1962).
34 Curtis, H. A.: Use of decomposition theory in the solution of the state assignment problem of sequential machines, *J. Assoc. Comp. Mach.*, vol. 10, pp. 386–411 (1963).
35 Dauber, P. S.: An analysis of errors in finite automata, *Inform. and Control*, vol. 8, pp. 295–303 (1965).

36 Davidow, W. H.: A state assignment technique for synchronous sequential networks, *Stanford Electron. Lab. Tech. Rept.* 1901-1 (July 20, 1961).

37 Davidow, W. H.: The selection problem for minimal-state sequential circuits, *Stanford Electron. Lab. Tech. Rept.* 1901-2 (July 20, 1961).

38 Davis, W. A.: On shift-register realizations for sequential machines, *Proc. Ann. Symp. Switching Theory and Logical Design,* pp. 71–83 (1965).

39 Dejean, F., and M. P. Schutzenberger: On a question of Egan, *Inform. and Control,* vol. 9, pp. 23–25 (1966).

40 Deuel, D. R., and A. Gill: Some decision problems associated with weighted, directed graphs, *SIAM J. Appl. Math.,* vol. 14, pp. 970–979 (1966).

41 Dolotta, T. A., and E. J. McCluskey: The coding of internal states of sequential circuits, *Trans. IEEE,* vol. EC-23, pp. 549–562 (1964).

42 Eggan, L. C.: Transition graphs and the star-height of regular expressions, *Mich. Math. J.,* vol. 10, pp. 385–397 (1963).

43 Elgot, C. C.: Decision problems of finite automata design and related arithmetics, *Trans. Am. Math. Soc.,* vol. 96, pp. 21–51 (1961).

44 Elgot, C. C.: A perspective view of discrete automata and their design, *Am. Math. Monthly,* vol. 72, pp. 125–134 (1965).

45 Elgot, C. C., and J. E. Mezei: Two-sided finite-state transduction, *IBM Res. Paper* RC-1017 (June 28, 1963).

46 Elgot, C. C., and J. D. Rutledge: Operations on finite automata, *Proc. 2d Ann. Symp. Switching Theory and Logical Design* (1961).

47 Elgot, C. C., and J. D. Rutledge: Machine properties preserved under state minimization, *Proc. 3d Ann. Symp. Switching Theory and Logical Design,* pp. 62–70 (1962).

48 Epley, D. L., and P. T. Wang: On state assignments and sequential machine decompositions from s.p. partitions, *Proc. 5th Ann. Symp. Switching Theory and Logical Design,* pp. 228–233 (1964).

49 Even, S.: Test for synchronizability of finite automata and variable length codes, *Trans. IEEE,* vol. IT-10, pp. 185–189 (1964).

50 Even, S.: On information lossless automata of finite order, *Trans. IEEE,* vol. EC-14, pp. 561–569 (1965).

51 Farr, H. E.: Lattice properties of sequential machines, *J. Assoc. Comp. Mach.,* vol. 10, pp. 365–385 (1963).

52 Feferman, S.: On partial and complete decomposition of autonomous sequential networks, *Stanford Res. Inst. Proj.* 3131 *Tech. Rept.* 3 (January, 1961).

53 Fitch, F. B.: Representation of sequential circuits in combinatory logic, *Phil. Sci.,* vol. 25, pp. 263–279 (1958).

54 Fleck, A. C.: Isomorphism groups of automata, *J. Assoc. Comp. Mach.,* vol. 9, pp. 469–476 (1962).

55 Fleck, A. C.: On the automorphism group of an automaton, *J. Assoc. Comp. Mach.,* vol. 12, pp. 566–569 (1965).

56 Friedman, A. D.: Feedback in synchronous sequential switching circuits, *Trans. IEEE,* vol. EC-15, pp. 354–367 (1966).

57 Friedman, J.: A decision procedure for computations of finite automata, *J. Assoc. Comp. Mach.,* vol. 9, pp. 315–323 (1962).

58 Gavrilov, M. A.: A sharpened estimate for finding the number of states in the composition of finite automata, *Automation and Remote Control,* vol. 25, pp. 1434–1440 (1964).

59 Gerace, G. B., and G. Gestr: State assignments for reducing the number of delay elements in sequential machines, *Inform. and Control,* vol. 10, pp. 223–256 (1964).

60 Ghiron, H.: Rules to manipulate regular expressions of finite automata, *Trans. IEEE*, vol. EC-11, pp. 574–575 (1962).
61 Gill, A.: Comparison of finite-state models, *Trans. IRE*, vol. CT-7, pp. 178–179 (1960).
62 Gill, A.: Characterizing experiments for finite-memory automata, *Trans. IRE*, vol. EC-9, pp. 469–471 (1960).
63 Gill, A.: A note on Moore's distinguishability theorem, *Trans. IRE*, vol. EC-10, pp. 290–291 (1961).
64 Gill, A.: Cascaded finite-state machines, *Trans. IRE*, vol. EC-10, pp. 366–370 (1961).
65 Gill, A.: State-identification experiments in finite-automata, *Inform. and Control*, vol. 4, pp. 132–154 (1961).
66 Gill, A.: "Introduction to the Theory of Finite-state Machines," McGraw-Hill, New York (1962).
67 Gill, A.: Time-varying sequential machines, *J. Franklin Inst.*, vol. 276, pp. 519–539 (1963).
68 Gill, A.: On the bound to the memory of sequential machines, *Trans. IEEE*, vol. EC-14, pp. 464–466 (1965).
69 Gill, A.: Realization of input-output relations by sequential machines, *J. Assoc. Comp. Mach.*, vol. 13, pp. 33–42 (1966).
70 Gillespie, R. G., and D. D. Aufenkamp: On the analysis of sequential machines, *Trans. IRE*, vol. EC-7, pp. 119–122 (1958).
71 Ginsburg, S.: On the length of the smallest uniform experiment which distinguishes the terminal states of a machine, *J. Assoc. Comp. Mach.*, vol. 5, pp. 266–280 (1958).
72 Ginsburg, S.: A synthesis technique for minimal-state sequential machines, *Trans. IRE*, vol. EC-8, pp. 13–24 (1959).
73 Ginsburg, S.: On the reduction of superfluous states in a sequential machine, *J. Assoc. Comp. Mach.*, vol. 6, pp. 259–282 (1959).
74 Ginsburg, S.: A technique for the reduction of a given machine to a minimal-state machine, *Trans. IRE*, vol. EC-8, pp. 346–355 (1959).
75 Ginsburg, S.: Synthesis of minimal-state machines, *Trans. IRE*, vol. EC-8, pp. 441–449 (1959).
76 Ginsburg, S.: Connective properties preserved in minimal-state machines, *J. Assoc. Comp. Mach.*, vol. 7, pp. 311–325 (1960).
77 Ginsburg, S.: Some remarks on abstract machines, *Trans. Am. Math. Soc.*, vol. 96, pp. 400–444 (1960).
78 Ginsburg, S.: Sets of tapes accepted by different types of automata, *J. Assoc. Comp. Mach.*, vol. 8, pp. 81–86 (1961).
79 Ginsburg, S.: Compatibility of states in input-independent machines, *J. Assoc. Comp. Mach.*, vol. 8, pp. 400–403 (1961).
80 Ginsburg, S.: Examples of abstract machines, *Trans. IRE*, vol. EC-11, pp. 132-135 (1962).
81 Ginsburg, S.: "An Introduction to Mathematical Machine Theory," Addison-Wesley, Reading, Mass. (1962).
82 Ginsburg, S.: Abstract machines: A generalization of sequential machines, in "Mathematical Theory of Automata," Polytechnic Press, Brooklyn, pp. 125–138 (1963).
83 Ginsburg, S., and T. N. Hibbard: Solvability of machine mappings of regular sets to regular sets, *J. Assoc. Comp. Mach.*, vol. 11, pp. 302–312 (1964).
84 Ginsburg, S., and E. H. Spanier: Distinguishability of a semigroup by a machine, *Proc. Am. Math. Soc.*, vol. 12, pp. 661–668 (1961).

85 Ginzburg, A.: About some properties of definite, reverse-definite and related automata, *Trans. IEEE*, vol. EC-15, pp. 806–810 (1966).
86 Ginzburg, A.: A procedure for checking equality of regular expressions, *J. Assoc. Comp. Mach.*, vol. 14, pp. 355–362 (1967).
87 Ginzburg, A., and M. Yoeli: Products of automata and the problem of covering, *Trans. Am. Math. Soc.*, vol. 116, pp. 256–266 (1965).
88 Giveon, J.: Boolean matrices and their application to finite automata, *Hebrew Univ. Jerusalem Tech. Rept.* 5 (1960).
89 Giveon, J.: Lattice matrices, *Inform. and Control*, vol. 7, pp. 477–484 (1964).
90 Glushkov, V. M.: The abstract theory of automata, *Russ. Math. Surv.*, vol. 16, pp. 1–53 (1961).
91 Glushkov, V. M.: Automata theory and its applications, *Proc. IFIP*, vol. 1, pp. 1–8 (1965).
92 Glushkov, V. M.: "Introduction to Cybernetics," Academic, New York (1966).
93 Grasseli, A.: Minimal closed partitions for incompletely specified flow tables, *Trans. IEEE*, vol. EC-15, pp. 245–249 (1966).
94 Grasseli, A., and F. Luccio: A method for minimizing the number of internal states in incompletely specified sequential networks, *Trans. IEEE*, vol. EC-14, pp. 350–359 (1965).
95 Grasseli, A., and F. Luccio: A method for the combined row-column reduction of flow tables, *Proc. 7th Ann. Symp. Switching and Automata Theory*, pp. 136–147 (1966).
96 Gray, J. N., and M. A. Harrison: The theory of sequential relations, *Inform. and Control*, vol. 9, pp. 435–468 (1966).
97 Hadlock, F. O., and C. L. Coates: Realization of sequential machines with threshold elements, *Proc. 7th Ann. Symp. Switching and Automata Theory*, pp. 172–183 (1966).
98 Haring, D. R.: Some aspects of the state assignment problem for sequential circuits, *U.S. Govt. Res. Rept.*, vol. 38, pp. 109–110(A) (Jan. 5, 1963).
99 Haring, D. R.: "Sequential-circuit Synthesis: State Assignment Aspects," MIT Press, Cambridge, Mass. (1966).
100 Harrison, M. A.: On the asymptotic number of automata, *Electron. Res. Lab. Univ. Calif. (Berkeley) Rept.* 64–8, pp. 61–63 (April, 1964).
101 Harrison, M. A.: A census of finite automata, *Can. J. Math.*, vol. 17, pp. 100–113 (1965).
102 Harrison, M. A.: On the error-correcting capacity of finite automata, *Inform. and Control*, vol. 8, pp. 430–450 (1965).
103 Harrison, M. A.: "Introduction to Switching and Automata Theory," McGraw-Hill, New York (1965).
104 Harrison, M. A.: On asymptotic estimates in switching and automata theory, *J. Assoc. Comp. Mach.*, vol. 13, pp. 151–157 (1966).
105 Hartmanis, J.: Symbolic analysis of a decomposition of information processing machines, *Inform. and Control*, vol. 3, pp. 154–178 (1960).
106 Hartmanis, J.: On the state assignment problem for sequential machines, *Trans. IRE*, vol. EC-10, pp. 157–165 (1961).
107 Hartmanis, J.: Loop-free structure of sequential machines, *Inform. and Control*, vol. 5, pp. 25–43 (1962).
108 Hartmanis, J.: Maximal autonomous clocks of sequential machines, *Trans. IEEE*, vol. EC-11, pp. 83–86 (1962).
109 Hartmanis, J.: Further results on the structure of sequential machines, *J. Assoc. Comp. Mach.*, vol. 10, pp. 78–88 (1963).

110 Hartmanis, J.: The equivalence of sequential machine models, *Trans. IEEE*, vol. EC-12, pp. 18–19 (1963).

111 Hartmanis, J.: Minimal feedback realizations of sequential machines, *Trans. IEEE*, vol. EC-15, pp. 931–933 (1966).

112 Hartmanis, J., and R. E. Stearns: Some dangers in state reduction of sequential machines, *Inform. and Control*, vol. 5, pp. 252–260 (1962).

113 Hartmanis, J., and R. E. Stearns: A study of feedback and errors in sequential machines, *Trans. IEEE*, vol. EC-12, pp. 223–232 (1963).

114 Hartmanis, J., and R. E. Stearns: Pair algebra and its application to automata theory, *Inform. and Control*, vol. 7, pp. 485–507 (1964).

115 Hartmanis, J., and R. E. Stearns: "Algebraic Structure of Sequential Machines," Prentice-Hall, Englewood Cliffs, N.J. (1966).

116 Hazeltine, B.: Regular expressions and variable length encoding, *Trans. IEEE*, vol. IT-6, p. 48 (1963).

117 Hennie, F. C.: Fault detecting experiments for sequential circuits, *Proc. 5th Ann. Symp. Switching Theory and Logical Design*, pp. 95–110 (1964).

118 Hibbard, T. N.: Least upper bounds on minimal terminal state experiments for two classes of sequential machines, *J. Assoc. Comp. Mach.*, vol. 8, pp. 601–612 (1961).

119 Hohn, F. E.: States of sequential machines whose logical elements involve delay, *Proc. 3d Ann. Symp. Switching Theory and Logical Design*, pp. 81–90 (1962).

120 Holland, J. H.: Cycles in logical nets, *J. Franklin Inst.*, vol. 273, pp. 202–226 (1960).

121 Huffman, D. A.: The synthesis of sequential switching circuits, *J. Franklin Inst.*, vol. 257, pp. 161–190, 275–303 (1954).

122 Huffman, D. A.: Information conservation in sequence transducers, *Proc. Symp. Inform. Networks Polytech. Inst. Brooklyn*, pp. 291–307 (1954).

123 Huffman, D. A.: Canonical forms for information-lossless finite-state logical machines, *Trans. IRE*, vol. CT-6, pp. 41–59 (1959).

124 Huzino, S.: On some sequential machines and experiments, *Mem. Fac. Sci. Kyushu Univ.*, ser. A, vol. 12, pp. 136–158 (1958).

125 Huzino, S.: Reduction theorems on sequential machines, *Mem. Fac. Sci. Kyushu Univ.*, ser. A, vol. 12, pp. 159–179 (1958).

126 Huzino, S.: Some properties of convolution machines and signal composite machines, *Mem. Fac. Sci. Kyushu Univ.*, ser. A, vol. 13, pp. 69–83 (1959).

127 Huzino, S.: On some sequential equations, *Mem. Fac. Sci. Kyushu Univ.*, ser. A, vol. 14, pp. 50–62 (1960).

128 Huzino, S.: Theory of finite automata, *Mem. Fac. Sci. Kyushu Univ.*, ser. A, vol. 15, pp. 97–159 (1961/62).

129 Ibarra, O. H.: On the equivalence of finite-state sequential machine models, *Trans. IEEE*, vol. EC-16, pp. 88–90 (1967).

130 Jeffrey, R. C.: Finite-state transformations, *Inform. and Control*, vol. 7, pp. 45–54 (1964).

131 Karatsuba, A. A.: Solution of a problem from the theory of finite automata, *Usp. Mat. Nauk*, vol. 15, pp. 157–159 (1960).

132 Karatsuba, A. A.: Solution of a problem from the theory of finite automata, *Usp. Mat. Nauk*, vol. 15, pp. 157–159 (1960); English translation K-218, Morris D. Friedman, West Newton, Mass.

133 Karp, R. M.: Some techniques of state assignments for synchronous sequential machines, *Trans. IEEE*, vol. EC-13, pp. 507–518 (1964).

134 Kautz, W. H.: State-logic relations in autonomous sequential networks, *Proc. EJCC*, paper T-114 (1959).

135 Kime, C. R.: An organization for checking experiments on sequential circuits, *Trans. IEEE*, vol. EC-15, pp. 113–115 (1966).

136 King, W. F.: Analysis of iterative NDR autonomous sequential machines, *Trans. IEEE*, vol. EC-15, pp. 509–577 (1966).

137 Kinoshita, K.: Some considerations on the fault diagnosis of sequential circuits, *J. Inst. Elec. Comm. Eng. Japan*, vol. 46, no. 9, pp. 4–6 (1963).

138 Kleene, S. C.: Representation of events in nerve nets and finite automata, in "Automata Studies" (C. E. Shannon, J. McCarthy, eds.), Princeton University Press, Princeton, N.J., pp. 3–41 (1956).

139 Klir, J.: A note on the basic block diagram of finite automata from the engineering point of view, *Trans. IEEE*, vol. EC-16, pp. 223–224 (1967).

140 Kobrinskii, N. E., and B. A. Trakhtenbrot: "Introduction to the Theory of Finite Automata," North Holland, Amsterdam (1965).

141 Kohavi, Z.: Minimizing of incompletely specified sequential switching circuits, *U.S. Govt. Res. Rept.*, vol. 38, p. 32(A), (Jan. 20, 1963).

142 Kohavi, Z.: Secondary state assignment for sequential machines, *Trans. IEEE*, vol. EC-13, pp. 193–203 (1964).

143 Kohavi, Z.: Decomposition and state assignment for sequential machines, *U.S. Govt. Res. Rept.*, vol. 40, p. 112(A) (Feb. 5, 1965).

144 Kohavi, Z.: Reduction of output dependency in sequential machines, *Trans. IEEE*, vol. EC-14, pp. 932–934 (1965).

145 Kohavi, Z., and E. J. Smith: Decomposition of sequential machines, *Proc. 6th Ann. Symp. Switching Theory and Logical Design*, pp. 52–61 (1965).

146 Krohn, K. B., and J. L. Rhodes: Algebraic theory of machines, in "Mathematical Theory of Automata," Polytechnic Press, Brooklyn, pp. 341–384 (1963).

147 Krohn, K. B., and J. L. Rhodes: Algebraic Theory of Machines (I), *Trans. Am. Math. Soc.*, vol. 116, pp. 450–464 (1965).

148 Krohn, K., R. Mateosian, and J. Rhodes: Methods of the algebraic theory of machines (I), *J. Comp. System Sci.*, vol. 1, pp. 55–85 (1967).

149 Kutti, A. K.: On a graphical representation of the operating regime of circuits, in "Sequential Machines" (E. F. Moore, ed.), Addison-Wesley, Reading, Mass., pp. 228–235 (1964).

150 Laemmel, A. E.: Application of lattice-ordered semigroups to codes and finite-state transducers, in "Mathematical Theory of Automata," Polytechnic Press, Brooklyn, pp. 241–256 (1963).

151 Lee, C. Y.: Automata and finite automata, *Bell System Tech. J.*, vol. 39, pp. 1267–1295 (1960).

152 Lee, C. Y.: Characterizing automata by W-machine programs, *J. Assoc. Comp. Mach.*, vol. 8, pp. 384–399 (1961).

153 Liu, C. L.: A property of partially specified automata, *Inform. and Control*, vol. 6, pp. 169–176 (1959).

154 Liu, C. L.: k'th order finite automaton, *Trans. IEEE*, vol. EC-16, pp. 470–475 (1963).

155 Liu, C. L.: Determination of the final state of an automaton whose initial state is unknown, *Trans. IEEE*, vol. EC-12, pp. 918–921 (1964).

156 Liu, C. L.: Sequential machine realization using feedback shift registers, *Proc. 5th Ann. Symp. Switching Theory and Logical Design*, pp. 209–227 (1964).

157 Liu, C. L.: The memory orders of states of an automaton, *J. Franklin Inst.*, vol. 277, pp. 37–49 (1964).

158 Liu, C. L.: Pair algebra and its applications, *Proc. 7th Ann. Symp. Switching and Automata Theory*, pp. 103–112 (1966).

159 Liu, C. N.: A state variable assignment method for asynchronous sequential switching circuits, *J. Assoc. Comp. Mach.*, vol. 10, pp. 209–226 (1963).

160 Luccio, F.: Reduction of the number of columns in flow chart minimization, *Trans. IEEE*, vol. EC-15, pp. 803–805 (1966).

161 Massey, J. L.: Note on finite-memory sequential machines, *Trans. IEEE*, vol. EC-15, pp. 658–659 (1966).

162 Masters, G. M., and R. L. Mattson: The application of threshold logic to the design of sequential machines, *Proc. 7th Ann. Symp. Switching and Automata Theory*, pp. 184–194 (1966).

163 McCluskey, E. J.: A comparison of sequential and iterative circuits, *Trans. AIEE*, vol. 78, pt. 1, pp. 1039–1044 (1959).

164 McCluskey, E. J.: Introduction to state tables, in "A Survey of Switching Circuit Theory" (E. J. McCluskey, T. C. Bartee, eds.), McGraw-Hill, New York, pp. 109–119 (1962).

165 McCluskey, E. J.: Reduction of feedback loops in sequential circuits and carry leads in iterative networks, *Inform. and Control*, vol. 6, pp. 99–118 (1963).

166 McCluskey, E. J., and S. H. Unger: A note on the number of internal variable assignments for sequential switching circuits, *Trans. IRE*, vol. EC-8, pp. 439–440 (1959).

167 McNaughton, R.: The theory of automata, a survey, in "Advances in Computers," vol. 2 (F. L. Alt, ed.), Academic, New York, pp. 379–421 (1961).

168 McNaughton, R.: Testing and generating infinite sequences by finite automata, *Inform. and Control*, vol. 9, pp. 521–530 (1966).

169 McNaughton, R., and H. Yamada: Regular expressions and state graphs for automata, *Trans. IRE*, vol. EC-9, pp. 39–47 (1960).

170 Mealy, G. H.: Method for synthesizing sequential circuits, *Bell System Tech. J.*, vol. 34, pp. 1045–1079 (1955).

171 Medvedev, Y. T.: On the class of events representable in a finite automaton, in "Sequential Machines" (E. F. Moore, ed.), Addison-Wesley, Reading, Mass., pp. 215–227 (1964).

172 Mezei, J. E.: Minimal characterizing experiments for finite memory automata, *Trans. IRE*, vol. EC-10, p. 288 (1961).

173 Mezei, J. E.: Structure of monoids with application to automata, in "Mathematical Theory of Automata," Polytechnic Press, Brooklyn, pp. 267–299.

174 Miller, R. E.: "Switching Theory (II)," Wiley, New York, 1965.

175 Miller, R. E., and S. Winograd: On the number of transitions entering the states of a finite automaton, *Trans. IEEE*, vol. EC-13, pp. 463–464 (1964).

176 Moore, E. F.: Gedanken-experiments on sequential machines, in "Automata Studies" (C. E. Shannon, J. McCarthy, eds.), Princeton University Press, Princeton, N.J., pp. 129–153 (1956).

177 Muller, D. E.: Infinite sequences and finite machines, *Proc. 4th Ann. Symp. Switching Theory and Logical Design*, pp. 3–42 (1963).

178 Muller, D. E., and S. Bartky: A theory of asynchronous circuits, *Ann. Computation Lab.*, Harvard Univ., Cambridge, Mass., vol. 29, pp. 204–243 (1959).

179 Myhill, J.: Finite automata and representation of events, in Fundamental concepts in the theory of systems, *WADC Tech. Rept.* 57-624, *ASTIA Doc.* AD1557 41 (1957).

180 Narasimhan, R.: Miminizing incompletely specified sequential switching functions, *Trans. IRE*, vol. EC-10, pp. 531–532 (1961).
181 Nerode, A.: Linear automaton transformations, *Proc. Am. Math. Soc.*, vol. 9, pp. 541–549 (1958).
182 Netherwood, D. B.: Minimal sequential machines, *Trans. IRE*, vol. EC-8, pp. 339–345 (1959).
183 Nichols, A. J.: Comments on Armstrong's state assignment techniques, *Trans. IEEE*, vol. EC-12, pp. 407–409 (1963).
184 Nichols, A. J.: Minimal shift-register realizations of sequential machines, *Trans. IEEE*, vol. EC-14, pp. 688–700 (1965).
185 Nichols, A. J.: Modular synthesis of sequential machines, *Proc. 6th Ann. Symp. Switching Theory and Logical Design*, pp. 62–70 (1965).
186 Nievergelt, J.: Partially ordered classes of finite automata, *Proc. 6th Ann. Symp. Switching Theory and Logical Design*, pp. 229–234 (1965).
187 Oehmke, R. H.: On the structure of an automaton and its input semigroup, *J. Assoc. Comp. Mach.*, vol. 10, pp. 521–525 (1963).
188 Ott, G., and N. F. Feinstein: Design of sequential machines from their regular expressions, *J. Assoc. Comp. Mach.*, vol. 8, pp. 585–600 (1961).
189 Paul, M.: On the automorphism group of reduced automata, *Proc. 7th Ann. Symp. Switching and Automata Theory*, pp. 298–304 (1966).
190 Paull, M. C., and S. H. Unger: Minimizing the number of states in incompletely specified sequential switching functions, *Trans. IRE*, vol. EC-8, pp. 356–367 (1959).
191 Paz, A.: Homomorphisms between finite automata, *Bull. Res. Council Israel*, vol. 10F, pp. 93–99 (1962).
192 Paz, A., and B. Peleg: Ultimate-definite and symmetric-definite events and automata, *J. Assoc. Comp. Mach.*, vol. 12, pp. 399–410 (1965).
193 Perles, M., M. O. Rabin, and E. Shamir: The theory of definite automata, *Trans. IEEE*, vol. EC-12, pp. 233–243 (1963).
194 Pickett, H. E.: Note concerning the algebraic theory of automata, *J. Assoc. Comp. Mach.*, vol. 14, pp. 382–388 (1967).
195 Poage, J. F., and E. J. McCluskey: Derivation of optimum test sequences for sequential machines, *Proc. 5th Ann. Symp. Switching Theory and Logical Design*, pp. 121–132 (1964).
196 Preparta, F. P.: State-logic relations for autonomous sequential networks, *Trans. IEEE*, vol. EC-13, pp. 542–548 (1964).
197 Preparta, F. P.: On the realizability of special classes of autonomous sequential networks, *Trans. IEEE*, vol. EC-14, pp. 791–797 (1965).
198 Pu, A. T.: Generalized decomposition of incomplete finite automata, *Proc. 7th Ann. Symp. Switching and Automata Theory*, pp. 113–126 (1966).
199 Rabin, M. O., and D. Scott: Finite automata and their decision problems, *IBM J. Res. Develop.*, vol. 3, pp. 114–125 (1959).
200 Radke, C. E.: Enumeration of strongly connected sequential machines, *Inform. and Control*, vol. 8, pp. 377–389 (1965).
201 Randolph, J. W.: The theory of finite automata, *Princeton Univ. Digital System Lab. Tech. Rept.* 6 (May, 1961).
202 Raney, G. N.: Sequential functions, *J. Assoc. Comp. Mach.*, vol. 5, pp. 177–180 (1958).
203 Reed, I. S.: Mathematical structure of sequential machines, in "A Survey of Switching Circuit Theory" (E. J. McCluskey, T. C. Bartee, eds.), McGraw-Hill, New York, pp. 187–196 (1962).

204 Reiffen, B., and H. L. Yudkin: On nonlinear binary sequential circuits and their inverses, *Trans. IEEE*, vol. EC-15, pp. 586–596 (1966).
205 Rosenkrantz, D. J.: Synchronizing sequences for incompletely specified flow tables, *Trans. IEEE*, vol. EC-15, pp. 104–105 (1966).
206 Roth, J. P.: Systematic design of automata, *Proc. IFIP*, pp. 1093–1100 (1965).
207 Runyon, J. P.: Derivation of completely and partially specified state tables, in "A Survey of Switching Circuit Theory" (E. J. McCluskey, T. C. Bartee, eds.), McGraw-Hill, New York, pp. 121–144 (1962).
208 Salomaa, A.: The complete axiom systems for the algebra of regular events, *J. Assoc. Comp. Mach.*, vol. 13, pp. 158–169 (1966).
209 Schneider, M. I.: State assignment algorithm for clocked sequential machines, *U.S. Govt. Res. Rept.*, vol. 28 (Jan. 20, 1963).
210 Schubert, E. J.: Matrix algebra for sequential logic, *Trans. AIEE*, vol. 78, pt. 1, pp. 1074–1079 (1960).
211 Schutzenberger, M. P.: A remark on finite transducers, *Inform. and Control*, vol. 4, pp. 185–196 (1961).
212 Schutzenberger, M. P.: On the definition of a family of automata, *Inform. and Control*, vol. 4, pp. 245–270 (1961).
213 Schutzenberger, M. P.: Finite counting automata, *Inform. and Control*, vol. 5, pp. 91–107 (1962).
214 Schutzenberger, M. P.: Certain elementary families of automata, in "Mathematical Theory of Automata," Polytechnic Press, Brooklyn, pp. 139–153.
215 Schutzenberger, M. P.: A remark on incompletely specified automata, *Inform. and Control*, vol. 8, pp. 373–376 (1965).
216 Seshu, S.: Mathematical models for sequential machines, *IRE Natl. Conv. Record*, vol. 7, pt. 2, pp. 4–16 (1959).
217 Seshu, S., and D. N. Freeman: The diagnosis of asynchronous sequential switching systems, *Trans. IRE*, vol. EC-11, pp. 459–465 (1962).
218 Seshu, S., R. E. Miller, and G. Metze: Transportation matrices of sequential machines, *Trans. IRE*, vol. CT-6, pp. 5–12 (1959).
219 Seshu, S., and M. B. Reed: "Linear Graphs and Electrical Networks," Addison-Wesley, Reading, Mass., pp. 250–260 (1961).
220 Simon, J. M.: Some aspects of the network analysis of sequence transducers, *J. Franklin Inst.*, vol. 265, pp. 439–450 (1958).
221 Simon, J. M.: A note on the memory aspects of sequence transducers, *Trans. IRE*, vol. CT-6, pp. 26–29 (1959).
222 Smith, E. J., and Z. Kohavi: Synthesis of multiple sequential machines, *Proc. 7th Ann. Symp. Switching and Automata Theory*, pp. 160–171 (1966).
223 Srinivasan, C. V., and R. Narasimhan: On the synthesis of finite sequential machines, *Proc. Indian Acad. Sci.*, vol. 50, pp. 68–82 (1959).
224 Stanciulescu, F. S.: Sequential logic and its applications to the synthesis of finite automata, *Trans. IEEE*, vol. EC-14, pp. 780–791 (1965).
225 Stearns, R. E., and J. Hartmanis: On the state assignment problem for sequential machines, *Trans. IRE*, vol. EC-10, pp. 593–603 (1961).
226 Stearns, R. E., and J. Hartmanis: Regularity preserving modifications of regular expressions, *Inform. and Control*, vol. 6, pp. 55–69 (1963).
227 Stearns, R. E., and J. Hartmanis: On the application of pair algebra to automata theory, *Proc. 5th Ann. Symp. Switching Theory and Logical Design*, pp. 192–196 (1964).
228 Sunaga, T.: An algebraic theory of the analysis and synthesis of automata, in "Mathematical Theory of Automata," Polytechnic Press, Brooklyn, pp. 385–414 (1963).

229 Tal', A. A.: Questionnaire language and the abstract synthesis of minimal sequential machines, *Automation and Remote Control*, vol. 25, pp. 846–859 (1965).
230 Tal', A. A.: The abstract synthesis of sequential machines from the answers to questions of the first kind in the questionnaire language, *Automation and Remote Control*, vol. 26, pp. 675–680 (1965).
231 Thorelli, L. E.: Finite synchronous automata, *BIT*, vol. 5, pp. 175–202 (1965).
232 Trashin, V. I.: Algebraic method for minimization of incompletely defined sequential machines, *Automation and Remote Control*, vol. 26, pp. 2101–2106 (1965).
233 Trauth, C. A.: Group-type automata, *J. Assoc. Comp. Mach.*, vol. 13, pp. 170–175 (1966).
234 Unger, S. H.: Simplification of state tables, in "A Survey of Switching Circuit Theory" (E. J. McCluskey, T. C. Bartee, eds.), McGraw-Hill, New York, pp. 145–170 (1962).
235 Unger, S. H.: Flow table simplification—some useful aids, *Trans. IEEE*, vol. EC-14, pp. 472–475 (1965).
236 Weeg, G. P.: The structure of an automaton and its operation-preserving transformation group, *J. Assoc. Comp. Mach.*, vol. 9, pp. 345–349 (1962).
237 Weeg, G. P.: The group and semigroup associated with automata, in "Mathematical Theory of Automata," Polytechnic Press, Brooklyn, pp. 257–266 (1963).
238 Weeg, G. P.: The automorphism group of the direct product of strongly related automata, *J. Assoc. Comp. Mach.*, vol. 12, pp. 187–195 (1965).
239 Weiner, P., and E. J. Smith: On the number of distinct state assignments for synchronous sequential machines, *Trans. IEEE*, vol. EC-16, pp. 220–221 (1967).
240 Winograd, S.: Bounded transient automata, *Proc. 3d Ann. Symp. Switching Theory and Logical Design*, pp. 138–141 (1962).
241 Winograd, S.: Input-error-limiting automata, *J. Assoc. Comp. Mach.*, vol. 11, pp. 338–351 (1964).
242 Yamada, H.: Disjunctively linear logic nets, *Trans. IRE*, vol. EC-11, pp. 623–639 (1962).
243 Yanov, Yu. I.: Identical transformation of regular expressions, *Sov. Math.*, vol. 3, pp. 1630–1634 (1963).
244 Yau, S. S.: Autonomous clocks in sequential machines, *Trans. IEEE*, vol. EC-14, pp. 467–472 (1965).
245 Yoeli, M.: The cascade decomposition of sequential machines, *Trans. IPE*, vol. EC-10, pp. 587–592 (1961).
246 Yoeli, M.: Cascade-parallel decomposition of sequential machines, *Trans. IEEE*, vol. EC-12, pp. 322–324 (1963).
247 Yoeli, M.: Generalized cascade decomposition of automata, *J. Assoc. Comp. Mach.*, vol. 12, pp. 411–422 (1965).
248 Yoeli, M.: Canonical representations of chain events, *Inform. and Control*, vol. 8, pp. 180–189 (1965).
249 Yoeli, M., and A. Ginzburg: On homomorphic images of transition graphs, *J. Franklin Inst.*, vol. 278, pp. 291–296 (1964).
250 Zadeh, L. A.: From circuit theory to system theory, *Proc. IRE*, vol. 50, pp. 856–865 (1962).
251 Zahle, T. U.: On coding the states of sequential machines with the use of partition pairs, *Trans. IEEE*, vol. EC-15, pp. 249–253 (1966).
252 Zeiger, H. P.: Cascade synthesis of finite-state machines, *Proc. 6th Ann. Symp. Switching Theory and Logical Design*, pp. 45–51 (1965).

3

State space theory of linear time-varying systems

A. V. Balakrishnan
College of Engineering
University of California, Los Angeles

1 *Introduction*

In this chapter we develop the theory of linear time-varying systems from the state space point of view. Significant differences arise in the time-varying case in contrast with the time-invariant case, and in this presentation additional assumptions were necessary to obtain state-input relations. Some generality has also been sacrificed in order not to obscure the main thread of development with too many qualifying technical details.

We begin in Sec. *2* with a general development of the theory patterned after the time-invariant case. Here no assumptions are made on the dimensionality of the state spaces which are topologized using the outputs. Illustrating one of the fundamental differences from the time-invariant case, the system need not be dynamic even if the state spaces are finite dimensional. The precise definitions of system and state used are those given in [3]. We illustrate the theory with a finite-dimensional example in Sec. *3*. Section *4* deals with the fundamental question of deriving state spaces from the input-output relations. By introducing a sufficient condition (weak null connectedness) we show how it is possible to deduce state spaces and state relations from input-output relations.

Since this is not a survey, the references at the end of the chapter provide no more than a minimal set on material directly related to the present treatment. The definitive work is the treatise by Zadeh [1] and contains additional references as well as much background and motivational material for the state space point of view. Precise definitions using generalized functions are given in [3]. For a treatment of the time-invariant case without restriction to dimensionality see [2, 3]. For related recent work on finite-dimensional systems with applications to circuit synthesis, see [7, 8].

2 *Definitions and general theory*

Definition of state

Even though the term is ill used, for engineering purposes there is no harm in thinking of a system as a *black box* [or boite noire of physics] on which we can make terminal measurements starting at some arbitrary (finite) time. The main point here is that we may label these terminal measurements *input* and *output* with the understanding that the inputs starting at any given time are under our control and may be chosen arbitrarily from a suitably large class. Specifically we shall assume that the inputs starting at any time a, denoted u_a, will *include* the class $\mathfrak{D}_a$ of all infinitely differentiable functions which vanish outside compact subsets of the half-open interval $[a, \infty)$. It is difficult to conceive of systems which cannot accept such functions as stimuli or inputs. Corresponding to each input, there will be many outputs: At each time a the measurements yield *input-output pairs* (u_a, v_a) where, whenever u_a is in $\mathfrak{D}_a$, the output v_a is assumed to be in $\mathfrak{D}_a'$, the class of Schwartz distributions[1] on the open interval (a, ∞). A system is then, from the external point of view, merely the collection of these input-output pairs but with one important proviso that is inherent in our physical description as measurements on a block box but not necessarily our mathematical description: If (u_a, v_a) is an input-output pair at time a, so that the corresponding functions $u_a(s)$, $v_a(s)$ are defined in $s \geq a$, so is $(S(a + \tau; a)u_a; S(a + \tau; a)v_a)$ where

1 $$S[a + \tau; a]u_a[s] = u_a[s] \qquad s \geq s + \tau$$

and what is crucial, every input-output pair at every instant of time $a + \tau$, with $u_{a+\tau}$ in $\mathfrak{D}_{a+\tau}$, can be obtained in this way.

We can now define the set of *states* at any instant a. Let $\Sigma(a)$

[1] Continuous linear functionals on the Schwartz space $\mathfrak{D}_a$ (see [3] for elaboration). It must be noted that the *test functions* are in $\mathfrak{D}_a$ and the definitions differ in this technical detail from [1].

be an abstract set for each a. The elements of $\Sigma(a)$ are called the states at time a if the following two conditions hold:

i. There is a transformation $A(.;;)$ mapping $\Sigma(a) \times \mathfrak{D}_a$ into $\mathfrak{D}'_a$ such that for each input-output pair (u_a,v_a), $v_a = A(a;S;u_a)$ for some $S \in \Sigma(a)$, and

2 $$[v_a(a;S;u_a)]$$

for each S in $\Sigma(a)$ and u_a in $\mathfrak{D}_a$ is an input-output pair at time a.

ii. Given any input $u_a{}^0$ in $\mathfrak{D}_a$ and fixed $\tau > 0$, let us denote the class of all functions in $\mathfrak{D}_a$ such that they agree with $u_a{}^0$ on the interval $[a, a + \tau]$ by $C[u_a{}^0; a + \tau]$.

Then for any state S in $\Sigma(a)$, and every input u_a in $C[u_a{}^0; a + \tau]$, there is an element y in $\Sigma(a + \tau)$ such that if

3 $$v_a = A(a;S;u_a)$$

then

4 $$S(a + \tau; a)u_a = A(a + \tau; y; S(a + \tau; a)v_a)$$

This is simply a precise way of saying that the state y depends only on S and the input on the interval $[a, a + \tau]$.

It should be noted that in these definitions we have only used inputs in $\mathfrak{D}_a$. One could instead have demanded this for every *admissible* input suitably defined. But this is really unnecessary since in the first place any class of admissible inputs for a physical system should surely include $\mathfrak{D}_a$; and on the other hand, any more general input—such as generalized functions in $\mathfrak{D}'_a$—can be "approximated" by inputs in $\mathfrak{D}_a$: Given any generalized function in $\mathfrak{D}'_a$ we can find a sequence of elements in $\mathfrak{D}_a$ such that they converge to the given function in the distribution sense. Suppose now (u_a,v_a) is an input-output pair with u_a in $\mathfrak{D}'_a$ (the output v_a may also be in $\mathfrak{D}'_a$). Then we simply impose the *continuity condition* (in all the systems to be considered here) that we can always find a sequence of pairs $(u_a{}^n,v_a{}^n)$ with $u_a{}^n$ in $\mathfrak{D}_a$ such that $u_a{}^n$ converges in the distribution sense to u_a and $v_a{}^n$ similarly to v_a.

By a system with a state space description we shall mean a system which has states defined at every instant satisfying the conditions specified as well as the continuity condition. In what follows we shall consider only such systems.

Linear systems

We can now define linearity. A system is *linear* if

i. The state space $\Sigma(a)$ at every instant may be defined to be a linear vector space.

ii. The mapping

$$v_a = A[a;S;u_a] \qquad S \in \Sigma(a)$$

is linear on the (linear) cross-product space $\Sigma(a) \times \mathfrak{D}_a$ and is a continuous map of $\mathfrak{D}_a$ into $\mathfrak{D}'_a$ for each S in $\Sigma(a)$, with the weak-star topology on $\mathfrak{D}'_a$, and the Schwartz topology on $\mathfrak{D}_a$.

An essential step in the derivation of state-input and output-state relations is the *reduction of the state spaces.* For this we define

5 **State equivalence** Two states at a given time a are equivalent if they have the same output for every input. More precisely, two states S_1, S_2 in $\Sigma(a)$ are said to be equivalent if

$$A[a;S_1;u_a] = A[a;S_2;u_a] \qquad \text{for every } u_a \text{ in } \mathfrak{D}_a$$

In a linear system, S_1, S_2 are clearly equivalent as soon as

6 $$A[a;\, S_1 - S_2;\, 0] = 0$$

Let

7 $$\Sigma_0(a) = [s \in \Sigma(a) | A[a;S;0] = 0]$$

Then clearly $\Sigma_0(a)$ is a linear subspace of $\Sigma(a)$. Let $\Sigma_1(a)$ be the space complementary to $\Sigma_0(a)$, so that every state S in $\Sigma(a)$ can be expressed uniquely as

8 $$S = S_a + S_r \qquad \begin{matrix} S_a \in \Sigma_0(a) \\ S_r \in \Sigma_r(a) \end{matrix}$$

and further $A[a;S;u_a] = A[a;S_r;u_a]$ for every u_a in $\mathfrak{D}_a$. We shall refer to $\Sigma_r(a)$ as the *reduced state space at time a.* $\Sigma_r(a)$ is then also isomorphic to the quotient space modulo $\Sigma_0(a)$. If we denote by P_a the projection operator projecting $\Sigma(a)$ onto $\Sigma_r(a)$, then we have

9 $$A[a;S;u_a] = A[a;P_a(S);u_a]$$

and in particular for any S in $\Sigma(a)$,

10 $$A[a;P_a(S);0] = 0$$

implies that $P_a(S)$ is the zero state. [The zero state is the zero element in the vector space $\Sigma(a)$, and we shall denote it by θ.] Note that $\Sigma_0(a)$ is equivalent to θ. Following Zadeh's terminology, it is natural to call

$$A[a;S;0]$$

the zero-input response (at time a). It is convenient to write

11 $$A[a;S;0] = Z_i[a;S]$$

since the zero function is an element of $\mathfrak{D}_a$, this maps $\Sigma(a)$ or $\Sigma_r(a)$ into $\mathfrak{D}'_a$. From the linearity of the system we can clearly write

12 $$v_a = A[a;S;0] + A[a;\theta;u_a]$$

and denoting the second term as the *zero-state response* following Zadeh's terminology [1], we have

13 $$v_a = Z_i[a;S] + Z_s[a;u_a]$$

where we have introduced the functional notation

14 $$Z_s[a;u_a] = A[a;\theta;u_a]$$

The zero-input response allows us to introduce a transformation on the reduced state spaces $\Sigma_r(a)$. Thus for each t_1, t_2, $-\infty < t_1 \leq t_2 < \infty$, we define a linear transformation $S(t_2,t_1)$ mapping $\Sigma_r(t_1)$ into $Z_r(t_2)$ in the following way: for each x in $\Sigma_r(t_1)$,

15 $$Z_i(t_1;x) \in \mathfrak{D}'_{t_1}$$

For the moment let us consider the case where this is a continuous function and denote it by $v_{t_1}(\cdot)$. Then since the input continues to be zero for $t \geq t_2$ as well, it follows that there must be some state y in $\Sigma(t_2)$ such that

16 $$V_{t_1}(t) = V_{t_2}(t) \qquad t \geq t_2$$

where

17 $$V_{t_2} = Z_i[t_2;y]$$

and of course

18 $$Z_i[t_2;y] = Z_i[t_2,P_{t_2}(t)]$$

We define

19 $$T(t_2;t_1)x = P_{t_2}(y)$$

Let us now drop the assumption of continuity on the output function. (We observe that in the time-invariant case the zero-input response is always continuous or can be taken to be so. This is no longer necessarily the case in the general time-varying case.) Thus $V_{t_1}(\cdot)$ is now an element of $\mathfrak{D}'_{t_1}$.

Now for $t_2 \geq t_1$,

20 $$\mathfrak{D}'_{t_2} \subset \mathfrak{D}'_{t_1}$$

since $\mathfrak{D}'_{t_2}$ may be identified as those elements of $\mathfrak{D}'_{t_1}$ which vanish in the interval $[t_1,t_2)$. $\mathfrak{D}'_{t_2}$ being thus a subspace of $\mathfrak{D}'_{t_1}$, we may define the relevant projection operator mapping $\mathfrak{D}'_{t_1}$ onto $\mathfrak{D}'_{t_2}$ by $P(t_2,t_1)$. Then there must exist a state y in $\Sigma(t_2)$ such that

21 $$P(t_2;t_1)Z_i(t_1;x) = Z_i(t_2;y) = Z_i(t_2;P_{t_2}y)$$

Thus the transformation $T(t_2,t_1)$ is more precisely defined by

22 $$Z_i(t_2;T(t_2,t_1)x) = P(t_2,t_1)Z_i(t_1;x)$$

Thus defined it is readily verified that $S(t_2;t_1)$ is linear and that

23 $$T(t_3;t_2) = T(t_3;t_2)T(t_2;t_1) \qquad t_1 \leq t_2 \leq t_3$$

making use of the fact that

24 $$P(t_3;t_1) = P(t_3;t_2)P(t_2;t_1) \qquad t_1 \leq t_2 \leq t_3$$

So far we have introduced no topology on $\Sigma_r(a)$. (In the earlier theory, the tacit assumption is made that the space is finite dimensional, in which case there is no need to specify any special topology since all topologies that make it a linear topological space would be equivalent.) We shall now indicate a natural topology for $\Sigma_r(a)$ which will make it a locally convex linear topological space. For this we simply identify $\Sigma_r(a)$ with its image under the (one-to-one) linear mapping

25 $$Z_i[a;\Sigma_r(a)]$$

which is a subspace of $\mathfrak{D}'_a$. We induce the topology on $\Sigma_r(a)$ which makes this mapping continuous, with the weak-star topology on $\mathfrak{D}'_a$: in other words a sequence x_n of states in $\Sigma_r(a)$ converges to a state x_0 if and only if the distributions

$$Z_i(a;x_n)$$

converge weakly to the distribution

$$Z_i(a;x_0)$$

This is a natural topology in the sense that it is based only on the response or output, since our description of the system has to rely only on the terminal measurements. $\Sigma_r(a)$ being a locally convex linear topological space, we may complete it, and we denote the completed space by $\overline{\Sigma_r(a)}$. We may have introduced new states in this process, but the zero-input responses are automatically defined for these states and the transformation $S(t_2,t_1)$ is automatically extended to be linear and continuous on the completed spaces. The significance of the completion will be apparent later.

The reduced state spaces $\Sigma_r(a)$ need not all have the same cardinality (see later for an example) and $T(t_2,t_1)$ need not have any continuity properties as a function of t_1, t_2. However, we now make the following assumption $[A_1]$:

26 $$T(t_2,t_1)\Sigma_r(t_1) = \Sigma_r(t_2) \qquad t_2 \geq t_1$$

(we emphasize that the right side is not the whole space $\overline{\Sigma_r(t_2)}$ although dense in it). An example of a system in which A_1 is not satisfied is given below (Sec. 4).

Let us next consider the zero-state response. We note that

$$Z_s[a;u_a]$$

is a continuous mapping of $\mathfrak{D}'_a$, the latter in the weak-star topology. For any $v_a \in \mathfrak{D}'_a$, let us denote the corresponding "value" as a functional for any f_a in $\mathfrak{D}_a$ by

$$[v_a,f_a]$$

Then

$$[Z_s(a;u_a),f_a]$$

is a bilinear functional on $\mathfrak{D}_a$ which is continuous in each of its arguments u_a and f. We have then the Schwartz kernel theorem (for a precise statement and proof see, for example, p. 18 of [10]) by which there exists a generalized function of two variables $F_a(t_2,t_2)$, $a \leq t_1$, $a \leq t_2$, such that

27 $$[F_a(t_2,t_1),u_a(t_1)f_a(t_2)] = \iint_a^\infty F_a(t_2,t_1)u_a(t_1)f_a(t_2)\,dt_1\,dt_2$$

$[F_a(\cdot,\cdot)]$ is a continuous linear functional on the Schwartz space of infinitely differentiable functions of two variables vanishing outside compact intervals in $(a,\infty) \times (a,\infty)$. Here, as usual, the integral representation is for pictorial purposes only. It is readily verified that as distributions

28 $$F_a(t_2,t_1) = F_b(t_2,t_1) \qquad t_2 \geq b \geq a;\ t_1 \geq b \geq a$$

Hence there is a Schwartz distribution $F(t_2,t_1)$, $-\infty < t_2$, $t_1 < \infty$ such that for every a

29 $$[v_a,f_a] = \iint_a^\infty F(t_2,t_1)u_a(t_1)f_a(t_2)\,dt_1\,dt_2 \qquad v_a,f_a \in \mathfrak{D}_a$$

We may now add the condition of physical realizability. For each a and each state x in $\Sigma(a)$, the output $A[a;x;u_a]$ is such that if $u_a{}^1$, $u_a{}^2$ are two inputs in $\mathfrak{D}_a$ that agree on the interval $[a,b]$, so do the corresponding outputs. However, the ensuing theory is still too general and to avoid some of the mathematical technicalities, we now make the simplifying assumption $[A_2]$

30 $$F(t,s) = F_0(t,s) + \sum_0^n a_k(t)\delta^k(t-s) \qquad t \geq s$$

where $F_0(t,s)$ is Lebesgue integrable on finite intervals and similarly

$\{a_k(\cdot)\}$, and

31 $$\int_a^t |F_0(t,\sigma)|\, d\sigma \to 0 \qquad \text{as } t \to a \text{ for every } a$$

and the $\delta^k(\cdot)$ is the kth derivative of the *delta function* functional in $\mathfrak{D}_0$, concentrated at zero. Now for any $f(\cdot)$ in $\mathfrak{D}_{a^+}$,

32 $$\int_a^\infty F_0(t,s)f(s)\, ds$$

is a measurable function of $t \geq a$ and is also integrable on finite intervals. Thus, in particular, the zero-state response has the same properties for inputs in $\mathfrak{D}_a$. Let us now invoke the condition of physical realizability. Let $f(\cdot) \in \mathfrak{D}_a$, and let E denote the Lebesgue set of the function

33 $$\int_a^\infty F_0(t,s)f(s)\, ds \qquad t \geq a$$

For any t in E let $f_n(\cdot)$ in $\mathfrak{D}_a$ be chosen so that

34 $$\begin{aligned} \hat{f}_n(s) &= f(s) && a \leq s \leq t \\ &= 0 && s < t + 1/n \end{aligned}$$

Then

35 $$\int_a^\infty F_0(t,s)f(s)\, ds = \int_a^t F_0(t,s)f(s)\, ds + \int_t^{t+1/n} F_0(t,s)\hat{f}_n(s)\, ds$$

We can clearly choose $\hat{f}_n$ so that

36 $$\int_t^{t+1/n} F_0(t,s)\hat{f}_n(s)\, ds \to 0 \qquad \text{as } n \to \infty$$

Hence we have that

37 $$\int_a^\infty F_0(t,s)f(s)\, ds = \int_a^t F_0(t,s)f(s)\, ds \qquad \text{ae in } t \geq a$$

Hence

$$Z_s[a;u_a]$$

is a Lebesgue measurable function, integrable on finite intervals and may be defined by

38 $$\int_a^t F_0(t,s)u_a(s)\, ds + \sum_0^n a_k(T)(-1)^k u_a^{(k)}(t) \qquad a \leq t$$

where the derivatives $u_a^{(k)}(\cdot)$ are *right-sided* derivatives for $t = a$. Next let $f_n(\cdot)$ be a delta-convergent sequence in $\mathfrak{D}_a$—that is, that $f_n(\cdot)$ converges weakly to the delta function concentrated at a. Then we observe that the functions

39 $$\int_a^{t_0} F_0(t,s)f_n(s)\, ds + \sum_0^n a_k(t)(-1)^k f_n^{(k)}(t)$$

converge weakly (as functionals over $\mathfrak{D}_a$) to the function

40 $$F_0(t,a) + \sum_0^n a_k(t)\delta^{k+1}(t - a) \qquad t \geq a$$

which is thus the zero-state response to the delta-function input at time a. But for each n, the input is zero in $[a + 1/n, \phi)$ so that by the state hypothesis there must be a state $S(a + 1/n)$ in $\Sigma_r(a + 1/n)$, such that for any $\phi(\cdot)$ in $\mathfrak{D}_{a+1/n}$

41 $$\int_{a+1/n}^{\infty} F_0(t,a)\phi(t)\,dt = [Z_i(a + 1/n); S(a + 1/n), \phi]$$

But by assumption A_1, we know that

42 $$S(a + 1/n) = T[a + 1/n; a]x_n \qquad x_n \in \Sigma_r(a)$$

for some x_n. But

43 $$Z_i[a + 1/n; T(a + 1/n; a)x_n] = P[a + 1/n; a]Z_i[a;x_n]$$

Hence for any $\phi(\cdot)$ in $\mathfrak{D}_a$, we must have that for a sufficiently large, so that $\phi(\cdot)$ vanishes in $[a, a + 1/n]$

44 $$[Z_i[a;x_n],\phi] = \int_{a+1/n}^{\infty} F_0(t,a)\phi(t)\,dt$$

Hence $\{x_n\}$ is a Cauchy sequence, and hence there is an element $B(a)$ in $\overline{\Sigma_r(a)}$ such that

45 $$[Z_i[a;B(a)],\phi] = \int_a^{\infty} F_0(t,a)\phi(t)\,dt$$

or that $Z_i[a;B(a)]$ coincides with the function

46 $$F_0(t,a) \qquad t \geq a$$

Let us next consider the abstract integral over $\overline{\Sigma_r(t)}$

47 $$\int_a^t T(t,s)B(s)f(s)\,ds \qquad f(\cdot) \in \mathfrak{D}_a$$

This is well defined as a Pettis integral; in fact, for any $\phi(\cdot)$ in $\mathfrak{D}_t$

48 $$\int_a^t [T(t,s)B(s),\phi]f(s)\,ds = \int_t^{\infty} \phi(y)\,dy \int_a^t F_0(y,s)f(s)\,ds$$

or

49 $$\int_a^t T(t,s)B(s)f(s)\,ds$$

may be identified with the function

50 $$\int_a^t F_0(y,s)f(s)\,ds \qquad y \geq t$$

which is clearly Lebesgue measurable and integrable on finite intervals.

Let

51 $$g(y) = \int_a^t F_0(y,s)f(s)\,ds$$

Let

52 $$h(y) = \int_a^y F_0(y,s)f(s)\,ds$$

Then $h(y)$ is Lebesgue measurable and integrable on finite intervals. Moreover

53 $$g(y) - h(y) = -\int_t^y F_0(y,s)f(s)\,ds$$

and goes to zero as y tends to t, by assumption A_2. Let $\phi_n(\cdot)$ be a delta-convergent sequence in $\mathfrak{D}_0$. Then

54 $$\int_t^\infty \phi_n(y-t)g(y)\,dy = \int_t^\infty \phi_n(y-t)[g(y) - h(y)]\,dy + \int_t^\infty \phi_n(t-y)h(y)\,dy$$

Hence

55 $$\int_t^\infty \phi_n(y-t)g(y)\,dy \to h(t) \qquad \text{ae in } t \geq a$$

We now introduce a linear functional $L(t)$ for each t, defined as a sub-domain of $\overline{\Sigma_r(t)}$ by

56 $$L(t)[x] = \lim_n L_n(t)[x]$$

57 $$L_n(t)[x] = [Z_i(t;x),\phi_n(\cdot - t)]$$

whenever the limit exists (the limit is then automatically unique). We thus have that

58 $$\int_a^t T(t,s)B(s)f(s)\,ds$$

belongs to the domain of $L(t)$ almost everywhere in $t \geq a$. For any x in $\overline{\Sigma_r(a)}$, let us define for $u_a \in \mathfrak{D}_{a^+}$

59 $$x(t) = \int_a^t T(t;s)B(s)u_a(s)\,ds + T(t,a)x$$

If x is such that

$$Z_i[a,x]$$

can be identified with a Lebesgue measurable function that is integral on finite intervals, so that the total response is then also similar, we have that $x(t)$ belongs to the domain of $L(t)$ almost everywhere, and

60 $$v_a(t) = L(t)[x(t)] + \sum_0^n a_k(t)(-1)^k u_a^{(k)}(t)$$

Thus *59* and *60* yield the state-input and output-state relations sought. Equation *59* is also true whenever the response $v_a(\cdot)$ is Lebesgue measurable (and integrable on finite intervals) since in that case

$$Z_i[a;x]$$

must also correspond to a measurable function integrable on finite intervals. In the case where the response function is not necessarily measurable, we have that

61 $$Z_i[a;x;u_a] = \lim_n L_n^{(t)}[x(t)] + \sum_0^n a_k(t)(-1)^k u_a^{(t)}(\cdot)$$

where the limit is now to be taken in the weak-star topology of $\mathfrak{D}'_a$.

Finite dimensional state space

Let us specialize to the case where the state spaces $\Sigma(t)$ are finite dimensional for each t. Then s_0 is $\Sigma_r(t)$, of course, and

62 $$\overline{\Sigma_r(t)} = \Sigma_r(t)$$

Also, under assumption A_1,

63 $$\dim\,(\Sigma_r(t_2)) \leq \dim\,(\Sigma_r(t_1)) \qquad t_2 \geq t_1$$

Now

64 $$B(s) \in \Sigma_r(a) \qquad \text{for } s \geq a, \text{ since } \Sigma_r(s) \subset \Sigma_r(a) \text{ for } s \geq a$$

Hence, for $u_a(\cdot)$ in $\mathfrak{D}_a$, we have, using assumption A_2,

65 $$[B(s),u_a(\cdot)] = \int_s^\infty F(t,s)u_a(t)\,dt$$

which is thus a Lebesgue measurable function. Hence it follows that $B(s)$ is a Lebesgue measurable function, integrable (in norm) on finite intervals. Similarly, we can readily verify that $T(t,s)B(s)$ is measurable and integrable on finite intervals for $a \leq s \leq t$, so that the integral

$$\int_a^t T(t,s)B(s)u_a(s)\,ds$$

is now well defined as a Lebesgue interval. Again, if we make the additional assumption that the response $A[a;x;u_a]$ is measurable and integrable on finite intervals for u_a in $\mathfrak{D}_a$, we have that $L(t)$ is a linear functional on $\Sigma_r(t)$ and hence, we have that

66 $$L(t)[x] = [C(t),x]$$

where $C(t)$ is an element of $\Sigma_r(t)$, and $[\cdot,\cdot]$ denotes the inner product in

$\Sigma_r(t)$. We have then that

67 $$v_a(t) = [C(t),x(t)] + \sum_0^n a_k(t)(-1)^k u_a^{(k)}(t)$$

where

68 $$x(t) = T(t,a)x + \int_a^t T(t,s)B(s)u_a(s)\,ds$$

However, we do not necessarily obtain dynamic equations (see Sec. *3*). But we have:

69 **Theorem** A sufficient condition that a linear system with a state space description satisfying A_1 and A_2 and with output measurable and integrable on finite intervals be dynamic is that the reduced state spaces $\Sigma_r(t)$ have the same finite dimension for every t.

Proof *Sufficiency* (see [10] for a similar proof) We have that

70 $$T(t,s)\Sigma_r(s) = \Sigma_r(t) \qquad t \geq s$$

and since $\Sigma_r(t)$ has the same finite dimension—say, n—as $\Sigma_r(s)$, it follows that $T(t,s)$ must be nonsingular. Let us define

71 $$T(s,t) = T(t,s)^{-1} \qquad s \leq t$$

Then we have that

72 $$T(t,s)T(s,a) = T(t,a) \qquad \text{for all } a,\ s,\ t$$

Let

73 $$\phi(t) = T(t,a) \qquad \text{for same } a \text{ and every } t,\ -\infty < t < \infty$$

Then

74 $$T(t,s) = \phi(t)\phi(s)^{-1}$$

Hence in *59* we can write

75 $$x(t) = \phi(t)\int_a^t \phi(s)^{-1}B(s)u_a(s)\,ds + \phi(t)\phi(a)^{-1}x = \phi(t)Y(t)$$

where

76 $$Y(t) = \int_a^t \phi(s)^{-1}B(s)u_a(s)\,ds + \phi(a)^{-1}x$$

Now from *60*,

77 $$v_a(t) = [C(t),\phi(t)Y(t)] + \sum_0^n a_k(t)(-1)^k u_a^{(k)}(t)$$

where

78 $$\dot{Y}(t) = \phi(t)^{-1}B(t)u_a(t)$$

which yields the dynamic system representation sought.

3 *A finite dimensional example*

As an example, suppose we consider a dynamic system, expressed in the usual way

1 $$\frac{dx}{dt} = A(t)x(t) + B(t)u(t)$$

2 $$v(t) = C(t)x(t) + \sum_{0}^{m} d_k(t)u^{(k)}(t)$$

where $x(t)$ is an $n \times 1$ matrix, $A(t)$ is an $n \times n$ matrix, $B(t)$ is $n \times 1$, $C(t)$ is $1 \times n$, the $d_k(t)$ are scalars, all functions being measurable and essentially bounded on bounded intervals. Here it is implicit that the state spaces

3 $$\Sigma(a) = E_n \qquad \text{euclidean } n\text{-space}$$

It is readily verified that we have a linear system satisfying condition A_2, the response v_a being measurable and also essentially bounded on bounded intervals for inputs u_a in $\mathfrak{D}_a$. Now

4 $$\Sigma_0(a) = [x \in E_n | C(t)\phi(t)\phi(a)^{-1}x = 0 \qquad \text{ae } t \geq a]$$

where $\phi(t)$ is the fundamental matrix solution of

5 $$\frac{d\phi(t)}{dt} = A(t)\phi(t)$$

The subspace $\Sigma_r(a)$, complementary to $\Sigma(a)$, is now of course the orthogonal complement of $\Sigma_0(a)$. Let $P(a)$ denote the corresponding projection operator, mapping E_n onto $\Sigma_r(a)$. To obtain a representation for the operator $P(a)$ [or, equivalently, the subspace (a)] we proceed as follows. Let

6 $$\Lambda(a,T) = \int_a^{a+T} \phi(a)^{*-1}\phi(t)^*C(t)^*C(t)\phi(t)\phi(a)^{-1}\,dt \qquad T > 0$$

Then $\Lambda(a,T)$ is nonnegative definite, the null space of $\Lambda(a,T)$ for fixed a is a monotone nondecreasing function of T, and the range space (and the rank) is thus a nonincreasing monotone function of T. Hence we can find T_0 such that

7 $$\operatorname{rank} \Lambda(a,T) = \operatorname{rank} \Lambda(a,T_0) \qquad \text{for } T \geq T_0$$

and hence, the subspace $\Sigma_0(a)$ is the null space of $\Lambda(a,T_0)$ and

8 $$\Sigma_r(a) = \Lambda(a,T_0)x \qquad x \in E_n$$

Let $y_1, \ldots, y_m$ be a basis among the columns of the matrix $\Lambda(a,T_0)$, the dimension of $\Sigma_r(a)$ being $m \leq n$. Then the y_i provide a basis for $\Sigma_r(a)$. If

9 $$P(a)x = \sum_1^m a_i y_j$$

then the column vector

$$\begin{bmatrix} a_1 \\ a_2 \\ \cdot \\ \cdot \\ \cdot \\ a_m \end{bmatrix}$$

has the representation

$$(\Lambda^*\Lambda)^{-1}\Lambda^*x$$

where Λ is the $n \times m$ matrix composed on the m column vectors $\{y_i\}$.

If the functions $C(t)$, $B(t)$, $A(t)$ are analytic, or can be expanded in a Taylor series at a, then

10 $$C(t)\phi(t)\phi(a)^{-1}x = 0 \qquad t \geq a$$

is clearly equivalent to

11 $$\frac{d^k}{dt^k}[C(t)\Phi(t)\Phi(a)^{-1}x] = 0 \qquad \text{at } t = a \text{ for every } k$$

or

12 $$\begin{aligned} &C(a)x = 0 \\ &[C(a) + C(a)A(a)]x = 0 \\ &\cdots\cdots\cdots\cdots \end{aligned}$$

where the nth-order derivative can be determined by using Leibnitz rule. If the dimension of $\Sigma_r(a)$ is denoted m, then we shall again find exactly m linearly independent (row) vectors among these (but not necessarily the first m in the order written), and denoting their transposes (or corresponding column vector) by y_i we can again obtain a representation for $\Sigma_r(a)$ in terms of the basis y_i as before. The main advantage here of course is that we do not need to have the fundamental matrix solution; on the other hand, the differentiability conditions may be too strong [8].

Let us next observe that the assumption A_1 is indeed satisfied in the present example. From

13 $$\begin{aligned} C(t)\phi(t)\phi(a)^{-1}x &= C(t)\phi(t)\phi(a)^{-1}P(a)x & t &\geq a \\ &= C(t)\phi(t)\phi(\tau)^{-1}[\phi(\tau)\phi(a)^{-1}P(a)x] & t &\geq \tau \geq a \\ &= C(t)\phi(t)\phi(\tau)^{-1}[P(\tau)\phi(\tau)\phi(a)^{-1}P(a)x] & t &\geq \tau \geq a \end{aligned}$$

it follows that

14 $$T(t,s) = P(t)\phi(t)\phi(s)^{-1}P(s)$$

Again for any x in E_n, for any $\tau \geq a$, we know that

15 $$x = \phi(\tau)\phi(a)^{-1}y \qquad \text{for some } y$$

and

16 $$\begin{aligned} C(t)\phi(t)\phi(a)^{-1}y &= C(t)\phi(t)\phi(\tau)^{-1}x && t \geq a \\ &= C(t)\phi(t)\phi(\tau)^{-1}P(\tau)x && t \geq \tau \\ &= C(t)\phi(t)\phi(\tau)^{-1}P(\tau)\phi(a)^{-1}P(a)y && t \geq \tau \end{aligned}$$

Or,

17 $$C(t)\phi(t)\phi(\tau)^{-1}P(\tau)x = C(t)\phi(t)\phi(\tau)^{-1}P(\tau)\phi(\tau)\phi(a)^{-1}P(a)y \qquad t \geq \tau$$

and hence

18 $$P(\tau)x = P(\tau)\phi(\tau)\phi(a)^{-1}P(a)y = T(\tau;a)y$$

Hence

19 $$T(t;s)\Sigma_r(s) = \Sigma_r(t) \qquad t \geq s$$

Next in the notation of Sec. *2*

20 $$L(t)x = C(t)P(t)x = C(t)x \qquad \text{ae}$$

and

21 $$\begin{aligned} F_0(t;s) &= C(t)\phi(t)\phi(s)^{-1}B(s) && t \geq s \\ &= C(t)P(t)\phi(t)\phi(s)^{-1}P(s)B(s) && \text{ae } t \geq s \\ &= C(t)T(t;s)P(s)B(s) && \text{ae } t \geq s \end{aligned}$$

Hence we have finally

22 $$v_a(t) = C(t)\left[T(t,a)P(a)x + \int_a^t T(t,s)[P(s)B(s)]u_a(s)\,ds\right]$$

However, we do not in general have any dynamic equation representation. A sufficient condition for this is that

23 $$\dim \Sigma_r(t) = \text{const}$$

as already indicated in Theorem *3.2.69*.

4 *Determining states and state relations from input-output relations*

So far we have been concerned with systems which were assumed to have a state space description. The question arises whether given an input-output description (satisfying the conditions we have imposed and suitable additional conditions perhaps) it is always possible to associate states with the properties we have required of them. In this section we shall study one such condition and show how to deduce state spaces and associated relations. We call this property weak null connectedness or weak null controllability.

We begin with a definition of weak null connectedness in terms of states for a linear dynamic system and discuss the relationship to complete controllability. It turns out that the two are equivalent in the time-invariant case, but neither necessarily implies the other in the time-varying case.

Definition of weak null connectedness

Let us first consider a linear dynamic system where the input $u(t)$ (assumed to be one-dimensional for simplicity of notation, the extension to the general finite-dimensional case being obvious), and the output $y(t)$ (also assumed one-dimensional), being related by the equations:

1 $$\frac{dX(t)}{dt} = A(t)X(t) + B(t)u(t)$$

2 $$y(t) = C(t)X(t) + \sum_{0}^{m} d_k(t)u^{(k)}(t)$$

where $X(t)$ is an $n \times 1$ matrix function, $A(t)$ is an $n \times n$ matrix function, $B(t)$ is $n \times 1$, $C(t)$ is $1 \times n$, and $d_k(t)$ are scalars, all functions being measurable and essentially bounded on finite intervals.

For such a system, the state space at any instant of time can be taken to be (isomorphic to) an n-dimensional vector space, denoted E_n. In fact, since the assumptions on $A(t)$ and $B(t)$ imply that *1* has a unique solution for each initial value (as a Cauchy problem), we may take *1* as the state-input relation and *2* as the state-input-output relation. With reference to *1*, we may state our definition for weak null connectedness (WNC).

3 **Definition** The system defined through *1* and *2* is said to be weakly null connected or weakly null controllable if, given any state X at any time t, it is possible to find an earlier instant of time t_0, $t_0 < t$, and an input starting at time t_0 such that *1* has a solution satisfying:

$$X(t_0) = 0 \qquad X(t) = X$$

To see why this definition is new and different, let us recall the usual definition of *complete controllability* or *complete connectedness* (CC) [1, 5]: Given any state X_1 at time t_1 and any other state X_2, it is possible to find an input which will transfer the state X_1 at time t_1 to the state X_2

at some $t > t_1$; that is, we can find a solution of *1* satisfying

$$X(t_1) = X_1 \qquad \text{and} \qquad X(t) = X_2 \qquad \text{for some } t > t_1$$

4 **Theorem** Suppose the system *1* is time invariant; that is

5
$$\frac{dA(t)}{dt} = 0 \qquad \frac{dB(t)}{dt} = 0$$

Then weak null controllability is equivalent to complete controllability.

Proof Since *3.2.74* holds, let

6
$$A(t) = A \qquad B(t) = B$$

The proof is immediate since we have that

7
$$\exp At = \sum_0^{n-1} Q_k(t) A^k$$

and

8
$$\int_{t_0}^t [\exp A(t-s)]Bu(s)\,ds = \sum_0^{n-1} \left(\int_{t_0}^t Q_k(t-s)u(s)\,ds \right) A^k B$$

so that weak null connectedness readily implies that A^kB be linearly independent for $k = 0, \ldots, n-1$. The latter being the well-known condition for complete controllability, the proof is complete, clearly.

However, Theorem *1* is false in general in the time-varying case, as the following simple counterexample shows. Thus let *1* have the special form

9
$$\frac{dX}{dt} = AX(t) + B(t)u(t)$$

where

10
$$\begin{aligned} B(t) &= 0 \qquad \text{for } t < \text{some fixed } t_0 \\ &= B \qquad t > t_0 \end{aligned}$$

and

11
$$\{A^kB\} \text{ are linearly independent} \qquad k = 0, \ldots, n-1$$

Then for any τ, fixed and less than t_0, we have

12
$$\int_\tau^t [\exp A(t-s)]B(s)u(s)\,ds = \int_{t_0}^t [\exp A(t-s)]Bu(s)\,ds$$

and by taking t larger than t_0, we see that any state can be reached, so that we have CC. On the other hand, no nonzero state can be reached at any time t, $t < t_0$ starting with the zero state at any earlier time; or we do not have WNC. By reversing the inequality in *10* it is clear that we can obtain a system that is WNC, but not CC.

However, a sufficient condition [essentially a sort of analyticity condition on $A(t)$ and $B(t)$] that has played a key role in optimal control theory and is invoked by Pontryagin et al. [6] may be given which implies CC and WNC simultaneously. (This is what Pontryagin et al. call the *general position condition.*) Thus let P denote the condition:

The vectors $B_k(t)$ are linearly independent for every t

13 $$B_k(t) = -A(t)B_{k-1}(t) + \frac{dB_{k-1}(t)}{dt} \qquad k = 1, \ldots, n-1$$

$$B_0(t) = B(t)$$

it being assumed, of course, that the necessary differentiability conditions are satisfied.

It may also be noted that if the system *1* is WNC, then for any t, any state at time t can be reached from the zero state starting at the fixed time t-L, for some fixed positive L; this is simply a consequence of the finite dimensionality of the state space. We can also give a set of necessary and sufficient conditions for a dynamic system (with the state-input relation *1*) to be WNC. For this let $Q_i(s)$ be the column vectors of the matrix $\psi(s)$ which is a fundamental matrix solution of the equation

14 $$\frac{dY(s)}{ds} = -A^*(s)Y(s)$$

Then we can state

15 **Theorem** A necessary and sufficient condition for the system *1* to be WNC is that

16 $$\sum_1^n a_i B(s)^* Q_i(s) = 0 \qquad s < t, \text{ for some (any) } t$$

implies that all $\{a_i\}$ are zero.

Proof Suppose the system is WNC. Then it is not possible to find a nonzero vector Y such that

17 $$Y^* \int_{-\infty}^{t} \psi(t)^{*-1}\psi(s)B(s)u(s)\, ds = 0$$

for every $u(\cdot)$, or equivalently, that

18 $$B(s)^*\psi(s)\psi(t)^{-1}Y = 0 \qquad s < t$$

and since $\psi(t)$ is nonsingular, this implies condition *16*. Conversely, if *16* holds, we obtain equivalently *17* and hence *18*, which would then yield WNC.

19 **Remark** It may be noted that no differentiability condition has been used in *16*; but the fundamental matrix solution is required. We can of course state a corresponding (one-sided) version of P in place of *16* with appropriate differentiability conditions. Also, we get CC by reversing the inequality in *16*.

Definition of WNC based on input-output relation

Weak null controllability (as well as complete controllability) has been defined in terms of the state-input relation for a linear dynamic system. Such a definition can be clearly extended to any system with a state space description even including those whose state spaces are not finite dimensional, but it requires the notion of state. We shall now give a definition of WNC which is based only on the input-output relation, and without reference to states. In particular therefore such a definition can be applied to systems which are described only in terms of the input-output relation. We shall show that for systems satisfying the new definition of WNC, it is possible to deduce states and associated state space description from the input-output relation and further that the states then will have the WNC property also.

Our definition of weak null connectedness is essentially that the output is uniquely specified for $t > t_0$ by specifying a previous input history prior to t_0. (See [4] where nonlinear time-invariant systems are considered.) There is, in other words, a previous input history, which may be unknown but which if given will determine the output corresponding to the input for all the future. More specifically, we define a system given in terms of input-output relations to be linear and weakly null controllable if the output $y(t)$, corresponding to the input $u(t)$ for $t > t_0$, can be expressed in the form

20 $$y(t) = \int_{t_0-L}^{t_0} W(t,s)u_0(s)\,ds + \int_{t_0}^{t} W(t,s)u(s)\,ds \qquad 0 < L \leqq \infty$$

for some $u_0(\cdot)$, where $W(t,s)$ is a fixed function of the two variables s, t $-\infty < s, t < +\infty$. The interpretation of the integral as well as the precise definition of $L = +\infty$ depends on the kind of restrictions placed on the function $W(\cdot,\cdot)$. If we allow $W(t,s)$ to be a generalized function, then the input functions have to be infinitely differentiable, and the output functions have to be generalized functions also. On the other hand, the class of input functions can be extended to integrable functions if we restrict $W(s,t)$ to be, say, Lebesgue measurable and essentially bounded on finite intervals. We shall assume this in what follows. In particular, then, the integral is defined almost everywhere in t for finite L for inputs integrable on finite intervals, and the limiting case of $L = \infty$ will be interpreted to mean that the integral converges almost uniformly in each interval of the form $[t_0, t_0 + \Delta]$, $0 < \Delta < \infty$.

If a linear dynamic system is WNC, then it is clearly also WNC in the new definition. For from *1* we have that

21 $$x(t) = \phi(t)\phi(s)^{-1}x(t_0) + \int_{t_0}^{t} \phi(t)\phi(s)^{-1}B(s)u(s)\,ds$$

where $\phi(t)$ is the fundamental matrix solution of

22 $$\phi(t) = A(t)\phi(t)$$

and if the system is WNC, we must have:

23 $$x(t_0) = \int_{t_0-L}^{t_0} \phi(t_0)\phi(s)^{-1}B(s)u_0(s)\,ds$$

for some (finite) $L > 0$ and appropriate $u_0(\cdot)$. Hence from *2*

24 $$y(t) = \int_{t_0-L}^{t_0} W(t,s)u_0(s)\,ds + \int_{t_0}^{t} W(t,s)u(s)\,ds$$

where

25 $$W(t,s) = C(t)\phi(t)\phi(s)^{-1}B(s) + \sum_{0}^{m} d_k(t)(-1)^k\delta^k(t-s)$$

and $\delta^k(\cdot)$ denotes the kth derivative of the delta function. The first term is measurable and essentially bounded on finite intervals whereas the second term requires that the generality of Schwartz distributions be allowed. By restricting ourselves to the former class we forego the inclusion of the derivatives of the input functions.

We shall now consider the problem of determining states for a system whose input-output relation satisfies the WNC criterion (*20*).

26 **Theorem** Let the input-output relation be specified by *20* where we assume that $W(t;s)$ is Lebesgue measurable and essentially bounded on finite intervals. Then it is possible to deduce state spaces for the system such that the reduced states are WNC. The reduced state spaces can be taken as locally convex spaces, with the state-input relation being given by

27 $$x(t) = \int_{t_0}^{t} T(t;s)B(s)u(s)\,ds + T(t;t_0)x(t_0)$$

where $T(t;s)$ is a family of linear continuous transformations such that

28 $$T(t;\tau)T(\tau;s) = T(t;s) \qquad s < \tau < t$$

$B(s)$ is a reduced state for each s, and the output-state relation is $y(t) = C(t)[x(t)]$, ae, where $C(t)$ is a linear functional on the reduced state space at time t.

Proof Because of our assumptions on the weight function $W(t,s)$, the class of inputs for which the output is defined as a measurable function includes the linear class of functions of bounded variation (or set functions countably additive on bounded Borel sets) with compact support in $(-\infty;+\infty)$. We shall denote this class by $\mathcal{B}$. For the input β in $\mathcal{B}$ the output is given by

29 $$y(t) = \int_{-\infty}^{t} W(t,s)\, d\beta(s)$$

defined almost everywhere in t, $-\infty < t < +\infty$. Since we will be dealing for the most part with absolutely continuous (set) functions and with (set) functions with purely atomic parts, we shall henceforth write *29* more simply as

30 $$y(t) = \int_{-\infty}^{t} W(t,s)u(s)\, ds$$

and allow for delta functions in $u(\cdot)$ as necessary. To obtain a state space representation we begin by rewriting *30* as:

31 $$\begin{aligned} y(t) &= \int_{-\infty}^{t_0} W(t;s)u(s)\, ds + \int_{t_0}^{t} W(t;s)u(s)\, ds \qquad t_0 < t = t_0 + \Delta \\ &= \int_{-\infty}^{0} W(t_0 + \Delta;\, t_0 + s)u(t_0 + s)\, ds + \int_{t_0}^{t_0+\Delta} W(t;s)u(s)\, ds \end{aligned}$$

Let us denote by Σ the subclass of functions in $\mathcal{B}$ whose support is confined to $(-\infty,0]$. We note that the past input with reference to *31*

32 $$u(t_0 + s) \qquad -\infty < s \leq 0$$

is an element of Σ. Let us now introduce a family of linear transformations $L(t)$, $-\infty < t < +\infty$, defined on Σ, mapping Σ into $\mathcal{L}$, the space of Lebesgue measurable functions on $(0,\infty)$ which are essentially bounded on finite intervals by means of

33 $$\begin{aligned} L(t)u &= v \\ v(\Delta) &= \int_{-\infty}^{0} W(t + \Delta;\, t + s)u(s)\, ds \qquad \Delta \geq 0 \end{aligned}$$

Then, of course, $L(t)$ is linear. We shall show that Σ can serve as a state space for inputs confined to $\mathcal{B}$. For this purpose let us denote by $S(t)$ the shift semigroup on Σ, mapping Σ into Σ, defined by

34 $$\begin{aligned} S(t)u = v;\, y(s) &= u(s + t) \qquad -\infty < s \leq -t \\ &= 0 \qquad -t < s < 0 \end{aligned}$$

We note that Σ can be considered as a subspace of the space of continuous linear functionals on the Banach space of continuous functions $C(-0,0]$. If we topologize Σ by the corresponding weak-star topology, $S(t)$ is a continuous linear transformation for each t. If we denote by δ

the delta function supported at the origin, for any $u(\cdot)$ in Σ the integral

35 $$\int_{t_0}^{t} S(t - s)\delta u(s)\, ds$$

is well defined as a Pettis integral, and in fact corresponds to the function:

36 $$\begin{array}{ll} u(t + s) & -t + t_0 < s < 0 \\ 0 & -\infty < s < -t + t_0 \end{array}$$

For given $u(\cdot)$ in Σ, and each a, $-\infty < a < +\infty$, the function

37 $$u(a + s) \qquad -\infty < s < 0$$

is an element of Σ. If we denote it by $x(a)$, we have the representation

38 $$x(t) = S(t - t_0)x(t_0) + \int_{t_0}^{t} S(t - s)\delta u(s)\, ds \qquad t \geq t_0$$

Next let

39 $$v(t) = L(t)x(t)$$

Then it is readily verified that the element $v(t)$ in $\mathfrak{L}$ corresponds to the function:

40 $$\int_{-\infty}^{t} W(t + \Delta; s)u(s)\, ds \qquad \text{ae } \Delta > 0$$

To relate *38* to the output let us define a linear functional on a nonempty linear subspace of α by:

41 $$f_0(g) = \lim_{\Delta \to 0} \frac{1}{\Delta} \int_0^{\Delta} g(s)\, ds$$

whenever this limit exists and is finite. Then because of our assumptions on the function $w(t,s)$, we note that for any $x \in \Sigma$, $L(t)x$ belongs to the domain of definition of $f_0(\cdot)$, omitting a set of Lebesgue measure zero (which is independent of x). Omitting this set of measure zero, we can define a family of linear (not necessarily continuous) functionals on Σ

42 $$c(t)(x) = f_0(L(t)x) \qquad x \in \Sigma$$

Moreover we have then that for $x(t)$ defined by *38*, the output is given by

43 $$y(t) = c(t)[x(t)] \qquad \text{ae}$$

We note that *38* and *43* describe the system in terms of state-input and output-state relations.

We proceed next to enlarge the state spaces and accommodate all inputs for which the output is defined as measurable functions essentially bounded on finite intervals. We can do this by first reducing the state spaces and then introducing a new topology—the *output-induced* topology—and completing the space in that topology. For each t let:

44 $$\Sigma_0(t) = [x \in \Sigma | L(t)x = 0]$$

The reduced states at time t are the elements of the subspace complementary to the subspace $\Sigma_0(t)$. Let us denote the complementary space by

$$\Sigma_R(t)$$

This space is of course (algebraically) isomorphic to the factor space modulo $\Sigma_0(t)$. We topologize $\Sigma_R(t)$ by inducing the minimal topology which makes $L(t)$ continuous, considering $\mathfrak{L}$ topologized by the denumerable seminorms

45 $$P_n(f) = \operatorname*{ess\,sup}_{0<t<n} |f(t)|$$

for each positive integer n. Alternatively one can use the topology of distributions, as indicated earlier. Since $\mathfrak{L}$ is then a locally convex space, so is $\Sigma_R(t)$ for each t. Let us denote the linear mapping defined on Σ mapping Σ onto $\Sigma_R(t)$. Suppose x is an element of $\Sigma_0(s)$. Then it is readily verified that

46 $$P(t)S(t - s)x = 0 \qquad \text{for } t \geq s$$

Hence we can define a two-parameter family of linear transformations $T(t;s)$, $-\infty < s \leq t < +\infty$, mapping $\Sigma_R(s)$ into $\Sigma_R(t)$, defined by

47 $$T(t;s)x = P(t)S(t - s)y$$

where y is any element in Σ such that

48 $$P(s)y = x$$

It will be convenient to write this as

49 $$T(t;s) = P(t)S(t - s)P(s)^{-1}$$

It is readily verified that $T(t;s)$ is a linear continuous transformation. Also we have the transition property:

50 $$T(t;s) = T(t;\tau)T(\tau;s) \qquad s \leq \tau \leq t$$

Next let

51 $$B(t) = P(t)\delta$$

Then from *38* we can write

52 $$P(t)x(t) = P(t)S(t - t_0)P(t_0)^{-1}P(t_0)x(t_0) + \int_{t_0}^{t} P(t)S(t - s)P(s)^{-1}B(s)u(s)\, ds$$

so that in terms of reduced states we have the relation

53 $$\hat{x}(t) = T(t;t_0)\hat{x}(t_0) + \int_{t_0}^{t} T(t;s)B(s)u(s)\,ds$$

where the caret ($\wedge$) indicates that the states are reduced at the indicated times. Also we obviously have in place of *43*:

54 $$\begin{aligned} y(t) &= C(t)[P(t)^{-1}\hat{x}(t)] && \text{ae} \\ &= \hat{C}(t)[\hat{x}(t)] && \text{ae} \end{aligned}$$

It is not difficult to see that relations *53* and *54* be extended to the completions of the spaces $\Sigma_R(t)$. We shall denote the completed spaces by $\overline{\Sigma_R(t)}$. Thus *53* and *54* are the state-input and output-state relations in terms of reduced states.

Next we shall show that the weak connectedness property holds for the completed reduced states. Thus let the reduced state $x(t)$ be given, and let us assume first that it is in $\Sigma_R(t)$. Let $u(\cdot)$ be in Σ such that

55 $$P(t)u = x(t)$$

Then we know that $u(s)$ vanishes for

$$s < -t_0$$

for some positive t_0. It is now readily verified that

56 $$u = \int_{t-t_0}^{t} S(t-s)\,\delta u(s-t)\,ds$$

and hence we have

57 $$\hat{x}(t) = \int_{t-t_0}^{t} T(t;s)B(s)v(s)\,ds$$

where

$$v(s) = u(s-t) \qquad t - t_0 < s < t$$

and *57* verifies the required property. If $\hat{x}(t)$ is in the completed space $\overline{\Sigma_R(t)}$ then it is clear from the definition that we can find a sequence $v_n(\cdot)$ such that

58 $$\hat{x}(t) = \lim \int_{t-t_n}^{t} T(t;s)B(s)v_n(s)\,ds$$

This completes the proof of the theorem.

Let us next consider the spaces $\Sigma_R(t)$. Since these need be only determined within an isomorphism, we can take

59 $$\Sigma_R(t) = L(t)\Sigma$$

with the topology as a subspace of $\mathfrak{L}$. The completion $\Sigma_R(t)$ is simply the closure of the subspace on the right of *59*. We now define Σ as the closed linear subspace in $\mathfrak{L}$ generated by the subspaces

$$\Sigma_R(t) \qquad -\infty < t < +\infty$$

and in particular, we can then discuss the continuity of

$$T(t;s)x \qquad x \in \Sigma_R(s)$$

as a function of t. Thus

60 $$\begin{aligned} T(t+\Delta;\, s)x - T(t;s)x &= [T(t+\Delta;\, t) - I]T(t;s)x \\ &= [T(t+\Delta;\, t) - I]x(t) \qquad x(t) \in \Sigma_R(t) \end{aligned}$$

Now for any x in $\Sigma_R(t)$,

61 $$T(t+\Delta;\, t)x - x = L(t+\Delta)S(\Delta)u - L(t)u \qquad x = L(t)u$$

and the element on the right is given by

62 $$\int_{-\infty}^{0} [W(t+\Delta;\, +\sigma;\, t+s) - W(t+\sigma;\, t+s)]u(s)\, ds \qquad 0 < \sigma < \infty$$

Since in particular we may take $u(\cdot)$ to be a delta function, it follows that $T(t,s)x$ is continuous in t, $t \geq s$, if and only if, for each nonpositive s, and each L,

63 $$\operatorname*{ess\,sup}_{0<\sigma<L} |W(t+\Delta+\sigma;\, t+s) - W(t+\sigma;\, t+s)|$$

goes to zero with Δ. To see that this is a sufficient condition we have also to make use of the fact that $W(t;s)$ is bounded on finite intervals.

Next let us consider the consequences of finite dimensionality of the reduced state spaces. First of all we shall consider a simple case to show that the situation is not the same as in the time-invariant case. Thus let $F(\cdot)$ denote a finitely additive set function defined on the field of finite unions of half-open intervals such that

64 $$g(t;s) = F([s,t))$$

is measurable in s, t and bounded (from above) on finite intervals. We note that such a function need not be countably additive. Let

65 $$\begin{aligned} W(t,s) &= \exp g(t,s) \qquad t > s \\ W(t,t) &= 1 \end{aligned}$$

Then we have:

66 $$W(t,s) = W(t,\tau)W(\tau,s) \qquad s < \tau < t$$

Hence for any u in Σ

67 $$L(t)u = a(t,u)L(t)\delta$$

where

68 $$a(t,u) = \int_{-\infty}^{0} W(t,s)u(s)\,ds$$

and $L(t)\delta$ is the function:

$$W(t+\sigma,\, t) \qquad 0 < \sigma < \infty$$

It follows that $\Sigma_R(t)$ is of dimension at most one for each t. But it can be of dimension zero for some t. For example, we have only to choose $g(\cdot,\cdot)$ so that

69 $$g(t,s) = -\infty \qquad \text{for } s \leq t_0 < t$$

but finite otherwise. Specifically, let

70 $$W(t,s) = \exp - \int_s^t \frac{1}{|x|}\,dx$$

Then $a(t,u)$ is zero for every u for $t = 0$, and hence $\Sigma_R(t)$ is of dimension zero, for $t = 0$, but of dimension one for $t \neq 0$. In particular condition A_1 is not satisfied. One consequence of this is that a system can have finite dimensional state spaces and yet need not be dynamic. To see this, let us pursue the same example with $W(t,s)$ given by *70*. Suppose the system were dynamic so that the input and output are related by equations of the form:

71 $$\dot{x}(t) = A(t)x(t) + B(t)u(t)$$
$$y(t) = C(t)x(t)$$

Let $\Phi(t)$ be the fundamental matrix solution of the homogeneous equation. Then it would follow that we must have

72 $$W(t,s) = C(t)\phi(t)\phi(s)^{-1}B(s) \qquad s < t$$

Taking the input $u(t)$ to be zero for $t > 0$, we have

73 $$y(t) = \int_{-\infty}^{0} W(t,s)u(s)\,ds = C(t)\phi(t)\phi(s)^{-1}x(0)$$
$$= 0 \qquad t > 0$$

But $x(0)$ can be chosen arbitrarily here, and for each such choice there must be WNC and a corresponding input $u(t)$ in $t \leq 0$. Hence

74 $$C(t)\phi(t)\phi(0)^{-1}x(0) = 0 \qquad t > 0$$

Hence $C(t)$ must be zero for positive t almost everywhere. But this contradicts the fact that:

75 $$0 \neq W(t,s) = C(t)\phi(t)\phi(s)^{-1}B(s) \qquad 0 < s < t$$

We can now state some necessary and sufficient conditions for the reduced state spaces to be finite dimensional.

76 **Theorem** A necessary and sufficient condition for the system given by the input-output relation *29* to have a reduced state space of finite dimension at any given time t is that the following relation holds

77
$$W(t + \Delta; t - s) = \sum_{j=1}^{n} b_j(s;t) W(t + \Delta; t - s_j)$$

for every Δ, s nonnegative and fixed s_j nonnegative.

Proof Suppose condition *77* is satisfied; then for any u in Σ, it follows readily that

78
$$L(t)u = \sum_{j=1}^{n} c_j L(t) \delta_j$$

where δ_j represents the delta function:

79
$$\delta_j(s) = \delta(s + s_j) \qquad s \leq 0$$

and hence $\Sigma_R(t)$ is of finite dimension. Conversely, suppose $\Sigma_R(t)$ is finite dimensional. Then let us consider the linear space generated by the elements of the form

$$L(t)\delta_\tau \qquad 0 \leq \tau$$

where

$$\delta_\tau(s) = \delta(s + \tau) \qquad 0 \geq s$$

Since this space has finite dimension, let $\{L(t)\delta_{\tau_j}\}$ be a basis. Then *77* follows, since $L(t)\delta_\tau$ corresponds to the function

$$W(t + \Delta; t - \tau) \qquad 0 < \Delta < \infty$$

Also it readily follows that $\{L(t)\delta_{\tau_j}\}$ provides a basis for $\Sigma_R(t)$ as well. This completes the proof of the theorem.

Let us note next that in a linear WNC system (whether WNC is defined in terms of states or by *20*), if the reduced state space $\Sigma_R(t_0)$ is finite dimensional for some t_0, and condition A_1 is satisfied, so is $\Sigma_R(t)$ clearly for every $t > t_0$, and the dimension of $\Sigma_R(t)$ cannot increase with t. However, condition A_1 need not be satisfied in general, even in a WNC system. For example, if we define the weighting function $W(t,s)$ as

80
$$\begin{aligned} W(t,s) &= \frac{s}{t} && -\infty < s < t < 0 \\ &= 0 && -\infty < s < 0 \leq t \\ &= g(t - s) && 0 < s < t \end{aligned}$$

it is seen (as in the previous example) that the dimension of $\Sigma_R(t)$ is one for t less than zero, zero for $t = 0$, whereas for $t > 0$,

$$y(t + \Delta) = \int_\infty^t W(t + \Delta,\, s)u(s)\, ds \qquad 0 < \Delta$$
$$= \int_0^t g(t + \Delta - s)u(s)\, ds$$

Hence by choosing $g(\cdot)$ suitably, for instance for

$$g(s) = \exp -s^2$$

the dimension of $\Sigma_R(t)$ for $t > 0$ is actually infinite (since *77* is not satisfied). However we have:

81 **Theorem** Suppose a linear system is WNC (whether in terms of states or in terms of input-output as in *20*), and suppose the dimension of the reduced state space at every instant is exactly the same and finite. Then the system may be represented as a dynamic system.

Proof The proof of Theorem *3.2.69* will apply provided we can show that condition A_1 is satisfied. We proceed to show this. Since $\Sigma_R(t)$ has the same finite dimension (for example, n) for every t, we may set $\Sigma_R(t) = E_n$, and it is enough to show that $T(t,s)$, which is now representable as an $n \times n$ matrix, is nonsingular for every t, s. Let us consider $T(t,s)$ as a function of s for fixed t. Suppose first that $T(t,s)$ is singular for every $s < t$. For any x in E_n, we have, by WNC, that

82 $$x = T(t,L)x_L + \int_L^t T(t,\sigma)B(\sigma)u(\sigma)\, d\sigma$$

for some $u(\cdot)$, and $L < t$. Now since the dimension of the range space of $T(t,s)$ is an integer-valued nondecreasing function of s, it follows that the dimension must be a constant (less than n) for $s_0 < s < t$, for some s_0. This means that the range space remains the same for $s_0 < s < t$. But we can write

83 $$x = T(t,\, t - t_n)y_n + \int_{t-t_n}^t T(t,\sigma)B(\sigma)\tilde{u}(\sigma)\, d\sigma + \gamma B(t)$$

where $\tilde{u}(\cdot)$ does not contain a delta function concentrated at t. Moreover, we can find a delta-convergent sequence $u_n(\cdot)$ converging to the delta function at t, and $u_n(\cdot)$ vanishing in $(t - 1/n,\, t)$ for n sufficiently large, such that

84 $$B(t) = \lim \int_{t-t_0}^t T(t,\sigma)B(\sigma)u_n(\sigma)\, d\sigma$$

the equality holding in the topology specified. For

85 $$B(t) \sim W(t + \Delta,\, t) \qquad \Delta > 0$$

and for each n,

86 $$\int_{t-t_0}^{t} T(t,\sigma)B(\sigma)u_n(\sigma)\,d\sigma \sim \int_{t-t_0}^{t} W(t+\Delta,\sigma)u_n(\sigma)\,d\sigma$$

and for each finite L, it follows from our assumptions on $W(t,s)$ that

87 $$\operatorname*{ess\,sup}_{0<\Delta<L}\left| W(t+\Delta,t) - \int_{t-t_0}^{t} W(t+\Delta,\sigma)u_n(\sigma)\,d\sigma \right|$$

goes to zero with n. Thus the range of

88 $$T(t,L)x_L + \int_L^t T(t,\sigma)B(\sigma)u(\sigma)\,d\sigma$$

is not n-dimensional, contradicting WNC. Hence it follows that we can find τ such that $T(t,s)$ is nonsingular for $\tau < s < t$. But we shall now show that $T(t,\tau)$ must itself be also nonsingular. For suppose there is an element x in E_n such that

89 $$T(t,\tau)x = 0$$

But for any $\Delta > 0$, $\tau + \Delta < t$, we have

90 $$T(t,\tau)x = T(t,\tau+\Delta)T(\tau+\Delta,\tau)x = 0$$

and $T(t,\tau+\Delta)$ is nonsingular, so that

91 $$T(\tau+\Delta,\tau)x = 0 \qquad \text{for } 0 < \Delta < t - \tau$$

But

92 $$T(\tau+\Delta,\tau)x \sim \int_{-\infty}^{\tau} W(\tau+\Delta+\sigma, s)u_0(s)\,ds \qquad \sigma > 0$$

for some $u_0(\cdot)$ implying that

93 $$\int_{-\infty}^{\tau} W(\tau+\gamma, s)u_0(s)\,ds = 0 \qquad \text{for every } \gamma > 0$$

which in turn means that x itself is zero. Hence $T(t,\tau)$ is nonsingular. But t being arbitrary, we can apply the same argument to τ, and thus we must have that $T(t,s)$ is nonsingular for every $s < t$. The second possibility is that $T(t,s)$ is not singular for every s, $s < t$. But again because of the finite dimensionality of the range spaces, and their nondecreasing nature, it follows that there must exist τ such that $T(t,s)$ is nonsingular for $\tau < s < t$ and by the second part of the argument above, it follows that $T(t,s)$ is again actually nonsingular for every $s < t$. But

94 $$T(t,s)\Sigma_R(s) \subseteq \Sigma_R(t)$$

and by nonsingularity, the equality must hold, or we have proved property A_1.

95 **Corollary** Under the conditions of Theorem *81*, the input-output rela-

tion may be expressed

96 $$y(t) = \left[\hat{C}(t), \int_{-\infty}^{t} D(s)u(s)\,ds\right]$$

where $\hat{C}(t)$, $D(s)$ are functions (Lebesgue measurable and essentially bounded on finite intervals) with values in E_n, and the range of the linear transformation

97 $$\int_{-\infty}^{0} D(t+s)u(s)\,ds$$

mapping Σ into E_n is all of E_n for each t. Conversely, any system whose input-output relation may be expressed by *96* is a linear dynamic system, provided *97* holds.

Proof Under the conditions of the theorem we have from WNS and *3.2.74* that

$$W(t,s) = [C(t), \psi(t)\psi(s)^{-1}\hat{P}(s)B(s)]$$

where $P(t)$ denotes the $|:|$ mapping of $\Sigma_r(t)$ onto the euclidean space E_n.

$$D(s) = \psi(s)^{-1}\hat{P}(s)B(s) \qquad \hat{C}(t) = \psi(t)^{*}C(t)$$

Again, for each $u(\cdot)$ in Σ, $L(t)u$ now corresponds to the function

$$\left[\hat{C}(t+\Delta), \int_{-\infty}^{0} D(t+s)u(s)\,ds\right] \qquad \Delta \geq 0$$

and the range of $L(t)$ is isomorphic to $\Sigma_R(t)$ which has dimension n for each t, by assumption and hence *97* follows. Conversely, if *96* and *97* hold, we can write

98 $$\dot{z}(t) = D(t)u(t)$$

99 $$y(t) = [\hat{C}(t), z(t)]$$

and the system will of course have the WNC property in addition. In fact *98* has the solution

100 $$z(t) = z(t_0) + \int_{t_0}^{t} D(s)u(s)$$

and by *97* we can write

101 $$z(t_0) = \int_{-\infty}^{0} D(t_0+s)u(s)\,ds = \int_{-\infty}^{t_0} D(s)u(s-t_0)\,ds$$

or *98* and *99* are equivalent to *96*.

102 **Remark** The condition that the reduced state spaces have the same dimension may be replaced by the condition that the reduced state spaces are finite dimensional and the transformation $T(t,s)$ is continuous in $t \geq s$ for each s. For, by a result given by Aczel [9], this would

imply that $T(t,s)$ is nonsingular for $t \geq s$ and hence the key result *74* may be deduced.

REFERENCES

1 Zadeh, L., and C. Desoer: "Linear System Theory," McGraw-Hill, New York, 1964.
2 Balakrishnan, A. V.: On the State Space Theory of Linear Systems, *J. Math. Analysis Appl.*, vol. 14, pp. 371–391, 1966.
3 Balakrishnan, A. V.: Foundations of the State Space Theory of Continuous Systems, *J. Computer Systems Sci.*, vol. 1, March, 1967.
4 Balakrishnan, A. V.: On the Controllability of a Nonlinear System, *Proc. Natl. Acad. Sci.*, pp. 365–368, March, 1966.
5 Kalman, R. E.: Mathematical Description of Linear Dynamic Systems, *J. SIAM Ser. Control*, pp. 159–192, 1963.
6 Pontryagin, L.: "The Mathematical Theory of Optimal Processes"; English translation, Wiley, New York, 1962.
7 Youla, D. C.: The Synthesis of Linear Dynamic Systems from Prescribed Weighting Functions, *SIAM J. Appl. Math.*, pp. 527–549, May, 1966.
8 Gilbert, E. G.: Controllability and Observability in Multivariable Control Systems, *J. SIAM Ser. Control*, vol. 1, pp. 128–151, 1963.
9 Aczel, J.: Lectures on Functional Equations and Their Applications, Academic, New York, 1966.
10 Gelfand, I. M., and N. Y. Vilenkin: "Generalized Functions," Academic, New York, 1964.

4

Some network interpretations of systems problems

T. E. Stern[1]
Department of Electrical Engineering
Columbia University

1 *Introduction*

One of the most important aspects of system theory is the problem of system optimization. An optimization requirement which involves extremizing a function of a finite number of variables subject to various types of constraints can usually be cast in the form of a mathematical programming problem. Similarly, a problem involving the extremum of a functional, such as that which occurs in optimal control, is essentially a variational problem. The purpose of this chapter is to demonstrate that these two basic types of system-optimization problems have natural interpretations in terms of network analogs. The former leads to a reciprocal nonlinear resistive network analog whereas the latter is associated with a *lagrangian* network analog, a generalization of a conservative network. Once an analog network is formulated it is possible to identify all of the characteristics of the extremum problem with physical properties of the network, and, in fact, it is often possible to deduce certain aspects of the mathematical structure of the problem from the physical structure of the network.

The minimum heat theorem of Maxwell [1] and its generalization to nonlinear networks by Millar [2] suggest the use of a reciprocal resistive network as an analog for mathematical programming problems. An

[1] This work was partially supported by the National Science Foundation under grants NSFG P533 and NSFG P14514 and by the Department of the Navy under Contract NONR 4259(04).

intensive study of the resistive network analog as a heuristic tool in the solution of programming problems can be found in Dennis [3]. Many of his results are incorporated in modified form in Sec. *4*. However, they are developed in the manner of [4] rather than following Dennis' procedure.

Hamilton's principle for conservative systems suggests the use of conservative networks as devices for generating extremals associated with variational problems. By defining a broader class of networks, the lagrangian networks, which satisfy Hamilton's principle, it is possible to synthesize a general class of network analogs for variational problems.

The first part of this chapter (Secs. *2*, *3*, *4*, *5*) is devoted to the discussion of the resistive network interpretation of mathematical programming problems, and the latter part (Secs. *6*, *7*, *8*) describes the role of the lagrangian network as an analog for variational problems.

2 *Properties of reciprocal networks*

In the development which follows, we shall make use of very general types of reciprocal resistive network elements. This section will, therefore, be devoted to defining such elements and exploring their properties.

A general n-port resistive element is shown schematically in Fig. *4.2.1*. If we represent the n terminal voltages by the vector $\mathbf{e}_R$, and the n

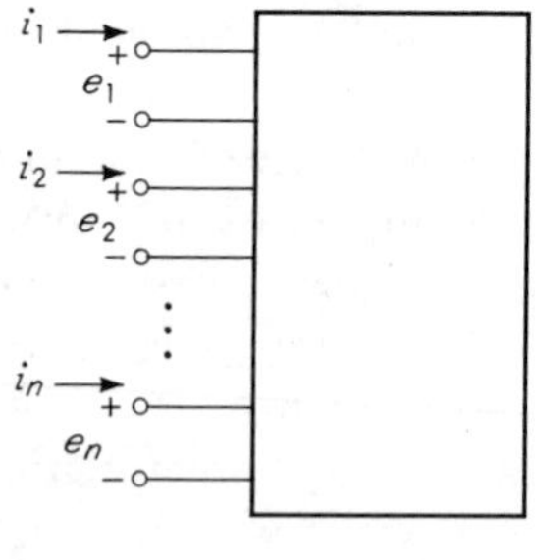

Fig. 4.2.1 n-port resistive element.

terminal currents by the vector $\mathbf{i}_R$, the element can be defined by the implicit relations

$$\mathbf{f}(\mathbf{e}_R,\mathbf{i}_R) = \mathbf{0}$$

where $\mathbf{f}$ is an n-vector. (In all that follows, only time-invariant elements will be considered. Hence the time t will not appear in the defining relations.) Generally it may be possible to write these relations in any one of several explicit forms. For example,

1 $$\mathbf{e}_R = \mathbf{e}_R(\mathbf{i}_R)$$

2 $$\mathbf{i}_R = \mathbf{i}_R(\mathbf{e}_R)$$

or, partitioning the variables, and letting

$$\mathbf{e}_1 = \begin{bmatrix} e_1 \\ \cdot \\ \cdot \\ \cdot \\ e_k \end{bmatrix} \qquad \mathbf{i}_1 = \begin{bmatrix} i_1 \\ \cdot \\ \cdot \\ \cdot \\ i_k \end{bmatrix}$$

$$\mathbf{e}_2 = \begin{bmatrix} e_{k+1} \\ \cdot \\ \cdot \\ \cdot \\ e_n \end{bmatrix} \qquad \mathbf{i}_2 = \begin{bmatrix} i_{k+1} \\ \cdot \\ \cdot \\ \cdot \\ i_n \end{bmatrix}$$

it may be possible to write the explicit form

3 $$\mathbf{i}_1 = \mathbf{i}_1(\mathbf{e}_1,\mathbf{i}_2)$$

$$\mathbf{e}_2 = \mathbf{e}_2(\mathbf{e}_1,\mathbf{i}_2)$$

In order to simplify diagrams, n-port elements will be represented schematically as shown in Fig. *4.2.2*, where many sets of terminal pairs

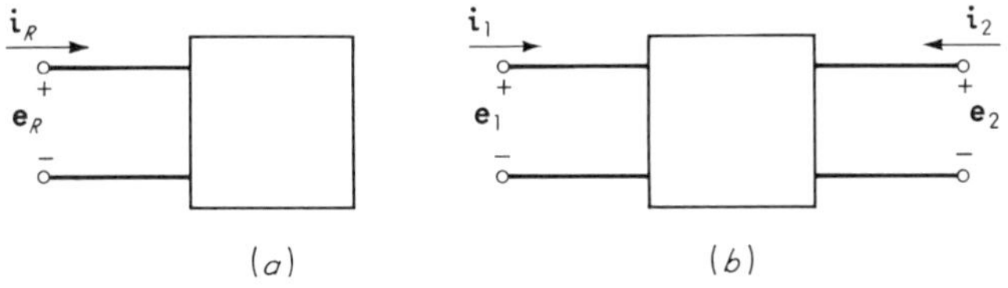

Fig. 4.2.2 Vector representation of n-port resistive element.

are grouped together, and the variables indicated in the diagram are vector variables. Expressions *1, 2, 3* will be termed branch relations for the element. Besides representing *individual* network elements, these relations could clearly characterize the behavior of an interconnection of several elements as viewed from a certain set of terminal pairs.

Since the derivatives of various types of functions will appear frequently, we digress for a moment to introduce some notation. Given a set of functions,

$$\mathbf{y} = \mathbf{y}(\mathbf{x})$$

where $\mathbf{y}$ is an n-vector and $\mathbf{x}$ an m-vector, we denote their partial derivatives by

4
$$\frac{\partial \mathbf{y}}{\partial \mathbf{x}} = \begin{bmatrix} \frac{\partial y_1}{\partial x_1} & \frac{\partial y_1}{\partial x_2} & \cdots & \frac{\partial y_1}{\partial x_m} \\ \frac{\partial y_2}{\partial x_1} & \frac{\partial y_2}{\partial x_2} & \cdots & \frac{\partial y_2}{\partial x_m} \\ \cdots & \cdots & \cdots & \cdots \\ \frac{\partial y_n}{\partial x_1} & \frac{\partial y_n}{\partial x_2} & \cdots & \frac{\partial y_n}{\partial x_m} \end{bmatrix}$$

Thus, for example, the gradient of a scalar function, $\phi(\mathbf{x})$, is written

5
$$\text{grad } \phi = \left(\frac{\partial \phi}{\partial \mathbf{x}}\right)^t$$

[where $(\cdot)^t$ denotes *transpose*].

Given a resistive element defined in terms of an explicit set of differentiable branch relations, we may associate with these relations an *incremental parameter matrix*. Thus, for branch relations of the form of *1*, we define the *incremental resistance matrix*,

6
$$R(\mathbf{i}_R) \triangleq \frac{\partial \mathbf{e}_R}{\partial \mathbf{i}_R}$$

Given the inverse relations of *2*, we define an *incremental conductance matrix*,

7
$$G(\mathbf{e}_R) \triangleq \frac{\partial \mathbf{i}_R}{\partial \mathbf{e}_R}$$

and, given the mixed relations of *3*, we define a *hybrid incremental resistance matrix*

8
$$H(\mathbf{e}_1,\mathbf{i}_2) \triangleq \frac{\partial(\mathbf{i}_1,\mathbf{e}_2)}{\partial(\mathbf{e}_1,\mathbf{i}_2)} \triangleq \begin{bmatrix} H_{11} & H_{12} \\ H_{21} & H_{22} \end{bmatrix} \triangleq \begin{bmatrix} \frac{\partial \mathbf{i}_1}{\partial \mathbf{e}_1} & \frac{\partial \mathbf{i}_1}{\partial \mathbf{i}_2} \\ \frac{\partial \mathbf{e}_2}{\partial \mathbf{e}_1} & \frac{\partial \mathbf{e}_2}{\partial \mathbf{i}_2} \end{bmatrix}$$

Reciprocity can now be defined in terms of the incremental parameter matrices.

9 **Definition** Given a resistive network element defined in terms of the explicit branch relations *1*, *2*, or *3*, the element is *reciprocal* if

$$R(\mathbf{i}_R) \text{ is symmetric for all } \mathbf{i}_R$$

or
$$G(\mathbf{e}_R) \text{ is symmetric for all } \mathbf{e}_R$$

or
$$\begin{bmatrix} H_{11} & H_{12} \\ -H_{21} & -H_{22} \end{bmatrix} \text{ is symmetric for all } \mathbf{e}_1, \mathbf{i}_2$$

It is easily shown that if any one of the three matrices in Definition *9* is symmetric so are any others which are *defined.* However, not all three forms may be definable. For example, a bank of ideal transformers can be defined by the branch relations,

10
$$\mathbf{i}_1 = -N^t\mathbf{i}_2$$
$$\mathbf{e}_2 = N\mathbf{e}_1$$

The pertinent matrix in definition *9* is

$$\begin{bmatrix} H_{11} & H_{12} \\ -H_{21} & -H_{22} \end{bmatrix} = \begin{bmatrix} 0 & -N^t \\ -N & 0 \end{bmatrix}$$

which is clearly symmetric. Hence this is a reciprocal element. Its incremental resistance and conductance matrices, however, cannot be defined.

A network composed of resistive elements and viewed from a particular set of ports will be called *reciprocal from these ports* if the appropriate symmetry conditions are met at these ports. (A network containing only reciprocal elements must be reciprocal from all sets of ports. However, a network may appear reciprocal from certain ports and yet contain nonreciprocal elements.)

Reciprocity is of central importance here because any reciprocal element can be concisely characterized in terms of one or more scalar *dissipation functions.* A particular dissipation function may be associated with each of the three types of explicit branch relations, as follows.

11 **Definition** Given a reciprocal resistive element defined by branch relations of the form of *1*, the *content*[1] function, $\mathfrak{F}(\mathbf{i}_R)$, is defined as

12
$$\mathfrak{F}(\mathbf{i}_R) = \int_{\mathbf{i}_{R0}}^{\mathbf{i}_R} \mathbf{e}_R{}^t(\mathbf{u})\, d\mathbf{u}$$

13 **Definition** Given a reciprocal resistive element defined by branch relations of the form of *2*, the *cocontent* function, $\mathfrak{F}'(\mathbf{e}_R)$, is defined as

14
$$\mathfrak{F}'(\mathbf{e}_R) = \int_{\mathbf{e}_{R0}}^{\mathbf{e}_R} \mathbf{i}_R{}^t(\mathbf{u})\, d\mathbf{u}$$

15 **Definition** Given a reciprocal resistive element defined by branch relations of the form of *3*, the *hybrid dissipation function,*[2] $\mathfrak{F}''(\mathbf{e}_1,\mathbf{i}_2)$, is defined as

16
$$\mathfrak{F}''(\mathbf{e}_1,\mathbf{i}_2) = \int_{\mathbf{e}_{10}}^{\mathbf{e}_1} \mathbf{i}_1{}^t(\mathbf{u})\, d\mathbf{u} - \int_{\mathbf{i}_{20}}^{\mathbf{i}_2} \mathbf{e}_2{}^t(\mathbf{v})\, d\mathbf{v}$$

A word of explanation is needed here. First, it will be noted that each dissipation function is defined in terms of a *line integral.* Thus, in

[1] The terms content and cocontent were originally coined by Millar [2] for 1-port elements.

[2] This was first defined by Moser [5].

order that these functions be uniquely defined, the integral must be independent of path, a condition which is guaranteed by the reciprocity property. Second, the lower limit of integration has been left arbitrary, introducing some ambiguity. Thus each function is only defined within an arbitrary constant. With minor exceptions, this constant will be of no consequence. In the exceptional cases, the lower limit of integration will be explicitly specified. These dissipation functions are generalizations of the well-known Rayleigh dissipation function which appears in classical dynamics.[1]

It can be seen from the above definitions that the branch relations can be recovered directly from the dissipation functions by differentiation. Thus

17
$$\begin{aligned} \mathbf{e}_R &= \left(\frac{\partial \mathfrak{F}}{\partial \mathbf{i}_R}\right)^t \\ \mathbf{i}_R &= \left(\frac{\partial \mathfrak{F}'}{\partial \mathbf{e}_R}\right)^t \\ \begin{bmatrix} \mathbf{i}_1 \\ -\mathbf{e}_2 \end{bmatrix} &= \left(\frac{\partial \mathfrak{F}''}{\partial \mathbf{e}_1,\mathbf{i}_2}\right)^t \end{aligned}$$

For illustration, Fig. *4.2.3* shows the content and cocontent functions for some 1-port elements. (All explicitly definable 1-port resistive elements are, by definition, reciprocal.) The branch relations for the elements shown in Fig. *4.2.3b* and *4.2.3c* will be of special interest. Figure *4.2.3b* represents a diode with zero reverse conductance and a small forward resistance μ. Its branch relation and cocontent function are also shown. Since functions of this form will be used often in the sequel, they shall henceforth be denoted with the aid of the following notation: Define

18
$$\delta(x) \triangleq \begin{cases} 0 & x \geq 0 \\ \dfrac{x}{\mu} & x < 0;\ \mu > 0 \end{cases}$$

19
$$\Delta(x) \triangleq \int_0^x \delta(u)\,du = \begin{cases} 0 & x \geq 0 \\ \dfrac{1}{2\mu}x^2 & x < 0 \end{cases}$$

Similarly, for a vector variable $\mathbf{x}$ we define

20
$$\boldsymbol{\delta}(\mathbf{x}) \triangleq \begin{bmatrix} \delta(x_1) \\ \delta(x_2) \\ \cdot \\ \cdot \\ \cdot \\ \delta(x_n) \end{bmatrix}$$

[1] See, for example, Whittaker [6], p. 230.

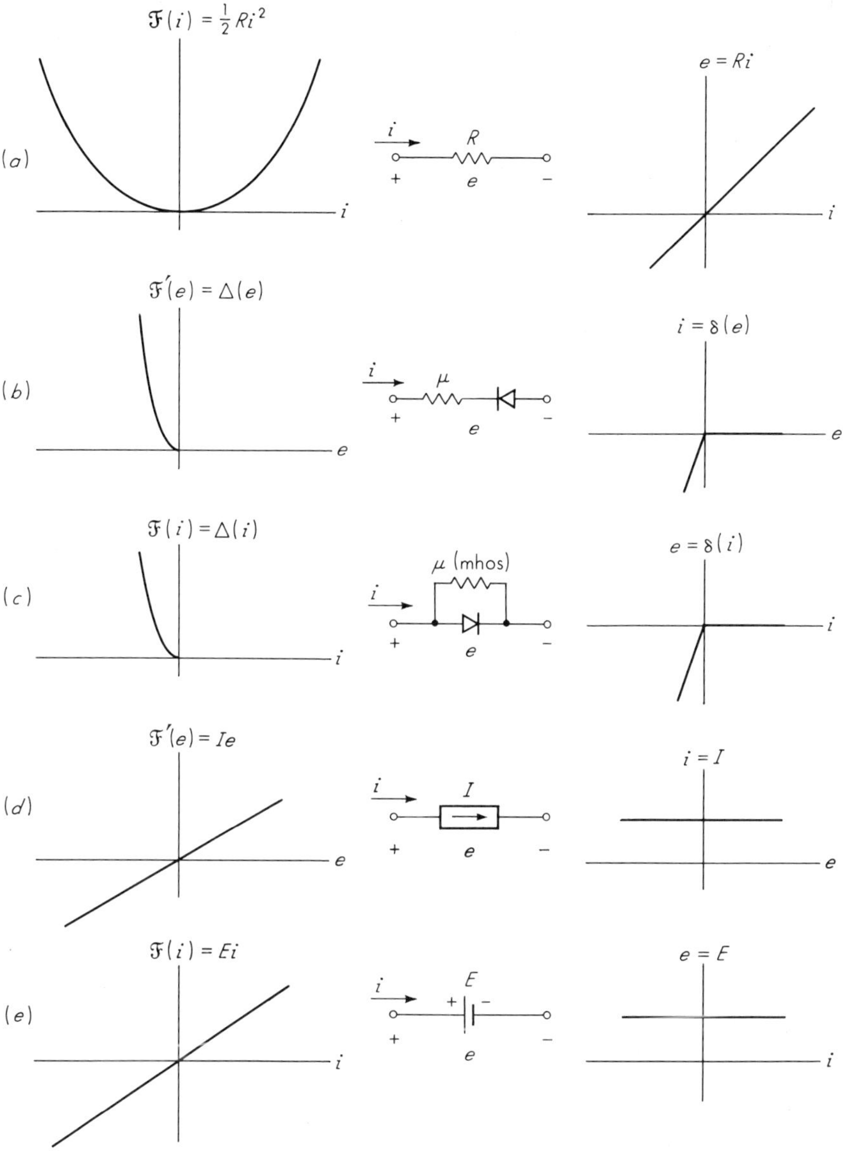

Fig. 4.2.3 Dissipation functions for some 1-port elements.

21 $$\Delta(\mathbf{x}) \triangleq \sum_{i=1}^{n} \Delta(x_i) = \int_{\mathbf{0}}^{\mathbf{x}} \boldsymbol{\delta}^t(\mathbf{u})\, d\mathbf{u}$$

The two functions $\boldsymbol{\delta}(\mathbf{x})$ and $\Delta(\mathbf{x})$ are related by

22 $$\boldsymbol{\delta}(\mathbf{x}) = \left(\frac{\partial \Delta}{\partial \mathbf{x}}\right)^t$$

The *i-e* relation for the diode of Fig. *4.2.3b* is then denoted as

23 $$i = \delta(e)$$

and its cocontent function is denoted as

24 $$\mathfrak{F}'(e) = \Delta(e)$$

Similarly, for the dual configuration of Fig. *4.2.3c* we have

25 $$e = \delta(i) \qquad \mathfrak{F}(i) = \Delta(i)$$

The transformer bank of *10* provides a simple illustration of the hybrid dissipation function of a multi-port element. For this element,

26 $$\mathfrak{F}''(\mathbf{e}_1,\mathbf{i}_2) = -\mathbf{i}_2{}^t N \mathbf{e}_1$$

All of the elements appearing in these illustrations will be used in constructing network analogs of mathematical programming problems.

Thus far, we have considered a network element as being defined by branch relations and have derived the dissipation functions from these relations. However, it will also be useful to reverse this sequence, i.e., to consider the network element as defined by a dissipation function and to derive the branch relations from this function. This is particularly convenient, since in this way any arbitrary scalar function of n variables can be considered as defining an n-port reciprocal network element. For example, the function

$$\mathfrak{F}(\mathbf{i}) = (i_1{}^2 + i_2{}^2)^{\frac{3}{2}}$$

defines a reciprocal network element having the following branch relations

$$e_1 = 3i_1(i_1{}^2 + i_2{}^2)^{\frac{1}{2}}$$
$$e_2 = 3i_2(i_1{}^2 + i_2{}^2)^{\frac{1}{2}}$$

If both the content and cocontent functions are *defined* for a given reciprocal element then their sum is

27 $$\mathfrak{F}(\mathbf{i}_R) + \mathfrak{F}'(\mathbf{e}_R) = \int_{\mathbf{i}_{R0}}^{\mathbf{i}_R} \mathbf{e}_R{}^t(\mathbf{u})\, d\mathbf{u} + \int_{\mathbf{e}_{R0}}^{\mathbf{e}_R} \mathbf{i}_R{}^t(\mathbf{v})\, d\mathbf{v}$$

If the lower limits on the integrals are chosen to satisfy the relation

$$\mathbf{e}_{R0}{}^t\mathbf{i}_{R0} = 0$$

then

$$\mathfrak{F}(\mathbf{i}_R) + \mathfrak{F}'(\mathbf{e}_R) = \mathbf{e}_R{}^t\mathbf{i}_R \tag{28}$$

Equation *28* indicates that the *sum of the content and cocontent functions for a reciprocal element equals the total power absorbed by the element.* If it is written in the form

$$\mathfrak{F}'(\mathbf{e}_R) = \mathbf{e}_R{}^t\mathbf{i}_R - \mathfrak{F}(\mathbf{i}_R) \tag{29}$$

it defines the *Legendre transformation* relating the two dissipation functions. In effect, the Legendre transformation represents a change of the coordinate system in which the dissipation function is defined. Thus, *29* provides a means of changing from $\mathbf{i}_R$ to $\mathbf{e}_R$ coordinates. In order to be able to effect this transformation it must be possible to solve the branch relations for $\mathbf{i}_R$ in terms of $\mathbf{e}_R$. A sufficient condition such that this can be accomplished is that the function $\mathfrak{F}(\mathbf{i}_R)$ be *strictly* convex.[1] (This condition assures that if the $\mathbf{i}_R$-space maps into a region R of the $\mathbf{e}_R$-space, then to every value of $\mathbf{e}_R \in R$, there corresponds one and only one value of $\mathbf{i}_R$. The transformed function, $\mathfrak{F}'(\mathbf{e}_R)$, can therefore be uniquely defined for all $\mathbf{e}_R \in R$.) It can also be shown that if a function is strictly convex, its Legendre transform is also strictly convex.

The dissipation functions provide a convenient means of writing the equations of a resistive network in compact form. Thus, suppose the network equations are written in terms of a set of independent node-pair voltages $\mathbf{e}$. If we interpret this set of node pairs as a set of external ports of the network (see Fig. *4.2.4a*), and if, further, the network is *reciprocal* as seen from these ports, then a *network cocontent function* $\mathfrak{F}'_N(\mathbf{e})$ can be defined with respect to these ports. The equilibrium

[1] A function $f(\mathbf{x})$ is *convex* if for any $\mathbf{x}_1 \neq \mathbf{x}_2$

$$\lambda f(\mathbf{x}_1) + (1 - \lambda)f(\mathbf{x}_2) \geq f[\lambda\mathbf{x}_1 + (1 - \lambda)\mathbf{x}_2] \qquad \text{for all } 0 < \lambda < 1$$

f is *strictly convex* if the strict inequality holds. f is (strictly) concave if $-f$ is (strictly) convex.

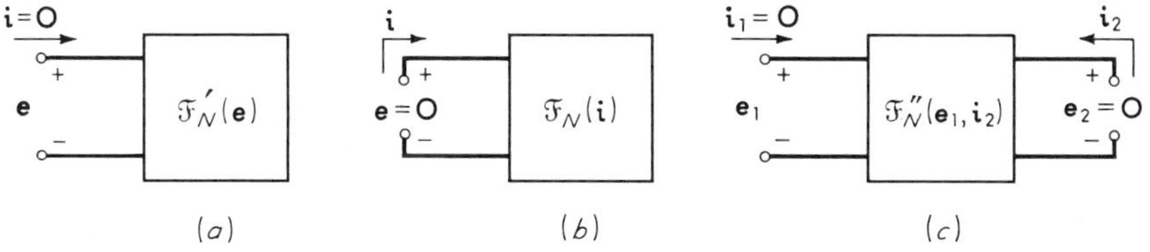

Fig. 4.2.4 Equilibrium conditions for reciprocal resistive networks.

conditions for the network then can be written,

30 $$\mathbf{i} = \left(\frac{\partial \mathfrak{F}_N'}{\partial \mathbf{e}}\right)^t = \mathbf{0}$$

where $\mathbf{i}$ represents the external current entering the ports. Similarly if the equations of a resistive network are defined in terms of an independent set of loop currents $\mathbf{i}$ and if the network is reciprocal as seen from these loops (viewed as short-circuited external ports, see Fig. *4.2.4b*), then a network content function $\mathfrak{F}_N(\mathbf{i})$ can be defined. The equilibrium conditions for the network can then be written

31 $$\mathbf{e} = \left(\frac{\partial \mathfrak{F}_N}{\partial \mathbf{i}}\right)^t = \mathbf{0}$$

Finally, defining the network equations in terms of an independent mixed set of variables $\mathbf{e}_1$, $\mathbf{i}_2$ (see Fig. *4.2.4c*), if the necessary reciprocity conditions hold at the appropriate ports, the equilibrium conditions can be stated in terms of a network hybrid dissipation function $\mathfrak{F}_N''(\mathbf{e}_1,\mathbf{i}_2)$ as

32 $$\begin{bmatrix} \mathbf{i}_1 \\ -\mathbf{e}_2 \end{bmatrix} = \left(\frac{\partial \mathfrak{F}_N''}{\partial \mathbf{e}_1,\mathbf{i}_2}\right)^t = \mathbf{0}$$

The above discussion can be summed up by the following:

33 **Theorem** If a network dissipation function can be defined as above for a resistive network, then the equilibrium conditions for the network correspond to the stationary values of the dissipation function.

Although Theorem *33* relates equilibria to stationary points of the dissipation functions, it does not indicate whether the equilibria are stable or unstable. In order to investigate stability of the equilibria of a resistive network it is necessary to take into account the effects of "stray" energy storage elements. The networks of Fig. *4.2.4* may be modified for purposes of stability analysis by adding sets of linear capacitances and inductances as indicated in Fig. *4.2.5*. With the addition of these elements, the algebraic equilibrium equations become

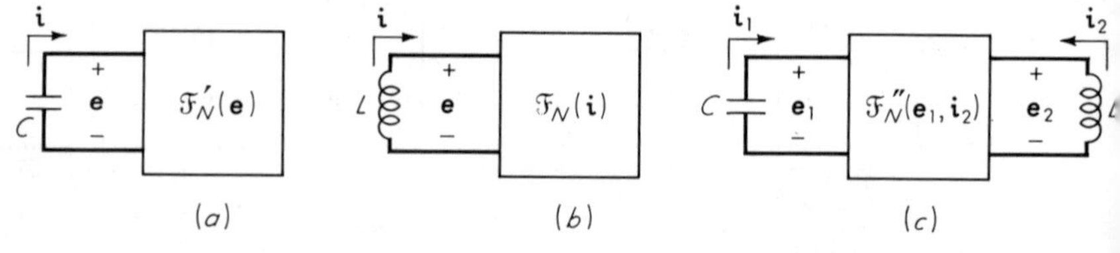

Fig. 4.2.5 Networks of Fig. *4.2.4* with stray elements added.

differential equations. Thus, *30*, representing the network of Fig. *4.2.4a*, becomes

34
$$C\frac{d\mathbf{e}}{dt} = -\left(\frac{\partial \mathfrak{F}'_N}{\partial \mathbf{e}}\right)^t$$

representing the modified network of Fig. *4.2.5a*. Similarly, *31* and *32* are replaced respectively by

35
$$L\frac{d\mathbf{i}}{dt} = -\left(\frac{\partial \mathfrak{F}_N}{\partial \mathbf{i}}\right)^t$$

and

36
$$C\frac{d\mathbf{e}_1}{dt} = -\left(\frac{\partial \mathfrak{F}''_N}{\partial \mathbf{e}_1}\right)^t$$

$$L\frac{d\mathbf{i}_2}{dt} = \left(\frac{\partial \mathfrak{F}''_N}{\partial \mathbf{i}_2}\right)^t$$

where L and C are positive definite diagonal inductance and capacitance matrices representing the stray energy storage elements. It will be noted that the equilibria of the networks are now the singular points of *34*, *35*, and *36* and that the stability of the equilibria can be determined by investigating the stability of these singular points. It turns out that stable singular points correspond to *minima* of the functions $\mathfrak{F}_N$ and $\mathfrak{F}'_N$ and *saddle points* of $\mathfrak{F}''_N$. We shall make use of the above differential equations in Sec. *5* when we examine questions of stability and convergence in mathematical programming problems.

3 *Mathematical programming*

In this section we shall briefly review the pertinent characteristics of the general mathematical programming problem. Our aim will be to point out certain special features which have direct counterparts in the network analogs to be described in Sec. *4*. Since the assertions and theorems stated herein are well-known results, we shall not include any proofs.

The general form of the problem will be considered first after which we shall point out some important special cases. The general mathematical programming problem is stated as follows:[1]

1 *Problem* Minimize the scalar function $\phi(\mathbf{e})$ subject to the inequality

[1] Of the several variants in formulation found in the literature we have chosen the form which lends itself best to the network interpretation.

constraints[1]

2 $$\mathbf{f}(\mathbf{e}) \geq \mathbf{0}$$
$$\mathbf{e} \geq \mathbf{0}$$

where $\mathbf{e}$ is an n-vector and $\mathbf{f}$ is an m-vector.

The function $\phi(\mathbf{e})$ is known as the *objective function* and the set S_c of points $\mathbf{e}$ satisfying the inequality constraints is known as the *constraint set*. Any vector $\mathbf{e} \in S_c$ is called a *feasible* vector. Clearly, S_c must be nonempty if the problem is to have a solution. Programming problems are simply extremum problems with special types of constraints, which set them apart from the "classical" variety.

In case ϕ is a nonlinear function (the *nonlinear programming problem*) the search for a minimum may be quite complicated, even without constraints, owing to the possibility of occurrence of more than one *relative* minimum (a relative minimum being a point $\mathbf{e}_0$ such that $\phi(\mathbf{e}_0) \leq \phi(\mathbf{e})$ for all $\mathbf{e}$ in a neighborhood of $\mathbf{e}_0$). Since practically all methods of minimization are equivalent to a search for points at which the partial derivatives of ϕ are zero, these methods correspond to the search for a relative minimum, although what is really sought is a *global* minimum. In order to avoid the difficulty of distinguishing between these two types of minima, and in order to simplify the ensuing development, we shall henceforth restrict discussion to cases in which the following assumptions hold:

3 ϕ is convex, continuous, and twice-differentiable
4 Each f_j is concave, continuous, and twice-differentiable
5 There exists a point $\mathbf{e}_0$ which corresponds to an *isolated* minimum of ϕ in S_c

Condition *4* implies that S_c is a convex set. Conditions *3* and *5* together imply that $\mathbf{e}_0$ is a unique local minimum, and hence the global minimum. Double differentiability is assumed merely to simplify some of the derivations to follow.

A program whose objective function is convex and whose constraint functions are concave is called a *concave program*. Within the class of concave programs, two subclasses are of special interest:

The linear program

6 *Problem* Minimize $\mathbf{c}^t\mathbf{e}$ with

$$A\mathbf{e} - \mathbf{b} \geq \mathbf{0}$$
$$\mathbf{e} \geq \mathbf{0}$$

[1] A vector expression of the form $\mathbf{x} \geq \mathbf{0}$ means $x_i \geq 0$ for all i.

where $\mathbf{c}$ and $\mathbf{e}$ are n-vectors, $\mathbf{b}$ is an m-vector, and A is an $m \times n$ matrix. Since we are minimizing a linear form subject to linear constraints, all functions are both concave and convex.

Positive semidefinite quadratic program

7 *Problem* Minimize $\frac{1}{2}\mathbf{e}^t Q \mathbf{e} + \mathbf{c}^t \mathbf{e}$ with

$$A\mathbf{e} - \mathbf{b} \geq \mathbf{0}$$
$$\mathbf{e} \geq \mathbf{0}$$

where Q is an $n \times n$ positive semidefinite matrix and the other symbols are as defined previously. (Because Q is positive semidefinite, the objective function is convex.)

A well-known method of treating equality-constrained extremum problems is the method of Lagrange multipliers. This consists, essentially, in forming a new objective function ψ which is equal to the sum of the original objective function plus a linear combination of the constraint functions, where the coefficients of the constraint functions are known as *Lagrange multipliers*. This technique can be extended to mathematical programming problems to convert a minimization problem to what is known as a saddle-point problem. This problem is formulated as follows. Associate with the general programming problem the function

8 $$\psi(\mathbf{e},\mathbf{i}) \triangleq \phi(\mathbf{e}) - \mathbf{i}^t\mathbf{f}(\mathbf{e})$$

called a *lagrangian form*, where the m-vector $\mathbf{i}$ denotes a set of Lagrange multipliers, and they are constrained by

$$\mathbf{i} \geq \mathbf{0}$$

A point $(\mathbf{e}_0,\mathbf{i}_0)$ is said to be a saddle point of $\psi(\mathbf{e},\mathbf{i})$ in $\mathbf{e} \geq \mathbf{0}$, $\mathbf{i} \geq \mathbf{0}$ if

9 $$\psi(\mathbf{e}_0,\mathbf{i}) \leq \psi(\mathbf{e}_0,\mathbf{i}_0) \leq \psi(\mathbf{e},\mathbf{i}_0) \qquad \text{for all } \mathbf{e}, \mathbf{i} \geq \mathbf{0}$$

The following basic theorem due to Kuhn and Tucker [7] indicates the equivalence of the minimization and saddle-point problems:

10 **Theorem** Let $\phi(\mathbf{e})$ be convex, $f_j(\mathbf{e})$ be concave for each j, and let there exist an $\mathbf{e}' > \mathbf{0}$ such that[1]

$$f_j(\mathbf{e}') > 0 \qquad \text{for all } j$$

Then a vector $\mathbf{e}_0$ is a solution of the programming problem *1* if and only if there exists a vector $\mathbf{i}_0$ such that $(\mathbf{e}_0,\mathbf{i}_0)$ is a saddle point of $\psi(\mathbf{e},\mathbf{i})$.

[1] This condition differs from the more complicated one appearing in Kuhn and Tucker's original statement of the theorem. (The theorem is still true as stated above.)

The significance of Theorem *10* is that we have converted a problem of searching for a minimum subject to various possibly nonlinear constraints to one of seeking a saddle point subject only to the constraints $\mathbf{e}, \mathbf{i} \geq \mathbf{0}$. Furthermore, the Lagrange multipliers $\mathbf{i}$ introduced in the saddle-point version of the problem often have useful physical or economic interpretations. (See, for example, Samuelson [8].)

A computational algorithm for locating the saddle point of $\psi(\mathbf{e},\mathbf{i})$ can be evolved as a natural generalization of the method of steepest descent for finding the minimum of a function. Since a saddle point corresponds to a minimum with respect to $\mathbf{e}$ and a maximum with respect to $\mathbf{i}$, it is reasonable to seek this point by moving in a direction of steepest *descent* in the $\mathbf{e}$ coordinates and steepest *ascent* in the $\mathbf{i}$ coordinates. This roughly defines the so-called *gradient method* for solving saddle-point problems. More precisely, the gradient method can be defined by the following set of differential equations:

11
$$\frac{de_i}{dt} = \begin{cases} 0 & \text{if } e_i = 0, \dfrac{\partial\psi}{\partial e_i} > 0 \\ -\dfrac{\partial\psi}{\partial e_i} & \text{otherwise} \end{cases}$$

$$\frac{di_j}{dt} = \begin{cases} 0 & \text{if } i_j = 0, \dfrac{\partial\psi}{\partial i_j} < 0 \\ \dfrac{\partial\psi}{\partial i_j} & \text{otherwise} \end{cases}$$

Note that the direction of the velocity $\frac{d\mathbf{e}}{dt}$ is made to correspond to the negative gradient of ψ with respect to $\mathbf{e}$, while the direction of $\frac{d\mathbf{i}}{dt}$ is made to correspond to the gradient with respect to $\mathbf{i}$, *except* when on a boundary of the constraint set. Special conditions are required on the boundaries so that the constraint conditions $\mathbf{e}, \mathbf{i} \geq \mathbf{0}$ are not violated. A saddle point is clearly a singular point of *11* and solutions would normally be expected to tend toward this point. However (assuming that the singular point is stable), the usefulness of the gradient method depends upon the *type* of stability exhibited.[1] Thus, for example, if the singular point is merely stable in the sense of Liapunov, it might be a *vortex point*, i.e., a point which is encircled by sets of closed trajectories. This means that solutions of *11* will tend to oscillate about the saddle point but never approach it. (This phenomenon occurs, for example, if the gradient method is applied to the solution of linear

[1] Usually *11* would be approximated numerically and integrated on a digital computer, in which case one would speak of convergence rather than stability.

programming problems.[1]) A somewhat stronger requirement is that of asymptotic stability. If a singular point is asymptotically stable one may at least be assured that initial values of **e** and **i** in *11* which are sufficiently close to the singular point will lead to solutions which approach it. This, however, is also far from satisfactory, since stable behavior is not assured unless an approximate answer to the problem is known in advance. The strongest requirement we can impose is that of global stability of the singular point. This will guarantee (1) that there are no other singular points and (2) that all initial conditions lead to solutions which approach the saddle point as $t \to \infty$. It can be shown[2] that (subject to certain other minor requirements), if the programming problem conforms to assumptions *3*, *4*, *5*, and if in addition $\phi(\mathbf{e})$ is *strictly* convex, then a unique singular point $(\mathbf{e}_0,\mathbf{i}_0)$ of *11* will exist and the **e** component of all solutions will tend toward $\mathbf{e}_0$ as $t \to \infty$. Note that the strict convexity condition rules out linear programs and that this condition is something less than global stability in that nothing has been said about the behavior of the **i** coordinate. We shall see in Sec. *5* that by taking into account the physical imperfections of an electrical network which simulates the gradient method, we can prove a *stronger* result for the network equations under conditions *weaker* than those indicated above. In particular, the strict convexity requirement can be changed to simple convexity.

One other feature of programming problems which has an interesting network interpretation is the notion of *duality*. Roughly speaking, when the roles of the variables **e** and the Lagrange multipliers **i** are interchanged in a given problem, a new problem results which is called the *dual* of the original one. (The original problem is then called the *primal* problem.) A detailed discussion of the duality principle would not be appropriate here so we shall simply state certain results which have their counterparts in electrical network analogs, and refer the reader to the literature[3] for further explanation.

Consider the following concave program (the primal program):

12 *Problem* Minimize $\varphi(\mathbf{e}_1) + \mathbf{c}^t\mathbf{e}_2$ with

$$A_1\mathbf{e}_1 + A_2\mathbf{e}_2 - \mathbf{b} \geq \mathbf{0}$$
$$\mathbf{e}_1 \geq \mathbf{0}$$
$$\mathbf{e}_2 \geq \mathbf{0}$$

where φ is strictly convex, $\mathbf{e}_2$ and $\mathbf{c}$ are p-vectors, $\mathbf{e}_1$ is a q-vector, A_2 is an $m \times p$ matrix, A_1 is an $m \times q$ matrix, and $\mathbf{b}$ is an m-vector. Note

[1] See, for example, Samuelson [8].
[2] Uzawa [9], p. 129.
[3] See, for example, Dennis [3], pp. 153ff.

that, because of the linear form $\mathbf{c}^t\mathbf{e}_2$ appearing in the objective function, it is not strictly convex.

Now consider a second program with linear constraints (the dual program):

13 *Problem* Minimize $\theta(\mathbf{i}_1) - \mathbf{b}^t\mathbf{i}_2$ with

$$A_1^t\mathbf{i}_2 - \mathbf{i}_1 \leq \mathbf{0}$$
$$A_2^t\mathbf{i}_2 - \mathbf{c} \leq \mathbf{0}$$
$$\mathbf{i}_2 \geq \mathbf{0}$$
$$\mathbf{i}_1 \quad \text{unrestricted}$$

where

$$\theta(\mathbf{i}_1) \triangleq \mathbf{e}_1^t\mathbf{i}_1 - \varphi(\mathbf{e}_1)$$

and

$$\mathbf{i}_1 \triangleq \left(\frac{\partial\varphi}{\partial\mathbf{e}_1}\right)^t$$

$\mathbf{i}_1$ is a q-vector, $\mathbf{i}_2$ is an m-vector, and the other quantities in *13* have been defined above. Note that $\theta(\mathbf{i}_1)$ is defined as the Legendre transform of $\varphi(\mathbf{e}_1)$, and hence is also strictly convex. The separation of the objective function into linear and strictly convex parts was necessary since a linear form cannot be Legendre transformed. The most well-known special case of this pair of dual programs is the linear case

Primal linear program

14 *Problem* Minimize $\mathbf{c}^t\mathbf{e}$ with

$$A\mathbf{e} - \mathbf{b} \geq \mathbf{0}$$
$$\mathbf{e} \geq \mathbf{0}$$

Dual linear program

15 *Problem* Minimize $-\mathbf{b}^t\mathbf{i}$ with

$$A^t\mathbf{i} - \mathbf{c} \leq \mathbf{0}$$
$$\mathbf{i} \geq \mathbf{0}$$

A fundamental property of a pair of dual programs as defined above is that *at a solution point, the objective functions of the two programs sum to zero.* It will be shown in the following sections that a nonlinear reciprocal network can be used as a network analog of a pair of dual mathematical programs, and that each property of the mathematical formulation has a direct physical interpretation in terms of the network dissipation functions.

4 *Network interpretation*

The formulation of the equations of a reciprocal network in terms of dissipation functions suggests the possibility of using a network as an analog for a mathematical programming problem. Since the stable equilibria of a reciprocal network occur at minima of the content or cocontent functions, if a network can be synthesized so that

$$\mathfrak{F}'_N(\mathbf{e}) = \phi(\mathbf{e})$$

where $\phi(\mathbf{e})$ represents the objective function of the programming problem, and if the appropriate inequality constraints can be incorporated into the network, the independent node-pair voltages $\mathbf{e}$ will automatically assume the values which minimize ϕ subject to the constraints. As an example, consider a linear programming problem of the form of *4.3.6*:

Minimize $\phi(\mathbf{e}) = -2e_1 + e_2$ with

1

$$\begin{aligned} -e_1 + 1 &\geq 0 \\ -e_2 + 3 &\geq 0 \\ e_1 + e_2 - 2 &\geq 0 \\ e_1 &\geq 0 \\ e_2 &\geq 0 \end{aligned}$$

It is illustrated graphically in Fig. *4.4.1*. The constraint set S_c is indicated by the trapezoidal area in the e_1-e_2 plane, and the solution

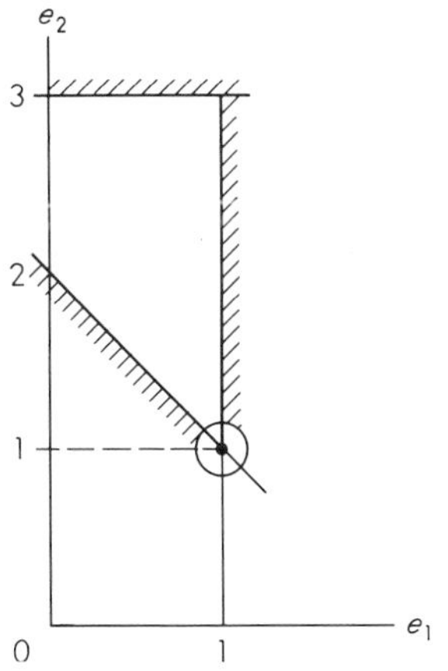

Fig. 4.4.1 Graphical illustration of linear programming problem.

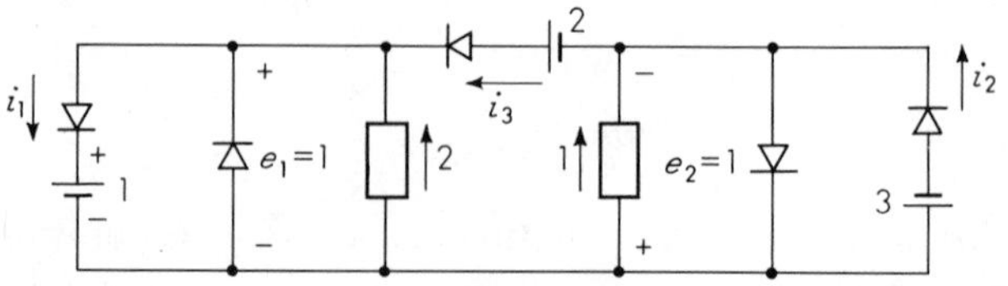

Fig. 4.4.2 Network analog for linear programming problem.

point (1,1) is encircled in the figure. The network of Fig. *4.4.2* has been constructed to simulate this problem. Note that the network cocontent function is given in terms of the node-pair voltages e_1 and e_2 as

$$\mathfrak{F}'_N(\mathbf{e}) = -2e_1 + e_2$$

for all values of e_1 and e_2 satisfying the constraints imposed by the ideal diodes. It is easily verified that the diodes constrain the variables to the values required by *1*. Note that within the constraint set, no elements except the current sources contribute to $\mathfrak{F}'_N$. The equilibrium values of voltages are readily seen to be $e_1 = e_2 = 1$, which is the correct solution to the programming problem. (It is worth noting that in cases where the constraints are contradictory, that is, S_c is empty, the network analog becomes degenerate, that is, no equilibrium exists.)

Now if we calculate a network content function in terms of a set of independent currents i_1, i_2, i_3 shown in the figure, we find

2 $$\mathfrak{F}_N(\mathbf{i}) = i_1 + 3i_2 - 2i_3$$

where the i_j are constrained to the set,

3 $$\begin{aligned} -i_1 + i_3 + 2 &\leq 0 \\ -i_2 + i_3 - 1 &\leq 0 \\ i_1,\ i_2,\ i_3 &\geq 0 \end{aligned}$$

Comparing *2* and *3* with *1* we find that these currents represent the variables in the dual problem. Furthermore, since $\mathfrak{F}_N(\mathbf{i})$ is minimized at equilibrium, the network solves the dual as well as the primal problem. It can be seen by inspection of the network of Fig. *4.4.2* that $\mathfrak{F}'_N(\mathbf{e})$ represents the sum of the cocontents of each network element whereas $\mathfrak{F}_N(\mathbf{i})$ represents the sum of the contents of each element. Thus if e_k, i_k, $\mathfrak{F}_k$, and $\mathfrak{F}'_k$ represent respectively the branch voltage, branch current, content, and cocontent for the kth element, we may write

4 $$\mathfrak{F}'_N(\mathbf{e}) + \mathfrak{F}_N(\mathbf{i}) = \sum_k \mathfrak{F}'_k + \sum_k \mathfrak{F}_k = \sum_k (\mathfrak{F}'_k + \mathfrak{F}_k)$$

But by *4.2.28* this reduces to[1]

5 $$\mathfrak{F}'_N(\mathbf{e}) + \mathfrak{F}_N(\mathbf{i}) = \sum_k e_k i_k = 0$$

Equation *5*, which is simply an expression of the principle of conservation of energy, verifies the fact that the sum of the primal and dual objective functions is zero at equilibrium.

Having exhibited a simple example of a network analog, let us now consider the general case.

The network of Fig. *4.4.3* represents a general analog for the mathematical programming problem *4.3.1*. Several features of this network

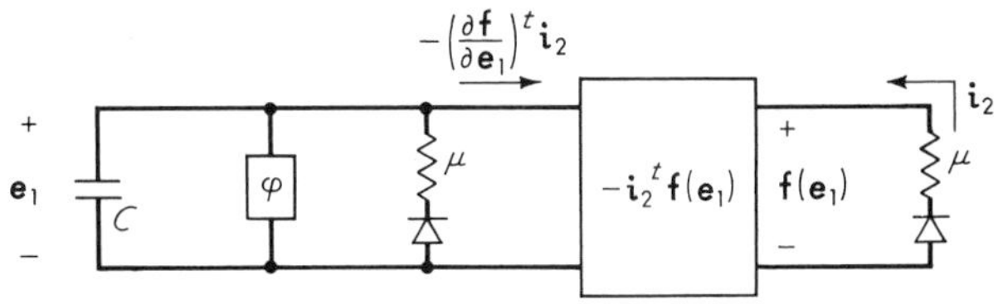

Fig. 4.4.3 General analog for mathematical program.

should be noted. First, the elements shown as black boxes represent reciprocal resistive multi-ports defined by the dissipation functions indicated in the figure. Thus, the element labelled φ, simulating the objective function, is defined by the cocontent function

6 $$\mathfrak{F}'(\mathbf{e}_1) = \phi(\mathbf{e}_1)$$

and the element labelled $-\mathbf{i}_2{}^t\mathbf{f}(\mathbf{e}_1)$, embodying the constraint relations, is defined by a hybrid dissipation function

7 $$\mathfrak{F}''(\mathbf{e}_1,\mathbf{i}_2) = -\mathbf{i}_2{}^t\mathbf{f}(\mathbf{e}_1)$$

The two sets of diodes in the network serve to mechanize the inequality constraints

$$\mathbf{e}_1 \geq \mathbf{0}$$
$$\mathbf{f}(\mathbf{e}_1) \geq \mathbf{0}$$

In order to circumvent certain mathematical difficulties,[2] small forward resistances μ have been included in series with each diode with the result that the inequality constraints are only satisfied approximately for any positive value of μ. Since these resistances are an accurate

[1] Provided that the lower limits of integration are chosen as in *4.2.27* et seq.

[2] When investigating the properties of the differential equations for the network it is mathematically convenient not to restrict the values $\mathbf{e}_1$ may assume. Addition of the resistances μ has this effect.

reflection of the situation which would exist in any real network analog, it is not unreasonable to include them in the network model. Furthermore, we shall show below that their inclusion does not significantly alter the network solution of the programming problem.

The capacitors C (positive) have been included for purposes of stability analysis (see Sec. *5*).

Looking at the network from the capacitor terminals, the network cocontent is found to be of the form

8 $$\mathfrak{F}'_N(\mathbf{e}_1) = \phi(\mathbf{e}_1) + \Delta(\mathbf{e}_1) + \Delta[\mathbf{f}(\mathbf{e}_1)] + K$$

where K is an arbitrary constant. From the definition of the function Δ in *4.2.21*, it can be seen that $\mathfrak{F}'_N$ is (within an arbitrary constant) exactly equal to the objective function of problem *4.3.1* for all $\mathbf{e}_1 \in S_c$. However, it increases sharply as $\mathbf{e}_1$ leaves S_c. In effect, the functions $\Delta(\mathbf{e}_1)$ and $\Delta[\mathbf{f}(\mathbf{e}_1)]$ confine $\mathbf{e}_1$ to S_c by introducing large penalties[1] for leaving the constraint set.

The differential equations for the network are written

9 $$C\frac{d\mathbf{e}_1}{dt} = -\left(\frac{\partial \mathfrak{F}'_N}{\partial \mathbf{e}_1}\right)^t$$

and hence solutions of problem *4.3.1* are (approximately) singular points of the network. We can, in fact, make a stronger statement:

10 **Theorem** Under assumptions *4.3.3*, *4.3.4*, *4.3.5*, any singular points of the network of Fig. *4.4.3* approach $\mathbf{e}_0$, the unique solution of problem *4.3.1*, as $\mu \to 0$.

Proof will be deferred to the appendix.

Theorem *10*, together with Theorem *4.5.1*, which settles the stability question, shows that the network analog will give an arbitrarily good approximation of the true solution of the programming problem. Of course, a practical question naturally arises as to whether the elements labelled $\phi(\mathbf{e}_1)$ and $-\mathbf{i}_2{}^t\mathbf{f}(\mathbf{e}_1)$ may easily be realized. Suppose we examine first the element simulating the objective function. While it is theoretically possible to construct an element which will exhibit terminal behavior defined by the function ϕ, it would be impractical to do so in most cases. There are, however, several simple special cases which are of considerable interest. The linear objective function $\mathbf{c}^t\mathbf{e}$ is synthesized as shown in Fig. *4.4.4a*, using only constant current sources. A quadratic objective function as appears in problem *4.3.7* is synthesized as in Fig. *4.4.4b* using current sources together with a

[1] The functions Δ are actually of the nature of "penalty" functions, introduced by Courant [10], pp. 270–280, and further exploited by Rubin and Ungar [11] and Kelley [12] in dealing with constrained extremum problems.

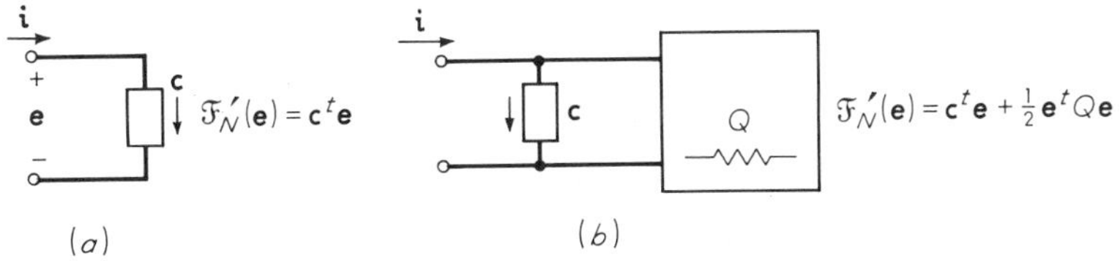

Fig. 4.4.4 Network analogs for linear and quadratic objective functions.

linear passive resistive network. Finally, given a general convex function $\phi(\mathbf{e})$, it is possible to approximate it arbitrarily closely by a piecewise-linear function of the form,

11 $$\phi(\mathbf{e}) \approx \phi'(\mathbf{e}') = \max_r [e_r']$$

where $\mathbf{e}'$ is an m-vector defined by

12 $$\mathbf{e}' = T\mathbf{e} - \mathbf{c}$$

T being an $m \times n$ matrix and $\mathbf{c}$ an m-vector. The network of Fig. *4.4.5* as seen from the terminals labelled $e_1, \ldots, e_n$ has the cocontent

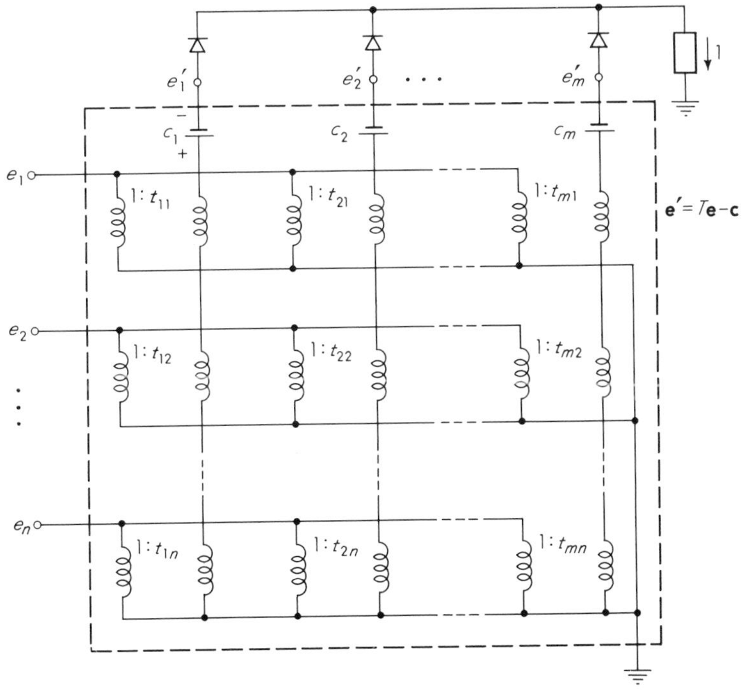

Fig. 4.4.5 Network analog for piecewise-linear convex objective function.

function *11*. Note that the affine transformation *12* is effected by the transformers and voltage sources within the dashed lines. The selection of the maximum of the e'_r is performed by the diodes, and the 1-amp current source is the only element contributing to the cocontent function.

We may make similar remarks concerning the realization of the element embodying the constraint relations. If these relations happen to be linear and of the form

13 $$\mathbf{f}(\mathbf{e}) = A\mathbf{e} - \mathbf{b}$$

then the hybrid dissipation function *7* becomes

14 $$\mathfrak{F}''_N(\mathbf{e}_1,\mathbf{i}_2) = -\mathbf{i}_2{}^t(A\mathbf{e}_1 - \mathbf{b})$$

which will be recognized as the sum of the hybrid dissipation function for a bank of ideal transformers, and the content function for a bank of voltage sources. The complete network is shown in Fig. *4.4.6*. (It is, in fact, precisely the same form of network as that appearing within the dashed lines in Fig. *4.4.5*.) Now, any constraint set defined by a set of concave inequalities (assumption *4.3.4*) can be approximated arbitrarily closely using a set of *linear* constraints of the form of *13*. This amounts to making piecewise-linear approximations of the bounding surfaces of S_c. Since we have just demonstrated how to synthesize linear constraint relations, the problem of realizing the constraint relation block is essentially solved.

We have thus shown that a network simulating a piecewise-linear approximation of any concave program may always be realized using only voltage sources, one current source, ideal diodes, and ideal transformers.

It will be noted that the example of Fig. *4.4.2* was realized without transformers. This was possible because the matrix A in the constraint equations happened to correspond to an *incidence* matrix (i.e., each column contained one element of value $+1$, one of -1, and the rest zero). There are several classes of programming problems which lend themselves naturally to transformerless analogs, in particular, the maximum flow problem and the minimum distance problem. Since ideal transformers are to be avoided if possible, problems which do not require them are especially well suited to network simulation.

Let us turn now to an interpretation of the gradient method in terms of the equations of the network analog. In order to exhibit this relationship, it is convenient to present the network analog in the modified form of Fig. *4.4.7*. The modifications are (1) the introduction of

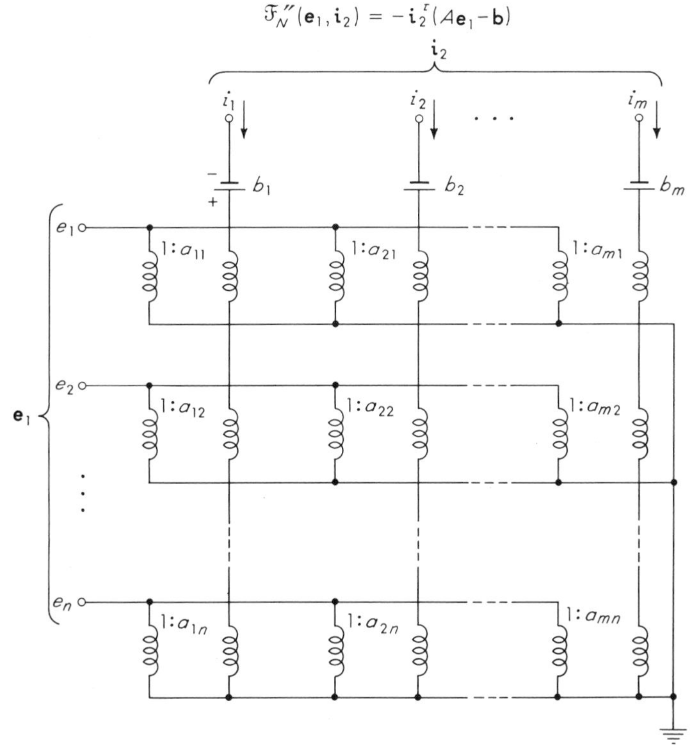

Fig. 4.4.6 Network analog for linear constraints.

a set of positive inductances L and (2) the replacement of the forward resistance μ by a reverse conductance μ in the right-hand set of diodes. (This replacement has been made for the reasons stated in footnote 1 on page 151.) Both the capacitances and inductances in Fig. 4.4.7 can be interpreted as approximating the small "stray" energy storage which is inevitably present in any real network. Their inclusion does not in any way affect the equilibrium values of the network variables.

A hybrid dissipation function for the network as seen from the

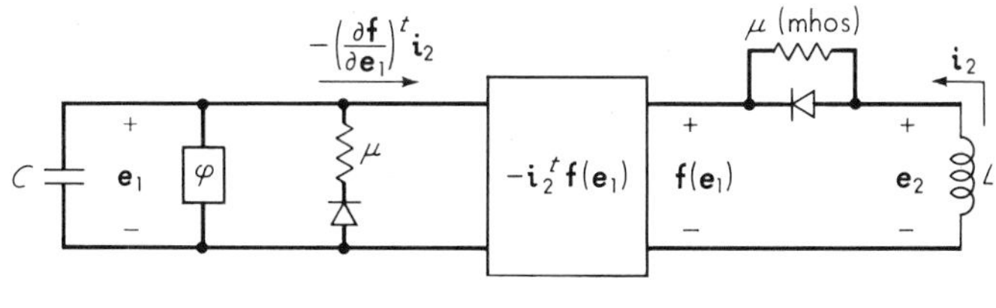

Fig. 4.4.7 Network analog for gradient method.

capacitor and inductor terminals can be written as

15 $$\mathfrak{F}''_N(\mathbf{e}_1,\mathbf{i}_2) = \phi(\mathbf{e}_1) + \Delta(\mathbf{e}_1) - \mathbf{i}_2{}^t\mathbf{f}(\mathbf{e}_1) - \Delta(\mathbf{i}_2)$$

We may, therefore, write the network differential equations as

16 $$C\frac{d\mathbf{e}_1}{dt} = -\left(\frac{\partial \mathfrak{F}''_N}{\partial \mathbf{e}_1}\right)^t$$
$$L\frac{d\mathbf{i}_2}{dt} = \left(\frac{\partial \mathfrak{F}''_N}{\partial \mathbf{i}_2}\right)^t$$

where L and C are positive definite diagonal matrices.

Except for the presence of functions Δ, the function $\mathfrak{F}''_N$ will be recognized as the lagrangian form *4.3.8* for the programming problem, where $\mathbf{i}_2$ plays the role of the Lagrange multipliers. Furthermore, equations *16* essentially define the gradient method *4.3.11* for locating a saddle point of *4.3.8*.[1] (The differences between the form of *16* and *4.3.11* are minor. The presence of the matrices C and L merely serves to modify the time scale. Also, since the functions Δ have been used here to incorporate the inequality constraints on $\mathbf{e}_1$ and $\mathbf{i}_2$, they implicitly approximate the special conditions which are required at the boundaries of the constraint set.)

Thus, when stray energy storage elements are considered, it can be seen that the *capacitor voltages* and *inductor currents* in the analog network simulate the gradient method of solution of the *saddle-point problem*. We shall discuss the stability of the network in Sec. *5*.

A final word on a general network analog for the pair of dual programs *4.3.12* and *4.3.13* is now in order. Since the network of Fig. *4.4.7* does not bring out the essential features of the duality principle, we show a special analog network in Fig. *4.4.8* for this purpose. All symbols in the figure correspond to those in *4.3.12* and *4.3.13*. The

[1] This fact was pointed out to the author by G. Fisher.

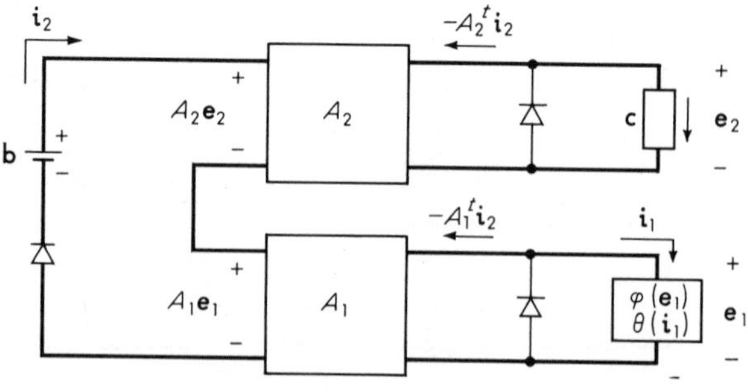

Fig. 4.4.8 Network analog for dual concave programs.

blocks labelled A_1 and A_2 represent banks of ideal transformers. Inspection of the figure shows that the cocontent for the network, expressed in terms of $\mathbf{e}_1$ and $\mathbf{e}_2$, corresponds to the objective function of the primal program, while the content, expressed in terms of $\mathbf{i}_1$ and $\mathbf{i}_2$, represents the objective function of the dual program. It is easily verified that the required constraints are satisfied in each case. Furthermore, by using conservation of energy arguments we find as before that the sum of the primal and dual objective functions is zero, as it must be.

5 *Stability*

In networks of a form as general as those discussed above, neither the local stability of an equilibrium nor the global stability of the system as a whole is obvious. Thus, a study of these network analogs is not complete without analysis of stability.[1] This section shall, therefore, be devoted to the investigation of stability in the two basic analog configurations of Figs. *4.4.3* and *4.4.7*. Since the latter configuration simulates the gradient method, our results will be equivalent to a proof of the convergence of this method, as simulated by a network analog. In particular we shall establish the fact that under fairly general conditions, the network variables will always approach, as $t \to \infty$, the solution of the problem they are simulating.

Consider first the network of Fig. *4.4.3*.

1 **Theorem** Let the network of Fig. *4.4.3* be constructed to simulate problem *4.3.1*. Then if assumptions *4.3.3*, *4.3.4*, *4.3.5* hold, all solutions of *4.4.9* tend toward singular points as $t \to \infty$.

[It is assumed in Theorem *1* that the diode resistances and conductances are small enough so that any singular point of *4.4.9* is within some arbitrarily small radius ϵ of the solution point $\mathbf{e}_0$ (Theorem *4.4.10*). Thus Theorem *4.4.10* together with Theorem *1* implies that the network analog does perform as desired.]

Proof We make use of the direct method of Liapunov, using $\mathfrak{F}'_N(\mathbf{e}_1)$

[1] It may at first seem irrelevant to bring up the question of stability of resistive networks, since this is a property associated with dynamic rather than static systems. It is, however, well known that in *static*, or *zero-memory*, systems which possess multiple equilibria, some are generally unstable, in the sense that the system will not by itself tend to remain in these configurations. The mechanism of instability in these cases can only be explained by inclusion into the mathematical model of the dynamic effects which determine stability. In the electrical network case, these effects can be represented by stray energy storage elements.

as a Liapunov function. It is sufficient to show that

$$\mathfrak{F}'_N(\mathbf{e}_1) \to \infty \qquad \text{as } \|\mathbf{e}_1\|\dagger \to \infty$$

and that its total time derivative along a solution of *4.4.9* is nonpositive, and zero only at a singular point. (See, for example, Lasalle and Lefschetz [13], theorem VIII.)

The appropriate behavior of $\mathfrak{F}'_N$ for large $\|\mathbf{e}_1\|$ can be deduced from the fact that $\mathfrak{F}'_N$ is convex and from condition *4.3.5*.

The time derivative of $\mathfrak{F}'_N(\mathbf{e}_1)$ is, from *4.4.9*,

2 $$\frac{d\mathfrak{F}'_N}{dt} = -\left(\frac{\partial \mathfrak{F}'_N}{\partial \mathbf{e}_1}\right) C^{-1} \left(\frac{\partial \mathfrak{F}'_N}{\partial \mathbf{e}_1}\right)^t$$

Since C^{-1} is positive definite, $d\mathfrak{F}'_N/dt$ is nonpositive and zero only at a point,

$$\left(\frac{\partial \mathfrak{F}'_N}{\partial \mathbf{e}_1}\right)^t = \mathbf{0}$$

which is a singular point of *4.4.9*. QED

Now let us consider the network of Fig. *4.4.7*, which simulates the gradient method. Because of the addition of the inductances this is a more complete, and in a sense, more realistic model for investigating stability. However, we have already pointed out that oscillations may occur in the gradient method under assumptions *4.3.3*, *4.3.4*, *4.3.5*. That the same difficulty is present in the network analog can be seen by investigating the behavior of the analog for the following simple linear program: Minimize $\phi(e) = e$ with

$$f(e) = e - 1 \geq 0$$
$$e \geq 0$$

Despite the fact that oscillations occur in the *mathematical model* of the network, they would *not* occur in a *real* analog network, because of the small dissipation present. Thus, a reasonable way of avoiding oscillations in the mathematical model of the general network without requiring the additional assumption of strict convexity of ϕ is to include additional small positive resistances and conductances as shown in Fig. *4.5.1*. These elements, together with the other small resistive elements introduced previously, may be considered as reflecting realistic approximations to the form of a diode characteristic. Their net effect is to damp out any oscillations which might occur.

† $\|\cdot\|$ denotes *norm*.

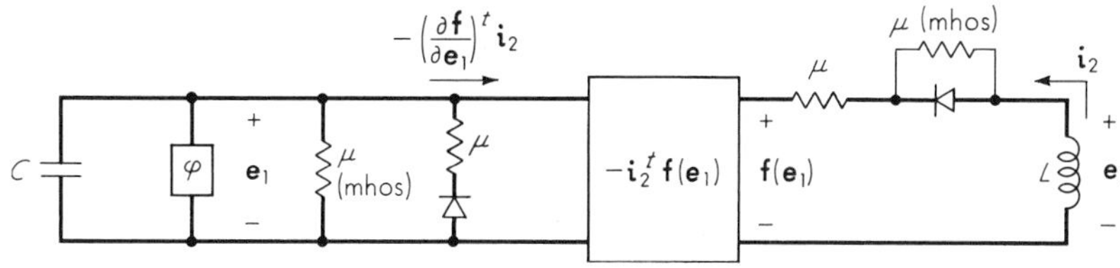

Fig. 4.5.1 Modified analog for gradient method.

In order to simplify the stability proof, we shall consider a somewhat restricted programming problem:

3 *Problem* Minimize $\phi(\mathbf{e})$ with

$$A\mathbf{e} - \mathbf{b} \geq \mathbf{0}$$
$$\mathbf{e} \geq \mathbf{0}$$

where assumptions *4.3.3*, *4.3.4*, *4.3.5* are satisfied and in addition,

4 $$\left(\frac{\partial \phi}{\partial \mathbf{e}}\right)^t \to Q\mathbf{e} + \mathbf{c} \qquad \text{as } \|\mathbf{e}\| \to \infty$$

where Q is a symmetric positive semidefinite matrix and $\mathbf{c}$ is a constant vector. The above requirements imply that this is an *asymptotically quadratic* program.

5 **Theorem** If the network of Fig. *4.5.1* is constructed to simulate problem *3*, then all solutions of the network equations tend toward a singular point as $t \to \infty$.

Since, for sufficiently small μ, any singular point corresponds (approximately) to the solution of problem *3*, Theorem *5* shows that the network analog behaves as desired.

Proof The network equations are in this case

6 $$C\frac{d\mathbf{e}_1}{dt} = -\left(\frac{\partial \mathfrak{F}_N''}{\partial \mathbf{e}_1}\right)^t = -\left(\frac{\partial \phi}{\partial \mathbf{e}_1}\right)^t - \mu\mathbf{e}_1 - \mathbf{\delta}(\mathbf{e}_1) + A^t\mathbf{i}_2 \triangleq -\mathbf{i}_1(\mathbf{e}_1,\mathbf{i}_2)$$

7 $$L\frac{d\mathbf{i}_2}{dt} = \left(\frac{\partial \mathfrak{F}_N''}{\partial \mathbf{i}_2}\right)^t = -\mu\mathbf{i}_2 - \mathbf{\delta}(\mathbf{i}_2) - A\mathbf{e}_1 + \mathbf{b} \triangleq -\mathbf{e}_2(\mathbf{e}_1,\mathbf{i}_2)$$

Choosing a Liapunov function,

8 $$V = \tfrac{1}{2}(\mathbf{i}_1{}^tC^{-1}\mathbf{i}_1 + \mathbf{e}_2{}^tL^{-1}\mathbf{e}_2)$$

we proceed as in the proof of Theorem *1*.

First let us prove that

$$V \to \infty \qquad \text{as } \left\|\begin{matrix}\mathbf{e}_1\\ \mathbf{i}_2\end{matrix}\right\| \to \infty$$

Suppose this is not the case. Then it must be possible for both $\|\mathbf{i}_1\|$ and $\|\mathbf{e}_2\|$ to remain finite as $\left\|\begin{matrix}\mathbf{e}_1\\ \mathbf{i}_2\end{matrix}\right\| \to \infty$. But

9 $$\|\mathbf{e}_2\| = \|\mu\mathbf{i}_2 + \boldsymbol{\delta}(\mathbf{i}_2) + A\mathbf{e}_1 - \mathbf{b}\|$$

For *9* to remain finite, there must exist a constant nonzero vector $\begin{bmatrix}\mathbf{k}_1\\ \mathbf{k}_2\end{bmatrix}$ such that if

10 $$\begin{bmatrix}\mathbf{e}_1\\ \mathbf{i}_2\end{bmatrix} = \lambda\begin{bmatrix}\mathbf{k}_1\\ \mathbf{k}_2\end{bmatrix}$$

11 then $$\frac{1}{\lambda}\|\mathbf{e}_2(\lambda\mathbf{k}_1,\lambda\mathbf{k}_2)\| \to 0 \qquad \text{as } \lambda \to \infty$$

12 or $$\frac{1}{\lambda}\|\mu\lambda\mathbf{k}_2 + \boldsymbol{\delta}(\lambda\mathbf{k}_2) + \lambda A\mathbf{k}_1 - \mathbf{b}\| \to 0 \qquad \text{as } \lambda \to \infty$$

13 But $$\boldsymbol{\delta}(\lambda\mathbf{k}_2) = \frac{\lambda}{\mu} D_2\mathbf{k}_2$$

where D_2 is a diagonal matrix with either 0 or 1 as diagonal elements.

Thus, *12* implies

14 $$\mu\mathbf{k}_2 + \frac{1}{\mu} D_2\mathbf{k}_2 + A\mathbf{k}_1 = \mathbf{0}$$

15 or $$\mathbf{k}_2 = \frac{-M(\mu)}{\mu(\mu^2+1)} A\mathbf{k}_1$$

where $M(\mu)$ is a positive definite diagonal matrix each of whose diagonal elements is either μ^2 or $(\mu^2 + 1)$.

Thus we have a linear relation between $\mathbf{k}_1$ and $\mathbf{k}_2$. Now in order that $\|\mathbf{i}_1\|$ also remain finite we must have

16 $$\frac{1}{\lambda}\left\|\left(\frac{\partial\phi}{\partial\mathbf{e}_1}\right)^t + \mu\lambda\mathbf{k}_1 + \boldsymbol{\delta}(\lambda\mathbf{k}_1) - \lambda A^t\mathbf{k}_2\right\| \to 0 \qquad \text{as } \lambda \to \infty$$

17 But $$\boldsymbol{\delta}(\lambda\mathbf{k}_1) = \frac{\lambda}{\mu} D_1\mathbf{k}_1$$

where D_1 is a diagonal matrix whose elements are either 0 or 1.

Using *17*, *4*, and *15*, we may rewrite *16* as

18 $$\left\| Q\mathbf{k}_1 + \frac{1}{\lambda}\mathbf{c} + \mu\mathbf{k}_1 + \frac{1}{\mu} D_1\mathbf{k}_1 + \frac{A^tM(\mu)A}{\mu(\mu^2+1)}\mathbf{k}_1 \right\| \to 0 \qquad \text{as } \lambda \to \infty$$

which requires that

19 $$\det\left[Q + \mu I + \frac{1}{\mu} D_1 + \frac{A^tM(\mu)A}{\mu(\mu^2+1)}\right] = 0$$

However this is impossible for any $\mu > 0$ since the matrix in brackets is positive definite.

Thus our original supposition was incorrect, and V has the required unbounded behavior.

Now to prove that $\frac{dV}{dt}$ is nonpositive and zero only at singular points we write from *6, 7, 8,*

20 $$\frac{dV}{dt} = -\begin{bmatrix} \mathbf{i}_1 \\ \mathbf{e}_2 \end{bmatrix}^t \begin{bmatrix} C^{-1} & 0 \\ 0 & L^{-1} \end{bmatrix} [H(\mathbf{e}_1,\mathbf{i}_2)] \begin{bmatrix} C^{-1} & 0 \\ 0 & L^{-1} \end{bmatrix} \begin{bmatrix} \mathbf{i}_1 \\ \mathbf{e}_2 \end{bmatrix}$$

where

21 $$H(\mathbf{e}_1,\mathbf{i}_2) = \begin{bmatrix} \frac{\partial}{\partial \mathbf{e}_1}\left(\frac{\partial \phi}{\partial \mathbf{e}_1}\right)^t & -A^t \\ A & 0 \end{bmatrix} + \mu I + \frac{1}{\mu} D$$

and D is a diagonal matrix with elements 0 or 1 depending upon the sign of the appropriate diode current. (Strictly speaking, H is not defined at the break points of the diodes, since their branch relations are not differentiable at these points. This is only a minor difficulty, however, since any physically realizable element will have a characteristic whose incremental resistance makes a smooth transition in the vicinity of the origin.)

Since ϕ is assumed convex, dV/dt is negative for all nonzero $\begin{bmatrix} \mathbf{i}_1 \\ \mathbf{e}_2 \end{bmatrix}$, and hence the theorem is proved. (Note that dV/dt is a negative-definite function of $\mathbf{i}_1$ and $\mathbf{e}_2$ *only* because of the presence of the matrix μI, which represents the diode resistances and conductances that were added to insure stability. Without these elements it would be possible for dV/dt to be zero at points other than singular points, which would invalidate the proof.)

6 *Properties of lagrangian networks*

In the remainder of this chapter we shall be concerned with the relations between problems in the calculus of variations and the structure of certain types of electrical networks. These networks, which will be called *lagrangian networks*, are characterized by the fact that they obey a variational principle. In order to define their characteristics, we digress for a moment to review the basic properties of variational problems.

A typical problem in the calculus of variations is:

1 *Problem* Find a continuous differentiable vector function $\mathbf{x}(t)$ which passes through the points

2 $$\mathbf{x}(t_0) = \mathbf{x}_0 \qquad \mathbf{x}(t_1) = \mathbf{x}_1$$

and which makes the functional

3 $$F[\mathbf{x}(t)] \triangleq \int_{t_0}^{t_1} \mathcal{L}(\mathbf{x},\dot{\mathbf{x}},t)\, dt$$

a minimum ($\dot{\mathbf{x}}$ denotes differentiation with respect to t). As is well known, a necessary condition for the functional *3* to possess an extremum (either maximum or minimum) along a function $\mathbf{x}(t)$ is that $\mathbf{x}(t)$ satisfy the *Euler-Lagrange equations*

4 $$\frac{d}{dt}\left(\frac{\partial \mathcal{L}}{\partial \dot{\mathbf{x}}}\right)^t - \left(\frac{\partial \mathcal{L}}{\partial \mathbf{x}}\right)^t = \mathbf{0}$$

(It is assumed throughout this discussion that all functions are suitably differentiable.) Solutions of *4* are termed *extremals*. In order to satisfy the conditions of problem *1*, a member of the family of extremals must be chosen which satisfies the boundary conditions *2*. Thus, one method of solving a variational problem (termed an *indirect* method) is to solve the boundary-value problem defined by *2* and *4*. Although any extremal will make the functional F *stationary*, there is no guarantee that a stationary value will be a local minimum, nor that a local minimum will correspond to a global minimum. Thus, this indirect approach to the variational problem leaves some questions unanswered. In spite of this, indirect methods are widely used and often successful in seeking solutions of variational problems. We shall show below that the solutions of certain classes of electric networks satisfy equations of the Euler-Lagrange type, and hence these networks can be used as analogs to generate families of extremals for variational problems.

To introduce the concept of a lagrangian network, we recall a basic principle from classical dynamics. If the state of a dynamic system is defined in terms of a set of independent generalized coordinates $\mathbf{x}$ and their velocities $\dot{\mathbf{x}}$, then, provided that the necessary energy functions exist, we may define a *lagrangian* $\mathcal{L}$ for this system as

5 $$\mathcal{L}(\mathbf{x},\dot{\mathbf{x}},t) = \mathcal{T}' - \mathcal{U}$$

where $\mathcal{T}'$ is the kinetic coenergy for the system, and $\mathcal{U}$ is the potential energy.[1] If the system is nondissipative, its motion is governed by *Hamilton's principle:*

If a nondissipative system with lagrangian $\mathcal{L}$ moves from a point $\mathbf{x}_0$ at time t_0 to a point $\mathbf{x}_1$ at time t_1, then among all possible paths between these end points, the path the system follows must be one which makes the functional

$$F \triangleq \int_{t_0}^{t_1} \mathcal{L}\, dt$$

stationary.

(In certain cases it can be shown that the functional is actually minimized; however, this is not generally true.)

In view of Hamilton's principle, the equations of motion of a nondissipative system with lagrangian $\mathcal{L}$ can be written in the Euler-Lagrange form *4*.

But if we choose to take Hamilton's principle as a *postulate,* we can expand our discussion to systems much more general than those described by lagrangians of the form *5*. We can, in fact, *define* a system in terms of an arbitrary lagrangian, in much the same manner as we defined resistive network elements in terms of arbitrary dissipation functions. This idea is embodied in the following.

6 **Definition** A system whose generalized coordinates and velocities are, respectively, $\mathbf{x}$ and $\dot{\mathbf{x}}$ will be termed a lagrangian system if there exists a scalar function $\mathcal{L}(\mathbf{x},\dot{\mathbf{x}},t)$ (the system lagrangian) such that the equations

$$\frac{d}{dt}\left(\frac{\partial \mathcal{L}}{\partial \dot{\mathbf{x}}}\right)^t - \left(\frac{\partial \mathcal{L}}{\partial \mathbf{x}}\right)^t = \mathbf{0}$$

define the motion of the system.

By definition, any lagrangian system satisfies Hamilton's principle. We shall be concerned mainly with lagrangian *networks,* which may be considered as a generalization of ordinary reactive networks, just as the reciprocal networks discussed in Sec. *2* are generalizations of ordinary resistive networks.

It will also be useful to characterize an individual element within a larger system in terms of a lagrangian. If such an element has n degrees of freedom $x_1, \ldots, x_n$, or, in network terminology, is an

[1] In an electric network, if the generalized coordinates $\mathbf{x}$ are interpreted as charges, then τ' becomes the magnetic coenergy and $\mathcal{U}$ the electric energy. Similarly, if the $\mathbf{x}$ are interpreted as flux linkages, then τ' becomes the electric coenergy and $\mathcal{U}$ the magnetic energy.

n-port, it may be acted on by an external force f_j associated with each coordinate x_j. Let us denote these forces by the vector $\mathbf{f}$ and the coordinates by $\mathbf{x}$. Now the device in question will generally be definable by terminal characteristics relating $\mathbf{f}$ and $\mathbf{x}$ of the form

7 $$\mathbf{f} = \mathbf{f}(\mathbf{x},\dot{\mathbf{x}},\ddot{\mathbf{x}},t)$$

We shall say that this is a lagrangian element if there exists a function,

8 $$\mathfrak{L}(\mathbf{x},\dot{\mathbf{x}},t)$$

such that

9 $$\frac{d}{dt}\left(\frac{\partial \mathfrak{L}}{\partial \dot{\mathbf{x}}}\right)^t - \left(\frac{\partial \mathfrak{L}}{\partial \mathbf{x}}\right)^t = \mathbf{f}(\mathbf{x},\dot{\mathbf{x}},\ddot{\mathbf{x}},t)$$

It is, of course, possible to conceive of an infinite variety of lagrangian elements, most of which will not correspond to any known physical devices. Without limiting ourselves to known devices, however, let us explore some of the possibilities, with particular reference to electric network elements. In a network, a generalized coordinate x_j may be interpreted either as a charge q_j or a flux linkage λ_j. In the former case, the variables must be identified as

10 $$\begin{aligned} x_j &\to q_j \\ \dot{x}_j &\to \dot{q}_j = i_j \\ f_j &\to e_j \end{aligned}$$

and in the latter case

11 $$\begin{aligned} x_j &\to \lambda_j \\ \dot{x}_j &\to \dot{\lambda}_j = e_j \\ f_j &\to i_j \end{aligned}$$

As an example, suppose we define a lagrangian element by the function

12 $$\mathfrak{L} = kx_1\dot{x}_2$$

Interpreting both coordinates as charges, we have the branch relations

13 $$\begin{aligned} \frac{d}{dt}\left(\frac{\partial \mathfrak{L}}{\partial \dot{q}_1}\right) - \frac{\partial \mathfrak{L}}{\partial q_1} &= -ki_2 = e_1 \\ \frac{d}{dt}\left(\frac{\partial \mathfrak{L}}{\partial \dot{q}_2}\right) - \frac{\partial \mathfrak{L}}{\partial q_2} &= ki_1 = e_2 \end{aligned}$$

which are the equations of a gyrator. (It is interesting to note that the gyrator, being a nonreciprocal element, cannot be defined by a dissipation function. Yet we see that it may be defined by a lagrangian.)

Now, if, instead of the above interpretation, we make the identification

14
$$x_1 \to \lambda_1$$
$$x_2 \to q_2$$

the branch relations become

15
$$-ki_2 = i_1$$
$$ke_1 = e_2$$

which define an ideal transformer.

We may formalize the definition of a lagrangian n-port network element as follows.

16 **Definition** Given a function $\mathcal{L}(\mathbf{x},\dot{\mathbf{x}},t)$, where $\mathbf{x}$ is an n-vector, a *lagrangian n-port* is defined by associating, say, $x_1, x_2, \ldots, x_k$ with charges $q_1, q_2, \ldots, q_k$, and $x_{k+1}, x_{k+2}, \ldots, x_n$ with flux linkages $\lambda_{k+1}, \lambda_{k+2}, \ldots, \lambda_n$. Letting

17
$$\mathcal{L}(\mathbf{x},\dot{\mathbf{x}},t) \to \mathcal{L}(\mathbf{q}_1,\boldsymbol{\lambda}_2,\dot{\mathbf{q}}_1,\dot{\boldsymbol{\lambda}}_2,t)$$

where

18
$$\mathbf{q}_1 \triangleq \begin{bmatrix} q_1 \\ q_2 \\ \cdot \\ \cdot \\ \cdot \\ q_k \end{bmatrix} \qquad \mathbf{i}_1 = \dot{\mathbf{q}}_1 \qquad \mathbf{e}_1 \triangleq \begin{bmatrix} e_1 \\ e_2 \\ \cdot \\ \cdot \\ \cdot \\ e_k \end{bmatrix}$$
$$\boldsymbol{\lambda}_2 \triangleq \begin{bmatrix} \lambda_{k+1} \\ \lambda_{k+2} \\ \cdot \\ \cdot \\ \cdot \\ \lambda_n \end{bmatrix} \qquad \mathbf{e}_2 \triangleq \dot{\boldsymbol{\lambda}}_2 \qquad \mathbf{i}_2 \triangleq \begin{bmatrix} i_{k+1} \\ i_{k+2} \\ \cdot \\ \cdot \\ \cdot \\ i_n \end{bmatrix}$$

the branch relations are defined as

19
$$\frac{d}{dt}\left(\frac{\partial \mathcal{L}}{\partial \dot{\mathbf{q}}_1}\right)^t - \left(\frac{\partial \mathcal{L}}{\partial \mathbf{q}_1}\right)^t = \mathbf{e}_1$$
$$\frac{d}{dt}\left(\frac{\partial \mathcal{L}}{\partial \dot{\boldsymbol{\lambda}}_2}\right)^t - \left(\frac{\partial \mathcal{L}}{\partial \boldsymbol{\lambda}_2}\right)^t = \mathbf{i}_2$$

As an example, consider the lagrangian,

20
$$\mathcal{L} = \mathbf{x}_1{}^t N^t \dot{\mathbf{x}}_2$$

where

21 $$\mathbf{x}_1 = \begin{bmatrix} x_1 \\ x_2 \\ \cdot \\ \cdot \\ \cdot \\ x_k \end{bmatrix} \qquad \mathbf{x}_2 = \begin{bmatrix} x_{k+1} \\ x_{k+2} \\ \cdot \\ \cdot \\ \cdot \\ x_n \end{bmatrix}$$

Making the identification

22 $$\mathbf{x}_1 \rightarrow \boldsymbol{\lambda}_1 \qquad \mathbf{x}_2 \rightarrow \mathbf{q}_2$$

we have the branch relations

23 $$-N^t\mathbf{i}_2 = \mathbf{i}_1 \qquad N\mathbf{e}_1 = \mathbf{e}_2$$

which define a bank of ideal transformers with turns-ratio matrix N. (Ideal transformers and gyrators are examples of special types of lagrangian elements, known as *traditors*,[1] which neither absorb, liberate, nor store energy.)

7 *Variational problems: optimal control*

We shall devote this section to the formulation of a class of variational problems in a manner suitable for network interpretation. The unconstrained variational problem has already been stated in *4.6.1*. As was pointed out, its solution by indirect methods requires the solution of the Euler-Lagrange equations. However, these are generally in the form of a set of second-order differential equations. Since it is usually preferable to work with first-order equations, it is more convenient to use another first-order formulation in dealing with variational problems, i.e., the canonical equations of Hamilton. The transformation to canonical form is accomplished as follows.

Let a system be defined by the lagrangian $\mathfrak{L}(\mathbf{x},\dot{\mathbf{x}},t)$, and let a new set of variables $\mathbf{p}$, called the *canonical momenta* (or conjugate momenta), be defined by

1 $$p_i \triangleq \frac{\partial \mathfrak{L}}{\partial \dot{x}_i} \qquad i = 1, 2, \ldots, n$$

[1] A word coined by Duinker [14].

p_i is said to be the momentum *conjugate* to the coordinate x_i, and the set of coordinates **x**, **p** are called the *canonical variables* for the system. Now, a new function $H(\mathbf{x},\mathbf{p},t)$, the *hamiltonian*, is defined as

2 $$H(\mathbf{x},\mathbf{p},t) \triangleq \mathbf{p}^t\dot{\mathbf{x}} - \mathcal{L}(\mathbf{x},\dot{\mathbf{x}},t)$$

Equation *2* represents a Legendre transformation from the $(\mathbf{x},\dot{\mathbf{x}})$ coordinate system to the $(\mathbf{x},\mathbf{p})$ system. In order to effect this transformation, *1* must be solvable for the $\dot{\mathbf{x}}$ in terms of the other variables. The Euler-Lagrange equations are now expressed in canonical form as

3 $$\dot{\mathbf{x}} = \left(\frac{\partial H}{\partial \mathbf{p}}\right)^t$$
$$\dot{\mathbf{p}} = -\left(\frac{\partial H}{\partial \mathbf{x}}\right)^t$$

If all n velocities $\dot{x}_i$ are present in $\mathcal{L}$, then the canonical equations will be a set of $2n$ first-order differential equations. However, if some of the velocities are missing, there will be fewer equations, and some will be of zero order (i.e., algebraic equations). We shall use the Euler-Lagrange equations and the canonical equations interchangeably in the sequel, the choice depending upon the context of the problem.

If a minimum of *4.6.3* is sought subject to general equality constraints of the form

4 $$g(\mathbf{x},\dot{\mathbf{x}}) = \mathbf{0}$$

where **g** is an m-vector, we introduce the constraints into the problem as is customary by the method of *Lagrange multipliers*. Consider a set of m auxiliary functions $\mathbf{y}(t)$, the Lagrange multipliers, and define a new functional

5 $$F^* \triangleq \int_{t_0}^{t_1} \mathcal{L}^*\, dt$$

6 where $$\mathcal{L}^* \triangleq \mathcal{L} + \mathbf{y}^t\mathbf{g}(\mathbf{x},\dot{\mathbf{x}})$$

Now, considering both **x** and **y** as independent arguments of F^*, the Euler-Lagrange equations associated with F^* are

7 $$\frac{d}{dt}\left[\left(\frac{\partial \mathcal{L}}{\partial \dot{\mathbf{x}}}\right)^t + \left(\frac{\partial \mathbf{g}}{\partial \dot{\mathbf{x}}}\right)^t \mathbf{y}\right] - \left(\frac{\partial \mathcal{L}}{\partial \mathbf{x}}\right)^t - \left(\frac{\partial \mathbf{g}}{\partial \mathbf{x}}\right)^t \mathbf{y} = \mathbf{0} \qquad -\mathbf{g}(\mathbf{x},\dot{\mathbf{x}}) = \mathbf{0}$$

It can be shown that a necessary condition for a functional F^* to have an extremum along $\mathbf{x}(t)$ subject to the constraints *4* is that there exist functions $\mathbf{y}(t)$, which, together with $\mathbf{x}(t)$, satisfy *7*.

The most general problem we shall consider may involve both equality and inequality constraints.

8 *Problem* Find a vector function $\mathbf{x}(t)$ which passes through the points

9 $$\mathbf{x}(t_0) = \mathbf{x}_0 \qquad \mathbf{x}(t_1) = \mathbf{x}_1$$

and minimizes the functional

10 $$F = \int_{t_0}^{t_1} \mathcal{L}\, dt$$

subject to the constraints,

11 $$\mathbf{g}(\mathbf{x},\dot{\mathbf{x}}) = \mathbf{0}$$

12 $$\mathbf{h}(\mathbf{x}) \geq \mathbf{0}$$

where $\mathbf{x}$ is an n-vector, $\mathbf{g}$ an m-vector, and $\mathbf{h}$ an r-vector.

Although the mathematical difficulties imposed by the inequality constraints take this problem outside the realm of the classical theory of the calculus of variations, we may, as in the case of programming problems, employ penalty functions to circumvent these difficulties. Thus, defining

13 $$\mathcal{L}' = \mathcal{L} + \Delta[\mathbf{h}(\mathbf{x})]$$

14 and $$\mathcal{L}^* = \mathcal{L}' + \mathbf{y}^t\mathbf{g}(\mathbf{x},\dot{\mathbf{x}})$$

where the $\mathbf{y}$ are Lagrange multipliers, we may substitute for F the modified functional

15 $$F^* = \int_{t_0}^{t_1} \mathcal{L}^*\, dt$$

Since the integrand of *15* becomes arbitrarily large when the inequality constraints are violated, F^* implicitly incorporates these constraints (at least approximately) as well as those of *11*. (We shall not in this case attempt any mathematical justification of the use of penalty functions, relying on the fact that intuitively they would seem to be reasonable engineering approximations.)

A special case of the general problem defined above is the optimal control problem which we shall phrase as follows:

16 *Problem* Let a dynamic system be represented by the equations,

17 $$\dot{\mathbf{x}} = \mathbf{f}(\mathbf{x},\mathbf{u})$$

where $\mathbf{x}$ is an n-vector representing the state of the system, and $\mathbf{u}$ is a k-vector, the *control function*, representing the input; let $\mathbf{u}$ be constrained to some limited region Ω of the k-space by the r inequalities

18 $$\mathbf{h}(\mathbf{u}) \geq \mathbf{0}$$

and let the *cost functional* F be defined as

19 $$F \triangleq \int_{t_0}^{t_1} \mathcal{L}(\mathbf{x},\mathbf{u})\, dt$$

Then, given an initial state $\mathbf{x}(t_0) = \mathbf{x}_0$ and a desired final state $\mathbf{x}(t_1) = \mathbf{x}_1$, determine an admissible control function $\mathbf{u}_0(t)$ which takes $\mathbf{x}$ from the initial state to the final state and in so doing minimizes the functional F. $\mathbf{u}_0(t)$ is termed an *optimal control function*. [Note that since $\mathbf{x}(t)$ is determined by the initial value $\mathbf{x}_0$ and the function $\mathbf{u}(t)$, the functional can be expressed in terms of $\mathbf{u}(t)$ alone.] By *admissible function* is meant any bounded piecewise-continuous function $\mathbf{u}(t) \in \Omega$ for all t.

The maximum principle of Pontryagin is particularly suited to the optimal control problem because, unlike classical variational techniques, it does not break down when inequality constraints are present. Formulating the optimal control problem in terms of the maximum principle,[1] we define a scalar function

20
$$H(\mathbf{x},\mathbf{u},\mathbf{m}) \triangleq \mathbf{m}^t\mathbf{f}(\mathbf{x},\mathbf{u}) - \mathcal{L}(\mathbf{x},\mathbf{u})$$

where $\mathbf{m}$ is an n-vector satisfying the *adjoint equations*

21
$$\dot{\mathbf{m}} = -\left(\frac{\partial \mathbf{f}}{\partial \mathbf{x}}\right)^t \mathbf{m} + \left[\frac{\partial \mathcal{L}}{\partial \mathbf{x}}(\mathbf{x},\mathbf{u})\right]^t$$

We shall refer to the $\mathbf{m}$ as the *momenta* conjugate to the state $\mathbf{x}$, and to H as the *hamiltonian*. This terminology is chosen deliberately in order to exhibit the similarity between the formulation of Pontryagin and the canonical equations of Hamilton. The maximum principle is then stated as follows.

If $\mathbf{u}_0(t)$ is an optimal control function for problem *16*, then there exists a corresponding function $\mathbf{x}(t)$ which with $\mathbf{u}_0(t)$ satisfies *17* with the appropriate boundary conditions, as well as a function $\mathbf{m}(t)$ which with $\mathbf{x}(t)$ and $\mathbf{u}_0(t)$ satisfies *21*, such that for all t in the interval $[t_0,t_1]$

22
$$H(\mathbf{x},\mathbf{u}_0,\mathbf{m}) = \max_{\mathbf{u}\in\Omega} H(\mathbf{x},\mathbf{u},\mathbf{m})$$

Note that the two equations *17* and *21* can be expressed respectively as

23
$$\dot{\mathbf{x}} = \left(\frac{\partial H}{\partial \mathbf{m}}\right)^t$$
$$\dot{\mathbf{m}} = -\left(\frac{\partial H}{\partial \mathbf{x}}\right)^t$$

The maximum principle and the Euler-Lagrange equations *4.6.4* are quite similar in that they both define indirect methods of solution of

[1] This is a slight modification of the original formulation in that it is based upon the Lagrange rather than Mayer form of the variational problem. For a detailed discussion of the maximum principle see Rozonoer [15].

variational problems, they both specify necessary but not sufficient conditions, and they both involve the solution of boundary-value problems.

To explore further the relation between the maximum principle and classical variational techniques, let us cast the optimal control problem as an equality-constrained variational problem, using penalty functions to eliminate the inequality constraints. Defining

24 $$\mathcal{L}'(\mathbf{x},\mathbf{u}) \triangleq \mathcal{L}(\mathbf{x},\mathbf{u}) + \Delta[\mathbf{h}(\mathbf{u})]$$

25 and $$\mathcal{L}^*(\mathbf{x},\dot{\mathbf{x}},\mathbf{y},\mathbf{u}) \triangleq \mathcal{L}'(\mathbf{x},\mathbf{u}) + \mathbf{y}^t[\dot{\mathbf{x}} - \mathbf{f}(\mathbf{x},\mathbf{u})]$$

where the $\mathbf{y}$ are Lagrange multipliers, the problem becomes (approximately) that of minimizing the functional

26 $$F^* \triangleq \int_{t_0}^{t_1} \mathcal{L}^*(\mathbf{x},\dot{\mathbf{x}},\mathbf{y},\mathbf{u})\, dt$$

subject to the usual end conditions. This can be treated by deriving a set of Euler-Lagrange equations associated with F^*, or, equivalently, by converting these equations to canonical form through the use of the hamiltonian. We shall take the latter course.

To form the hamiltonian, we first calculate the canonical momenta $\mathbf{p}_x$ conjugate to $\mathbf{x}$. (Since $\dot{\mathbf{y}}$ and $\dot{\mathbf{u}}$ are not present in $\mathcal{L}^*$, the momenta conjugate to these coordinates are zero.) The nonzero momenta in this case are seen to be just the Lagrange multipliers $\mathbf{y}$. Using *2*, the hamiltonian corresponding to $\mathcal{L}^*$ is

27 $$H^* = \mathbf{p}_x{}^t\dot{\mathbf{x}} - \mathcal{L}^* = \mathbf{p}_x{}^t\mathbf{f}(\mathbf{x},\mathbf{u}) - \mathcal{L}'(\mathbf{x},\mathbf{u})$$

Differentiating with respect to the variables which appear in H^* we obtain the canonical equations,

28 $$\dot{\mathbf{x}} = \left(\frac{\partial H^*}{\partial \mathbf{p}_x}\right)^t = \mathbf{f}(\mathbf{x},\mathbf{u})$$

29 $$\dot{\mathbf{p}}_x = -\left(\frac{\partial H^*}{\partial \mathbf{x}}\right)^t = -\left(\frac{\partial \mathbf{f}}{\partial \mathbf{x}}\right)^t \mathbf{p}_x + \left(\frac{\partial \mathcal{L}'}{\partial \mathbf{x}}\right)^t$$

30 $$\dot{\mathbf{p}}_u = \mathbf{0} = -\left(\frac{\partial H^*}{\partial \mathbf{u}}\right)^t$$

These equations generate a family of extremals for the optimal control problem (to a degree of approximation consistent with the form of the penalty functions), and therefore the control function $\mathbf{u}(t)$ satisfying them satisfies necessary conditions for a minimum of F^*. It should be noted that although the first two canonical equations are sets of first-order differential equations, the third represents a set of n implicit algebraic equations in $\mathbf{x}$, $\mathbf{u}$, and $\mathbf{p}_x$. If it is possible to solve these explicitly in the form

31 $$\mathbf{u} = \mathbf{U}(\mathbf{x},\mathbf{p}_x)$$

then *31* would constitute a *control law* for the system, determining $\mathbf{u}$ at each instant as a function of the other coordinates $\mathbf{x}$ and $\mathbf{p}_x$.

Now, comparing the maximum principle to the preceding development, we note that if the identification $\mathbf{m} \Leftrightarrow \mathbf{p}_x$ is made, the hamiltonian H defined by Pontryagin is almost identical to H^*, with the difference that H^* incorporates penalty functions to account for the inequality constraints on $\mathbf{u}$. Furthermore, the first two canonical equations *28* and *29* are identical in form to *23* which appear in the statement of the maximum principle. The third canonical equation *30*, providing a necessary condition for a maximum of H^* with respect to $\mathbf{u}$, is analogous to but somewhat weaker than the maximum condition stated in *22*.

8 *Network interpretation*

Network analogs for variational problems may be developed in a manner similar to those for mathematical programming problems. Since the evolution of the variables in a lagrangian network satisfies Hamilton's principle, i.e., makes the functional,

1 $$F = \int_{t_0}^{t_1} \mathcal{L}\, dt$$

stationary (where $\mathcal{L}$ is the network lagrangian), these networks are an obvious choice as analogs for variational problems. Indeed, we shall show that, in principle, it is always possible to construct an analog network which will generate a family of extremals for a given variational problem. (Also, it appears that a dual variational problem is always solved along with the original problem. However, we shall not explore the duality principle for variational problems here.) In general, the complete solution of the problem, i.e., the selection of the extremal which matches the required boundary conditions, requires the calculation of a set of appropriate initial conditions for charges and flux linkages in the network.

Before deriving a general network analog it is instructive to consider a simple example:

2 *Example* Find a function $x(t)$ which passes through the points $x(0) = \frac{7}{4}$, $x(1) = \frac{5}{4}$, and which minimizes the functional

3 $$F = \int_0^1 \mathcal{L}\, dt \qquad \mathcal{L} = \frac{x^2}{2}$$

subject to the velocity constraint

4 $$|\dot{x}| \leq 1$$

The inequality constraint may be (approximately) incorporated into the functional F by defining a new function

5 $$\mathfrak{L}'(x,\dot{x}) = \Delta(1 - |\dot{x}|) + \frac{x^2}{2}$$

and minimizing the modified functional

6 $$F' = \int_0^1 \mathfrak{L}' \, dt$$

Now, in order to synthesize a network which generates extremals for this problem we identify x as, say, a charge q (the choice is arbitrary) and then take $\mathfrak{L}'(q,\dot{q})$ as the lagrangian of the analog network. In this case the network elements can be identified by inspection. The term $x^2/2$ corresponds to the electric energy function for a -1-farad (negative) capacitor, and the term $\Delta(1 - |\dot{q}|)$ represents a nonlinear inductor having the magnetic coenergy function

7 $$W'_m(\dot{q}) \triangleq \int \lambda(\dot{q}) \, d\dot{q} = \Delta(1 - |\dot{q}|)$$

where λ represents the inductor flux linkages. The network is shown in Fig. *4.8.1*, and the inductor branch relation $\lambda(i)$ in Fig. *4.8.2*. Upon

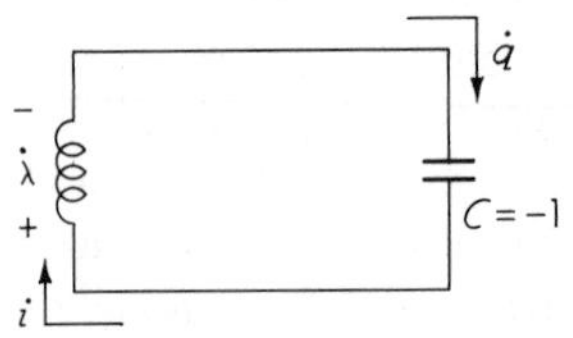

Fig. 4.8.1 Network analog for Example *4.8.2*.

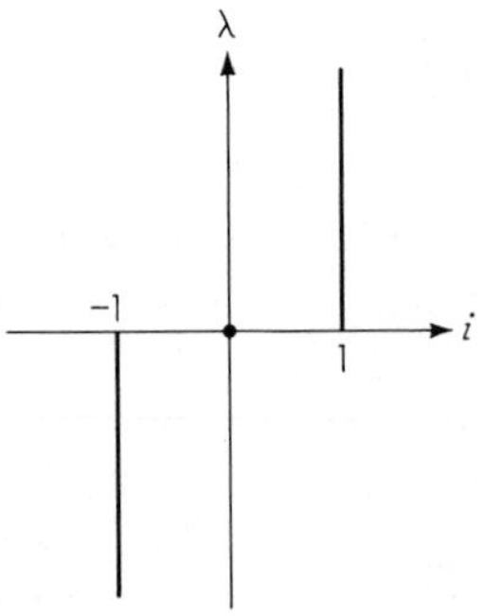

Fig. 4.8.2 Inductor branch relation for network of Fig. *4.8.1*.

differentiation of *5*, the Euler-Lagrange equation is found to be

8 $$\frac{d}{dt}[\lambda(\dot{q})] - q = 0$$

All extremals must satisfy *8* which is the Kirchhoff voltage law equation for the network. Note that the form of the inductor characteristic requires that the current $\dot{q}$ remain (approximately) at the extreme values ± 1 for all time except those isolated points where λ changes sign. If we prefer to write the equations in canonical form, it is found that

9 $$p \triangleq \frac{\partial \mathfrak{L}'}{\partial \dot{q}} = \lambda(\dot{q})$$

and thus the canonical equations become

10 $$\begin{aligned} \dot{q} &= i(\lambda) \\ \dot{\lambda} &= q \end{aligned}$$

where the function $i(\lambda)$ is the inverse of $\lambda(i)$. With the equations in this form no difficulty is encountered if the small parameter μ in the penalty function is allowed to shrink to zero producing perfect limiting of $|\dot{q}|$. (A minor annoyance remains in that the function $i(\lambda)$ is discontinuous at the origin. However, this does not cause any difficulties in solving the network equation.) A little geometric reasoning shows that the correct extremal is selected by choosing the initial conditions in *10* as

$$\begin{aligned} q(0) &= \tfrac{7}{4} \\ \lambda(0) &= \tfrac{33}{32} \end{aligned}$$

The resultant waveforms $q(t)$ and $\lambda(t)$ appear in Fig. *4.8.3*. The locus of the operating point on the inductor characteristic is also indicated in the figure. (The circled numbers relate corresponding points on the three curves.) Note that the initial value $\lambda(0)$ determines the time at which the inductor current switches from $+1$ to -1. By correct choice of this initial condition, any final value which satisfies the inequality,

$$|q(1) - q(0)| \leq 1$$

can be reached.

It is a straightforward matter to extrapolate the results of this example to a general variational problem. Thus consider problem *4.7.8*. The modified integrand $\mathfrak{L}^*$ for this problem may be considered as a function of generalized coordinates $\mathbf{x}$ and $\mathbf{y}$ (as well as the velocities $\dot{\mathbf{x}}$). These coordinates may be interpreted as network variables in

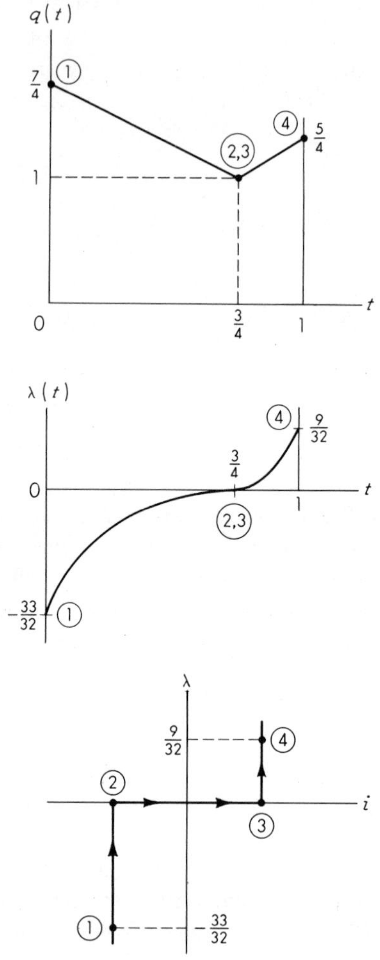

Fig. 4.8.3 Waveform for Example *4.8.2*.

various possible ways. Let us make the arbitrary identification

11
$$\mathbf{x} \to \mathbf{q}_1$$
$$\mathbf{y} \to \mathbf{q}_2$$

Then, from *4.7.13*, and *4.7.14*, the lagrangian defining the network analog becomes

12
$$\mathcal{L}^*(\mathbf{q}_1,\mathbf{q}_2,\dot{\mathbf{q}}_1,t) = \mathcal{L}(\mathbf{q}_1,\dot{\mathbf{q}}_1,t) + \Delta[\mathbf{h}(\mathbf{q}_1)] + \mathbf{q}_2{}^t\mathbf{q}(\mathbf{q}_1,\dot{\mathbf{q}}_1)$$

Each term in *12* can be identified as the lagrangian for a particular multi-port network element with the following branch relations

13 $\mathcal{L}(\mathbf{q}_1,\dot{\mathbf{q}}_1,t)$: $$\mathbf{e}_{\mathcal{L}} = \frac{d}{dt}\left(\frac{\partial \mathcal{L}}{\partial \dot{\mathbf{q}}_1}\right)^t - \left(\frac{\partial \mathcal{L}}{\partial \mathbf{q}_1}\right)^t$$

$\Delta[\mathbf{h}(\mathbf{q}_1)]$: $$\mathbf{e}_{\Delta} = -\left\{\frac{\partial}{\partial \mathbf{q}_1}[\Delta(\mathbf{h})]\right\}^t$$

$\mathbf{q}_2{}^t\mathbf{g}(\mathbf{q}_1,\dot{\mathbf{q}}_1)$: $$\mathbf{e}_1 = \frac{d}{dt}\left[\frac{\partial}{\partial \dot{\mathbf{q}}_1}(\mathbf{q}_2{}^t\mathbf{g})\right]^t - \left[\frac{\partial}{\partial \mathbf{q}_1}(\mathbf{q}_2{}^t\mathbf{g})\right]^t$$
$$\mathbf{e}_2 = \mathbf{g}(\mathbf{q}_1,\dot{\mathbf{q}}_1)$$

(In the above equations, the voltages $\mathbf{e}_{\mathcal{L}}$, $\mathbf{e}_{\Delta}$, and $\mathbf{e}_1$ are all n-vectors and $\mathbf{e}_2$ is an m-vector.) The complete analog network is shown in block form in Fig. *4.8.4*. (The elements are identified by their lagrangians.) Since the network is defined by the lagrangian $\mathcal{L}^*$, it must generate extremals for the problem in question. Figure *4.8.4* does not serve par-

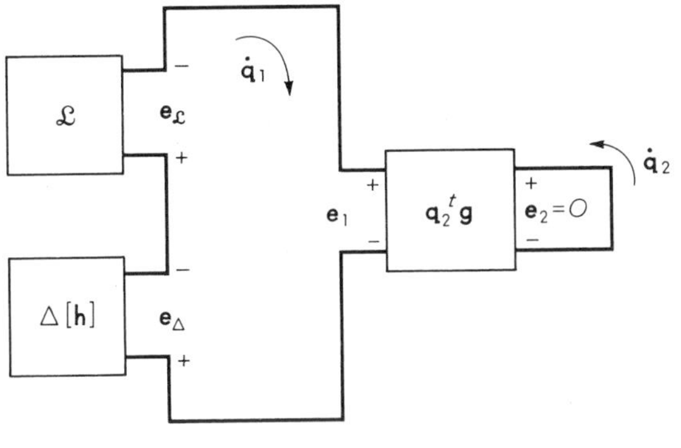

Fig. 4.8.4 Network analog of general variational problem.

ticularly well as an illustration of the form of a network analog since it is too general in nature. Let us therefore specialize our thinking to the optimal control problem. In order to simplify matters further, discussion will be restricted to problems involving the control of linear systems with linear inequality constraints on $\mathbf{u}$. Let the equations of the controlled system be

14 $$\dot{\mathbf{x}} = \mathbf{f}(\mathbf{x},\mathbf{u}) = A\mathbf{x} + B\mathbf{u}$$

and the constraint equations be

15 $$C\mathbf{u} - \mathbf{d} \geq \mathbf{0}$$

where A is an $n \times n$ matrix, B an $n \times k$ matrix, C an $r \times k$ matrix, and $\mathbf{d}$ an r-vector. This implies no lack of generality, since the networks we shall derive can be generalized in a straightforward way to nonlinear systems.

The lagrangian associated with this problem is, from *4.7.24* and *4.7.25*,

16 $$\mathfrak{L}^* = \mathfrak{L} + \mathbf{y}^t(\mathbf{x} - A\mathbf{x} - B\mathbf{u}) + \Delta(C\mathbf{u} - \mathbf{d})$$

If all variables in $\mathfrak{L}^*$ are identified with charges so that

17 $$\begin{aligned} &\mathbf{x} \rightarrow \mathbf{q}_x \qquad \dot{\mathbf{x}} \rightarrow \dot{\mathbf{q}}_x = \mathbf{i}_x \\ &\mathbf{y} \rightarrow \mathbf{q}_y \\ &\mathbf{u} \rightarrow \mathbf{q}_u \end{aligned}$$

the resultant form for $\mathfrak{L}^*$ is

18 $$\mathfrak{L}^*(\mathbf{q}_x,\dot{\mathbf{q}}_x,\mathbf{q}_y,\mathbf{q}_u) = \mathfrak{L}_G + \mathfrak{L}_A + \mathfrak{L}_B + \mathfrak{L} + \mathfrak{L}_\Delta$$

where

19 $$\begin{aligned} \mathfrak{L}_G &\triangleq \mathbf{q}_y{}^t\dot{\mathbf{q}}_x & \mathfrak{L} &\triangleq \mathfrak{L}(\mathbf{q}_x,\mathbf{q}_u) \\ \mathfrak{L}_A &\triangleq -\mathbf{q}_y{}^tA\mathbf{q}_x & \mathfrak{L}_\Delta &\triangleq \Delta[C\mathbf{q}_u - \mathbf{d}] \\ \mathfrak{L}_B &\triangleq -\mathbf{q}_y{}^tB\mathbf{q}_u \end{aligned}$$

Each of the above terms represents the lagrangian for a particular multi-port network element. For example, $\mathfrak{L}_G$ represents a bank of gyrators (cf. *4.6.12*). The remaining terms represent capacitive elements; however elements of a highly unusual type. Using *4.6.19* the branch relations for each element may be written

20 $\mathfrak{L}_G$:
$$-\dot{\mathbf{q}}_x = \mathbf{e}_{Gy}$$
$$\dot{\mathbf{q}}_y = \mathbf{e}_{Gx}$$

$\mathfrak{L}_A$:
$$A^t\mathbf{q}_y = \mathbf{e}_{Ax}$$
$$A\mathbf{q}_x = \mathbf{e}_{Ay}$$

$\mathfrak{L}_B$:
$$B^t\mathbf{q}_y = \mathbf{e}_{Bu}$$
$$B\mathbf{q}_u = \mathbf{e}_{By}$$

$\mathfrak{L}$:
$$-\left(\frac{\partial \mathfrak{L}}{\partial \mathbf{q}_x}\right)^t = \mathbf{e}_{\mathfrak{L}x}$$
$$-\left(\frac{\partial \mathfrak{L}}{\partial \mathbf{q}_u}\right)^t = \mathbf{e}_{\mathfrak{L}u}$$

$\mathfrak{L}_\Delta$:
$$-\left[\frac{\partial \Delta}{\partial \mathbf{q}_u}(C\mathbf{q}_u - \mathbf{d})\right] = \mathbf{e}_{\Delta u}$$

Figure *4.8.5* contains a complete diagram of the analog network, wherein each element (except that labeled δ) is denoted by its lagrangian. It will be noted that $\mathfrak{L}_A$ and $\mathfrak{L}_B$ represent banks of elements each of which

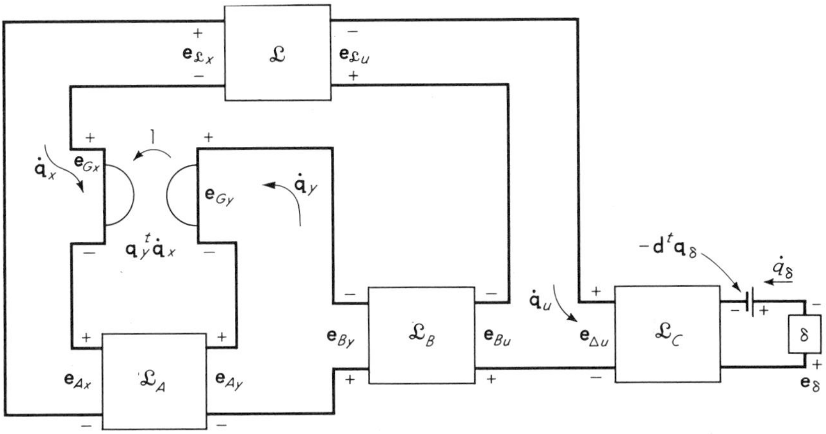

Fig. 4.8.5 Network analog for optimal control of linear system.

may be considered as a linear 2-port capacitor. These devices have the property that a charge applied at one port causes a proportional voltage to appear at another port; i.e., they represent mutual capacitances unaccompanied by any self-capacitance. $\mathfrak{L}$ is also a capacitive element but cannot be described more specifically without specifying the nature of its lagrangian. The element $\mathfrak{L}_\Delta$ has been synthesized using a combination of elements defined by the indicated lagrangians, where

21 $$\mathfrak{L}_C = \mathbf{q}_\delta{}^t C \mathbf{q}_u$$

denotes another bank of mutual capacitances.

Note that the element denoted in the figure by the lagrangian $-\mathbf{d}^t\mathbf{q}_\delta$ is simply a bank of voltage sources, and that denoted by δ is a bank of *capacitive diodes* defined by branch relations $\mathbf{q}_\delta = \boldsymbol{\delta}(\mathbf{e}_\delta)$. (The combination of capacitive elements representing the linear constraints in Fig. *4.8.5* has its direct counterpart in the combination of resistive elements representing the linear constraints in the mathematical programming analog of Fig. *4.4.6*.)

To show that the network of Fig. *4.8.5* does generate extremals for the problem being considered, we merely write the Euler-Lagrange equations associated with the function $\mathfrak{L}^*$ as follows

22 $$\begin{aligned} -\dot{\mathbf{q}}_x + A\mathbf{q}_x + B\mathbf{q}_u &= \mathbf{0} \\ \dot{\mathbf{q}}_y + A^t\mathbf{q}_y - \left(\frac{\partial\mathfrak{L}}{\partial\mathbf{q}_x}\right)^t &= \mathbf{0} \\ B^t\mathbf{q}_y - \left(\frac{\partial\mathfrak{L}}{\partial\mathbf{q}_u}\right)^t - \left[\frac{\partial\Delta}{\partial\mathbf{q}_u}(C\mathbf{q}_u - \mathbf{d})\right]^t &= \mathbf{0} \end{aligned}$$

Using *20*, these take the form

23
$$\begin{aligned}\mathbf{e}_{Gy} + \mathbf{e}_{Ay} + \mathbf{e}_{By} &= \mathbf{0}\\ \mathbf{e}_{Gx} + \mathbf{e}_{Ax} + \mathbf{e}_{\mathfrak{L}x} &= \mathbf{0}\\ \mathbf{e}_{Bu} + \mathbf{e}_{\mathfrak{L}u} + \mathbf{e}_{\Delta u} &= \mathbf{0}\end{aligned}$$

But by inspection of Fig. *4.8.5* it can be seen that *23* are just the Kirchhoff voltage law equations for the analog network. The network equations may be identified with those occurring in the maximum principle by noting that the controlled system *4.7.17* is simulated in loop $\mathbf{x}$, the adjoint equations *4.7.21* in loop $\mathbf{y}$, and the control law equations *4.7.22*, *4.7.30*, or *4.7.31* are solved in loop $\mathbf{u}$.

To generate an extremal corresponding to a particular set of boundary values, the correct initial charges $\mathbf{q}_x(t_0)$, $\mathbf{q}_y(t_0)$, $\mathbf{q}_u(t_0)$ must be established. $\mathbf{q}_x(t_0)$ corresponds to $\mathbf{x}_0$ and is hence known. $\mathbf{q}_y(t_0)$ corresponds to the initial values of the momenta $\mathbf{m}$ in the maximum principle (or the Lagrange multipliers in the lagrangian formulation). These must be calculated in some way so as to lead to the correct final value $\mathbf{q}_x(t_1) = \mathbf{x}_1$. Having established these two sets of initial charges it can be seen from Fig. *4.8.5* that $\mathbf{e}_{\Delta u}(t_0)$ is thereby determined, and hence $\mathbf{q}_u(t_0)$ is fixed, provided that a unique relation exists between $\mathbf{e}_{\Delta u}$ and $\mathbf{q}_u$. (We assume throughout this discussion that all elements in series in a loop have the same values of charges.)

Consider now a specific example.

24 *Example* A well-known problem in optimal control (a form of the *bang-bang* problem) is:

Given a system defined by *14* with

25
$$\mathbf{x} = \begin{bmatrix} x_1 \\ x_2 \end{bmatrix} \qquad A = \begin{bmatrix} 0 & 1 \\ -1 & 0 \end{bmatrix} \qquad B = \begin{bmatrix} 0 \\ 1 \end{bmatrix} \qquad \mathbf{u} = u$$

with the constraint

26
$$|u| \le 1$$

Find a control function $u(t)$ which brings the system from some initial point $\mathbf{x}_0$ to the origin in minimum time.

The functional to be minimized can be taken in this case to be

27
$$\mathbf{F} = \int_{t_0}^{t_1} dt$$

that is, $\mathfrak{L} = 1$. (This is a slight variant of the optimal control problem as we originally stated it, since the time t_1 is unspecified. However, the form of the analog remains the same.) Modifying $\mathfrak{L}$ to include the amplitude constraint on u we have

28 $$\mathcal{L}' = 1 + \Delta(1 - |u|)$$

and finally, including the equality constraints,

29 $$\mathcal{L}^* = 1 + \Delta(1 - |u|) + y_1(\dot{x}_1 - x_2) + y_2(\dot{x}_2 + x_1 - u)$$

where y_1 and y_2 are Lagrange multipliers.

An analog network associated with $\mathcal{L}^*$ is shown in Fig. *4.8.6*. In the

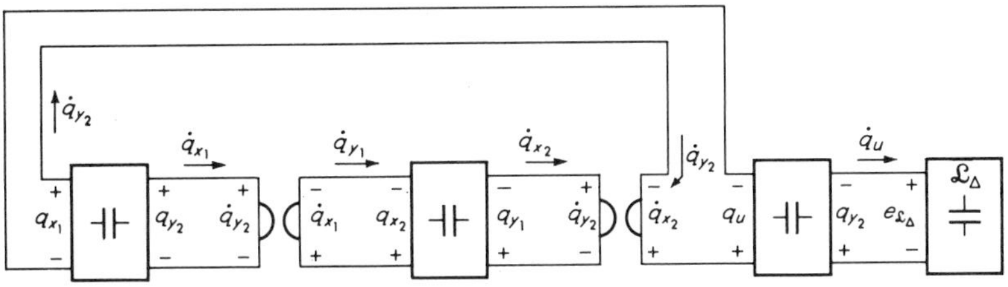

Fig. 4.8.6 Network analog for the bang-bang problem.

figure each gyrator has unity gain, and each 2-port capacitive element is defined by branch relations of the general form

30 $$q_1 = e_2$$
$$q_2 = e_1$$

The only nonlinear element is the 1-port capacitor derived from the lagrangian $\mathcal{L}_\Delta = \Delta(1 - |q_u|)$, which accounts for the amplitude limiting of q_u. Its branch relation is similar in form to that shown in Fig. *4.8.2* except for a sign reversal. (Methods of calculating the initial conditions on $\mathbf{q}_y$ which are necessary to bring $\mathbf{q}_x$ to zero in minimum time can be found in the literature. See, for example, Desoer [16].)

9 *Conclusions*

We have set forth certain special properties of networks which can be exploited in synthesizing network analogs for two basic types of extremum problems. On the one hand, the fact that the equilibria of resistive reciprocal networks can be identified with stationary points of their associated dissipation functions leads in a natural way to the construction of network analogs for mathematical programming problems. On the other hand, the fact that lagrangian networks behave in such a manner as to make a certain functional stationary leads to the formulation of networks which generate extremals for variational problems. It should be emphasized that these analogs are meant simply as network interpretations of extremum problems. The actual use to which they are put must depend upon the inclination of the individual and on the particular problem being analyzed. Among their possible uses are (1) as a heuristic tool to promote a better "physical" understanding of a problem, (2) as a means of suggesting more efficient computational schemes for solving extremum problems, and (3) as a direct analog to be used either alone or in conjunction with other devices for the solution of an extremum problem.

APPENDIX

Proof of Theorem 4.4.10 We wish to prove that, given any $\epsilon > 0$, there exists a $\mu_0 > 0$ such that for all

$$0 < \mu \leq \mu_0$$

any stationary point $\mathbf{e}_N$, of $\mathfrak{F}'_N(\mathbf{e}_1)$, satisfies the relation,

1 $$\|\mathbf{e}_N - \mathbf{e}_0\| < \epsilon$$

where $\mathbf{e}_0$ is the unique minimum of $\varphi(\mathbf{e}) \in S_c$.

To facilitate the proof we note the following properties of $\mathfrak{F}'_N$:

2 $$\mathfrak{F}'_N(\mathbf{e}_1) = \varphi(\mathbf{e}_1) \qquad \mathbf{e}_1 \in S_c$$

3 $$\mathfrak{F}'_N(\mathbf{e}_1) > \varphi(\mathbf{e}_1) \qquad \mathbf{e}_1 \notin S_c$$

4 $$\mathfrak{F}'_N(\mathbf{e}_1) \text{ is convex}$$

Now consider two cases:

1. $\mathbf{e}_0$ is an interior point of S_c
2. $\mathbf{e}_0$ is a boundary point of S_c

In case 1, the above properties of $\mathfrak{F}'_N$ show that $\mathbf{e}_0$ can be its only stationary point, and hence the proof is trivial.

To complete the proof in case 2, choose any $\epsilon > 0$ and define the set D:

5 $$\|\mathbf{e}_1 - \mathbf{e}_0\| = \epsilon$$

Since D is compact, $\varphi(\mathbf{e}_1)$ has a glb m at a point $\mathbf{e}_m \in D$. Also there exists an $\alpha > 0$ such that

6 $$\varphi(\mathbf{e}_1) \geq \alpha + \varphi(\mathbf{e}_0) \qquad \text{for all } \mathbf{e}_1 \in D \cap S_c$$

Now given an $\eta > 0$ we define S_η:

7 $$\|\mathbf{e}_1 - \mathbf{e}_c\| < \eta \qquad \text{for all } \mathbf{e}_c \in S_c$$

By continuity there exists an $\eta > 0$ such that

8 $$\varphi(\mathbf{e}_1) > \varphi(\mathbf{e}_0) + \frac{\alpha}{2} \qquad \text{for all } \mathbf{e}_1 \in D \cap S\eta$$

Thus

$$\mathfrak{F}'_N(\mathbf{e}_1) > \varphi(\mathbf{e}_0) + \frac{\alpha}{2} \qquad \text{for all } \mathbf{e}_1 \in D \cap S_\eta \tag{9}$$

Let $E \triangleq D \cap S_\eta{}^c$ (where $S_\eta{}^c$ denotes the complement of S_η), and let

$$F(\mathbf{e}_1) \triangleq \min_{i,\,j} \, [e_i, f_j(\mathbf{e}_1)] \tag{10}$$

Since E is compact, $F(\mathbf{e}_1)$ has a lub $M < 0$ on E.
Now if we choose any $\mu_0 > 0$ such that

$$\frac{M^2}{2\mu_0} \geq \left[\varphi(\mathbf{e}_0) - \varphi(\mathbf{e}_m) + \frac{\alpha}{2} \right] \tag{11}$$

then from the definition of $\mathfrak{F}'_N(\mathbf{e}_1)$ we find that

$$\mathfrak{F}'_N(\mathbf{e}_1) \geq \varphi(\mathbf{e}_0) + \frac{\alpha}{2} \qquad \begin{array}{l} \text{for all } 0 < \mu \leq \mu_0 \\ \text{and all } \mathbf{e}_1 \in D \end{array} \tag{12}$$

But because of the convexity of $\mathfrak{F}'_N$ this implies that any stationary point $\mathbf{e}_N$ must satisfy

$$\|\mathbf{e}_N - \mathbf{e}_0\| < \epsilon \tag{13}$$

which completes the proof.

REFERENCES

1 Maxwell, J. C.: "A Treatise on Electricity and Magnetism," 3d ed., vol. 1, Clarendon Press, Oxford, p. 407, 1892.

2 Millar, W.: Some General Theorems for Nonlinear Systems Possessing Resistance, *Phil. Mag.* ser. 7, vol. 13, p. 1150, October, 1951.

3 Dennis, J. B.: "Mathematical Programming and Electrical Networks," Technology Press and Wiley, New York, 1959.

4 Stern, T. E.: Extremum Relations in Nonlinear Networks and Their Applications to Mathematical Programming, *Journées d'Études sur le Contrôle Optimum et les Systèmes Nonlinéaires*, Institut National des Sciences et Techniques Nucléaires, Saclay, France, pp. 135–156, June, 1962.

5 Moser, J.: On the Differential Equations of Electrical Circuits and the Global Nature of the Solutions, *Intern. Symp. Nonlinear Differential Equations and Nonlinear Mechanics* (J. P. Lasalle and S. Lefschetz, eds.), Academic, New York, pp. 147–154, 1963.

6 Whittaker, E. T.: "Analytical Dynamics," 3d ed., Cambridge University Press, Cambridge, 1927.

7 Kuhn, H. W., and A. W. Tucker: Nonlinear Programming, *Proc. Second Berkeley Symp. Math. Statistics and Probability* (J. Neyman, ed.), University of California Press, Berkeley, pp. 481–492, 1951.

8 Samuelson, P. A.: Market Mechanisms and Maximizations, *RAND* Corp. P-69, 1949.

9 Uzawa, H.: Gradient Method for Concave Programming, II: Global Stability in the Strictly Concave Case, in "Studies in Linear and Nonlinear Program-

ming" (K. J. Arrow, L. Hurwicz, H. Uzawa, eds.), Stanford University Press, Stanford, 1958.

10 Courant, R.: Calculus of Variations and Supplementary Notes and Exercises, 1945–46, revised and amended by J. Moser, N.Y.U. Institute of Mathematical Sciences, 1956–57 (mimeographed lecture notes).

11 Rubin, H., and P. Ungar: Motion under a Strong Constraining Force, *Commun. Pure Appl. Math.*, vol. 10, pp. 65–87, 1957.

12 Kelley, H. J.: Method of Gradients, in "Optimization Techniques" (G. Leitmann, ed.), Academic, New York, pp. 205–254, 1962.

13 Lasalle, J. P., and S. Lefschetz: "Stability by Liapunov's Direct Method with Applications," Academic, New York, 1961.

14 Duinker, S.: Traditors, A New Class of Nonenergic Nonlinear Network Elements, *Philips Res. Rept.*, vol. 14, pp. 29–51, 1959.

15 Rozonoer, L. I.: L. S. Pontryagin Maximum Principle in the Theory of Optimum Systems; English translation, *Automation and Remote Control*, pp. 1288–1302, 1405–1421, 1517–1532 (1960).

16 Desoer, C. A.: The Bang Bang Servo Problem Treated by Variational Techniques, *Inform. and Control*, vol. 2, pp. 333–348, 1959.

Part Two

LINEAR SYSTEMS

5

Linear modular systems

A. Gill[1]
Department of Electrical Engineering and Computer Sciences
University of California, Berkeley

1 *Introduction*

Linear modular systems (abbreviated LMS) are of interest to the system theorist for two important reasons. First, these systems constitute a subclass of the class of finite-state systems (introduced in Chap. *2*) where powerful theories of finite groups, rings and fields, and of linear vector spaces can be exploited to advantage. As such, LMS constitute a bridge between the general finite-state system and the general linear system and offer insight into the operation of both. Secondly, LMS have found wide application in computer control circuitry, implementation of error-correction codes, random-number generation, and other digital tasks, which provide ample justification for their study from the practical point of view.

2 *Mathematical prerequisites*

The study of the analysis, synthesis, and applications of linear modular systems requires wide background in the theories of finite groups, finite

[1] The writing of this chapter was supported in part by the Air Force Office of Scientific Research, Office of Aerospace Research, United States Air Force, under AFOSR Grant AF-AFOSR-639-67, and by the United States Department of the Navy, Office of Naval Research, under Contract Nonr-222(53).

fields, and linear algebra. Sections *3* to *11* present a brief summary of definitions and results (without proofs) which pertain directly to the material in subsequent sections. This summary is included to establish notation and serve as an easy reference, and by no means constitutes adequate preparation for the subject at hand. The reader may refer to any of many good textbooks on modern algebra for more complete coverage.

Notation and terminology

Vectors and matrices are printed boldface. The element appearing in row i and column j of a matrix is called the (i,j) *element* of the matrix. An $m \times n$ matrix $\mathbf{M}$ whose (i,j) element is m_{ij} will sometimes be written as $[m_{ij}]_{m\times n}$. The determinant of $\mathbf{M}$ is written as $|\mathbf{M}|$, the transpose as $\mathbf{M}'$, and the adjoint as $\mathbf{M}^{\mathrm{ADJ}}$. $\mathbf{I}$ will denote the identity matrix and $\mathbf{0}$ the null matrix (or vector).

A time function $f(t)$, defined for nonnegative integral values of t only, will be written as $\alpha_0\alpha_1\alpha_2 \cdots$, where $\alpha_t = f(t)$. If $f(t) = f(t + T)$ for all $t \geq r$ [that is, if after r symbols $f(t)$ becomes periodic with period T], $f(t)$ will be written as

$$\alpha_0\alpha_1 \cdots \alpha_{r-1}.\alpha_r\alpha_{r+1} \cdots \alpha_{r+T-1}, \alpha_r\alpha_{r+1} \cdots \alpha_{r+T-1}, \ldots$$

The greatest common divisor and the least common multiple of the integers $\nu_1, \nu_2, \ldots, \nu_k$, will be written, respectively, as

$$\gcd(\nu_1,\nu_2, \ldots ,\nu_k) \qquad \text{and} \qquad \operatorname{lcm}(\nu_1,\nu_2, \ldots ,\nu_k)$$

The remaining notation and terminology will be developed as needed.

3 Groups

The set G is a *group* if a single operation $*$ is defined for every pair of elements in G, and if it satisfies the following four postulates:

1 *Closure* For all α, β in G, $\alpha * \beta$ is in G.

2 *Associativity* For all α, β, γ in G, $\alpha * (\beta * \gamma) = (\alpha * \beta) * \gamma$.

3 *Identity* G contains an element i, called the *identity* of G, such that for every α in G, $i * \alpha = \alpha * i = \alpha$.

4 *Inverse* For every α in G there is an element α^{-1} in G, called the *inverse* of α, such that $\alpha * \alpha^{-1} = \alpha^{-1} * \alpha = i$.

G is an *Abelian group* if, in addition to *1*, *2*, *3*, and *4*, the following is satisfied:

5 *Commutativity* For all α, β in G, $\alpha * \beta = \beta * \alpha$.

When the operation $*$ is $+$, G is an *additive group*, i is the *zero* of G (commonly denoted by 0), α^{-1} is written as $-\alpha$ and $\alpha + (-\beta)$ is written as $\alpha - \beta$. When the operation is $\cdot$ ($\alpha \cdot \beta$ is also written as $\alpha\beta$), G is a *multiplicative group*.

4 *Rings*

The set R is a *ring* if addition and multiplication are defined for every pair of elements in R, and if it satisfies the following four postulates:

1 R is an additive Abelian group.

2 *Closure* For all α, β in R, $\alpha\beta$ is in R.

3 *Associativity* For all α, β, γ in R, $\alpha(\beta\gamma) = (\alpha\beta)\gamma$.

4 *Distributivity* For all α, β, γ in R, $\alpha(\beta + \gamma) = \alpha\beta + \alpha\gamma$ and $(\beta + \gamma)\alpha = \beta\alpha + \gamma\alpha$.

R is a *commutative ring* if, in addition to *1*, *2*, *3*, and *4*, the following is satisfied:

5 *Commutativity* For all α, β in R, $\alpha\beta = \beta\alpha$.

5 *Fields*

The commutative ring F is called a *field* if it satisfies the following two postulates:

1 *Identity* F contains an element 1 such that for every α in F $1\alpha = \alpha 1 = \alpha$.

2 *Inverse* For every nonzero α in F there is an element α^{-1} such that $\alpha\alpha^{-1} = \alpha^{-1}\alpha = 1$.

3 *Example* The set of integers $\{0, 1, \ldots, p - 1\}$, where p is prime and where addition and multiplication are defined mod p, is a field. It is denoted by $GF(p)$.

6 Polynomials over a field

A *polynomial over a field F* is an expression of the form

$$f(x) = \alpha_0 + \alpha_1 x + \cdots + \alpha_n x^n$$

where the coefficients α_i are from F. The *degree* of $f(x)$, denoted $\partial(f(x))$, is the highest power of x with a nonzero coefficient; this coefficient is called the *leading coefficient* of $f(x)$. $f(x)$ is called a *monic polynomial* if its leading coefficient is 1. A polynomial $f(x)$ is irreducible if its only divisors are α and $\alpha f(x)$ (where α is any element in F).

1 *Prime factorization theorem* $f(x)$ can be written in the form

$$f(x) = [p_1(x)]^{e_1}[p_2(x)]^{e_2} \cdots [p_r(x)]^{e_r}$$

where the $p_i(x)$ are distinct and irreducible. The factors $[p_i(x)]^{e_i}$ are called the *prime factors* of $f(x)$, and are unique up to a constant multiplier.

2 *Division algorithm* For any $a(x)$ and $b(x)$ one can uniquely write

$$a(x) = q(x)b(x) + r(x) \qquad \text{where } 0 \leq \partial(r(x)) < \partial(b(x)) \text{ or } r(x) = 0$$

3 *Euclidean algorithm* Given $a_0(x)$ and $a_1(x)$ where $\partial(a_0(x)) \geq \partial(a_1(x))$, construct the equations:

$$\begin{aligned}
a_0(x) &= q_1(x)a_1(x) + a_2(x) & \partial(a_2(x)) &< \partial(a_1(x)) \\
a_1(x) &= q_2(x)a_2(x) + a_3(x) & \partial(a_3(x)) &< \partial(a_2(x)) \\
a_2(x) &= q_3(x)a_3(x) + a_4(x) & \partial(a_4(x)) &< \partial(a_3(x)) \\
&\cdots\cdots\cdots \\
a_{r-2}(x) &= q_{r-1}(x)a_{r-1}(x) + a_r(x) & \partial(a_r(x)) &< \partial(a_{r-1}(x)) \\
a_{r-1}(x) &= q_r(x)a_r(x)
\end{aligned}$$

Then $a_r(x) = \gcd(a_0(x), a_1(x))$.

4 Every polynomial $f(x)$ (not divisible by x) over a finite field is a factor of $1 - x^i$ for some i. The least such i is called the *period* of $f(x)$. If $f(x) = p(x)$ is an irreducible polynomial (other than x) of degree n over $GF(p)$, its period must divide $p^n - 1$. The period of $[p(x)]^e$ is p^jT, where j is the least integer such that $p^j \geq e$, and T is the period of $p(x)$.

5 An irreducible polynomial of degree n over $GF(p)$ exists for every p

and n. At least one such polynomial has the period $p^n - 1$. (Tables of irreducible polynomials over $GF(2)$ are included in Peterson [85].)

6 The *reciprocal* of $f(x) = \alpha_0 + \alpha_1 x + \cdots + \alpha_n x^n$ is defined by $[f(x)]^* = x^n f(1/x)$. The prime factors of $[f(x)]^*$ are the reciprocals of the prime factors of $f(x)$.

7 The set of all polynomials over F forms a ring, denoted by $F[x]$.

7 *Modular ring of polynomials*

Consider the set of all polynomials over F for which the following is postulated: Two polynomials are equal if and only if their difference is a multiple of $m(x)$. This set constitutes a ring [in which addition and multiplication are defined mod $m(x)$], called the *ring of polynomials over F mod m(x)*. $m(x)$ is called the *modulus polynomial* of this ring. If $\partial(m(x)) = k$, the elements of the ring can be represented by the set of all polynomials of degrees $k - 1$ or less over F. To differentiate these polynomials from those of $F[x]$ (for which the new postulate does not hold), they will be expressed as functions of the indeterminate ξ rather than x. Thus, in the ring of polynomials over F mod $m(x)$, $m(\xi) = 0$ and every element is equivalent to some polynomial of the form

$$f(\xi) = \alpha_0 + \alpha_1 \xi + \cdots + \alpha_{k-1} \xi^{k-1}$$

8 *Galois fields*

1 The ring of polynomials over $GF(p)$ mod an irreducible polynomial $p(x)$ can be shown to be a field. If $\partial(p(x)) = k$, this field is represented by the set of all p^k polynomials in ξ of degrees $k - 1$ or less over $GF(p)$. It is called a *Galois field of order* p^k and denoted by $GF(p^k)$.

2 Every element in $GF(p^k)$ satisfies the equation $x - x^{p^k} = 0$. Also, every element can be expressed as a power of some element, called the *primitive element* of $GF(p^k)$.

3 Every finite field F is isomorphic to some Galois field $GF(p^k)$ [i.e., every element in F can be placed in one-to-one correspondence with an element in $GF(p^k)$ in the following manner: If α and β in F correspond to $\bar{\alpha}$ and $\bar{\beta}$ in $GF(p^k)$, then $\alpha + \beta$ and $\alpha\beta$ in F correspond to $\bar{\alpha} + \bar{\beta}$ and $\bar{\alpha}\bar{\beta}$, respectively, in $GF(p^k)$].

9 Vector spaces

Let V be an additive Abelian group and let F be a field. Then V is called a *vector space over* F if the following four postulates are satisfied:

1 *Closure* For all α in F and $\mathbf{v}$ in V, $\alpha\mathbf{v}$ is defined and in V.

2 *Associativity* For all α, β in F and $\mathbf{v}$ in V, $(\alpha\beta)\mathbf{v} = \alpha(\beta\mathbf{v})$.

3 *Distributivity* For all α, β in F and $\mathbf{u}$, $\mathbf{v}$ in V, $\alpha(\mathbf{u} + \mathbf{v}) = \alpha\mathbf{u} + \alpha\mathbf{v}$ and $(\alpha + \beta)\mathbf{v} = \alpha\mathbf{v} + \beta\mathbf{v}$.

4 *Identity* For all $\mathbf{v}$ in V, $1\mathbf{v} = \mathbf{v}$.

Elements of V are called *vectors*, and those of F *scalars*. $\mathbf{0}$ denotes the zero of V, called the *null vector*.

A *linear combination* of the vectors $\mathbf{v}_1, \mathbf{v}_2, \ldots, \mathbf{v}_n$ is a vector of the form $\alpha_1\mathbf{v}_1 + \alpha_2\mathbf{v}_2 + \cdots + \alpha_n\mathbf{v}_n$, where the α_i are scalars. $\mathbf{v}_1, \mathbf{v}_2, \ldots, \mathbf{v}_n$ are *linearly independent* if $\alpha_1\mathbf{v}_1 + \alpha_2\mathbf{v}_2 + \cdots + \alpha_n\mathbf{v}_n = \mathbf{0}$ implies $\alpha_1 = \alpha_2 = \cdots = \alpha_n = 0$. If $\mathbf{v}_1, \mathbf{v}_2, \ldots, \mathbf{v}_n$ are linearly independent, and if every vector in V can be expressed as their linear combination, they form a *basis* for V. V is then said to be *n-dimensional.*

10 Matrices over a field

1 A *matrix over a field* F is a matrix with elements from F. All matrices under discussion will be assumed to be of this type.

2 The *elementary divisors* of a square matrix $\mathbf{M}$ over F is a set of polynomials over F which can be uniquely computed from the elements of $\mathbf{M}$. These polynomials are of the form:

$$
\begin{array}{llcll}
[p_1(x)]^{e_{11}} & [p_1(x)]^{e_{12}} & \cdots & [p_1(x)]^{e_{1l_1}} & 0 < e_{11} \le e_{12} \le \cdots \le e_{1l_1} \\
[p_2(x)]^{e_{21}} & [p_2(x)]^{e_{22}} & \cdots & [p_2(x)]^{e_{2l_2}} & 0 < e_{21} \le e_{22} \le \cdots \le e_{2l_2} \\
\cdots & \cdots & \cdots & \cdots & \\
[p_r(x)]^{e_{r1}} & [p_r(x)]^{e_{r2}} & \cdots & [p_r(x)]^{e_{rl_r}} & 0 < e_{r1} \le e_{r2} \le \cdots \le e_{rl_r}
\end{array}
$$

where the $p_i(x)$ are monic, irreducible, and of degree at least 1. The elementary divisors $[p_i(x)]^{e_{il_i}}$ are called the *leading divisors* of $\mathbf{M}$.

3 The *characteristic polynomial* of $\mathbf{M}$, denoted by $\varphi_M(x)$, is defined by

$$\varphi_M(x) = |\mathbf{M} - x\mathbf{I}|$$

Except possibly for sign, $\varphi_M(x)$ equals the product of all the elementary divisors of **M**. **M** satisfies $\varphi_M(x) = 0$ [that is, $\varphi_M(\mathbf{M}) = \mathbf{0}$]. **M** is singular if and only if $\varphi_M(x)$ is divisible by x.

4 The *minimum polynomial* of **M** is the least-degree monic polynomial over F, denoted by $m_M(x)$, such that $m_M(\mathbf{M}) = \mathbf{0}$. $m_M(x)$ is unique, and a divisor of every polynomial $f(x)$ such that $f(\mathbf{M}) = \mathbf{0}$. $m_M(x)$ equals the product of all leading divisors of **M**.

11 *The rational canonical form*

1 Two square matrices **M** and $\bar{\mathbf{M}}$ over F are said to be similar if a nonsingular matrix **P** exists such that $\bar{\mathbf{M}} = \mathbf{PMP}^{-1}$. **P** is called the *similarity transformation matrix from* **M** *to* $\bar{\mathbf{M}}$. Two matrices are similar if and only if they have the same set of elementary divisors.

2 Let $d(x) = \alpha_0 + \alpha_1 x + \cdots + \alpha_{k-1}x^{k-1} + x^k$ be a monic polynomial of degree k over F. The *companion matrix of* $d(x)$, denoted by $\mathbf{M}_{d(x)}$, is a $k \times k$ matrix given by

3
$$\mathbf{M}_{d(x)} = \begin{bmatrix} 0 & 0 & \cdots & 0 & -\alpha_0 \\ 1 & 0 & \cdots & 0 & -\alpha_1 \\ 0 & 1 & \cdots & 0 & -\alpha_2 \\ \cdot & \cdot & \cdots & \cdot & \cdot \\ 0 & 0 & \cdots & 1 & -\alpha_{k-1} \end{bmatrix}$$

$d(x)$ is the minimum polynomial and $(-1)^k d(x)$ the characteristic polynomial of $\mathbf{M}_{d(x)}$. $\mathbf{M}_{d(x)}$ is similar to its transpose $\mathbf{M}'_{d(x)}$.

4 Let **M** be a square matrix with the elementary divisors $d_1(x)$, $d_2(x)$, . . . , $d_w(x)$. Then **M** (and every matrix similar to **M**) is similar to

5
$$\mathbf{M}^* = \begin{bmatrix} \mathbf{M}_{d_1(x)} & \mathbf{0} & \cdots & \mathbf{0} \\ \mathbf{0} & \mathbf{M}_{d_2(x)} & \cdots & \mathbf{0} \\ \cdot & \cdot & \cdots & \cdot \\ \mathbf{0} & \mathbf{0} & \cdots & \mathbf{M}_{d_w(x)} \end{bmatrix}$$

$\mathbf{M}^*$ is called the *rational canonical form* of $\mathbf{M}^*$. The submatrices $\mathbf{M}_{d_i(x)}$ are called the *elementary blocks* of $\mathbf{M}^*$.

Due to the key role that elementary divisors and similarity transformation matrices play in the analysis and synthesis of linear modular systems, and due to the fact that algorithms for their determination rarely appear in algebra textbooks, these algorithms are included as appendixes at the end of this chapter.

12 *LMS—definition*

An LMS $\mathcal{A}$ is defined mathematically by the following:

1 A finite field $GF(p^k)$.

2 An l-dimensional vector space (called the *input space* of $\mathcal{A}$), an m-dimensional vector space (called the *output space* of $\mathcal{A}$), and an n-dimensional vector space (called the *state space* of $\mathcal{A}$)—all defined over $GF(p^k)$. Vectors in the input, output, and state spaces are called *inputs, outputs,* and *states,* respectively, of $\mathcal{A}$; they are functions of discrete values of time and denoted by $\mathbf{u}(t)$, $\mathbf{y}(t)$, and $\mathbf{s}(t)$, respectively, where t can assume integral values only. Whenever understood or immaterial, (t) will be omitted from the notation; $\mathbf{s}(t+1)$ will be written as $\mathbf{s}'$.

3 Four *characterizing matrices* over $GF(p^k)$

$$\mathbf{A} = [a_{ij}]_{n\times n} \qquad \mathbf{B} = [b_{ij}]_{n\times l} \qquad \mathbf{C} = [c_{ij}]_{m\times n} \qquad \mathbf{D} = [d_{ij}]_{m\times l}$$

4 A rule relating the state at time $t+1$ and output at time t to the state and input at time t

5 $$\mathbf{s}(t+1) = \mathbf{As}(t) + \mathbf{Bu}(t) \qquad \text{or} \qquad \mathbf{s}' = \mathbf{As} + \mathbf{Bu}$$

6 $$\mathbf{y}(t) = \mathbf{Cs}(t) + \mathbf{Du}(t) \qquad \text{or} \qquad \mathbf{y} = \mathbf{Cs} + \mathbf{Du}$$

An LMS as defined above is said to be *over* $GF(p^k)$ and of *order* n. $\mathbf{A}$ is called the *characteristic matrix* of the LMS.

13 *Primitive components*

As will be seen shortly, an LMS over $GF(p^k)$ can be simulated by an interconnection of components called *adders, scalers,* and *delayers,* defined as follows:

1 *Adders* An adder has two or more input terminals and a single output terminal. If the inputs to these terminals are $u_1(t), u_2(t), \ldots, u_r(t)$, then the output is $y(t) = u_1(t) + u_2(t) + \cdots + u_r(t)$, with addition performed as per rules of $GF(p^k)$.

2 *Scalers* A scaler with a *constant* α [taken from $GF(p^k)$] has a single input $u(t)$ and a single output $y(t) = \alpha u(t)$, with multiplication performed as per rules of $GF(p^k)$.

3 *Delayers* A delayer has a single input $u(t)$ and a single output $y(t) = u(t - 1)$.

The above components are referred to as *primitive components over* $GF(p^k)$. The symbology used for these components is shown in Fig. *5.13.1*.

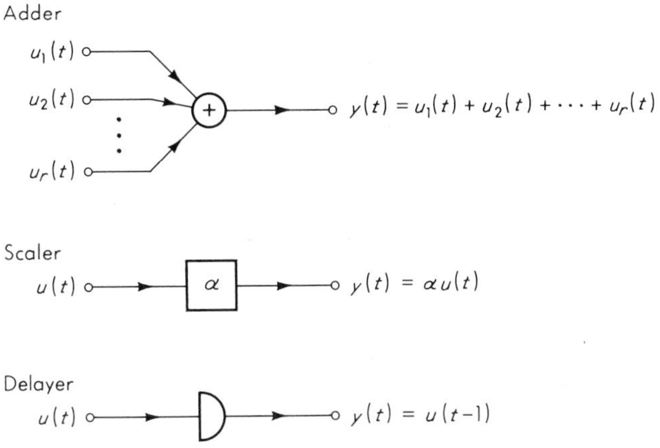

Fig. 5.13.1 Primitive components.

14 *Realization of LMS*

The diagram of a circuit simulating the operation of the LMS $\mathcal{A}$, as defined in Sec. *12*, can be constructed as follows: Draw l input terminals, m output terminals, and n delayers. Number all terminals and delayers. Label the νth input terminal u_ν, the νth output terminal y_ν; label the output and input of the νth delayer s_ν and s'_ν, respectively. Insert an adder in front of each output terminal y_ν and each delayer input s'_ν. The inputs to the adder associated with delayer i $(i = 1,2, \ldots ,n)$ are the outputs s_j, each applied via a scaler with constants a_{ij} $(j = 1,2, \ldots ,n)$ and the inputs u_j, each applied via a scaler with the constant b_{ij} $(j = 1,2, \ldots ,l)$. The inputs to the adder associated with output terminal y_i $(i = 1,2, \ldots ,m)$ are the outputs s_j, each applied via a scaler with the constant c_{ij} $(j = 1,2, \ldots ,n)$, and the inputs u_j, each applied via a scaler with the constant d_{ij} $(j = 1,2, \ldots ,l)$. The general interconnection is indicated in Fig. *5.14.1*.

One can imagine elements from $GF(p^k)$ being fed into the y_i terminals at integral-valued instants of time, and the circuit components per-

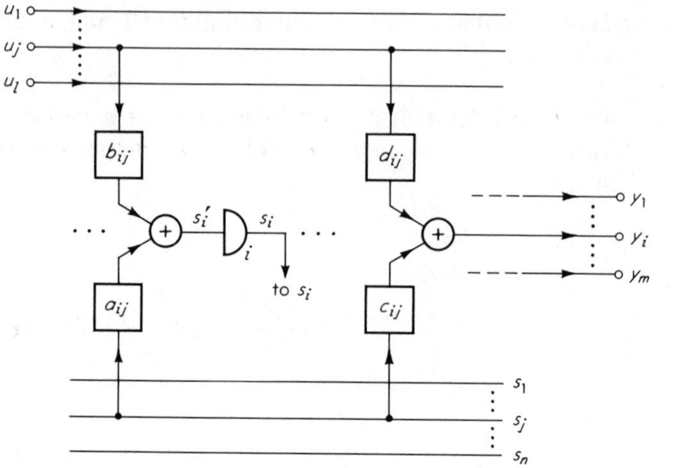

Fig. 5.14.1 Realization of LMS.

forming their function in unison at these same instants. If one now defines

1 $$\mathbf{u} = \begin{bmatrix} u_1 \\ u_2 \\ \cdot \\ \cdot \\ \cdot \\ u_l \end{bmatrix} \qquad \mathbf{y} = \begin{bmatrix} y_1 \\ y_2 \\ \cdot \\ \cdot \\ \cdot \\ y_m \end{bmatrix} \qquad \mathbf{s} = \begin{bmatrix} s_1 \\ s_2 \\ \cdot \\ \cdot \\ \cdot \\ s_n \end{bmatrix} \qquad \mathbf{s}' = \begin{bmatrix} s_1' \\ s_2' \\ \cdot \\ \cdot \\ \cdot \\ s_n' \end{bmatrix}$$

then the operation of the circuit represented by the diagram is precisely

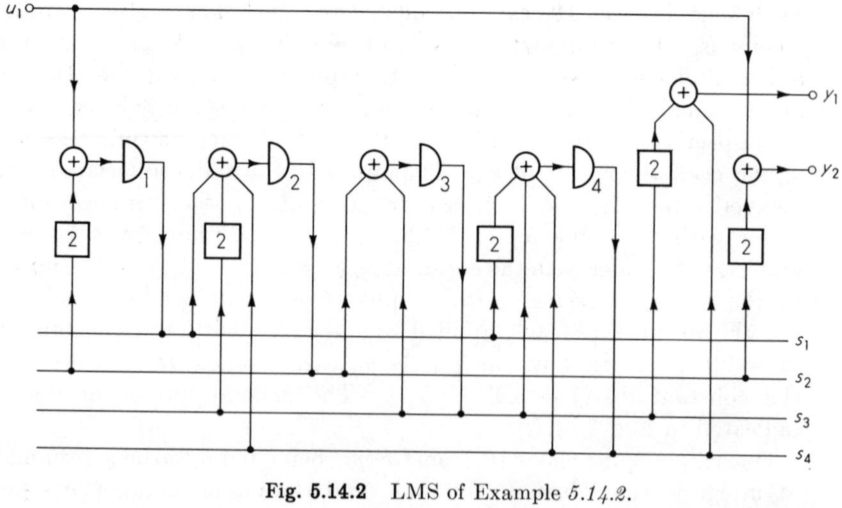

Fig. 5.14.2 LMS of Example *5.14.2*.

that described by *5.12.5* and *5.12.6*. This circuit will be referred to as the *realization* of $\mathfrak{A}$.

2 *Example* The following are the characterizing matrices of a fourth-order LMS over $GF(3)$:

$$\mathbf{A} = \begin{bmatrix} 0 & 2 & 0 & 0 \\ 1 & 0 & 2 & 1 \\ 0 & 1 & 1 & 0 \\ 2 & 0 & 1 & 1 \end{bmatrix} \qquad \mathbf{B} = \begin{bmatrix} 1 \\ 0 \\ 0 \\ 0 \end{bmatrix}$$

$$\mathbf{C} = \begin{bmatrix} 0 & 0 & 2 & 1 \\ 0 & 2 & 0 & 0 \end{bmatrix} \qquad \mathbf{D} = \begin{bmatrix} 0 \\ 1 \end{bmatrix}$$

Its realization is shown in Fig. *5.14.2*.

15 *Matrix characterization of circuits*

An arbitrary circuit consisting of a finite number of adders, scalers, and delayers over $GF(p^k)$ (provided every closed loop contains at least one delayer, to avoid indeterminancy) can be described mathematically as an LMS over $GF(p^k)$. This can be done as follows: Extract from the given circuit all delayers and all terminals assigned as external input and output terminals; label these as shown in Fig. *5.14.1*. Trace the paths leading from s_j to s_i'; compute the product of the scaler constants encountered along each path and add the products [as per rules of $GF(p^k)$]; let a_{ij} denote the resulting sum. Let b_{ij} denote the corresponding quantity for the paths from u_j to s_i'; c_{ij} for the paths from s_j to y_i; d_{ij} for the paths from u_j to y_i. Then the circuit is the realization of an LMS of order n over $GF(p^k)$, whose characterizing matrices are **A**, **B**, **C**, and **D** as defined in Sec. *12*.

Thus, every LMS over $GF(p^k)$ can be modeled by a circuit of adders, scalers, and delayers over $GF(p^k)$, and every such circuit (subject to the delayer-in-every-loop clause) can be described abstractly as an LMS. Henceforth, the term LMS will refer to both the abstract system and to any circuit realizing this system.

16 *Multiplication of elements in $GF(p^k)$*

α and β, elements in $GF(p^k)$, can be represented as polynomials in ξ over $GF(p)$ (see Sec. *8*):

1 $$\alpha(\xi) = \alpha_0 + \alpha_1\xi + \cdots + \alpha_{k-1}\xi^{k-1}$$

2 $$\beta(\xi) = \beta_0 + \beta_1\xi + \cdots + \beta_{k-1}\xi^{k-1}$$

or, alternatively, as k-dimensional vectors over $GF(p)$:

3 $$\boldsymbol{\alpha} = \begin{bmatrix} \alpha_0 \\ \alpha_1 \\ \cdot \\ \cdot \\ \cdot \\ \alpha_{k-1} \end{bmatrix} \qquad \boldsymbol{\beta} = \begin{bmatrix} \beta_0 \\ \beta_1 \\ \cdot \\ \cdot \\ \cdot \\ \beta_{k-1} \end{bmatrix}$$

If the modulus polynomial of $GF(p^k)$ is

4 $$p(x) = \eta_0 + \eta_1 x + \cdots + \eta_{k-1}x^{k-1} + x^k$$

we have

5 $$\begin{aligned}\xi\beta(\xi) &= \beta_0\xi + \beta_1\xi^2 + \cdots + \beta_{k-2}\xi^{k-1} + \beta_{k-1}(-\eta_0 - \eta_1\xi - \cdots \\ &\qquad - \eta_{k-1}\xi^{k-1}) \\ &= -\eta_0\beta_{k-1} + (\beta_0 - \eta_1\beta_{k-1})\xi + \cdots + (\beta_{k-2} - \eta_{k-1}\beta_{k-1})\xi^{k-1}\end{aligned}$$

Denoting the vector representing $\xi^i\beta(\xi)$ by $\boldsymbol{\gamma}_i$, *5* implies

6 $$\boldsymbol{\gamma}_1 = \mathbf{M}_{p(x)}\boldsymbol{\beta}$$

where $\mathbf{M}_{p(x)}$ is the companion matrix of $p(x)$ (see Sec. *11*). By induction

7 $$\boldsymbol{\gamma}_i = \mathbf{M}^i_{p(x)}\boldsymbol{\beta} \qquad i = 1, 2, \ldots$$

Now, denote the vector representation of $\pi(\xi) = \alpha(\xi)\beta(\xi)$ by $\boldsymbol{\pi}$. Then

8 $$\pi(\xi) = \alpha_0\beta(\xi) + \alpha_1\xi\beta(\xi) + \cdots + \alpha_{k-1}\xi^{k-1}\beta(\xi)$$

9 $$\begin{aligned}\boldsymbol{\pi} &= \alpha_0\boldsymbol{\gamma}_0 + \alpha_1\boldsymbol{\gamma}_1 + \cdots + \alpha_{k-1}\boldsymbol{\gamma}_{k-1} \\ &= (\alpha_0 + \alpha_1\mathbf{M}_{p(x)} + \cdots + \alpha_{k-1}\mathbf{M}^{k-1}_{p(x)})\boldsymbol{\beta} \\ &= \alpha(\mathbf{M}_{p(x)})\boldsymbol{\beta}\end{aligned}$$

where $\alpha(\mathbf{M}_{p(x)})$ is the matrix obtained by replacing every ξ in $\alpha(\xi)$ with $\mathbf{M}_{p(x)}$.

10 *Example* $\alpha(\xi) = 1 + \xi^2$, $\beta(\xi) = 1 + \xi + \xi^3$ are elements in $GF(2^4)$, where the modulus polynomial is $p(x) = 1 + x + x^4$. In this case:

$$\mathbf{M}_{p(x)} = \begin{bmatrix} 0 & 0 & 0 & 1 \\ 1 & 0 & 0 & 1 \\ 0 & 1 & 0 & 0 \\ 0 & 0 & 1 & 0 \end{bmatrix} \qquad \alpha(\mathbf{M}_{p(x)}) = \begin{bmatrix} 1 & 0 & 1 & 0 \\ 0 & 1 & 1 & 1 \\ 1 & 0 & 1 & 1 \\ 0 & 1 & 0 & 1 \end{bmatrix}$$

$$\boldsymbol{\beta} = \begin{bmatrix} 1 \\ 1 \\ 0 \\ 1 \end{bmatrix} \qquad \boldsymbol{\pi} = \begin{bmatrix} 1 \\ 0 \\ 0 \\ 0 \end{bmatrix}$$

Hence, $\alpha(\xi)\beta(\xi) = 1$.

17 *Realization with components over GF(p)*

Given an LMS $\mathfrak{A}$ over $GF(p^k)$, consider an LMS $\mathfrak{A}'$ over $GF(p)$, constructed as follows: Replace every line in $\mathfrak{A}$ with a bundle of k lines, numbered 1, 2, . . . , k; if the original line carries $\alpha(\xi)$, then line i in the bundle carries the ith coordinate of $\boldsymbol{\alpha}$. Replace every adder with

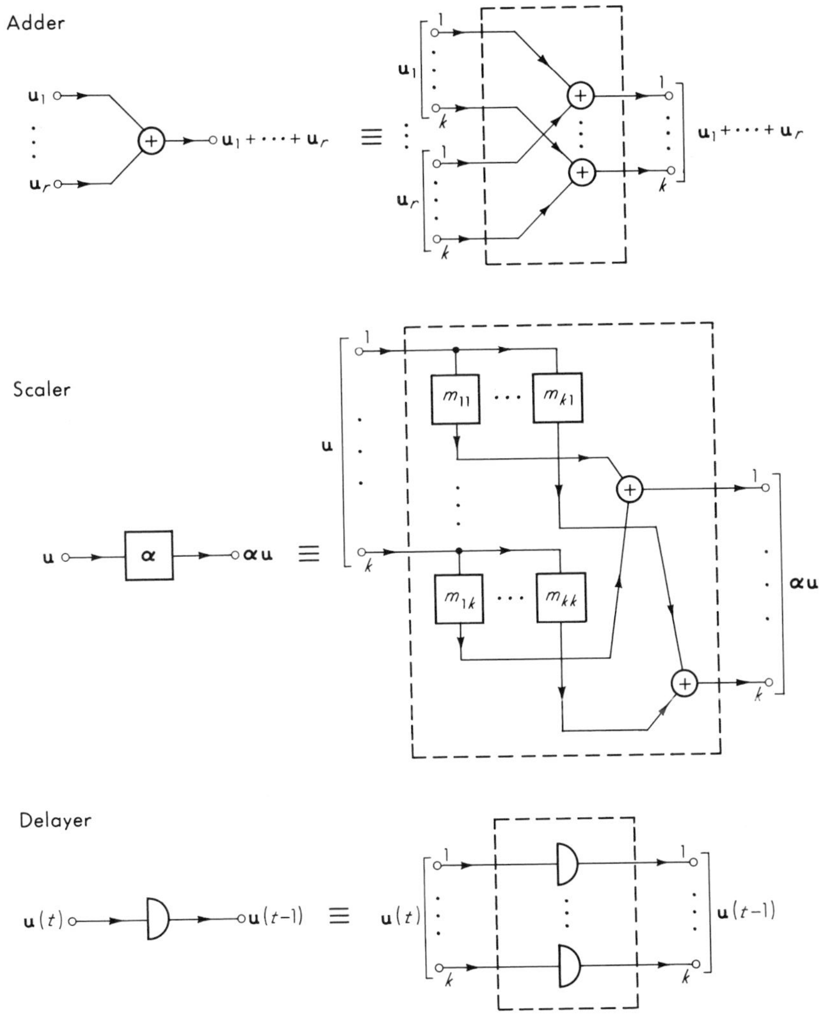

Fig. 5.17.1 Realization of components over $GF(p^k)$ with components over $GF(p)$.

k adders over $GF(p)$, numbered 1, 2, . . . , k; the inputs to adder i are the input lines labeled i, and its output is the output line labeled i. Replace every scaler whose constant is α with a network of adders and scalers over $GF(p)$, in the following manner: If m_{ij} is the (i,j) element of $\alpha(\mathbf{M}_{p(x)})$, then line j of the input is connected to line i of the output via a scaler with the constant m_{ij}. Finally, replace every delayer with k delayers over $GF(p)$, numbered 1, 2, . . . , k; both the input and output lines of delayer i are labeled i. These substitutions are summarized in Fig. *5.17.1*.

By design, the sole difference between $\mathcal{A}$ and $\mathcal{A}'$ is that in $\mathcal{A}$ the variables [elements in $GF(p^k)$] are transmitted via single lines and in $\mathcal{A}'$ the variables [elements in $GF(p)$] are transmitted via bundles of k lines. The corresponding difference in the matrix representation *5.12.5* and *5.12.6* is that, for $\mathcal{A}$, the components of any vector variable $\mathbf{v}$ are polynomials, while for $\mathcal{A}'$ the components of $\mathbf{v}$ are themselves vectors [with each component $\alpha(\xi)$ replaced with $\boldsymbol{\alpha}$]. Hence, insofar as the analysis and synthesis of $\mathcal{A}$ is concerned, no loss in generality is incurred and a great deal of convenience is earned by consistently replacing it with $\mathcal{A}'$. Accordingly, we shall henceforth make the tacit assumption that *every LMS is an LMS over GF(p)*.

18 *The general response formula*

1 **Theorem**

$$\mathbf{s}(t) = \mathbf{A}^t\mathbf{s}(0) + \sum_{\nu=0}^{t-1} \mathbf{A}^{t-\nu-1}\mathbf{B}\mathbf{u}(\nu)$$

Proof (by induction on t) Setting $t = 0$ in *5.12.5*, we have

$$\mathbf{s}(1) = \mathbf{A}\mathbf{s}(0) + \mathbf{B}\mathbf{u}(0)$$

which proves *1* for $t = 1$. Hypothesizing that *1* is true, *5.12.5* yields

2
$$\mathbf{s}(t+1) = \mathbf{A}\left[\mathbf{A}^t\mathbf{s}(0) + \sum_{\nu=0}^{t-1} \mathbf{A}^{t-\nu-1}\mathbf{B}\mathbf{u}(\nu)\right] + \mathbf{B}\mathbf{u}(t)$$
$$= \mathbf{A}^{t+1}\mathbf{s}(0) + \sum_{\nu=0}^{t} \mathbf{A}^{t-\nu}\mathbf{B}\mathbf{u}(\nu)$$

which proves *1* for $t + 1$.

3 **Theorem**

$$\mathbf{y}(t) = \mathbf{C}\mathbf{A}^t\mathbf{s}(0) + \sum_{\nu=0}^{t} \mathbf{H}(t-\nu)\mathbf{u}(\nu)$$

4 where
$$\mathbf{H}(t) = \begin{cases} \mathbf{D} & t = 0 \\ \mathbf{CA}^{t-1}\mathbf{B} & t > 0 \end{cases}$$

Proof Substituting *1* in *5.12.6*:

$$\mathbf{y}(t) = \mathbf{C}\left[\mathbf{A}^t\mathbf{s}(0) + \sum_{\nu=0}^{t-1} \mathbf{A}^{t-\nu-1}\mathbf{Bu}(\nu)\right] + \mathbf{Du}(t)$$
$$= \mathbf{CA}^t\mathbf{s}(0) + \sum_{\nu=0}^{t} \mathbf{H}(t - \nu)\mathbf{u}(\nu)$$

where $\mathbf{H}(t - \nu) = \mathbf{CA}^{t-\nu-1}\mathbf{B}$ when $t - \nu - 1 \geq 0$, and $\mathbf{H}(t - \nu) = \mathbf{D}$ when $t - \nu - 1 = -1$.

19 *Free and forced responses*

From *5.18.3* one can see that the response of an LMS can be decomposed into two components: The *free response*

1
$$\mathbf{y}(t)\Big|_{\text{free}} = \mathbf{CA}^t\mathbf{s}(0)$$

obtained by setting $\mathbf{u}(t) = \mathbf{0}$ for all $t \geq 0$, and the *forced response*

2
$$\mathbf{y}(t)\Big|_{\text{forced}} = \sum_{\nu=0}^{t} \mathbf{H}(t - \nu)\mathbf{u}(\nu)$$

obtained by setting $\mathbf{s}(0) = \mathbf{0}$. Given any input sequence $\mathbf{u}(t)$ and initial state $\mathbf{s}(0)$, these two components can be found separately and then added up. This is a fortunate circumstance, as there are excellent techniques for finding the components individually (state-graph methods for the free response and d-transform methods for the forced response), but no satisfactory method for finding them simultaneously.

Depending on the function for which the LMS is intended, one often finds that only one of the two response components is actually of interest. If the LMS is used as a *sequence generator*, its performance is described by the free response; if the LMS is used as a *sequence transformer*, its performance is described by the forced response.

20 *State graphs*

Let $\mathcal{A}$ be an LMS of order n over $GF(p)$, with the characteristic matrix $\mathbf{A}$. The *state graph* of $\mathcal{A}$ (or of $\mathbf{A}$) is an oriented graph with p^n vertices, one for each state of $\mathcal{A}$ (the terms *vertex* and *state* will be used interchangeably); an arrow points from state $\mathbf{s}_1$ to state $\mathbf{s}_2$ if and only if

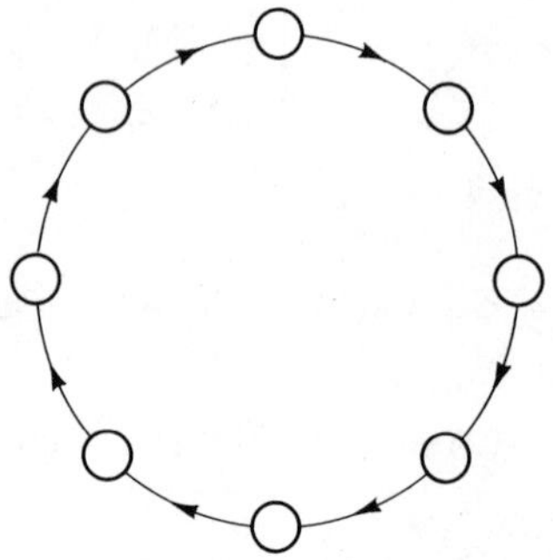

Fig. 5.20.1 Pure cycle of length 8.

$\mathbf{s}_2 = \mathbf{A}\mathbf{s}_1$ (in this case we say that $\mathbf{s}_1$ *leads to* $\mathbf{s}_2$ or $\mathbf{s}_2$ is *reachable from* $\mathbf{s}_1$). Thus, the state graph displays the sequence of states pursued by the input-free $\mathcal{A}$, given any specified initial state. As seen from *5.19.1*, the free response at any time is merely a fixed linear transformation of the state at that time; thus, the state graph (as a concept as well as a visual aid) constitutes a tool for determining the input-free behavior of the LMS.

A *path* of *length* r in a state graph is a sequence of r branches $b_1, b_2, \ldots, b_r$ and $r + 1$ vertices $v_1, v_2, \ldots, v_{r+1}$, such that b_i points from v_i to v_{i+1} $(i = 1,2, \ldots, r)$. If the v_i are distinct except $v_{r+1} = v_1$, the

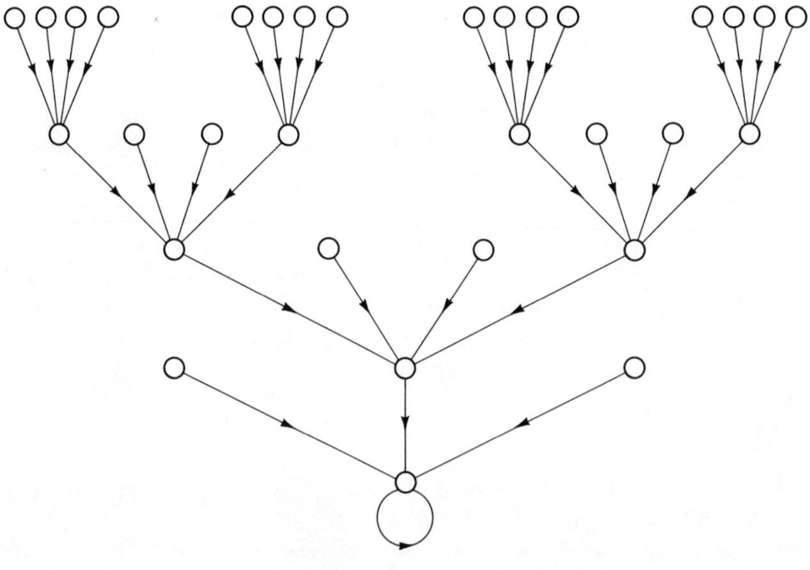

Fig. 5.20.2 Tree of height 4.

path is a *cycle* of length r. If the only vertex leading to v_{i+1} is v_i ($i = 1,2, \ldots ,r - 1$) and the only vertex leading to v_1 is v_r, then the cycle is called a *pure cycle*.

A *tree* is a subgraph with the following properties: (*a*) One vertex, called the *root* of the tree, is reachable from all other vertices (and possibly from itself). (*b*) There are no cycles in the subgraph (except, possibly, for a cycle of length 1 touching the root). The tree vertices reaching the root via a path of length ν (in ν steps) but not less than ν, form the νth *level* of the tree. A tree whose highest level is the Lth is said to be a tree of *height* L.

Figure *5.20.1* shows a pure cycle of length 8, and Fig. *5.20.2* a tree of height 4.

21 *Isomorphism of state graphs*

Two state graphs, say S and $\bar{S}$, are *isomorphic* if a one-to-one correspondence can be established between the states of S and $\bar{S}$ in the following manner: If $\mathbf{s}$ of S corresponds to $\bar{\mathbf{s}}$ of $\bar{S}$, then the successor of $\mathbf{s}$ corresponds to the successor of $\bar{\mathbf{s}}$. Thus, except for state labeling, isomorphic state graphs are identical. The same definition applies to isomorphism among state subgraphs.

1 **Theorem** The state graphs of similar characteristic matrices are isomorphic.

Proof Let $\mathbf{A}$ and $\bar{\mathbf{A}} = \mathbf{PAP}^{-1}$ be similar characteristic matrices of $\mathfrak{A}$ and $\bar{\mathfrak{A}}$, respectively. Establish the correspondence $\mathbf{s} \rightarrow \bar{\mathbf{s}} = \mathbf{P}\bar{\mathbf{s}}$. Since $\mathbf{P}$ is nonsingular, this correspondence is one to one. Moreover $\bar{\mathbf{A}}\bar{\mathbf{s}} = (\mathbf{PAP}^{-1})(\mathbf{Ps}) = \mathbf{P}(\mathbf{As})$, and hence the successor of $\bar{\mathbf{s}}$ corresponds to the successor of $\mathbf{s}$.

Thus, if one is interested only in the structural properties of the state graph, the graph of $\bar{\mathbf{A}}$ is just as adequate as that of $\mathbf{A}$. In particular, $\mathbf{A}$ can be replaced with its rational canonical form $\mathbf{A}^*$ (see Sec. *11*)—a step which results in a great deal of simplification in both the analysis and synthesis of LMS.

22 *Nonsingular LMS*

An LMS is *nonsingular* if its characteristic matrix is nonsingular (i.e., if $|\mathbf{A}| \neq 0$). The elementary divisors of a nonsingular LMS, then, are indivisible by x, and the elementary blocks of $\mathbf{A}^*$ are all nonsingular (see Secs. *6*, *10*, and *11*).

1 **Theorem** The state graph of a nonsingular LMS consists of pure cycles only.

Proof Since $\mathbf{A}$ is nonsingular, every state $\mathbf{s}$ has exactly one predecessor, namely $\mathbf{A}^{-1}\mathbf{s}$. Since $\mathbf{s}$ necessarily has exactly one successor, namely $\mathbf{As}$, the theorem follows.

Note that a state graph must contain at least one cycle of length 1—the cycle containing the null state $\mathbf{0}$.

In Secs. *23* to *31* our discussion will be confined entirely to nonsingular LMS. In this discussion, the term *cycle* will be understood to mean *pure cycle*.

23 *State period and matrix period*

The *period* of a given state $\mathbf{s}$ is the least integer T such that $\mathbf{A}^T\mathbf{s} = \mathbf{s}$. Thus, the period of $\mathbf{s}$ is the length of the cycle which includes $\mathbf{s}$.

The *period* of $\mathbf{A}$ is the least integer T such that $\mathbf{A}^T = \mathbf{I}$.

1 **Theorem** If $T_1, T_2, \ldots, T_w$ are state periods realized by an LMS whose characteristic matrix is $\mathbf{A}$, then the period of $\mathbf{A}$ is

$$\operatorname{lcm}(T_1, T_2, \ldots, T_w)$$

Proof Let T denote the period of $\mathbf{A}$ and let T' denote

$$\operatorname{lcm}(T_1, T_2, \ldots, T_w)$$

Since $\mathbf{A}^T\mathbf{s} = \mathbf{s}$ for every $\mathbf{s}$, T must be a multiple of each T_i and hence a multiple of T'. On the other hand, $(\mathbf{A}^{T'} - \mathbf{I})\mathbf{s} = \mathbf{0}$ for all $\mathbf{s}$, and hence $(\mathbf{A}^{T'} - \mathbf{I})\mathbf{I} = \mathbf{0}$ or $\mathbf{A}^{T'} = \mathbf{I}$. Thus, $T' \geq T$. Therefore we must have $T = T'$.

2 **Theorem** Suppose $\mathbf{A}$ has the form

3
$$\mathbf{A} = \begin{bmatrix} \mathbf{A}_1 & \mathbf{0} \\ \mathbf{0} & \mathbf{A}_2 \end{bmatrix}$$

and let $\begin{bmatrix} \mathbf{s}_1 \\ \mathbf{0} \end{bmatrix}$ and $\begin{bmatrix} \mathbf{0} \\ \mathbf{s}_2 \end{bmatrix}$ be two states partitioned in accordance with $\mathbf{A}$ in *3*, having the periods T_1 and T_2, respectively. Then the period of $\mathbf{s} = \begin{bmatrix} \mathbf{s}_1 \\ \mathbf{s}_2 \end{bmatrix}$ is $\operatorname{lcm}(T_1, T_2)$.

Proof If T is the period of **s**, then T is the least integer such that $\mathbf{A}^T\mathbf{s} = \mathbf{s}$, or such that

4 $$\begin{bmatrix} \mathbf{A}_1{}^T\mathbf{s}_1 \\ \mathbf{A}_2{}^T\mathbf{s}_2 \end{bmatrix} = \begin{bmatrix} \mathbf{s}_1 \\ \mathbf{s}_2 \end{bmatrix}$$

Hence, T must be a multiple of T_1 and T_2. Since *4* holds when

$$T = \text{lcm}\,(T_1,T_2)$$

the theorem follows.

24 *Cycle sets*

Let $\mathcal{A}$ be a nonsingular LMS with the characteristic matrix **A**. Up to isomorphism, the state graph of $\mathcal{A}$ can be described by a set of integer pairs

1 $$\Sigma = \{N_1[T_1],N_2[T_2], \ . \ . \ . \ ,N_q[T_q]\}$$

where N_i is the number of cycles of length T_i. Σ is called the *cycle set* of $\mathcal{A}$ (or of **A**), and each integer pair $N_i[T_i]$ a *cycle term.*

Now consider a matrix **A** of the form *5.23.3*. Suppose the state graph of $\mathbf{A}_1$ has N_1 cycles of length T_1, and the state graph of $\mathbf{A}_2$ has N_2 cycles of length T_2. Hence there are N_1T_1 states of the form $\begin{bmatrix} \mathbf{s}_1 \\ \mathbf{0} \end{bmatrix}$ and period T_1, and N_2T_2 states of the form $\begin{bmatrix} \mathbf{0} \\ \mathbf{s}_2 \end{bmatrix}$ and period T_2. By *5.23.2*, the state graph of **A** must contain $N_1N_2T_1T_2$ states of period lcm (T_1,T_2), and hence $N_1N_2T_1T_2/\text{lcm}\,(T_1,T_2) = N_1N_2\,\text{gcd}\,(T_1,T_2)$ cycles of length lcm (T_1,T_2). (There may be other cycles of this length due to other T_1, T_2 pairs with the same least common multiple.)

We shall now define the *product* of two cycle terms as a third cycle term, obtained by the following rule

2 $$N_1[T_1] \cdot N_2[T_2] = N_1N_2\,\text{gcd}\,(T_1,T_2)\,[\text{lcm}\,(T_1,T_2)]$$

If $\Sigma_1 = \{a_1,a_2, \ . \ . \ . \ ,a_{q_1}\}$ and $\Sigma_2 = \{b_1,b_2, \ . \ . \ . \ ,b_{q_2}\}$, where the a_i and b_j are cycle terms, then the product $\Sigma_1\Sigma_2$ is defined as a cycle set whose cycle terms are all possible products a_ib_j. In view of the preceding paragraph and on the basis of these definitions, the following can now be stated:

3 **Theorem** Let

4 $$\mathbf{A} = \begin{bmatrix} \mathbf{A}_1 & \mathbf{0} \\ \mathbf{0} & \mathbf{A}_2 \end{bmatrix}$$

If the cycle sets of $\mathbf{A}_1$ and $\mathbf{A}_2$ are Σ_1 and Σ_2, respectively, then the cycle set of $\mathbf{A}$ is $\Sigma_1\Sigma_2$.

5 *Example* Given:

6 $$\Sigma_1 = \{2[1], 3[2], 7[8]\}$$

7 $$\Sigma_2 = \{4[1], 2[6]\}$$

we have

8 $$\begin{aligned}\Sigma_1\Sigma_2 &= \{2[1], 3[2], 7[8]\}\{4[1], 2[6]\}\\ &= \{2[1]\cdot 4[1],\ 2[1]\cdot 2[6],\ 3[2]\cdot 4[1],\ 3[2]\cdot 2[6],\ 7[8]\cdot 4[1],\ 7[8]\cdot 2[6]\}\\ &= \{8[1], 4[6], 12[2], 12[6], 28[8], 28[24]\}\\ &= \{8[1], 12[2], 16[6], 28[8], 28[24]\}\end{aligned}$$

25 *Cycle set computation—strategy*

The characteristic matrix of an LMS can be replaced with its rational canonical form without impairing its cycle set. For purposes of computing cycle sets, therefore, this matrix can be assumed to have the form

1 $$\mathbf{A} = \begin{bmatrix} \mathbf{M}_{d_1(x)} & \mathbf{0} & \cdots & \mathbf{0} \\ \mathbf{0} & \mathbf{M}_{d_2(x)} & \cdots & \mathbf{0} \\ \cdots & \cdots & \cdots & \cdots \\ \mathbf{0} & \mathbf{0} & \cdots & \mathbf{M}_{d_w(x)} \end{bmatrix}$$

From *5.24.3*, by induction, we thus have:

2 **Theorem** Let $d_1(x), d_2(x), \ldots, d_w(x)$ be the elementary divisors of $\mathbf{A}$, and let Σ_i be the cycle set of $\mathbf{M}_{d_i(x)}$. Then the cycle set Σ of $\mathbf{A}$ is given by

3 $$\Sigma = \Sigma_1\Sigma_2 \cdots \Sigma_w$$

What remains to be done is the formulation of a procedure for determining the cycle set of a typical elementary block $\mathbf{M}_{d_i(x)}$, where

$$d_i(x) = [p_i(x)]^{e_i}$$

Once the cycle set is determined for each such block in $\mathbf{A}$, the cycle set of the entire matrix can be computed by a straightforward application of *2*.

26 *States as ring elements*

Consider an LMS $\mathfrak{M}$ of order n over $GF(p)$, with the characteristic matrix $\mathbf{M}_{d(x)}$, where

1 $$d(x) = \alpha_0 + \alpha_1 x + \cdots + \alpha_{n-1}x^{n-1} + x^n = [p(x)]^e \qquad \alpha_0 \neq 0$$

For reasons to become apparent shortly, it is convenient to regard every state of $\mathfrak{M}$ as an element in the ring of polynomials over $GF(p)$ mod $d(x)$. The state

2 $$\mathbf{s} = \begin{bmatrix} \sigma_0 \\ \sigma_1 \\ \cdot \\ \cdot \\ \cdot \\ \sigma_{n-1} \end{bmatrix}$$

will correspond to the ring element

3 $$s(\xi) = \sigma_0 + \sigma_1\xi + \cdots + \sigma_{n-1}\xi^{n-1}$$

4 **Theorem** If $s(\xi)$ represents the initial state $\mathbf{s}$ of $\mathfrak{M}$, then the state attained in i steps (i.e., the state $\mathbf{M}^i_{d(x)}\mathbf{s}$) is represented by $\xi^i\mathbf{s}(\xi)$.
Proof

5 $$\mathbf{s}' = \mathbf{M}_{d(x)}\mathbf{s} = \begin{bmatrix} 0 & 0 & \cdots & 0 & -\alpha_0 \\ 1 & 0 & \cdots & 0 & -\alpha_1 \\ 0 & 1 & \cdots & 0 & -\alpha_2 \\ \cdot & \cdot & \cdots & \cdot & \cdot \\ 0 & 0 & \cdots & 1 & -\alpha_{n-1} \end{bmatrix} \begin{bmatrix} \sigma_0 \\ \sigma_1 \\ \sigma_2 \\ \cdot \\ \cdot \\ \cdot \\ \sigma_{n-1} \end{bmatrix} = \begin{bmatrix} -\alpha_0\sigma_{n-1} \\ \sigma_0 - \alpha_1\sigma_{n-1} \\ \sigma_1 - \alpha_2\sigma_{n-1} \\ \cdot \\ \cdot \\ \cdot \\ \sigma_{n-2} - \alpha_{n-1}\sigma_{n-1} \end{bmatrix}$$

Hence

6 $$\begin{aligned} s'(\xi) &= -\alpha_0\sigma_{n-1} + (\sigma_0 - \alpha_1\sigma_{n-1})\xi + (\sigma_1 - \alpha_2\sigma_{n-1})\xi^2 + \cdots \\ &\qquad + (\sigma_{n-2} - \alpha_{n-1}\sigma_{n-1})\xi^{n-1} \\ &= \sigma_0\xi + \sigma_1\xi^2 + \cdots + \sigma_{n-2}\xi^{n-1} - \sigma_{n-1}(\alpha_0 + \alpha_1\xi + \cdots \\ &\qquad + \alpha_{n-1}\xi^{n-1}) \\ &= \xi s(\xi) - \sigma_{n-1}d(\xi) = \xi s(\xi) \end{aligned}$$

4 then follows by induction.

27 *Cycle set of an elementary block*

We have now converted the problem of finding the period of a state $\mathbf{s}$ of $\mathfrak{M}$ into that of finding the least integer T such that

1 $$\xi^T s(\xi) = s(\xi)$$

2 or

$$(1 - \xi^T)s(\xi) = 0$$

In the ring of polynomials over $GF(p)$, *2* implies

3

$$(1 - x^T)s(x) = g(x)[p(x)]^e$$

for some polynomial $g(x)$. In what follows, h will denote the degree of $p(x)$, and T_i the period of $[p(x)]^i$.

4 **Lemma** If $s(x)$ is divisible by $[p(x)]^{e-1}$ but not by $[p(x)]^{e-i+1}$, then the period of $\mathbf{s}$ is T_i.
Proof By the prime factorization theorem (see *5.6.1*), the conditions in *4* imply that T is the least integer such that $1 - x^T$ is to be a multiple of $[p(x)]^i$. Since T_i, too, is the least integer such that $1 - x^{T_i}$ is a multiple of $[p(x)]^i$, $T_i = T$.

5 **Lemma** $\mathfrak{M}$ has $p^{ih} - p^{(i-1)h}$ states of period T_i $(i = 1,2, \ldots ,e)$.
Proof The number of distinct polynomials $s(x)$ of degree n divisible by $[p(x)]^{e-i}$ is $p^{n-h(e-i)} = p^{ih}$. These include all polynomials of degree n divisible by $[p(x)]^{e-i+1}$, which number $p^{n-h(e-i+1)} = p^{(i-1)h}$. Hence, the number of distinct states $\mathbf{s}$ satisfying the conditions in *4* (and thus having the period T_i) is $p^{ih} - p^{(i-1)h}$.

6 **Corollary** The state graph of $\mathfrak{M}$ has $(p^{ih} - p^{(i-1)h})/T_i$ cycles of length T_i.

Now, since

7

$$\sum_{i=1}^{e} (p^{ih} - p^{(i-1)h}) = p^{eh} - 1 = p^n - 1$$

the cycles counted via *6* account for all states save one. The state unaccounted for is the null state—the only one not satisfying the conditions in *4* with any i. Hence, the cycles described in *6* plus one cycle of length 1 constitute the entire graph of $\mathfrak{M}$. In conclusion, we have:

8 **Theorem** Let $p(x)$ be an irreducible polynomial (other than x) of degree h, and let T_i denote the period of $[p(x)]^i$. Then the cycle set of $\mathbf{M}_{[p(x)]^e}$ is given by

$$\left\{1[1], \frac{p^h - 1}{T_1}[T_1], \frac{p^{2h} - p^h}{T_2}[T_2], \frac{p^{3h} - p^{2h}}{T_3}[T_3], \ldots, \frac{p^{eh} - p^{(e-1)h}}{T_e}[T_e]\right\}$$

28 *Cycle set computation—summary*

We can now summarize the procedure for obtaining the cycle set of a nonsingular LMS $\mathcal{A}$ over $GF(p)$, with the characteristic matrix $\mathbf{A}$:

1 Find the elementary divisors of $\mathbf{A}$, say, $d_1(x), d_2(x), \ldots, d_w(x)$.

2 Suppose $d_i(x) = [p_i(x)]^{e_i}$, where $p_i(x)$ is of degree h_i. Find the period $T_1^{(i)}$ from tables or by trial ($T_1^{(i)}$ must divide $p^{h_i} - 1$), for $i = 1, 2, \ldots, w$.

3 Evaluate $T_j^{(i)}$, the period of $[p_i(x)]^j$ for $i = 1, 2, \ldots, w$ and $j = 1, 2, \ldots, e_i$: $T_j^{(i)} = p^{k_j}T_1^{(i)}$, where k_j is the least integer such that $p^{k_j} \geq j$.

4 Determine the cycle set of $\mathbf{M}_{d_i(x)}$ for $i = 1, 2, \ldots, w$:

5 $$\Sigma_i = \left\{1[1], \frac{p^{h_i} - 1}{T_1^{(i)}}[T_1^{(i)}], \frac{p^{2h_i} - p^{h_i}}{T_1^{(i)}}[T_2^{(i)}], \ldots, \frac{p^{e_ih_i} - p^{(e_i-1)h_i}}{T_{e_i}^{(i)}}[T_{e_i}^{(i)}]\right\}$$

6 The cycle set of $\mathbf{A}$ is given by

7 $$\Sigma = \Sigma_1\Sigma_2 \cdots \Sigma_w$$

8 *Example* Consider the following characteristic matrix over $GF(2)$:

9 $$\mathbf{A} = \mathbf{A}^* = \left[\begin{array}{ccc|cc} 0 & 0 & 1 & 0 & 0 \\ 1 & 0 & 1 & 0 & 0 \\ 0 & 1 & 1 & 0 & 0 \\ \hline 0 & 0 & 0 & 0 & 1 \\ 0 & 0 & 0 & 1 & 1 \end{array}\right]$$

In this case

10 $$d_1(x) = 1 + x + x^2 + x^3 = (1 + x)^3 \qquad p_1(x) = 1 + x \qquad h_1 = 1 \qquad e_1 = 3$$

11 $$d_2(x) = 1 + x + x^2 \qquad p_2(x) = 1 + x + x^2 \qquad h_2 = 2 \qquad e_2 = 1$$

12 $$T_1^{(1)} = 1 \qquad T_2^{(1)} = 2 \qquad T_3^{(1)} = 4$$

13 $$T_1^{(2)} = 3$$

14 $$\Sigma_1 = \left\{1[1], \frac{2-1}{1}[1], \frac{2^2-2}{2}[2], \frac{2^3-2^2}{4}[4]\right\}$$

$$= \{1[1],1[1],1[2],1[4]\} = \{2[1],1[2],1[4]\}$$

15 $$\Sigma_2 = \left\{1[1], \frac{2^2-1}{3}[3]\right\} = \{1[1],1[3]\}$$

16 $$\Sigma = \Sigma_1\Sigma_2 = \{2[1],1[2],1[4]\}\{1[1],1[3]\}$$

$$= \{2[1],1[2],2[3],1[4],1[6],1[12]\}$$

The state graph of $\mathbf{A}$ is shown in Fig. *5.28.1*.

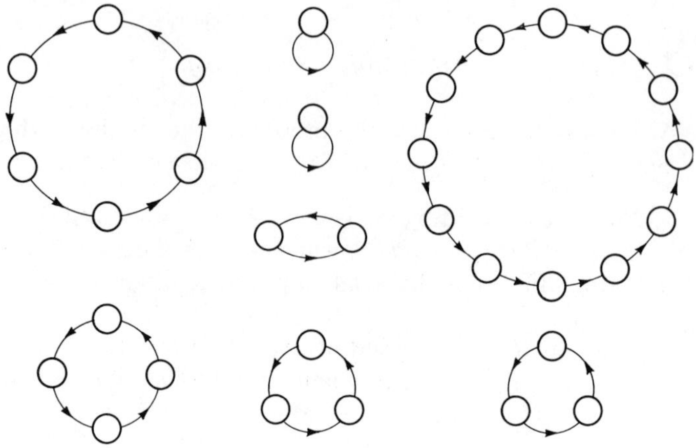

Fig. 5.28.1 State graph of LMS of Example *5.28.8*.

29 *Fundamental periods of an LMS*

Let us list the periods associated with each Σ_i, as given in *5.28.5* (with $T_0^{(1)} = 1$ for all i):

1

$$\begin{matrix} T_0^{(1)}, & T_1^{(1)}, & \dots, & T_{e_1}^{(1)} \\ T_0^{(2)}, & T_1^{(2)}, & \dots, & T_{e_2}^{(2)} \\ \dots & \dots & \dots & \dots \\ T_0^{(w)}, & T_1^{(w)}, & \dots, & T_{e_w}^{(w)} \end{matrix}$$

From *5.28.7* it follows that the state periods realizable by $\mathcal{A}$ are given by

2

$$\operatorname{lcm}\,(T_{j_1}^{(1)}, T_{j_2}^{(2)}, \dots, T_{j_w}^{(w)})$$

for every combination of integers $j_1, j_2, \dots, j_w$ $(0 \le j_\nu \le e_\nu)$. Now, if $d_{i_1}(x)$ divides $d_{i_2}(x)$, Σ_{i_1} is certainly included in Σ_{i_2}; moreover, the least common multiple of a period in Σ_{i_1} and a period in Σ_{i_2} is some period in Σ_{i_2}. Hence, if one wishes to compute all possible periods realizable by $\mathcal{A}$ (without computing its cycle set), only the leading elementary divisors (see Sec. *10*) need to be considered. We thus have:

3 **Theorem** Let $\mathcal{A}$ be a nonsingular LMS with the characteristic matrix **A**. Let the minimum polynomial of **A** be

4

$$m_A(x) = [p_1(x)]^{e_1}[p_2(x)]^{e_2} \cdots [p_r(x)]^{e_r}$$

and denote the period of $[p_i(x)]^j$ by $T_j^{(i)}$. List the periods

5

$$\begin{array}{l} T_0^{(1)}, T_1^{(1)}, \ldots, T_{e_1}^{(1)} \\ T_0^{(2)}, T_1^{(2)}, \ldots, T_{e_2}^{(2)} \\ \cdots\cdots\cdots\cdots \\ T_0^{(r)}, T_1^{(r)}, \ldots, T_{e_r}^{(r)} \end{array}$$

Then the state periods realizable by $\mathcal{A}$ are given by all integers of the form

6 $$\text{lcm}\,(T_{j_1}^{(1)}, T_{j_2}^{(2)}, \ldots, T_{j_r}^{(r)}) \qquad 0 \le j_\nu \le e_\nu$$

The periods listed in *6* are called the *fundamental periods* of $\mathcal{A}$.

7 *Example* Suppose the characteristic matrix **A** over $GF(2)$ has the minimum polynomial

8 $$m_A(x) = (1 + x)^5(1 + x + x^3)^3$$

The fundamental periods in this case are

9 $$\begin{array}{l} 1, 1, 2, 4, 4, 8 \\ 1, 7, 14, 28 \end{array}$$

Hence, the state periods realizable by $\mathcal{A}$ are

10 $$1, 2, 4, 7, 8, 14, 28, 56$$

30 *Computation of state period*

In view of *5.23.2* and *5.27.4*, we can now formulate a procedure for determining the period of any state **s** in the nonsingular LMS $\mathcal{A}$ with the characteristic matrix **A** (notation follows Sec. *28*):

1 Find the rational canonical form $\mathbf{A}^* = \mathbf{PAP}^{-1}$ of **A**.

2 Compute

$$\mathbf{s}^* = \mathbf{Ps} = \begin{bmatrix} \mathbf{s}_1 \\ \mathbf{s}_2 \\ \cdot \\ \cdot \\ \cdot \\ \mathbf{s}_w \end{bmatrix}$$

where $\mathbf{s}_i$ consists of the coordinates corresponding to the rows of $\mathbf{M}_{d_i(x)}$ in $\mathbf{A}^*$. Let $s_i(\xi)$ be the polynomial representation of s_i as a ring element.

3 Let $d_i(x) = [p_i(x)]^{e_i}$. For every nonzero $\mathbf{s}_i$ find the highest power of $p_i(x)$ which divides $s_i(x)$. If this power is μ_i, the period of $\mathbf{s}_i$ is the period of $[p_i(x)]^{e_i-\mu_i}$ (that is, $T^{(i)}_{e_i-\mu_i}$). If $\mathbf{s}_i = \mathbf{0}$, its period is 1.

4 If T_i denotes the period of $\mathbf{s}_i$, then the period of $\mathbf{s}$ is given by

5 $$T = \text{lcm}\ (T_1, T_2, \ldots, T_w)$$

6 *Example* Consider the LMS specified in *5.28.8*, and the state

7 $$\mathbf{s} = \begin{bmatrix} 0 \\ 1 \\ 1 \\ 0 \\ 1 \end{bmatrix}$$

In this case:

8 $$\mathbf{s}_1 = \begin{bmatrix} 0 \\ 1 \\ 1 \end{bmatrix} \qquad \mathbf{s}_2 = \begin{bmatrix} 0 \\ 1 \end{bmatrix}$$

9 $$s_1(x) = x + x^2 \qquad s_2(x) = x$$

10 $$d_1(x) = (1 + x)^3 \qquad d_2(x) = 1 + x + x^2$$

11 $$\mu_1 = 1 \qquad \mu_2 = 0$$

12 $$T^{(1)}_{3-1} = 2 \qquad T^{(2)}_{1-0} = 3$$

Hence, the period of $\mathbf{s}$ is given by

13 $$T = \text{lcm}\ (2,3) = 6$$

31 *Initiation of a specified cycle*

We can also formulate a procedure for finding a state $\mathbf{s}$ in $\mathfrak{A}$ which initiates a cycle of specified length T realizable by $\mathfrak{A}$ (notation follows Sec. *30*):

1 Find $\mathbf{A}^* = \mathbf{PAP}^{-1}$.

2 Find any set of periods $T^{(1)}_{j_1}, T^{(2)}_{j_2}, \ldots, T^{(w)}_{j_w}$ such that

$$T = \text{lcm}\ (T^{(1)}_{j_1}, T^{(2)}_{j_2}, \ldots, T^{(w)}_{j_w})$$

3 For each $T^{(\nu)}_{j_\nu}$ select a polynomial $s_\nu(\xi)$ in the following manner: If $T^{(\nu)}_{j_\nu} = 1$, choose $s_\nu(\xi) = 0$; if $T^{(\nu)}_{j_\nu}$ is the period of $[p_\nu(x)]^{j_\nu}$, choose $s_\nu(\xi) = [p_\nu(\xi)]^{e_\nu - j_\nu}$.

4 If $\mathbf{s}_i$ is the vector represented by $s_\nu(\xi)$, then

5
$$\mathbf{s} = \mathbf{P}^{-1}\begin{bmatrix} \mathbf{s}_1 \\ \mathbf{s}_2 \\ \cdot \\ \cdot \\ \cdot \\ \mathbf{s}_w \end{bmatrix}$$

6 *Example* Consider the following characteristic matrix over $GF(2)$:

7
$$\mathbf{A} = \mathbf{A}^* = \begin{bmatrix} \mathbf{M}_{(1+x)^3} & \mathbf{0} & \mathbf{0} \\ \mathbf{0} & \mathbf{M}_{1+x+x^2} & \mathbf{0} \\ \mathbf{0} & \mathbf{0} & \mathbf{M}_{(1+x+x^3)^3} \end{bmatrix}$$

The polynomials and periods of interest can be summarized as follows:

8

i	$d_i(x)$	$p_i(x)$	e_i	Fundamental periods
1	$(1+x)^3$	$1+x$	3	1, 1, 2, 4
2	$1+x+x^2$	$1+x+x^2$	1	1, 3
3	$(1+x+x^3)^3$	$1+x+x^3$	3	1, 7, 14, 28

The realizable periods are

9
$$1, 2, 3, 4, 6, 7, 12, 14, 21, 28, 42, 84$$

Suppose we wish to initiate a cycle of length $T = 42$. We can write

10
$$42 = \text{lcm}\,(2,3,7) \qquad 2 = T_2^{(1)};\ 3 = T_1^{(2)};\ 7 = T_1^{(3)}$$

Hence:

11
$$s_1(\xi) = (1+\xi)^{3-2} = 1+\xi$$

12
$$s_2(\xi) = (1+\xi+\xi^2)^{1-1} = 1$$

13
$$s_3(\xi) = (1+\xi+\xi^3)^{3-1} = 1+\xi^2+\xi^6$$

Hence, a state which initiates a cycle of length 42 is given by

14
$$\mathbf{s} = \begin{bmatrix} \mathbf{s}_1 \\ \mathbf{s}_2 \\ \mathbf{s}_3 \end{bmatrix}$$

where
$$\mathbf{s}_1 = \begin{bmatrix} 1 \\ 1 \\ 0 \end{bmatrix} \qquad \mathbf{s}_2 = \begin{bmatrix} 1 \\ 0 \end{bmatrix} \qquad \mathbf{s}_3 = \begin{bmatrix} 1 \\ 0 \\ 1 \\ 0 \\ 0 \\ 0 \\ 1 \\ 0 \\ 0 \end{bmatrix}$$

32 *Nilpotent LMS*

An LMS is *nilpotent* if its characteristic matrix is nilpotent (i.e., if for some t, $\mathbf{A}^t = \mathbf{0}$). The elementary divisors of a nilpotent LMS, then, are of the form x^r. An elementary block $\mathbf{M}_{x^r}$ of $\mathbf{A}^*$ has the form

1
$$\mathbf{M}_{x^r} = \begin{bmatrix} 0 & 0 & \cdots & 0 & 0 \\ 1 & 0 & \cdots & 0 & 0 \\ 0 & 1 & \cdots & 0 & 0 \\ \cdot & \cdot & \cdots & \cdot & \cdot \\ 0 & 0 & \cdots & 1 & 0 \end{bmatrix}$$

Let $\mathfrak{M}$ be the LMS whose characteristic matrix is $\mathbf{M}_{x^r}$. If

$$s(\xi) = \sigma_0 + \sigma_1\xi + \cdots + \sigma_{r-1}\xi^{r-1}$$

represents the initial state $\mathbf{s}$ of $\mathfrak{M}$, then the sequence of states traversed by $\mathfrak{M}$ is given by

2
$$\begin{aligned} \mathbf{s} &\to \sigma_0 + \sigma_1\xi + \sigma_2\xi^2 + \cdots + \sigma_{r-2}\xi^{r-2} + \sigma_{r-1}\xi^{r-1} \\ \mathbf{M}_{x^r}\mathbf{s} &\to \sigma_0\xi + \sigma_1\xi^2 + \cdots + \sigma_{r-3}\xi^{r-2} + \sigma_{r-2}\xi^{r-1} \\ \mathbf{M}_{x^r}^2\mathbf{s} &\to \sigma_0\xi^2 + \cdots + \sigma_{r-4}\xi^{r-2} + \sigma_{r-1}\xi^{r-1} \\ &\cdot \\ &\cdot \\ &\cdot \\ \mathbf{M}_{x^r}^{r-2}\mathbf{s} &\to \sigma_0\xi^{r-2} + \sigma_1\xi^{r-1} \\ \mathbf{M}_{x^r}^{r-1}\mathbf{s} &\to \sigma_0\xi^{r-1} \\ \mathbf{M}_{x^r}^{r}\mathbf{s} &\to 0 \end{aligned}$$

The sequence *2* reveals immediately that no nonzero state of $\mathfrak{M}$ can reach itself in one or more steps. Also, every state reaches the null state in r steps or less, and remains in the null state thereafter. [If $s(\xi)$ is divisible by ξ^ν, it reaches 0 in exactly $r - \nu$ steps.]

33 *State graph of a nilpotent LMS*

From the preceding remarks it follows that the state graph of the nilpotent LMS $\mathfrak{M}$ is a tree whose root is the null state. Further examination of *5.32.2* yields the following characterization of this tree:

1 The tree is of height r.
2 Level ν contains $(p - 1)p^{\nu-1}$ states.

3 The number of states reaching any given state (not in level r) in i steps is exactly p^i.

Now, consider a general nilpotent LMS $\mathcal{A}$, whose characteristic matrix $\mathbf{A}$ has the rational canonical form

4
$$\mathbf{A}^* = \begin{bmatrix} \mathbf{M}_{x^{r_1}} & \mathbf{0} & \cdots & \mathbf{0} \\ \mathbf{0} & \mathbf{M}_{x^{r_2}} & \cdots & \mathbf{0} \\ \cdot & \cdot & \cdots & \cdot \\ \mathbf{0} & \mathbf{0} & \cdots & \mathbf{M}_{x^{r_w}} \end{bmatrix}$$

By writing a sequence exemplified by *5.32.2* for each elementary block $\mathbf{M}_{x^{r_\nu}}$, one can arrive at the following conclusions:

5 The state graph of $\mathcal{A}$ is a tree whose root is the null state, and whose height L equals the greatest r_ν.

6 If N_i denotes the number of states in level i, and m_j the number of $j \times j$ elementary blocks in $\mathbf{A}^*$, then

7
$$N_i = p^{m_1+2m_2+3m_3+\cdots+(i-1)m_{i-1}+i(m_i+m_{i+1}+\cdots+m_L)} - (1 + N_1 + N_2 + \cdots + N_{i-1})$$

8 The number of states reaching any given state in i steps is either 0 or $1 + N_1 + N_2 + \cdots + N_i$.

The integers $r_1, r_2, \ldots, r_w$ (or, equivalently, $m_1, m_2, \ldots, m_L$), together with properties *5*, *6*, and *8* are sufficient to construct the tree for $\mathcal{A}$, starting at the root and proceeding level by level toward the top.

9 *Example* Consider the nilpotent LMS $\mathcal{A}$ over $GF(2)$, with the characteristic matrix

10
$$\mathbf{A} = \mathbf{A}^* = \left[\begin{array}{cccc|cc|c} 0 & 0 & 0 & 0 & 0 & 0 & 0 \\ 1 & 0 & 0 & 0 & 0 & 0 & 0 \\ 0 & 1 & 0 & 0 & 0 & 0 & 0 \\ 0 & 0 & 1 & 0 & 0 & 0 & 0 \\ \hline 0 & 0 & 0 & 0 & 0 & 0 & 0 \\ 0 & 0 & 0 & 0 & 1 & 0 & 0 \\ \hline 0 & 0 & 0 & 0 & 0 & 0 & 0 \end{array}\right]$$

In this case $r_1 = 4$, $r_2 = 2$, $r_3 = 1$. Hence the state graph of $\mathcal{A}$ is a tree of height 4. $m_1 = m_2 = m_4 = 1$, but otherwise $m_\nu = 0$. By *7*

11
$$\begin{aligned} N_1 &= 2^{1(1+1+1)} - 1 = 7 \\ N_2 &= 2^{1+2(1+1)} - (1 + 7) = 24 \\ N_3 &= 2^{1+2+3(1)} - (1 + 7 + 24) = 32 \\ N_4 &= 2^{1+2+4(1)} - (1 + 7 + 24 + 32) = 64 \end{aligned}$$

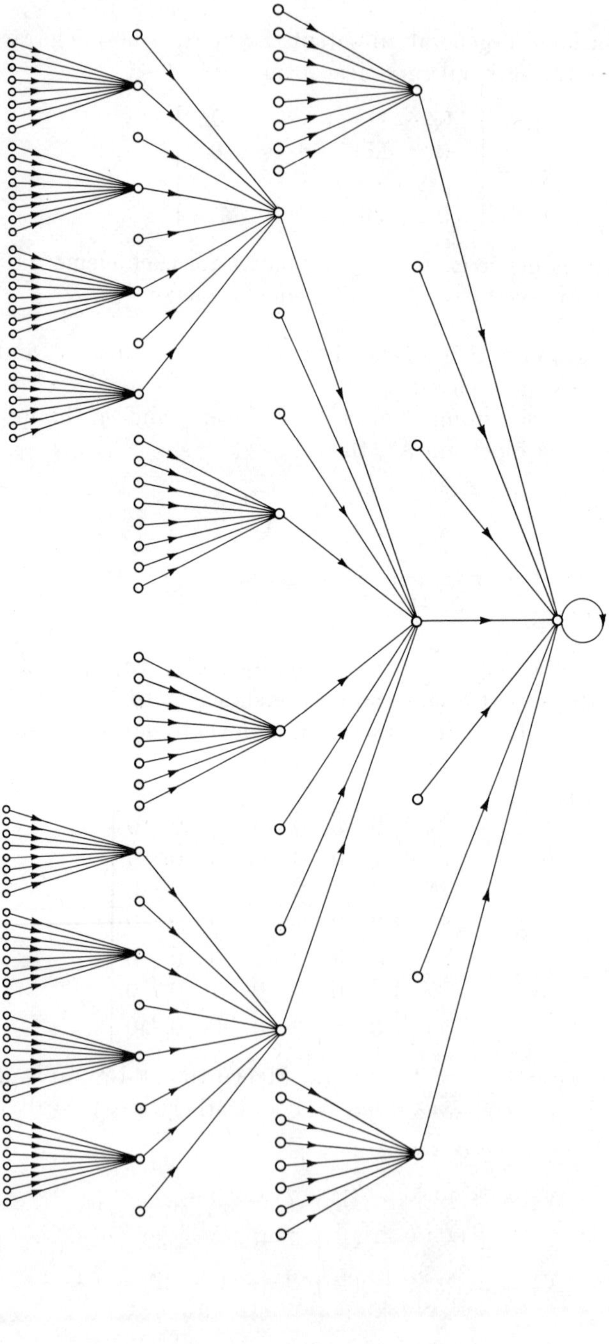

Fig. 5.33.1 State graph of LMS of Example *5.33.9*.

which accounts for all $2^7 = 128$ states of $\mathfrak{A}$, save the null state. By *8*, the number of states reaching any given state in one step is either 0 or 8; in two steps either 0 or 32; in three steps either 0 or 64; in four steps either 0 or 128. The tree constructed on the basis of these results is shown in Fig. *5.33.1*.

34 *General LMS*

In general, the elementary divisors of the characteristic matrix $\mathbf{A}$ of an LMS may include divisors of the following two types:

1 $$d(x) = \alpha_0 + \alpha_1 x + \cdots + \alpha_{k-1}x^{k-1} + x^k = [p(x)]^e \qquad \alpha_0 \neq 0$$

2 $$d(x) = x^k$$

The elementary blocks of $\mathbf{A}^*$ corresponding to type 1 are nonsingular, while those corresponding to type 2 are nilpotent. Thus, the rational canonical form $\mathbf{A}^*$ of $\mathbf{A}$ can be put in the form

3 $$\mathbf{A}^* = \begin{bmatrix} \mathbf{A}_0 & \mathbf{0} \\ \mathbf{0} & \mathbf{A}_1 \end{bmatrix}$$

where $\mathbf{A}_0$ is nilpotent and $\mathbf{A}_1$ is nonsingular.

Let $\mathbf{s}$ be any state $\begin{bmatrix} \mathbf{s}_0 \\ \mathbf{s}_1 \end{bmatrix}$, partitioned in accordance with $\mathbf{A}^*$ in *3*. Then, for any t,

4 $$(\mathbf{A}^*)^t\mathbf{s} = \begin{bmatrix} \mathbf{A}_0 & \mathbf{0} \\ \mathbf{0} & \mathbf{A}_1 \end{bmatrix}^t \begin{bmatrix} \mathbf{s}_0 \\ \mathbf{s}_1 \end{bmatrix} = \begin{bmatrix} \mathbf{A}_0{}^t\mathbf{s}_0 \\ \mathbf{A}_1{}^t\mathbf{s}_1 \end{bmatrix}$$

Hence, the set of all states of the form $\begin{bmatrix} \mathbf{s}_0 \\ \mathbf{0} \end{bmatrix}$ constitutes a tree (with the root $\mathbf{0}$) in the state graph of $\mathbf{A}^*$; this tree, called the *null tree* of $\mathbf{A}^*$, is precisely the state graph of $\mathbf{A}_0$, constructed as per rules of Sec. *33*. Similarly, all states of the form $\begin{bmatrix} \mathbf{0} \\ \mathbf{s}_1 \end{bmatrix}$ constitute cycles in the state graph of $\mathbf{A}^*$; these cycles are precisely the state graph of $\mathbf{A}_1$, constructed as per rules of Sec. *28*. States of the form $\begin{bmatrix} \mathbf{0} \\ \mathbf{s}_1 \end{bmatrix}$ will be referred to as *cyclic states*.

35 *State graphs of general LMS*

1 **Lemma** Every cyclic state in the state graph of $\mathbf{A}^*$ is the root of a tree isomorphic to the null tree of $\mathbf{A}^*$.

Proof Let $\begin{bmatrix} \mathbf{0} \\ \boldsymbol{\theta} \end{bmatrix}$ be any cyclic state, and $\begin{bmatrix} \mathbf{s}_0 \\ \mathbf{0} \end{bmatrix}$ any state which reaches $\mathbf{0}$ in ν steps. Establish the following correspondence

2 $$\mathbf{s} = \begin{bmatrix} \mathbf{s}_0 \\ \mathbf{0} \end{bmatrix} \rightarrow \bar{\mathbf{s}} = \begin{bmatrix} \mathbf{s}_0 \\ (\mathbf{A}_1{}^{\nu})^{-1}\boldsymbol{\theta} \end{bmatrix}$$

which is, clearly, one to one. Since

3 $$\mathbf{s}' = \mathbf{A}^*\mathbf{s} = \begin{bmatrix} \mathbf{A}_0\mathbf{s}_0 \\ \mathbf{0} \end{bmatrix} \qquad \bar{\mathbf{s}}' = \mathbf{A}^*\bar{\mathbf{s}} = \begin{bmatrix} \mathbf{A}_0\mathbf{s}_0 \\ (\mathbf{A}_1^{\nu-1})^{-1}\boldsymbol{\theta} \end{bmatrix}$$

it follows that $\mathbf{s}'$ and $\bar{\mathbf{s}}'$ also bear this correspondence. Hence, the null tree of $\mathbf{A}^*$ is isomorphic to the subgraph consisting of all states of the form $\bar{\mathbf{s}}$ (with any fixed $\boldsymbol{\theta}$). Since none of the states $\bar{\mathbf{s}}$ where $\mathbf{s}_0 \neq \mathbf{0}$ can be a cyclic state, and since $(\mathbf{A}^*)^{\nu}\bar{\mathbf{s}} = \begin{bmatrix} \mathbf{0} \\ \boldsymbol{\theta} \end{bmatrix}$, the latter subgraph is a tree isomorphic to the null tree, with $\begin{bmatrix} \mathbf{0} \\ \boldsymbol{\theta} \end{bmatrix}$ as a root.

A procedure can now be summarized for constructing the state graph of a general LMS $\mathcal{A}$ whose characteristic matrix is $\mathbf{A}$:

4 Find $\mathbf{A}^*$ and partition it as in *5.34.3*.
5 Construct the state graphs of $\mathbf{A}_0$ (a tree) and of $\mathbf{A}_1$ (cycles).
6 The state graph of $\mathbf{A}$ consists of the cycles of $\mathbf{A}_1$, with the tree of $\mathbf{A}_0$ tacked to every state in every cycle (see Fig. *5.35.1*, where the boxes signify identical trees).

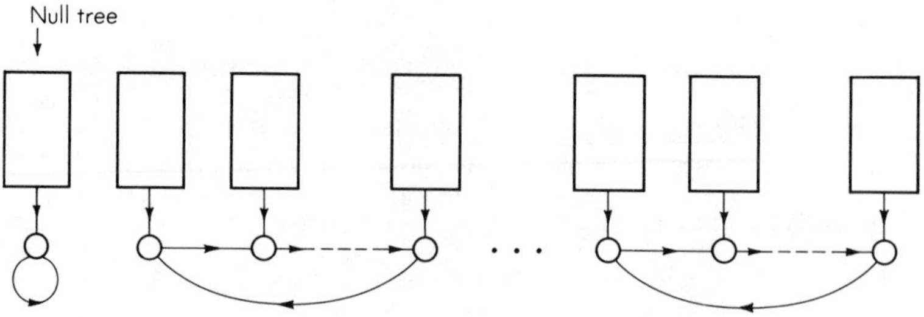

Fig. 5.35.1 State graph of general LMS.

7 *Example* Consider an LMS over $GF(2)$, where the elementary divisors of the characteristic matrix $\mathbf{A}$ are x, x^2, and $(1 + x)^3$. In this case, then:

8 $$\mathbf{A}_0 = \left[\begin{array}{c:cc} 0 & 0 & 0 \\ \hdashline 0 & 0 & 0 \\ 0 & 1 & 0 \end{array}\right] \qquad \mathbf{A}_1 = \begin{bmatrix} 0 & 0 & 1 \\ 1 & 0 & 1 \\ 0 & 1 & 1 \end{bmatrix}$$

The state graph of $\mathbf{A}_0$ is a tree of height 2, with $N_1 = 3$, $N_2 = 4$; the number of states reaching any given state in one step is either 0 or 4. The cycle set of $\mathbf{A}_1$ (see *5.28.14*) is $\{2[1],1[2],1[4]\}$. The resulting state graph of $\mathbf{A}$ is shown in Fig. *5.35.2*.

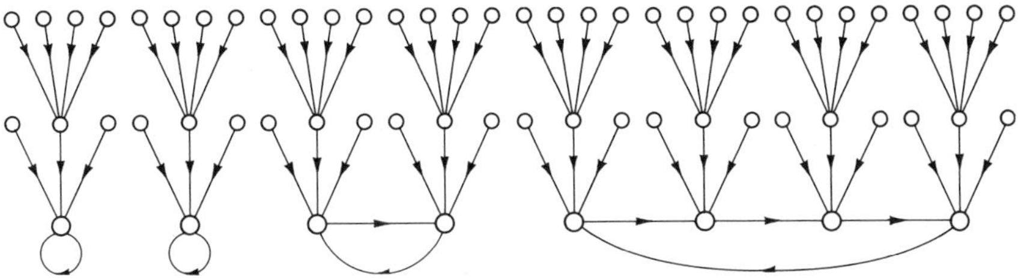

Fig. 5.35.2 State graph of LMS of Example *5.35.7*.

36 *State-graph realization—shift registers*

Given an LMS whose characteristic matrix is $\mathbf{A}$, we wish to construct a circuit which realizes the state graph of $\mathbf{A}$ up to isomorphism. $\mathbf{A}$, then, can be replaced with its rational canonical form $\mathbf{A}^*$; since $\mathbf{A}^*$ and its transpose are similar, we can assume that each elementary block in $\mathbf{A}^*$ is in the form

1
$$\mathbf{M}'_{d(x)} = \begin{bmatrix} 0 & 1 & 0 & \cdots & 0 \\ 0 & 0 & 1 & \cdots & 0 \\ \cdot & \cdot & \cdot & \cdots & \cdot \\ 0 & 0 & 0 & \cdots & 1 \\ -\alpha_0 & -\alpha_1 & -\alpha_2 & \cdots & -\alpha_{k-1} \end{bmatrix}$$

A circuit realizing the state graph of $\mathbf{M}'_{d(x)}$ is shown in Fig. *5.36.1*. It is

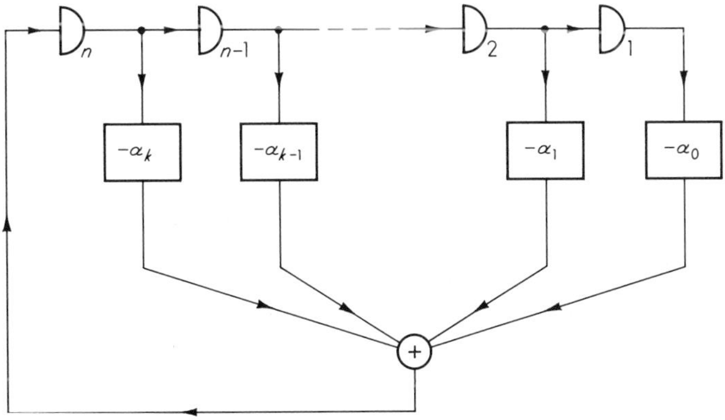

Fig. 5.36.1 Shift register.

called a *shift register* and has a number of practical advantages which make it a useful building block in the synthesis of LMS. Thus, if **A** has w elementary divisors, its state graph can be realized with w shift registers, one for each divisor. The scaler constants in the feedback loops of each register can be obtained directly from the coefficients of the corresponding divisor. Note that divisors of the form x^k correspond to feedback-free registers, while all other divisors must have at least one feedback loop, extending from the last to the first delayer. The feedback-free registers, therefore, serve to realize the trees (or the *transient* component of the free response) while the feedback registers serve to realize the cycles (or the *steady-state* component of the free response).

2 *Example* **A** is the characteristic matrix of an LMS over $GF(3)$, whose elementary divisors are

3 $$x,\ x^2,\ x^4,\ 2 + x^3,\ 1 + 2x + x^3 + x^4$$

Figure *5.36.2* shows the shift-register realization of this LMS.

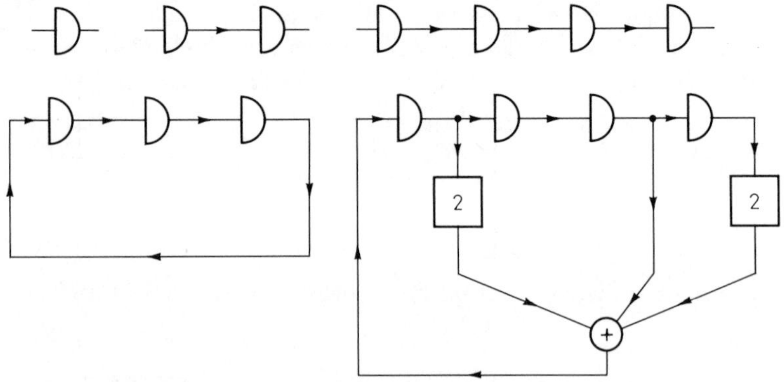

Fig. 5.36.2 Realization of LMS of Example *5.36.2*.

37 *Computation of forced response—preliminaries*

As defined in Sec. *19*, the forced response of an LMS is the component of the output obtained under the assumption $\mathbf{s}(0) = \mathbf{0}$. This assumption will tacitly prevail for the remainder of this chapter. Correspondingly, *output* will mean the forced component, and all variables will be taken as 0 for all $t < 0$.

In accordance with *5.19.2*, we can write

1 $$\mathbf{y}(t) = \sum_{\nu=0}^{t} \mathbf{H}(t - \nu)\mathbf{u}(\nu)$$

where $\mathbf{H}(t)$ is as given in *5.18.4*. $\mathbf{H}(t)$ will be called the *transfer matrix* of the LMS. If $h_{ij}(t)$ denotes the (i,j) element of $\mathbf{H}(t)$, and if $\mathbf{u}$ and $\mathbf{y}$ are as given in *5.14.1*, then

2 $$y_i(t) = \sum_{\nu=0}^{t} h_{i1}(t - \nu)u_1(\nu) + \sum_{\nu=0}^{t} h_{i2}(t - \nu)u_2(\nu) + \cdots + \sum_{\nu=0}^{t} h_{il}(t - \nu)u_l(\nu)$$

Hence, computing the output of an l-input m-output LMS, whose transfer matrix is $\mathbf{H}(t)$, is equivalent to computing the output of an lm two-terminal LMS whose transfer matrices are the elements $h_{ij}(t)$ of $\mathbf{H}(t)$. With no loss in generality, therefore, we shall assume that all LMS under analysis are two-terminal LMS. Correspondingly, *1* will be written as

3 $$y(t) = \sum_{\nu=0}^{t} h(t - \nu)u(\nu)$$

38 *Superposition and the impulsive response*

5.37.3 implies the *superposition property* of LMS:

1 **Theorem** If $y^{(1)}(t)$ and $y^{(2)}(t)$ are the responses of an LMS to $u^{(1)}(t)$ and $u^{(2)}(t)$, respectively, then the response of the LMS to $\alpha_1 u^{(1)}(t) + \alpha_2 u^{(2)}(t)$, for any α_1, α_2 in $GF(p)$, is $\alpha_1 y^{(1)}(t) + \alpha_2 y^{(2)}(t)$.

A *unit impulse*, denoted by $i(t)$, is a sequence defined by

2 $$i(t) = \begin{cases} 1 & t = 0 \\ 0 & t \neq 0 \end{cases}$$

The impulsive response of an LMS is its output when the input is $i(t)$. From *5.37.3* we have:

3 **Theorem** The impulsive response of an LMS with the transfer matrix $h(t)$ is $h(t)$.

Thus, the response of an LMS to any input can be computed by adding up impulsive responses, appropriately weighted and delayed.

4 *Example* Consider the LMS over $GF(3)$, specified in *5.14.3* (and Fig. *5.14.2*), with the output y_2 omitted. The characterizing matrices

of the revised LMS are

5
$$\mathbf{A} = \begin{bmatrix} 0 & 2 & 0 & 0 \\ 1 & 0 & 2 & 1 \\ 0 & 1 & 1 & 0 \\ 2 & 0 & 1 & 1 \end{bmatrix} \qquad \mathbf{B} = \begin{bmatrix} 1 \\ 0 \\ 0 \\ 0 \end{bmatrix}$$
$$\mathbf{C} = [0 \quad 0 \quad 2 \quad 1] \qquad \mathbf{D} = [0]$$

By *5.18.4*, the impulsive response can be computed as follows:

6
$$h(0) = \mathbf{D} = 0 \qquad h(1) = \mathbf{CB} = 0 \qquad h(2) = \mathbf{CAB} = 2$$
$$h(3) = \mathbf{CA}^2\mathbf{B} = 1 \qquad h(4) = \mathbf{CA}^3\mathbf{B} = 1 \qquad h(5) = \mathbf{CA}^4\mathbf{B} = 0$$
$$h(6) = \mathbf{CA}^5\mathbf{B} = 1 \qquad h(7) = \mathbf{CA}^6\mathbf{B} = 2 \qquad h(8) = \mathbf{CA}^7\mathbf{B} = 2$$
$$h(9) = \mathbf{CA}^8\mathbf{B} = \mathbf{CB} = h(1), \ldots$$

Hence

7
$$h(t) = 0.02110122,02110122, \ldots$$

Now suppose

8
$$u(t) = 1022000 \cdots$$

The corresponding output can be computed as follows:

9

ν	$u(\nu)$	$u(\nu)h(t-\nu)$
0	1	00211012202110122021 $\cdots$
1	0	
2	2	001220211012202110 $\cdots$
3	2	00122021101220211 $\cdots$
4	0	
.	.	
.	.	
.	.	
		$y(t) = 0021.20211012,20211012, \ldots$

39 *The d transform*

The *d transform* of a sequence $f(t)$, denoted by $\mathfrak{D}[f(t)]$ or F, is defined as follows:

1
$$\mathfrak{D}[f(t)] = F = \sum_{t=0}^{\infty} f(t)d^t$$

$f(t)$ is called the *inverse transform* of F.

Consider a rational function in d

$$A(d) = \frac{q(d)}{r(d)} = \frac{\beta_0 + \beta_1 d + \cdots + \beta_m d^m}{\alpha_0 + \alpha_1 d + \cdots + \alpha_n d^n}$$

If, after cancellation of all factors common to $q(d)$ and $r(d)$, the denominator has no factor d, $A(d)$ can be expanded in a Taylor series about $d = 0$:

2 $$A(d) = \rho_0 + \rho_1 d + \rho_2 d^2 + \cdots$$

Under these conditions, $A(d)$ is said to be *invertible;* the inverse transform of $A(d)$ is defined as the sequence $\rho_0\rho_1\rho_2 \cdots$. Clearly, if $q(d)/r(d)$ is invertible, its inverse is the same as that of $z(d)q(d)/z(d)r(d)$ with any nonzero $z(d)$.

3 *Example* Consider the following ratio of polynomials over $GF(3)$:

4 $$A(d) = \frac{2d^2 + d^3 + d^4 + d^6 + 2d^7 + 2d^8}{1 + 2d^8}$$

The highest common factor of the numerator and denominator of $A(d)$ can be found via the euclidean algorithm (see *5.6.3*) to be $1 + 2d + 2d^2 + 2d^4 + d^5 + d^6$. After the cancellation of this factor we have:

5 $$A(d) = \frac{2d^2}{1 + d + 2d^2}$$

The expansion of $A(d)$ into a power series in d can be done by long division

6 $$\begin{array}{r|l} & 2d^2 + d^3 + d^4 + d^6 + 2d^7 + 2d^8 + \cdots \\ \hline 1 + d + 2d^2 & 2d^2 \\ & \underline{2d^2 + 2d^3 + d^4} \\ & \quad d^3 + 2d^4 \\ & \quad \underline{d^3 + d^4 + 2d^5} \\ & \qquad d^4 + d^5 \\ & \qquad \underline{d^4 + d^5 + 2d^6} \\ & \qquad\qquad d^6 \\ & \qquad\qquad \underline{d^6 + d^7 + 2d^8} \\ & \qquad\qquad\quad 2d^7 + d^8 \\ & \qquad\qquad\quad \underline{2d^7 + 2d^8 + d^9} \\ & \qquad\qquad\qquad 2d^8 + 2d^9 \\ & \qquad\qquad\qquad \vdots \end{array}$$

Hence

7 $$\mathfrak{D}^{-1}[A(d)] = a(t) = 00211022 \cdots$$

40 *Transform pairs*

A time sequence $f(t)$ and its d transform F are called a *transform pair*. Table *5.40.1* lists some commonly encountered transform pairs. Finding the d transform of a given sequence and the inverse of a given function of d is often facilitated by reference to this table.

Table 5.40.1

$f(t)$	F
1. $\sum_{\nu=1}^{r} \alpha_\nu f_\nu(t)$	$\sum_{\nu=1}^{r} \alpha_\nu F_\nu$
2. $f(t-\nu)$	$d^\nu F$
3. $f_1(t) * f_2(t)$	F_1F_2
4. $f(t) = f(t+T)$	$\dfrac{f(0) + f(1)d + \cdots + f(T-1)d^{T-1}}{1-d^T}$
5. $\sum_{\nu=0}^{t} f(\nu)$	$\dfrac{F}{1-d}$
6. $\alpha^t f(t)$	$F(\alpha d)$
7. $i(t)$	1
8. α^t	$\dfrac{1}{1-\alpha d}$
9. $\left[\binom{r}{t}\right]_p$	$(1+d)^r$
10. $(-1)^t \left[\binom{r+t-1}{t}\right]_p$	$\dfrac{1}{(1+d)^r}$

1. α_ν are elements of $GF(p)$.

3. $f_1(t) * f_2(t) = \sum_{\nu=0}^{t} f_1(\nu) f_2(t-\nu)$ is the *convolution* of $f_1(t)$ and $f_2(t)$.

4. $f(t)$ is periodic with period T.

6, 8. α is a nonzero element of $GF(p)$.

7. $i(t)$ is a unit impulse, as defined in *5.38.2*.

9, 10. $\left[\binom{b}{a}\right]_p$ is the binomial coefficient $\binom{b}{a}$ reduced mod p.

1 *Example* Consider the following function over $GF(3)$:

2 $$F = \frac{d^2 + d^3}{1 + d^3}$$

We can write

3 $$F = d^2 \left[\frac{1 + 2(2d)}{1 - (2d)^3}\right]$$

By (6) of the table

4 $$\mathfrak{D}^{-1} \left[\frac{1 + 2(2d)}{1 - (2d)^3}\right] = 2^t \mathfrak{D}^{-1} \left(\frac{1 + 2d}{1 - d^3}\right)$$

By (4) of the table

5 $$\mathfrak{D}^{-1} \left(\frac{1 + 2d}{1 - d^3}\right) = 120,120,120,120, \ . \ . \ .$$

Hence

6 $$\mathfrak{D}^{-1} \left[\frac{1 + 2(2d)}{1 - (2d)^3}\right] = 110220,110220, \ . \ . \ .$$

Finally, by (2) of the table

7 $$\mathfrak{D}^{-1} \left\{d^2 \left[\frac{1 + 2(2d)}{1 - (2d)^3}\right]\right\} = 00.110220,110220, \ . \ . \ .$$

41 *The transfer function*

Let $\mathcal{A}$ be an LMS of order n whose characterizing matrices are **A**, **B**, **C**, and **D**. As $\mathcal{A}$ is a two-terminal LMS, equations *5.12.5* and *5.12.6* can be written in the form

1 $$\mathbf{s}(t) = \mathbf{A}\mathbf{s}(t - 1) + \mathbf{B}u(t - 1)$$

2 $$y(t) = \mathbf{C}\mathbf{s}(t) + \mathbf{D}u(t)$$

If **S** is an n-dimensional vector whose ith coordinate is the d transform of $s_i(t)$, the d transform of the system of equations *1* and *2* is given by

3 $$\mathbf{S} = \mathbf{A}d\mathbf{S} + \mathbf{B}dU$$

4 $$\mathbf{Y} = \mathbf{C}\mathbf{S} + \mathbf{D}U$$

3 yields

5 $$(d\mathbf{A} - \mathbf{I})\mathbf{S} = -d\mathbf{B}U$$

Now, $|d\mathbf{A} - \mathbf{I}|$ is some polynomial in d of degree at most n:

6 $$|d\mathbf{A} - \mathbf{I}| = \beta_0' + \beta_1' d + \cdots + \beta_n' d^n$$

When $d = 0$, $|d\mathbf{A} - \mathbf{I}| = (-1)^n$, hence $\beta_0' \neq 0$ and $|d\mathbf{A} - \mathbf{I}| \neq 0$.

Thus we can write:

7 $$\mathbf{S} = -(d\mathbf{A} - \mathbf{I})^{-1} d\mathbf{B} U = \frac{-(d\mathbf{A} - \mathbf{I})^{\mathrm{ADJ}} d\mathbf{B}}{|d\mathbf{A} - \mathbf{I}|} U$$

Substituting in *4*, we have:

8 $$Y = \left[-\mathbf{C} \frac{(d\mathbf{A} - \mathbf{I})^{\mathrm{ADJ}} d\mathbf{B}}{|d\mathbf{A} - \mathbf{I}|} + \mathbf{D} \right] U$$

The rational function Y/U is called the *transfer function* of $\mathcal{A}$, denoted by τ:

9 $$\tau = \frac{Y}{U} = \frac{\mathfrak{D}[y(t)]}{\mathfrak{D}[u(t)]} = \mathbf{D} - \frac{\mathbf{C}(d\mathbf{A} - \mathbf{I})^{\mathrm{ADJ}} d\mathbf{B}}{|d\mathbf{A} - \mathbf{I}|}$$

As a ratio of two polynomials, τ has the form

10 $$\tau = \frac{q'(d)}{r'(d)} = \frac{\alpha_0' + \alpha_1' d + \cdots + \alpha_n' d^n}{\beta_0' + \beta_1' d + \cdots + \beta_n' d^n} \qquad \beta_0' \neq 0$$

Multiplying and dividing τ by $(\beta_0')^{-1}$ yields the *normalized form* of the transfer function

11 $$\tau = \frac{q(d)}{r(d)} = \frac{\alpha_0 + \alpha_1 d + \cdots + \alpha_n d^n}{1 + \beta_1 d + \cdots + \beta_n d^n}$$

Note that

12 $$r'(x) = |x\mathbf{A} - \mathbf{I}| = x^n \left| \mathbf{A} - \frac{1}{x}\mathbf{I} \right|$$

Hence, the reciprocal of $r'(x)$ (see *5.6.6*) is given by

13 $$[r'(x)]^* = x^n r' \left(\frac{1}{x} \right) = |\mathbf{A} - x\mathbf{I}| = \varphi_A(x)$$

where $\varphi_A(x)$ is the characteristic polynomial of $\mathbf{A}$. Thus

14 $$r(d) = (\beta_0')^{-1} [\varphi_A(d)]^*$$

and hence the irreducible factors of $r(d)$ can be obtained directly from those of $\varphi_A(x)$.

42 *Response computation from transfer function*

We can now formulate a general procedure for computing the forced response of a two-terminal LMS:

1 Compute the transfer function τ of the LMS.
2 Compute the d transform of the input, $U = \mathfrak{D}[u(t)]$.

3 Then $y(t) = \mathfrak{D}^{-1}[\tau U]$.

4 *Example* For the LMS of example *5.38.4*, *5.41.7* yields:

5 $$\mathbf{S} = \begin{bmatrix} d(1 + d + 2d^2 + d^3)/(1 + d + d^3 + 2d^4) \\ d^2(1 + 2d^2)/(1 + d + d^3 + 2d^4) \\ d^3(1 + d)/(1 + d + d^3 + 2d^4) \\ d^2(2 + d)/(1 + d + d^3 + 2d^4) \end{bmatrix} U$$

Hence, by *5.41.9*:

6 $$\tau = \frac{2d^2}{1 + d + 2d^2}$$

The response of the LMS to $u(t) = 1022000 \cdots$ is given by

7 $$y(t) = \mathfrak{D}^{-1}\left[\frac{2d^2}{1 + d + 2d^2}(1 + 2d^2 + 2d^3)\right] = \mathfrak{D}^{-1}\left(\frac{2d^2 + d^4 + d^5}{1 + d + 2d^2}\right)$$
$$= \mathfrak{D}^{-1}(2d^2 + d^3 + 2d^4 + 2d^6 + d^7 + d^8 + d^{10} + 2d^{11} + \cdots)$$
$$= 0021.20211012, \ldots$$

which checks with *5.38.9*.

43 *Transfer function and impulsive response*

Since $\mathfrak{D}[i(t)] = 1$, τ is precisely the d transform of the impulsive response, and hence

1 $$h(t) = \mathfrak{D}^{-1}[\tau]$$

Thus, if $\tau = q(d)/r(d)$, $h(t)$ can be obtained by a long division of $q(d)$ by $r(d)$.

Since the impulsive response is a free response for all $t > 0$, $h(t)$ must become periodic after $t \leq n$, and hence have the form

2 $$h(t) = \rho_0\rho_1 \cdots \rho_{k-1}.\rho_k\rho_{k+1} \cdots \rho_{k+T-1}, \ldots$$

τ can be constructed directly from $h(t)$ with the aid of (4) of Table *5.40.1*:

3 $$\tau = H = \rho_0 + \rho_1 d + \cdots \rho_{k-1}d^{k-1} + \frac{d^k(\rho_k + \rho_{k+1}d + \cdots + \rho_{k+T-1}d^{k+T-1})}{1 - d^T}$$

4 *Example* Given the transfer function of $\mathfrak{A}$:

5 $$\tau = \frac{2d^2}{1 + d + 2d^2}$$

the impulsive response can be found by long division

6 $$h(t) = \mathfrak{D}^{-1}\left(\frac{2d^2}{1 + d + 2d^2}\right) = \mathfrak{D}^{-1}(2d^2 + d^3 + d^4 + d^6 + 2d^7 + 2d^8 + \cdots) = 0.02110122, \ldots$$

which checks with *5.38.7*. Conversely, given $h(t)$ as in *6*, τ can be found as follows:

7 $$\tau = H = \frac{2d^2 + d^3 + d^4 + d^6 + 2d^7 + 2d^8}{1 - d^8} = \frac{2d^2}{1 + d + 2d^2}$$

where cancellation of common factors is carried out via the euclidean algorithm.

44 *Flow-graph techniques*

Computation of the transfer function τ of an LMS directly from the circuit configuration can be often facilitated through the use of flow-graph techniques. The key of these techniques is the following fact: Let $\pi_1, \pi_2, \pi_3, \ldots$ be all the paths leading from input terminal to output terminal, and let τ_i denote the transfer function of the path π_i (if π_i contains k_i delayers and if the product of scaler constants encountered along π_i is α_i, then $\tau_i = \alpha_i d^{k_i}$). Then

1 $$\tau = \tau_1 + \tau_2 + \tau_3 + \cdots$$

(there may be an infinite number of terms).

2 *Example* The transfer function of the LMS shown in Fig. *5.44.1* is

3 $$\begin{aligned}\tau &= \tau_1 + \tau_1\tau_2\tau_1 + \tau_1\tau_2\tau_1\tau_2\tau_1 + \tau_1\tau_2\tau_1\tau_2\tau_1\tau_2\tau_1 + \cdots \\ &= \tau_1[1 + \tau_1\tau_2 + (\tau_1\tau_2)^2 + (\tau_1\tau_2)^3 + \cdots] \\ &= \frac{\tau_1}{1 - \tau_1\tau_2}\end{aligned}$$

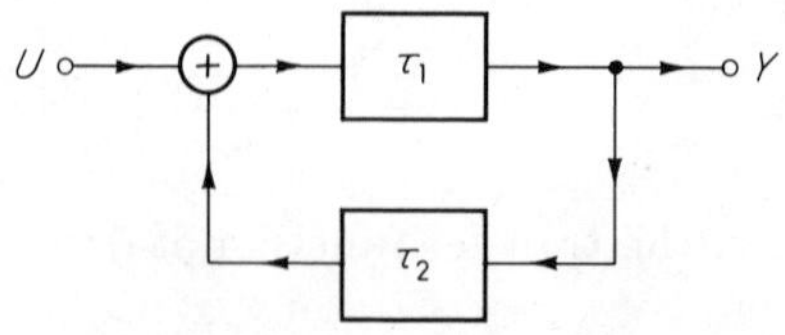

Fig. 5.44.1 LMS of Example *5.44.2*.

4 *Example* For the LMS over $GF(3)$ shown in Fig. *5.44.2*:

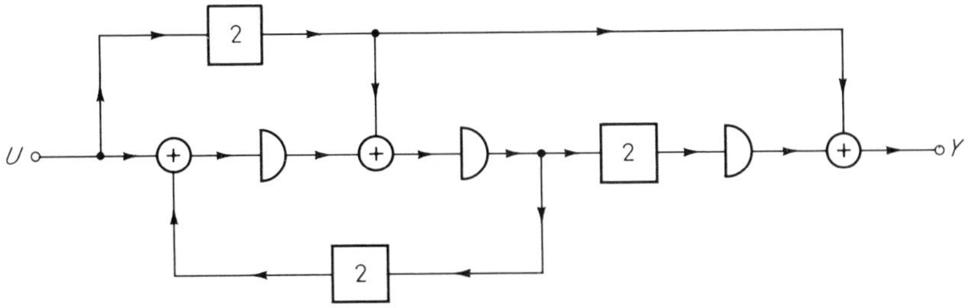

Fig. 5.44.2 LMS of Example *5.44.4*.

5
$$\tau = 2 + \left(\frac{d^2}{1 - 2d^2}\right) 2d + 2\left(\frac{d}{1 - 2d^2}\right) 2d = \frac{2 + 2d^3}{1 + d^2}$$

The thorough development of flow-graph techniques is beyond the scope of this chapter. The reader is referred to any of a number of textbooks available on this subject.

45 *Realization of transfer functions*

Using flow-graph techniques, the d transform of the output of the LMS shown in Fig. *5.45.1* can be expressed as follows:

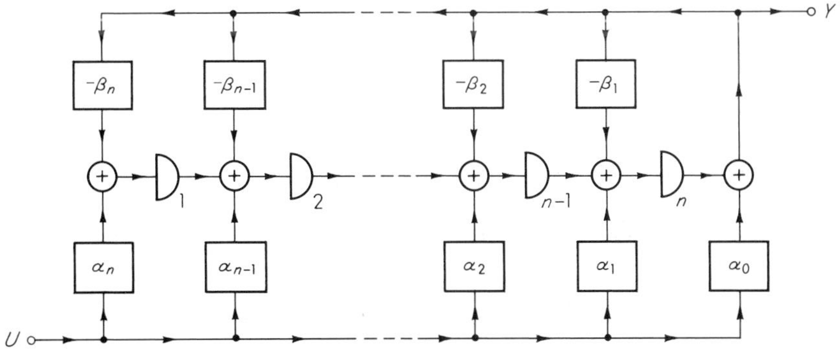

Fig. 5.45.1 General realization of a transfer function.

1 $$\begin{aligned} Y &= \alpha_0 U + S_n \\ &= \alpha_0 U + \alpha_1 dU - \beta_1 dY + dS_{n-1} \\ &= \alpha_0 U + \alpha_1 dU + \alpha_2 d^2 U - \beta_1 dY - \beta_2 d^2 Y + d^2 S_{n-2} \\ &\quad \cdots\cdots\cdots\cdots\cdots\cdots \\ &= \alpha_0 U + \alpha_1 dU + \cdots + \alpha_n d^n U - \beta_1 dY - \beta_2 d^2 Y - \cdots - \beta_n d^n Y \end{aligned}$$

where S_i denotes the d transform of the output of delayer i. Hence:

2 $$\tau = \frac{Y}{U} = \frac{\alpha_0 + \alpha_1 d + \cdots + \alpha_n d^n}{1 + \beta_1 d + \cdots + \beta_n d^n}$$

We thus have a circuit which realizes an arbitrary transfer function directly from the normalized form of this function.

3 *Example* Figure *5.45.2* shows the realization of an LMS over $GF(3)$,

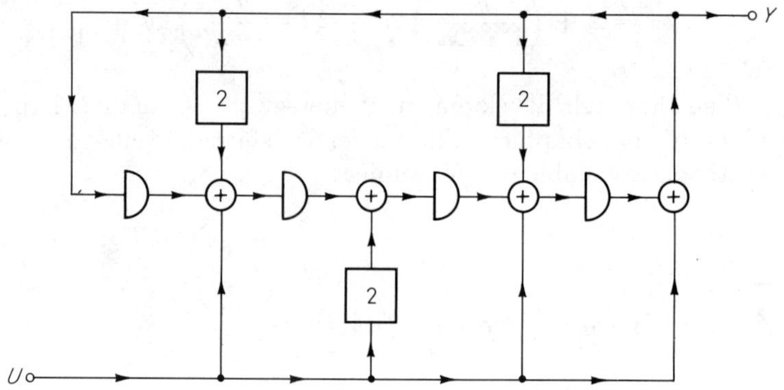

Fig. 5.45.2 Realization of LMS of Example *5.45.3*.

whose transfer function is

4 $$\tau = \frac{1 + d + 2d^2 + d^3}{1 + d + d^3 + 2d^4}$$

APPENDIX A DETERMINATION OF ELEMENTARY DIVISORS OF A SQUARE MATRIX

Given an $n \times n$ matrix $\mathbf{M}$ over a field F, we shall define three *elementary row (column) operations*, abbreviated ero (eco), which can be performed on

$$\mathbf{M}_1 = \mathbf{M} - x\mathbf{I}$$

1 The interchange of any two rows (columns).
2 The multiplication of a row (column) by a nonzero element of F.

3 The addition of any polynomial-multiplied row (column) to another row (column).

Let $a_1(x)$ be a least-degree nonzero element in $\mathbf{M}_1$. If $a_1(x)$ does not divide every other element, let $b_1(x)$ be any element in $\mathbf{M}_1$ not divisible by $a_1(x)$. Suppose $a_1(x)$ and $b_1(x)$ share the same column:

4
$$\begin{array}{c} \\ i \\ \\ j \\ \\ \end{array} \begin{bmatrix} & \overset{k}{} & \\ \hline & a_1(x) & \\ \hline \\ \hline & b_1(x) & \\ \hline & & \end{bmatrix}$$

By the division algorithm (see *5.6.2*):

5
$$b_1(x) = q_1(x)a_1(x) - a_2(x) \qquad \partial(a_2(x)) < \partial(a_1(x))$$

Hence, if by ero *3*, $-q_1(x)$ times row i is added to row j, $b_1(x)$ is replaced with $a_2(x)$ whose degree is less than that of $a_1(x)$. A similar operation can be performed when $a_1(x)$ and $b_1(x)$ share the same row rather than the same column. If $a_1(x)$ and $b_1(x)$ share neither row nor column, the replacement of $b_1(x)$ with an element $a_2(x)$, whose degree is less than that of $a_1(x)$, can be done via a third element which shares its row with $a_1(x)$ and column with $b_1(x)$ (or conversely). Now, if $a_2(x)$ does not divide every other element in the new matrix, find $b_2(x)$ not divisible by $a_2(x)$ and, by a similar process, replace $b_2(x)$ with $a_3(x)$ whose degree is less than that of $a_2(x)$. In this manner the least degree in the matrix can be successively reduced until an element $a_r(x)$ is obtained which divides every other element in the matrix (this situation is always attainable since, at worst, the degree can always be reduced to 0, in which case the matrix contains a constant which divides all other elements). By eros and ecos of type *1*, $a_r(x)$ can be placed in the upper left-hand corner of the matrix. Subsequently, by eros and ecos of type *3*, $a_r(x)$ can be used to replace all other entries in row 1 and column 1 with 0. Finally, by ero *2*, $a_r(x)$ can be replaced with a monic polynomial $f_1(x)$. At this point the matrix has the form

6
$$\left[\begin{array}{c|c} f_1(x) & 0 \cdots 0 \\ \hline 0 & \\ \vdots & \mathbf{M}_2 \\ 0 & \end{array}\right]$$

where $f_1(x)$ is a monic polynomial dividing all elements of $\mathbf{M}_2$. $\mathbf{M}_2$ can undergo a similar process, at the end of which the original matrix assumes the form

7
$$\left[\begin{array}{cc|c} f_1(x) & 0 & 0 \cdots 0 \\ 0 & f_2(x) & 0 \cdots 0 \\ \hline 0 & 0 & \\ \cdots & \cdots & \mathbf{M}_3 \\ 0 & 0 & \end{array}\right]$$

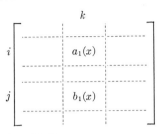

where $f_2(x)$ is a monic polynomial dividing all elements in $\mathbf{M}_3$. If $f_1(x)$ is a common factor of all elements in $\mathbf{M}_2$, it clearly remains so after eros and ecos of types *1*, *2*, *3* have been performed on $\mathbf{M}_1$. Hence, $f_2(x)$ is a multiple of $f_1(x)$. Continuing in this fashion, $\mathbf{M}_1$ can be converted into its *Smith's canonical form* $\tilde{\mathbf{M}}_1$ given by

8 $$\tilde{\mathbf{M}}_1 = \begin{bmatrix} f_1(x) & 0 & \cdots & 0 \\ 0 & f_2(x) & \cdots & 0 \\ \cdots & \cdots & \cdots & \cdots \\ 0 & 0 & \cdots & f_n(x) \end{bmatrix}$$

where $f_i(x)$ divides $f_{i+1}(x)$ for $i = 1, 2, \ldots, n-1$, and where every $f_i(x)$ is monic. The elements $f_i(x)$ in $\tilde{\mathbf{M}}_1$ are called the *similarity invariants of* $\mathbf{M}$. It can be shown that two matrices are similar if and only if they have the same similarity invariants.

9 *Example* Find the similarity invariants of

10 $$\mathbf{M} = \begin{bmatrix} 0 & 0 & 0 \\ 0 & 0 & 1 \\ 2 & 1 & 2 \end{bmatrix}$$

over $GF(3)$. In the following, R_i and C_i stand for row i and column i, respectively, $a \to b$ stands for a replaces b.

11 $$\mathbf{M}_1 = \begin{bmatrix} 2x & 1 & 0 \\ 0 & 2x & 1 \\ 2 & 1 & 2+2x \end{bmatrix} C_1 \rightleftarrows C_2 \begin{bmatrix} 1 & 2x & 0 \\ 2x & 0 & 1 \\ 1 & 2 & 2+2x \end{bmatrix} xC_1 + C_2 \to C_2$$

$$\begin{bmatrix} 1 & 0 & 0 \\ 2x & 2x^2 & 1 \\ 1 & 2+x & 2+2x \end{bmatrix} \begin{matrix} xR_1 + R_2 \to R_1 \\ 2R_1 + R_3 \to R_3 \end{matrix} \begin{bmatrix} 1 & 0 & 0 \\ 0 & 2x^2 & 1 \\ 0 & 2+x & 2+2x \end{bmatrix} C_2 \rightleftarrows C_3$$

$$\begin{bmatrix} 1 & 0 & 0 \\ 0 & 1 & 2x^2 \\ 0 & 2+2x & 2+x \end{bmatrix} x^2C_2 + C_3 \to C_3 \begin{bmatrix} 1 & 0 & 0 \\ 0 & 1 & 0 \\ 0 & 2+2x & 2+x+2x^2+2x^3 \end{bmatrix}$$

$$(1+x)R_2 + R_3 \to R_3$$

$$\begin{bmatrix} 1 & 0 & 0 \\ 0 & 1 & 0 \\ 0 & 0 & 2+x+2x^2+2x^3 \end{bmatrix} 2R_3 \to R_3 \begin{bmatrix} 1 & 0 & 0 \\ 0 & 1 & 0 \\ 0 & 0 & 1+2x+x^2+x^3 \end{bmatrix} = \tilde{\mathbf{M}}_1$$

The similarity invariants of $\mathbf{M}$, then, are $1, 1, 1 + 2x + x^2 + x^3$.

In a factored form, the similarity invariants of $\mathbf{M}$ can be written as

12 $$\begin{aligned} f_n(x) &= [p_1(x)]^{e_{11}}[p_2(x)]^{e_{21}} \cdots [p_r(x)]^{e_{r1}} \\ f_{n-1}(x) &= [p_1(x)]^{e_{12}}[p_2(x)]^{e_{22}} \cdots [p_r(x)]^{e_{r2}} \\ &\cdots\cdots\cdots\cdots\cdots\cdots \\ f_1(x) &= [p_1(x)]^{e_{1n}}[p_2(x)]^{e_{2n}} \cdots [p_r(x)]^{e_{rn}} \end{aligned}$$

where the $p_i(x)$ are irreducible monic polynomials and where

13 $$e_{i1} \geq e_{i2} \geq \cdots \geq e_{in} \geq 0 \qquad e_{i1} > 0$$

The *elementary divisors* of **M** are all nonconstant factors $[p_i(x)]^{e_{ij}}$.

14 *Example* The similarity invariants of

15 $$\mathbf{M} = \begin{bmatrix} 0 & 0 & 1 & 1 & 1 & 1 & 1 & 1 \\ 0 & 1 & 0 & 0 & 0 & 0 & 0 & 0 \\ 0 & 1 & 1 & 1 & 1 & 1 & 1 & 1 \\ 0 & 0 & 0 & 0 & 1 & 1 & 1 & 1 \\ 0 & 0 & 0 & 0 & 1 & 0 & 0 & 0 \\ 0 & 0 & 0 & 0 & 0 & 1 & 0 & 1 \\ 0 & 0 & 0 & 0 & 0 & 0 & 1 & 1 \\ 0 & 0 & 0 & 0 & 0 & 0 & 1 & 0 \end{bmatrix}$$

over $GF(2)$ are

16 $$\begin{aligned} f_8(x) &= (1 + x)^2 x(1 + x + x^2) \\ f_7(x) &= (1 + x)x \\ f_6(x) &= 1 + x \\ f_5(x) &= 1 \\ &\cdots\cdots \\ f_1(x) &= 1 \end{aligned}$$

Hence, the elementary divisors are

17 $$\begin{aligned} &(1 + x)^2,\ 1 + x,\ 1 + x \\ &x,\ x \\ &1 + x + x^2 \end{aligned}$$

APPENDIX B DETERMINATION OF SIMILARITY TRANSFORMATION MATRIX OF TWO SIMILAR MATRICES

Given an $n \times n$ matrix **M** over a field F, the similarity transformation matrix **P** from **M** to its rational canonical form $\mathbf{M}^*$ (that is, **P** such that $\mathbf{M}^* = \mathbf{PMP}^{-1}$) can be found as follows:

1 Perform on an $n \times n$ identity matrix **I** every column operation undergone by $\mathbf{M}_1 = \mathbf{M} - x\mathbf{I}$ in reducing $\mathbf{M}_1$ to its Smith's canonical form $\tilde{\mathbf{M}}_1$ (see Appendix A). Denote the final form of **I** by $\mathbf{Q}_1$.

2 Construct the rational canonical form $\mathbf{M}^*$ of **M** (see Sec. *11*), and let $\check{\mathbf{M}}$ denote the transpose of $\mathbf{M}^* - x\mathbf{I}$.

3 Perform on an $n \times n$ identity matrix **I** every column operation undergone by $\check{\mathbf{M}}$ in reducing it to its Smith's canonical form. Denote the final form of **I** by $\mathbf{Q}_2$.

4 Compute $\mathbf{Q} = \mathbf{Q}_1\mathbf{Q}_2^{-1}$, and write **Q** as a matrix polynomial $\mathfrak{q}(x)$ (that is, as a polynomial in x with matrices over F as coefficients).

5 Then $\mathbf{P}^{-1} = \mathfrak{q}(\mathbf{M}^*)$.

6 *Example* Consider the following matrix, over $GF(2)$.

7 $$\mathbf{M} = \begin{bmatrix} 0 & 1 & 1 \\ 0 & 0 & 1 \\ 1 & 0 & 0 \end{bmatrix}$$

In this case

8 $$\tilde{\mathbf{M}}_1 = \begin{bmatrix} 1 & 0 & 0 \\ 0 & 1 & 0 \\ 0 & 0 & 1 + x + x^3 \end{bmatrix} \qquad \mathbf{Q}_1 = \begin{bmatrix} 0 & 1 & x \\ 0 & x & 1 + x^2 \\ 0 & 0 & 1 \end{bmatrix}$$

9 $$(\mathbf{M}^*)' = \begin{bmatrix} 0 & 1 & 0 \\ 0 & 0 & 1 \\ 1 & 1 & 0 \end{bmatrix} \qquad \mathbf{Q}_2 = \begin{bmatrix} 0 & 0 & 1 \\ 1 & 0 & x \\ 0 & 1 & x^2 \end{bmatrix}$$

10 $$\mathbf{Q} = \mathbf{Q}_1\mathbf{Q}_2^{-1} = \begin{bmatrix} 0 & 1 & x \\ 0 & x & 1 + x^2 \\ 0 & 0 & 1 \end{bmatrix} \begin{bmatrix} x & 1 & 0 \\ x^2 & 0 & 1 \\ 1 & 0 & 0 \end{bmatrix} = \begin{bmatrix} x + x^2 & 0 & 1 \\ 1 + x^2 + x^3 & 0 & x \\ 1 & 0 & 0 \end{bmatrix}$$

11 $$\mathbf{q}(x) = \begin{bmatrix} 0 & 0 & 1 \\ 1 & 0 & 0 \\ 1 & 0 & 0 \end{bmatrix} + \begin{bmatrix} 1 & 0 & 0 \\ 0 & 0 & 1 \\ 0 & 0 & 0 \end{bmatrix} x + \begin{bmatrix} 1 & 0 & 0 \\ 1 & 0 & 0 \\ 0 & 0 & 0 \end{bmatrix} x^2 + \begin{bmatrix} 0 & 0 & 0 \\ 1 & 0 & 0 \\ 0 & 0 & 0 \end{bmatrix} x^3$$

12 $$\mathbf{q}(\mathbf{M}^*) = \begin{bmatrix} 0 & 0 & 1 \\ 1 & 0 & 0 \\ 1 & 0 & 0 \end{bmatrix} + \begin{bmatrix} 1 & 0 & 0 \\ 0 & 0 & 1 \\ 0 & 0 & 0 \end{bmatrix} \mathbf{M}^* + \begin{bmatrix} 1 & 0 & 0 \\ 1 & 0 & 0 \\ 0 & 0 & 0 \end{bmatrix} (\mathbf{M}^*)^2 + \begin{bmatrix} 0 & 0 & 0 \\ 1 & 0 & 0 \\ 0 & 0 & 0 \end{bmatrix} (\mathbf{M}^*)^3$$

13 $$\mathbf{P}^{-1} = \begin{bmatrix} 0 & 1 & 0 \\ 1 & 0 & 1 \\ 1 & 0 & 0 \end{bmatrix} \qquad \mathbf{P} = \begin{bmatrix} 0 & 0 & 1 \\ 1 & 0 & 0 \\ 0 & 1 & 1 \end{bmatrix}$$

Given two similar matrices $\mathbf{M}_a$ and $\mathbf{M}_b$ over a field F, the similarity transformation matrix $\mathbf{P}$ from $\mathbf{M}_a$ to $\mathbf{M}_b$ (that is, $\mathbf{P}$ such that $\mathbf{M}_b = \mathbf{P}\mathbf{M}_a\mathbf{P}^{-1}$) can be found as follows:

14 Find the similarity transformation matrix $\mathbf{P}_a$ from $\mathbf{M}_a$ to its normal canonical form $\mathbf{M}_a^*$.

15 Find the similarity transformation matrix $\mathbf{P}_b$ from $\mathbf{M}_b$ to its rational canonical form $\mathbf{M}_b^*$.

16 Then $\mathbf{P} = \mathbf{P}_b^{-1}\mathbf{P}_a$.

REFERENCES

1 Ash, R.: "Information Theory," chap. 5, Wiley, New York, 1965.

2 Bacon, G.: Analysis of p-nary Time Series, series 60, issue 436, Electronics Research Laboratory, University of California, Berkeley, pp. 1–5, Feb. 15, 1962.

3 Bacon, G.: Linear Modular Circuits as Automata, Department of Electrical Engineering, University of California, Berkeley, 1962 (mimeographed notes).

4 Bailey, J. S.: Generalized Single-ended Counter, *J. Assoc. Comp. Mach.*, vol. 13, pp. 412–418, 1966.

5 Bartee, T. C., and D. I. Schneider: Computation with Finite Fields, *Inform. and Control*, vol. 6, pp. 79–98, 1963.

6 Birdsall, T. G., and M. P. Ristenbatt: Introduction to Linear Shift-register Generated Sequences, *Tech. Rept.* 90, Cooley Electronics Laboratory, University of Michigan, Ann Arbor, October, 1958.

7 Bollman, D. A.: "On the Periodicity of States in Linear Sequential Machine Having a Composite Modulus," unpublished doctoral dissertation, University of Illinois, Urbana, 1963.

8 Bollman, D. A.: Some Periodicity Properties of Transformations on Vector

Spaces over Residue Class Rings, *J. Soc. Ind. Appl. Math.*, vol. 13, pp. 902–912, 1965.

9 Bollman, D. A.: Some Periodicity Properties of Modules over the Ring of Polynomials with Coefficients in a Residue Class Ring, *J. SIAM Appl. Math.*, vol. 14, pp. 237–241, 1966.

10 Booth, T. L.: "Representation of Signal Flow through Linear and Nonlinear Sequential Networks," unpublished doctoral dissertation, University of Connecticut, Storrs, 1962.

11 Booth, T. L.: Nonlinear Sequential Networks, *Trans. IEEE*, vol. CT-10, pp. 279–281, 1963.

12 Booth, T. L.: An Analytic Representation of Signals in Sequential Networks, *Proc. Symp. on Math. Theory of Automata*, Polytechnic Institute of Brooklyn, vol. 12, pp. 301–340, 1963.

13 Brenner, J. L.: Linear Recurrence Relations, *Amer. Math. Monthly*, vol. 61, pp. 171–173, 1954.

14 Bryant, P. R., and R. D. Killick: Nonlinear Feedback Shift Registers, *Trans. IRE*, vol. EC-11, pp. 410–412, 1962.

15 Bryant, P. R., F. G. Heath, and R. D. Killick: Counting with Feedback Shift Registers by Means of a Jump Technique, *Trans. IRE*, vol. EC-11, pp. 285–286, 1962.

16 Brzozowski, J. A.: Regular Expressions for Linear Sequential Circuits, *Trans. IEEE*, vol. EC-14, pp. 148–156, 1965.

17 Brzozowski, J. A., and W. A. Davis: On the Linearity of Autonomous Sequential Machines, *Trans. IEEE*, vol. EC-13, pp. 673–678, 1964.

18 Bussey, W. H.: Galois Field Tables for $p^n \leq 169$, *Bull. Am. Math. Soc.*, vol. 12, pp. 22–38, 1905.

19 Bussey, W. H.: Galois Field Tables of Order Less Than 1000, *Bull. Am. Math. Soc.*, vol. 16, pp. 188–206, 1909.

20 Campbell, L. L.: Two Properties of Pseudo-random Sequences, *Trans. IRE*, vol. IT-5, p. 32, 1959.

21 Church, R.: Tables of Irreducible Polynomials for the First Four Prime Moduli, *Ann. Math.*, vol. 36, pp. 198–209, 1935.

22 Cohn, M.: Controllability in Linear Sequential Networks, *Trans. IRE*, vol. CT-9, pp. 74–78, 1962.

23 Cohn, M.: A Theorem on Linear Automata, *Trans. IEEE*, vol. EC-13, pp. 52–53, 1964.

24 Cohn, M.: Properties of Linear Machines, *J. Assoc. Comp. Mach.*, vol. 11, pp. 296–301, 1964.

25 Cohn, M., and S. Even: Identification and Minimization of Linear Machines, *Trans. IEEE*, vol. EC-14, pp. 367–376, 1965.

26 Colley, L. E.: Computation of Time-phase Displacements of Binary Linear Sequence Generators, *Trans. IEEE*, vol. EC-16, pp. 357–359, 1967.

27 Crowell, R. H.: Graphs of Linear Transformations over Finite Fields, *J. Soc. Indust. Appl. Math.*, vol. 10, pp. 103–112, 1962.

28 Davies, A. C.: Signal-flow Graphs and Linear Feedback Shift Registers, *Trans. IEEE*, vol. IT-13, pp. 119–120, 1967.

29 Davies, N. G.: Some Properties of Linear Recursive Sequences, *Tech. Rept.* 1031, Defence Research Telecom. Establishment, Ottawa, December, 1959.

30 Davis, W. A.: An Introduction to Linear Sequential Machines, *Tech. Rept.* 63-2, Electrical Engineering Department, University of Ottawa, February, 1963.

31 Davis, W. A.: "On the Linearity of Sequential Machines," unpublished master's thesis, Electrical Engineering Department, University of Ottawa, September, 1963.
32 Davis, W. A., and J. A. Brzozowski: On the Linearity of Sequential Machines, *Proc. Fifth Symp. Switching Theory and Logical Design*, Institute of Electrical and Electronics Engineers, pp. 197–208, October, 1964.
33 Davis, W. A., and J. A. Brzozowski: On the Linearity of Sequential Machines, *Trans. IEEE*, vol. EC-15, pp. 21–29, 1966.
34 Elspas, B.: The Theory of Autonomous Linear Sequential Networks, *Trans. IRE*, vol. CT-6, pp. 45–60, 1959.
35 Even, S.: An Extension of Linear Sequential Machines, *Rept.* BL-30, *Sec.* 7, *Comp. Lab.*, Harvard University, Cambridge, Mass., pp. 1–9, 1962.
36 Fitzpatrick, G. B.: Synthesis of Binary Ring Counters of Given Periods, *J. Assoc. Comp. Mach.*, vol. 7, pp. 287–297, 1960.
37 Friedland, B.: Linear Modular Sequential Circuits, *Trans. IRE*, vol. CT-6, pp. 61–68, 1959.
38 Friedland, B., and T. E. Stern: Linear Modular Sequential Circuits and Their Application to Multiple Level Coding, *IRE Natl. Conv. Record*, vol. 7, pt. 2, pp. 40–48, 1959.
39 Friedland, B., and T. E. Stern: On Periodicity of States in Linear Modular Sequential Circuits, *Trans. IRE*, vol. IT-5, pp. 136–137, 1959.
40 Fukunaga, K.: A Theory of Nonlinear Autonomous Sequential Nets Using *z*-Transforms, *Trans. IEEE*, vol. EC-13, pp. 310–312, 1964.
41 Gill, A.: "Introduction to the Theory of Finite-state Machines," chap. 6, McGraw-Hill, New York, 1962.
42 Gill, A.: Analysis of Linear Sequential Circuits by Confluence Sets, *Trans. IEEE*, vol. EC-13, pp. 226–231, 1964.
43 Gill, A.: Analysis and Synthesis of Stable Linear Sequential Circuits, *J. Assoc. Comp. Mach.*, vol. 12, pp. 141–149, 1965.
44 Gill, A.: The Minimization of Linear Sequential Circuits, *Trans. IEEE*, vol. CT-12, pp. 292–294, 1965.
45 Gill, A.: The Reduced Form of a Linear Automaton, in E. R. Caianiello (ed.), "Automata Theory," pp. 164–175, Academic, New York, 1966.
46 Gill, A.: State Graphs of Autonomous Linear Automata, in E. R. Caianiello (ed.), "Automata Theory," pp. 176–180, Academic, New York, 1966.
47 Gill, A.: On the Series-to-Parallel Transformation of Linear Sequential Circuits, *Trans. IEEE*, vol. EC-15, pp. 107–108, 1966.
48 Gill, A.: Graphs of Affine Transformations, with Applications to Sequential Circuits, *IEEE Conf. Record. 7th Ann. Symp. Switching and Automata Theory*, pp. 127–135, 1966.
49 Gill, A.: "Linear Sequential Circuits: Analysis, Synthesis and Applications," McGraw-Hill, New York, 1967.
50 Gill, A., and J. P. Jacob: On a Mapping Polynomial for Galois Fields, *Quart. Appl. Math.*, vol. 24, pp. 57–62, 1966.
51 Gill, A., and C. J. Tan: The Factorization of Linear Cycle Sets, *Trans. IEEE*, vol. CT-12, pp. 630–632, 1965.
52 Gold, R.: Characteristic Linear Sequences and Their Coset Functions, *J. SIAM Appl. Math.*, vol. 14, pp. 980–985, 1966.
53 Golomb, S. W.: Sequences with Randomness Properties, *Terminal Progress Rept.*, Glenn L. Martin Co., 1955.
54 Golomb, S. W.: Linear Recurring Sequences, Jet Propulsion Laboratory, Pasadena, Calif., February, 1961 (dittoed notes).

55 Golomb, S. W. (ed.): "Digital Communication with Space Applications," Prentice-Hall, Englewood Cliffs, N.J., 1964.

56 Golomb, S. W., L. R. Welch, and R. M. Goldstein: Cycles from Non-linear Shift Registers, *Progress Rept.* 20-389, Jet Propulsion Laboratory, Pasadena, Calif., August, 1959.

57 Gorenstein, D., and E. Weiss: An Acquirable Code, *Inform. and Control,* vol. 7, pp. 315–319, 1964.

58 Hall, M.: An Isomorphism between Linear Recurring Sequences and Algebraic Rings, *Trans. Am. Math. Soc.*, vol. 44, pp. 196–218, 1938.

59 Hartmanis, J.: Linear Multivalued Sequential Coding Networks, *Trans. IRE,* vol. CT-6, pp. 69–74, 1959.

60 Hartmanis, J.: Two Tests for the Linearity of Sequential Machines, *Trans. IEEE,* vol. EC-14, pp. 781–786, 1965.

61 Heath, F. G., and M. W. Gribble: Chain Codes and Their Electronic Applications, *Proc. IEE,* vol. 108C, pp. 50–57, 1961.

62 Hotz, G.: On the Mathematical Theory of Linear Sequential Networks, in H. Aiken and W. F. Main (eds.), "Switching Theory in Space Technology," pp. 11–19, Stanford University Press, Stanford, 1963.

63 Hsiao, M. Y., and K. Y. Sih: Series to Parallel Transformation of Linear-feedback Shift-Register Circuit, *Trans. IEEE,* vol. EC-13, pp. 738–740, 1964.

64 Huffman, D. A.: A Linear Circuit Viewpoint of Error-correcting Codes, *Trans. IRE,* vol. IT-2, pp. 20–28, 1956.

65 Huffman, D. A.: The Synthesis of Linear Sequential Coding Networks, in C. Cherry (ed.), "Information Theory," pp. 77–95, Academic, New York, 1956.

66 Huffman, D. A.: An Algebra for Periodically Time-varying Linear Binary Sequence Transducers, *Ann. Comp. Lab.*, Harvard University, Cambridge, Mass., vol. 29, pp. 189–203, 1959.

67 Jacob, J. P.: The Design of Circuits for Performing Operations and Computing Functions over Finite Fields, *Tech. Mem.* M-106, Electronics Research Laboratory, University of California, Berkeley, Nov. 30, 1964.

68 Jury, E. I.: "Theory and Application of the z-Transform Method," sec. 8.5, Wiley, New York, 1964.

69 Kaneko, H.: A Few Probabilistic Properties of Modular Circuits, series 60, issue 448, Electronics Research Laboratory, University of California, Berkeley, Apr. 30, 1962.

70 Kautz, W. H. (ed.): "Linear Sequential Switching Circuits—Selected Technical Papers," Holden-Day, San Francisco, 1965.

71 Kwakernaak, H.: The Autocorrelation Function of a Complete Recurrent Sequence and the Cross Correlation Function of Two Complete Recurrent Sequences with Mutually Prime Periods, series 60, issue 436, Electronics Research Laboratory, University of California, Berkeley, pp. 37–42, Feb. 15, 1962.

72 Lavallee, P.: Some Further Group Properties of Singular Linear Sequential Circuits and Their Synthesis, *Rept.* 1250, Polytechnic Institute of Brooklyn, October, 1964.

73 Lavallee, P.: Nonstable Cycle and Level Sets for Linear Sequential Machines, *Trans. IEEE,* vol. EC-14, pp. 957–959, 1965.

74 Lavallee, P.: Some New Group Theoretic Properties of Singular Linear Sequential Machines, *Trans. IEEE,* vol. EC-14, pp. 959–961, 1965.

75 Lechner, R. J.: "Affine Equivalence of Switching Functions," unpublished doctoral dissertation, Harvard University, Cambridge, Mass., January, 1963.

76 Lerner, R. M.: "Signals with Uniform Ambiguity Functions," *IRE Natl. Conv. Record*, vol. 6, pt. 4, p. 27, 1958.
77 Lunelli, L.: Matrices in Theory of Autonomous Sequential Networks, *Trans. IRE*, vol. CT-6, pp. 392–393, 1959.
78 Magleby, K. B.: The Synthesis of Nonlinear Feedback Shift Registers, *Tech. Rept.* 6207-1, Stanford Electronics Laboratories, Stanford University, Stanford, October, 1963.
79 Mandelbaum, D.: A Comparison of Linear Sequential Circuits and Arithmetic Sequences, *Trans. IEEE*, vol. EC-16, pp. 151–157, 1967.
80 Marcovitz, A. B.: On Time-varying Coding Networks, *Proc. WESCON, Paper* 34/1, 1961.
81 Marsh, R. W.: Tables of Irreducible Polynomials over *GF*(2) through Degree 19, National Security Agency, Washington, D.C., Oct. 24, 1957.
82 Massey, J. L., and R. W. Liu: Equivalence of Nonlinear Shift Registers, *Trans. IEEE*, vol. IT-10, pp. 378–379, 1964.
83 Meggitt, J. E.: The Mathematical Theory of Sequential Systems, with Particular Reference to Two-element Systems, *IBM British Lab.*, Winchester, Hants October, 1960.
84 Ormsby, J. F. A.: A Note on Linear Recurring Sequences, series 60, issue 436, Electronics Research Laboratory, University of California, Berkeley, pp. 62–74, Feb. 15, 1962.
85 Peterson, W. W.: "Error-correcting Codes," The M.I.T. Press, Cambridge, Mass., 1961.
86 Preparata, F. P.: On the Realizability of Special Classes of Autonomous Sequential Circuits, *Trans. IEEE*, vol. EC-14, pp. 791–797, 1965.
87 Pugsley, J. H.: Sequential Functions and Linear Sequential Machines, *Trans. IEEE*, vol. EC-14, pp. 376–382, 1965.
88 Radchenko, A. N., and V. I. Filipov: Shift Registers with Logical Feedback and Their Use as Counting and Coding Devices, *Automation and Remote Control*, vol. 20, pp. 1467–1473, 1959.
89 Richalet, J.: Operational Calculus for Finite Rings, *Trans. IEEE*, vol. CT-12, pp. 558–570, 1965.
90 Robinson, I. J. W.: A Study of the Generation of Linear Recursive Sequences, *Tech. Rept.* 1082, Defence Research Telecom. Establishment, Ottawa, November, 1961.
91 Roth, H. H.: Linear Binary Shift Register Circuits Utilizing a Minimum Number of Mod-2 Adders, *Trans. IEEE*, vol. IT-11, pp. 215–220, 1965.
92 Solomon, G.: Linear Recursive Sequences as Finite Difference Equations, *Group Rept.* 47.37, Lincoln Laboratory, Lexington, Mass., March, 1960.
93 Srinivasan, C. V.: State Diagrams of Linear Sequential Machines, *J. Franklin Inst.*, vol. 273, pp. 383–418, 1962.
94 Stern, T. E., and B. Friedland: The Linear Modular Sequential Circuit Generalized, *Trans. IRE*, vol. CT-8, pp. 79–80, 1961.
95 Tang, D. T.: Transfer Function Synthesis of Linear Shift-Register Circuits, *Proc. Third Ann. Allerton Conf. Circuit and System Theory*, pp. 63–72, 1965.
96 Toda, I.: A Theory of Linear Machines, *ARPA Contract* SD-185, University of California, Berkeley, 1965 (dittoed notes.)
97 Toda, I.: The Tree Set of a Linear Machine, *Trans. IEEE*, vol. EC-14, pp. 954–957, 1965.
98 Van Heerden, P. J.: Analysis of Binary Time Series in Periodic Functions, *Trans. IRE*, vol. EC-8, pp. 228–229, 1959.

99 Van Heerden, P. J.: Periodic Binary Time Series and Their Relation to Boolean Functions, *Trans. IRE*, vol. EC-9, p. 510, 1960.

100 Wang, K. C.: "On the Linearity of Sequential Machines," unpublished doctoral dissertation, Northwestern University, Evanston, Ill., September, 1965.

101 Ward, M.: The Arithmetical Theory of Linear Recurring Series, *Trans. Am. Math. Soc.*, vol. 35, pp. 600–628, 1933.

102 Watson, E. J.: Primitive Polynomials (mod 2), *Math. of Computation*, vol. 16, pp. 368–369, 1962.

103 Yau, S. S., and K. C. Wang: Linearity of Sequential Machines, *Trans. IEEE*, vol. EC-15, pp. 337–354, 1966.

104 Young, F. H.: Analysis of Shift Register Counters, *J. Assoc. Comp. Mach.*, vol. 5, pp. 385–388, 1958.

105 Zierler, N.: Several Binary Sequence Generators, *Tech. Rept.* No. 95, Lincoln Laboratories, Lexington, Mass., Sept. 12, 1955.

106 Zierler, N.: Linear Recurring Sequences, *J. Soc. Indust. Appl. Math.*, vol. 7, pp. 31–48, 1959.

6

Linear time-invariant systems

E. Polak[1]
Department of Electrical Engineering and Computer Sciences
University of California, Berkeley

1 *Introduction*

As the name implies, linear differential systems are systems whose input-output relations can be expressed in the form of a set of linear differential equations. The intrinsic importance of such systems stems from two facts. First, many of the systems encountered in the real world are governed, at least approximately, by linear differential equations. Second, linear differential systems are particularly susceptible to analytical treatment on a very general level.

Obviously, in the process of its development, the state space approach to linear differential systems has built on known results from the theory of differential equations. It has also absorbed a great deal from several older disciplines such as analytical mechanics, stability theory, circuit theory, and control theory. For the sake of completeness some of these results will be reviewed in this chapter. However, the main concern of this chapter will be with certain system theoretic concepts which are not directly traceable either to the classical theory of differential equations or to the other disciplines mentioned above.

To be specific, the chapter is roughly divided into three parts. In Secs. *2* to *6* we shall examine the classical properties of the solutions to the so-called standard, or canonical, form of the state equations of linear, time-invariant differential systems. In Secs. *7* to *9* we shall

[1] The research reported herein was supported in part by the National Aeronautics and Space Administration under Grant NsG-354 (S-4).

study the specifically system-theoretic concepts of controllability, observability, equivalence, and minimality of representation. Finally, in Secs. *10* to *12*, we shall consider the possibility of obtaining alternate representations for a system.

2 *The standard form*

As will be shown in Secs. *10*, *11*, and *12*, the state equations of a linear, finite-dimensional, time-invariant differential system S can be expressed in the form

1 $$\dot{x}(t) = Ax(t) + Bu(t)$$

S:

2 $$y(t) = Cx(t) + Du(t)$$

where $x = (x^1, \ldots, x^n)$† is the state of the system, whose components are real or complex functions of time; $u = (u^1, \ldots, u^m)$ is the input to the system, whose components are real functions of time;

$$y = (y^1, \ldots, y^k)$$

is the output of the system, whose components are real functions of time; and A, B, C, and D are constant matrices with complex or real elements, of dimension $n \times n$, $n \times m$, $k \times n$, and $k \times m$, respectively. The dot on $\dot{x}(t)$ denotes differentiation with respect to time. We shall refer to *1* and *2* as the *standard*, or *canonical*, form of state equations. We now focus our attention on the solution of equations of the form of *1*.

We recall that the derivative and integral of a time-dependent matrix $Z(t)$, with elements $z_{ij}(t)$, are defined to be

3 $$\dot{Z}(t) \triangleq [\dot{z}_{ij}(t)]$$

$$\int Z(t)\, dt \triangleq \left[\int z_{ij}(t)\, dt\right]$$

that is, the indicated operation is performed on each element of the matrix $Z(t)$ individually. We also recall that the most elementary way in which a function mapping scalars into scalars can be extended to a function mapping matrices into matrices is as follows:

4 **Definition** Let $\sum_{k=0}^{\infty} a_k z^k$ be a scalar power series and let $f(\cdot)$ be the

† It will usually be clear from the context whether a vector z is a column or row vector. In the few cases where ambiguity may arise, we shall resort to Dirac notation and write $\langle z$ when we use z as a row vector and $z\rangle$ when we use z as a column vector.

function defined by

5 $$f(z) \triangleq \sum_{k=0}^{\infty} a_k z^k$$

for all real or complex z for which the series converges. The extension of $f(\cdot)$ to $n \times n$ matrices, where $n = 1, 2, 3, \ldots$, is a matrix-valued function, also denoted by $f(\cdot)$, which is defined by

6 $$f(Z) \triangleq \sum_{k=0}^{\infty} a_k Z^k \qquad \text{where } Z^0 = I$$

for all real or complex square matrices Z for which the series converges componentwise (I is the identity matrix).

We can now obtain expressions for the solutions of *1* and *2*. Let $x(t;t_0,x_0,u)$ denote the solution of *1* at time t, from the initial state x_0 at the time t_0, corresponding to the input u. Let $y(t;t_0,x_0,u)$ denote the corresponding output at time t. When there is no ambiguity involved, we shall denote these simply by $x(t)$ and $y(t)$, respectively. We now claim that

7 $$x(t;t_0,x_0,u) = e^{(t-t_0)A}\left[x_0 + \int_{t_0}^{t} e^{(t_0-\tau)A}Bu(\tau)\, d\tau\right]$$

To verify that *7* is indeed the solution of *1*, we first observe that according to the definition *4*,

8 $$e^{tA} = I + tA + \frac{t^2}{2!}A^2 + \frac{t^3}{3!}A^3 + \cdots$$

It can be shown that this series converges for all square matrices A. Differentiating the right-hand side of *8* term by term with respect to t, we get

9 $$\frac{d}{dt}e^{tA} = A + tA^2 + \frac{t^2}{2!}A^3 + \cdots = Ae^{tA}$$

Now, let us compute the product $e^{t_1A}e^{t_2A}$ as follows:

10 $$e^{t_1A}e^{t_2A} = \left(I + t_1A + \frac{t_1^2}{2!}A^2 + \cdots\right)\left(I + t_2A + \frac{t_2^2}{2!}A + \cdots\right) = I + (t_1 + t_2)A + \frac{(t_1+t_2)^2}{2!}A^2 + \cdots = e^{(t_1+t_2)A}$$

Consequently, $e^{t_1A}e^{t_2A} = e^{t_2A}e^{t_1A}$, and also

11 $$e^{-tA} = (e^{tA})^{-1} \qquad \text{for all } t$$

Computing $\dot{x}(t)$ from *7* and making use of the differentiation rule for products of functions, which remains valid for the matrix case, we get

12 $$\begin{aligned}\dot{x}(t) &= Ae^{(t-t_0)A}\left[x_0 + \int_{t_0}^{t} e^{(t_0-\tau)A}Bu(\tau)\,d\tau\right] + e^{(t-t_0)A}[e^{(t_0-t)A}Bu(t)] \\ &= Ax(t) + Bu(t)\end{aligned}$$

Thus, $x(t)$, as given by *7*, satisfies *1*. Letting $t = t_0$, we find that $x(t_0) = x_0$, which completes the proof.

Substituting for $x(t)$ in *2*, we get

13 $$y(t;t_0,x_0,u) = Ce^{(t-t_0)A}\left[x_0 + \int_{t_0}^{t} e^{(t_0-\tau)A}Bu(\tau)\,d\tau\right] + Du(t)$$

Since the matrix e^{tA} was defined in *4* in series form, it is not clear that we can obtain closed-form expressions for $x(t)$ and $y(t)$. We shall now present an alternative definition of a function of a matrix which subsumes the series definition of *4* and which leads to closed-form expressions in *7* and *13*.

3 *Evaluation of the matrix* e^{tA}

The definition of a function of a matrix $f(\cdot)$ by means of a power series as in Sec. *2* is very natural, but it is somewhat restricted and not particularly suitable for computing the matrix $f(Z)$.

We shall now introduce an alternative definition for extending a function mapping scalars into scalars to a function of the same name mapping matrices into matrices, which is equivalent to *6.2.4* but which applies to a larger class of square matrices than the first definition and results in closed-form expressions.

1 **Definition** Let Z be an $n \times n$ matrix with distinct eigenvalues $\lambda_1, \ldots, \lambda_s$, of respective multiplicity m_j (as a root of the characteristic polynomial), $j = 1, \ldots, s$; let $f(\cdot)$ be a function analytic in an open set containing $\lambda_1, \ldots, \lambda_s$; and let

$$p_Z(\lambda) = \alpha_0 + \alpha_1\lambda + \cdots + \alpha_{n-1}\lambda^{n-1}$$

be the polynomial of degree $n - 1$ whose coefficients are determined uniquely by the set of equations

2 $$p_Z^{(l)}(\lambda_j) = f^{(l)}(\lambda_j) \qquad l = 0, 1, \ldots, m_{j-1}; j = 1, 2, \ldots, s$$

where $p_Z^{(l)}$ denotes the lth derivative of p_Z.

Then we define the function $f(\cdot)$ by

3 $$f(Z) = p_Z(Z) \triangleq \sum_{j=0}^{n-1} \alpha_j Z^j$$

where $p_Z(Z)$ is a polynomial in Z obtained from $p_Z(\lambda)$ by replacing λ^j by Z^j, $j = 0, 1, \ldots, n-1$. We shall refer to *3* as *the interpolation formula*, and to p_Z as *the interpolation polynomial.*

4 *Comment* Note that we can use the Cayley-Hamilton theorem to express powers Z^{n-1+k}, $k = 1, 2, \ldots,$ of an $n \times n$ matrix in terms of polynomials in Z of degree $n - 1$, and therefore we can reduce any convergent power series *6.2.6* to the finite form *3.*

From *3* we see that if $e_i\rangle$, $i = 1, 2, \ldots, s$, is an eigenvector of Z; that is, $Ze_i\rangle = \lambda_i e_i\rangle$, then $e_i\rangle$ is also an eigenvector of $f(Z)$, but the corresponding eigenvalue is $f(\lambda_i) = \sum_{j=0}^{n-1} \alpha_j \lambda_i^j$; that is,

5 $$f(Z)e_i\rangle = f(\lambda_i)e_i\rangle$$

Thus, to compute $f(Z)$ in closed form, we simply find the interpolating polynomial $p_Z(\lambda)$. For example, let A be an $n \times n$ matrix with *distinct* eigenvalues $\lambda_1, \lambda_2, \ldots, \lambda_n$. To compute e^{tA}, we find the interpolation polynomial

$$p(\lambda) = \alpha_0(t) + \lambda\alpha_1(t) + \lambda^2\alpha_2(t) + \cdots + \lambda^{n-1}\alpha_{n-1}(t)$$

by solving the following set of equations for the coefficients $\alpha_i(t)$, $i = 0, 1, \ldots, n-1$:

6 $$e^{\lambda_i t} = \alpha_0(t) + \lambda_i\alpha_1(t) + \lambda_i^2\alpha_2(t) + \cdots + \lambda_i^{n-1}\alpha_{n-1}(t) \qquad i = 1, 2, \ldots, n-1$$

This set of functional equations always has a unique solution, and hence

7 $$e^{tA} = \sum_{i=0}^{n-1} \alpha_i(t) A^i$$

Obviously, expressions such as *7* lead to closed-form solutions $x(t)$, $y(t)$ in *6.2.7* and *6.2.13*. They are also much more suitable than the series form *6.2.6* for the study of the properties of e^{tA}.

4 *Spectral decomposition of matrices*

We shall restrict ourselves in this section to $n \times n$ matrices with *distinct* eigenvalues, and we shall examine the properties of matrices and of functions of matrices, which will be needed for a discussion of modes in the next section.

Thus, let A be an $n \times n$ matrix with distinct eigenvalues $\lambda_1, \ldots, \lambda_n$, and let $e_1\rangle, \ldots, e_n\rangle$, where $e_i = (e_i^1, \ldots, e_i^n)$, be the corresponding (right) eigenvectors of A; that is, $Ae_i\rangle = \lambda_i e_i\rangle$, for $i = 1, 2, \ldots, n$. The eigenvectors $e_i\rangle$ can be shown to be linearly independent, and therefore they form a basis for the n-dimensional, complex vector space C^n. Let the row vectors $\langle f_1, \ldots, \langle f_n$, where $f_i = (f_i^1, \ldots, f_i^n)$, be the *reciprocal basis vectors;* i.e., the vectors $\langle f_i$ satisfy the set of equations

1 $$\langle f_i, e_j\rangle \triangleq \delta_{ij} \qquad i, j = 1, 2, \ldots, n$$

where δ_{ij} is the Kronecker delta and $\langle f_i, e_j\rangle = \sum_{l=1}^{n} \bar{f}_i^l e_j^l$ is the usual *complex scalar product* (the bar here denotes complex conjugation). It is readily seen from the defining relation *1* that for $i = 1, 2, \ldots, n$ the vector $\langle f_i$ is the ith row of the matrix $\bar{E}^{-1}$, where $\bar{E} \triangleq [\bar{e}_j\rangle]$ is a matrix whose jth column is the complex conjugate of the vector $e_j\rangle$.

The vectors $\langle \bar{f}_i$ can also be shown to be the left eigenvectors of the matrix A; that is,

2 $$\langle \bar{f}_i A = \lambda_i \langle \bar{f}_i \qquad i = 1, 2, \ldots, n$$

To show this, let E be an $n \times n$ matrix whose ith column is $e_i\rangle$, and let F be an $n \times n$ matrix with rows $\langle f_i$. Then, because of *1*, and the fact that the vectors $e_i\rangle$ are right eigenvectors of A, we have

3 $$\bar{F}AE = D$$

where D is an $n \times n$ diagonal matrix with elements $d_{ii} = \lambda_i$, $i = 1, 2, \ldots, n$. But we have seen that $\bar{F} = E^{-1}$, hence

4 $$\bar{F}A = D\bar{F}$$

and, examining the ith row of *4*, for $i = 1, 2, \ldots, n$, we find that *2* holds. Relation *3* is important in itself since it shows how to transform the matrix A into the diagonal Jordan canonical form D.

5 **Definition** Let $a = (a^1, a^2, \ldots, a^r)$ and $b = (b^1, b^2, \ldots, b^s)$ be any two vectors. We shall call the $r \times s$ matrix $a\rangle\,\langle \bar{b}$ a *dyad*. Note that for any vector $x = (x^1, x^2, \ldots, x^s)$, $[a\rangle\,\langle \bar{b}]x = a\rangle\,\langle b, x\rangle$.†

We now make an important observation. The sum of the dyads formed by the right eigenvectors $e_i\rangle$ and left eigenvectors $\langle f_i$ of the

† Since eigenvectors may have complex elements, we shall always use the complex scalar product; that is, $\langle x, y\rangle = \sum_{i=1}^{n} \bar{x}^i y^i$, with $\bar{x}$ being the complex conjugate of x.

matrix A is the identity matrix, provided they have been normalized to satisfy $\langle e_i, f_j\rangle = \delta_{ij}$ for $i, j = 1, 2, \ldots, n$. Thus,

6 $$\sum_{i=1}^{n} e_i\rangle \langle \bar{f}_i = I$$

Clearly, the dyads $e_i\rangle \langle \bar{f}_i$ in *6* are $n \times n$ matrices, with $\alpha\beta$ elements $e_i^\alpha \bar{f}_i^\beta$. To prove the truth of *6*, let us take any vector $x\rangle$ and express it in the form

7 $$x\rangle = \sum_{i=1}^{n} \xi^i e_i\rangle$$

The decomposition *7* is always possible and is unique, since the vectors $e_i\rangle$ form a basis. Now,

8 $$\left(\sum_{i=1}^{n} e_i\rangle \langle \bar{f}_i\right) x\rangle = \sum_{i=1}^{n} e_i\rangle \langle f_i, x\rangle$$
$$= \sum_{i=1}^{n} e_i\rangle \langle f_i, \sum_{j=1}^{n} \xi^j e_j\rangle = \sum_{i=1}^{n} \sum_{j=1}^{n} \xi^j e_i\rangle \langle f_i, e_j\rangle = \sum_{i=1}^{n} \xi^i e_i\rangle = x\rangle$$

which proves the assertion *6*.

The result *6* is fundamental, since it enables us to decompose a matrix, or a function of a matrix, into spectral components (the set of all the eigenvalues of a square matrix A is referred to as the spectrum of A). Thus, for the matrix A, we get the spectral decomposition

9 $$A = A\left(\sum_{i=1}^{n} e_i\rangle \langle \bar{f}_i\right) = \sum_{i=1}^{n} Ae_i\rangle \langle \bar{f}_i = \sum_{i=1}^{n} \lambda_i e_i\rangle \langle \bar{f}_i$$

Similarly, if $f(A)$, the value of the function f at A, is given by the interpolation formula *6.3.3* as

10 $$f(A) = \sum_{i=0}^{n-1} \alpha_i A^i$$

then the spectral decomposition of $f(A)$ is seen to be

11 $$f(A) = f(A)\left(\sum_{i=1}^{n} e_i\rangle \langle \bar{f}_i\right) = \sum_{i=1}^{n} f(\lambda_i) e_i\rangle \langle \bar{f}_i$$

Thus, for example, the spectral decomposition of e^{tA} is

12 $$e^{tA} = \sum_{i=1}^{n} e^{\lambda_i t} e_i\rangle \langle \bar{f}_i$$

Expression *11*, which is obviously consistent with *6.3.3*, can be used as an independent definition of a function of a matrix, whose domain of definition is the set of all $n \times n$ matrices with distinct eigenvalues. We can also obtain a decomposition similar to *11*, but much more complicated, for the case in which the eigenvalues are not distinct.[1] However, we shall omit this in the present treatment.

The reader may verify that *11* leads to the following useful spectral decomposition formulas:

13 $$A^{-1} = \sum_{i=1}^{n} \frac{1}{\lambda_i} e_i\rangle \langle \bar{f}_i \qquad (\text{if } \lambda_i \neq 0 \text{ for } i = 1, 2, \ldots, n)$$

14 $$e^{-tA} = \sum_{i=1}^{n} e^{-\lambda_i t} e_i\rangle \langle \bar{f}_i$$

The eigenvectors $e_i\rangle$ and the reciprocal basis vectors $\langle \bar{f}_i$ of the matrix A have yet another interesting property. Let T be any constant, nonsingular $n \times n$ matrix and let $\tilde{A}$ be defined by

15 $$\tilde{A} = T^{-1}AT$$

The matrix $\tilde{A}$ is then said to be similar to the matrix A. We may easily verify that the eigenvalues and eigenvectors of the matrices A and $\tilde{A}$ are related as follows. For $i = 1, 2, \ldots, n$, let $\tilde{\lambda}_i$ be the eigenvalues of $\tilde{A}$; let $\tilde{e}_i\rangle$ be the right eigenvectors of $\tilde{A}$; and let $\langle \tilde{\bar{f}}_i$ be the reciprocal basis vectors of $\tilde{A}$. Then

16 $$\tilde{e}_i\rangle = T^{-1}e_i\rangle \qquad \text{for } i = 1, 2, \ldots, n$$

17 $$\langle \tilde{\bar{f}}_i = \langle \bar{f}_i T \qquad \text{for } i = 1, 2, \ldots, n$$

18 $$\tilde{\lambda}_i = \lambda_i \qquad \text{for } i = 1, 2, \ldots, n$$

We therefore conclude from the preceding development that *similar* matrices have identical eigenvalues and that any function f which can be evaluated on A can also be evaluated on $\tilde{A}$, assuming the value

19 $$f(\tilde{A}) = T^{-1}f(A)T$$

5 *Spectral decomposition of the state*

Let us now return to our system S defined by *6.2.1* and *6.2.2*; that is,

1 $$\dot{x}(t) = Ax(t) + Bu(t)$$

S:

2 $$y(t) = Cx(t) + Du(t)$$

[1] See Zadeh and Desoer (Ref. 1), p. 604.

and let us assume again that the eigenvalues $\lambda_1, \ldots, \lambda_n$ of the matrix A are distinct. Again, let $e_i\rangle$, $i = 1, 2, \ldots, n$, be the eigenvectors of A, and let $\langle f_i$, $i = 1, 2, \ldots, n$, be the reciprocal basis vectors determined by *6.4.1*. Then (see *6.4.6* and *6.4.8*)

3 $$x(t) = \sum_{i=1}^{n} e_i\rangle \langle f_i, x(t)\rangle$$

that is,

4 $$x(t) = \sum_{i=1}^{n} \xi^i(t)e_i\rangle$$

where we define $\xi^i(t) = \langle f_i, x(t)\rangle$. As a result of *6.4.9* and *4*, Eq. *1* may now be decomposed as follows:

5 $$\sum_{i=1}^{n} \dot{\xi}^i(t)e_i\rangle = \sum_{i=1}^{n} \lambda_i\xi^i(t)e_i\rangle + \sum_{i=1}^{n} e_i\rangle \langle f_i, Bu(t)\rangle$$

We observe that $\xi^i(t)$ describes the motion of the system "along" the eigenvector $e_i\rangle$, and that each $\xi^i(t)$ is independent of the others; i.e., the motion of the system along any eigenvector is unaffected by its motion along any other eigenvector. This fact is made particularly clear when we write from *5* the scalar differential equations for the coefficients $\xi^i(t)$. Thus,

6 $$\begin{aligned} \dot{\xi}^i(t) &= \lambda_i\xi^i(t) + \langle f_i, Bu(t)\rangle \\ &= \lambda_i\xi^i(t) + \langle B^*f_i, u(t)\rangle \qquad i = 1, 2, \ldots, n \end{aligned}$$

where B^* is the complex-conjugate transpose of B.

We may think of the vectors $\langle B^*f_i$ as the "weights" which determine the magnitude of the effect of the input $u(t)$ on the motion of $x(t)$ in the "direction" $e_i\rangle$.

The solution of the system *6* may be written in the form

7 $$\xi^i(t) = e^{(t-t_0)\lambda_i}\left[\xi^i(t_0) + \int_{t_0}^{t} e^{(t_0-s)\lambda_i}\langle B^*f_i, u(s)\rangle\, ds\right]$$

where the $\xi^i(t_0) = \langle f_i, x(t_0)\rangle$ are determined from the given initial state $x(t_0) = \sum_{i=1}^{n} \xi^i(t_0)e_i\rangle$. Thus, the solution *6.2.7* of *6.2.1* is seen to have the following *spectral expansion:*

8 $$x(t) = \sum_{i=1}^{n} e^{(t-t_0)\lambda_i}e_i\rangle \langle f_i, x(t_0)\rangle + \sum_{i=1}^{n} e^{(t-t_0)\lambda_i}e_i\rangle \int_{t_0}^{t} e^{(t_0-s)\lambda_i}\langle B^*f_i, u(s)\rangle\, ds$$

Alternatively, the expansion *8* could have been obtained directly from *6.2.7* by substituting $x(t_0) = \sum_{i=1}^{n} \xi^i(t_0)e_i\rangle$ and

$$e^{sA} = \sum_{i=1}^{n} e^{s\lambda_i}e_i\rangle\langle \bar{f}_i$$

with $s = t - t_0$. Expression *8* is called the *spectral decomposition of the state.* It is usual to refer to the vector-valued functions of time $e^{\lambda_i t}e_i\rangle$, where $i = 1, 2, \ldots, n$, as the *modes of the system 1.* We see that expression *8* decomposes the state $x(t)$ into a sum of modes, with time-varying coefficients. We can obtain a similar decomposition for the output by substituting for $x(t)$ from *8* into *2*; that is,

9 $$y(t) = \sum_{i=1}^{n} e^{(t-t_0)\lambda_i}Ce_i\rangle\langle f_i, x(t_0)\rangle + \sum_{i=1}^{n} \int_{t_0}^{t} e^{(t-s)\lambda_i}Ce_i\rangle\langle B^*f_i, u(s)\rangle\, ds + Du(t)$$

The preceding development could have been substantially shortened by introducing a formalism which, however, may have obscured the important features of the spectral decomposition. It is proper for us to present this formalism now.

As in Sec. *4*, let E be an $n \times n$ matrix whose ith column is $e_i\rangle$, and let F be an $n \times n$ matrix whose ith row is $\langle f_i$, where, for $i = 1, 2, \ldots, n$, the $e_i\rangle$ are the eigenvectors of the system matrix A and the vectors $\langle f_i$ form the reciprocal basis. (We continue to assume that the matrix A has no repeated eigenvalues.)

Let $\xi(t) = (\xi^1(t), \ldots, \xi^n(t))$ be a vector determined by

10 $$x(t) = E\xi(t)$$

The matrix E, whose columns are the linearly independent eigenvectors $e_i\rangle$ of A, is clearly nonsingular. Substituting for $x(t)$ in *1*, we get

11 $$E\dot{\xi}(t) = AE\xi(t) + Bu(t)$$

and since $\bar{F}E = I$, the identity matrix, we get

12 $$\dot{\xi}(t) = \bar{F}AE\xi(t) + \bar{F}Bu(t)$$

where $\bar{F}AE$ is seen by *6.4.3* to be a diagonal matrix. We see at a glance that *12* and *5* express exactly the same relationship.

6 *Transfer function of the standard form*

Consider again the system S given by *6.2.1* and *6.2.2*. Let $\tilde{x}(s) \triangleq \int_{0-}^{\infty} x(t)e^{-st}\,dt$ be the Laplace transform of the state x, let $\tilde{y}(s) \triangleq \int_{0-}^{\infty} y(t)e^{-st}\,dt$ be the Laplace transform of the output y, and let $\tilde{u}(s) \triangleq \int_{0-}^{\infty} u(t)e^{-st}\,dt$ be the Laplace transform of the input u. Then, taking the Laplace transform of Eqs. *6.2.1* and *6.2.2*, we get

1 $$(sI - A)\tilde{x}(s) = x(0-) + B\tilde{u}(s)$$

2 $$\tilde{y}(s) = C\tilde{x}(s) + D\tilde{u}(s)$$

To obtain the *system transfer function matrix* (see Sec. *11*), we let $x(0-) = 0$, upon which we obtain

3 $$\tilde{y}(s) = [C(sI - A)^{-1}B + D]\tilde{u}(s)$$

where $\tilde{W}(s) \triangleq [C(sI - A)^{-1}B + D]$ is the transfer function matrix. The inverse of the matrix $(sI - A)$ is defined for all s for which det $(sI - A) \neq 0$, that is, for all $s \neq \lambda_i$, $i = 1, 2, \ldots, n$, where the λ_i are the eigenvalues of the matrix A. Comparing *3* with *6.2.13*, we observe that the Laplace transform of e^{tA} is $(sI - A)^{-1}$, and we conclude that it is possible to compute e^{tA} by finding the inverse transform of $(sI - A)^{-1}$.

When the eigenvalues of A are distinct, we can obtain for *3* a spectral decomposition by utilizing the spectral analysis given in Sec. *4*. We note that the eigenvectors $e_i\rangle$, $i = 1, 2, \ldots, n$, of the matrix A are also eigenvectors of the matrix $(sI - A)$. Thus

4 $$(sI - A)e_i\rangle = (s - \lambda_i)e_i\rangle \qquad i = 1, 2, \ldots, n$$

and we see that the corresponding eigenvalues of $(sI - A)$ are $(s - \lambda_i)$. Clearly, the reciprocal basis vectors $\langle f_i$, $i = 1, 2, \ldots, n$, of A (see *6.4.1*) are also the reciprocal basis vectors of $(sI - A)$, and hence we obtain

5 $$(sI - A) = \sum_{i=1}^{n} (s - \lambda_i)e_i\rangle\langle\bar{f}_i$$

Similarly (see *6.4.13*),

6 $$(sI - A)^{-1} = \sum_{i=1}^{n} \frac{1}{s - \lambda_i} e_i\rangle\langle\bar{f}_i \qquad \text{for } s \neq \lambda_i,\ i = 1, 2, \ldots, n$$

Expression *6* can be verified by direct multiplication with *5*. Hence *3* becomes

7
$$\begin{aligned}\tilde{y}(s) &= \sum_{i=1}^{n} \frac{1}{s-\lambda_i} Ce_i\rangle \langle f_i, B\tilde{u}(s)\rangle + D\tilde{u}(s) \\ &= \sum_{i=1}^{n} \frac{1}{s-\lambda_i} Ce_i\rangle \langle B^*f_i, \tilde{u}(s)\rangle + D\tilde{u}(s)\end{aligned}$$

Computing the inverse Laplace transform of *7*, we obtain

8
$$y(t) = \sum_{i=1}^{n} \int_0^t e^{\lambda_i(t-\tau)} Ce_i\rangle \langle B^*f_i, u(\tau)\rangle \, d\tau + Du(t)$$

We see that *8* and *6.5.9* are identical, as they should be, for $t_0 = 0$ and $x(0) = 0$ in *6.5.9*.

7 *Controllability*

Up to this point we have been primarily concerned with the study of various basic properties of the solutions of state equations. We now turn our attention to some of the important system-theoretic aspects of the behavior of linear systems. We begin with the concept of controllability which arises in two-point boundary-value problems when it is necessary to determine for a given initial state x_0 at time t_0 and a terminal state $x_1 \neq x_0$ whether it is possible to find a finite time $t_1 > t_0$ and an input u which takes a system from the initial state x_0 at t_0 to the final state x_1 at t_1. Mathematically, we can answer the question of controllability only for the *representations* of a system. Since some representations of a system may be completely controllable, whereas others are not, we shall have to be careful from now on not to confuse a system with its representation. Equivalence between representations will be discussed in Sec. *9* (also see Chap. *1*, Sec. *6*).

1 **Definition** The linear, time-invariant system representation

$$\dot{x}(t) = Ax(t) + Bu(t)\dagger$$

6.2.1 is said to be *completely controllable* if for any initial state x_0 at time zero and final state x_1 there exists a finite time $t_1 > 0$ and a real

† The reader will recall that the matrices A and B may be real or complex, that $\langle\cdot,\cdot\rangle$ denotes the complex scalar product, and that the superscript * denotes the complex-conjugate transpose of a matrix.

input u defined on $[0,t_1]$ such that

2 $$x(t_1) = e^{tA}\left[x_0 + \int_0^{t_1} e^{-tA}Bu(t)\,dt\right] = x_1$$

Since the representation of *6.2.1* is time-invariant, it should be clear that we can always assume that the initial time $t_0 = 0$.

When the matrix A in *6.2.1* has distinct eigenvalues, it is very easy to obtain necessary and sufficient conditions for the controllability of the representation $\dot{x}(t) = Ax(t) + Bu(t)$ (*6.2.1*), by examining the spectral decomposition of the state $x(t)$, which was shown in *6.5.8* to be

$$x(t) = \sum_{i=1}^{n} e^{(t-t_0)\lambda_i}e_i\rangle\,\langle f_i,\, x(t_0)\rangle + \sum_{i=1}^{n} e^{(t-t_0)\lambda_i}e_i\rangle \int_{t_0}^{t} \langle B^*f_i,\, u(\tau)\rangle e^{(t_0-\tau)\lambda_i}\,d\tau$$

These conditions are as follows:

3 **Theorem** Suppose that the eigenvalues of A in *6.2.1* are distinct. Then the system representation *6.2.1* is completely controllable if and only if the n vectors $\langle B^*f_i$ $(i = 1, 2, \ldots, n)$ are not zero.

Since this theorem follows directly from the more general conditions we are about to give, we leave its proof as an exercise for the reader, with the following hint. The fact that the representation is not completely controllable when some $\langle B^*f_i = 0$ is obvious, since $\langle B^*f_i = 0$ implies that the mode $e^{t\lambda_i}e_i\rangle$ cannot be excited. Hence, $\langle B^*f_i \neq 0$ is a necessary condition. Sufficiency is somewhat harder to prove.

4 **Theorem** Consider the linear time-invariant system representation,

5 $$\dot{x}(t) = Ax(t) + Bu(t)$$

where A is an $n \times n$ matrix and B is an $n \times m$ matrix. The representation *5* is completely controllable if and only if for every time $t_1 > 0$ the rows of the matrix $e^{-tA}B$ are linearly independent (as functions of time) on the interval $[0,t_1]$.

Proof We begin by proving sufficiency. Let $t_1 > 0$ be a time such that the rows of $e^{-tA}B$ are linearly independent on $[0,t_1]$. Let x_0 and x_1 be any given initial and terminal states for *5*. Then we must find a u satisfying the equation

6 $$x_1 = e^{t_1A}\left[x_0 + \int_0^{t_1} e^{-tA}Bu(t)\,dt\right]$$

which is equivalent to

7 $$e^{-t_1A}x_1 - x_0 = \int_0^{t_1} e^{-tA}Bu(t)\,dt$$

Now let

8 $$u(t) = (e^{-tA}B)^*k \qquad \text{for } t \in [0,t_1]$$

where $k = (k^1,k^2, \ldots ,k^n)$ is a constant vector. Substituting for $u(t)$ in *7*, we obtain

9 $$e^{-t_1A}x_1 - x_0 = \left[\int_0^{t_1} e^{-tA}B(e^{-tA}B)^*\,dt\right]k$$

Now, since the rows of the matrix $e^{-tA}B$ are linearly independent on $[0,t_1]$, the real $n \times n$ matrix

10 $$N(t_1) = \int_0^{t_1} e^{-tA}B(e^{-tA}B)^*\,dt$$

is nonsingular. Hence we can solve *9* by setting

11 $$k = N(t_1)^{-1}(e^{-t_1A}x_1 - x_0)$$

Equation *8* now defines a control u which takes the representation *5* from x_0 to x_1 in time t_1.

Next, we prove necessity. For a proof by contradiction, suppose that the rows of the matrix $e^{-tA}B$ are linearly dependent on every time interval $[0,t_1]$, with $t_1 > 0$. Then there must exist an initial state $x_0 \neq 0$ such that

$$B^*(e^{-tA})^*x_0 \equiv 0 \qquad \text{for } t \in [0,\infty)$$

Now, suppose that there is a time $t_1 > 0$ and an input u which take the system from x_0 to the origin in time t_1; that is, by *7*,

12 $$-x_0 = \int_0^{t_1} e^{-tA}Bu(t)\,dt$$

Taking the scalar product of *12* with x_0, we obtain

13 $$-\langle x_0, x_0\rangle = -\|x_0\|^2 = \int_0^{t_1} \langle u(t), B^*(e^{-tA})^*x_0\rangle\,dt = 0$$

But $\|x_0\| \neq 0$, and hence there is no $t_1 > 0$ and no u which satisfy *12*; that is, when the rows of the matrix $e^{-tA}B$ are linearly dependent on the interval $[0,\infty)$, the representation *5* is not completely controllable. This completes our proof.

In the form stated, the conditions of the above theorem seem difficult to verify. We therefore give a simple test for establishing whether the rows of the matrix $e^{-tA}B$ are linearly independent on any interval $[0,t_1]$, with $t_1 > 0$.

14 **Theorem** Consider the linear, time-invariant system representation

15 $$\dot{x}(t) = Ax(t) + Bu(t)$$

where A is an $n \times n$ matrix and B is an $n \times m$ matrix. The representation *15* is completely controllable if and only if the $(n \times nm)$ *controllability matrix* Q_c, defined by

16 $$Q_c = [B, AB, \ldots, A^{n-1}B]$$

has rank n (that is, it has n linearly independent columns).

Proof We first prove necessity. Suppose that the rank of Q_c is less than n. Then there must exist a vector $x_0 = (x_0^1, x_0^2, \ldots, x_0^n) \neq 0$ such that

17 $$Q_c^* x_0 = 0$$

that is,

18 $$B^* x_0 = B^* A^* x_0 = \cdots = B^*(A^{n-1})^* x_0 = 0$$

Now, by *6.3.3*,

19 $$e^{-tA} = \sum_{i=0}^{n-1} \alpha_i(t) A^i$$

and hence, from *19* and *18*,

20 $$B^*(e^{-tA})^* x_0 = \sum_{i=0}^{n-1} \alpha_i(t) B^*(A^i)^* x_0 \equiv 0$$

which implies that the rows of $e^{-tA}B$ are not linearly independent and hence *15* is not controllable.

We proceed to prove sufficiency. Suppose that the representation *15* is not completely controllable. Then there exists a vector $x_0 = (x_0^1, x_0^2, \ldots, x_0^n) \neq 0$ such that

21 $$B^*(e^{-tA})^* x_0 \equiv 0 \qquad \text{for all } t \in [0, \infty)$$

Differentiating *21* $n - 1$ times, we obtain

22 $$B^*(e^{-tA})^* x_0 = -B^* A^*(e^{-tA})^* x_0 = \cdots = (-1)^{n-1} B^*(A^{n-1})^*(e^{-tA})^* x_0 = 0$$

Now let $t = 0$ in *22*, and recall that e^{-tA} is the identity matrix for $t = 0$; hence,

23 $$B^* x_0 = B^* A^* x_0 = \cdots = B^*(A^{n-1})^* x_0 = 0$$

which implies that $Q_c^* x_0 = 0$, that is, that the rank of Q_c is less than n.

We observe that theorem *14* depended in no way on the terminal time t_1. This leads us to the following important conclusion.

24 **Corollary** If the representation *15* is completely controllable, then for any initial state x_0 at time 0 and any final state x_1 at a specified time

$t_1 > 0$, there exists an input u such that

25 $$x_1 = e^{t_1 A}\left[x_0 + \int_0^{t_1} e^{-tA}Bu(t)\,dt\right]$$

Proof Since the representation *15* is completely controllable by assumption and the rank of the controllability matrix Q_c is independent of t_1, the rows of the matrix $e^{-tA}B$ must be linearly independent on all intervals $[0,t_1]$, $t_1 > 0$. Hence for any $t_1 > 0$, the matrix $N(t_1)$ defined in *10* is nonsingular and *8*, *10*, and *11* define a control u which satisfies *25*.

26 *Example* Consider the system representation

27 $$\begin{bmatrix}\dot{x}_1(t)\\ \dot{x}_2(t)\end{bmatrix} = \begin{bmatrix}1 & 2\\ 0 & 3\end{bmatrix}\begin{bmatrix}x_1(t)\\ x_2(t)\end{bmatrix} + \begin{bmatrix}1\\ 1\end{bmatrix}u(t)$$

In this case B is the vector $(1,1)$, and AB is the vector $(3,3)$. Clearly, B and AB are linearly dependent, and hence the controllability matrix

$$Q_c = \begin{bmatrix}1 & 3\\ 1 & 3\end{bmatrix}$$

does not have rank 2; that is, *27* is not completely controllable. The reader can readily verify that the slightly modified representation

28 $$\begin{bmatrix}\dot{x}_1(t)\\ \dot{x}_2(t)\end{bmatrix} = \begin{bmatrix}1 & 2\\ 0 & 3\end{bmatrix}\begin{bmatrix}x_1(t)\\ x_2(t)\end{bmatrix} + \begin{bmatrix}2\\ 1\end{bmatrix}u(t)$$

is completely controllable.

8 *Observability*

Since usually we observe only the input u and output y of a system, with a representation such as

1 $$\dot{x}(t) = Ax(t) + Bu(t)$$

S:

2 $$y(t) = Cx(t) + Du(t)$$

(where A is an $n \times n$ matrix, B is an $n \times m$ matrix, C is a $k \times n$ matrix, and D is a $k \times m$ matrix), we are naturally interested in whether everything that goes on inside the system representation has a detectable effect on the output y. About the only thing that goes on in the system representation that we do not observe directly are changes in the state $x(t)$. Hence we are led to the following concept.

3 **Definition** The system representation[1] *1* and *2* is said to be *completely observable* if for every initial state x_0 at time zero, with input $u \equiv 0$, there exists a finite time $t_1 \geq 0$ such that the knowledge of the output over the interval $[0,t_1]$ suffices to determine the initial state x_0. (The reason for assuming that $u \equiv 0$ is that if we can determine x_0 for $u \equiv 0$, we can obviously also find it for arbitrary u.)

Consider first the case in which the matrix A has distinct eigenvalues. Then the output can be seen from *6.5.9* to have the spectral decomposition

4 $$y(t) = \sum_{i=1}^{n} e^{(t-t_0)\lambda_i} Ce_i\rangle \langle f_i, x(t_0)\rangle + \sum_{i=1}^{n} e^{(t-t_0)\lambda_i} Ce_i\rangle \int_{t_0}^{t} \langle B^* f_i, u(\tau)\rangle e^{(t_0-\tau)\lambda_i}\, d\tau + Du(t)$$

Obviously, if $Ce_i\rangle = 0$ for some i, then initial states of the form $x_0 = \alpha e_i\rangle$ would result in zero output (with zero input) and would not be distinguishable from the zero state $x = 0$. Hence, we obtain the following result.

5 **Theorem** Suppose that the eigenvalues of A in *1* are distinct. Then the representation *1* and *2* is completely observable if and only if for $i = 1, 2, \ldots, n$, the vectors $Ce_i\rangle$ are not zero (thus S is completely controllable if and only if every mode is observable).

This theorem is a consequence of the following more general result, and we therefore leave its proof as an exercise for the reader.

6 **Theorem** Consider the linear time-invariant system representation

7 $$\dot{x}(t) = Ax(t) + Bu(t)$$

S:

8 $$y(t) = Cx(t) + Du(t)$$

where A is an $n \times n$ matrix, B is an $n \times m$ matrix, C is a $k \times n$ matrix, and D is a $k \times m$ matrix. The representation S is completely observable if and only if the $nk \times n$ observability matrix Q_0, defined by

9 $$Q_0^* = [C^*, A^*C^*, \ldots, (A^{n-1})^*C^*]$$

has rank n.

[1] As in the preceding section, we must again distinguish between a system and its representation since there may be two representations of a given system, one completely observable and one not completely observable. Equivalence between representations will be discussed in Sec. *9* (also see Chap. *1*, Sec. *6*).

Proof We begin by proving necessity. Suppose that the rank of Q_0 is less than n. Then there must exist an initial state $x_0 \neq 0$ such that

10 $$Q_0 x_0 = 0$$

Now, from *6.2.13*, for $u \equiv 0$ and $t_0 = 0$,

11 $$y(t) = Ce^{tA}x_0$$

However, by *6.3.7*, $e^{tA} = \sum_{i=0}^{n-1} \alpha^i(t)A^i$, and hence *11* becomes

12 $$y(t) = \sum_{i=0}^{n-1} \alpha^i(t)CA^i x_0$$

However, by *10*, $Q_0 x_0 = 0$, and therefore

13 $$Cx_0 = CAx_0 = CA^2x_0 = \cdots = CA^{n-1}x_0 = 0$$

which leads to $y(t) \equiv 0$ in *12*. Thus, x_0 is indistinguishable from the zero state, and hence S is not completely observable.

We now prove sufficiency. Suppose that the representation S is not completely observable. Then there must be at least two initial states x' and x'', $x' \neq x''$, which are indistinguishable; that is,

14 $$Ce^{tA}x' \equiv Ce^{tA}x''$$

Let $x_0 = x' - x''$; then the output resulting from this initial state, with $u \equiv 0$, is

15 $$y(t) = Ce^{tA}x_0 \equiv 0$$

that is, there is an initial state x_0 which is indistinguishable from the zero state.

Differentiating the expression *15* $n - 1$ times, we obtain

16 $$Ce^{tA}x_0 = CAe^{tA}x_0 = \cdots = CA^{n-1}e^{tA}x_0 = 0$$

Setting $t = 0$ in *16*, we obtain

17 $$Cx_0 = CAx_0 = \cdots = CA^{n-1}x_0 = 0$$

that is, $Q_0 x_0 = 0$. Thus, if S is not completely observable, the rank of Q_0 is less than n. This completes our proof.

The reader may be curious as to whether there exist methods for computing the initial state x_0 from the observed output. The answer is that there are, with the most obvious one being as follows.

By comparing the above theorem with the theorems on controllability in the preceding section, we conclude that S is completely observable if and only if the matrix Ce^{tA} has linearly independent columns as functions of time. Hence, if S is completely observable and $u \equiv 0$,

18 $$y(t) = Ce^{tA}x_0$$

and for any $t_1 > 0$,

19 $$\int_0^{t_1} (Ce^{tA})^* y(t)\, dt = \left[\int_0^{t_1} (Ce^{tA})^* Ce^{tA}\, dt\right] x_0$$

But the columns of Ce^{tA} are linearly independent, and hence the matrix

20 $$M(t_1) = \int_0^{t_1} (Ce^{tA})^* Ce^{tA}\, dt$$

is nonsingular. Consequently,

21 $$x_0 = M(t_1)^{-1} \int_0^{t_1} (Ce^{tA})^* y(t)\, dt$$

It should now be amply clear from *6.2.13* that if $u \not\equiv 0$, we could still find x_0 by replacing $y(t)$ with

22 $$\hat{y}(t) = y(t) - Du(t) - Ce^{tA} \int_0^t e^{-sA} Bu(s)\, ds$$

23 *Example* Consider the system

24 $$\begin{bmatrix} \dot{x}_1(t) \\ \dot{x}_2(t) \end{bmatrix} = \begin{bmatrix} 1 & 2 \\ 0 & 3 \end{bmatrix} \begin{bmatrix} x_1(t) \\ x_2(t) \end{bmatrix} + \begin{bmatrix} 2 \\ 1 \end{bmatrix} u(t)$$

25 $$y(t) = [1, -1] \begin{bmatrix} x_1(t) \\ x_2(t) \end{bmatrix}$$

Here the matrix $C = [1, -1]$, and the matrix $CA = [1, -1]$ also; hence the observability matrix

26 $$Q_0 = \begin{bmatrix} 1 & -1 \\ 1 & -1 \end{bmatrix}$$

has rank less than 2; that is, the system is not completely observable.

9 *Equivalent representations*

We recall from the previous section that the representation *6.2.1* may have modes which are never observed in the output $y(t)$, defined by *6.2.2*. Thus, in such cases, there appears to exist a "smaller" representation defining the same input-output relation. Also, we know from experience that the choice of the state x in defining a system representation is not unique, and we therefore may expect representations such as *6.2.1* and *6.2.2*, having different matrices A, B, and C, to yield the same outputs $y(t)$ for the same inputs $u(t)$. These questions are best dealt with in terms of system equivalence (see Chap. *1*, Sec. *6*).

Let S and $\hat{S}$ be two systems, whose outputs y and $\hat{y}$ are vectors of the same dimension and to which the same inputs $u(t)$ can be applied, described by

1 $$\dot{x}(t) = Ax(t) + Bu(t)$$
S:
2 $$y(t) = Cx(t) + Du(t)$$

and

3 $$\dot{\hat{x}}(t) = \hat{A}\hat{x}(t) + \hat{B}u(t)$$
$\hat{S}$:
4 $$\hat{y}(t) = \hat{C}\hat{x}(t) + \hat{D}u(t)$$

where the quantities in *1* and *2* are defined as in *6.2.1* and *6.2.2*; the quantities in *3* and *4* are also defined as in *6.2.1* and *6.2.2* except that the dimension of the state $\hat{x}$ is $\hat{n}$.

5 **Definition** We say that the representation $\hat{S}$ in *3* and *4* is *equivalent*[1] to the representation S in *1* and *2* if to any initial state x_0 of S at any initial time t_0 there corresponds an initial state $\hat{x}_0$ of $\hat{S}$, also at time t_0, such that for any admissible input u

6 $$y(t;t_0,x_0,u) \equiv \hat{y}(t;t_0,\hat{x}_0,u)\dagger$$

Clearly, t_0 may be taken to be zero in the above definition.

A sufficient condition for the equivalence of two representations S and $\hat{S}$ is that they be images of one another under a change of coordinates. We may state this as follows.

7 **Theorem** Consider the representations S and $\hat{S}$ defined by *1* and *2* and *3* and *4*, respectively. If $D = \hat{D}$ and there exists a nonsingular matrix T such that

8 $$\begin{aligned} A &= T^{-1}\hat{A}T \\ B &= T^{-1}\hat{B} \\ C &= \hat{C}T \end{aligned}$$

then S is equivalent to $\hat{S}$.

Proof The outputs of the representations S and $\hat{S}$ corresponding to

[1] Note that this definition of equivalence corresponds to that of strong equivalence in Chap. *1*, Sec. *6*.

† Note that for the representation $\hat{S}$ to be equivalent to S, the matrix $\hat{D}$ must be equal to D.

some input $u(t)$ are given by

9 $$y(t) = Ce^{(t-t_0)A}\left[x_0 + \int_{t_0}^{t} e^{(t_0-\tau)A}Bu(\tau)\,d\tau\right] + Du(t)$$

10 $$\hat{y}(t) = \hat{C}e^{(t-t_0)\hat{A}}\left[\hat{x}_0 + \int_{t_0}^{t} e^{(t_0-\tau)\hat{A}}\hat{B}u(\tau)\,d\tau\right] + \hat{D}u(t)$$

Now from the relations *8*, and the fact that (see *6.4.19*)

11 $$e^{tA} = T^{-1}e^{t\hat{A}}T$$

we obtain

12 $$y(t) = \hat{C}e^{(t-t_0)\hat{A}}\left[Tx_0 + \int_{t_0}^{t} e^{(t_0-\tau)\hat{A}}\hat{B}u(\tau)\,d\tau\right] + \hat{D}u(t)$$

If we choose $\hat{x}_0 = Tx_0$ (or $x_0 = T^{-1}\hat{x}_0$), then

13 $$y(t) \equiv \hat{y}(t) \qquad \text{for } t \geq t_0$$

which completes the proof.

Note that if we let $x(t) = T\hat{x}(t)$, we get *1* and *2* from *3* and *4*, provided the relations *8* hold.

14 **Definition** We shall say that the two representations S and $\hat{S}$, defined by *1* to *4*, are *similar* if the relations *8* hold and $D = \hat{D}$.

15 **Remark** It follows from the theorem above that any two similar representations are equivalent. The converse is not true because two equivalent representations may have state vectors of different dimensions.

Now suppose that the $n \times n$ matrix A in *1* has distinct eigenvalues. Then from *6.5.8* and *6.2.13* the spectral decomposition of the output $y(t)$ is

16 $$y(t) = \sum_{i=1}^{n} e^{(t-t_0)\lambda_i}Ce_i\rangle\,\langle f_i, x(t_0)\rangle + \sum_{i=1}^{n} e^{(t-t_0)\lambda_i}Ce_i\rangle \int_{t_0}^{t} e^{(t_0-s)\lambda_i}\langle B^*f_i, u(s)\rangle\,ds + Du(t)$$

Furthermore, suppose that $Ce_i\rangle = 0$ for some $i \in \{1,2, \ldots ,n\}$. Then it would seem that one should be able to delete the corresponding modes $e^{t\lambda_i}e_i\rangle$ from Eq. *1* without affecting the input-output characteristics of the representation S. In other words, one suspects that there must be a representation $\hat{S}$, as in *3* and *4*, with dimension $\hat{n} < n$, equivalent to S and such that the matrix $\hat{A}$ in *3* has all the eigenvalues of A in *1* except those λ_i for which $e^{t\lambda_i}Ce_i\rangle \equiv 0$. This brings us to the topic of minimal equivalents of a representation.

17 **Definition** We shall say that a representation $\hat{S}$, defined as in *3* and *4*, is a *minimal equivalent* of a representation S, defined as in *1* and *2*, if $\hat{S}$ is equivalent to S and $\hat{S}$ is completely observable.

Note that if a representation S, defined as in *1* and *2*, is completely observable, then in any representation $\hat{S}$, defined as in *3* and *4*, which is equivalent to S, we must have $\hat{n} \geq n$. This is so because with $\hat{n} < n$ the representation $\hat{S}$ could not reproduce all the "modes" of the representation S. Thus, a representation $\hat{S}$ which is equivalent to S has minimum dimension $\hat{n}$ if and only if $\hat{S}$ is completely observable.

We shall now show how one can find a minimal equivalent for a representation S, defined as in *1* and *2*.

18 **Theorem** Consider the time-invariant system representation

$$S: \quad \begin{aligned} \dot{x}(t) &= Ax(t) + Bu(t) \\ y(t) &= Cx(t) + Du(t) \end{aligned}$$

defined in *1* and *2*. If the observability matrix Q_0, defined by

19 $$Q_0^* = [C^* \mid A^*C^* \mid \cdots \mid (A^{n-1})^*C^*]$$

has rank $q < n$, then the representation S is similar (and, therefore, equivalent) to a representation S' of the form

20 $$\begin{bmatrix} \dot{\hat{x}}_1(t) \\ \dot{\hat{x}}_2(t) \end{bmatrix} = \begin{bmatrix} \hat{A}_{11} & 0 \\ \hat{A}_{21} & \hat{A}_{22} \end{bmatrix} \begin{bmatrix} \hat{x}_1(t) \\ \hat{x}_2(t) \end{bmatrix} + \begin{bmatrix} \hat{B}_1 \\ \hat{B}_2 \end{bmatrix} u(t)$$

S':

21 $$y(t) = \hat{C}_1\hat{x}_1(t) + Du(t)$$

where $\hat{A}_{11}$ is a $q \times q$ matrix, $\hat{A}_{22}$ is an $(n-q) \times (n-q)$ matrix, $\hat{A}_{21}$ is an $(n-q) \times q$ matrix, $\hat{B}_1$ is a $q \times m$ matrix, $\hat{B}_2$ is an $(n-q) \times m$ matrix, and $\hat{C}_1$ is a $k \times q$ matrix.

Furthermore, the representation $\hat{S}$,

22 $$\dot{\hat{x}}_1(t) = \hat{A}_{11}\hat{x}_1(t) + \hat{B}_1u(t)$$

$\hat{S}$:

23 $$y(t) = \hat{C}_1\hat{x}_1(t) + Du(t)$$

is a minimal equivalent of the representation S.

Proof Consider the $n \times n(k+1)$ matrix (in partitioned form)

24 $$[Q_0^* \mid I]$$

where I is an $n \times n$ identity matrix.

Since the rank of Q_0 is $q < n$, we can use elementary row operations† on *24* to reduce it to a matrix of the form,

25 $$\left[\begin{array}{c|c} \hat{Q}_0{}^{1*} & \\ \hline 0 & T^* \end{array}\right]$$

where $\hat{Q}_0{}^{1*}$ is a $q \times nk$ matrix of rank q and T is a nonsingular $n \times n$ matrix.

Now let

26 $$x = T\hat{x}$$

with $\hat{x} = (\hat{x}_1,\hat{x}_2)$, $\hat{x}_1 = (\hat{x}_1{}^1,\hat{x}_1{}^2, \ldots ,\hat{x}_1{}^q)$, and $\hat{x}_2 = (\hat{x}_2{}^1,\hat{x}_2{}^2, \ldots ,\hat{x}_2^{n-q})$. Then by *7*, the representation

27 $$\begin{bmatrix} \dot{\hat{x}}_1(t) \\ \dot{\hat{x}}_2(t) \end{bmatrix} = \left[\begin{array}{c|c} \hat{A}_{11} & \hat{A}_{12} \\ \hline \hat{A}_{21} & \hat{A}_{22} \end{array}\right] \begin{bmatrix} \hat{x}_1(t) \\ \hat{x}_2(t) \end{bmatrix} + \left[\begin{array}{c} \hat{B}_1 \\ \hline \hat{B}_2 \end{array}\right] u(t)$$

S':

28 $$y(t) = \hat{C}_1\hat{x}_1(t) + \hat{C}_2\hat{x}_2(t) + Du(t)$$

with

29 $$\hat{A} = \left[\begin{array}{c|c} \hat{A}_{11} & \hat{A}_{12} \\ \hline \hat{A}_{21} & \hat{A}_{22} \end{array}\right] = T^{-1}AT$$

30 $$\hat{B} = \left[\begin{array}{c} \hat{B}_1 \\ \hline \hat{B}_2 \end{array}\right] = T^{-1}B$$

and

31 $$\hat{C} = [\hat{C}_1 \,|\, \hat{C}_2] = CT$$

is equivalent to S (since obviously, S' is similar to S). Now *25* was obtained from *24* by premultiplying *24* by the matrix T^*. Hence

32 $$\left[\begin{array}{c} \hat{Q}_0{}^{1*} \\ \hline 0 \end{array}\right] = [T^*C^* \,|\, T^*A^*(T^*)^{-1}T^*C^* \,|\, \cdots \,|\, T^*(A^{n-1})^*(T^*)^{-1}T^*C^*]$$
$$= [\hat{C}^* \,|\, \hat{A}^*\hat{C}^* \,|\, \cdots \,|\, (\hat{A}^{n-1})^*\hat{C}^*]$$

Comparing *32* with *31*, we conclude that $\hat{C}_2 = 0$.

Now multiplying *32* by $\hat{A}^*$, we obtain

33 $$\left[\begin{array}{c|c} \hat{A}_{11}^* & \hat{A}_{21}^* \\ \hline \hat{A}_{12}^* & \hat{A}_{22}^* \end{array}\right] \left[\begin{array}{c} \hat{Q}_0{}^{1*} \\ \hline 0 \end{array}\right] = \left[\begin{array}{c} \hat{A}_{11}^*\hat{Q}_0{}^{1*} \\ \hline \hat{A}_{12}^*\hat{Q}_0{}^{1*} \end{array}\right] = [\hat{A}^*\hat{C}^* \,|\, (\hat{A}^2)^*\hat{C}^* \,|\, \cdots \,|\, (\hat{A}^n)^*\hat{C}^*]$$

† By an elementary row operation on the matrix *24*, we mean one of the following three operations: (1) interchange of any two rows, (2) multiplication of a row by a *nonzero* constant, or (3) multiplication of a row by a constant and the addition of this row to a *different* row. The reader may verify for himself that each of these operations can be carried out by premultiplying the matrix *24* by a nonsingular $n \times n$ matrix. This premultiplying matrix can be obtained by performing the desired operation on the identity matrix (also see *6.10.4*, *6.10.5*, and *6.10.6*).

From *32*, the last $n - q$ rows of $[\hat{C}^* \vdots \hat{A}^*\hat{C}^* \vdots \cdots \vdots (\hat{A}^{n-1})^*\hat{C}^*] \cdots$ are zero. Also since we can always express $\hat{A}^n$ in the form $\hat{A}^n = \sum_{i=0}^{n-1} \alpha_i \hat{A}^i$, it follows that the last $n - q$ rows of $(\hat{A}^n)^*\hat{C}^*$ are also zero. We now see from *33* that this implies that $\hat{A}_{12}^* = 0$, since $\hat{Q}_0{}^{1*}$ is a $q \times nk$ matrix of rank q, that is, of maximal rank. Thus we have shown that the representation S is equivalent to a representation S' of the form *20* and *21*.

Now,

34 $$\hat{Q}_0{}^{1*} = [\hat{C}_1^* \vdots \hat{A}_{11}^*\hat{C}_1^* \vdots \cdots \vdots (\hat{A}_{11}^{n-1})^*\hat{C}_1^*]$$

By inspection, it contains the complex-conjugate transpose of the observability matrix of the representation $\hat{S}$ *22* and *23*, and since the rank of $\hat{Q}_0^1$ is q, it follows that $\hat{S}$ is completely observable.

Let (u,y) be any input-output pair for the representation S, defined for $t \geq 0$ and corresponding to an initial state x_0. Then (u,y) also satisfies *22* and *23* with initial state $\hat{x}_{01} = PT^{-1}x_0$, where

35 $$P = [I \vdots 0]$$

with I a $q \times q$ identity matrix and 0 a $q \times (n - q)$ zero matrix.

Conversely, let (u,y) be an input-output pair for the representation $\hat{S}$ *22* and *23*, defined for $t \geq 0$ and corresponding to an initial state $\hat{x}_{01}$. Then (u,v) also satisfies *1* and *2*, with

36 $$x_0 = T \begin{bmatrix} \hat{x}_{01} \\ \hdashline 0 \end{bmatrix}$$

Thus, $\hat{S}$ is equivalent to S, and since it is completely observable, $\hat{S}$ is a minimal equivalent of S.

37 *Example* Consider the system representation S in *6.8.24* and *6.8.25* again; that is,

38 $$\begin{bmatrix} \dot{x}_1(t) \\ \dot{x}_2(t) \end{bmatrix} = \begin{bmatrix} 1 & 2 \\ 0 & 3 \end{bmatrix} \begin{bmatrix} x_1(t) \\ x_2(t) \end{bmatrix} + \begin{bmatrix} 2 \\ 1 \end{bmatrix} u(t)$$

S:

39 $$y(t) = [1, -1] \begin{bmatrix} x_1(t) \\ x_2(t) \end{bmatrix}$$

From *6.8.26*, the matrix $[Q_0^* \vdots I]$ is

40 $$[Q_0^* \vdots I] = \left[\begin{array}{cc:cc} 1 & 1 & 1 & 0 \\ -1 & -1 & 0 & 1 \end{array}\right]$$

Adding the first row to the last, we obtain

41 $$\left[\begin{array}{cc:cc} 1 & 1 & 1 & 0 \\ 0 & 0 & 1 & 1 \end{array}\right]$$

Hence the matrix T is

42 $$T = \begin{bmatrix} 1 & 1 \\ 0 & 1 \end{bmatrix}$$

Putting $x = T\hat{x}$, we obtain

43 $$\begin{bmatrix} \dot{\hat{x}}_1(t) \\ \dot{\hat{x}}_2(t) \end{bmatrix} = \begin{bmatrix} 1 & 0 \\ 0 & 3 \end{bmatrix} \begin{bmatrix} \hat{x}_1(t) \\ \hat{x}_2(t) \end{bmatrix} + \begin{bmatrix} 1 \\ 1 \end{bmatrix} u(t)$$

S':

44 $$y(t) = \hat{x}_1(t)$$

with S' similar to S. Finally, the minimal equivalent of S is seen to be the system representation

45 $$\dot{\hat{x}}_1(t) = \hat{x}_1(t) + u(t)$$

$\hat{S}$:

46 $$y(t) = \hat{x}_1(t)$$

There is also a possibility that the representation S is not completely controllable, and we may wish to extract from it the controllable part. For this purpose we need the following concept, which will lead to the desired construction.

47 **Definition** The representation $\hat{S}$ *3* and *4* is *zero-state equivalent* to the representation S *1* and *2*, if for any admissible input u and any initial time t_0,

48 $$\hat{y}(t;t_0,0,u) \equiv y(t,t_0,0,u)$$

In other words, their outputs corresponding to the same input are identical provided that at the initial time t_0 both representations are in the zero state. Since S and $\hat{S}$ are assumed to be time-invariant, we may always take $t_0 = 0$ in *48*.

49 **Theorem** Consider the time-invariant system representation

50 $$\dot{x}(t) = Ax(t) + Bu(t)$$

S:

51 $$y(t) = Cx(t) + Du(t)$$

defined in *1* and *2*. If the controllability matrix

52 $$Q_c = [B \vdots AB \vdots A^2B \vdots \cdots \vdots A^{n-1}B]$$

has rank $q < n$, then the representation S is similar to a system of the form

53 $$\begin{bmatrix} \dot{\hat{x}}_1(t) \\ \dot{\hat{x}}_2(t) \end{bmatrix} = \left[\begin{array}{c:c} \hat{A}_{11} & \hat{A}_{12} \\ \hdashline 0 & \hat{A}_{22} \end{array}\right] \begin{bmatrix} \hat{x}_1(t) \\ \hat{x}_2(t) \end{bmatrix} + \begin{bmatrix} \hat{B}_1 \\ 0 \end{bmatrix} u(t)$$

S':

54 $$y(t) = \hat{C}_1\hat{x}_1(t) + \hat{C}_2\hat{x}_2(t) + Du(t)$$

where $\hat{x}_1 = (\hat{x}_1{}^1, \hat{x}_1{}^2, \ldots, \hat{x}_1{}^q)$, $\hat{x}_2 = (\hat{x}_2{}^1, \hat{x}_2{}^2, \ldots, \hat{x}_2^{n-q})$, and the matrices $\hat{A}_{11}$, $\hat{A}_{12}$, $\hat{A}_{22}$, $\hat{B}_1$, $\hat{C}_1$, and $\hat{C}_2$ are dimensioned accordingly.

Furthermore, the representation

55 $$\dot{\hat{x}}_1(t) = \hat{A}_{11}\hat{x}_1(t) + \hat{B}_1u(t)$$

$\hat{S}$:

56 $$y(t) = \hat{C}_1\hat{x}_1(t) + Du(t)$$

is completely controllable and is zero-state equivalent to S.

We omit the details of proof for this theorem, since it follows essentially the same lines as the proof of theorem *18*. The reader who wishes to construct the proof for himself should begin by constructing the partitioned matrix

57 $$[Q_c \vdots I]$$

and then reduce it by elementary transformations to the form

58 $$\left[\begin{array}{c:c} \hat{Q}_c{}^1 & \\ \hdashline 0 & T \end{array}\right]$$

Then he should set $x = T^{-1}\hat{x}$.

It is now clear that if we are interested in constructing a *smallest* representation $\hat{S}'$ which is zero-state equivalent to S (that is, the dimension $\hat{n}$ of $\hat{S}'$ is minimal), then we can first construct a minimal equivalent $\hat{S}$ of S by Theorem *18* and then construct a completely controllable zero-state equivalent $\hat{S}'$ for $\hat{S}$ by Theorem *49*. It may be helpful to give such an equivalent a name.

59 **Definition** A representation $\hat{S}'$ will be said to be a *reduced minimal equivalent* of a representation S if $\hat{S}'$ is zero-state equivalent to S and $\hat{S}'$ is completely observable and completely controllable.

60 **Remark** It can be shown that the degree (i.e., the dimension n of the A matrix) of the reduced minimal equivalent is equal to the rank of the matrix Q_0Q_c.

This concludes our discussion of equivalent representations.

10 An algorithm for reducing a differential system to state form[1]

For the standard form *6.2.1* and *6.2.2* to have much value, it is essential that other descriptions of a linear time-invariant system be reducible to it. In the present section we shall consider this question with regard to systems described by simultaneous differential equations, and in the next section we shall consider systems described by transfer function matrices.

Thus, consider the differential system S with input

$$u(t) = (u^1(t),u^2(t), \ldots ,u^r(t))$$

and output $y(t) = (y^1(t),y^2(t), \ldots ,y^n(t))$, described by the system of differential equations

1 $$S: \qquad L(p)y(t) = M(p)u(t)$$

where $L(p)$ is an $n \times n$ matrix and $M(p)$ is an $n \times r$ matrix, whose respective elements $l_{ij}(p)$ and $m_{ij}(p)$ are finite polynomials in $p = d/dt$, the differentiation operator, with constant coefficients. We assume that $\det L(s)$ is not identically zero. Hence the transfer function matrix $\tilde{W}(s) = L^{-1}(s)M(s)$ (see Sec. *11*) exists, and its elements $\tilde{w}_{ij}(s)$ are rational functions. We assume that for all $\tilde{w}_{ij}(s)$, the degree of the denominator is not smaller than the degree of the numerator.

We wish to construct from S an equivalent system representation $\hat{S}$, with input $u(t) = (u^1(t),u^2(t), \ldots ,u^r(t))$ and output

$$y(t) = (y^1(t),y^2(t), \ldots ,y^n(t))$$

of the form

2 $$\dot{x}(t) = Ax(t) + Bu(t)$$

$$\hat{S}:$$

3 $$y(t) = Cx(t) + Du(t)$$

where $x(t) = (x^1(t),x^2(t), \ldots ,x^N(t))$ is a state vector, and A, B, C, and D are constant matrices of dimension $N \times N$, $N \times r$, $n \times N$, and $n \times r$, respectively. In our construction, the dimension of the state, N, will be equal to the degree of the polynomial $\det L(s)$, and $\hat{S}$ will be a minimal state representation of S. It will be recalled that for the representation $\hat{S}$ to be equivalent to S, it must have the following property. Let $u(t)$ be any input defined on $[t_0, \infty)$, and let $y(t)$ be any output of $\hat{S}$

[1] Please note that we depart in this section from the previously used symbols for the dimension of the various quantities involved.

satisfying the equations of $\hat{S}$ for this $u(t)$. Then $y(t)$ also satisfies the equations of S for this $u(t)$. Conversely, let $y(t)$ be any output of S satisfying the equations of S for this $u(t)$. Then there exists an initial state $x(t_0)$ such that $y(t)$ also satisfies the equations of $\hat{S}$ for this $u(t)$.

Thus, we propose to construct a completely observable representation $\hat{S}$ in state form which is equivalent to S (i.e., it is a minimal equivalent). The algorithm about to be given consists of two parts: in the first part S is reduced to a specific triangular form using the Gauss elimination method, and in the second part the state equations are constructed. The first step is not required when Eq. *1* is scalar.

Triangularization of the representation S

To triangularize S, we shall use the following three $n \times n$ matrices: the matrix $T_{ij}[f(p)]$, whose principal diagonal elements are unity and whose off-diagonal elements are zero with the exception of the ijth, which is equal to $f(p)$, a polynomial in p; the matrix U_{ij}, whose principal diagonal elements are unity except for the ith and the jth, which are zero, and whose off-diagonal elements are zero with the exception of the ijth and the jith, which are unity; and the matrix $V_{ii}(c)$ whose off-diagonal elements are zero and whose diagonal elements are unity except for the ith, which is equal to c, a nonzero scalar.

Thus,

4
$$T_{ij}[f(p)] = \begin{array}{c} \\ \\ \\ \\ i \\ \\ \\ \\ \end{array} \left[\begin{array}{ccccccc} 1 & 0 & 0 & \cdots & 0 & 0 & 0 \\ 0 & 1 & 0 & \cdots & 0 & 0 & 0 \\ 0 & 0 & 1 & \cdots & 0 & 0 & 0 \\ \cdot & \cdot & \cdot & \cdots & \cdot & \cdot & \cdot \\ 0 & 0 & f(p) & \cdots & 0 & 0 & 0 \\ 0 & 0 & 0 & \cdots & 1 & 0 & 0 \\ 0 & 0 & 0 & \cdots & 0 & 1 & 0 \\ 0 & 0 & 0 & \cdots & 0 & 0 & 1 \end{array}\right] \\ \qquad\qquad\qquad\qquad j$$

5
$$U_{ij} = \begin{array}{c} \\ \\ i \\ \\ \\ \\ j \\ \\ \\ \end{array} \left[\begin{array}{ccccccccc} 1 & 0 & 0 & 0 & \cdots & 0 & 0 & 0 & 0 \\ 0 & 1 & 0 & 0 & \cdots & 0 & 0 & 0 & 0 \\ 0 & 0 & 0 & 0 & \cdots & 0 & 1 & 0 & 0 \\ 0 & 0 & 0 & 1 & \cdots & 0 & 0 & 0 & 0 \\ \cdot & \cdot & \cdot & \cdot & \cdots & \cdot & \cdot & \cdot & \cdot \\ 0 & 0 & 0 & 0 & \cdots & 1 & 0 & 0 & 0 \\ 0 & 0 & 1 & 0 & \cdots & 0 & 0 & 0 & 0 \\ 0 & 0 & 0 & 0 & \cdots & 0 & 0 & 1 & 0 \\ 0 & 0 & 0 & 0 & \cdots & 0 & 0 & 0 & 1 \end{array}\right] \\ \qquad\qquad\qquad i \qquad\qquad\qquad j$$

6
$$V_{ii}(c) = i\begin{bmatrix} 1 & 0 & 0 & \cdot & \cdot & \cdot & 0 & 0 & 0 \\ 0 & 1 & 0 & \cdot & \cdot & \cdot & 0 & 0 & 0 \\ 0 & 0 & 1 & \cdot & \cdot & \cdot & 0 & 0 & 0 \\ \cdots & & & & & & & & \cdots \\ \cdot & \cdot & \cdot & 1 & 0 & 0 & \cdot & \cdot & \cdot \\ \cdot & \cdot & \cdot & 0 & c & 0 & \cdot & \cdot & \cdot \\ \cdot & \cdot & \cdot & 0 & 0 & 1 & \cdot & \cdot & \cdot \\ \cdots & & & & & & & & \cdots \\ 0 & 0 & 0 & \cdot & \cdot & \cdot & 1 & 0 & 0 \\ 0 & 0 & 0 & \cdot & \cdot & \cdot & 0 & 1 & 0 \\ 0 & 0 & 0 & \cdot & \cdot & \cdot & 0 & 0 & 1 \end{bmatrix}$$
$$i$$

When $L(p)$ is premultiplied by $T_{ij}[f(p)]$, the jth row of $L(p)$ is multiplied by $f(p)$ and added to the ith row of $L(p)$. Otherwise, the product has the same rows as $L(p)$. The effect of premultiplication of $L(p)$ by U_{ij} is to exchange the ith and jth rows, and the effect of premultiplication by $V_{ii}(c)$ is to multiply the ith row by c, leaving the rest of $L(p)$ intact.

Thus, the matrices T_{ij}, V_{ii}, and V_{ij} perform elementary row operations of exactly the same kind as described in the preceding section (except that now the matrices are defined on the ring of polynomials), and hence, they may be constructed by performing the corresponding row operations on the identity matrix.

7 **Theorem** Consider the representation S: $L(p)y = M(p)u$. Let $f(p)$ be any finite, nonzero polynomial in p, let c be any nonzero scalar, and let $i \neq j$, $k \neq l$ be any integers in $\{1,2, \ldots ,n\}$. Then the representations S_1: $T_{ij}[f(p)]L(p)y = T_{ij}[f(p)]M(p)u$; S_2: $U_{kl}L(p)y = U_{kl}M(p)u$; and S_3: $V_{ii}(c)L(p)y = V_{ii}(c)M(p)u$ are all equivalent to S.

Proof Since the determinants of $T_{ij}[f(p)]$, U_{ij}, and $V_{ii}(c)$ are *nonzero constants*, their inverses exist and have elements which are either constants (for U_{ij} and $V_{ii}(c)$) or polynomials in p. Since we can multiply the representation S by these matrices and their inverses in succession, it follows trivially that the representations $S_\alpha(\alpha = 1,2,3)$ are all equivalent to S.

8 **Algorithm** To triangularize the representation S, perform the following operations on its matrices.

STEP 1. Find, among the nonzero elements in the first column of the matrix $L(p)$, one which is of least degree. Suppose this element is in the ith row. Premultiply $L(p)$ and $M(p)$ by U_{1i} to obtain new matrices $L'(p)$ and $M'(p)$, with the element in question in the first row and column of $L'(p)$. Rename the matrices $L'(p)$ and $M'(p)$ as $L(p)$ and $M(p)$.

STEP 2. For $i = 2, 3, \ldots, n$, divide $l_{11}(p)$ into $l_{i1}(p)$ to obtain

9 $$l_{i1}(p) = l_{11}(p)q_{i1}(p) + r_{i1}(p) \qquad i = 2, 3, \ldots, n$$

where $q_{i1}(p)$ is the quotient polynomial and $r_{i1}(p)$ is the remainder polynomial, with degree strictly less than the degree of $l_{11}(p)$. Now, multiply both sides of *1* in succession by the matrices $T_{i1}[-q_{i1}(p)]$, for $i = 2, 3, \ldots, n$. This results in a matrix $M'(p)$ and in a matrix $L'(p)$ whose first column is

10 $$(l_{11}, r_{21}, r_{31}, \ldots, r_{n1})^T$$

in terms of the quantities appearing in *9*. Rename the matrices $L'(p)$ and $M'(p)$ as $L(p)$ and $M(p)$.

STEP 3. If the elements $l_{21}, l_{31}, \ldots, l_{n1}$ are not identically zero, repeat step 1 and step 2 again and again until the remainders $r_{i1}(p)$, as given by *9*, are identically zero for $i = 2, 3, \ldots, n$. Since all the polynomials are of finite degree and since each iteration of step 1 and step 2 lowers the degree of the element $l_{11}(p)$, it is clear that this is a finite procedure. Again rename the matrices as $L(p)$ and $M(p)$.

STEP 4. Find a nonzero element among $l_{22}, l_{32}, \ldots, l_{n2}$ which is of least degree (second column, last $n - 1$ rows). Suppose it is in the ith row. Premultiply both sides of *1* by U_{2i} to bring it to the second row, and rename the matrices of the products as $L(p)$ and $M(p)$, respectively. Carry out steps 2 and 3 with the index 2 replacing the index 1 in all operations. We now have a matrix $L(p)$ whose elements in the first two columns, below the principal diagonal, are zero. Proceed in a similar fashion to obtain a representation S whose matrix $L(p)$ has only zero elements below the principal diagonal; that is,

11 $$\begin{bmatrix} l_{11}(p) & l_{12}(p) & l_{13}(p) & \cdots & l_{1n}(p) \\ 0 & l_{22}(p) & l_{23}(p) & \cdots & l_{2n}(p) \\ 0 & 0 & l_{33}(p) & \cdots & l_{3n}(p) \\ \cdots & \cdots & \cdots & \cdots & \cdots \\ 0 & 0 & 0 & \cdots & l_{nn}(p) \end{bmatrix} \begin{bmatrix} y^1 \\ y^2 \\ \cdot \\ \cdot \\ \cdot \\ y^n \end{bmatrix} = \begin{bmatrix} m_{11}(p) & \cdots & m_{1r}(p) \\ \cdots & \cdots & \cdots \\ m_{n1}(p) & \cdots & m_{nr}(p) \end{bmatrix} \begin{bmatrix} u^1 \\ \cdot \\ \cdot \\ \cdot \\ u^r \end{bmatrix}$$

STEP 5. Now force, in each column, the off-diagonal elements of the matrix $L(p)$ to be lower-degree polynomials than the diagonal element.

To achieve this in the second column, divide $l_{22}(p)$ into $l_{12}(p)$ to obtain

12 $$l_{12}(p) = l_{22}(p)q_{12}(p) + r_{12}(p)$$

where $q_{12}(p)$ is the quotient polynomial and $r_{12}(p)$ is the remainder polynomial, with degree strictly less than the degree of $l_{22}(p)$. Now multiply both sides of *11* by the matrix $T_{12}[-q_{12}(p)]$, and rename the respective matrix products as $L(p)$ and $M(p)$. Next, divide $l_{33}(p)$ into $l_{13}(p)$ and $l_{23}(p)$ to obtain

13 $$l_{i3}(p) = l_{33}(p)q_{i3}(p) + r_{i3}(p) \qquad i = 1, 2$$

where q_{i3} is the quotient polynomial and r_{i3} is the remainder polynomial with degree strictly less than $l_{33}(p)$. Now multiply both sides of *11* by $T_{i3}[-q_{i3}(p)]$, $i = 1, 2$, and rename the matrix products as $L(p)$ and $M(p)$, respectively. Proceed in a similar fashion to reduce the degree of the off-diagonal elements in the remaining $n - 3$ columns of the matrix $L(p)$.

With the representation S reduced to the equivalent form in which the matrix $L(p)$ is upper triangular, with the degree of the off-diagonal elements in each column lower than the degree of the corresponding diagonal element, we are ready to derive the state equations of S.

Reduction of the representation S to its state equivalent $\hat{S}$

Let ν_i be the degree of the polynomial $l_{ii}(p)$, where $i = 1, 2, \ldots, n$. Since, by assumption, the transfer function $\tilde{W}(s) = L^{-1}(s)M(s)$ exists and has elements which are rational functions with the degree of the denominator no smaller than the degree of the numerator, it follows that the degree of the polynomials $m_{ij}(p)$, $j = 1, 2, \ldots, r$, is no greater than ν_i, $i = 1, 2, \ldots, n$. Hence, we may assume that the elements of the matrices $L(p)$ and $M(p)$ in *11* may be written in the form

14 $$l_{ji}(p) = a_{ji}^0 + a_{ji}^1 p + \cdots + a_{ji}^{\nu_i} p^{\nu_i} \qquad i = 1, 2, \ldots, n; j = 1, 2, \ldots, i$$

15 $$m_{ij}(p) = b_{ij}^0 + b_{ij}^1 p + \cdots + b_{ij}^{\nu_i} p^{\nu_i} \qquad i = 1, 2, \ldots, n; j = 1, 2, \ldots, r$$

Referring back to *11*, we see that

16 $$\det L(p) = l_{11}(p)l_{22}(p) \cdots l_{nn}(p)$$

and hence the order of the representation S is $\nu_1 + \nu_2 + \cdots + \nu_n$. We now show how to obtain ν_i state variables, $x_i^1, x_i^2, \ldots, x_i^{\nu_i}$, from the scalar equation for the output y^i, where $i = 1, 2, \ldots, n$.

Again referring to *11*, we see that the scalar differential equation for y^n is

17 $$(a_{nn}^0 + a_{nn}^1 p + \cdots + a_{nn}^{\nu_n} p^{\nu_n}) y^n(t) = \sum_{j=1}^{r} (b_{nj}^0 + b_{nj}^1 p + \cdots + b_{nj}^{\nu_n} p^{\nu_n}) u^j(t)$$

(Obviously, when $n = 1$, the notation can be greatly simplified by omitting n both as a subscript and as a superscript.) We now use a standard algorithm ([1], p. 231) to associate states with the output y^n. Let $x_n^1, x_n^2, \ldots, x_n^{\nu_n}$ be defined as follows:

18 $$x_n^1 = a_{nn}^{\nu_n} y^n - \sum_{j=1}^{r} b_{nj}^{\nu_n} u^j$$

$$x_n^2 = a_{nn}^{\nu_n} p y^n - \sum_{j=1}^{r} b_{nj}^{\nu_n} p u^j + a_{nn}^{\nu_n - 1} y^n - \sum_{j=1}^{r} b_{nj}^{\nu_n - 1} u^j$$

$$\cdots\cdots\cdots\cdots\cdots\cdots\cdots\cdots$$

$$x_n^{\nu_n} = a_{nn}^{\nu_n} p^{\nu_n - 1} y^n - \sum_{j=1}^{r} b_{nn}^{\nu_n} p^{\nu_n - 1} u^j + a_{nn}^{\nu_n - 1} p^{\nu_n - 2} y^n - \sum_{j=1}^{r} b_{nj}^{\nu_n - 1} p^{\nu_n - 2} u^j + \cdots + a_{nn}^1 y^n - \sum_{j=1}^{r} b_{nj}^1 u^j$$

Solving the above system of equations, we obtain

19 $$\dot{x}_n(t) = A_{nn} x_n(t) + B_n u(t)$$

20 $$y^n(t) = C_{nn} x_n(t) + D_n u(t)$$

where $x_n = (x_n^1, x_n^2, \ldots, x_n^{\nu_n})$, A_{nn} is a $\nu_n \times \nu_n$ matrix, B_n is a $\nu_n \times r$ matrix, C_{nn} is a $1 \times \nu_n$ matrix, and D_n is a $1 \times r$ matrix, each with components as follows:

21 $$A_{nn} = \frac{1}{a_{nn}^{\nu_n}} \begin{bmatrix} -a_{nn}^{\nu_n - 1} & a_{nn}^{\nu_n} & 0 & \cdots & 0 \\ -a_{nn}^{\nu_n - 2} & 0 & a_{nn}^{\nu_n} & \cdots & 0 \\ \cdots & \cdots & \cdots & \cdots & \cdots \\ -a_{nn}^1 & 0 & 0 & \cdots & a_{nn}^{\nu_n} \\ -a_{nn}^0 & 0 & 0 & \cdots & 0 \end{bmatrix}$$

22 $$B_n = a_{nn}^{\nu_n} \begin{bmatrix} a_{nn}^{\nu_n} b_{n1}^{\nu_n - 1} - a_{nn}^{\nu_n - 1} b_{n1}^{\nu_n} & a_{nn}^{\nu_n} b_{n2}^{\nu_n - 1} - a_{nn}^{\nu_n - 1} b_{n2}^{\nu_n} & \cdots & a_{nn}^{\nu_n} b_{nr}^{\nu_n - 1} - a_{nn}^{\nu_n - 1} b_{nr}^{\nu_n} \\ \cdots & \cdots & \cdots & \cdots \\ a_{nn}^{\nu_n} b_{n1}^0 - a_{nn}^0 b_{n1}^{\nu_n} & a_{nn}^{\nu_n} b_{n2}^0 - a_{nn}^0 b_{n2}^{\nu_n} & \cdots & a_{nn}^{\nu_n} b_{nr}^0 - a_{nn}^0 b_{nr}^{\nu_n} \end{bmatrix}$$

23 $$C_{nn} = \left[\frac{1}{a_{nn}^{\nu_n}}, 0, \ldots, 0 \right] \qquad D_n = \frac{1}{a_{nn}^{\nu_n}} [b_{n1}^{\nu_n}, b_{n2}^{\nu_n}, \ldots, b_{nr}^{\nu_n}]$$

The reader should verify at this stage that the eigenvalues of the matrix A_{nn} are the zeros of the polynomial $l_{nn}(p)$.

Now let us proceed to the next scalar differential equation in *11*; that is,

24
$$l_{n-1,\,n-1}(p)y^{n-1} = -l_{n-1,\,n}(p)y^n + \sum_{j=1}^{r} m_{n-1,\,j}(p)u^j$$

The set of equations *18* is now used to eliminate y^n and its derivatives from *24*, resulting in an expression of the form

25
$$l_{n-1,\,n-1}(p)y^{n-1} = \sum_{i=1}^{\nu^n} e^i_{n-1,\,n}x_n{}^i + \sum_{j=1}^{r} [\bar{m}_{n-1,\,j}(p) + m_{n-1,\,j}(p)]u^j$$

where the $e^i_{n-1,\,j}$ are scalars and the $\bar{m}_{n-1,\,j}(p)$ are polynomials in p with degree no greater than that of $l_{n-1,\,n-1}(p)$. The fact that no derivatives of previous state variables occur in *25* was ensured by forcing the degree of the off-diagonal elements in each column to be less than the degree of the corresponding diagonal element, whereas the property of the degrees of $m_{n-1,\,j}(p)$ is due to the assumption on $W(s) = L^{-1}(s)M(s)$. Now treating the variables $x_n{}^i$ in *25* as additional inputs, we use a substitution similar to *18* to introduce ν_{n-1} state variables x^1_{n-1}, x^2_{n-1}, . . . , $x^{\nu_{n-1}}_{n-1}$, which satisfy a set of equations of the form

26
$$\dot{x}_{n-1}(t) = A_{n-1,\,n-1}x_{n-1}(t) + A_{n-1,\,n}x_n(t) + B_{n-1}u(t)$$

27
$$y^{n-1} = C_{n-1,\,n-1}x_{n-1}(t) + C_{n-1,\,n}x_n(t) + D_{n-1}u(t)$$

where $A_{n-1,\,n-1}$ is a $\nu_{n-1} \times \nu_{n-1}$ matrix, $A_{n-1,\,n}$ is a $\nu_{n-1} \times \nu_n$ matrix, B_{n-1} is a $\nu_{n-1} \times r$ matrix, and $C_{n-1,\,n-1}$, $C_{n-1,\,n}$, and D_{n-1} are matrices of respective dimensions $1 \times \nu_{n-1}$, $1 \times \nu_n$, and $1 \times r$.

The same process is now applied to the third line from the bottom of *11* and continued until all the n equations of *11* are similarly treated. Putting it all together into a single matrix form, we get the following desired minimal equivalent of our original representation S:

28
$$\begin{bmatrix} \dot{x}_1(t) \\ \dot{x}_2(t) \\ \cdot \\ \cdot \\ \cdot \\ \dot{x}_{n-1}(t) \\ \dot{x}_n(t) \end{bmatrix} = \begin{bmatrix} A_{11} & A_{12} & \cdots & A_{1n} \\ 0 & A_{22} & \cdots & A_{2n} \\ \cdots & \cdots & \cdots & \cdots \\ 0 & 0 & \cdots & A_{n-1,\,n} \\ 0 & 0 & \cdots & A_{nn} \end{bmatrix} \begin{bmatrix} x_1(t) \\ x_2(t) \\ \cdot \\ \cdot \\ \cdot \\ x_{n-1}(t) \\ x_n(t) \end{bmatrix} + \begin{bmatrix} B_1 \\ B_2 \\ \cdot \\ \cdot \\ \cdot \\ B_{n-1} \\ B_n \end{bmatrix} u(t)$$

29
$$\begin{bmatrix} y^1(t) \\ y^2(t) \\ \cdot \\ \cdot \\ \cdot \\ y^n(t) \end{bmatrix} = \begin{bmatrix} C_{11} & C_{12} & C_{13} & \cdots & C_{1n} \\ 0 & C_{22} & C_{23} & \cdots & C_{2n} \\ \cdots & \cdots & \cdots & \cdots & \cdots \\ 0 & 0 & 0 & \cdots & C_{nn} \end{bmatrix} \begin{bmatrix} x_1(t) \\ x_2(t) \\ \cdot \\ \cdot \\ \cdot \\ x_n(t) \end{bmatrix} + \begin{bmatrix} D_1 \\ D_2 \\ \cdot \\ \cdot \\ \cdot \\ D_n \end{bmatrix} u(t)$$

Note that the dimension of the representation *28* is $\sum_{i=1}^{n} \nu_i$, the same as the dimension of S. The matrices in *28* and *29* are defined in an obvious manner. This terminates the exposition of the algorithm. The reader should verify that the eigenvalues of the matrix A in *28* are the zeros of the polynomial $\det L(p)$.

We conclude this subsection with an example to demonstrate the application of the algorithm.

30 *Example* Consider the system described by

$$S\colon \begin{bmatrix} p^2 + 3p + 1 & 2p + 3 \\ p^3 + 3p^2 + p & 3p^2 + 3p + 6 \end{bmatrix} \begin{bmatrix} y^1 \\ y^2 \end{bmatrix} = \begin{bmatrix} 1 & 0 \\ p + 1 & p + 3 \end{bmatrix} \begin{bmatrix} u^1 \\ u^2 \end{bmatrix}$$

Multiplying through by $T_{21}[-p]$ (that is, multiplying the first equation by $-p$ and adding the result to the second equation), we get

31 $$S\colon \qquad \begin{bmatrix} p^2 + 3p + 1 & 2p + 3 \\ 0 & p^2 + 6 \end{bmatrix} \begin{bmatrix} y^1 \\ y^2 \end{bmatrix} = \begin{bmatrix} 1 & 0 \\ 1 & p + 3 \end{bmatrix} \begin{bmatrix} u^1 \\ u^2 \end{bmatrix}$$

We note that the representation now is of the form *11* and that step 5 of the algorithm in the previous subsection has been carried out. Hence, we may proceed to construct the state equations. We have, for y^2,

32 $$p^2y^2 + 0py^2 + 6y^2 = u^1 + (p + 3)u^2$$

Therefore, following the formulas just obtained, we let

33 $$\dot{x}_2{}^1 = x_2{}^2 + u^2$$

34 $$\dot{x}_2{}^2 = -6x_2{}^1 + 3u^2 + u^1$$

35 $$y^2 = x_2{}^1$$

We note that this is consistent with *32*. Now, proceeding to the next equation, we find that

36 $$(p^2 + 3p + 1)y^1 = -(2p + 3)y^2 + u^1$$

From *33* to *35* we obtain

37 $$-(2p + 3)y^2 = -(2x_2{}^2 + 3x_2{}^1) - 2u^2$$

Hence,

38 $$(p^2 + 3p + 1)y^1 = (2x_2{}^2 + 3x_2{}^1) - 2u^2 + u^1$$

Now, let

39 $$\dot{x}_1{}^1 = -3x_1{}^1 + x_1{}^2$$

40 $$\dot{x}_1{}^2 = -x_1{}^1 + u^1 - 2u^2 - (3x_2{}^1 + 2x_2{}^2)$$

41 $$y^1 = x_1{}^1$$

We see again that the last three equations are consistent with *36*. We may now write down the state equations of the system as follows:

42
$$\begin{bmatrix} \dot{x}_1{}^1 \\ \dot{x}_1{}^2 \\ \dot{x}_2{}^1 \\ \dot{x}_2{}^2 \end{bmatrix} = \begin{bmatrix} -3 & +1 & 0 & 0 \\ -1 & 0 & -3 & -2 \\ 0 & 0 & 0 & 1 \\ 0 & 0 & -6 & 0 \end{bmatrix} \begin{bmatrix} x_1{}^1 \\ x_1{}^2 \\ x_2{}^1 \\ x_2{}^2 \end{bmatrix} = \begin{bmatrix} 0 & 0 \\ 1 & -2 \\ 0 & 1 \\ 1 & 3 \end{bmatrix} \begin{bmatrix} u^1 \\ u_2 \end{bmatrix}$$

43
$$\begin{bmatrix} y^1 \\ y^2 \end{bmatrix} = \begin{bmatrix} 1 & 0 & 0 & 0 \\ 0 & 0 & 1 & 0 \end{bmatrix} \begin{bmatrix} x_1{}^1 \\ x_1{}^2 \\ x_2{}^1 \\ x_2{}^2 \end{bmatrix}$$

44 **Remark** The assumption that the transfer function

$$\tilde{W}(s) = L^{-1}(s)M(s)$$

of the differential system has elements with numerator polynomials of degree no higher than the corresponding denominator polynomials is only necessary to ensure that the resulting state representation be of the form *2* and *3*. When this assumption is not satisfied, the algorithm can be extended, in an obvious manner, to obtain state representations of the form $\dot{x}(t) = Ax(t) + Bu(t)$, $y(t) = Cx(t) + Du(t) + E\dot{u}(t) + F\ddot{u}(t) + \cdots$.

The algorithm we presented in this section was written in a form particularly suitable for digital computer implementation. The reader using it for hand calculation may find it helpful to refer to *17* and *18* at each step following Eq. *24*.

11 *Realization of a transfer function matrix*

We say that a $k \times m$ matrix function of time $W(t)$ is the *weighting matrix* of a time-invariant linear system S with input

$$u(t) = (u^1(t),u^2(t), \ldots ,u^m(t))$$

and output $y(t) = (y^1(t),y^2(t), \ldots ,y^k(t))$ if the system output from zero state at time t_0 is given by the convolution integral

1 S:
$$y(t) = \int_{t_0}^{t} W(t - \tau)u(\tau)\, d\tau$$

for all admissible $u(t)$. Note that this description of S enables us to compute the zero-state response only. Thus, we shall have to restrict ourselves to zero-state equivalents in our discussion of S.

We now suppose that all we know about a linear, differential, finite-dimensional, time-invariant system is its $k \times m$ *weighting matrix* $W(t)$, or preferably, the Laplace transform of $W(t)$, $\tilde{W}(s) \triangleq \int_0^\infty W(t)e^{-st}\,dt$, that is, the *system transfer function matrix*. For finite-dimensional systems, the elements of the matrix $\tilde{W}(s)$ are ratios of polynomials in s. [We assume again that the input $u(t)$ and the output $y(t)$ are m and k vectors, respectively.]

The *problem of realizing a transfer function matrix* $\tilde{W}(s)$ is that of finding a representation in $\hat{S}$ state form,

2 $$\dot{x}(t) = Ax(t) + Bu(t)$$

$\hat{S}$:

3 $$y(t) = Cx(t) + Du(t)$$

such that for $x(0) = 0$, the Laplace transforms of the input and output of $\hat{S}$ satisfy

4 $$\tilde{y}(s) = [C(sI - A)^{-1}B + D]\tilde{u}(s) = \tilde{W}(s)\tilde{u}(s)$$

that is, we wish to find a representation $\hat{S}$ with matrices A, B, C, and D which satisfy the identity equation

5 $$[C(sI - A)^{-1}B + D] \equiv \tilde{W}(s)$$

6 **Definition** We shall say that a representation $\hat{S}$ of the form *2* and *3* is a *realization* of the representation *1* if its matrices satisfy the identity *5*.

7 **Definition** We shall say that a representation $\hat{S}$ of the form *2* and *3* is a *minimal realization* of the system *1* if its matrices satisfy *5* and there is no other realization of *1* whose state vector x is of lower dimension than in $\hat{S}$.

Note that $\hat{S}$ is a minimal realization of *1* if and only if it is completely observable and completely controllable.

In this section we shall show how to construct a realization $\hat{S}$ for a transfer matrix $\tilde{W}(s)$, which is completely observable only. A minimal realization can then be obtained by making use of the algorithms outlined in Sec. *9*.

Case 1: the matrix $\tilde{W}(s)$ has simple poles only

As we pointed out before, the $k \times m$ matrix $\tilde{W}(s)$ has elements

8 $$\tilde{w}_{ij}(s) = \frac{p_{ij}(s)}{q_{ij}(s)}$$

where $p_{ij}(s)$ and $q_{ij}(s)$ are polynomials in s. We begin by assuming, for each $\tilde{w}_{ij}(s)$ separately, that the zeros of $q_{ij}(s)$ are all distinct, that is, that there are no multiple poles in any of the matrix elements $\tilde{w}_{ij}(s)$. Now, let us suppose that each $\tilde{w}_{ij}(s)$ has been expanded in partial fractions and that the poles of $\tilde{W}(s)$ (assumed to be distinct) are

$\lambda_1, \lambda_2, \ldots, \lambda_h$. We may therefore rewrite $\tilde{W}(s)$ as a sum of $k \times m$ matrices as follows:

9 $$\tilde{W}(s) = \sum_{i=1}^{h} \frac{1}{s - \lambda_i} R_i + D$$

where the R_i are constant $k \times m$ matrices (possibly with complex coefficients), whose jth column will be denoted by $r_{ij}\rangle$, and D is a constant $k \times m$ matrix.

For the moment, let us assume that $h = 1$. Then the Laplace transform of *1*, with $t_0 = 0$, takes on the form

10 $$\tilde{y}(s) = \frac{1}{s - \lambda_1} R_1\tilde{u}(s) + D\tilde{u}(s)$$

Not all the columns $r_{1j}\rangle$, $j = 1, 2, \ldots, m$, of R_1 need be independent; i.e., the rank of R_1 may be less than m. Suppose that the columns of R_1 (which are k-vectors) span an α-dimensional subspace of C^k. Let $c_1, \ldots, c_\alpha$, with $c_i = (c_i^1, \ldots, c_i^k)$, be any basis for this subspace, which will be denoted by $\mathcal{R}(R_1)$, since it is the range space of R_1. Then, for each $r_{1j}\rangle$, $j = 1, \ldots, m$, there exist scalars ρ_i^j, with $i = 1, 2, \ldots, \alpha$, such that

11 $$r_{1j}\rangle = \sum_{i=1}^{\alpha} \rho_i^j c_i\rangle \qquad j = 1, 2, \ldots, m$$

Now, the product $R_1\tilde{u}(s)$ can be written as

12 $$R_1\tilde{u}(s) = \sum_{j=1}^{m} \tilde{u}^j(s) r_{1j}\rangle$$

Substituting from *11*, we obtain

13 $$R_1\tilde{u}(s) = \sum_{j=1}^{m} \tilde{u}^j(s) \left(\sum_{i=1}^{\alpha} \rho_i^j c_i\rangle \right) = \sum_{i=1}^{\alpha} \left(\sum_{j=1}^{m} \tilde{u}^j(s) \rho_i^j \right) c_i\rangle$$

Now, let $b_i = (\bar{\rho}_i^1, \ldots, \bar{\rho}_i^m)$,† $i = 1, 2, \ldots, \alpha$. Then *13* becomes

14 $$R_1\tilde{u}(s) = \sum_{i=1}^{\alpha} c_i\rangle \langle b_i, \tilde{u}(s)\rangle$$

We see immediately that by picking any basis in the range space of R_1 we can construct a dyadic decomposition of R_1; that is,

15 $$R_1 = \sum_{i=1}^{\alpha} c_i\rangle \langle \bar{b}_i$$

Inspecting *15*, we see that the vectors $b_i\rangle$, $i = 1, 2, \ldots, \alpha$, span

† As before, the bar over a symbol denotes its complex conjugate, $\langle \cdot, \cdot \rangle$ denotes the complex scalar product; that is, $\langle x, y\rangle = \Sigma \bar{x}^i y^i$, and the superscript * denotes the complex-conjugate transpose of a matrix.

$\mathcal{R}(R_1^*)$, the range space of the complex-conjugate transpose of R_1. Note that as a basis for $\mathcal{R}(R_1)$ we may take the first α linearly independent columns of R_1.

Let us return to *10*. Substituting for R_1 its dyadic expansion *15*, we obtain

16
$$\tilde{y}(s) = \frac{1}{s - \lambda_1} \sum_{i=1}^{\alpha} c_i\rangle \langle b_i, \tilde{u}(s)\rangle + D\tilde{u}(s)$$

Now let

17
$$\dot{x}^i(t) = \lambda_1 x^i(t) + \langle b_i, u(t)\rangle \qquad \text{for } i = 1, \ldots, \alpha$$

and let

18
$$y(t) = \sum_{i=1}^{\alpha} x^i(t) c_i\rangle + Du(t)$$

Obviously, the representation *17* and *18* can be written in the form

19
$$\dot{x}(t) = Ax(t) + Bu(t)$$

$\hat{S}$:

20
$$y(t) = Cx(t) + Du(t)$$

where A is an $\alpha \times \alpha$ matrix whose main diagonal elements are equal to λ_1 and whose off-diagonal elements are zero. B is a matrix with rows $\langle \bar{b}_i$, and C is a matrix with columns $c_i\rangle$. We also see that the representation *19* and *20* is a realization of the transfer function given by *10*. It is left as an exercise for the reader to show that the representation $\hat{S}$ of *19* and *20* is completely observable.

Let us now return to the general form *9*. We proceed exactly as before, decomposing each R_i into dyads as follows:

21
$$R_i = \sum_{\beta=1}^{\alpha_i} c_{i\beta}\rangle \langle \bar{b}_{i\beta}$$

where α_i is the dimension of $\mathcal{R}(R_i)$ and the $\bar{b}_{i\beta}$, $\beta = 1, 2, \ldots, \alpha_i$, span $\mathcal{R}(R_i^*)$, where R_i^* is the complex-conjugate transpose of R_i. We then obtain, from *9*,

22
$$\tilde{y}(s) = \sum_{i=1}^{h} \frac{1}{s - \lambda_i} \sum_{\beta=1}^{\alpha_i} c_{i\beta}\rangle \langle b_{i\beta}, \tilde{u}(s)\rangle + D\tilde{u}(s)$$

By proceeding as before, we get again a completely observable realization in the standard form *2* and *3*, where, using partitioning of matrices,

23
$$x(t) = [x_1(t) \mid \cdots \mid x_h(t)]$$

with

24
$$x_i(t) = (x_i^1, \ldots, x_i^{\alpha_i}) \qquad i = 1, 2, \ldots, h$$

The matrix A is a $\sum_{i=1}^{h} \alpha_i \times \sum_{i=1}^{h} \alpha_i$ diagonal matrix with elements a_{ij}, such that $a_{ij} = 0$ for $i \neq j$ and

25
$$\begin{aligned} a_{ii} &= \lambda_1 \qquad \text{for } i = 1, 2, \ldots, \alpha_1 \\ &= \lambda_2 \qquad \text{for } i = \alpha_1 + 1, \ldots, \alpha_1 + \alpha_2 \\ &\cdots\cdots\cdots\cdots\cdots\cdots\cdots \\ &= \lambda_h \qquad \text{for } i = \alpha_1 + \alpha_2 + \cdots + \alpha_{h-1} + 1, \ldots, \alpha_1 + \alpha_2 + \cdots + \alpha_h \end{aligned}$$

The matrix $B = [B_1^* \vdots B_2^* \cdots \vdots B_h^*]^*$, where the B_i are matrices with rows $\langle \bar{b}_{i\beta}$, and the matrix $C = [C_1 \vdots C_2 \vdots \cdots \vdots C_h]$, where the C_i are matrices with columns $c_{i\beta}\rangle$.

For the particular case in which $\tilde{W}(s)$ is a scalar function; i.e., both $y(t)$ and $u(t)$ are scalars, we obtain

26
$$\tilde{W}(s) = \sum_{i=1}^{h} \frac{R_i}{s - \lambda_i} + D$$

and a completely observable realization for it is given by

27
$$\begin{bmatrix} \dot{x}_1(t) \\ \dot{x}_2(t) \\ \cdot \\ \cdot \\ \cdot \\ \dot{x}_h(t) \end{bmatrix} = \begin{bmatrix} \lambda_1 & 0 & \cdots & 0 & 0 \\ 0 & \lambda_2 0 & \cdots & & 0 \\ 0 & 0 & \cdots & & 0 \\ \cdots & \cdots & \cdots & \cdots & \cdots \\ 0 & 0 & \cdots & & \lambda_h \end{bmatrix} \begin{bmatrix} x_1(t) \\ x_2(t) \\ \cdot \\ \cdot \\ \cdot \\ x_h(t) \end{bmatrix} + \begin{bmatrix} R_1 \\ R_2 \\ \cdot \\ \cdot \\ \cdot \\ R_n \end{bmatrix} u(t)$$

28
$$y(t) = [1, 1, \ldots, 1] \begin{bmatrix} x_1(t) \\ \cdot \\ \cdot \\ \cdot \\ x_k(t) \end{bmatrix} + Du(t)$$

Case 2: the matrix $\tilde{W}(s)$ has multiple poles

As soon as the matrix $\tilde{W}(s)$ has multiple poles, the complexity and difficulty of constructing a completely observable realization increases tremendously. Let us confine ourselves to the case in which $\tilde{W}(s)$ has poles of multiplicity 2, but not greater. In this event, proceeding as before, a partial-fraction expansion of the elements of $\tilde{W}(s)$ leads to the decomposition

29
$$\tilde{W}(s) = \sum_{i=1}^{h} \left(\frac{1}{s - \lambda_i} R_i' + \frac{1}{(s - \lambda_i)^2} R_i'' \right) + D$$

where the R_i' and R_i'' are $k \times m$ constant matrices (possibly with complex coefficients) and D is a $k \times m$ constant matrix.

Let us begin by considering the simplest case of *29*; that is,

30 $$\tilde{W}(s) = \frac{1}{s - \lambda_1} R_1' + \frac{1}{(s - \lambda_1)^2} R_i''$$

For $j = 1, 2, \ldots, n$, let $r_{ij}'\rangle$ be the jth column of R_1' and let $r_{ij}''\rangle$ be the jth column of R_1''. We note that the range spaces $\mathcal{R}(R_1')$ and $\mathcal{R}(R_1'')$, which are spanned by the columns of R_1' and R_1'', respectively, are subspaces whose dimensions are equal to the ranks of R_1' and R_1''. Now, let $c_1, \ldots, c_\alpha$, with $c_i = (c_i^1, \ldots, c_i^k)$, be any basis for the subspace $\mathcal{R}(R_1') \cap \mathcal{R}(R_1'')$. Let $c_1, \ldots, c_\alpha, c_{\alpha+1}', \ldots, c_\gamma'$ be a basis for $\mathcal{R}(R_1')$, and let $c_1, \ldots, c_\alpha, c_{\alpha+1}'', \ldots, c_\delta''$ be a basis for $\mathcal{R}(R_1'')$. Note that we have taken a maximal set of independent vectors common to both $\mathcal{R}(R_1')$ and $\mathcal{R}(R_1'')$ and have added to it so as to form two bases. As was done in *11*, we express the columns of R_1' and R_1'' in terms of these bases as follows:

31 $$r_{ij}'\rangle = \sum_{i=1}^{\gamma} \rho_i'^j c_i'\rangle \qquad j = 1, 2, \ldots, m$$

32 $$r_{ij}''\rangle = \sum_{i=1}^{\delta} \rho_i''^j c_i''\rangle \qquad j = 1, 2, \ldots, m$$

where $c_i' = c_i'' = c_i$ for $i = 1, 2, \ldots, \alpha$.

Following the procedure shown in *12* and *13*, for $i = 1, 2, \ldots, \gamma$ and $j = 1, 2, \ldots, \delta$, we let $b_i' = (\bar{\rho}_i'^1, \ldots \bar{\rho}_i'^m)$ and

$$b_j'' = (\bar{\rho}_j''^1, \ldots, \bar{\rho}_j''^m)$$

and hence, with $\tilde{W}(s)$ given by *30*, the Laplace transform of *1* yields

33 $$\tilde{y}(s) = \tilde{W}(s)\tilde{u}(s) = \sum_{i=1}^{\alpha} c_i\rangle \left(\frac{1}{s - \lambda_1} \langle b_i', \tilde{u}(s)\rangle + \frac{1}{(s - \lambda_1)^2} \langle b_i'', \tilde{u}(s)\rangle \right) + \sum_{i=\alpha+1}^{\gamma} \frac{1}{s - \lambda_1} c_i'\rangle \langle b_i, \tilde{u}(s)\rangle + \sum_{i=\alpha+1}^{\delta} \frac{1}{(s - \lambda_1)^2} c_i''\rangle \langle b_i'', \tilde{u}(s)\rangle + D\tilde{u}(s)$$

We are now ready to construct our state equations. By referring to the sums in *33*, we see that we can choose for the state the vector

$$x(t) = (v_1, z_1, v_2, z_2, \ldots, v_\alpha, z_\alpha \,\vdots\, v_{\alpha+1}, v_{\alpha+2}, \ldots, v_\gamma \,\vdots\, v_{\gamma+1}, z_{\gamma+1}, v_{\gamma+2}, z_{\gamma+2}, \ldots, v_\delta, z_\delta)$$

whose components satisfy the following differential equations (with zero initial conditions): for $i = 1, 2, \ldots, \alpha$,

34 $$\dot{v}_i(t) = \lambda_1 v_i(t) + \langle b_i'', u(t) \rangle$$

35 $$\dot{z}_i(t) = v_i(t) + \lambda_1 z_i(t) + \langle b_i', u(t) \rangle$$

for $i = \alpha + 1, \alpha + 2, \ldots, \gamma$,

36 $$\dot{v}_i(t) = \lambda_1 v_i(t) + \langle b_i', u(t) \rangle$$

for $i = \lambda + 1, \lambda + 2, \ldots, \delta$,

37 $$\dot{v}_i(t) = z_i(t)$$

38 $$\dot{z}_i(t) = -\lambda_1^2 v_i(t) + 2\lambda_1 z_i(t) + \langle b_i'', u(t) \rangle$$

When the states are assigned as above, we find that the matrix A for the standard form of *2* and *3* is given by

39 $$A = \left[\begin{array}{c|c|c}
\longleftarrow 2\alpha \longrightarrow & \longleftarrow \gamma - \alpha \longrightarrow & \longleftarrow 2(\delta - \alpha) \longrightarrow \\
\begin{array}{c:c:c}
\begin{matrix}\lambda_1 & 0 \\ 1 & \lambda_1\end{matrix} & 0 & \\ \hdashline
0 & \begin{matrix}\lambda_1 & 0 \\ 1 & 0\end{matrix} & 0 \\ \hdashline
 & 0 &
\end{array} &
\begin{matrix} 0 & \cdots & 0 \\ & \cdots & \\ 0 & \cdots & 0 \end{matrix} &
\begin{matrix} 0 & \cdots & 0 \\ & \cdots & \\ 0 & \cdots & 0 \end{matrix} \\ \hline
\begin{matrix} 0 & \cdots & 0 \\ & \cdots & \\ 0 & \cdots & 0 \end{matrix} &
\begin{matrix} \lambda_1 & & & \\ & \lambda_1 & & \\ & & \ddots & \\ & 0 & & \lambda_1 \end{matrix} &
\begin{matrix} 0 & \cdots & 0 \\ & \cdots & \\ 0 & \cdots & 0 \end{matrix} \\ \hline
\begin{matrix} 0 & \cdots & 0 \\ & \cdots & \\ 0 & \cdots & 0 \end{matrix} &
\begin{matrix} 0 & \cdots & 0 \\ & \cdots & \\ 0 & \cdots & 0 \end{matrix} &
\begin{array}{c:c}
\begin{matrix} 0 & 1 \\ -\lambda_1^2 & 2\lambda \end{matrix} & 0 \\ \hdashline
0 & \begin{matrix} 0 & 1 \\ -\lambda_1^2 & 2\lambda_1 \end{matrix}
\end{array}
\end{array}\right]$$

The matrix B has the form

40
$$B = \left[\begin{array}{c} \langle b_1'' \\ \langle b_1' \\ \cdot \\ \cdot \\ \cdot \\ \langle b_\alpha'' \\ \langle b_\alpha' \\ \hdashline \langle b_{\alpha+1}' \\ \langle b_{\alpha+2}' \\ \cdot \\ \cdot \\ \cdot \\ \langle b_\gamma' \\ \hdashline 0 \\ \langle b_{\alpha+1}'' \\ 0 \\ \langle b_{\alpha+2}'' \\ \cdot \\ \cdot \\ \cdot \\ 0 \\ \langle b_\delta'' \end{array}\right] \begin{array}{l} \left.\begin{array}{c} \\ \\ \\ \\ \\ \\ \\ \end{array}\right\} 2\alpha \\ \left.\begin{array}{c} \\ \\ \\ \\ \\ \\ \end{array}\right\} \gamma - \alpha \\ \left.\begin{array}{c} \\ \\ \\ \\ \\ \\ \\ \\ \\ \end{array}\right\} 2(\delta - \alpha) \end{array}$$

Finally, the matrix C is seen to be one with columns as follows:

41
$$C = [0\rangle, c_1\rangle, \ . \ . \ . \ , 0\rangle, c_\alpha\rangle \,\vdots\, c'_{\alpha+1}\rangle, \ . \ . \ . \ , c'_\gamma\rangle \,\vdots\, c''_{\alpha+1}\rangle, 0\rangle, \ . \ . \ . \ , c''_\delta\rangle, 0\rangle]$$

It should be reasonably clear that the general expression *1* can be used to construct a state space representation for the linear system by repeating the above procedure for each $i = 1, \ . \ . \ . \ , k$. An alternate procedure for realizing a transfer function matrix will be presented in the next section, following the discussion of techniques for reducing input-output relations of differential systems. This procedure will, in some respects, be simpler and computationally more effective than the procedure described in this section.

12 *Reduction of input-output relations*

Suppose we are given a linear time-invariant differential system in the form

1 S:
$$L(p)y(t) = M(p)u(t)$$

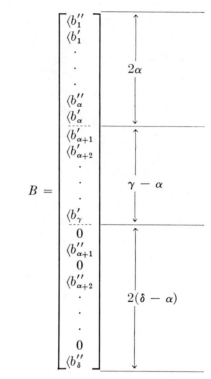

where $y = (y^1,y^2, \ldots ,y^n)$ is the output of the system,

$$u = (u^1,u^2, \ldots ,u^r)$$

is the input of the system, $L(p)$ is an $n \times n$ matrix whose $l_{ij}(p)$ elements are finite polynomials in $p = d/dt$, and $M(p)$ is an $n \times r$ matrix whose elements $m_{ij}(p)$ are also finite polynomials in $p = d/dt$, as in Sec. *10*. As in Sec. *10*, we again assume that $\det L(s) \not\equiv 0$ and that $\tilde{W}(s) \triangleq L^{-1}(s)M(s)$ has rational elements with numerators whose degree does not exceed that of the corresponding denominators.

Now, suppose that we are only interested in a subset of the components of the output, say, the last k components of y, that is, $y^{n-k+1}, \ldots ,y^n, y^{n-1}$. Thus, we may wish to extract from *1* a set of equations which involve only the input u and the last k components of the vector y.

Let $y_1 = (y^1,y^2, \ldots ,y^{n-k})$, and let $y_2 = (y^{n-k+1},y^{n-k+2}, \ldots ,y^n)$. Then *1* can be written in partitioned form, as follows:

2 $$S: \qquad \left[\begin{array}{c|c} L_{11}(p) & L_{12}(p) \\ \hline L_{21}(p) & L_{22}(p) \end{array}\right] \left[\begin{array}{c} y_1(t) \\ \hline y_2(t) \end{array}\right] = \left[\begin{array}{c} \tilde{M}_1(p) \\ \hline M_2(p) \end{array}\right] u(t)$$

Now triangularize the matrix $L(p)$ in *2* by means of the algorithm *6.10.8* to obtain the representation

3 $$\tilde{S}: \qquad \left[\begin{array}{c|c} \tilde{L}_{11}(p) & \tilde{L}_{12}(p) \\ \hline 0 & \tilde{L}_{22}(p) \end{array}\right] \left[\begin{array}{c} y_1(t) \\ \hline y_2(t) \end{array}\right] = \left[\begin{array}{c} \tilde{M}_1(p) \\ \hline \tilde{M}_2(p) \end{array}\right] u(t)$$

where $\tilde{L}_{11}(p)$ and $\tilde{L}_{22}(p)$ are both upper triangular matrices. Clearly, $\tilde{S}$ is equivalent to S, and the relation between y_2, the output components of interest, and the input is obviously given by

4 $$\hat{S}: \qquad \tilde{L}_{22}(p)y_2(t) = \tilde{M}_2(p)u(t)$$

This observation can now be applied to reverse the algorithm described in Sec. *10*. Thus, suppose we are given a system in the form of the following state equations:

5 $$\dot{x}(t) = Ax(t) + Bu(t)$$

S:

6 $$y(t) = Cx(t) + Du(t)$$

where A is an $n \times n$ matrix, B is an $n \times m$ matrix, C is a $k \times n$ matrix, and D is a $k \times m$ matrix. Furthermore, suppose we want a description for S which does not involve the state explicitly. Then, write S as

7 $$\left[\begin{array}{c|c} pI_n - A & 0 \\ \hline -C & I_k \end{array}\right] \left[\begin{array}{c} x(t) \\ y(t) \end{array}\right] = \left[\begin{array}{c} B \\ D \end{array}\right] u(t)$$

where $p = d/dt$, I_n is an $n \times n$ identity matrix, and I_k is a $k \times k$

identity matrix. Now triangularize *7* to obtain a form such as *3* with $y_1 = x$ and $y_2 = y$. Then, *4* gives the required relation

8 $$\hat{S}: \qquad \tilde{L}_{22}(p)y(t) = \tilde{M}_2(p)u(t)$$

We leave it as an exercise for the reader to show that $\hat{S}$ of *8* and S of *5* and *6* are indeed equivalent.

9 *Example* Consider the system

10 $$\begin{bmatrix} \dot{x}_1(t) \\ \dot{x}_2(t) \end{bmatrix} = \begin{bmatrix} 1 & 2 \\ 0 & 3 \end{bmatrix} \begin{bmatrix} x_1(t) \\ x_2(t) \end{bmatrix} + \begin{bmatrix} 1 & 1 \\ 2 & 1 \end{bmatrix} \begin{bmatrix} u^1(t) \\ u^2(t) \end{bmatrix}$$

S:

11 $$y(t) = [1,1] \begin{bmatrix} x_1(t) \\ x_2(t) \end{bmatrix}$$

and suppose we want to find the differential equation for y. Writing S in the form *7* we obtain

12 $$S: \qquad \begin{bmatrix} p-1 & -2 & 0 \\ 0 & p-3 & 0 \\ -1 & -1 & 1 \end{bmatrix} \begin{bmatrix} x_1(t) \\ x_2(t) \\ y(t) \end{bmatrix} = \begin{bmatrix} 1 & 1 \\ 2 & 1 \\ 0 & 0 \end{bmatrix} \begin{bmatrix} u^1(t) \\ u^2(t) \end{bmatrix}$$

Triangularizing *12*, we get

13 $$\tilde{S}: \begin{bmatrix} 1 & 1 & -1 \\ 0 & -4 & p-1 \\ 0 & 0 & (p-1)(p-3) \end{bmatrix} \begin{bmatrix} x_1(t) \\ x_2(t) \\ y(t) \end{bmatrix} = \begin{bmatrix} 0 & 0 \\ 3 & 2 \\ 3p-1 & 2p-2 \end{bmatrix} \begin{bmatrix} u^1(t) \\ u^2(t) \end{bmatrix}$$

and hence

14 $$\hat{S}: \quad \frac{d^2y(t)}{dt^2} - 4\frac{dy(t)}{dt} + 3y(t) = 3\frac{du^1(t)}{dt} - u^1(t) + 2\frac{du^2(t)}{dt} - 2u^2(t)$$

is equivalent to S and is described in terms of the input and output alone.

Our second observation pertains to the realization of transfer function matrices. Thus, suppose that we are given the system S in transfer function form, as in Sec. *11*; that is,

15 $$S: \qquad \tilde{y}(s) = \tilde{W}(s)\tilde{u}(s)$$

where $\tilde{y}(s)$ and $\tilde{u}(s)$ are the Laplace transforms of the output

$$y(t) = (y^1(t), y^2(t), \ldots, y^n(t))$$

and the input $u(t) = (u^1(t), \ldots, u^r(t))$, respectively, and $\tilde{W}(s)$ is an $n \times r$ transfer function matrix.

Now, there is a polynomial in s of least degree $\Delta(s)$, such that

16 $$\tilde{W}(s) = \frac{1}{\Delta(s)} M(s)$$

and $M(s)$ is an $n \times r$ matrix whose elements are polynomials in s. Observe that the representation

17 $$\hat{S}: \qquad \Delta(p) I y(t) = M(p) u(t)$$

where I is an $n \times n$ identity matrix, has transfer function $\tilde{W}(s)$, and hence it is zero-state equivalent to S. We can now obtain an equivalent state representation $\hat{S}'$ for $\hat{S}$ by the algorithm presented in Sec. *10*, and then, in turn, we can compute a reduced minimal equivalent $\hat{S}''$ for the representation $\hat{S}'$ by the algorithm outlined in Sec. *9*. The representation $\hat{S}''$ will have transfer function $\tilde{W}(s)$ and will be a minimal realization for the representation S. The advantage of this apparently most inelegant approach is that it is computationally quite efficient and simple to program.

This concludes our excursion into the world of time-invariant linear systems. We hope that our rather compact presentation will act as a map for the reader through the vast maze of related literature.

REFERENCES

1 Zadeh, L. A., and C. A. Desoer: "Linear System Theory," McGraw-Hill, New York, 1963.

2 Kalman, R. E.: On the General Theory of Control Systems, *Proc. 1st Intern. Cong. Automatic Control*, vol. 1, pp. 481–492, Butterworth, London, 1961.

3 Kalman, R. E., Y. C. Ho, and K. S. Narendra: Controllability of Linear Dynamical Systems, *Contrib. Differential Equations*, vol. 1, pp. 189–213, 1962.

4 Kalman, R. E.: Canonical Structure of Linear Dynamical Systems, *Proc. Nat'l Acad. Sci., U.S.*, vol. 48, pp. 596–600, April, 1962.

5 Kalman, R. E.: Mathematical Description of Linear Dynamical Systems, *J. SIAM Control*, vol. 1, pp. 152–192, 1963.

6 Gilbert, E. G.: Controllability and Observability in Multi-Variable Control Systems, *J. SIAM Control*, vol. 1, pp. 128–151, 1963.

7 Kreindler, E., and P. E. Sarachik: On the Concepts of Controllability and Observability of Linear Systems, *IEEE Trans. Autom. Control*, vol. AC-9, pp. 129–136, April, 1964.

8 Brockett, R. W.: Poles, Zeroes, and Feedback: State Space Interpretation, *IEEE Trans. Autom. Control*, vol. AC-10, pp. 129–134, April, 1965.

9 Chang, A.: An Algebraic Characterization of Controllability, *IEEE Trans. Autom. Control*, vol. AC-10, pp. 112–113, January, 1965.

10 Silverman, L. M., and H. E. Meadows: Controllability and Observability in Time-Variable Linear Systems, *J. SIAM Control*, vol. 5, pp. 64.73, 1967.

11 Kwakernaak, H., and E. Polak: On the Reduction of the System $x = Ax + Bu$, $y = c'x$ to Its Minimal Equivalent, *IEEE Trans.*, vol. CT-10, no. 4, 1963.

12 Silverman, L. M., and H. E. Meadows: Degrees of Controllability in Time-Variable Linear Systems, *Proc. Nat'l. Electronics Conf.*, vol. 21, pp. 689–693, 1965.

13 Anderson, B. D. O., R. W. Newcomb, R. E. Kalman, and D. C. Youla: Equivalence of Linear Time-Invariant Systems, *J. Franklin Inst.*, vol. 281, pp. 371–378, 1966.

14 Silverman, L. M., and H. E. Meadows: Equivalence and Syntheses of Time-Variable Linear Systems, *Proc. 4th Allerton Conf. Circuit and Systems Theory*, pp. 776–784, 1966.

15 Polak, E.: An Algorithm for Reducing a Linear, Time-Invariant Differential System to State Form, *IEEE Trans. Autom. Control*, vol. AC-11, pp. 557–579, 1966.

16 Brown, F. M.: State Equations Corresponding to a Time-Varying Linear Differential System, *IEEE Proc.*, vol. 55, no. 6, p. 1123, 1967.

17 Kalman, R. E.: Irreducible Realizations and the Degree of a Rational Matrix, *J. SIAM Control*, vol. 13, pp. 520–545, June, 1965.

18 Ho, B. L., and R. E. Kalman: Effective Construction of Linear State-Variable Models from Input/Output Data, *Proc. 3rd Allerton Conf. Circuit and Systems Theory, Univ. of Illinois, Urbana*, pp. 449–459, October, 1965.

19 Youla, D. C., and P. Tissi: *n*-Port Synthesis via Reactance Extraction—Part 1, *IEEE Conv. Record*, vol. 14, part 7, pp. 183–205, 1966.

20 Weiss, L., and R. E. Kalman: Contributions to Linear System Theory, *Int. J. Eng. Sci.*, vol. 3, pp. 141–171, 1965.

21 Youla, D. C.: The Synthesis of Linear Dynamical Systems from Prescribed Weighting Patterns, *J. SIAM Control*, vol. 14, pp. 527–549, 1966.

22 Silverman, L. M.: Stable Realization of Impulse Response Matrices, *IEEE Intern. Conv. Record*, vol. 15, part 5, pp. 32–36, 1967.

23 Johnson, C. D., and W. M. Wonham: A Note on the Transformation to Canonical (Phase-Variable) Form, *IEEE Trans. Autom. Control*, vol. AC-9, pp. 312–313, July, 1964.

24 Mufti, I. H.: On the Reduction of a System to Canonical (Phase-Variable) Form, *IEEE Trans. Autom. Control*, vol. AC-10, pp. 206–207, April, 1965.

25 Chidambara, M. R.: The Transformation to (Phase-Variable) Canonical Form, *IEEE Trans. Autom. Control*, vol. AC-10, pp. 492–494, October, 1965.

26 Silverman, L. M.: Transformation of Time-Variable Systems to Canonical (Phase-Variable) Form, *IEEE Trans. Autom. Control*, vol. AC-11, pp. 300–302, 1966.

27 Luenberger, D. G.: Canonical Forms for Linear Multivariable Systems, *IEEE Trans. Autom. Control*, vol. AC-12, pp. 290–293, 1967.

7

Large-scale linear systems

B. K. Harrison[1]
Department of Physics
Brigham Young University

1 *Introduction*

In any practical application of system theory, the size of the system under consideration is crucial in determining feasibility of solution. By "size" we mean, usually, the dimension of the state space (here taken to be a finite-dimensional vector space). A rough meaning of "size" is the number of "elements" in the system, where "elements" is understood intuitively.

The practicability of solution of the equations of a system depends markedly on its size. This fact can be illustrated by the simple example of a system whose solution requires inversion of an $n \times n$ matrix; such an inversion requires n^3 multiplications in general, according to a rule of thumb of Von Neumann cited in [1]. For very large systems, such an inversion becomes impractical even for machine computation. For systems requiring more than simple matrix inversion—requiring, say, a time integration of the input vector—the problem is aggravated.

[1] The author would like to acknowledge the assistance of Franklin H. Branin, Jr., and J. Paul Roth, both of International Business Machines Corp., in conversations and communications, and that of Thomas C. Doyle of Los Alamos Scientific Laboratory, in many discussions. He also wishes to thank the Society for Industrial and Applied Mathematics for permission to use material from an article published in the Society Journal [39], on which article the present one is based. This work was performed under the auspices of the United States Atomic Energy Commission while the author was a staff member at the Los Alamos Scientific Laboratory, Los Alamos, New Mexico.

Hence, there is a need for efficient methods of treating large systems and for as much simplification of such systems as possible.

A powerful method for treating large systems is Kron's method of "tearing" [2], which will be discussed in this chapter. In order to apply this method, one must first express the system as a discrete graph (or network). This is possible for a large variety of physical systems: electrical, mechanical, hydraulic, etc. [3, 4]. One can also construct graphical models of systems represented by partial differential equations [5–10]. This wide range of possible representations by graphs is one reason that Kron's method can be of great usefulness (see Sec. *9*).

After expressing the system as a graph, one figuratively "tears" the graph into smaller subgraphs, solves the equations of the subgraphs, and "interconnects" the solutions of the pieces (in several steps if necessary) in order to obtain the solution for the original system. The graph plays two roles: first, as an essential element in setting up the equations for the original system, and second, as an aid for outlining the tearing procedure. It is possible to outline the tearing without use of the graph; however, the graph is very useful for picturing the system and for selecting the most efficient scheme to use. Much of the method consists of straightforward mathematics; the actual tearing and organizing the interconnection of solutions is, however, more of an art, and use of the graph may be found to be desirable.

Under certain conditions, Kron's method can be used to treat very large systems with considerable saving in time over older methods of analysis. Such conditions are as follows:

1 The possibility of subdividing the system into parts with little or no coupling between separate parts.
2 The possibility of some parts being identical to each other, so that solution of the equations for one part suffices for others.

The reasons for these conditions will be made clear later in the chapter.

Unfortunately, at the present time, Kron's method is most useful only under two other special conditions: the requirements that the system be

3 Linear
4 In a state such that the equations for the system can be written in an algebraic form (with no derivatives occurring)

Requirement *4* is equivalent to requiring either that the system be in a constant state or that it be in a sinusoidal oscillation with a single frequency ω, so that the common factor $e^{i\omega t}$ may be divided out.

In terms of the state equations for a differential system [11],

$$\dot{s}(t) = f(s(t),u(t)) \tag{5}$$

$$y(t) = g(s(t),u(t)) \tag{6}$$

where u, s, and y are the input, state, and output, respectively, these requirements may be stated as follows. Condition *4* implies either that $\dot{s}(t)$ is zero or that $\dot{s}(t)$ is proportional to $s(t)$, so that *5* becomes

$$h(s(t),u(t)) = 0 \tag{7}$$

or, in view of *3*,

$$s(t) = Mu(t) \tag{8}$$

When $s(t)$ and $u(t)$ are elements of finite-dimensional vector spaces, M may be expressed as a matrix. Relation *6* now becomes, from *8* and *3*,

$$y(t) = Ns(t) \tag{9}$$

Thus, the general input-output relation [11],

$$y(t) = B(s(t_0);u_{[t_0,t]}) \tag{10}$$

becomes simply

$$y(t) = NMu(t) \tag{11}$$

The output is now a simple linear function of the input, not a functional, as in *10*. Furthermore, the initial state $s(t_0)$ does not occur in *11*; this results from the fact that, under the requirement of a constant state or a pure sinusoidal oscillation, there is effectively no initial state. The main problem in such a treatment is to calculate the matrix M. In the sinusoidal case, M will be a function of the frequency ω.

Some investigation has been carried out to try to remove these restrictions. Malmberg and Cornwell [12] have devised a machine code using Kron's method for treatment of electric circuits containing nonlinear elements (such as transistors). The solution of the equations of such circuits is accomplished in this code by a series of successive approximations to the correct result. Furthermore, there have been several recent articles in the literature concerning nonlinear electrical circuits (for example [13–15]), and it may be possible to use these in developing an application of Kron's method to graphs of nonlinear systems. See also Kron's work on nonlinear problems [16–17].

Little is known concerning the application of Kron's method to the problem of finding transients of differential systems. The main difficulty arises from the fact that one must invert an operator containing both derivatives and large matrices. If this is done formally, one obtains an input-output relation of the general form of *10*, with the functional dependence of u occurring in a time integral from t_0 to t.

The kernel of the integral is an exponential $e^{P\tau}$, where P is a matrix determined by the system. To make use of this form, one must know the characteristic equation of P, which in turn requires knowledge of the eigenvalues of P. It may be possible to use Kron's method to calculate the eigenvalues of P and then to use the eigenvalues and characteristic equation to evaluate the exponential $e^{P\tau}$. An essentially equivalent method consists of taking the Laplace transform of the general matrix equation; the eigenvalues are then the roots of a special determinant. Kron has done some work on these programs; see Ref. 24, vol. 161, pp. 1371, 1727.

The discussion in this chapter will be limited to treatment of systems satisfying requirements *3* and *4*.

There have been, in the literature, many different discussions of Kron's method [1, 18–20]. It is often difficult to compare one treatment with another because of the different procedures and notations used. Much of this confusion arises from the varying emphasis put on sections of Kron's work by different authors.

A few brief comments are in order to aid the reader who looks into the literature on Kron's work. It must be recognized that there are at least two distinct parts to Kron's work: first, his work on tensor analysis of networks (for example [21]) and second, his work on tearing [2, 22–24] (termed by Kron, "diakoptics"). The first part is concerned mainly with the equations of a graph (or network) themselves and with the fact that they have certain tensor properties. It comprises a very general method for setting up the differential equations for many systems (including rotating electrical machines, to which Kron has applied his theory extensively). The second part is concerned with the solution of the equations, as outlined earlier in this section, in which use is made of the earlier results on tensors.

The equations in this chapter are based primarily on the works of two authors in the field, F. H. Branin, Jr. [18] and J. P. Roth [1, 25, 26]. Discussions of the treatments of both authors are given.

For the reader interested in delving further into Kron's method, a good bibliography is given in Ref. 27.

2 *Description of system graph*

As noted in Sec. *1*, one must express the system under consideration in the form of a *graph*. This may have the form of an electrical network, or alternatively, a signal-flow graph. The graph need not be planar. One can then define several quantities which serve to characterize the graph completely. For discussions of graph theory with applications to system theory, see Refs. 3, 18, 20, and 40 to 43.

The primitive features of a graph are *branches*, *nodes* (or vertices), and *meshes* (or closed paths). A branch, crudely speaking, is a line segment together with its endpoints. A node or vertex is the endpoint of a branch (any point of a graph where two or more branches come together will thus be a node). A graph is a finite collection of branches such that no two branches have a point in common that is not a vertex.

A *subgraph* is any subset of the branches of a graph. A mesh or closed path is a subgraph in which every vertex has exactly two branches incident (touching) to it. An open path is similar to a mesh, except that it is "open," i.e., two of the branches have isolated endpoints instead of being connected to each other. A *connected graph* is a graph such that any two of its nodes may be connected by an open path lying in the graph [a disconnected graph has several (>1) *components*, each of which is a connected subgraph]. An *oriented branch* is a branch to which a direction has been assigned. An *oriented graph* is a graph composed of oriented branches. Closed and open paths may also be oriented. Such orientations are completely arbitrary. Graphs considered in this chapter will be oriented. Finally, we may assign one (arbitrary) node from each component of a graph to be a *reference* or *datum node.*

The above definitions provide a simple intuitive picture of a graph. For topological purposes, many of the above definitions can be generalized; however, we shall not be concerned with such generalizations.

We may form *basic sets* of branches, nodes, and meshes for any given graph. The basic sets of the branches and nodes are the sets containing all of the branches and nodes, which are thus complete and have linearly independent elements. A basic set of meshes is any linearly independent collection of meshes such that any mesh in the graph can be expressed as a linear combination of elements in the basic set. The three basic sets thus serve as bases for finite-dimensional vector spaces. We denote the number of linearly independent branches, nodes, and meshes (the dimensions of the corresponding vector spaces) as b, n, and m, respectively. We write k for the number of components, and define

1 $$p = n - k$$

p is thus the number of node pairs (a node pair is any nondatum node paired with the datum node of its component). It may be shown from elementary topology [42, 43] that

2 $$b = p + m$$

We now define a number of incidence matrices [18, 40–43] for the network. The first of these is the branch-node matrix $\bar{A}$. Its elements are given by

3 $$\bar{a}_{ij} = (+1, -1, 0)$$

if the ith branch is (positively, negatively, not) incident on the jth node. Here "incident" means "touching" and "positive incidence" means "pointing away from." We may see by inspection that the columns of $\bar{A}$ are linearly dependent, so we form a new matrix A from $\bar{A}$ by deleting all columns corresponding to datum nodes. $\bar{A}$ has dimensions $b \times n$, A has dimensions $b \times p$, and it can be shown that

4 $$\text{Rank } A = p$$

We define the branch-mesh matrix C as follows:

5 $$c_{ij} = (+1, -1, 0)$$

if the ith branch is (positively, negatively, not) included in the jth mesh. Here "positive" will be taken to mean "pointing in the same direction." The dimensions of C are $b \times m$. We also know from elementary topology that

6 $$\text{Rank } C = m$$

and that

7 $$A_t C = 0$$

where t denotes transpose [28, 43]. (In Ref. 42, A and C are called *junction* and *connection* matrices, respectively.)

Equation 4 implies that we may always construct a tree from the graph. A tree is any collection of p branches of the graph which includes all n nodes. Necessarily, it contains no meshes. The branches remaining in a graph after a tree has been chosen are called *links* or *chords*. If we number the tree branches first, and then the links, we can partition A and C as follows:

8 $$A = \begin{bmatrix} A^T \\ A^L \end{bmatrix}$$

9 $$C = \begin{bmatrix} C^T \\ C^L \end{bmatrix}$$

($T \triangleq$ tree and $L \triangleq$ link). A^T and C^L have dimensions $p \times p$ and $m \times m$, respectively, and can be shown to be nonsingular.

We may define another matrix B^T, called the *node-to-datum-path matrix* [18], by

10 $$b_{ij} = (+1, -1, 0)$$

if the ith branch is (positively, negatively, not) included in the jth node-to-datum path. Such a path is the unique path from a given node to the datum in its component which traverses only tree branches. Thus, B^T is a $p \times p$ matrix.

It may be shown [18] that

11 $$B^T = (A^T)_t^{-1}$$

Thus, the usefulness of B^T arises from the fact that $(A^T)^{-1}$ may be determined merely by inspection of the graph and computation of B^T. Computation of $(C^L)^{-1}$ may be avoided by choosing the meshes so that $C^L = 1_m$ (the symbol 1_a will be used to denote the unit matrix of dimensions $a \times a$).

From Eqs. *4* and *6*, we note that A and C possess left inverses [29]. We denote these by F_t and G_t, of dimensions $p \times b$ and $m \times b$, respectively. Then

12 $$F_t A = 1_p$$

13 $$G_t C = 1_m$$

There is some arbitrariness in the choice of F and G; however, a convenient choice is

14 $$F = \begin{bmatrix} (A^T)_t^{-1} \\ 0 \end{bmatrix} = \begin{bmatrix} B^T \\ 0 \end{bmatrix}$$

and

15 $$G = \begin{bmatrix} 0 \\ (C^L)_t^{-1} \end{bmatrix}$$

Then, in addition, we have

16 $$F_t G = 0$$

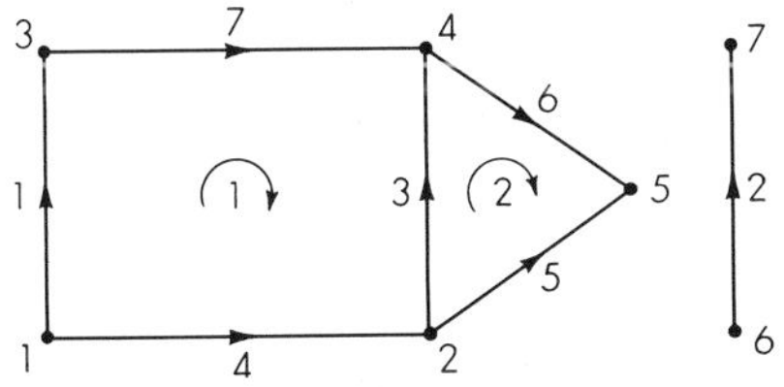

Fig. 7.2.1

To illustrate these definitions, we consider the graph shown in Fig. *7.2.1*. We see that $b = 7$, $n = 7$, $m = 2$, $k = 2$, and $p = 5$. We choose nodes 5 and 7 as datum nodes, and branches 1, 2, 3, 4, and 5 as a tree. Then the matrices corresponding to this graph are

$$\bar{A} = \begin{bmatrix} 1 & 0 & -1 & 0 & 0 & 0 & 0 \\ 0 & 0 & 0 & 0 & 0 & 1 & -1 \\ 0 & 1 & 0 & -1 & 0 & 0 & 0 \\ 1 & -1 & 0 & 0 & 0 & 0 & 0 \\ 0 & 1 & 0 & 0 & -1 & 0 & 0 \\ 0 & 0 & 0 & 1 & -1 & 0 & 0 \\ 0 & 0 & 1 & -1 & 0 & 0 & 0 \end{bmatrix}$$

$$A = \begin{bmatrix} 1 & 0 & -1 & 0 & 0 \\ 0 & 0 & 0 & 0 & 1 \\ 0 & 1 & 0 & -1 & 0 \\ 1 & -1 & 0 & 0 & 0 \\ 0 & 1 & 0 & 0 & 0 \\ 0 & 0 & 0 & 1 & 0 \\ 0 & 0 & 1 & -1 & 0 \end{bmatrix}$$

$$C = \begin{bmatrix} 1 & 0 \\ 0 & 0 \\ -1 & 1 \\ -1 & 0 \\ 0 & -1 \\ 0 & 1 \\ 1 & 0 \end{bmatrix}$$

$$A^T = \begin{bmatrix} 1 & 0 & -1 & 0 & 0 \\ 0 & 0 & 0 & 0 & 1 \\ 0 & 1 & 0 & -1 & 0 \\ 1 & -1 & 0 & 0 & 0 \\ 0 & 1 & 0 & 0 & 0 \end{bmatrix}$$

$$B^T = \begin{bmatrix} 0 & 0 & -1 & 0 & 0 \\ 0 & 0 & 0 & 0 & 1 \\ 0 & 0 & 0 & -1 & 0 \\ 1 & 0 & 1 & 0 & 0 \\ 1 & 1 & 1 & 1 & 0 \end{bmatrix}$$

3 *Formulation and formal solution of system equations*

We now must specify the physical quantities associated with the abstract graph of the system in order to form a complete picture of the graphical model of the system.

We first define a *system element*. This is, crudely speaking, an elemental structure of the system, broken down into simplest practical form. There is some ambiguity in this definition, since there is sometimes no clear-cut criterion of the point at which one should stop breaking the system down into elements. However, in most cases the choice will be clear. We consider a system element to be a two-terminal device, connecting two "points" or regions. Devices with more than two terminals (such as transistors) we assume to be representable as an appropriate combination of two-terminal elements (such as the equivalent circuit of a transistor). Examples of system elements are resistors, springs, dashpots, and hydraulic reservoirs with one inlet and one outlet. Elements are called *components* in Ref. 3, but the term "element" is used here to avoid confusion with components of disconnected graphs (Sec. *2*).

We now list the types of variables we expect in the model. There are two types, referred to in the literature as *through* and *across* variables [3]. They are characterized by the fact that to measure a through variable in a system element, the measuring device (meter) must be placed in series with the element, as shown in Fig. *7.3.1*. To measure an across

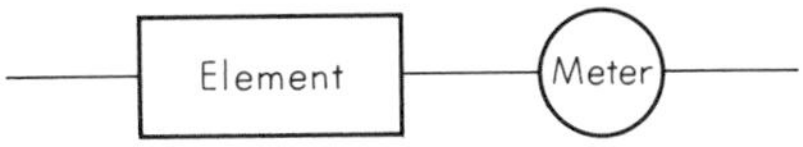

Fig. 7.3.1

variable, the element and meter are placed in parallel, as in Fig. *7.3.2*. Examples of through variables are current, force, torque, fluid flow, and heat transfer. Examples of across variables are voltage, displacement, rotation, pressure, and temperature. We shall denote across variables by symbols u, v, U, and V; we shall denote through variables by i, j, I, and J.

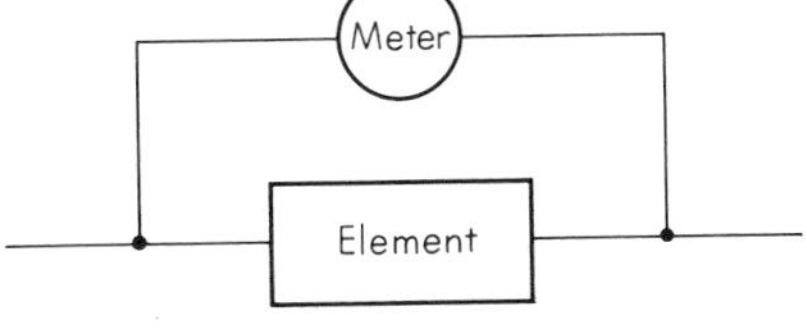

Fig. 7.3.2

We now note that there is usually a relation which is taken to exist between the through and across variables in an element of the system. The three usual types of relations are summarized in Table *7.3.1* [3].

Table 7.3.1

Name of relation	*Name of element*	*Through*		*Across*
Inductive	Inductor	$\frac{dj(t)}{dt}$	related to	$v(t)$
Dissipative or resistive	Resistor	$j(t)$	related to	$v(t)$
Capacitive	Capacitor	$j(t)$	related to	$\frac{dv(t)}{dt}$

In our case, these relations are assumed to be linear. Thus, in a capacitor,

1 $$\frac{dv(t)}{dt} = \frac{1}{c} j(t)$$

in a resistor,

2 $$v(t) = rj(t)$$

in an inductor,

3 $$v(t) = l \frac{dj(t)}{dt}$$

In the constant-state case, inductors and capacitors are assumed not to exist. In the sinusoidal variation case, with all quantities proportional to $e^{i\omega t}$, we may write

4 $$v(t) = zj(t)$$

where

5 $$z = \begin{cases} \dfrac{1}{i\omega c} & \text{Capacitive case} \\ r & \text{Resistive case} \\ i\omega l & \text{Inductive case} \end{cases}$$

z may be called an *impedance;* y, the reciprocal of z, is called an *admittance.*

It is apparent that *4* applies also to the constant-state case, with $z = r$ only. It should be noted that *2* for electric networks is merely Ohm's law.

The set of across variables and the set of through variables will be used as alternative expressions of the state of the system. We must now consider the input. This will be taken to be a collection of sources, either of the across or the through variety.

To achieve generality, we assume the system to be represented by a graph, of which each branch contains (1) an element, (2) an across-variable source, and (3) a through-variable source. The typical branch will then appear as in Fig. *7.3.3*. The polarity of the various

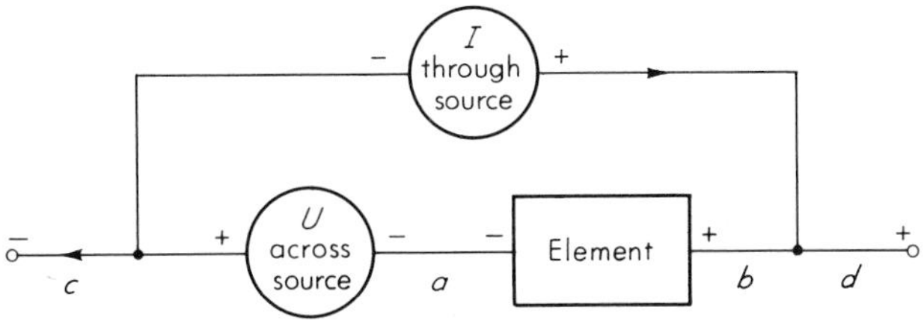

Fig. 7.3.3

parts is chosen for later convenience. If U and I are the strengths of the sources, u and i the measured variable values between points c and d, and V and J the measured variable values in the element (between points a and b), then, with polarity assumed as in Fig. *7.3.3*, we have

6 $$V = u + U$$

and

7 $$J = i + I$$

We now let the symbols V, u, U, J, i, and I stand for b-dimensional vectors whose vector components are the corresponding quantities in the individual branches of the given network. Equations *6* and *7* now become vector equations. We generalize Eq. *4* to

8 $$V = ZJ$$

where now Z is a matrix, called the *impedance matrix*, whose elements are the individual impedances between element across and through variables. In order to incorporate coupling between across and through variables of different branches (as with mutual impedance), we allow nonzero elements of Z off the main diagonal. In most cases Z will be symmetric.

In some applications, the elements of Z may be taken to be quantities which are not physically realizable in systems; this is permissible if necessary for the mathematical (or graphical) model.

The inverse of Z, if it exists, is called the *admittance matrix* Y. Equation *8* can thus be written

9 $$J = YV$$

Two more relations, of the nature of conservation laws, are required. These are called the *circuit and vertex laws for systems* [3]. Their analogs in electrical network theory are Kirchhoff's voltage and current laws. They may be stated as follows:

10 *Circuit law* As one moves around any closed path in the system graph, the sum of the across variables, taken with the proper sign, is zero.

11 *Vertex law* The sum of all the through variables at a node in the system graph, taken with the proper sign, is zero.

The mathematical expressions of these laws are simple, and they connect the graphical quantities with the physical variables. The circuit law is easily seen to become

12 $$C_t u = 0$$

and the vertex law becomes

13 $$A_t i = 0$$

Equations *6*, *7*, *8*, or *9*, *12*, and *13* now comprise the basic equations for the considered system. The state vectors are u and i; we wish to find either or both of these in terms of the input vectors U and I. The output vectors may be any desired linear combination of the individual components of u and i. The analysis follows Ref. 18.

Equations *12* and *13* imply, respectively,

14 $$u = Au'$$

and

15 $$i = Ci'$$

where u' and i' are new vectors, as yet arbitrary, of dimensions p and m, respectively. This is easily seen from Eqs. *7.2.2*, *7.2.4*, *7.2.6*, and *7.2.7*. u' represents sums of across variables along a node-to-datum path; i' represents sums of through variables around a mesh. Equations *6*, *7*, and *8* yield

16 $$u + U = Z(i + I)$$

Multiplication by C_t yields (see *12*)

$$C_t U = C_t Z(i + I)$$

or

17 $$C_t Z i = C_t(U - ZI)$$

Equation *15* now gives

18 $$C_t Z C i' = C_t(U - ZI)$$

A similar treatment yields

19 $$A_tYAe' = A_t(I - YU)$$

Thus,

20 $$i' = (Z')^{-1}C_t(U - ZI)$$

and

21 $$e' = (Y')^{-1}A_t(I - YU)$$

where

22 $$Z' \triangleq C_tZC$$

and

23 $$Y' \triangleq A_tYA$$

The question of the nonsingularity of Z' or Y' remains. Roth [1] has answered this question with the following definition:

24 *An ohmic matrix* L is a matrix such that the matrix-vector product $(Lw)_t^*w$ is nonzero for every nonzero w, where w is an element of a complex vector space ($* \triangleq$ complex conjugate).

Then Roth shows that the system equations always have a unique solution, regardless of how the elements are connected, if the system impedance matrix Z is ohmic. This implies the nonsingularity of Z' and Y'. It can be proved that if Z is ohmic, Y is ohmic, and vice versa.

What if Z is not ohmic? Such a case can arise if, for example, we wish to include branches with sources, but with no impedance. In this case, we can still find a solution to the system equations if we are careful always to allow acceptable connections, i.e., connections of the elements made in such a way that no variables become infinite. (For example, we cannot place a resistanceless short across the terminals of a voltage generator.) This question is discussed to some extent in Ref. 33.

In summary, then, we see that the solution of the system equations involves primarily the inversion of a certain matrix, either Z' or Y'. However, if the problem should be that only one set of source quantities I and U is used, then simple solution of the equations, by Gauss elimination, say, will be more efficient than matrix inversion.

4 *The basic auxiliary equation*

We now wish to prove an important equation, here called the *basic auxiliary equation*. We assume given an $a \times d$ matrix M, with $a \geq d$, such that

1 $$\text{Rank } M = d$$

If

2 $$c = a - d$$

there are d linearly independent rows of M and c linearly independent equations of the form

3 $$\sum_{i=1}^{a} \alpha_i V_i = 0$$

where the V_i represent the rows of M and the α_i are pure numbers. These facts show that there exist matrices R and N, of dimensions $a \times d$ and $a \times c$, respectively, such that

4 $$R_t M = 1_d$$

and

5 $$N_t M = 0$$

R_t is a left inverse for M. Since, for any matrices A and B,

6 $$\text{Rank}\ (AB) \leq \min\ (\text{rank}\ A,\ \text{rank}\ B)$$

[30], *4* shows that

7 $$\text{Rank}\ R = d$$

We require that

8 $$\text{Rank}\ N = c$$

in order that *5* express all independent equations of the form of *3*.

Since N has dimensions $a \times c$, with $a \geq c$, *8* shows that N also has a left inverse S_t; thus

9 $$S_t N = 1_c$$

S has dimensions $a \times c$, and

10 $$\text{Rank}\ S = c$$

From *4*, we have

11 $$M R_t M = M$$

or

12 $$(1_a - M R_t) M = 0$$

Now, *5* contains all the linear dependencies of the rows of M of the form of *3*; therefore *12* can be expressed in terms of these linear dependencies. Thus, we see that we may write

13 $$1_a - M R_t = Q N_t$$

where Q is an $a \times c$ matrix. Using *9* and *13*, we obtain

14 $$Q = S - M R_t S$$

Equations *13* and *14* now yield

15 $$1_a = MR_t + SN_t - MR_tSN_t$$

Equation *15* is the basic auxiliary equation. Note that it exists for any matrices M, R, N, and S satisfying *1, 4, 5, 7, 8, 9,* and *10,* and having the stated dimensions.

Gauge transformations exist for this system of equations. Equations *4, 5, 9,* and *15* are invariant under the transformations

16 $$R = R' + N\alpha$$

17 $$S = S' + M\beta$$

where α and β are $c \times d$ and $d \times c$, respectively. Since

18 $$R_tS = R'_tS' + \alpha_t + \beta$$

we can require

19 $$R'_tS' = 0$$

by putting

20 $$\beta = R_tS - \alpha_t$$

The transformation

21 $$R' = R'' + N\gamma$$

22 $$S' = S'' - M\gamma_t$$

now leaves *4, 5, 9, 15,* and *19* invariant.

We now note that A and C (Sec. *2*) satisfy the requirements made of M and N if we replace a, d, and c of this section with b, p, and m of Sec. *2*. Furthermore, we see that F and G are analogous to R and S. Thus, an equation of the type of *15* holds for A, C, F, and G; since $F_tG = 0$ by *7.2.16*, it reduces to

23 $$1_b = AF_t + GC_t$$

This equation will not be used here; however, it is useful in treating Roth's version of Kron's method, and an equivalent equation has been used in Ref. 20.

We may construct another important equation, of importance to Kron's method, by a few simple transformations. We introduce two $a \times a$ matrices W and X and require that

24 $$W' \triangleq M_tWM$$

and

25 $$X' \triangleq N_tXN$$

be nonsingular. (It is sufficient, but not necessary, for this requirement that W and X be ohmic. However, if W and X are not ohmic, there will be corresponding restrictions on M and N.)

We also define

26 $$P \triangleq M(W')^{-1}M_t$$

27 $$L \triangleq N(X')^{-1}N_t$$

and choose the following values for R and S:

28 $$R = W_tM(W')_t^{-1}$$

29 $$S = XN(X')^{-1}$$

These values satisfy *4* and *9*. We must require

30 $$\text{Rank}\ (W_tM) = d$$

31 $$\text{Rank}\ (XN) = c$$

(these equations are trivial if W and X are nonsingular). Then *15* holds, in the form

32 $$1_a = PW + XL - PWXL$$

If X is nonsingular and $W = X^{-1}$, then by *32* and *5* ($\Rightarrow PL = 0$),

33 $$1_a = PW + XL$$

and, from *33*,

34 $$P = X - XLX$$

and

35 $$L = W - WPW$$

Now if M, N, W, and X are replaced by A, C, Y, and Z, respectively, and if

36 $$H = C(Z')^{-1}C_t$$

37 $$K = A(Y')^{-1}A_t$$

we get from *33*,

38 $$1_b = KY + ZH$$

Equation *38* now yields

39 $$K = Z - ZHZ$$

and

40 $$H = Y - YKY$$

Equations *36*, *37*, *39*, *40*, *7.2.12*, and *7.2.13* result in

41 $$(Y')^{-1} = F_t(Z - ZHZ)F$$

42 $$(Z')^{-1} = G_t(Y - YUY)G$$

These equations show that if one of the quantities $(Y')^{-1}$ or $(Z')^{-1}$ is calculated, the other can be obtained by a series of simple matrix multiplications. It can be shown that the existence of one of $(Y')^{-1}$ or $(Z')^{-1}$ implies the existence of the other. $(Y')^{-1}$ and $(Z')^{-1}$ are called the *nodal* and *mesh solution matrices*, respectively.

As will be seen later, equations similar to the above equations form the heart of Kron's method. It should be mentioned that Eqs. *41* and *42* were probably first derived by Branin [18] by a different method; they are equivalent to Eqs. (79) and (80) in the reference cited. Equation *38* is equivalent to Eqs. (6.36) and (6.37) of Ponstein [20].

5 *The fundamentals of Kron's method of tearing*

In solving the system equations, one wishes the calculation to be as efficient as possible. The maximum efficiency attainable depends on such things as the method used, the sparseness of Z or Y (relative number of zero elements), and the repetitiveness of Z or Y. The value of Kron's method is the fact that it takes advantage of these special features and of the extra leverage obtained from *7.4.41* and similar equations, incorporating them into a graphical scheme which simplifies computation.

In the use of Kron's method, the graph itself is used extensively. This is not necessary, for after construction of the matrices A, B^T, and C, with their divisions into tree and link parts, it is possible to proceed with Kron's method by consideration of the various matrices alone. In other words, the topology of the graph is completely specified by A and C. The quantities Z, I, and U then complete the description of the problem. However, the graph serves as a very useful aid in tearing and in setting up the calculation. It may be wise to employ it frequently, especially since setting up the calculation using Kron's method is not just a mechanical procedure, but has several features of an art. In the following, various principles used in Kron's method will be outlined.

Numbering

As pointed out before, there is considerable freedom in defining and numbering the branches, nodes, and meshes of the graph. For example, Branin [18] defines the tree and the meshes so that $C^L = 1_m$. If numbering and definitions are chosen properly, later steps in the procedure will be simplified. Proper numbering is usually aided by reference to the system graph.

Tearing and interconnecting

After one has set up the system matrices A, B^T, C, and Z or Y, one outlines a tearing and interconnection procedure. This is essentially equivalent to (1) partitioning the matrix Z' and then (2) setting up an iterative scheme to calculate the solution in steps. Such a scheme will be outlined in the next section. It will be seen that the calculation is most efficient if there is no coupling between the parts of the graph after it has been torn. This is manifest in the form of Z or Y; if this form is block-diagonal, there is no coupling between the parts represented by the blocks. Thus, Z (or Y) is "sparse"; i.e., it contains a relatively large number of zeros. For an alternative method of utilizing sparseness, see Ref. 31.

Calculations

The calculations are facilitated by the use of equations of the form of *7.4.41*. Another aid to calculation is the use of known matrix inverses wherever possible. One usually must invert a Z' or a Y' matrix in each of several subgraphs in the course of a problem, and if the needed inverse is already known—either from a previously solved problem or from calculations for an identical subgraph in the same problem—the calculation time is correspondingly reduced. This feature is best employed in Roth's method [1] or in Branin's "elimination-backsubstitution" method [18] (see Sec. 7).

Another calculational aid is the use of matrix-vector multiplications instead of matrix-matrix multiplications where possible. This is perhaps of most use when only one or a few sets of source data is given; if a large number of such sets is given, it may be more efficient to calculate the needed inverse matrices and then to apply them to the source vectors. This method is most useful when combined with the other techniques discussed here.

6 *Iterative procedures in Kron's method*

In this section we shall discuss some of the elementary procedures used in Kron's method by Branin [18], with slightly different notation than is used by Branin. These are best used in connection with Branin's elimination-backsubstitution technique (Sec. 7).

In setting up the calculation, one first selects a tree for the full graph, numbering its branches from 1 to p. (If the graph consists of several unconnected subgraphs, each will have a subtree and a datum node.) Tearing is performed by separating the links of the graph from the tree. Interconnection is then performed by adding the links successively in N sets, with μ_i (≥ 1) links in the ith set. We denote the tree with its connected links, after the ith set has been connected, by E_i. The full graph is thus E_N. The number of branches and meshes in E_i will be written as l_i and m_i; thus,

1 $$l_i = p + m_i$$

The number s_i of unconnected branches is given by

2 $$s_i = b - l_i$$

Note that

3 $$m_i = \sum_{j=1}^{i} \mu_j$$

4 $$s_i = \sum_{j=i+1}^{N} \mu_j$$

5 $$m = m_i + s_i$$

6 $$m_i = m_{i-1} + \mu_{i-1} \qquad i \geq 1$$

7 $$l_i = l_{i-1} + \mu_i \qquad i \geq 1$$

and

8 $$s_{i-1} = s_i + \mu_i \qquad i \geq 1$$

The incidence matrices for E_i will be denoted as A_i and C_i. (Since the tree for all E_i is the same, all A^T and B^T will be the same.) Their dimensions are $l_i \times p$ and $l_i \times m_i$, respectively. We may partition them in analogy to *7.2.8* and *7.2.9* as follows:

9 $$A_i = \begin{bmatrix} A^T \\ A_i^L \end{bmatrix}$$

10 $$C_i = \begin{bmatrix} C_i^T \\ C_i^L \end{bmatrix}$$

Furthermore, from the assumed method of interconnection, we know that

11 $$A_i^L = \begin{bmatrix} A_{i-1}^L \\ \alpha_i \end{bmatrix}$$

12 $$C_i^T = [C_{i-1}^T \quad \beta_i]$$

and

13 $$C_i^L = \begin{bmatrix} C_{i-1}^L & \gamma_i \\ 0 & \delta_i \end{bmatrix}$$

A combination of *9* to *13* now yields

14 $$A_i = \begin{bmatrix} A_{i-1} \\ \alpha_i \end{bmatrix}$$

15 $$C_i = \begin{bmatrix} C_{i-1} & \lambda_i \\ 0 & \delta_i \end{bmatrix}$$

where

16 $$\lambda_i = \begin{bmatrix} \beta_i \\ \gamma_i \end{bmatrix}$$

α_i, λ_i, δ_i, have dimensions $\mu_i \times p$, $l_{i-1} \times \mu_i$, and $\mu_i \times \mu_i$, respectively. (Branin chooses $C_i{}^L = 1_{m_i}$, so that $\delta_i = 1_{\mu_i}$ and $\gamma_i = 0$.) We also have

17 $$(A_i)_t C_i = 0$$

Equations *14*, *15*, and *17* yield

18 $$(A_{i-1})_t C_{i-1} = 0$$

as expected, and

19 $$(A_{i-1})_t \lambda_i + (\alpha_i)_t \delta_i = 0$$

which reduces to

20 $$\alpha_i = (\sigma_i)_t A_{i-1}$$

where

21 $$\sigma_i \triangleq -\lambda_i \delta_i^{-1}$$

We now wish an iteration procedure to calculate $(Y')^{-1}$ for the entire graph, so that we can use Eq. *7.3.21*. We should like to do this by calculating $(Y_i')^{-1}$ in terms of previously known quantities; in particular, we should like to find $(Y_i')^{-1}$ in terms of $(Y_{i-1}')^{-1}$, so that we may proceed by steps (interconnection procedure). Here,

22 $$Y_i' \triangleq (A_i)_t Y_i A_i$$

and Y_i is the admittance matrix for E_i. It will be seen in the following calculation that the calculation is efficient only if Y is block-diagonal, one block corresponding to the tree and the others to the sets of links.

We define

23 $$Q_i = A_i (Y_i')^{-1} (A_i)_t$$

and

24 $$F_i = \begin{bmatrix} (A^T)_t{}^{-1} \\ 0 \end{bmatrix}$$

where the 0 has dimensions $m_i \times p$. Then

25 $$(F_i)_t A_i = 1_p$$

26 $$F_i = \begin{bmatrix} F_{i-1} \\ 0 \end{bmatrix}$$

in which the 0 has dimensions $\mu_i \times p$, and

27 $$(Y'_i)^{-1} = (F_i)_t Q_i F_i$$

To find Q_i, we define

28 $$k_i = (Y_i)^{-1}$$

29 $$k'_i = (C_i)_t k_i C_i$$

and

30 $$w_i = C_i (k'_i)^{-1} (C_i)_t$$

Note that k_i is not equal to Z_i, the impedance matrix for E_i, in the event that there is coupling between sets of links or between the links and the tree. One can now write an equation of the form *7.4.34* as follows:

31 $$Q_i = k_i - k_i w_i k_i$$

If we define

32 $$f_i = \begin{bmatrix} 1_{l_{i-1}} \\ 0 \end{bmatrix}$$

where the 0 is $\mu_i \times l_{i-1}$, then

33 $$F_i = f_i F_{i-1}$$

and *27* becomes

34 $$(Y'_i)^{-1} = (F_{i-1})_t V_i F_{i-1}$$

where

35 $$\begin{aligned} V_i &= (f_i)_t Q_i f_i \\ &= (f_i)_t [k_i - k_i C_i (k'_i)^{-1} (C_i)_t k_i] f_i \end{aligned}$$

by *30* and *31*. We must now calculate V_i.

We partition Z in three different ways as follows:

36 $$Z = \begin{bmatrix} Z_i & b_i \\ d_i & e_i \end{bmatrix}$$

with row and column dimensions equal to l_i and s_i;

37 $$Z = \begin{bmatrix} Z_{i-1} & b_{i-1} \\ d_{i-1} & e_{i-1} \end{bmatrix}$$

(*36* with $i \to i - 1$); and

38 $$Z = \begin{bmatrix} Z_{i-1} & q_i & u_i \\ r_i & t_i & v_i \\ w_i & x_i & e_i \end{bmatrix}$$

with row and column dimensions l_{i-1}, μ_i, and s_i. Then

39 $$Z_i = \begin{bmatrix} Z_{i-1} & q_i \\ r_i & t_i \end{bmatrix}$$

40 $$b_i = \begin{bmatrix} u_i \\ v_i \end{bmatrix}$$

41 $$d_i = [w_i \quad x_i]$$

42 $$b_{i-1} = [q_i \quad u_i]$$

43 $$d_{i-1} = \begin{bmatrix} r_i \\ w_i \end{bmatrix}$$

and

44 $$e_{i-1} = \begin{bmatrix} t_i & v_i \\ x_i & e_i \end{bmatrix}$$

From *28*, *36*, and *4* (Appendix) with $M = Z = Y^{-1}$ (Y_i corresponds to Y as Z_i does to Z in *36*),

45 $$k_i = (Y_i)^{-1} = Z_i - b_i e_i^{-1} d_i$$

or

46 $$k_i = \begin{bmatrix} \xi_i & \eta_i \\ \zeta_i & \rho_i \end{bmatrix}$$

where

47 $$\xi_i = Z_{i-1} - u_i e_i^{-1} w_i$$

48 $$\eta_i = q_i - u_i e_i^{-1} x_i$$

49 $$\zeta_i = r_i - v_i e_i^{-1} w_i$$

50 $$\rho_i = t_i - v_i e_i^{-1} x_i$$

Also, we have

51 $$k_{i-1} = Z_{i-1} - b_{i-1}(e_{i-1})^{-1} d_{i-1}$$

which gives

52 $$k_{i-1} = \xi_i - \eta_i \rho_i^{-1} \zeta_i$$

Now, from *15*, *29*, and *46*, we obtain

53 $$k'_i = \begin{bmatrix} \theta_i & -(D_i)_t \xi_i R_i \delta_i \\ -(\delta_i)_t S_i \xi_i D_i & (\delta_i)_t(\psi_i + S_i \xi_i R_i)\delta_i \end{bmatrix}$$

where

54 $$R_i = \sigma_i - \xi_i^{-1} \eta_i$$

55 $$s_i = (\sigma_i)_t - \zeta_i \xi_i^{-1}$$

56 $$\psi_i = \rho_i - \zeta_i \xi_i^{-1} \eta_i$$

57 $$D_i = C_{i-1}$$

and

58 $$\theta_i = (D_i)_t \xi_i D_i$$

(assuming ξ_i^{-1} to exist). Also,

59 $$k'_{i-1} = (D_i)_t k_{i-1} D_i$$

Inverting *53* by *2* (Appendix) we find

60 $$(k_i')^{-1} = \begin{bmatrix} \beta_i & \nu_i(\delta_i)_t^{-1} \\ \delta_i^{-1}\phi_i & \delta_i^{-1}\omega_i^{-1}(\delta_i)_t^{-1} \end{bmatrix}$$

where

61 $$\beta_i = \theta_i^{-1} + \theta_i^{-1}(D_i)_t\xi_i R_i\omega_i^{-1}S_i\xi_i D_i\theta_i^{-1}$$

62 $$\nu_i = \theta_i^{-1}(D_i)_t\xi_i R_i\omega_i^{-1}$$

63 $$\phi_i = \omega_i^{-1}S_i\xi_i D_i\theta_i^{-1}$$

64 $$\omega_i = \psi_i + S_i M_i R_i$$

in which

65 $$M_i = \xi_i - \xi_i D_i\theta_i^{-1}(D_i)_t\xi_i$$

if θ_i^{-1} exists.

We can now find V_i. We substitute *60* into *35*; making use of *32*, *46*, *15*, *54*, *55*, *57*, and *61* to *65*, we obtain the following:

66 $$V_i = M_i - M_i R_i\omega_i^{-1}S_i M_i$$

Also, from *30* and *31* (with $i \to i - 1$) and *57*, we have

67 $$Q_{i-1} = k_{i-1} - k_{i-1}D_i(k_{i-1}')^{-1}(D_i)_t k_{i-1}$$

We now wish to obtain $(Y_i')^{-1}$ in terms of $(Y_{i-1}')^{-1}$. In view of *23*, with $i \to i - 1$, and *34*, it appears that we should find V_i in terms of Q_{i-1}. Furthermore, since $R_i\omega_i^{-1}S_i$ is a function of σ_i and Q_{i-1} is not, we may expect the dependence of V_i on Q_{i-1} to reside in the M_i. But, from *67* and *59*,

68 $$Q_{i-1} = k_{i-1} - k_{i-1}D_i[(D_i)_t k_{i-1}D_i]^{-1}(D_i)_t k_{i-1}$$

where, from *52*,

69 $$k_{i-1} = \xi_i - \eta_i\rho_i^{-1}\zeta_i$$

and, from *65* and *58*

70 $$M_i = \xi_i - \xi_i D_i[(D_i)_t\xi_i D_i]^{-1}(D_i)_t\xi_i$$

There is no clear-cut dependence of M_i on Q_{i-1} unless

71 $$k_{i-1} = \xi_i$$

in which case

72 $$\eta_i\rho_i^{-1}\zeta_i = 0$$

Then

73 $$M_i = Q_{i-1}$$

and

74 $$V_i = Q_{i-1} - Q_{i-1}R_i\omega_i^{-1}S_i Q_{i-1}$$

We are not yet out of the woods. ω_i is a small matrix, and its inversion should be trivial. However, its computation is another matter. From *64*, *65*, and *54* to *58*, we have

75 $$\omega_i = \rho_i - \zeta_i\xi_i^{-1}\eta_i + [(\sigma_i')_t - \zeta_i\xi_i^{-1}]M_i(\sigma_i - \xi_i^{-1}\eta_i)$$

and we are faced with the problem of calculating ξ_i^{-1}, which is a large matrix. It may be that ξ_i^{-1} is already known in some way, in which case we may proceed. However, in most cases we must require

76 $$\zeta_i = 0$$

and

77 $$\eta_i = 0$$

Equation *72* is then automatically satisfied. Equations *46*, *71*, *76*, and *77* show that

78 $$k_i = \begin{bmatrix} k_{i-1} & 0 \\ 0 & \rho_i \end{bmatrix}$$

so that

79 $$Y_i = \begin{bmatrix} Y_{i-1} & 0 \\ 0 & \rho_i^{-1} \end{bmatrix}$$

By induction, Y is block-diagonal, so that Z is also. It then follows that $Y_i = (Z_i)^{-1}$, and *39* becomes

80 $$Z_i = \begin{bmatrix} Z_{i-1} & 0 \\ 0 & t_i \end{bmatrix}$$

Equation *75* becomes

81 $$\begin{aligned} \omega_i &= t_i + (\sigma_i)_t M_i \sigma_i \\ &= t_i + (\sigma_i)_t Q_{i-1}\sigma_i \\ &= t_i + (\sigma_i)_t A_{i-1}(Y_{i-1}')^{-1}(A_{i-1})_t\sigma_i \end{aligned}$$

by *23* with $i \to i - 1$. Equation *20* now yields

82 $$\omega_i = t_i + \alpha_i(Y_{i-1}')^{-1}(\alpha_i)_t$$

From *34*, *74*, *23*, *54*, *55*, and *20*, we now obtain the final iteration formula

83 $$(Y_i')^{-1} = (Y_{i-1}')^{-1} - (Y_{i-1}')^{-1}(\alpha_i)_t\omega_i^{-1}\alpha_i(Y_{i-1}')^{-1}$$

Little calculation is needed in using this, because ω_i is a small matrix. Had we known ahead of time that we needed to choose a block-diagonal Z, we could have derived this formula very simply from *79* (with $\rho_i = t_i$), *24*, *22*, and *6* (Appendix). (For an a priori indication of this, see Weinzweig [19].)

The above result justifies the statement made previously that there should be no coupling between sets of links or between the links and the tree.

It will be noted in the above iteration scheme that in order to begin, one must calculate $(Y'_0)^{-1}$, that is, the nodal solution matrix corresponding to the tree itself. To do this, we note that E_0 is merely the tree, so that

84 $$A_0 = A^T$$

and

85 $$Y_0 = Y^T$$

the admittance matrix for the tree. Then, from *22*, *84*, and *85*,

86 $$Y'_0 = (A^T)_t Y^T A^T$$

so that

87 $$(Y'_0)^{-1} = (A^T)^{-1}(Y^T)^{-1}(A^T)_t^{-1}$$

or, in view of *7.2.11*,

88 $$(Y'_0)^{-1} = (B^T)_t Z^T B^T$$

Since Z^T and B^T are presumed known, $(Y'_0)^{-1}$ is easily calculated.

If there is no coupling between any two links, i.e., if Z can be written

89 $$Z = \begin{bmatrix} Z^T & 0 \\ 0 & Z^L \end{bmatrix}$$

where Z^L is diagonal, then we may choose all $\mu_i = 1$, so that one link is connected at a time. Equation *83* becomes the following formula, first derived by Branin [18], if the ith link (impedance z_i^L) is connected between the pth and qth nodes of the graph:

90 $$(Y'_i)^{-1} = (Y'_{i-1})^{-1} - \frac{(Z^{i-1}_{\cdot p} - Z^{i-1}_{\cdot q})(Z^{i-1}_{p\cdot} - Z^{i-1}_{q\cdot})}{Z^{i-1}_{pp} + Z^{i-1}_{qq} - Z^{i-1}_{pq} - Z^{i-1}_{qp} + z_i{}^L}$$

where $Z^{i-1}_{\cdot p}$, $Z^{i-1}_{p\cdot}$, Z^{i-1}_{pp}, etc., are the pth column, pth row, and element (p,p), etc., of $(Y'_{i-1})^{-1}$. Zeros are substituted for quantities corresponding to datum nodes. This is called the *link-at-a-time* (LAT) *algorithm*.

If the matrix Z is not ohmic, then one can still use the above technique, if care is taken that the matrices used in each step are well behaved. In other words, no subgraph occurring anywhere in the problem can be nonphysical; i.e., it must not be such as to allow infinite currents, for example.

7 *Interconnecting on a large scale*

The real power of Kron's method lies in further techniques [18], used in conjunction with the method outlined in Sec. *6*. A convenient device

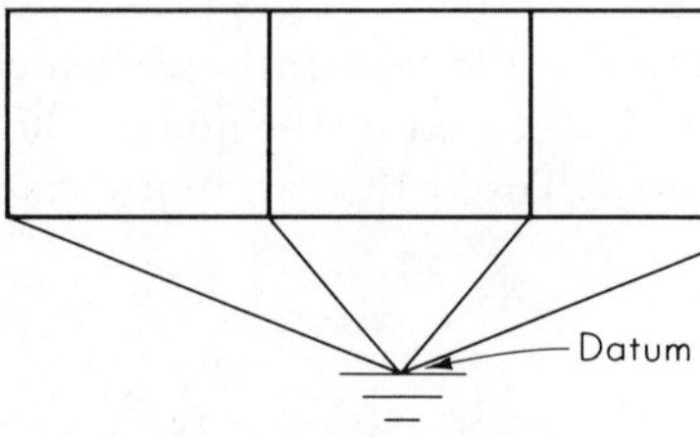

Fig. 7.7.1

used in these further techniques is that of the equivalent radial tree. If one is given any graph, for example the one shown in Fig. *7.7.1*, one may replace it with its equivalent radial tree, as shown in Fig. *7.7.2*. The virtue of this is that the nodal solution matrix $(Y')^{-1}$ of Fig. *7.7.1* is the same as the simple impedance matrix Z of Fig. *7.7.2*. This is used in the following discussion.

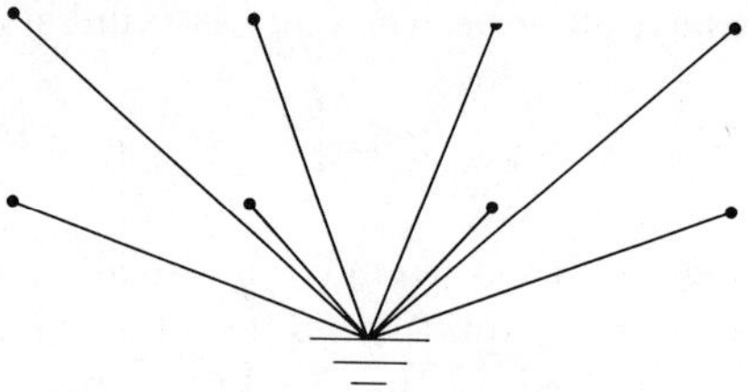

Fig. 7.7.2

In the "doubling" technique, we consider, for example, the graph shown in Fig. *7.7.3*. We tear it as shown in Fig. *7.7.4* and compute the nodal solution matrices for the subgraphs A. If we now replace these subgraphs by their equivalent radial trees, the impedance matrix Z for these subgraphs is of a simple block-diagonal form, with the blocks being the matrices $(Y')^{-1}$ for the subgraphs. The links marked a may

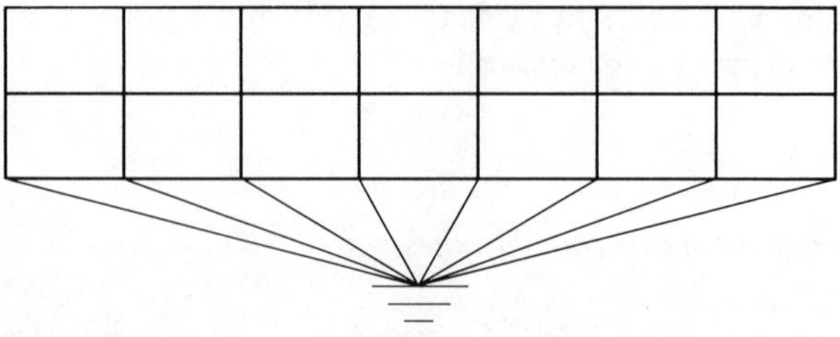

Fig. 7.7.3

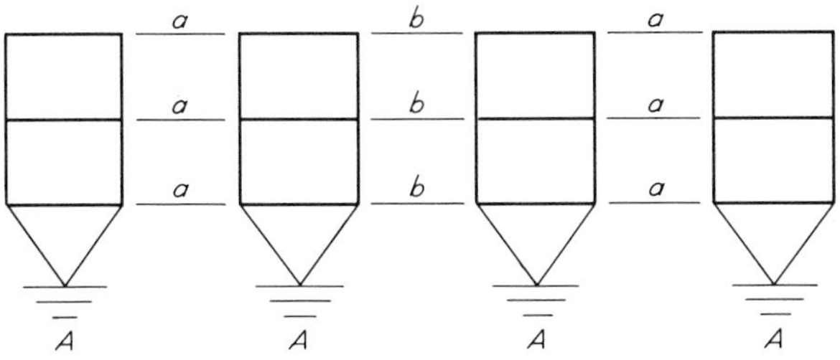

Fig. 7.7.4

then be connected. The transformed system with connected links looks like Fig. 7.7.5.

If we repeat the process, we can connect the links b in the next step. The process can obviously be extended to arbitrary large graphs, torn in any manner. There is probably an optimal method of organizing

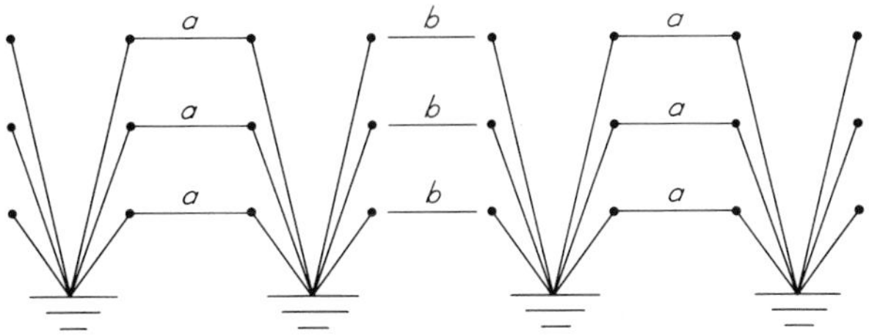

Fig. 7.7.5

such a calculation for a given graph; finding such a method does not seem to be straightforward and will presumably be aided by the experience of the system analyst.

For very large systems, the size of the matrices used will probably become unmanageable. For such cases, the elimination-backsubstitution method may be applicable. This method is based on the fact that certain nodes in a graph never participate in a calculation after a certain step. For example in Fig. 7.7.5 the nodes at the ends of branches a do not participate in the step in which branches b are connected.

One may make use of this fact in the following way. If we put

1 $$I' = A_t(I - YU)$$

then 7.3.21 may be written

2 $$e' = (Y')^{-1}I'$$

We separate the boundary nodes of a subgraph from the internal nodes and partition *2* accordingly; thus

3 $$\begin{bmatrix} e'_1 \\ e'_2 \end{bmatrix} = \begin{bmatrix} Z_a & Z_b \\ Z_c & Z_d \end{bmatrix} \begin{bmatrix} I'_1 \\ I'_2 \end{bmatrix}$$

Then e'_1, referring to the boundary nodes only, is given by

4 $$e'_1 = Z_a \tilde{I}$$

where

5 $$\tilde{I} = I'_1 + Z_a^{-1} Z_b I'_2$$

Equation *4* is exactly the same type of equation as *2*, except that it refers to the boundary nodes only. Now, the Z_a and $\tilde{I}$ for each subnetwork are used in the LAT algorithm to calculate $(Y')^{-1}$ for the next step. This procedure (elimination) is carried out for each step. After all steps have been completed, e'_1 for the last stage is computed from *4*. Then e'_2 for the last stage is computed from

6 $$e'_2 = (Z_d - Z_c Z_a^{-1} Z_b) I'_2 + Z_c Z_a^{-1} e'_1$$

We work back through the stages, computing e'_2 for each stage from *6* (backsubstitution). Note that this requires storage of the matrices Z_d, Z_c, Z_b, and Z_a^{-1} and of the vector I'_2 at each step of the earlier procedure of elimination. Note also that this requires computation of Z_a^{-1} from Z_a at each step. This is feasible because the number of boundary nodes at each stage is relatively small.

It will be noted that the important feature of this procedure is the fact that the matrices are kept small and are used as much as possible in matrix-vector multiplications instead of in matrix-matrix multiplications. This latter feature is essentially the "factored-form" technique originally introduced by Kron. Its use may be illustrated in *6* above; instead of computing $Z_d - Z_c Z_a^{-1} Z_b$, one first computes $Z_b I'_2$, then $Z_a^{-1} Z_b Z'_2$, and then $Z_c Z_a^{-1} Z_b I'_2$, which is then subtracted from $Z_2 I'_2$. No time-consuming matrix-matrix multiplications have been performed.

If one wishes to use the same graph, but with different input (source) values, one merely programs the computer to store all pertinent matrices at each step. Then the problem can be run for several inputs with use of only matrix-vector multiplications.

It may happen in some problems (for example, boundary-value problems) that the formulation of the problem may yield some of the e' known and some of the I' unknown. In that case, the solution equation is partitioned as in *3*, with e'_1 and I'_2 known and e'_2 and I'_1 unknown. Then expansion yields

7 $$I'_1 = Z_a^{-1}(e'_1 - Z_b I'_2)$$

and

8 $$e'_2 = (Z_d - Z_c Z_a^{-1} Z_b) I'_2 + Z_c Z_a^{-1} e'_1$$

much like *4* and *6*. This technique can be used with Kron's method to yield a solution.

8 *Roth's version of Kron's method*

Roth [1] has treated Kron's method from a viewpoint rather different from that of Branin. The point stressed in his work is that the mapping of the branch-vector space (one-chain group in Roth's treatment, which is based on algebraic topology) of the original graph into that of the term graph is an isomorphism. This allows construction of a nonsingular matrix S_i (related to C_i) for each step which provides relationships between the quantities J, V, and Z for succeeding steps:

1 $$J_{i-1} = S_i J_i$$

2 $$V_i = (S_i)_t V_{i-1}$$

3 $$Z_i = (S_i)_t Z_{i-1} S_i$$

(The basis of the branch vector space chosen here is composed of tree branches and meshes, in contrast to Branin's basis of tree branches and links.) Partitioning of these equations and of

4 $$V = ZJ$$

plus some algebra, eventually yields an iteration scheme similar to Branin's. Some very useful examples have been provided by Roth in his paper. Similar treatments based on the above-mentioned isomorphism have been provided by Weinzweig and Ponstein [19, 20]. All of these treatments are recommended as aids to understanding of Kron's method. It should be mentioned, however, that no counterpart of the elimination-backsubstitution method appears in these treatments.

9 *Conclusions*

In certain calculations, Kron's method of tearing should be very useful. Its generality results from the fact that it can be applied to graphical models of systems, regardless of the type of system (electrical, mechanical, etc.). At present, however, its greatest usefulness comes from applications to systems that are (1) linear, (2) in a constant state or in a sinusoidal oscillation state, (3) separable into uncoupled components. Even with these restrictions, however, its range of applicability is wide.

The properties of the graph, as expressed in the incidence matrices, are used in deriving the solution equations. The method of tearing, however, uses the graph in a rather different way. It has seemed to this author that it need not be necessary to refer to the graph in order to set up a tearing and interconnection procedure, but that such a procedure could be organized through proper numbering and judicious partitioning of matrices. From a practical standpoint, however, this is probably possible only for one extremely skilled in such work, and most users of the method will surely find use of the graph very valuable for preparing a tearing and interconnection procedure.

It seems to this author that the philosophy behind Kron's method—the realization that there are certain invariant properties of graphs under transformation—can provide a very useful and profound approach to the general theory of systems. Certainly this approach, in the form of tensor analysis, has provided much insight in other disciplines of thought, primarily in the fields of mechanics, fluid dynamics, relativity, and electromagnetism. It certainly is to be desired that this philosophy will be applied in other fields, as an aid to more fundamental understanding. (This important feature of Kron's work has scarcely been touched on here; the interested reader is referred to other works in the field [1, 25, 26, 19, 32, 33].)

A question related to Kron's method is this: what systems can be represented by a graphical model? Probably most discrete systems with lumped elements can be so represented. The question is harder to answer in the case of continuous systems. Most of these can be described by partial differential equations. Branin has investigated this question [10]; some of his results, based on a correspondence of the matrices A and C and their transposes to the vector differential operators grad, div, and curl, state that the following two general equations allow a graphical model representation:

1 $$\text{div}\,(Y \text{ grad } \phi) = I + a_0\phi + a_1 \frac{\partial \phi}{\partial t} + a_2 \frac{\partial^2 \phi}{\partial t^2}$$

2 $$\text{curl}\,(Z \text{ curl } \psi) = E + b_0\psi + b_1 \frac{\partial \psi}{\partial t} + b_2 \frac{\partial^2 \psi}{\partial t^2}$$

These two equations are not exhaustive; there are many other types of equations which admit of such representations. The reader should see Roth's comments on this question [1] and see also the models constructed for explicit systems by Kron [5–9].

In connection with the above comments, the following question arises: what topological and/or algebraic structure is most appropriate for a given system? Some controversy has developed over this point, especially between Kron and others writing on his method [34]. The author feels that the mathematical disciplines of algebraic topology and of differential forms may both shed light on the above question. Kron's method is probably susceptible to considerable generalization. See, for example, Kron's paper of Ref. 38. (The theoretically inclined reader may be interested in reading the treatment of Maxwell's equations in the article by Misner and Wheeler [35], which uses both algebraic topology and differential forms.) In any case, it seems apparent that much remains to be discovered about Kron's method, its variations, and its philosophy, at all levels of sophistication. Some of the recent work relating to Kron's method is found in Refs. 44 to 55.

APPENDIX MATRIX INVERSION EQUATIONS

The following schemes of matrix inversion were used in this chapter. Schur's formula, used in the "escalator" method of inversion [36], is as follows: If

1 $$M = \begin{bmatrix} A & B \\ C & D \end{bmatrix}$$

then

2 $$M^{-1} = \begin{bmatrix} A^{-1} + A^{-1}BFCA^{-1} & -A^{-1}BF \\ -FCA^{-1} & F \end{bmatrix}$$

where

3 $$F = (D - CA^{-1}B)^{-1}$$

or

4 $$M^{-1} = \begin{bmatrix} E & -EBD^{-1} \\ -D^{-1}CE & D^{-1} + D^{-1}CEBD^{-1} \end{bmatrix}$$

where

5 $$E = (A - BD^{-1}C)^{-1}$$

The required matrix inverses are assumed to exist. Simple multiplication of M and M^{-1} provides proof of the formulas. The second method merely employs the following formula, due to Householder [37]:

6 $$(F + GHK)^{-1} = F^{-1} - F^{-1}G(H^{-1} + KF^{-1}G)^{-1}KF^{-1}$$

Equation *6* may be proved by comparing elements in *2* and *4*.

REFERENCES

1 Roth, J. Paul: An Application of Algebraic Topology: Kron's Method of Tearing, *Quart. Appl. Math.*, vol. 17, pp. 1–24, 1959.

2 Kron, Gabriel: A Set of Principles to Interconnect the Solutions of Physical Systems, *J. Appl. Phys.*, vol. 24, pp. 965–980, 1953.

3 Koenig, Herman E., and William A. Blackwell: "Electromechanical System Theory," McGraw-Hill, New York, 1961.

4 Alexander, J. Eugene, and J. Milton Bailey: "Systems Engineering Mathematics," Prentice-Hall, Englewood Cliffs, N.J., 1962.

5 Kron, Gabriel: Equivalent Circuit of the Field Equations of Maxwell-I, *Proc. IRE*, vol. 32, pp. 289–299, 1944.

6 Kron, Gabriel: Equivalent Circuits of the Elastic Field, *J. Appl. Mech.*, vol. 11, pp. A149–A161, 1944.

7 Kron, Gabriel: Equivalent Circuits of Compressible and Incompressible Fluid Flow Fields, *J. Aero. Sci.*, vol. 12, pp. 221–231, 1945.

8 Kron, Gabriel: Electric Circuit Models of the Nuclear Reactor, *Communication and Electronics*, no. 13, pp. 259–265, July, 1954.

9 Kron, Gabriel: Electric Circuit Models of the Schrodinger Equation, *Phys. Rev.*, vol. 67, pp. 39–43, 1945.

10 Branin, F. H., Jr.: An Abstract Mathematical Basis for Network Analogies and Its Significance in Physics and Engineering, *IBM Report No. TR* 00.781, 23 pages, 1961.

11 Zadeh, L. A.: From Circuit Theory to System Theory, *Proc. IRE*, vol. 50, pp. 856–865, 1962; see also Zadeh, L. A., and C. A. Desoer: "Linear System Theory: The State Space Approach," pp. 39–41, McGraw-Hill, New York, 1963.

12 Malmberg, Allan F., and Fred L. Cornwell: NET-1 Network Analysis of Networks, *Los Alamos Scientific Laboratory Report No.* LA-2853, 1963.

13 Birkhoff, Garrett, and J. B. Diaz: Non-linear Network Problems, *Quart. Appl. Math.*, vol. 13, pp. 431–443, 1956.

14 Clauser, Francis H.: The Transient Behavior of Nonlinear Systems, *Trans. IRE*, vol. CT-7, pp. 446–458, 1960.

15 Bellman, Richard: Directions of Mathematical Research in Nonlinear Circuit Theory, *Trans. IRE, Circuit Theory*, vol. CT-7, pp. 542–553, 1960.

16 Kron, Gabriel: Tensor Analysis of Multielectrode-tube Circuits, *Elec. Eng.*, vol. 55, pp. 1220–1242, 1936.

17 Kron, Gabriel: Solution of Complex Nonlinear Plastic Structures by the Method of Tearing, *J. Aero. Sci.*, vol. 23, pp. 557–562, 1956.

18 Branin, F. H., Jr.: The Relation between Kron's Method and the Classical Methods of Network Analysis, 1959 *WESCON Conv. Record*, part 2, 29 pages; *IBM Report No. TR* 00.686.

19 Weinzweig, A. J.: The Kron Method of Tearing and the Dual Method of Identification, *Quart. Appl. Math.*, vol. 18, pp. 183–190, 1960.

20 Ponstein, J.: Matrix Description of Networks, *J. Soc. Indust. Appl. Math.*, vol. 9, pp. 233–268, 1961.

21 Kron, Gabriel: "Tensor Analysis of Networks," Wiley, New York, 1939.

22 Kron, Gabriel: A Method of Solving Very Large Physical Systems in Easy Stages, *Proc. IRE*, vol. 42, pp. 680–686, 1954.

23 Kron, Gabriel: Improved Procedure for Interconnecting Piece-wise Solutions, *J. Franklin Inst.*, vol. 262, pp. 385–392, 1956.

24 Kron, Gabriel: Diakoptics, the Piecewise Solution of Large-scale Systems, *The Electrical J.* (*London*), a series of articles in vols. 159–161, 1957–1959.

25 Roth, J. Paul: An Application of Algebraic Topology to Numerical Analysis: On the Existence of a Solution to the Network Problem, *Proc. Nat. Acad. Sci.*, vol. 41, pp. 518–521, 1955.

26 Roth, J. Paul: The Validity of Kron's Method of Tearing, *Proc. Nat. Acad. Sci.*, vol. 41, pp. 599–600, 1955.

27 Higgins, Thomas J.: Electroanalogic Methods, part VI, *Appl. Mech. Rev.*, vol. 11, pp. 203–206, 1958.

28 Guillemin, E. A.: "Introductory Circuit Theory," Wiley, New York, 1958.

29 Perlis, Sam: "Theory of Matrices," p. 58, Addison-Wesley, Cambridge, Mass., 1952.

30 Bodewig, E.: "Matrix Calculus," p. 19, North Holland, Amsterdam, and Interscience, New York, 1959.

31 Parter, S.: The Use of Linear Graphs in Gauss Elimination, *Soc. Indust. Appl. Math. Rev.*, vol. 3, pp. 119–130, 1961.

32 Hoffmann, Banesh: Kron's Non-Riemannian Electrodynamics, *Rev. Mod. Phys.*, vol. 21, pp. 535–540, 1949.

33 Hoffmann, Banesh: Nature of the Primitive System in Kron's Theory, *Am. J. Phys.*, vol. 23, pp. 341–355, 1955.

34 Kron, Gabriel: Camouflaging Electrical 1-networks as Graphs, *Quart. Appl. Math.*, vol. 20, pp. 161–174, 1962.

35 Misner, C. W., and J. A. Wheeler: Classical Physics as Geometry, *Ann. Phys.*, vol. 2, pp. 525–603, 1957.

36 Grabbe, E. M., S. Ramo, and D. E. Wooldridge: "Handbook of Automation, Computation, and Control," vol. 1, pp. 14-13–14-27, Wiley, New York, 1958.

37 Householder, A. S.: "Principles of Numerical Analysis," p. 79, McGraw-Hill, New York, 1953.

38 Kron, Gabriel: Multidimensional Curve-fitting with Self-organizing Automata, *J. Math. Anal. Appl.*, vol. 5, pp. 46–69, 1962.

39 Harrison, B. Kent: A Discussion of Some Mathematical Techniques Used in Kron's Method of Tearing, *J. Soc. Indust. Appl. Math.*, vol. 11, pp. 258–280, 1963.

40 Reza, J.: Some Topological Considerations in Network Theory, *Trans. IRE Circuit Theory*, vol. CT-5, pp. 30–42, 1958.

41 Reed, M. B.: "Foundation for Electric Network Theory," Prentice-Hall, Englewood Cliffs, N.J., 1961.

42 Ley, B. J., S. G. Luty, and C. F. Rehberg: "Linear Circuit Analysis," McGraw-Hill, New York, 1959.

43 Veblen, O.: "Analysis Situs," 2d ed., vol. V, part II, Am. Math. Soc. Colloquium Publications, New York, 1931.

44 Kron, G.: Invisible Dual (n − 1)-networks Induced by Electric 1-networks, *IEEE Trans. Circuit Theory*, vol. CT-12, pp. 464–470, 1965.

45 Kron, G.: Tensorial and Topological Foundations of Electric Networks, in B. Hoffmann (ed.), "Perspectives in Geometry and Relativity," Indiana University Press, Bloomington, Ind., 1966.

46 Kron, G.: The Misapplication of Graph Theory to Electric Networks, *AIEE Trans.*, part 1, vol. 81, pp. 257–267, 1962.

47 Happ, H. H.: Orthogonal Networks, *IEEE Trans. Power Apparatus Systems*, vol. PAS-85, pp. 281–294, 1966.

48 Happ, H. H.: Special Cases of Orthogonal Networks—Tree and Link, *IEEE Trans. Power Apparatus Systems*, vol. PAS-85, pp. 880–891, 1966.

49 Baumann, R.: Some New Aspects on Load-flow Calculation: I-Impedance Matrix Generation Controlled by Network Topology, *IEEE Trans. Power Apparatus Systems*, vol. PAS-85, pp. 1164–1176, 1966.

50 Amari, Shun-ichi: Topological Foundations of Kron's Tearing of Electric Networks, and Information-Theoretical Foundations of Diakoptics and Codiakoptics, *RAAG Memoirs Unifying Study Basic Problems Eng. Physical Sci. Means Geom.*, vol. 3, pp. 322–371, 1962.

51 Franksen, O. I.: The Uses of Macroprogramming Languages in Power System Design and Operation, *Proc. Power Systems Computation Conf.*, Queen Mary College, London, 1963.
52 Franksen, O. I.: Kron's Method of Tearing, *Fourth Power Industry Computer Application Conf.*, Clearwater, Fla., 1965.
53 Pestel, Edward C., and Frederick A. Keckie: "Matrix Methods in Electromechanics," McGraw-Hill, New York, 1963.
54 Lewis, W. E., and D. G. Pryce: "The Application of Matrix Theory to Electrical Engineering," Spon, London, 1965.
55 Kuo, Benjamin C.: "Linear Networks and Systems," McGraw-Hill, New York, 1967.

Part Three

NONLINEAR SYSTEMS

8

A survey of the theory of some systems governed by nonlinear functional equations

I. W. Sandberg
Bell Telephone Laboratories
Murray Hill, New Jersey

1 *Introduction*

In many respects, the classical results and methods of nonlinear analysis, such as the existence and uniqueness theorems of ordinary nonlinear differential equations, phase-plane techniques, pertubation techniques, the describing-function technique, and the second method of Liapunov, are valuable engineering tools, but they by no means provide a definitive theory of operation for even the simplest nontrivial frequency-dependent nonlinear systems.

During the past few years, some functional-analytic techniques have proven to be of value in connection with several aspects of the general problem of obtaining an understanding of the manner in which a nonlinear system acts on an input signal to produce an output signal. These techniques are particularly well suited to problems in which distributed parameters must be taken into consideration. The primary purpose of this chapter is to survey some of the results that have been obtained in this area. The survey is in no sense intended to be exhaustive; it is concerned almost exclusively with some of the analytical problems with which the author has been concerned during the past few years, and in the presentation of much of the material, only the nature of the results is indicated.

We devote a good deal of space here to a discussion of some properties of an important type of nonlinear integral equation that arises, for example, in the study of nonlinear feedback systems. Nyquist-like frequency-domain conditions are described under which a solution to this type of equation possesses a given property, such as asymptotic exponential decay, boundedness, or asymptotic periodicity with a given period. To illustrate the character of these results, consider a single-loop feedback system containing a linear subsystem with transfer function $K(i\omega)$ and a nonlinear element represented by the function $\psi(x)$. Let $\psi(0) = 0$, and let α and β be positive constants such that $\alpha \leq \psi(x)x^{-1} \leq \beta$ for all real $x \neq 0$. It can be shown by experiment, as well as by analytical means (see Sec. 6), that, under certain conditions, this type of feedback system can exhibit subharmonic response properties. Suppose, however, that the Nyquist locus of $K(i\omega)$ lies outside, and does not encircle, the disk of radius $\frac{1}{2}(\alpha^{-1} - \beta^{-1})$ centered on the real axis of the complex plane at $[-\frac{1}{2}(\alpha^{-1} + \beta^{-1}),0]$. Then, subject to some very reasonable additional assumptions, it can be proved that if the input signal to the feedback system is asymptotically periodic with period T, the output is also asymptotically periodic with period T.

This survey includes also some material concerned with the steady-state analysis of nonlinear systems, the validity of models for evaluating the effect of "nearly linear" elements, and signal-recovery problems.

2 The frequency-domain disk condition

One of the most fundamental problems of engineering interest is the determination of the properties of systems formed by the interconnection of relatively simple subsystems.

In contrast with the theory of linear time-invariant structures, which has been extensively developed, extremely little in the way of a reasonably complete mathematical theory is known about the properties of structures that contain elements which are not all linear[1] and time-invariant.

Feedback systems occupy a central position in the study of systems, not only because many systems of interest are feedback structures, but also because, as is well known, the types of equations that govern feedback systems also govern many other types of systems.

In connection with feedback systems, although the now well-known techniques of Liapunov (see, for example, LaSalle and Lefschetz [1],

[1] Of course, there are some important special results such as, for example, the Manley-Rowe equations.

Hahn [2], or Kalman and Bertram [3]) have led to many interesting results concerning the stability of time-varying nonlinear systems governed by ordinary differential equations (see the bibliography of Aizerman and Gantmacher [4] which cites 105 papers), these methods have by no means led to definitive stability results for even the simplest nontrivial time-varying nonlinear feedback systems. Consider, for instance, that with few exceptions the known explicit global stability conditions for nonlinear systems are concerned with undriven systems (i.e., with systems which are excited only by virtue of initial conditions).

In this section we focus attention on a certain frequency-domain disk condition which plays a central role in some recent results concerned with input-output properties of a class of time-varying nonlinear systems.

The feedback system

Consider the nonlinear feedback system of Fig. *8.2.1*. We restrict our discussion to cases in which g_1, f, u, and v denote real-valued functions of t, defined for $t \geq 0$.

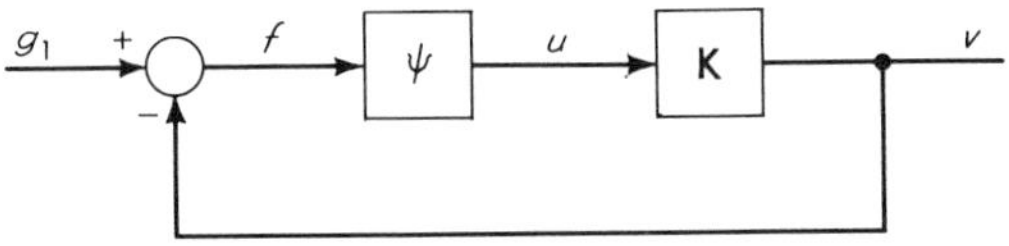

Fig. 8.2.1 Nonlinear feedback system.

It is assumed that the equations governing the system are

1 $$f(t) = g_1(t) - v(t)$$

2 $$u(t) = \psi[f(t),t]$$

3 $$v(t) = \int_0^t k(t-\tau)u(\tau)\,d\tau - g_2(t)$$

for $t \geq 0$, in which (1) $\psi(x,t)$ is a real-valued function of x and t with the properties that $\psi(0,t) = 0$ for $t \geq 0$ and that there exist a positive constant β and a real constant α such that

4 $$\alpha \leq \frac{\psi(x,t)}{x} \leq \beta \qquad t \geq 0$$

for all real $x \neq 0$ [observe that for each t the graph of $\psi(x,t)$ is restricted to lie between the two straight lines passing through the origin with slopes α and β]; and (2) k and g_2 are real-valued functions such that *a.* for $q = 1$ and $q = 2$

5 $$\int_0^\infty |k(t)t^p|^q \, dt < \infty$$

for $p = 0$, 1, and 2.

b. g_2 has finite energy, that is,

6 $$\int_0^\infty |g_2(t)|^2 \, dt < \infty$$

c. g_2 is bounded [i.e., there is a constant c such that $|g_2(t)| \leq c$ for all $t \geq 0$].

d. $g_2(t) \to 0$ as $t \to \infty$.

The function g_2 takes into account the initial conditions.

Conditions (*a*)–(*d*) are quite reasonable from the engineering viewpoint; they are satisfied if, as is often the case, u and v are related by a differential equation and both k and g_2 are finite sums of the form

7 $$\Sigma a_m(t)e^{-b_m t}$$

in which the $a_m(t)$ are polynomials in t and all of the b_m are positive. However, it is *not required* that u and v be related by a differential equation.

The governing integral equation

The signal f of Fig. *8.2.1* satisfies the integral equation

8 $$g(t) = f(t) + \int_0^t k(t - \tau)\psi[f(\tau),\tau] \, d\tau \qquad t \geq 0$$

with $g(t) = g_1(t) + g_2(t)$.

In order to study Eq. *8*, it is of course necessary to make some assumptions concerning g. It is certainly reasonable to assume that g is a member of the set $\mathcal{E}$ of all functions u with the property that

9 $$\int_0^t |u(t)|^2 \, dt < \infty$$

for all *finite* $t \geq 0$. Under this condition on g and a very weak additional assumption[1] concerning ψ, it follows (see Tricomi [5]) that $\mathcal{E}$ contains exactly one solution f of *8*. It is therefore reasonable to study *8* under the assumption that both g and f belong to $\mathcal{E}$. This assumption is used in the proofs of the results described in the next section. From the engineering viewpoint, it is clearly a trivial restriction.

[1] It would suffice to assume that ψ satisfies a "Lipshitz condition" [i.e., that there exists a constant γ such that $|\psi(x_1,t) - \psi(x_2,t)| \leq \gamma|x_1 - x_2|$ for all real $x_1 \neq x_2$ and all $t \geq 0$].

The more complicated feedback system of Fig. *8.2.2*, in which $\mathbf{K}_1$, $\mathbf{K}_2$, and $\mathbf{K}_3$ introduce constraints similar to the constraint introduced by $\mathbf{K}$ in Fig. *8.2.1*, also gives rise to an equation for f such as *8*. Of course, in this case, k depends on the impulse response functions of $\mathbf{K}_1$, $\mathbf{K}_2$, and $\mathbf{K}_3$, and g depends on u as well as on both the initial-condition functions and impulse response functions of $\mathbf{K}_1$, $\mathbf{K}_2$, and $\mathbf{K}_3$.

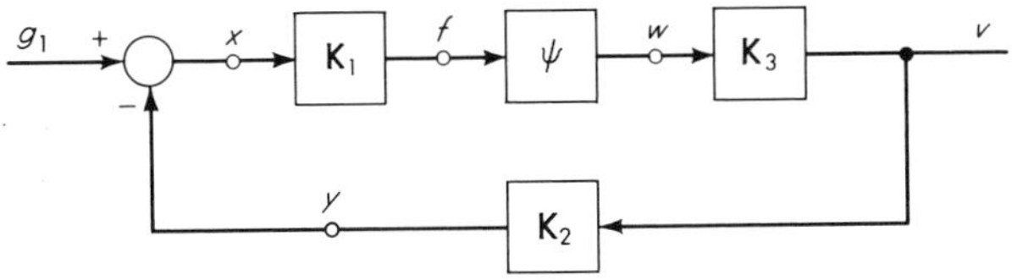

Fig. 8.2.2 Nonlinear feedback system containing three linear subsystems.

Input-output properties of the feedback system of Fig. *8.2.1*

Let $K(i\omega)$ be the transfer function associated with $\mathbf{K}$; that is, let

10
$$K(i\omega) = \int_0^\infty k(t)e^{-i\omega t}\,dt$$

for all real ω, and suppose that one of the following three conditions is satisfied.

11 $\alpha > 0$; and the locus of $K(i\omega)$ for $-\infty < \omega < \infty$ (*a*) lies outside the circle C_1 of radius $\frac{1}{2}(\alpha^{-1} - \beta^{-1})$ centered on the real axis of the complex plane at $[-\frac{1}{2}(\alpha^{-1} + \beta^{-1}),0]$ and (*b*) does not encircle C_1 (see Fig. *8.2.3*).

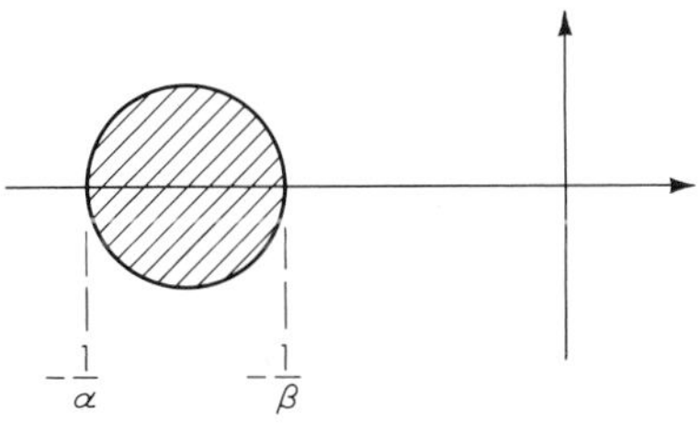

Fig. 8.2.3 Location of the "critical circle" C_1 in the complex plane ($\alpha > 0$); condition *11* is satisfied if the locus of $K(i\omega)$ for $-\infty < \omega < \infty$ lies outside C_1 and does not encircle C_1.

12 $\alpha = 0$, and $\mathrm{Re}\,[K(i\omega)] > -\beta^{-1}$ for all real ω.

13 $\alpha < 0$, and the locus of $K(i\omega)$ for $-\infty < \omega < \infty$ is contained within the circle C_2 of radius $\frac{1}{2}(\beta^{-1} - \alpha^{-1})$ centered on the real axis of the complex plane at $[-\frac{1}{2}(\alpha^{-1} + \beta^{-1}),0]$ (see Fig. *8.2.4*).

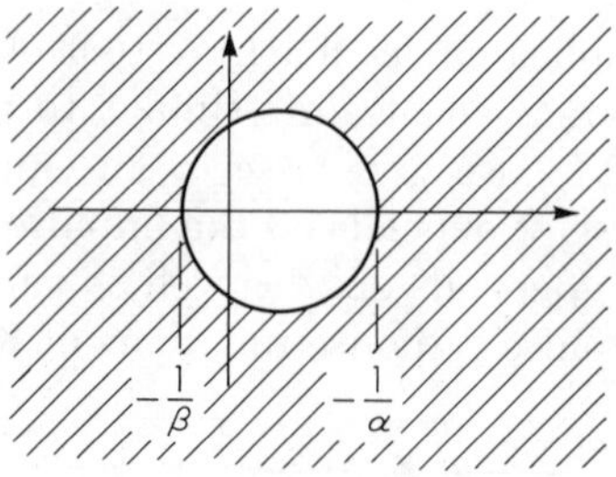

Fig. 8.2.4 Location of the "critical circle" C_2 in the complex plane ($\alpha > 0$); condition *13* is satisfied if the locus of $K(i\omega)$ for $-\infty < \omega < \infty$ is contained within C_2.

Under this assumption[1] concerning k, it has been proved[2] that the feedback system is stable in the sense that g_1 bounded and $g_1(t) \to 0$ as $t \to \infty$ imply that v is bounded and $v(t) \to 0$ as $t \to \infty$ and g_1 of finite energy implies that v has finite energy.

In addition, under this assumption on k, it has been proved that bounded inputs g_1 produce bounded outputs v, and that there is a positive constant ζ (which depends only on k, α, and β) such that if g_{a1} and g_{b1} denote two bounded inputs, then the corresponding outputs v_a and v_b satisfy[3]

14
$$\sup_{t \geq 0} |v_a(t) - v_b(t)| \leq \zeta \sup_{t \geq 0} |g_{a1}(t) - g_{b1}(t)|$$

provided that ψ satisfies the "slope condition"

15
$$\alpha \leq \frac{\psi(x_1,t) - \psi(x_2,t)}{x_1 - x_2} \leq \beta$$

for all real $x_1 \neq x_2$. In particular, if *15* holds, then the feedback system cannot exhibit jump phenomena.

Results have also been obtained concerning the growth rate or rate of decay of f, under certain assumptions (see Sec. *6*).

Finally, under the assumption on k, it has been proved that if the input g_1 is asymptotically periodic (i.e., is of the form $g_{1a} + g_{1b}$ with g_{1a} bounded and periodic and g_{1b} bounded and such that $g_{1b}(t) \to 0$ as $t \to \infty$), then the output v is also asymptotically periodic with the

[1] Observe that if $\alpha > 0$ and $\alpha = \beta$, then the circle C_1 degenerates to a point and the criterion becomes the usual Nyquist criterion.

[2] The presentation of results of this subsection has been simplified at the expense of the introduction of assumptions concerning k and g_2 which are actually not necessary in all cases.

[3] Recall that "sup" is the abbreviation for "supremum" which means "least upper bound."

same period as that of g_{1a} (and the *periodic part* of v is independent of g_{1b}), provided that $\psi(x,t)$ is independent of t, and *15* is satisfied for all real $x_1 \neq x_2$.

Each result stated above[1] is a specialization to $N = 1$ of a result which has been proved for systems containing an arbitrary number N of nonlinear elements of the type considered above (see Sec. *6*). On the strength of the N-nonlinear-element results, it has been possible to draw some quite general conclusions. For example, consider a nonlinear network obtained by terminating a linear time-invariant (but not necessarily lumped) N-port network $\tilde{N}$ by N time-invariant nonlinear resistors which have monotonic increasing characteristics which pass through the origin. Assume that all of the sources in $\tilde{N}$ are asymptotically periodic with period T. Then, under some reasonable assumptions, it has been proved that the voltages across the nonlinear elements are also asymptotically periodic with period T (and that the periodic parts of the voltages depend on the asymptotically periodic sources only through their periodic parts) if a certain (somewhat involved) condition is met. In particular, this condition is always met if $\tilde{N}$ is passive. It is not difficult to give examples in which the condition is not met and the voltages across the nonlinear elements contain *subharmonic* components (see Sec. *6*).

Systems with a time-invariant nonlinearity—results of the Popov type

Referring to Fig. *8.2.1*, let us assume now that ψ is a time-invariant nonlinearity with the properties that $\psi(0) = 0$ and that there exists a positive constant c such that

16 $$0 \leq \frac{\psi(x)}{x} \leq c$$

for all real $x \neq 0$. We assume, as above, that v and u are related by

17 $$v(t) = \int_0^t k(t - \tau)u(\tau)\, d\tau - g_2(t) \qquad t \geq 0$$

Here we suppose that g_2 and k satisfy certain reasonable conditions (see the references cited below for complete details), including in particular that g_2 is bounded and of finite energy, that $g_2(t) \to 0$ as $t \to \infty$, and that

18 $$\int_0^\infty |k(t)|\, dt < \infty \qquad \text{and} \qquad \int_0^\infty |\dot{k}(t)|\, dt < \infty$$

[1] The material presented above is a modification of some of the results of Refs. 6 and 7. For related material, see Ref. 8 and the work of Bongiorno [9, 10], Narendra and Goldwyn [11], Naumov and Tsypkin [12], Kudrewicz [13], Zames [14], and Yacubovich [15].

Under the assumption that the input g_1 is the zero function, the celebrated Popov result[1] (for the so-called *principal case*) asserts that $v(t) \to 0$ as $t \to \infty$, provided that there exists a real constant q and a positive constant ϵ such that

19 $$\operatorname{Re}\,[(1 + qi\omega)K(i\omega) + c^{-1}] \geq \epsilon$$

for all real ω, in which, of course, $K(i\omega)$ is the Fourier transform of k. Although it was assumed in early proofs of this result that v and u were related by a system of first-order (ordinary) differential equations, this assumption is not necessary; that is, k can take into account the presence of distributed elements (see, for example, Desoer [16]).

It has recently been proved[2] [17] that if *19* is satisfied and both the input g_1 and its derivative are bounded, then the output v is bounded. Alternatively, if *19* is met (and k satisfies certain integrability conditions) and the blocks labeled $\mathbf{K}$ and ψ in Fig. *8.2.1* are interchanged, then g_1 bounded implies that v is bounded even if $\dot{g}_1$ is not bounded.

If instead of *16* we have

20 $$\alpha \leq \frac{\psi(x)}{x} \leq \beta$$

then by a transformation it can be shown that the condition of *19* can be replaced by the requirement that there exists a real constant q such that one of the conditions of *11*, *12*, or *13* is satisfied with $K(i\omega)$ replaced by $(1 + qi\omega)K(i\omega)$.

There has been a good deal of interest in generalizing the result of Popov by exploiting further assumptions concerning the nonlinear function ψ (see, for example, the survey of Brockett [18]). For instance, if ψ is a monotone function that satisfies *16*, then a weaker (but considerably more involved) frequency-domain condition on $K(i\omega)$ suffices for stability.

3 *Steady-state analysis of networks containing resistors that are time-varying or nonlinear*

The preceding section is concerned with some general qualitative properties of systems. We consider now some problems that arise in the

[1] See, for example, the excellent treatment of Aizerman and Gantmacher [4].

[2] The proof of Ref. 17 actually considers only the case in which the constant q is positive. However, this restriction can be removed with the aid of an elementary transformation such as is employed by Aizerman and Gantmacher [4], p. 58.

steady-state analysis of networks[1] containing independent voltage and current sources, linear (not necessarily lumped) time-invariant elements and some resistors that are time-varying or nonlinear. As is well known, all currents and voltages within such a network can be determined by standard techniques once the voltages (or currents) associated with the time-varying or nonlinear elements are known.

Let $i_n(t)$ and $v_n(t)$ $(1 \leq n \leq N)$ denote, respectively, the current through and voltage across the nth not necessarily time-invariant, not necessarily linear resistor, and let this resistor introduce the constraint

1 $$i_n(t) = g_n(v_n(t),t)$$

in which $g_n(\cdot,\cdot)$ is a real-valued function. Let

2 $$i = (i_1,i_2, \ldots ,i_N)' \qquad v = (v_1,v_2, \ldots ,v_N)'$$

where $(\ \ )'$ denotes the transpose of $(\ \ )$, and define $\mathbf{G}$ by the condition that

3 $$(\mathbf{G}v)(t) = (g_1(v_1,t),g_2(v_2,t), \ldots ,g_N(v_N,t))'$$

so that $i = \mathbf{G}v$.

We assume that the Thévenin-type relation between v and i introduced by the linear time-invariant portion of the network is

4 $$e(t) = v(t) + (\mathbf{Z}i)(t)$$

in which $e(t)$ is independent of $v(t)$ and $i(t)$, and that $\mathbf{Z}$ is the linear operator defined by

5 $$(\mathbf{Z}i)(t) = \int_{-\infty}^{t} z(t-\tau)i(\tau)\,d\tau$$

where $z(t)$ is a real $N \times N$ (not necessarily symmetric) matrix of functions of t.

From *4* and $i = \mathbf{G}v$,

6 $$v + \mathbf{ZG}v = e$$

Concerning $\{z_{jk}\}$, the set of elements of z, it is assumed that

7 $$\int_0^\infty |z_{jk}(t)|\,dt < \infty$$

for $j, k = 1, 2, \ldots, N$. This assumption implies that the open-circuit impedance matrix

8 $$Z(j\omega) = \int_0^\infty z(t)e^{-j\omega t}\,dt$$

possesses the property that $Z(j\omega) \to 0_N$ as $|\omega| \to \infty$. Thus, in this

[1] The type of problem and the mathematical results that we describe here relate equally well to other types of systems. In the case of networks, the results possess some particularly illuminating physical interpretations.

sense, the linear time-invariant portion of the network is assumed to behave at infinity as would a network with each port shunted by a capacitor.

Notation and definitions

Let $\mathcal{K}$ denote the set of all complex periodic N-vector-valued functions $f(t)$, with period T, such that[1]

9 $$\|f\| \triangleq \left(\frac{1}{T}\int_0^T f^*(t)f(t)\,dt\right)^{\frac{1}{2}} < \infty$$

in which $f^*(t)$ denotes the complex-conjugate transpose of $f(t)$.

If f belongs to $\mathcal{K}$, then, as is well known,

10 $$f(t) = \sum_{n=-\infty}^{\infty} \hat{f}_n e^{jn\omega_0 t}$$

where $\omega_0 = 2\pi/T$, and the vector Fourier coefficients $\hat{f}_n$ are given by

11 $$\hat{f}_n = \frac{1}{T}\int_0^T f(t)e^{-jn\omega_0 t}\,dt$$

Let Σ denote any finite set of integers, and let $\mathbf{P}$ denote the linear operator with the property that

12 $$\frac{1}{T}\int_0^T (\mathbf{P}f)(t)e^{-jn\omega_0 t}\,dt = \begin{cases} \hat{f}_n & n \in \Sigma \\ 0 & n \notin \Sigma \end{cases}$$

for all $f \in \mathcal{K}$. (Clearly, $\mathbf{P}$ behaves as an ideal filter which passes certain frequencies and rejects others.)

We use the symbol $\mathcal{K}_{\mathcal{R}}$ to denote the set of all *real-valued* elements of $\mathcal{K}$.

A linear problem

Suppose that all N resistors are linear, positive, and periodically time-varying with the same period T; that is, suppose that for all $v_n(t)$

13 $$g_n(v_n(t),t) = g_n(1,t)v_n(t) \qquad n = 1, 2, \ldots, N$$

in which $g_n(1,t) > 0$ and $g_n(1,t) = g_n(1, t + T)$.

The basic problem here is to determine the N-vector of voltages $v(t)$ when $e(t) = e_0 e^{j\omega_1 t}$, where e_0 is an arbitrary constant N-vector and ω_1 is an arbitrary real constant. It is well known that the linearity and periodically time-varying character of the system imply that if a unique solution $v(t)$ exists, $v(t) = u(t)e^{j\omega_1 t}$, in which $u(t) = u(t + T)$.

[1] We use the symbol "$\triangleq$" to denote "equals by definition."

Equation *6* implies that $u(t)$ must satisfy

14 $$e_0 = u + \mathbf{Z}_1\mathbf{G}u$$

in which $\mathbf{Z}_1$ is obtained from $\mathbf{Z}$ by replacing $z(t)$ by $z(t)e^{-j\omega_1 t}$.

A well-known technique for obtaining an approximate solution of *14* is to solve a "suitably large" finite set of linear equations obtained by truncating the infinite system of equations involving the Fourier coefficients of $u(t)$ implied by *14*; that is, it is assumed that *14* possesses one and only one solution belonging to $\mathcal{K}$ and that it is approximately $\tilde{u}$, the exact solution of

15 $$e_0 = \tilde{u} + \mathbf{P}\mathbf{Z}_1\mathbf{G}\tilde{u}$$

for some finite Σ. The set Σ, which is ordinarily chosen in accordance with some intuitive criterion, must be such that $Z(\omega_1 + p\omega_0)$ is "suitably small" if $p \notin \Sigma$. Although this technique is of considerable practical utility, the following rather basic questions can be raised.

1. Does $\mathcal{K}$ contain one and only one solution of *14*?
2. Does the truncated set of equations possess a unique solution? More specifically, for a given $\mathbf{P}$ (that is, for a given Σ), does $\mathcal{K}$ contain one and only one solution of *15*?
3. Assuming that *14* and *15* possess unique solutions belonging to $\mathcal{K}$, is the solution of *15* close to that of *14*? In particular, what is an upper bound on the error[1] involved; and for an arbitrary positive constant γ, does there exist a finite subset Ξ of the integers such that the mean-square truncation error $\|u - \tilde{u}\|^2$ is at most γ whenever $\Xi \subseteq \Sigma$?

In connection with question 1, observe that Eq. *6 does not* possess a solution belonging to $\mathcal{K}$ if, say, $N = 1$, $e(t) = \sin(2\pi t/T)$,

16 $$g_1(v_1(t),t) = v_1(t)$$

(that is, the one-port termination is a unit time-invariant linear resistor), and $Z(j(2\pi/T)) = -1$, since then for every $v \in \mathcal{K}$, the Fourier coefficients associated with the radian frequencies $\pm 2\pi/T$ of the left side of *6* vanish.

A nonlinear problem

Let us now consider a different but analogous situation. Suppose that all N resistors are time-invariant but nonlinear; that is, suppose that

[1] Questions of this type have been considered for a special class of infinite systems of equations, the so-called *regular* systems. See Kantorovich and Krylov [19].

for all t

17 $$g_n(v_n(t),t) = g_n(v_n(t),0) \qquad n = 1, 2, \ldots, N$$

Assume also that there exist two positive constants σ_1 and σ_2 such that

18 $$\sigma_1(x_1 - x_2) \leq g_n(x_1,0) - g_n(x_2,0) \leq \sigma_2(x_1 - x_2)$$

$(n = 1,2, \ldots, N)$ for all real $x_1 \geq x_2$.

Here an important problem is the determination of the N-vector $v(t)$ when $e(t)$ is a given real-valued periodic function with period T. The problem is often treated by assuming that there exists a unique exact solution $v \in \mathcal{K}_{\mathcal{R}}$ and, as in the linear problem, choosing a finite Σ such that there is reason to believe that $\tilde{v}$, the exact solution of

19 $$e = \tilde{v} + \mathbf{PZG}\tilde{v}$$

is an acceptable approximation to v. We assume here that $\mathbf{P}$ is chosen so that it maps $\mathcal{K}_{\mathcal{R}}$ into itself; that is, we assume here that $n \in \Sigma$ if $-n \in \Sigma$.

With regard to $\tilde{v}$, the Fourier coefficients that correspond to frequencies $n\omega_0$ for $n \notin \Sigma$ are equal to the corresponding coefficients of e, whereas the remaining coefficients satisfy a finite set of nonlinear equations.[1]

It is clear that the questions analogous to those raised in connection with the linear problem are equally pertinent here. Indeed, the present situation perhaps appears to be even more uncertain because of the nonlinear character of the problem.

Results

Under certain assumptions, which are satisfied whenever the linear time-invariant portion of the network is passive [i.e., whenever[2] $[Z(j\omega) + Z^*(j\omega)]$ is nonnegative definite for all real ω] but which by no means require passivity, the questions raised in the preceding two subsections have been answered.

In particular, under these assumptions it has been proved (see Ref. 21) that for either the linear or nonlinear problem $\mathcal{K}$ ($\mathcal{K}_{\mathcal{R}}$ for the nonlinear problem) contains one and only one solution, that any corresponding finite set of truncated equations possesses a unique solution, and that for any $\gamma > 0$ there exists a finite subset Ξ of the

[1] This is essentially the describing-function technique. A rigorous examination of the validity of this method for predicting the existence of self-sustained oscillations is given in the paper by Bass [20].

[2] The complex-conjugate transpose of $Z(j\omega)$ is denoted by $Z^*(j\omega)$.

integers such that the mean-square truncation error is at most γ whenever $\Xi \subseteq \Sigma$. Explicit bounds on the truncation error have been obtained.

Some related work

The relation between the steady-state component of a transient solution and the complete transient solution of integral equations that govern systems of the type considered here is discussed in Sec. *6* (see the proof of Theorem *6.4.4*).

For further recent results concerned with the existence of solutions of nonlinear functional equations, see, for example, the book edited by Anselone [22] and paper of Minty [23].

4 *Some further applications of functional-analytic methods*

Properties of solutions of systems of second-order differential equations with variable coefficients

The methods used to obtain the results of Sec. *2* are useful also in studies of the behavior of the solutions of the inhomogeneous equation

1 $$\frac{d^2f}{dt^2} + A\frac{df}{dt} + B(t)f = g$$

in which f is an N-vector-valued function of t, A is a constant $N \times N$ matrix, and $B(t)$ is an $N \times N$ matrix-valued function of t. In particular, the following result [7] has been proved concerning a subclass of equations of this type of direct engineering interest.

Let A denote a constant positive-definite $N \times N$ hermitian matrix. Let $B(t)$ denote an $N \times N$ positive-definite hermitian-matrix-valued function of t for $t \geq 0$, and let the elements of $B(t)$ be piecewise-continuous and uniformly bounded for $t \geq 0$. Let f be a complex N-vector-valued function of t defined and twice differentiable on $[0, \infty)$, such that

2 $$\frac{d^2f(t)}{dt^2} + A\frac{df(t)}{dt} + B(t)f(t) = g(t) \qquad t \geq 0$$

with each component of ge^{c_1t} of finite energy on $[0, \infty)$ for some positive constant c_1.

Let $\underline{\lambda}\{A\}$, $\underline{\lambda}\{B(t)\}$, and $\bar{\lambda}\{B(t)\}$ denote, respectively, the smallest eigenvalue of A, the smallest eigenvalue of $B(t)$, and the largest eigenvalue of $B(t)$. Suppose that[1]

3 $$\inf_{t \geq 0} \underline{\lambda}\{B(t)\} > 0$$

and that

4 $$\underline{\lambda}\{A\} > (\sup_{t \geq 0} \bar{\lambda}\{B(t)\})^{\frac{1}{2}} - (\inf_{t \geq 0} \underline{\lambda}\{B(t)\})^{\frac{1}{2}}$$

Then there exist positive constants c_2 and c_3 such that (with f_j the jth component of f)

5 $$|f_j(t)| \leq c_2 e^{-c_3 t} \qquad t \geq 0$$

for $j = 1, 2, \ldots, N$.

In the study of parametrically excited dynamic systems, attention is frequently focused on the properties of differential equations of the form described above, with g the zero vector. Usually, $B(t)$ varies periodically with t and one is primarily interested in determining whether or not the trivial solution $f = 0$ is stable.

The matrix A is often associated with the damping present in a physical system. For a given $B(t)$ it is reasonable to expect that the system will be stable if the damping is sufficiently large in some sense, and it is frequently desirable to actually determine the amount of damping necessary for stabilization. The result presented in the previous paragraph provides a simple upper bound on the required damping for a large class of systems.

Models for evaluating the effect of "nearly linear" elements

Studies of the properties of nonlinear functional equations have led to results concerning the extent to which other well-known engineering approximation techniques are valid.

For example, the flow graph of Fig. *8.4.1* is a representation of a general transmission system containing linear time-invariant elements

[1] Recall that "inf" is the abbreviation for "infimum" which means greatest lower bound.

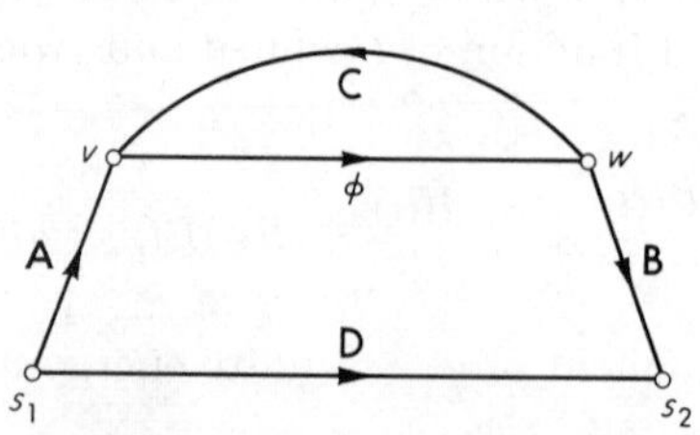

Fig. 8.4.1 Flow-graph representation of a general transmission system containing linear elements and a single time-variable nonlinear element ϕ.

and a single nonlinear element ϕ. The linear convolution operators **A**, **B**, **C**, and **D** can be determined by standard techniques in any specific situation.

Insofar as the effect of ϕ is concerned, it clearly suffices to consider the analysis of the flow graph of Fig. *8.4.2*. Let us suppose that ϕ represents a nearly linear element which behaves essentially as a unit gain amplifier for sufficiently small input signals, and that we wish to determine its influence in Fig. *8.4.2*.

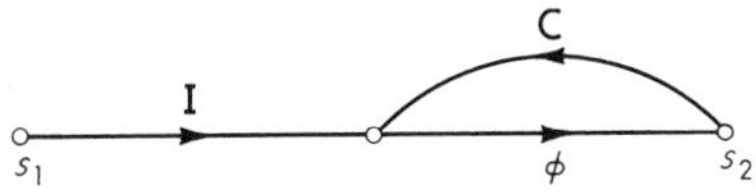

Fig. 8.4.2 Basic flow graph for studying the influence of ϕ.

Under certain precise conditions, and to within a certain error for which bounds have been obtained (see Ref. 24 and Desoer [25]), the output signal s_{21} of the *cascade* flow graph of Fig. *8.4.3* is a good approximation to s_2. This flow graph, in which $\tilde{\phi}$ denotes the nonlinear part[1] of ϕ, characterizes the essence of a well-known engineering technique (see Bode [26]) for approximately determining the effect of feedback on nonlinear distortion introduced in one stage of an amplifier, when the distortion is "small." In particular, observe that if, as indicated in Fig. *8.4.3*, $u(t)$ denotes the distortion[2] produced by the open-loop

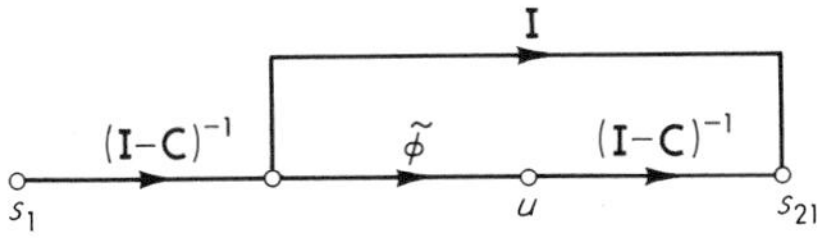

Fig. 8.4.3 Cascade flow graph for approximately determining the output signal in Fig. *8.4.2* (s_{21} is the approximation to s_2).

system with the same "small-signal transmission" and the same output stage as the feedback system in Fig. *8.4.2*, then the output distortion in Fig. *8.4.2* is approximately $(\mathbf{I} - \mathbf{C})^{-1}u$. In engineering terms, feedback is said to reduce the nonlinear distortion by the amount of the "return difference" $[1 - C(\omega)]$ [that is, by the formal frequency-domain representation of the operator $(\mathbf{I} - \mathbf{C})$].

[1] In other words, $\phi(x) = x + \tilde{\phi}(x)$ for all real x.

[2] The "distortion generator" referred to in the usual engineering arguments produces the signal $u(t)$.

The techniques and results can be extended to cases in which there are more than one nonlinear element.

Signal-recovery problems

Some interesting network theoretic problems arise in the study of the recoverability of signals passed through networks containing frequency-selective elements as well as nonlinear elements.

For example, it is well known that, because of the inherent nonlinear character of physical devices, there is a basic tendency for the large-amplitude portions of transmitted signals to be distorted. Similarly, there is a basic tendency for the low-amplitude portions of the signals to be corrupted by noise. For these reasons, it is natural to consider the possibility of transmitting the signal $\psi[f(t)]$, where $f(t)$ is the message function and $\psi(x)$ is a fixed monotonic-increasing function of x such as is shown in Fig. *8.4.4*.

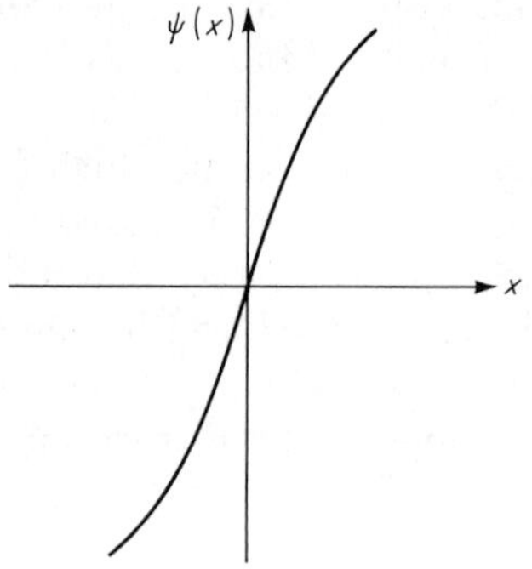

Fig. 8.4.4 Graph of $\psi(x)$.

Referring to Fig. *8.4.4* we see that the large slope of $\psi(x)$ near the origin reduces the effect of noise by providing amplification for the low-level part of the message; the saturationlike behavior reduces the large-amplitude portion of the message in order to decrease the nonlinear distortion of the transmitted signal. This process is often referred to as "instantaneous companding" (compand = compress + expand).

A difficulty with instantaneous companding is that if $f(t)$ is band-limited to a band Ω, in which Ω is a "low-pass" interval $[-\omega_0,\omega_0]$, then $\psi[f(t)]$ need not be band-limited to Ω, or, indeed, to any low-pass interval. Thus, with the exception of some very special cases, if $f(t)$ is band-limited to Ω and $\psi[f(t)]$ is transmitted through a channel represented by an ideal low-pass filter with passband Ω, then the output, which we shall call $g(t)$ (see Fig. *8.4.5*), will be a distorted version of $\psi[f(t)]$. However, it is an interesting fact that (subject to some reasonable qualifications) g completely determines f; that is, $f(t)$ can be determined if only the part of the spectrum of $\psi[f(t)]$ that lies in Ω is known.[1] Convergent iteration schemes for actually determining f from g are considered by Landau and Miranker [27].

A generalization of the main result of Landau and Miranker has been obtained in the form of a theorem concerning the solvability of a certain type of nonlinear functional equation defined on a Hilbert space (see Ref. 28). This theorem shows that the signal-recovery results are a quite special case of a mathematical proposition that is of use in connection with several problems. For example, a specialization of the theorem is the basis of a computer program for solving the equilibrium equations of networks containing an arbitrary finite number of monotonic resistors (see Katzenelson and Seitelman [29]).

Conditions have also been obtained [30] under which recovery is possible by an iteration scheme when ψ in Fig. *8.4.5* is replaced with a

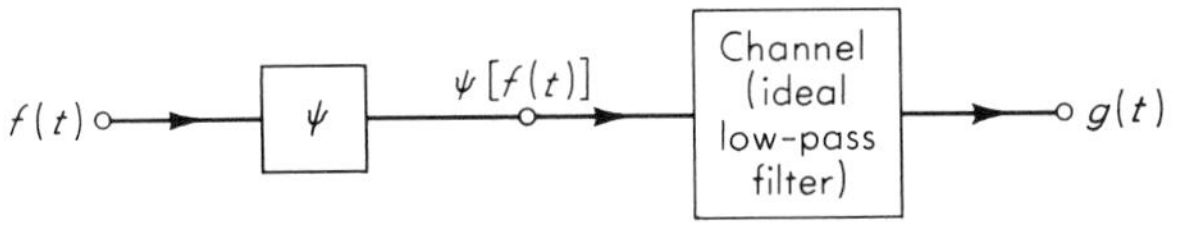

Fig. 8.4.5 The relationship of $g(t)$ to $f(t)$.

rather general system containing linear time-invariant elements and a single nonlinear element such as ψ. In that case it is, of course, by no means always true that recovery is possible.

5 *Causality and passivity*

The external properties of a physical system can frequently be characterized by an operator relation of the form

1 $$g = \mathbf{T}f$$

in which g and f are real N-vector-valued functions of t such that $g'f$ represents the total instantaneous power entering the system. For example, for an electromechanical system, the jth component of f might be the voltage or force at the jth accessible point of the system, in which case g would be the corresponding N-vector of currents and velocities.

[1] This early result was proved by A. Beurling. His proof was published for the first time in Ref. 27.

The notions of energy and causality play a central role in the study of the properties of physical systems. It is therefore of some theoretical interest to consider the relation between energy-type properties of a general operator **T** and the causality or lack of causality of **T**.

Let us agree to say that **T** is *causal* if for every $\delta > -\infty$, $\mathbf{T}f_1$ and $\mathbf{T}f_2$ agree on the interval $(-\infty,\delta)$ whenever the N-vector-valued functions f_1 and f_2 are permissible inputs to the system represented by **T**, and f_1 and f_2 agree on $(-\infty,\delta)$.

Let us say also that **T** is *passive* if

2 $$\int_{-\infty}^{x} (\mathbf{T}f)'f\,dt \geq 0$$

for all real x and every permissible f.

Youla, Castriota, and Carlin [31] have proved the interesting result that, under some weak assumptions, if an operator **T** is linear and passive, it is also causal.

Recently, necessary and sufficient energy-type conditions which imply causality have been obtained (see Ref. 32) for a large class of nonlinear operators.

The simplest result of this study is that, under certain weak assumptions, a nonlinear operator **T** is causal if the linearization of **T** (defined in a quite reasonable manner from the engineering viewpoint) about an arbitrary permissible input yields a passive (linear) operator.

6 *Results for an n-vector generalization of equation 2.8*

Notation and definitions

The set of real N-vector-valued functions of the real variable t defined on $[0,\infty)$ is denoted by $\mathcal{H}_N(0,\infty)$ and the jth component of $f \in \mathcal{H}_N(0,\infty)$ is denoted by f_j.

The sets $\mathfrak{L}_{\infty N}(0,\infty)$ and $\mathfrak{L}_{2N}(0,\infty)$ are defined by

1 $$\mathfrak{L}_{\infty N}(0,\infty) = \{f \mid f \in \mathcal{H}_N(0,\infty),\ \sup_{t\geq 0}\,[f'(t)f(t)] < \infty\}$$

2 $$\mathfrak{L}_{2N}(0,\infty) = \left\{f \mid f \in \mathcal{H}_N(0,\infty),\ \int_0^{\infty} f'(t)f(t)\,dt < \infty\right\}$$

in which $f'(t)$ denotes the transpose of $f(t)$. In order to be consistent with standard notation, we let $\mathfrak{L}_2(0,\infty) = \mathfrak{L}_{2N}(0,\infty)$ when $N = 1$.

Let $y \in (0,\infty)$, define f_y by

3 $$f_y(t) = \begin{cases} f(t) & \text{for } t \in [0,y] \\ 0 & \text{for } t > y \end{cases}$$

for any $f \in \mathcal{H}_N(0,\infty)$, and let

4 $$\mathcal{E}_N = \{f | f \in \mathcal{H}_N(0,\infty), f_y \in \mathcal{L}_{2N}(0,\infty) \text{ for } 0 < y < \infty\}$$

With A an arbitrary real $N \times N$ matrix-valued function of t with elements $\{a_{nm}\}$ defined on $[0,\infty)$, let $\mathcal{K}_{pN}$ $(p = 1,2)$ denote

5 $$\left\{A \;\middle|\; \int_0^\infty |a_{nm}(t)|^p \, dt < \infty \quad (n,m = 1,2, \ldots ,N)\right\}$$

For an arbitrary $f \in \mathcal{H}_N(0,\infty)$, let $\psi[f(t),t]$ denote

$$(\psi_1[f_1(t),t], \psi_2[f_2(t),t], \ldots ,\psi_N[f_N(t),t])'$$

where $\psi_1(w,t)$, $\psi_2(w,t)$, . . . , $\psi_N(w,t)$ are real-valued functions of the real variables w and t for $w \in (-\infty,\infty)$ and $t \in [0,\infty)$ such that $\psi_n(0,t) = 0$ for $t \in [0,\infty)$ and $n = 1, 2, \ldots, N$.

Let α and β denote real numbers such that $\alpha \leq \beta$. We shall say that $\psi[\cdot,\cdot] \in \Psi_0(\alpha,\beta)$ if and only if

6 $$\alpha \leq \frac{\psi_n(w,t)}{w} \leq \beta \qquad n = 1, 2, \ldots, N$$

for $t \in [0,\infty)$ and all real $w \neq 0$; and we shall say that $\psi[\cdot,\cdot] \in \Psi(\alpha,\beta)$ if and only if

7 $$\alpha \leq \frac{\psi_n(w_1,t) - \psi_n(w_2,t)}{w_1 - w_2} \leq \beta \qquad n = 1, 2, \ldots, N$$

for $t \in [0,\infty)$ and all real w_1 and w_2 such that $w_1 \neq w_2$.

In this section we consider the equation

8 $$g(t) = f(t) + \int_0^t k(t-\tau)\psi[f(\tau),\tau] \, d\tau \qquad t \geq 0$$

in which $g \in \mathcal{E}_N$, $f \in \mathcal{E}_N$, $k \in \mathcal{K}_{1N}$, and $\psi[\cdot,\cdot] \in \Psi_0(\alpha,\beta)$ for some α and β. This type of equation arises, for example, in the study of multi-input multi-output generalizations of the system of Fig. *8.2.2*. In order to state our results it is convenient to introduce the following further notation and definitions.

Let M denote an arbitrary matrix. We shall denote by M', M^*, and M^{-1}, respectively, the transpose, the complex-conjugate transpose, and the inverse of M. The positive square root of the largest eigenvalue of M^*M is denoted by $\Lambda\{M\}$, and 1_N denotes the identity matrix of order N.

The norm of $f \in \mathcal{L}_{2N}(0,\infty)$ is denoted by $\|f\|$ and is defined by

9 $$\|f\| = \left(\int_0^\infty f'(t)f(t) \, dt\right)^{\frac{1}{2}}$$

The symbol s denotes a scalar complex variable with $\sigma = \text{Re}\,[s]$ and $\omega = \text{Im}\,[s]$.

We shall say that k is an element of the set $\Phi(\alpha,\beta)$ if and only if $k \in \mathcal{K}_{1N}$ and, with

10 $$K(s) = \int_0^\infty k(t)e^{-st}\,dt \qquad \text{for } \sigma \geq 0$$

1. $\det\,[1_N + \frac{1}{2}(\alpha + \beta)K(s)] \neq 0 \qquad \text{for } \sigma \geq 0$
2. $\frac{1}{2}(\beta - \alpha) \sup\limits_{-\infty<\omega<\infty} \Lambda\{[1_N + \frac{1}{2}(\alpha + \beta)K(i\omega)]^{-1}K(i\omega)\} < 1$

Comments It can be shown that conditions (1) and (2) above are satisfied if $\alpha \geq 0$ and $[K(i\omega) + K(i\omega)^*]$ is nonnegative definite for all real ω.

For $N = 1$, conditions 1 and 2 above are met if $\beta > 0$ and one of the conditions *11*, *12*, or *13* of Sec. *2* is satisfied.

Results [6, 7]

Our first theorem, which is proved in Ref. 6 (see also the next two subsections) as an application of a proposition concerning the "norm boundedness" of solutions f of abstract functional equations of the form $g = f + Tf$, is the key result of this subsection. It is of direct interest in the theory of stability of dynamic systems, and it plays an important role in the proof of each of the other theorems stated below.

11 **Theorem** Let $k \in \Phi(\alpha,\beta)$, let $\psi[\cdot,\cdot] \in \psi_0(\alpha,\beta)$, and let

12 $$g(t) = f(t) + \int_0^t k(t-\tau)\psi[f(\tau),\tau]\,d\tau \qquad t \geq 0$$

where $g \in \mathcal{L}_{2N}(0,\infty)$ and $f \in \mathcal{E}_N$. Then $f \in \mathcal{L}_{2N}(0,\infty)$, and there exists a positive constant ρ, which depends only on k, α, and β, such that

13 $$\|f\| \leq \rho\|g\|$$

14 **Corollary** Let $k \in \Phi(\alpha,\beta)$, let $\psi[\cdot,\cdot] \in \psi(\alpha,\beta)$, and let

15 $$g_1(t) = f_1(t) + \int_0^t k(t-\tau)\psi[f_1(\tau),\tau]\,d\tau \qquad t \geq 0$$

16 $$g_2(t) = f_2(t) + \int_0^t k(t-\tau)\psi[f_2(t),\tau]\,d\tau \qquad t \geq 0$$

where $g_1, g_2, f_1, f_2 \in \mathcal{E}_N$, and $(g_1 - g_2) \in \mathcal{L}_{2N}(0,\infty)$. Then $(f_1 - f_2) \in \mathcal{L}_{2N}(0,\infty)$, and there exists a positive constant ρ, which depends only on k, α, and β, such that

17 $$\|f_1 - f_2\| \leq \rho\|g_1 - g_2\|$$

Proof of Corollary Let $q_j(t)$ be defined on $[0,\infty)$ by

18
$$q_j(t) = \begin{cases} \dfrac{\psi_j[f_{1j}(t),t] - \psi_j[f_{2j}(t),t]}{f_{1j}(t) - f_{2j}(t)} & t \in \{t|t \geq 0, f_{1j}(t) \neq f_{2j}(t)\} \\ \frac{1}{2}(\alpha + \beta) & t \in \{t|t \geq 0, f_{1j}(t) = f_{2j}(t)\} \end{cases}$$

for $j = 1, 2, \ldots, N$; and let $q(t)$ denote the diagonal matrix

$$\text{diag}\,[q_1(t),q_2(t), \ldots ,q_N(t)]$$

Then $\alpha \leq q_j(t) \leq \beta$ for $j = 1, 2, \ldots, N$, and

19
$$g_1(t) - g_2(t) = f_1(t) - f_2(t) + \int_0^t k(t-\tau)q(\tau)[f_1(\tau) - f_2(\tau)]\,d\tau \qquad t \geq 0$$

The conclusion of the corollary follows from this equation and the theorem.

20 **Remarks** A direct application of the Schwarz inequality and the Riemann-Lebesgue lemma shows that if the hypotheses of Theorem *11* are satisfied and $g(t) \to 0$ as $t \to \infty$ [that is, $g_j(t) \to 0$ as $t \to \infty$ for $j = 1, 2, \ldots, N$], then $f(t) \to 0$ as $t \to \infty$, provided that $k \in \mathcal{K}_{2N}$ [observe that $k \in \mathcal{K}_{2N}$ if $k \in \mathcal{K}_{1N}$ and the elements of k are uniformly bounded on $[0,\infty)$]. Similarly, if the hypotheses of Corollary *14* are met and $[g_1(t) - g_2(t)] \to 0$ as $t \to \infty$, then $[f_1(t) - f_2(t)] \to 0$ as $t \to \infty$, provided that $k \in \mathcal{K}_{2N}$.

Theorem 8 of Ref. 7 leads to a result for the integral equation of *12* that is actually somewhat stronger than that stated as Theorem *11*. If k, $\psi[\cdot,\cdot]$, and f are as defined in Theorem *11* and if $g \in \mathcal{E}_N$ satisfies the integral equation, then it can be shown that there exists a positive constant ρ which depends only on k, α, and β such that $\|f_y\| \leq \rho\|g_y\|$ for all $y > 0$.

21 **Theorem** Let

22
$$g(t) = f(t) + \int_0^t k(t-\tau)\psi[f(\tau),\tau]\,d\tau \qquad t \geq 0$$

in which $\psi[\cdot,\cdot] \in \Psi_0(\alpha,\beta)$, $f \in \mathcal{E}_N$, and there exists a real constant c_1 such that

1. $ge^{c_1t} \in \mathfrak{L}_{2N}(0,\infty)$
2. $ke^{c_1t} \in \mathcal{K}_{1N} \cap \mathcal{K}_{2N}$
3. $ke^{c_1t} \in \Phi(\alpha,\beta)$

Then there exists a positive constant c_2 such that

23
$$|f_j(t)| \leq |g_j(t)| + c_2e^{-c_1t} \qquad t \geq 0$$

for $j = 1, 2, \ldots, N$.

24 **Corollary** Let

25 $$g(t) = f(t) + \int_0^t k(t-\tau)\psi[f(\tau),\tau]\,d\tau \qquad t \geq 0$$

in which $\psi[\cdot,\cdot] \in \Psi_0(\alpha,\beta)$, $k \in \Phi(\alpha,\beta)$, $f \in \mathcal{E}_N$, and there exists a positive constant c_1 such that

1. $ge^{c_1 t} \in \mathcal{L}_{2N}(0,\infty)$
2. $ke^{c_1 t} \in \mathcal{K}_{1N} \cap \mathcal{K}_{2N}$

Then there exist positive constants c_2 and c_3 such that

26 $$|f_j(t)| \leq |g_j(t)| + c_2 e^{-c_3 t} \qquad t \geq 0$$

Proof of Theorem 21 From the fact that f and g satisfy *22* we have

27 $$e^{c_1 t}g(t) = \hat{f}(t) + \int_0^t e^{c_1(t-\tau)}k(t-\tau)e^{c_1\tau}\psi[e^{-c_1\tau}\hat{f}(\tau),\tau]\,d\tau \qquad t \geq 0$$

in which $\hat{f}(t) = f(t)e^{c_1 t}$. Since

28 $$\alpha \leq \frac{e^{c_1 t}\psi_n[e^{-c_1 t}x,t]}{x} \leq \beta \qquad n = 1, 2, \ldots, N$$

for all real $x \neq 0$ and $t \geqq 0$, it follows from Theorem *11* that $\hat{f} \in \mathcal{L}_{2N}(0,\infty)$. Thus $e^{c_1 t}\psi[f(\cdot),\cdot] \in \mathcal{L}_{2N}(0,\infty)$, and by the Schwarz inequality, there exists a positive constant c_2 such that the modulus of the jth component of

29 $$\int_0^t e^{c_1(t-\tau)}k(t-\tau)e^{c_1\tau}\psi[f(t),\tau]\,d\tau$$

does not exceed c_2 for $t \geq 0$ and $j = 1, 2, \ldots, N$. Thus, using *27*, we obtain

30 $$|f_j(t)| \leq |g_j(t)| + c_2 e^{-c_1 t} \qquad t \geq 0$$

for $j = 1, 2, \ldots, N$.

Proof of Corollary 24 Let

31 $$K(i\omega - \rho) = \int_0^\infty k(t)e^{-(i\omega-\rho)t}\,dt$$

for $\rho \leq c_1$ and $-\infty < \omega < \infty$. It clearly suffices to prove that there exists a positive constant $c_4 \leq c_1$ such that $ke^{\rho t} \in \Phi(\alpha,\beta)$ for $0 \leq \rho \leq c_4$. The existence of such a constant follows easily from the fact that each element of $[K(s) - K(s-\rho)]$ approaches zero uniformly in $\sigma \geq 0$ as $\rho \to 0+$. The details are omitted.

The following theorem has been proved with the aid of Theorem *11*.

32 **Theorem** Let $k \in \Phi(\alpha,\beta)$ with $t^p k \in \mathcal{K}_{1N} \cap \mathcal{K}_{2N}$ for $p = 0, 1, 2$. Let $\psi[\cdot,\cdot] \in \Psi_0(\alpha,\beta)$, and let

33 $$g(t) = f(t) + \int_0^t k(t-\tau)\psi[f(\tau),\tau]\, d\tau \qquad t \geq 0$$

where $g \in \mathfrak{L}_{\infty N}(0,\infty)$ and $f \in \mathcal{E}_N$. Then $f \in \mathfrak{L}_{\infty N}(0,\infty)$, and there exists a positive constant ρ which depends only on k, α, and β such that

34 $$\max_j \sup_{t \geq 0} |f_j(t)| \leq \rho \max_j \sup_{t \geq 0} |g_j(t)|$$

and $f_j(t) \to 0$ as $t \to \infty$ for $j = 1, 2, \ldots, N$ whenever $g_j(t) \to 0$ as $t \to \infty$ for $j = 1, 2, \ldots, N$.

35 **Corollary** Let $k \in \Phi(\alpha,\beta)$ with $t^p k \in \mathcal{K}_{1N} \cap \mathcal{K}_{2N}$ for $p = 0, 1, 2$. Let $\psi[\cdot,\cdot] \in \Psi(\alpha,\beta)$, and let

36 $$g_1(t) = f_1(t) + \int_0^t k(t-\tau)\psi[f_1(\tau),\tau]\, d\tau \qquad t \geq 0$$

37 $$g_2(t) = f_2(t) + \int_0^t k(t-\tau)\psi[f_2(\tau),\tau]\, d\tau \qquad t \geq 0$$

where $g_1, g_2, f_1, f_2 \in \mathcal{E}_N$ and $(g_1 - g_2) \in \mathfrak{L}_{\infty N}(0,\infty)$. Then $(f_1 - f_2) \in \mathfrak{L}_{\infty N}(0,\infty)$, and there exists a positive constant ρ which depends only on k, α, and β such that

38 $$\max_j \sup_{t \geq 0} |f_{1j}(t) - f_{2j}(t)| \leq \rho \max_j \sup_{t \geq 0} |g_{1j}(t) - g_{2j}(t)|$$

and $[f_{1j}(t) - f_{2j}(t)] \to 0$ as $t \to \infty$ for $j = 1, 2, \ldots, N$ whenever $[g_{1j}(t) - g_{2j}(t)] \to 0$ as $t \to \infty$ for $j = 1, 2, \ldots, N$.

Comments If the hypotheses of Theorem *32* are altered to the extent that the integrability condition on $t^p k$ is replaced with the assumption that there exists a positive constant c_1 such that $e^{c_1 t}k \in \mathcal{K}_{1N} \cap \mathcal{K}_{2N}$, then it is possible to give a relatively simple proof of the fact that $f \in \mathfrak{L}_{\infty N}(0,\infty)$. Specifically, under the new assumptions, it can be easily verified that for any positive constant $c_2 < c_1$, there exists a positive constant c_3 such that the modulus of the jth component of

39 $$\int_0^y k(y-\tau)\psi[f(\tau),\tau]\, d\tau$$

does not exceed $c_3 e^{-c_2 y}\|e^{c_2 t} f_y\|$ for all $y > 0$ and $j = 1, 2, \ldots, N$. It can be shown that there exist positive constants ρ and c_4 such that $c_4 < c_1$ and

40 $$\|e^{c_4 t} f_y\| \leq \rho \|e^{c_4 t} g_y\|$$

for all $y > 0$. Since $g \in \mathcal{L}_{\infty N}(0,\infty)$ and for $y > 0$

41
$$f(y) = g(y) - \int_0^y k(y-\tau)\psi[f(\tau),\tau]\,d\tau$$

and

42
$$\|e^{c_4 t} g_y\| \leq \left(\frac{N}{2c_4}\right)^{\frac{1}{2}} e^{c_4 y} \max_j \sup_{t \geq 0} |g_j(t)|$$

it follows that $f \in \mathcal{L}_{\infty N}(0,\infty)$. This type of approach, when coupled with the techniques of Sec. V of Ref. 7, can be used to establish the $\mathcal{L}_{\infty N}(0,\infty)$-boundedness of solutions of more general functional equations.

Results similar to Theorems *11* and *32* concerning the discrete analog of *8.2.8* have also been obtained.

43 **Definition** Let T be a real positive constant, and let

$$\mathfrak{D} = \{f | f \in \mathcal{L}_{\infty N}(-\infty,\infty), f(t) = f(t+T) \text{ for } -\infty < t < \infty\}$$

where $\mathcal{L}_{\infty N}(-\infty,\infty)$ is the natural extension of the space $\mathcal{L}_{\infty N}(0,\infty)$ to N-vector-valued functions defined on the entire real line.

44 **Theorem** Let $k \in \Phi(\alpha,\beta)$ with $t^p k \in \mathcal{K}_{1N} \cap \mathcal{K}_{2N}$ for $p = 0, 1, 2$. Let $g_1 \in \mathfrak{D}$, $g_2 \in \mathcal{L}_{\infty N}(0,\infty)$, $g_2(t) \to 0$ as $t \to \infty$, and $\psi[\cdot,\cdot] \in \Psi(\alpha,\beta)$ with $\psi_n(w,t) = \psi_n(w, t+T)$ for all real w and $t \geq 0$. Let $f \in \mathcal{E}_N$ satisfy

45
$$g_1(t) + g_2(t) = f(t) + \int_0^t k(t-\tau)\psi[f(\tau),\tau]\,d\tau \qquad t \geq 0$$

Then $\mathfrak{D}$ contains an element $\hat{f}$, which does not depend on g_2, such that $[f(t) - \hat{f}(t)] \to 0$ as $t \to \infty$.

If, in addition to the hypotheses stated above, there exist positive constants c_1, c_2, and c_3 such that

46
$$e^{c_1 t} k \in \mathcal{K}_{1N} \cap \mathcal{K}_{2N} \qquad \int_t^\infty |k_{mn}(x)|\,dx \leqq c_2 e^{-c_3 t} \qquad t \geq 0$$

for $m, n = 1, 2, \ldots, N$, and

47
$$|g_{2j}(t)| \leq c_2 e^{-c_3 t} \qquad t \geq 0$$

for $m, n = 1, 2, \ldots, N$, then there exist positive constants c_4 and c_5 such that

48
$$|f_j(t) - \hat{f}_j(t)| \leq c_4 e^{-c_5 t} \qquad t \geq 0$$

for $j = 1, 2, \ldots, N$.

Proof Assume that the hypotheses of the first part of Theorem *44* are satisfied. Let $\psi_n(w,t)$ be defined for $t < 0$ by the condition that $\psi_n(w,t) = \psi_n(w, t+T)$ for *all* real t, all real w, and $n = 1, 2, \ldots, N$.

We need the following result, which can be proved with the aid of Theorem 4 of Ref. 21 and the remarks relating to its proof.

49 **Lemma** The set $\mathfrak{D}$ contains a unique element $\hat{f}$ such that

50 $$g_1(t) = \hat{f}(t) + \int_{-\infty}^{t} k(t-\tau)\psi[\hat{f}(\tau),\tau]\,d\tau \qquad -\infty < t < \infty$$

Thus, we have

51 $$g_1(t) - \int_{-\infty}^{0} k(t-\tau)\psi[\hat{f}(\tau),\tau]\,d\tau = \hat{f}(t) + \int_{0}^{t} k(t-\tau)\psi[\hat{f}(\tau),\tau]\,d\tau \qquad t \geq 0$$

52 $$g_1(t) + g_2(t) = f(t) + \int_{0}^{t} k(t-\tau)\psi[f(\tau),\tau]\,d\tau \qquad t \geq 0$$

Since

53 $$g_2(t) + \int_{-\infty}^{0} k(t-\tau)\psi[\hat{f}(\tau),\tau]\,d\tau \to 0 \qquad \text{as} \qquad t \to \infty$$

by Corollary *35*, $[f(t) - \hat{f}(t)] \to 0$ as $t \to \infty$.

The second part of the theorem follows at once from Corollary *24* and the fact that here

54 $$g_2(t) + \int_{-\infty}^{0} k(t-\tau)\psi[\hat{f}(\tau),\tau]\,d\tau = [f(t) - \hat{f}(t)] + \int_{0}^{t} k(t-\tau)\{\psi[f(\tau),\tau] - \psi[\hat{f}(\tau),\tau]\}\,d\tau \qquad t \geq 0$$

with $\psi[\cdot,\cdot] \in \Psi(\alpha,\beta)$.

Comments Under the additional assumptions that $g_1(t)$ is a constant N-vector and that $\psi_n(w,t)$ is independent of t for $n = 1, 2, \ldots, N$, it can be shown that $f(t)$ of Theorem *44* approaches a limit as $t \to \infty$.

It is a simple matter to construct examples, involving f's not contained in $\mathfrak{L}_{\infty N}(0,\infty)$, which illustrate that the conclusion of the first part of Theorem *44* can be false if k does not belong to $\Phi(\alpha,\beta)$ (with the understanding that the remaining hypotheses are satisfied). The following example shows that the conclusion can be false in some relatively simple situations in which $f \in \mathfrak{L}_{\infty N}(0,\infty)$, if k does not belong to $\Phi(\alpha,\beta)$.

Let $N = 1$, and for $t \geq 0$ let

55 $$\psi(w,t) = \begin{cases} w & -\infty < w \leq 1 \\ w^{\frac{1}{2}} & 1 \leq w \leq 9 \\ \frac{1}{6}w + \frac{3}{2} & w \geq 9 \end{cases}$$

Let $t^p k \in \mathcal{K}_{11} \cap \mathcal{K}_{21}$ for $p = 0, 1, 2$, and let $K(0) = 0$ and $K(i) = -4$. Here $\psi[\cdot,\cdot] \in \Psi(\frac{1}{6},1)$ and, since $K(i)$ is a point on the real-axis diameter of the disk of Fig. *8.2.3* when $\alpha = \frac{1}{6}$ and $\beta = 1$, it is clear that k does not belong to $\Phi(\frac{1}{6},1)$.

For $t \geq 0$, let

56 $$g_1(t) = \tfrac{9}{2} - \tfrac{1}{2}\cos 2t$$

57 $$g_{2a}(t) = e^{-t} + \int_0^t k(t-\tau)\{\psi[\tfrac{9}{2} + 4\sin\tau - \tfrac{1}{2}\cos 2\tau + e^{-\tau}, 0] - \psi[\tfrac{9}{2} + 4\sin\tau - \tfrac{1}{2}\cos 2\tau, 0]\}\, d\tau - \int_{-\infty}^{0} k(t-\tau)\{\psi[\tfrac{9}{2} + 4\sin\tau - \tfrac{1}{2}\cos 2\tau, 0]\}\, d\tau$$

[Observe that $g_{2a}(t)$ is uniformly bounded on $[0,\infty)$ and that $g_{2a}(t) \to 0$ as $t \to \infty$.] Then, using the identity

$$2 + \sin t = (\tfrac{9}{2} + 4\sin t - \tfrac{1}{2}\cos 2t)^{\frac{1}{2}}$$

which is valid for all real t, it can be verified that

$$f_1(t) = \tfrac{9}{2} + 4\sin t - \tfrac{1}{2}\cos 2t + e^{-t}$$

satisfies

58 $$g_1(t) + g_{2a}(t) = f_1(t) + \int_0^t k(t-\tau)\psi[f_1(\tau),0]\, d\tau \qquad t \geq 0$$

Note that although f_1 is ultimately periodic, it contains a component of one-half the frequency of g_1.

At this point it is convenient to comment on the necessity for the hypotheses of Corollaries *14* and *35*. Let g_1, f_1, k, and ψ be as defined in the preceding two paragraphs, and assume that

59 $$\int_t^\infty |k(\tau)|\, d\tau \in \mathfrak{L}_2(0,\infty)$$

For $t \geq 0$, let

60 $$g_{2b}(t) = e^{-t} + \int_0^t k(t-\tau)\{\psi[\tfrac{9}{2} - 4\sin\tau - \tfrac{1}{2}\cos 2\tau + e^{-\tau}, 0] - \psi[\tfrac{9}{2} - 4\sin\tau - \tfrac{1}{2}\cos 2\tau, 0]\}\, d\tau - \int_{-\infty}^{0} k(t-\tau)\psi[\tfrac{9}{2} - 4\sin\tau - \tfrac{1}{2}\cos 2\tau, 0]\, d\tau$$

Then, using the identity mentioned above, we can verify that

$$f_2(t) = \tfrac{9}{2} - 4\sin t - \tfrac{1}{2}\cos 2t + e^{-t}$$

satisfies

61 $$g_1(t) + g_{2b}(t) = f_2(t) + \int_0^t k(t-\tau)\psi[f_2(\tau),0]\, d\tau \qquad t \geq 0$$

Although $[g_{2a}(t) - g_{2b}(t)]$ approaches zero at infinity and belongs to both $\mathfrak{L}_{\infty 1}(0,\infty)$ and $\mathfrak{L}_2(0,\infty)$, it is obvious that $[f_1(t) - f_2(t)]$ (that is, $8\sin t$) does not approach zero at infinity and does not belong to $\mathfrak{L}_2(0,\infty)$.

An abstract proposition

In this subsection, we describe one abstract proposition [33] from which Theorem *11* can be obtained. The general character of the proposition can be exploited to obtain many other results concerning specific equations.

Let $\mathcal{K}$ denote an abstract linear space, over the real or complex field $\mathfrak{F}$, that contains a normed linear space $\mathcal{L}$ with norm $\|\cdot\|$. Let Ω denote a set of real numbers, and let P_y denote a linear mapping of $\mathcal{K}$ into $\mathcal{L}$ for each $y \in \Omega$, such that $\|P_y h\| \leq \|h\|$ for all $h \in \mathcal{L}$ and all $y \in \Omega$. We say that a (not necessarily linear) operator T is an element of the set Θ if and only if T maps $\mathcal{K}$ into itself and $P_y T = P_y T P_y$ on $\mathcal{K}$ for all $y \in \Omega$. The symbol I denotes the identity operator on $\mathcal{K}$.

62 **Proposition**[1] Let A belong to Θ, and assume that A maps the zero element of $\mathcal{L}$ into itself. Let B map $\mathcal{K}$ into itself. Let $f \in \mathcal{K}$, and let $g = f + ABf$. Suppose that there exists $\lambda \in \mathfrak{F}$ such that

1. $I + \lambda A$ is invertible on $\mathcal{K}$, $(I + \lambda A)^{-1} \in \Theta$, and $A(I + \lambda A)^{-1}$ maps $\mathcal{L}$ into itself
2. $\eta_\lambda \triangleq \sup \{\|A(I + \lambda A)^{-1}h\|/\|h\| : h \in \mathcal{L}, h \neq 0\} < \infty$
3. there exists a nonnegative constant k_λ and a function $p_\lambda(y)$ with the property that

$$\|P_y(B - \lambda I)f\| \leq k_\lambda \|P_y f\| + p_\lambda(y) \text{ for all } y \in \Omega$$

4. $\eta_\lambda k_\lambda < 1$

Then

63 $$\|P_y f\| \leq (1 - \eta_\lambda k_\lambda)^{-1}[(1 + |\lambda|\eta_\lambda)\|P_y g\| + \eta_\lambda p_\lambda(y)]$$

for all $y \in \Omega$.

Proof Let $y \in \Omega$. Then, since $Bf = (I + \lambda A)^{-1}[(B - \lambda I)f + \lambda g]$, we have

64 $$\begin{aligned} P_y f &= P_y g - P_y A(I + \lambda A)^{-1}[(B - \lambda I)f + \lambda g] \\ &= P_y g - P_y A(I + \lambda A)^{-1} P_y[(B - \lambda I)f + \lambda g] \end{aligned}$$

and hence

65 $$\begin{aligned} \|P_y f\| &\leq \|P_y g\| + \eta_\lambda \|P_y[(B - \lambda I)f + \lambda g]\| \\ &\leq \|P_y g\| + \eta_\lambda \|P_y(B - \lambda I)f\| + |\lambda|\eta_\lambda \|P_y g\| \\ &\leq (1 + |\lambda|\eta_\lambda)\|P_y g\| + \eta_\lambda k_\lambda \|P_y f\| + \eta_\lambda p_\lambda(y) \end{aligned}$$

[1] This proposition is a generalization of a result proved in Ref. 7.

which establishes the proposition.

Direct proof[1] of Theorem *11* for $N = 1$ Let y be an arbitrary positive constant. Then, using

66 $$g(t) = f(t) + \int_0^t k(t-\tau)\psi[f(\tau),\tau]\,d\tau \qquad t \geq 0$$

we have

67 $$\int_0^y g(t)e^{-i\omega t}\,dt = \int_0^y f(t)e^{-i\omega t}\,dt + \int_0^y \left[\int_0^t k(t-\tau)\psi[f_y(\tau),\tau]\,d\tau\right] e^{-i\omega t}\,dt$$

for $-\infty < \omega < \infty$, in which

68 $$f_y(t) = \begin{cases} f(t) & \text{for } 0 \leq t \leq y \\ 0 & \text{for } t > y \end{cases}$$

(In view of the Schwarz inequality and our assumptions concerning f and g, it is clear that the integrals exist.)

Let

69 $$G_y(i\omega) = \int_0^y g(t)e^{-i\omega t}\,dt \qquad -\infty < \omega < \infty$$

70 $$F_y(i\omega) = \int_0^y f(t)e^{-i\omega t}\,dt \qquad -\infty < \omega < \infty$$

71 $$h_y(t) = \psi[f_y(t),t] \qquad t \geq 0$$

72 $$H_y(i\omega) = \int_0^y h_y(t)e^{-i\omega t}\,dt \qquad -\infty < \omega < \infty$$

Then, from *67*

73 $$G_y(i\omega) = F_y(i\omega) + K(i\omega)H_y(i\omega) - X(i\omega) \qquad -\infty < \omega < \infty$$

in which

74 $$X(i\omega) = \int_y^\infty \left[\int_0^t k(t-\tau)\psi[f_y(\tau),\tau]\,d\tau\right] e^{-i\omega t}\,dt$$

Equation *73* implies that

75 $$\begin{aligned} F_y(i\omega) &- [1 + \tfrac{1}{2}(\alpha+\beta)K(i\omega)]^{-1}X(i\omega) \\ &= -K(i\omega)[1 + \tfrac{1}{2}(\alpha+\beta)K(i\omega)]^{-1}[H_y(i\omega) - \tfrac{1}{2}(\alpha+\beta)F_y(i\omega)] \\ &\quad + [1 + \tfrac{1}{2}(\alpha+\beta)K(i\omega)]^{-1}G_y(i\omega) \qquad -\infty < \omega < \infty \end{aligned}$$

Since, by assumption, $|k(\cdot)|$ is integrable on $(0,\infty)$ and

$$1 + \tfrac{1}{2}(\alpha+\beta)K(s) \neq 0$$

for $\sigma \geq 0$, there exists (see Paley and Wiener [35]) a function $w(\cdot)$ such that

76 $$\int_0^\infty |w(t)|\,dt < \infty$$

[1] This proof is given in Ref. 34.

and

77 $$\tfrac{1}{2}(\alpha+\beta)K(i\omega)[1+\tfrac{1}{2}(\alpha+\beta)K(i\omega)]^{-1} = \int_0^\infty w(t)e^{-i\omega t}\,dt \qquad -\infty<\omega<\infty$$

It follows that

78 $$[1+\tfrac{1}{2}(\alpha+\beta)K(i\omega)]^{-1}X(i\omega)$$

is the Fourier transform of the square-integrable function $\hat{f}_y(t)$ defined by

79 $$\hat{f}_y(t) = \begin{cases} 0 & t\in(-\infty,y) \\ u(t) - \int_y^t w(t-\tau)u(\tau)\,d\tau & t\in[y,\infty) \end{cases}$$

in which

80 $$u(t) = \int_0^t k(t-\tau)\psi[f_y(\tau),\tau]\,d\tau \qquad t\in[y,\infty)$$

(The square-integrability of $\hat{f}_y$ can be established with the aid of the Schwarz inequality.) We now exploit the fact that $\hat{f}_y(t)$ vanishes for $t<y$.

Using Parseval's identity, *75*, and Minkowski's inequality, we obtain

81 $$\left(\int_0^y |f_y(t)|^2\,dt\right)^{\frac{1}{2}} \le \left(\int_0^\infty |f_y(t)-\hat{f}_y(t)|^2\right)^{\frac{1}{2}}$$
$$\le (2\pi)^{-\frac{1}{2}}\left(\int_{-\infty}^{\infty} |K(i\omega)[1+\tfrac{1}{2}(\alpha+\beta)K(i\omega)]^{-1}[H_y(i\omega) - \tfrac{1}{2}(\alpha+\beta)F_y(i\omega)]|^2\,d\omega\right)^{\frac{1}{2}}$$
$$+ (2\pi)^{-\frac{1}{2}}\left(\int_{-\infty}^{\infty} |[1+\tfrac{1}{2}(\alpha+\beta)K(i\omega)]^{-1}G_y(i\omega)|^2\,d\omega\right)^{\frac{1}{2}}$$

Thus,

82 $$\left(\int_0^y |f_y(t)|^2\,dt\right)^{\frac{1}{2}} \le \sup_\omega |K(i\omega)[1+\tfrac{1}{2}(\alpha+\beta)K(i\omega)]^{-1}|$$
$$(2\pi)^{-\frac{1}{2}}\left(\int_{-\infty}^{\infty} |H_y(i\omega) - \tfrac{1}{2}(\alpha+\beta)F_y(i\omega)|^2\,d\omega\right)^{\frac{1}{2}}$$
$$+ \sup_\omega |[1+\tfrac{1}{2}(\alpha+\beta)K(i\omega)]^{-1}| \left(\int_0^\infty |g(t)|^2\,dt\right)$$

However, since $|x^{-1}\psi(x,t) - \tfrac{1}{2}(\alpha+\beta)| \le \tfrac{1}{2}(\beta-\alpha)$ for all real $x\ne 0$ and $t\ge 0$, we have

83 $$\left(\int_{-\infty}^{\infty} |H_y(i\omega) - \tfrac{1}{2}(\alpha+\beta)F_y(i\omega)|^2\,d\omega\right)^{\frac{1}{2}}$$
$$= (2\pi)^{\frac{1}{2}}\left(\int_0^y |\psi[f_y(t),t] - \tfrac{1}{2}(\alpha+\beta)f_y(t)|^2\,dt\right)^{\frac{1}{2}}$$

84 $$\le \tfrac{1}{2}(\beta-\alpha)(2\pi)^{\frac{1}{2}}\left(\int_0^y |f_y(t)|^2\,dt\right)^{\frac{1}{2}}$$

It follows that

85 $$\left(\int_0^y |f_y(t)|^2\,dt\right)^{\frac{1}{2}} \le (1 - r)^{-1} \sup_{\omega} |[1 + \tfrac{1}{2}(\alpha + \beta)K(i\omega)]^{-1}| \left(\int_0^\infty |g(t)|^2\,dt\right)^{\frac{1}{2}}$$

in which

86 $$r = \tfrac{1}{2}(\beta - \alpha) \sup_{-\infty<\omega<\infty} |K(i\omega)[1 + \tfrac{1}{2}(\alpha + \beta)K(i\omega)]^{-1}|$$

The continuity of $K(i\omega)$, the fact that it approaches zero as $|\omega| \to \infty$, and our assumption that $[1 + \frac{1}{2}(\alpha + \beta)K(i\omega)] \neq 0$ for all ω imply that

87 $$q = \sup_{\omega} |[1 + \tfrac{1}{2}(\alpha + \beta)K(i\omega)]^{-1}| < \infty$$

Thus, since *85* is valid for all $y > 0$, it follows that

88 $$\int_0^\infty |f(t)|^2\,dt < \infty$$

and, with $\rho = q(1 - r)^{-1}$,

89 $$\left(\int_0^\infty |f(t)|^2\,dt\right)^{\frac{1}{2}} \le \rho \left(\int_0^\infty |g(t)|^2\,dt\right)^{\frac{1}{2}}$$

This completes the proof of Theorem *11* for $N = 1$.

7 *Final remarks*

The results we have discussed are illustrative of various efforts in the direction of building an analytical theory for nonlinear systems which will eventually be of value in connection with a wide variety of engineering problems. Relative to our understanding of the mathematical properties of nonlinear systems as of a few years ago, a good deal of progress has been made. The true nature of this progress is not adequately characterized by the results that have been obtained; it lies in the fact that approaches and techniques have been developed which have permitted the analyst to come to grips with a class of nonlinear problems which, until recently, appeared to be almost impenetrable.

REFERENCES

1 LaSalle, J., and S. Lefschetz: "Stability by Liapunov's Direct Method," Academic, New York, 1961.
2 Hahn, W.: "Theory and Application of Liapunov's Direct Method," Prentice-Hall, Englewood Cliffs, N.J., 1963.
3 Kalman, R. E., and J. E. Bertram: Control System Design via the Second

Method of Liapunov, Part I, Continuous-time Systems, *ASME J. of Basic Eng.*, vol. 82, p. 371, 1960.
4 Aizerman, M. A., and F. R. Gantmacher: "Absolute Stability of Regulator Systems," Holden-Day, San Francisco, 1964.
5 Tricomi, F. G.: "Integral Equations," p. 42, Interscience, New York, 1957.
6 Sandberg, I. W.: A Frequency-domain Condition for the Stability of Feedback Systems Containing a Single Time-varying Nonlinear Element; On the $\mathcal{L}_2$-boundedness of Solutions of Nonlinear Functional Equations, *Bell System Tech. J.*, vol. 43, pp. 1601–1608 and 1581–1600, 1964.
7 Sandberg, I. W.: Some Results on the Theory of Physical Systems Governed by Nonlinear Functional Equations, *Bell System Tech. J.*, vol. 44, p. 871, 1965.
8 Sandberg, I. W.: On the Stability of Solutions of Linear Differential Equations with Periodic Coefficients, *SIAM J.*, vol. 12, p. 487, 1964.
9 Bongiorno, J. J., Jr.: An Extension of the Nyquist-Barkhausen Stability Criterion to Linear Lumped-parameter Systems with Time-varying Elements, *IEEE Trans. Automatic Control*, vol. AC-8, p. 166, 1963.
10 Bongiorno, J. J., Jr.: Real-frequency Stability Criteria for Linear Time-varying Systems, *Proc. IEEE*, vol. 52, p. 832, 1964.
11 Narendra, K. S., and R. M. Goldwyn: A Geometrical Criterion for the Stability of Certain Nonlinear Nonautonomous Systems, *IEEE Trans. Circuit Theory*, vol. CT-11, p. 406, 1964.
12 Naumov, B. N., and Y. Z. Tsypkin: Frequency Criterion for Absolute Process Stability in Nonlinear Automatic Control Systems, *Automation and Remote Control*, vol. 25, p. 765, 1965.
13 Kudrewicz, J.: Stability of Nonlinear Feedback Systems, *Automation and Remote Control*, vol. 25, p. 1145, 1965.
14 Zames, G.: On the Stability of Nonlinear, Time-varying Feedback Systems, *Proc. Nat. Electronics Conf.*, p. 725, 1964.
15 Yacubovich, V. A.: The Matrix-inequality Method in the Theory of Stability of Nonlinear Control Systems: I. The Absolute Stability of Forced Vibrations, *Automation and Remote Control*, vol. 25, p. 905, 1965.
16 Desoer, C. A.: A Generalization of the Popov Criterion, *IEEE Trans. Automatic Control*, vol. AC-10, p. 182, 1965.
17 Sandberg, I. W.: Some Stability Results Related to Those of V. M. Popov, *Bell System Tech. J.*, vol. 44, p. 2133, 1965.
18 Brockett, R. W.: The Status of Stability Theory for Deterministic Systems, *IEEE Intern. Conv. Record*, vol. 6, 1966.
19 Kantorovich, L. V., and V. I. Krylov: "Approximate Methods of Higher Analysis," Interscience, New York, 1958.
20 Bass, R. W.: Mathematical Legitimacy of Equivalent Linearization by Describing Functions, in J. F. Coates (ed.) "Automation and Remote Control," p. 895, Butterworth, London, 1961.
21 Sandberg, I. W.: On Truncation Techniques in the Approximate Analysis of Periodically Time-varying Nonlinear Networks, *IEEE Trans. Circuit Theory*, vol. CT-11, p. 195, 1964.
22 Anselone, P. M. (ed.): "Nonlinear Integral Equations," University Press, Madison, Wis., 1964.
23 Minty, G. J.: Monotone Operators and Certain Systems of Ordinary Differential Equations, *Proc. Symp. System Theory*, vol. 15, p. 39, Polytechnic Institute of Brooklyn, N.Y., 1965.
24 Sandberg, I. W.: Signal Distortion in Nonlinear Feedback Systems, *Bell System Tech. J.*, vol. 42, p. 2533, 1963.

25 Desoer, C. A.: Nonlinear Distortion in Feedback Systems, *IRE Trans. Circuit Theory,* vol. CT-9, p. 6, 1962.

26 Bode, H. W.: "Network Analysis and Feedback Amplifier Design," Van Nostrand, Princeton, N.J., 1945.

27 Landau, H. J., and W. L. Miranker: The Recovery of Distorted Band-limited Signals, *J. Math. Anal. Appl.,* vol. 2, p. 97, 1961.

28 Sandberg, I. W.: On the Properties of Some Systems That Distort Signals—I, *Bell System Tech. J.*, vol. 42, p. 2033, 1963.

29 Katzenelson, J., and L. Seitelman: An Iterative Method for Solution of Nonlinear Resistive Networks, *Proc. Third Ann. Allerton Conf. on Circuit and System Theory, Univ. of Illinois, Urbana, Illinois,* 1965, p. 647.

30 Sandberg, I. W.: On the Properties of Some Systems That Distort Signals—II, *Bell System Tech. J.*, vol. 43, p. 91, 1964.

31 Youla, D. C., L. J. Castriota, and H. J. Carlin: Bounded Real Scattering Matrices and the Foundations of Linear Passive Network Theory, *IRE Trans., Circuit Theory,* vol. CT-6, 1959.

32 Sandberg, I. W.: Conditions for the Causality of Nonlinear Operators Defined on a Function Space, *Quart. Appl. Math.,* vol. 23, p. 87, 1965.

33 Sandberg, I. W.: An Observation Concerning the Application of the Contraction-mapping Fixed-point Theorem, and a Result Concerning the Norm-boundedness of Solutions of Nonlinear Functional Equations, *Bell System Tech. J.*, vol. 44, p. 1809, 1965.

34 Sandberg, I. W.: Frequency-domain Criteria for the Stability of Nonlinear Feedback Systems, *Proc. Nat. Electronics Conf.,* 1964, p. 737.

35 Paley, R. E., and N. Wiener: "Fourier Transforms in the Complex Domain," p. 62, American Mathematical Society, Providence, R.I., 1934.

9

Stability theory

A. M. Letov

Institute of Automatics and Telemechanics
Moscow

In lieu of a historical survey

Alexander Mikhailovich Liapunov's famous doctoral dissertation, "On the General Problem of Stability of Motion" [1], was published for the first time in 1892 by the Kharkov Mathematical Society. This dissertation contained the fundamental concept of perturbed-unperturbed motion as well as methods for solving the problem of stability of motion. Among these methods, the so-called *direct method* has acquired particular importance at the present time because of its extreme generality.

For some 50 years the direct method found no practical applications. The arbitrariness in the choice of Liapunov functions, as well as a prevalent inability to construct such functions, was found to be extremely discouraging. The founder of the Kazan School of Liapunov stability theory, Nikolai Gur'evitch Chetaev [2], was mainly responsible for overcoming this feeling of discouragement and the accompanying static period. He was the first one to show the effectiveness of the direct method for the solution both of purely theoretical problems and applied problems.

N. G. Chetaev produced a series of magnificent examples for which he constructed Liapunov functions. The methods of Liapunov have further been significantly developed in the Union of Soviet Socialist Republics in a number of papers published by Soviet scientists and scholars. Their contribution, in its most substantial aspects, can be found in the monographs [2–6].

Over a period of many years, there has been little interest in the stability problem outside the Soviet Union. However, in recent years, an increasing concern with the stability problem has arisen in a number of countries (the United States, Mexico, Japan, Germany, Czechoslovakia, Italy, etc.), and many interesting results have since been published in these countries [7–10].[1]

Although Liapunov himself for the most part studied local stability in special cases, his definition of the concept of stability encompasses the problem in a substantially broader sense. In connection with this, a substantial contribution to the direct method was made by E. A. Barbashin and N. N. Krassovskii [3], who extended the direct method to the stability problem in the wider sense.

The direct method was first applied to a control problem in a technical note published by A. I. Lur'e and V. N. Postnikov [11] and was further discussed in the light of control theory in A. I. Lur'e's book [12]. The original idea for constructing Liapunov functions, presented in Refs. 11 and 12, was substantially explored and extended in a number of papers by other scientists in the field. Other forms of Liapunov functions have been found, and the classes of systems for which these functions solve the stability problem have been extended. It has also been shown that it is possible to obtain effective bounds on the transient processes of regulator systems, thus solving the problem of transient process quality [6, 8–10, 12–22].

Finally, quite recently, a connection has been established between the direct method of Liapunov and Bellman's dynamic programming method [23, 31, 33]. This has made it possible to solve the synthesis problem of optimal regulators. As a result, many quantitative aspects of the theory of stability of motion have been clarified.

One may now boldly assert that the classical theory of regulator systems, as an exact science, can be constructed on the basis of Liapunov's single concept of perturbed-unperturbed motion, his direct method, and Bellman's dynamic programming method.

This chapter presents an effort at summing up the various methods for constructing Liapunov functions and their utilization in the solution of three major problems in regulator theory: stability, transient process quality, and synthesis of regulator systems.

1 *The concept of perturbed-unperturbed motion* [1–6]

Let us assume that the differential equation

1 $$\dot{z} = Z(z,u,t)$$

[1] We do not refer to numerous other interesting papers which were written by outstanding scientists in the indicated countries. However, the reader will find a more extensive bibliography in Ref. 10.

represents the mathematical model of the plant to be controlled. Here $z = (z_1, \ldots, z_n)$ is the state vector of the plant, u is the controller output, and $t \in [t_0, T]$ or $t \in [t_0, \infty)$, $Z = (Z_1, \ldots, Z_n)$ is the vector of the generalized forces acting on the plant.

Equation *1* is a vector representation of the physical law governing the behavior of the plant. The properties of this law are either exactly or approximately reflected by the character of the function Z. The function $Z(z,u,t)$ is defined in a closed or open region $N(z,u) \geq 0$ of the variables z and u, in which the validity of the physical law applies.

We shall assume that the control $u(t)$ belongs to a given class of functions U and that *1* is such that for any $u(t) \in U$ it has a unique solution.

Suppose we choose some control $u^*(t) \in U$ and an initial state of the plant z_0^*. To these corresponds the solution

2 $$z = z^*(t, u^*(t), z_0^*)$$
$$u = u^*(t)$$

The motion of *2* will be called the *unperturbed motion.* Any other motion, corresponding to any $z_0 \neq z_0^*$, will be called a *perturbed motion,* and the differences $z - z^* = y$ and $u - u^* = \zeta$ will be called *perturbations.* These satisfy the equations

3 $$\dot{y} = Y(y, \zeta, t)$$

4 $$Y = Z(z^* + y,\ u^* + \zeta,\ t) - \dot{z}^*$$

The above equations are called the *equations of perturbed motion.*

We now add to the equations of the plant *3* the equations of the controller. The controller consists of a single programmable element which realizes the control $u^*(t)$, and a regulator which describes an appropriate differential equation

5 $$F(\cdots \dot{\zeta}, \zeta, y, t) = 0$$

(or a system of equations). Equation *5* has the property that when $y = 0$, $\zeta = 0$, $\dot{\zeta} = 0, \ldots, F(0,0,0,t) \equiv 0$.

We now define a vector x with components $y_1, \ldots, y_n, \zeta_1, \dot{\zeta}, \ldots$. Combining Eqs. *3* and *5*, we obtain the equations of perturbed motion for the closed-loop system in the Cauchy normal form; thus

6 $$\dot{x} = X(x,t)$$

Here $x \in N$, and N may be the entire space.

If *2* is an exact solution of Eq. *1*, then the function $X(x,t)$ always has the property

7 $$X(0,t) \equiv 0$$

This means that the function

8 $$x^* = 0$$

is a particular solution of Eq. *6*. Also, it happens to be an *unperturbed motion*.

We formulate the problem of its stability with the assumption that $t \in [t_0, \infty)$. As a result of a one-to-one correspondence, the latter signifies that if the motion of *8* is stable, then the unperturbed motion of *2* will also be stable.

9 **Definition** The unperturbed motion of *8* is said to be stable in the Liapunov sense if, for any arbitrary given number $A > 0$, no matter how small, there exists a number $\lambda(A) > 0$ such that if the inequality

10 $$\|x_0\|^2 \leq \lambda(A)$$

holds, then so does the inequality

11 $$\|x(t)\|^2 < A$$

for any $t > t_0$. If this is not the case, the unperturbed motion is unstable. If, in addition to the inequalities of *10* and *11*, the equality

12 $$\lim_{t \to \infty} \|x(t)\|^2 = 0$$

is also satisfied, then the unperturbed motion is asymptotically stable.

This definition has been the object of much study by mathematicians who would like to extend it to include more general forms of motion, including stability in the presence of constantly acting disturbances, stability of invariant sets (in particular the work of T. Yoshizava), "eventual stability" which was proposed by LaSalle, stability on a finite time interval, etc. None of these extensions of the concept of stability, nor the extensions of the Liapunov methods which go with them, fall into the framework of this chapter. The reader may get some idea of their nature from the monographs [1–10].

2 *The main theorems of the direct method of Liapunov*

The main theorems are based on the properties of one large class of scalar-valued functions V of the variables x and t, which will now be defined.

1 1. The function $V(x)$ is said to be *positive-definite* if

$$V(x) = 0 \text{ only for } x = 0$$
$$V(x) > 0 \text{ everywhere in } N \text{ for all } x \neq 0$$

Example: $V_1(x) = x_1^2 + x_2^2$ $(n = 2)$.

2. The function $V(x)$ is called *positive-semidefinite* if it is nonnegative in N.

Example: $V_2(x) = (x_1 + x_2)^2$.

3. The function $V(x,t)$ is said to be *positive-definite* if there exists a function $W^*(x)$ satisfying the conditions of definition 1 and such that the inequality

2 $$V(x,t) \geq W^*(x) > 0$$

is satisfied for all $x \in N$ and $t \geq t_0$.

Example: $V_3(x) = (1 + e^{-\alpha t})V_1(x)$, $\alpha > 0$, $W^*(x) = V_1(x)$.

4. A function $V(x,t)$ is said to have a *least upper bound* if there exists a function $W_*(x)$ satisfying the conditions of definition 1 and such that the inequality

3 $$0 < V(x,t) \leq W_*(x)$$

is satisfied for all $x \in N$ and $t \geq t_0$.

Example: $V_4 = V_3(x)$, $\alpha > 0$, $W_*(x) = 2V_1(x)$.

Negative-definite functions $V(x,t)$ or negative-semidefinite functions $V(x,t)$ are defined analogously. Positive-definite functions $V(x)$ have the property that the equation

4 $$V(x) = C \qquad C > 0$$

defines a C-parametric family of closed surfaces enclosing the point of *9.1.8*, provided that the constant C is sufficiently small.

For the enclosure property to be preserved for any value of C, it is *necessary and sufficient* [3] that the function $V(x)$ have the property

5 $$V(x) \to \infty \qquad \text{for } \|x\|^2 \to \infty$$

For example, the function

$$V(x) = x_1^2 + \frac{x_2^2}{1 + x_2^2}$$

does not have this property; when $C \geq 1$, the surface is no longer closed [13].

If, however, V depends explicitly on t, then the inequalities of *2* and *3* bound the variations of the surface $V(x,t) = C$ both from the outside and the inside. This means that the surface $V(x,t) = C$ will lie in the region enclosed between the surfaces $W^*(x) = C$ and $W_*(x) = C$.

When C decreases to zero, the surfaces $V(x,t) = C$ contract. Indeed, they contract to the origin O with the surface $W^*(x) = C$.

Positive-definite functions $V(x,t)$ have the property that the surfaces $V(x,t) = C$ intersect all paths leading from the origin into the outer space, and vice versa.

From now on we shall limit ourselves to the discussion of only such positive-definite, continuous, functions $V(x,t)$ which are differentiable in all their arguments and have the property of *5*. Then the Liapunov theorems take on the form in which they were cast by E. A. Barbashin and N. N. Krassovskii [3]. Together with $V(x,t)$ we shall consider

6
$$\dot{V} = (\text{grad } V) \cdot X(x,t) + \frac{\partial V}{\partial t}$$

computed along trajectories of the system of *9.1.6*.

7 **Theorem** If the differential equations of *9.1.6* of perturbed motion are such that it is possible to find a positive-definite function $V(x,t) > 0$, whose derivative of *6*, computed by means of these equations, is either a negative-semidefinite function or is identically zero, then the unperturbed motion of *9.1.8* is stable.

Proof We shall give a simple proof of the theorem for the case in which the system of *9.1.6* is time-invariant and the function V does not depend explicitly on t.

Consider the vector $X(x,t)$. It defines the velocity of the state along a trajectory of the system of *9.1.6*. Then the expression

$$\dot{V} = (\text{grad } V) \cdot X$$

is the length of the projection of the velocity X onto the outward normal of the surface of *4*.

By assumption, $\dot{V}$ is either negative or zero; consequently, the trajectories of the system either intersect the surfaces of *4* from outside in an inward direction, or else they lie in these surfaces.

In either event, for any given $A > 0$, it is always possible to choose a $\delta(A) \leq C < A$ such that if the inequality of *9.1.10* is satisfied and $\dot{V} \leq 0$ by assumption (that is, a trajectory of the system can leave the surface of *4*) only in a direction corresponding to a decreasing C, then the inequality of *9.1.11* is also satisfied for any $t > t_0$. This completes the proof of the theorem.

The following theorem is also true.

8 **Theorem** If the differential equations *9.1.6* of the perturbed motion are such that it is possible to find a positive-definite function $V(x,t)$ whose derivative *4* computed by means of *9.1.6* is negative-definite, then the unperturbed motion of *9.1.8* is asymptotically stable.

Proof The proof of this theorem becomes obvious as soon as we realize that since $\dot{V}$ becomes zero only at the origin, no trajectory of the system will have trajectory arcs located on the surfaces of *4*. All the trajectories will intersect these surfaces in an inward direction.

Since it is possible to choose the number A arbitrarily small, it is possible to follow this inward motion of a trajectory almost to the instant when it arrives at the point of *9.1.8*. Hence the conclusion about asymptotic stability follows.

The reader may now try to obtain an equally simple geometric proof of the Liapunov theorem for the time-varying case.

9 The functions $V(x,t)$ used in solving the stability problem are called *Liapunov* functions.[1]

10 **Remark 1** Let us assume that $\dot{V} = U(x,t)$ and that $U(x,t)$ is a negative-semidefinite function. Then the first theorem also guarantees asymptotic stability of the unperturbed motion of *9.1.8*, provided that the surface $U(x,t) = 0$ does not contain an entire trajectory.

11 **Remark 2** If the system of *9.1.6* is defined only for $t \in [t_0,T]$, then the inequalities of *9.1.10* and *9.1.11* can always be satisfied because of the theorem on the continuous dependence of the solutions of the equations of *9.1.6* on x_0. Hence, in such cases, it would be better to think in terms of bounds for the solutions $x(t,x_0)$.

However, after transforming time to the new variable

$$\tau = \frac{T}{T - t}$$

and using the fact that $d/dt = (\tau^2/T)(d/d\tau)$, it becomes possible, at least formally, in this case also to talk of stability, since $\tau \in [\tau_0, \infty)$. As a matter of fact the formally stable solution of *9.1.8* there corresponds to either a nonincrease or a monotonic decrease of a positive-definite function $V(x,t)$, such that for any given number A, no matter how small, one can always find a number $\lambda(A) = A$, such that if the equation

12 $$V(x_0,t_0) = \lambda$$

is satisfied, then the inequality

13 $$V(x,t) \leq A$$

[1] For a treatment of the existence of such functions, see Refs. 3 to 6.

is also satisfied for any $t \in [t_0,T]$. The conditions of *11* and *12* allow us to obtain suitable bounds for the function $V(x,t)$ (see for example Sec. *15*) and, consequently, also for $x(t)$.

3 Perturbed motion equations for regulator systems

The remainder of this chapter will be devoted to discussing the various methods for constructing Liapunov functions for systems of the form

1
$$\dot{y} = By + hf(\sigma)$$
$$\sigma = p'y$$

Here $B = \|b_{k\alpha}\|$ is an $n \times n$ matrix, h is a vector, and p is a vector.† The elements of the matrix B and vector h are either given constants or given functions of time, determined by the unperturbed behavior of *9.1.2*; the elements of the vector p are the adjustable parameters of the controller.

The function $f(\sigma)$ is bounded; it is almost everywhere continuous and differentiable with respect to σ. It has the properties

2
$$f(\sigma) = 0 \qquad \text{for } |\sigma| \le \sigma_*$$
$$\sigma f(\sigma) > 0 \qquad \text{for } |\sigma| > \sigma_*$$
$$\int_0^\sigma f(\sigma)\, d\sigma \to \infty \qquad \text{for } |\sigma| \to \infty$$

Here σ_* is a fixed nonnegative number[1] which characterizes the dead zone of the controller with respect to σ. Either the function $f(\sigma)$ or its derivative $df/d\sigma$ may be discontinuous for $\sigma = \pm\sigma_*$. Such functions, for the sake of brevity, will be called class A functions (Fig. *9.3.1*).

† If p is a vector (column vector), p' is a transpose vector or row vector p' $\{p_1, p_2, \ldots, p_n\}$.

[1] For simplicity it is better to put $\sigma_* = 0$.

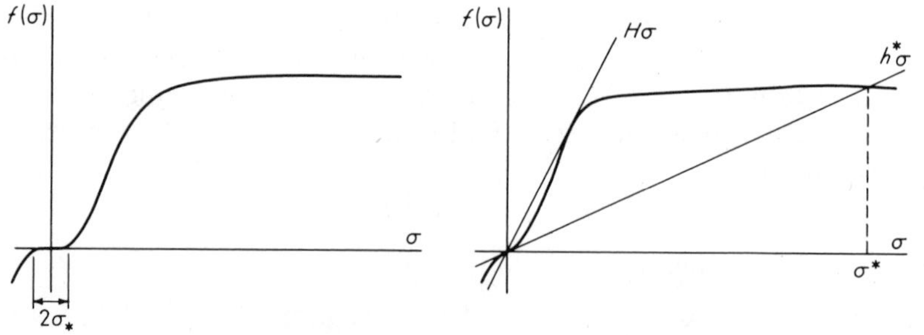

Fig. 9.3.1 Class A and class A′ curves.

The characteristics of linear servomotors are class A functions.

Whenever we discuss the stability of systems which are open-loop unstable, we shall require, in addition to *2*, that

3 $$\sigma_* = 0, \left[\frac{df}{d\sigma}\right]_{\sigma=0} \geq h^* > 0$$

be satisfied, where h^* is some constant.

We shall say that such functions form a subclass A' of the functions in the class A. We introduce this subclass to single out those servomotors which have a sufficiently fast response time with respect to changes in the variable σ. As an example, we might point out a servomotor that has relay-type characteristics.

The variable σ is the mathematical description of the control law.

4 *Formulation of the absolute stability problem*

We assume that B is a nonsingular matrix. Then, the equation

1 $$By + hf(\sigma) = 0$$

has the solution

2 $$y = -B^{-1}hf(\sigma)$$

and the number of singular points of the system of *9.3.1* depends on the number of roots of the equation

3 $$\sigma = p'(-B^{-1}h)f(\sigma)$$

In a system which has been intelligently designed [13], we expect to find that

4 $$p'(-B^{-1}h) \leq 0$$

In this case, Eq. *3* has the single root $\sigma = 0$, while Eq. *2* has the unique solution

5 $$y^* = 0$$

If, however, the inequality of *4* is not satisfied, then Eq. *3* has several solutions, including some which are not zero. As a result, the system of *9.3.1* will have several singular points, and the formulation of the absolute stability problem ceases to make sense.

From now on, we assume that the condition of *4* is satisfied. Furthermore, we assume that the system of *9.3.1* is completely controllable [23, 24].

6 *The problem now consists in finding a nonempty set S of the parameters*

of the controller, p, such that the system of 9.3.1 is stable for any $p \in S$, any $y \in N$, and any $f(\sigma) \in A$ or $f(\sigma) \in A'$. We shall call stability of this kind absolute stability.

5 *The canonical transformation*

The canonical transformation facilitates the construction of Liapunov functions. Let us consider time-invariant systems. The equation

1 $$D(\lambda) = |B - \lambda I| = 0$$

defines the eigenvalues λ_k of the matrix B, which we assume to be all nonzero. Equation *9.3.1* is then said to describe a system of *direct control*. For the sake of simplicity, we further assume that all the λ_k are distinct, that $\lambda_1, \ldots, \lambda_s$ form complex-conjugate pairs, that $\lambda_{s+1}, \ldots, \lambda_n$ are real numbers, and that

2 $$\operatorname{Re} \lambda_k < 0 \qquad k = 1, \ldots, n$$

We now transform from y_k to the new variables [12]; thus

3 $$x_k = \frac{1}{H_m(\lambda_k)} \sum D_{\alpha m}(\lambda_k) y_\alpha \qquad k = 1, 2, \ldots, n$$

Here $D_{\alpha m}$ are the minors of the determinant $D(\lambda)$, and the numbers H_j are defined by the equations

4 $$H_j(\lambda) = \Sigma h_k D_{kj}(\lambda) \qquad j = 1, \ldots, n$$

The index m is chosen from the set $1, \ldots, n$ in such a way that $H_m(\lambda_k) \neq 0$ $(k = 1, \ldots, n)$. When the λ_k are distinct, the transformation *3* is nonsingular, and

5 $$y_k = -\sum \frac{H_k(\lambda_\alpha)}{D'(\lambda_\alpha)} x_\alpha \qquad D' = \frac{dD}{d\lambda}$$

In terms of the new variables $x_1, \ldots, x_n$, the equations of perturbed motion acquire the canonical form

6 $$\dot{x} = \lambda x + e f(\sigma)$$
$$\sigma = p' x$$

Here $\lambda = \operatorname{diag}(\lambda_1, \ldots, \lambda_n)$ is a matrix, e is a vector whose elements are all 1, and γ is a vector whose elements are

7 $$\gamma_k = -\sum p_j \frac{H_j(\lambda_k)}{D'(\lambda_k)} \qquad k = 1, \ldots, n$$

Clearly, the variables $x_1, \ldots, x_s$ and the constants $\gamma_1, \ldots, \gamma_s$ form complex-conjugate pairs, whereas $x_{s+1}, \ldots, x_n$ and $\gamma_{s+1}, \ldots, \gamma_n$ are real quantities.

We shall later need an expression for $\dot{\sigma}$. As can be seen from *6*,

8 $$\dot{\sigma} = \beta' x - \tau f(\sigma)$$

where $\beta = (\beta_1, \ldots, \beta_n)$ is a vector and

9 $$\beta_k = \lambda_k \gamma_k \qquad \tau = -\Sigma \gamma_\alpha \qquad k = 1, \ldots, n$$

We now consider a particular case of the above transformation when one of the λ_k defined by *1* and *2*, for example λ_n, is zero. It is then said that the equations of *9.3.1* describe a system of *indirect control*. Clearly, $\beta_n = 0$.

Two cases are possible. In the first case, one can express σ in terms of the canonical variables x and then use the equations of *6*. In the second case it is not possible to express σ in terms of the canonical variables [13]. It is then necessary to drop the equation for x_n and in its stead use Eq. *8*. The equations for the problem now become

10 $$\dot{x} = \Lambda x + ef(\sigma)$$
$$\dot{\sigma} = \beta' x - \tau f(\sigma)$$

where $\Lambda = \text{diag}\,(\lambda_1, \ldots, \lambda_m)$ is a matrix, $x = (x_1, \ldots, x_m)$ is a vector, e is a vector, $\beta = (\beta_1, \ldots, \beta_m)$ is a vector and $m = n - 1$.

Clearly if a system is open-loop unstable $[f(\sigma) \equiv 0]$, then it is impossible to stabilize it with any $f(\sigma) \in A$ [13].

Let $h^*\sigma$ be the linear part of $f(\sigma) \in A'$. We shall denote by $\pm\sigma^*$ the roots of the equation $f(\sigma) = h^*\sigma$. Then the function

$$\phi(\sigma) = f(\sigma) - h^*\sigma$$

belongs to the class A for $\sigma \in [-\sigma^*, +\sigma^*]$ (except perhaps for the last of the conditions of *9.3.2* which is not satisfied).

Let $\mu_1, \ldots, \mu_n$ be the eigenvalues of the matrix

$$\bar{B} = B + h^* h p' = \|\bar{b}_{k\alpha}\|$$

they are the roots of the equation

11 $$\bar{D}(\mu) = |\bar{B} - \mu I|$$

We now choose p so that the conditions

12 $$\text{Re}\, \mu_k < 0 \qquad k = 1, \ldots, n$$

are satisfied. Furthermore, we shall assume that $\mu_1, \ldots, \mu_s$ form complex-conjugate pairs and that $\mu_{s+1}, \ldots, \mu_n$ are real distinct numbers. Then the transformations *3* to *5* remain valid provided the elements of $\bar{D}(\mu)$ are substituted for the elements of $D(\lambda)$.

The canonical equations then acquire the form

13 $$\dot{x} = \mu x + e\phi(\sigma) \qquad \sigma = \bar{\gamma}x$$

Here $\mu = \text{diag}(\mu_1, \ldots, \mu_n)$ is a square matrix, e is a vector whose elements are unity, and the vector $\bar{\gamma}$ is defined by the equations

14 $$\bar{\gamma}_k = -\sum p_j \frac{H_j(\mu_k)}{\bar{D}'(\mu_k)}$$

Analogous to *8* we have

15 $$\dot{\sigma} = \bar{\beta}'x - \bar{\tau}\phi(\sigma)$$

16 $$\beta_k = \mu_k\bar{\gamma}_k \qquad \tau = -\Sigma\bar{\gamma}_k \qquad k = 1, \ldots, n$$

From now on, we shall always assume that the necessary inequalities

17 $$\Sigma\gamma_k \leq 0$$

18 $$\Sigma\bar{\gamma}_k \leq 0$$

are satisfied. These ensure the nonnegativity of τ and $\bar{\tau}$.

6 *Stability of systems of direct control: the method of resolving equations* [13, 16, 25]

Let us return to the equations of *9.5.6* and consider a constant vector a, whose components $a_1, \ldots, a_s$ are arbitrary complex-conjugate pairs and whose components $a_{s+1}, \ldots, a_n$ are real nonzero numbers. The vector a will be called a *completely nonzero vector*. We now form the matrix

1 $$A = \left\| \frac{a_k a_j}{\rho_k + \rho_j} \right\| \qquad \rho_k = -\lambda_k$$

and associate with it the quadratic form

2 $$V = x'Ax$$

If all the ρ_k are distinct, then

$$V = \int_0^\sigma \left[\sum a_k x_k e^{-\rho_k \tau}\right]^2 d\tau$$

The form V is positive-definite for any completely nonzero vector a.

We now form the function

3 $$V = x'Ax + \int_0^{\sigma} f(\xi)\, d\xi$$

Usually, in order to be able to decide as to the asymptotic stability of systems of indirect control, one adds to the right-hand side of *3* a positive-definite function $\Phi(x)$ [12, 13, 16]. Further on it will be shown that, generally speaking, there is no need to do it for systems of direct control.

Computing the derivative *9.5.6*, we obtain

4 $$\dot{V} = [\lambda x + ef(\sigma)]'Ax + x'A[\lambda x + ef(\sigma)] + f(\sigma)[\beta' x - \tau f(\sigma)]$$

Let us now take the identity

5 $$0 = 2\sqrt{\tau}\, f(\sigma)[a'x - a'x]$$

and add it term by term to *4*.

If there exists a completely nonzero vector a, satisfying the equations

6 $$\beta_k + 2\sqrt{\tau}\, a_k + 2a_k \sum \frac{a_j}{\rho_k + \rho_j} = 0 \qquad k = 1, \ldots, n$$

then

7 $$\dot{V} = -[a'x + \sqrt{\tau}\, f(\sigma)]^2$$

is a negative-semidefinite function. Thus, absolute stability is ensured if *6* is satisfied.

We may now formulate this result in the form of the following theorem.

8 **Theorem** The state of a system of direct control corresponding to the solution *9.4.5* is absolutely stable if there exists a nonempty set S of the parameters p of the controller, such that one can find in this set a completely nonzero vector a which is also a solution of *6*.

7 *On the solvability of the equations of 9.6.6*

In solving an applied problem there is really no need to search for a vector a. It is sufficient to find criteria for the existence of solutions of the equations of *9.6.6* which define a completely nonzero vector a.

Such a criterion has not been found for the general case. Nevertheless it is possible to indicate certain necessary conditions for the solvability of the equations of *9.6.6*.

Let us divide each one of the equations of *9.6.6* by ρ_k and add them term by term. We find that

1 $$\sum_{k=1}^{n} b_k = -\sqrt{\tau}$$

Here $a_k = \rho_k b_k$. We now substitute the expression for $\sqrt{\tau}$ from *1* in the equations of *9.6.6* and write them in the form

2 $$\frac{\beta_k}{{\rho_k}^2} = 2b_k \sum_{j=1}^{n} \frac{b_j}{\rho_k + \rho_j}$$

Adding the equations of *2* term by term, we find that a necessary condition for the solvability of the equations of *9.6.6* is

3 $$\sum_{k=1}^{n} \frac{\gamma_k}{\rho_k} < 0$$

This condition coincides exactly with the condition of *9.4.4*.

We now divide each of the equations of *2* by ρ_k and, after adding term by term, we obtain

4 $$\sum_{k=1}^{n} \frac{b_k}{\rho_k} = \pm D$$

Here D^2 denotes the number

5 $$D^2 = -\sum_{k=1}^{n} \frac{\gamma_k}{{\rho_k}^2}$$

which must be positive.

Multiplying *2* by ρ_k and adding term by term, we obtain *9.5.17*.

Thus, we have *three necessary conditions for the existence of a Liapunov function of the form of 9.6.3* for direct control as follows:

6 $$\sum_{k=1}^{n} \gamma_k < 0 \qquad \sum_{k=1}^{n} \frac{\gamma_k}{\rho_k} < 0 \qquad \sum_{k=1}^{n} \frac{\gamma_k}{{\rho_k}^2} < 0$$

In a number of cases of practical importance, the satisfaction of these inequalities is sufficient for the solution of the problem.

For example, for $n = 3$, Eqs. *1* and *4* are easily solved for b_1 and b_2, independently of the actual real or complex values of $\rho_1 \neq \rho_2$. Then the problem reduces to finding real solutions for the single quadratic equation

7 $$(\rho_3 - \rho_2)(\rho_1 - \rho_3)b_3^2 + 2\rho_3[\pm\rho_1\rho_2 D - \rho_3\sqrt{\tau}]b_3 + \gamma_3(\rho_2 + \rho_3)(\rho_3 + \rho_1) = 0$$

Such solutions must exist if

8 $$\Delta_3^2 = \rho_3^2[\pm\rho_1\rho_2 D - \rho_3\sqrt{\tau}]^2 - \gamma_3(\rho_3^2 - \rho_2^2)(\rho_1^2 - \rho_3^2) \geq 0$$

For $n = 4$, the equations are again solvable in general terms.

8 *Is this asymptotic stability?*

In practical applications, once absolute stability has been established, it is important to determine whether or not it is a case of asymptotic absolute stability.

Let us assume that there exists a nonempty controller parameter set S, in which there is a completely nonzero vector a satisfying the equations of *9.6.6*.

Then there exists a Liapunov function of the form of *9.6.3* whose derivative is determined by *9.6.7*. This derivative may become identically zero if there exists at least one entire trajectory which lies simultaneously in the surfaces

1 $$V = C \qquad C > 0$$

2 $$ax + \sqrt{\tau}f(\sigma) = 0$$

Such a trajectory must satisfy the equation

3 $$\dot{x}_k = -\rho_k x_k - \frac{1}{\sqrt{\tau}}\sum a_k x_k$$

Consequently, the question of asymptotic stability is solved by examining the solutions of the equation of *3* lying in the manifolds of *1* and *2*.

Therefore, whenever we can show that the characteristic polynomial has no pure imaginary roots, we know that there does not exist an entire trajectory lying in the above manifolds.

This characteristic polynomial has the form

4 $$D_n(\lambda) = \phi(\lambda) + \psi(\lambda)$$

Here

5 $$\phi = (\lambda + \rho_1) \cdots (\lambda + \rho_n)$$

$$\psi = \sum_{k=1}^{n} (\lambda + \rho_1) \cdots (\lambda + \rho_{k-1}) \frac{a_k}{\sqrt{\tau}} (\lambda + \rho_{k+1}) \cdots (\lambda + \rho_n)$$

Obviously, as a result of *9.7.1*, $D_n(0) = 0$ and also the equation $D_n(\lambda) = 0$ always has at least one zero root. If this is a simple root, then the solution which corresponds to it is $x^* = 0$.

Let us now address ourselves to the particular cases $n = 2$ and $n = 3$. The equations of *9.7.1* and *9.7.4* yield

6 $$D_2 = \lambda \left[\lambda \pm \frac{\rho_1 \rho_2}{\sqrt{\tau}} D \right] = 0$$

7 $$D_3 = \lambda \left[\lambda^2 \pm \frac{\Delta_3}{\rho_3 \sqrt{\tau}} \lambda \pm \frac{\rho_1 \rho_2 \rho_3}{\sqrt{\tau}} \cdot D \right] = 0$$

It is hence clear that both for $n = 2$ and for $n = 3$ (provided only that $\Delta_3 \neq 0$), any trajectory defined by Eq. *3* tends asymptotically either to zero or to ∞. It is true at least for the second-order system without additional conditions. This therefore is an indication [46, p. 26] that equation *9.6.6*, ". . . ineligible for solution of the problem stability of direct control," is not correct.

An examination of examples indicates that there exists a multitude of cases for which it is possible to construct a Liapunov function of the form of *9.6.3*, which guarantees absolute stability for the system.

There are various other methods for differentiating between asymptotic and nonasymptotic stability. However, it is not possible to discuss these in the scope of this chapter.

9 *The Bulgakov problem* [13]

As an illustrative example we shall consider the system

1 $$T^2 \ddot{\psi} + U \dot{\psi} + k\psi + \mu = 0$$

$$\dot{\mu} = -\mathcal{H}\mu + f^*(\sigma)$$

$$\sigma = a\psi + E\dot{\psi} + G^2 \ddot{\psi} - \frac{1}{e}\mu$$

With some assumptions, Eqs. *1* may be considered to be the equations for the roll stabilization of the ocean liner "Queen Mary" [26].

Let

2
$$\psi = y_1 \qquad \dot{\psi} = \sqrt{s}\, y_2 \qquad \mu = iy_3 \qquad t = \frac{\tau}{\sqrt{s}}$$

$$p = \frac{U}{T^2} \qquad q = \frac{k}{T^2} \qquad s = \frac{l}{T^2 + lG^2} \qquad i = sT^2$$

$$h_1 = h_2 = 0 \qquad h_3 = 1 \qquad b_{21} = \frac{-q}{s} \qquad b_{22} = \frac{-p}{\sqrt{s}}$$

$$b_{23} = -1 \qquad b_{33} = -\frac{\mathcal{K}}{\sqrt{s}} \qquad f(\sigma) = \frac{1}{i\sqrt{s}} f^*(\sigma)$$

$$p_1 = a - qG^2 \qquad p_2 = (E - pG^2)\sqrt{s} \qquad p_3 = -1$$

$$\rho_1 + \rho_2 = b_{22} \qquad \rho_1\rho_2 = -b_{21}$$

We may now rewrite the original equations in the normal form of *9.3.1*.
The transformation

3
$$x = \begin{bmatrix} \rho_1\rho_2 & \rho_1 & 1 \\ \rho_1\rho_2 & \rho_2 & 1 \\ 0 & 0 & 1 \end{bmatrix} \begin{bmatrix} y_1 \\ y_2 \\ y_3 \end{bmatrix}$$

now takes these equations into the canonical form of *9.5.6*, where

4
$$\gamma_1 = \frac{1}{\rho_1(\rho_2 - \rho_1)}(p_1 - \rho_1 p_2)$$

$$\gamma_2 = \frac{1}{\rho_2(\rho_2 - \rho_1)}(-p_1 + \rho_2 p_2)$$

$$\gamma_3 = -1 - \frac{p_1}{\rho_1\rho_2}$$

We now only have to show that the set S is nonempty. This is determined by means of the inequalities of *9.7.6* and *9.7.8*. It is easy to verify that the inequality *9.5.17* is trivially satisfied; the other two inequalities of *9.7.6* are

5
$$[\rho_3(\rho_1 + \rho_2) - \rho_1\rho_2]p_1 \leq \rho_1^2\rho_2^2 + \rho_1\rho_2\rho_3 p_2$$

6
$$[\rho_3^2(\rho_1^2 + \rho_2^2 + \rho_1\rho_2) - \rho_1^2\rho_2^2]p_1 \leq \rho_1^3\rho_2^3 + \rho_1\rho_2\rho_3^2(\rho_1 + \rho_2)p_2$$

By adjoining to these inequalities the inequality *9.7.3*, we find the region S which guarantees asymptotic absolute stability. The inequalities can obviously be satisfied by the parameters a, l, E, and G^2.

10 Method of resolving equations: the simplified variant

In the form $x'Ax$ a term containing, for example, x_n, may be absent. In that event the function of *9.6.3* does not cease to be positive-definite. Let us denote by $\bar{A}$ the matrix of *9.6.1* in which the elements $a_n a_j$ and $a_k a_n$ $(k,j = 1, \ldots, n)$ do not appear, and by $\bar{a} = (a_1, \ldots, a_{n-1}, 0)$ the completely nonzero vector. We now compute the derivative *9.2.5* in which the term $a_n x_n$ will no longer appear, but which will have the term $\beta_n x_n$. We eliminate $\beta_n x_n$ by making use of the equation

1 $$\beta_n x_n = -\rho_n \left(\sigma - \sum_{j=1}^{n-1} \gamma_j x_j\right)$$

We then add to the right-hand side of $\dot{V}$ the expression

2 $$2\sqrt{\tau}\, f(\sigma)[\bar{a}'x - \bar{a}'x]$$

which is identically zero. We obtain

3 $$\dot{V} = -[\bar{a}'x + \sqrt{\tau}\, f(\sigma)]^2 - \rho_n \sigma f(\sigma)$$

provided the components of the vector $\bar{a}$ satisfy the equations

4 $$\bar{\beta}_k = \beta_k + \rho_n \gamma_k$$

$$\bar{\beta}_k + 2\sqrt{\tau}\, a_k + 2a_k \sum_{j=1}^{n-1} \frac{a_j}{\rho_j} = 0 \qquad k = 1, 2, \ldots, n-1$$

We now formulate a result in the form of the following theorem.

5 **Theorem** The state of a system of direct control, corresponding to the solution *9.4.5*, is absolutely stable if there exists a nonempty set S, having controller parameters p_k and containing a completely nonzero vector $\bar{a}$ which satisfies Eqs. *4*.

It is possible to obtain one necessary condition for the existence of a solution of Eqs. *4*. For this purpose, we divide each one of them by ρ_k and then add them together to obtain

6 $$\sum_{k=1}^{n-1} \frac{a_k}{\rho_k} + \sqrt{\tau} = \pm\Gamma$$

where

7 $$\Gamma^2 = \tau - \sum_{k=1}^{n-1} \frac{\bar{\beta}_k}{\rho_k}$$

Using the notation of *9.5.9*, we can put the inequality *7* into the form

8 $$\Gamma^2 = -\rho_n \sum_{k=1}^{n} \frac{\gamma_k}{\rho_k} > 0$$

If this inequality is satisfied, then

9 $$\sum_{k=1}^{n-1} \frac{a_k}{\rho_k} = -\sqrt{\tau} \pm \Gamma$$

For the case of $n = 3$, Eqs. *4* can be solved completely. Indeed, after multiplying *4* by ρ_k and adding, we obtain

10 $$[a_1 + a_2 + \sqrt{\tau}\,(\rho_1 + \rho_2)] = \pm D$$
$$D^2 = \tau(\rho_1^2 + \rho_2^2) - \bar{\beta}_1\rho_1 - \bar{\beta}_2\rho_2 \pm 2\rho_1\rho_2\sqrt{\tau}\,\Gamma > 0$$

The existence of the set S is guaranteed by the satisfaction of only two inequalities, that is,

11 $$\Gamma^2 \geq 0 \qquad D^2 \geq 0$$

Let us consider the second of these inequalities. We find that

$$\tau(\rho_1^2 + \rho_2^2) - p_1 + (\rho_1 + \rho_2 - \rho_3)p_2 \pm 2\sqrt{\tau}\,\rho_1\rho_2\Gamma \geq 0$$

or, using the notation of *9.9.2*, that

12 $$\frac{p^2 - 2q}{s} - p_1 + \frac{p - \mathcal{H}}{\sqrt{s}}\,p_2 \pm 2\,\frac{q}{s}\,\Gamma \geq 0$$

Thus, whenever the inequality $\Sigma\gamma_k < 0$ is trivially satisfied, the simplified form of the method of resolving equations yields the two conditions *9.9.5* and *9.10.12* which determine the set S for the problem stated in Sec. *9*.

For $n = 4$, 5, this variant of the method may also lead to equations which can be solved explicitly. For $n > 5$, the solution of Eqs. *4* becomes extremely difficult. In connection with this, one may find further simplifications for the function of *9.6.3*. Indeed, let n be an odd integer. We now introduce $(n - 1)/2$ pairs of vectors $\{a_1,a_2\}$, $\{a_3,a_4\}$, . . . , $\{a_{n-2},a_{n-1}\}$ and construct a function V of the form

13 $$V = \sum V_j + \int_0^\sigma f(\sigma)\,d\sigma$$

Here each V_j is a positive-definite quadratic form depending on two variables only. The V_j have the form

14 $$V_j = \frac{a_j}{2\rho_j}\,x_j^2 + \frac{2a_ja_{j+1}}{\rho_j + \rho_{j+1}}\,x_jx_{j+1} + \frac{a_{j+1}^2}{2\rho_{j+1}}\,x_{j+1}^2$$

where the index j takes on the values $j = 1, 3, \ldots, n-1$. Then, instead of the simultaneous set of $n - 1$ Eqs. *4*, we obtain $(n-1)/2$ pairs of quadratic equations. Each pair is then solved explicitly by means of the method described below [13].

One may proceed analogously for the case in which n is even. We leave this to the reader.

In terminating our presentation of the method of resolving equations, we should like to remark that this method is equally well applicable to both systems of the form of *9.5.13* and systems of indirect control (the nonsimplified form).[1] The method of resolving equations may be applied successfully also to considerably more complex control systems in which, for instance, one takes into account the dependence of the velocity of displacement of the servomotor on time or loading.

For the last described case, the problem of stability can be solved only by means of Liapunov functions [13, 45].

11 The method of separation of variables

This method is due to E. A. Barbashin [27]. We shall assume that the system of equations for perturbed motion can be written in the form

1 $$\dot{y}_k = \Sigma p_{kj} f_j(\sigma_j) \qquad k = 1, \ldots, n$$

where the p_{kj} are known functions depending on the state, time, and the parameters of the controller. The $f_j(\sigma_j)$ are class A′ functions whose argument

2 $$\sigma_j = \Sigma a_{jm} y_m$$

where the a_{jm} are constants.

In particular, any linear system may be reduced to the form *1*. E. A. Barbashin has suggested a Liapunov function of the form

3 $$V = \sum C_j \int_0^{\sigma_i} f_j(\sigma)\, d\sigma$$

where the C_j are arbitrary positive constants. Its derivative computed by means of *1* is a quadratic form of the functions $f_k(\sigma_k)$, and the conditions for its negativity constitute stability criteria for the system. To give an example, we return to the equations of *9.5.6*.

In order to put these equations into the form of *1*, we let

4 $$f_k(\sigma_k) = -\rho_k x_k \qquad \sigma_k = x_k \qquad k = 1, 2, \ldots, n$$

[1] It is suggested that the reader consult [8, 16, 17, 25].

We then obtain

5
$$\dot{x}_k = f_k(\sigma_k) + f(\sigma)$$
$$\sigma = -\sum \frac{\gamma_k}{\rho_k} f_k(\sigma_k)$$

The function V can be taken to be

6
$$V = -\sum_{j=1}^{n-1} C_j \int_0^{\sigma_j} f_j(\sigma)\, d\sigma - \int_0^{\sigma} f(\sigma)\, d\sigma$$

It is negative-definite provided that all the C_j are given positive numbers. Clearly, just as in Sec. *10*, we obtain

7
$$\dot{V} = \sum_{j=1}^{n-1} C_j f_j^2(\sigma_j) + \tau f^2(\sigma) + f(\sigma) \sum_{j=1}^{n-1} \left(C_j - \gamma_j + \rho_n \frac{\gamma_j}{\rho_j} \right) f_j(\sigma_j) + \rho_n \sigma f(\sigma)$$

In order that *6* be a Liapunov function, it is necessary and sufficient that the last of the Sylvester inequalities, for the positive-definiteness of the form $\dot{V}$, be satisfied together with the inequality $\tau > 0$. These two conditions guarantee absolute asymptotic stability.

Thus, for the problem stated in Sec. *9*, we find ($C_1 = C_2 = 1$)

8
$$\left(\frac{\rho_1 + (\rho_3 - \rho_1)\gamma_1}{2\rho_1} \right)^2 + \left(\frac{\rho_2 + (\rho_3 - \rho_2)\gamma_2}{2\rho_2} \right)^2 < 1$$

12 *The method of squares*

The method of resolving equations is quite specific and does not have general applicability. This shortcoming is avoided in the method for constructing Liapunov functions, which was proposed by N. N. Krassovskii [3]. His method reduces to the following: suppose that we have equations of perturbed motion of the form of *9.1.6*, that the X_k are once differentiable in $x_1, \ldots, x_n$, and that these derivatives are continuous functions of the variables. Clearly, the function V defined by

1
$$V = \tfrac{1}{2}\|X\|^2$$

can be regarded as a Liapunov function under certain conditions. These conditions are easy to find. We have

2
$$\dot{V} = \sum_j \sum_k \left(\frac{\partial X_k}{\partial x_j} \right) X_k X_j + \sum X_j \frac{\partial X_j}{\partial t}$$

Let us suppose that X does not depend on t. Then the complete derivative is a quadratic form of the variables X_k and X_j. Hence, for the function V of *1* to be a Liapunov function for any system of the form of *9.1.6*, it is necessary and sufficient that there exist a region $G(x)$ containing the point $x = 0$ such that, for all points in G, the matrix

3 $$J = \left\| -\left(\frac{\partial X_k}{\partial x_j} + \frac{\partial X_j}{\partial x_k}\right) \right\|$$

satisfies the Sylvester inequalities for all $t \geq t_0$. *We shall call such a matrix a Sylvester matrix.* These inequalities actually form a sufficient criterion of stability and enable us to find the region of attraction of the system.

We shall now demonstrate the effectiveness of the method by means of an application; we therefore return to Eq. *9.5.13*. In our case

$$X_k = \mu_k x_k + \phi(\sigma) \qquad \sigma = \bar{\gamma}' x$$

It is hence clear that

4 $$\frac{\partial X_k}{\partial x_j} = \psi \bar{\gamma}_j + \mu_k \delta_{kj} \qquad \psi = \frac{\partial \phi}{\partial \sigma}$$

The form $-V$ is defined by the matrix

5 $$(-1)^n \begin{bmatrix} \mu_1 + \psi\bar{\gamma}_1 & \cdots & \frac{\psi}{2}(\bar{\gamma}_1 + \bar{\gamma}_n) \\ \cdots & \cdots & \cdots \\ \frac{\psi}{2}(\gamma_1 + \bar{\gamma}_n) & \cdots & \mu_n + \psi\bar{\gamma}_n \end{bmatrix}$$

The criterion of stability for the case in which the μ_k are real is then obtained in the form of the inequality

6 $$(-1)^k \begin{bmatrix} \mu_1 + \psi\bar{\gamma}_1 & \cdots & \frac{\psi}{2}(\bar{\gamma}_1 + \bar{\gamma}_k) \\ \cdots & \cdots & \cdots \\ \frac{\psi}{2}(\bar{\gamma}_1 + \bar{\gamma}_k) & \cdots & \mu_k + \psi\bar{\gamma}_k \end{bmatrix} > 0 \qquad k = 1, 2, \ldots, n$$

The effectiveness of the Krassovskii method can be seen immediately from the inequalities of *6*. For a strictly linear system $\phi(\sigma) = 0$ the inequalities of *6* are equivalent to the Hurwitz inequalities for the given system. The larger ψ, the more different the inequalities of *6* from Hurwitz inequalities.

If the function ψ is continuous and sufficiently small in magnitude and the parameters of the controller are so chosen that the linear system ($\psi \equiv 0$) is stable, then there always exists a region $G(x) > 0$ containing the origin for which the inequalities of *6* are satisfied. The existence of this region is a simple consequence of the above assumptions. The region G is the region of attraction.

If X depends explicitly on t, then it is necessary to require that the inequality

$$-\sum_k \sum_j \frac{\partial X_k}{\partial x_j} X_k X_j \geq \left| \sum \frac{\partial X_k}{\partial t} X_k \right|$$

be satisfied. The simultaneous satisfaction of the above inequality and the Sylvester inequalities guarantees stability.

The function of *1* can be taken in a substantially more general form. For example

7 $$V = X'C(x)X$$

Then, if $C(x)$ is a given Sylvester matrix, we can follow the above described procedure and obtain stability criteria.

In other cases we may hope to determine the elements of the matrix $C(x)$ in such a way that in some neighborhood $G(x)$ containing the origin, the function of *7* is a Liapunov function. This approach was proposed by G. Szegö [19] in his extension of the Zubov method.

13 *The method of virtual linearization*

This method was proposed by V. I. Zubov [21, 28]. The differential equations for the system are written in the form

1 $$\dot{x} = F(x,t)x \qquad F(x,t) = \|f_{kj}\|$$

where the f_{kj} are, generally speaking, some functions of time and the state. In case f_{kj} = a constant, we have linear equations with constant coefficients. In general, the functions f_{kj} allow us to take into account the presence of nonlinearities.

We shall assume that the system of *1* is defined in some region $N(x)$ containing the origin and that it has a unique solution for any initial state belonging to N.

In the simplest case, we define the function V by

2 $$2V = \|x\|^2$$

Its derivative, computed using *9.12.1*, is

3 $$\dot{V} = x'Bx$$

where

4 $$B = \|B_{kj}\| \qquad B_{kj} = \tfrac{1}{2}(f_{kj} + f_{jk})$$

The basic idea of the method is that expression *3* can be considered as a quadratic form whose coefficients are known functions of time and state. Hence, if the functions f_{kj} are such that there exists a region $G(x) \geq 0$ containing the origin, in which the form $\dot{V}$ is negative for any $t > 0$ and x in G, then the system is stable. The stability will be asymptotic if $\dot{V}$ is negative-definite. The criteria of stability are either the Sylvester inequalities for the form $\dot{V}$ or the Hurwitz inequalities for the equation

5 $$|B - \lambda I| = 0$$

which determines the eigenvalues of the form $\dot{V}$, defined over G and $t > 0$. Clearly, when this criterion is satisfied, all the $\lambda_k = \lambda_k(x,t)$ must be negative for $x \in G$ and $t \geq t_0$.

In a more general case, instead of *2*, we could use a full quadratic form with constant coefficients or a form such as

6 $$V = x'C(x)x$$

as was proposed by G. Szegö [19]. Computing the derivative of this form, we obtain

7 $$\dot{V} = x'[F'C + CF + \dot{C}]x$$

Let $D(x)$ be a Sylvester matrix defined for $x \in G$. We now define a matrix C in such a way that the equations

8 $$\dot{C} + CF + F'C = -D$$

are satisfied along the trajectories of the system of *1*. Then the task of constructing a Liapunov function reduces to choosing a solution C of Eq. *8* such that (1) there exists a region $G(x)$ containing the point $x = 0$ and (2) for any $x \in G(x)$, the matrix $C(x)$, defined as a solution of *8*, is a Sylvester matrix.

The application of a method as general as this to the construction of Liapunov functions is limited by its obvious difficulty. It can be successful only when special-purpose digital computers are available, the machines being specially adapted for Liapunov function computations. For a large number of cases however, only the above method seems possible, and hence it becomes unavoidable for a rigorous solution of the stability problem.

14 *A nonlinear transformation* [13, 29]

Let us consider a control system of the form

1 $$\dot{y} = By + f(y,t)$$

in which B is a given matrix with time-varying elements, $f(f_1, \ldots, f_n)$ is a given, nonlinear, vector-valued function. We now introduce the nonlinear transformation

2 $$R^2 = \|y\|^2$$
$$y_k = x_k \cdot R \qquad k = 1, \ldots, n$$

The new variables satisfy the equations

3 $$\dot{R} = -WR + \frac{\Phi}{R}$$

4 $$\dot{x} = X^*(x,R,t)$$

where

5 $$-W = x'Bx \qquad \frac{\Phi}{R} = x'f$$

whereas the form of the function X^* is easily found in the process of carrying out the transformation. Since we shall not need the exact form of X^*, we do not determine it here.

It is easily seen that Eqs. *3* and *4* have the following first integral:

6 $$\|x\|^2 = 1$$

Transformation *2* is attractive because of its geometric clarity; in the space y the function R defines a quadratic metric, whereas the x_k are direction cosines of the radius vector from the origin to the given state.

Transformation *2* is one-to-one; if y is known, then so are the R and x which satisfy Eq. *6*, and conversely. Hence to solution *9.4.5* there corresponds uniquely the solution

7 $$R = 0 \qquad x = 0$$

15 *The problem of stability* [13, 29]

We shall assume that the functions f_k are continuous in all their arguments and that they satisfy the conditions

1 $$f(0,t) \equiv 0$$

2 $$|f_k(y,t)| \leq L_k^{(N)} R$$

where $L_k^{(N)}$ are some constants depending on the form of the functions f_k and the form of the region $N(y)$ over which the equations of perturbed motion are defined.

We shall consider R^2, given by *9.14.2*, as a V function. Its derivative is given by *9.14.3*, where W and Φ are known functions of the variables x, defined on the sphere of *9.14.6*. Consequently [28],

3 $$R(t) = \left[R(0) + \int_0^t \exp\left(\int_0^s W\,dr\right) \frac{\Phi(s)}{R(s)}\,ds \right] \exp\left(-\int_0^t W\,dt\right)$$

Hence it follows that

4 $$R(t)\exp\left(\int_0^t W\,dt\right) \leq R(0) + \int_0^t \frac{|\Phi(s)|}{R^2(s)} R \exp\left(\int_0^s W\,dr\right) ds$$

We now make use of the following lemma [7]. Let u, $v \geq 0$, and let C be a positive constant related by

5 $$u \leq C + \int_0^t uv\,dt$$

Then the inequality

6 $$u \leq C \exp\left[\int_0^t v(s)\,ds\right]$$

is always satisfied. Comparing *4* and *5*, we find that

7 $$R(t) \leq R(0) \exp\left[-\int_0^t \left(W - \frac{|\Phi|}{R^2}\right) ds\right.$$

Let us examine the inequality of *7*. First we assume that the system of *9.14.1* is strictly linear. Then $\Phi \equiv 0$, and asymptotic stability is ensured if W is a positive-definite function on the sphere of *9.14.6*. Consequently, the Sylvester inequalities

8 $$B_{kj} = -b_{kj} \qquad \begin{bmatrix} B_{11} & \cdots & B_{1k} \\ \cdots & \cdots & \cdots \\ B_{k1} & \cdots & B_{kk} \end{bmatrix} > 0 \qquad k = 1, \ldots, n$$

must be satisfied for any $t > 0$.

In this case the roots of the equation

9 $$|B - \lambda(t)I| = 0$$

are positive and define the extremal values of W on the sphere *9.14.6*. Let $0 < \lambda_1 \leq \lambda_2, \ldots \leq \lambda_n$. Asymptotic stability is a consequence of the fact that

10 $$R(t) \leq R(0) \exp\left(-\int_0^t W\,dt\right) \leq R(0) \exp\left[-\int_0^t \lambda_1(t)\,dt\right]$$

where $\lambda_1(t) > 0$ for any $t > 0$.

When the system is nonlinear, as a result of *2*, we find that

$$\frac{|\Phi|}{R^2} \leq \sum |x_k| L_k^{(N)}$$

However it follows from the Cauchy-Buniakovsky inequality that

11 $$\frac{|\Phi|}{R^2} \leq E = \sqrt{\sum (L_k^{(N)})^2}$$

We therefore find that

12 $$R(t) \leq R(0) \exp \left\{ - \int_0^t [\lambda_1(t) - E]\, dt \right\}$$

Asymptotic stability is guaranteed for any $f_k(x,t)$ satisfying the conditions of *1* and *2* for which the difference $\lambda_1(t) - E$ is such that

13 $$\int_0^t [\lambda_1(t) - E]\, dt \to \infty \qquad \text{for } t \to \infty$$

In practice the utilization of the above obtained bounds is quite simple for time-invariant systems.

Thus, if the system is linear, it may always be transformed into the Jordan canonical form by means of a nonsingular transformation. For such a system, the criterion of *8* becomes equivalent to the Hurwitz criterion.

In case of a nonlinear system, for example, such as *13*, using the notation of Fig. *9.3.1*, we find

14 $$\phi(\sigma) \leq (H - h) \sqrt{\Sigma \gamma_k^2}\, R = ER$$

Let us assume that the μ_k are real numbers, such that $\mu_n < \cdots < \mu_1$. The problem now reduces to the determination of a set of the controller parameters S in which condition *13* is satisfied for $\lambda_1 = \mu_1$. For time-varying systems, in order to apply the above method it is first necessary to transform the original equations into a special form.

16 *The problem of quality of control* [13, 29]

The problem of the quality of control is concerned with finding bounds for the rate of decay of the transient process $y(t)$ and is formulated as follows: we assume that we are given a set of vectors $p \in S$, for which the system of *9.14.1* is asymptotically stable.

Consequently, for each $p \in S$ there exists a number $\lambda^* > 0$ such that

1 $$R(t) \leq R(0) \exp(-\lambda^* t)$$

Let a be a given positive number. We shall call t^* the time of conditional decay of the transient process, if

2 $$\frac{R(t^*)}{R(0)} \leq e^{-a}$$

assuming that $R(t)$ satisfies condition *1*.

In case of asymptotic stability there always exists such a number t^*, and it is bounded as follows:

3 $$t^* \leq \frac{a}{\lambda^*}$$

It follows from Sec. *14* that for the linear time-invariant systems of *9.15.3*, $\phi(\sigma) \equiv 0$, and hence we may put $|\mu_1| = \lambda^*$. Thus, for linear time-invariant systems we have

4 $$\lambda^* \cdot t^* = a = \int_0^{t^*} \lambda_1(t)\, dt$$

For nonlinear systems we obtain

5 $$a = \int_0^{t^*} [\lambda_1(t) - E]\, dt$$

Obviously, the problem of the quality of control is solved by finding a vector $p \in S$ for which the difference $\lambda_1(t) - E$ is as large as possible for every $t \in [t_0, t^*]$.

17 A general method for solving the problems of stability and quality of control

We shall assume that the right-hand side of Eq. *9.1.6* can be expanded in a series as follows:

1 $$\dot{y} = A(t)y + y'B(t)y + \cdots$$

Let $N(y)$ be the region of its convergence for any $t \geq t_0$.

We consider some function $V(y,t)$, and compute $\dot{V}$ according to *9.2.5*. The method under discussion then reduces to examining the solution $V(y,t)$ of the partial differential equation

2 $$(\text{grad } V)(Ay + y'By + \cdots) + \frac{\partial V}{\partial t} = -W(y,t)$$

where $W(y,t)$ is either a positive-definite or a positive-semidefinite function. This method follows from Liapunov's work [1] and it has been used to some extent by N. G. Chetaev [2].

We assume that $W(y,t)$ can be expanded into a series convergent everywhere in $N(y)$ for any $t \geq t_0$. We may now seek a solution of Eq. *2* in the form

3 $$V = y'C(t)y + \cdots$$

The problem of constructing this solution reduces to

1. The determination of the coefficients of the series of *3*
2. The establishing of uniform convergence of the series of *3* and of its region of convergence, $G(y)$
3. The determination of the sign of the function of *3* in the region $G(y)$

Problem 1 can be solved by means of the method of undetermined coefficients after substituting *3* into *2*. The coefficients of the series of *3* are then found as solutions of a system of recurrent differential equations. This method is particularly valuable in case

4 $$W(y,t) = k\Theta(V)$$

where $k > 0$, and $\Theta(V)$ is a positive-definite function of V. We then have

5 $$\dot{V} = -k\Theta(V)$$

A function thus constructed [2, 21, 22] will solve also the problem of quality of control. For example, when $\Theta(V) = V$, we have

6 $$V(t) = V(t_0)e^{-k(t-t_0)}$$

and consequently $\lambda^* = k$.

18 *Synthesis of optimal control systems* [30–36]

Two problems arise when the controller of *9.1.5* is given: the problem of stability and the problem of quality of control. Instead of specifying the controller equations, one may formulate the requirements on the transient process resulting from the perturbed motion of *9.1.3* by means of a single indicator, such as the functional

1 $$\mathfrak{F}(\zeta) = \int_0^\infty W(y,\zeta,t)\,dt$$

The following optimal control synthesis problem may then be formulated on the basis of the Liapunov concept of perturbed-unperturbed motion [34].

Let us consider an arbitrary given undisturbed motion of *9.1.2*.

The exact knowledge of the control u^* does not enable us to realize it because of the initial perturbation y_0.

Let A be a given positive number. The inequality

2 $$\|y_0\|^2 \leq A$$

defines a region in which perturbed motions may originate. A controller is necessary to make such motions decay.

For any given $u^* + \zeta \in U$, Eqs. *9.1.3* have the unique solution $y(t,y_0)$, where y_0 is any point in region *2*. The set of these solutions will be called the set of all *admissible comparison curves* for the functional *1*.

3 The synthesis problem consists of the following: *it is necessary to determine the equation*

4 $$F(\zeta,y,t) = 0$$

defined on the set of admissible curves, which represents a control law such that the corresponding controller, together with the plant, should result in a stable system and that the functional 1 should thereby be minimized over all the motions originating in the region 2.

Clearly, in case of asymptotic stability, the integral of *1* always converges. It is supposed that the object of control is completely controllable and completely observable.

19 *Solution of the synthesis problem*

The problem may be solved by means of Bellman's principle of optimality [37].

We now introduce the function

1 $$\psi[y(t),t] = \int_t^\infty W(y,\zeta,t)\,dt$$

The problem consists in choosing a ζ, defined in *9.18.3* for which ψ takes on a minimum at each instant of time t. Let $s > 0$ be some number. Then, according to the principle of optimality,

2 $$\psi[y(t+s),\,t+s] = \int_{t+s}^\infty W(y,\zeta,t)\,dt$$

and, at the instant $t + s$, the function of *2* also takes on a minimum value with respect to ζ. Consequently,

3 $$\psi[y(t),t] = \int_t^{t+s} W\,dt + \psi[y(t+s),\,t+s]$$

From the Lagrange theorem on finite increments it follows that

4 $$y(t+s) = y(t) + \dot{y}^* s$$

$$\psi[y(t+s), t+s] = \psi[y(t),t] + \sum \left(\frac{\partial \psi}{\partial y_k}\right)^* \dot{y}_k^* s + \left(\frac{\partial \psi}{\partial t}\right)^* s$$

Here * denotes only that the corresponding derivatives of the functions y_k and ψ are computed at suitable interior points of the intervals.

Making use of the mean-value theorem for integrals, we get

5 $$\int_t^{t+s} W\, dt = W^* s$$

Then the necessary condition for ζ to minimize $\mathfrak{F}(\zeta)$ (*9.18.1*) may be written in the form

6 $$0 = W(y,\zeta,t) + (\text{grad } \psi) \cdot Y + \frac{\partial \psi}{\partial t}$$

7 $$0 = \inf \left[W(y,\zeta,t) + (\text{grad } \psi) \cdot Y + \frac{\partial \psi}{\partial t} \right]$$

We arrive at these conditions by introducing *4* and *5* into Eq. *3*, then dividing through by s and taking the limit for $s \to 0$. These conditions must be satisfied for any t.

Suppose that somehow we have found the functions $\psi(y,t)$ and $\zeta(y,t)$ satisfying Eqs. *6* and *7*.

In order that such a function $\zeta(y,t)$ satisfy the conditions of the synthesis problem, it is sufficient that $\psi(y,t)$ be a Liapunov function for the closed-loop system. Indeed, after substituting the function $\zeta(y,t)$ into *6*, we obtain

8 $$\dot{\psi} = -W[y,\zeta(y,t),t]$$

along trajectories of the closed-loop system.

Then the closed-loop system is stable, and the integral of *1* converges for $t \in [t_0, \infty)$.

We now formulate our result in the form of the following theorem.

9 **Theorem** If there exist two functions, $\psi(y,t)$ and $\zeta(y,t)$, such that Eqs. *6* and *7* are satisfied and $\psi(y,t)$ is a Liapunov function for the system of *9.1.3* with the controller $\zeta = \zeta(y,t)$, then this controller is a solution of the synthesis problem [38].

In the case in which

10 $$W = y' a(t) y + c(t) \zeta^2$$

where $a(t)$ is a positive-definite matrix, $c(t) > 0$, and Eq. *9.1.3* is linear; that is,

11 $$\dot{y} = By + m\zeta$$

Then the function $\psi = y'Ay$ is a quadratic form. The matrix A is a positive-definite matrix whose elements A_{kj} are the solutions of the Ricatti equation

$$-\dot{A}_{\alpha\beta} = a_{\alpha\beta} + \sum_k b_{k\alpha}(A_{k\beta} + A_{\beta k}) - \frac{1}{4c}\sum_k m_k(A_{k\alpha} + A_{\alpha k})\sum_k m_k(A_{k\beta} + A_{\beta k})$$

with the appropriate boundary condition [39].

20 The inverse optimal control problem

It was shown that if the functional to be optimized in the synthesis problem is given, the optimal control is obtained from a Liapunov function which satisfies the Bellman principle of optimality. It is also interesting to consider the role of the Liapunov function from a different point of view and ask the following question: *Can we not consider any system for which a Liapunov function is known to be optimal in some sense?*

We shall now explain the inverse optimal control problem more carefully. We assume that in the region $N(z)$ are defined the differential equations

1 $$\dot{z} = Z(z,t,p)$$

of perturbed motion of the closed-loop system. Here

$$p = (p_1, \ldots, p_q)$$

are the parameters which can be adjusted. These parameters belong to some region S such that for any $p \in S$ the state

2 $$z^* = 0$$

is asymptotically stable.

For a broad class of functions $Z(z,t,p)$, there exist an infinite number of Liapunov functions which enable one to determine asymptotic stability [3].

Let $V(z,t)$ be one of these Liapunov functions. Its derivative, computed using *1*,

3 $$\dot{V} = (\text{grad } V) \cdot Z + \frac{\partial V}{\partial t} = -U(z,t,p)$$

is a negative-definite function (or a negative-semidefinite function, if this is sufficient for asymptotic stability). We now ask whether for any $p \in S$, one can consider the system of *1* to be optimal, i.e., to be the result of solving the synthesis problem of some other, auxiliary system, with a minimization functional whose value is

4 $$V(z_0,0) = \int_0^\infty U(z,t,p)\, dt$$

What is the possible form of the auxiliary system and the minimization functional?

We note that the inverse optimal control problem is a typical inverse variational problem first introduced by Darboux [40].

Three functions are used in the synthesis problem: V, W, ζ. If W is given, we have the basic problem of Sec. *18*. By specifying V or ζ, we obtain two different forms of the inverse optimal control problem. The first of these is the more general.

Let us consider the surface $V(z,t) = C$ together with the vector

5 $$\text{grad } V = \sqrt{\sum \left(\frac{\partial V}{\partial z_k}\right)^2}\, \bar{n}$$

It is directed along the inward normal $\bar{n}$ of the surface $V = C$. We now define the nonzero vector $m(z,t)$ by means of the equation

6 $$(\text{grad } V) \cdot m(zt) = 0$$

Such a vector always exists if the surface $V = C$ has no singular points for any $t > 0$ and C.

We now consider the synthesis problem for the auxiliary system

7 $$\dot{z} = Z(z,t) + m\zeta$$

8 $$\mathfrak{F}(\zeta) = \int_0^\infty (U + \alpha\zeta^2)\, dt$$

Here $\alpha(z,t)$ is positive for all z,t. The Liapunov-Bellman method leads to the following equations which solve the synthesis problem of the auxiliary system

9 $$-\frac{\partial \psi}{\partial t} = U + \alpha\zeta^2 + (\text{grad } \psi)(Z + m\zeta)$$

$$0 = 2\alpha\zeta + (\text{grad } \psi) \cdot m$$

Here ψ denotes the Liapunov function

10 $$\psi = \int_t^\infty (U + \alpha\zeta^2)\, dt$$

This function satisfies the following partial differential equation:

11 $$-\frac{\partial\psi}{\partial t} = U + (\text{grad } \psi) \cdot Z - \frac{1}{4\alpha} (\text{grad } \psi \cdot m)^2$$

Because of *6*, this equation is satisfied for $\psi = V(z,t)$, and the control $\zeta \equiv 0$. Hence the following theorem arises.

12 **Theorem** Any system of differential equations of the form of *1* which has been shown to be asymptotically stable by means of some Liapunov function $V(z,t)$ can be interpreted to be optimal, i.e., to be the result of solving the synthesis problem for some auxiliary system *7* which is optimized with respect to the functional of *8*, provided there exists at least one nonzero vector $m(z,t)$ which is orthogonal to grad V.

13 **Remark** The fact that the control ζ is identically zero is immaterial since it is always possible to shift the role of controller to a new function ξ which will not be identically zero.

A different approach to the inverse problem may be formulated in terms of an explicit elimination of the control $\zeta(z,t)$.

Thus, there are given the equations of perturbed motion

14 $$\dot{y} = Y(y,t,\zeta)$$

and also the control law

15 $$\zeta = \zeta(y,t)$$

It is required to find all the functions $W(y,\zeta,t)$ for which the integral

16 $$\mathfrak{F}(\zeta) = \int_0^\infty W(y,\zeta,t)\, dt$$

is a minimum.

The inverse optimal control problem for the case when the equations *14*, *15* are linear and time-invariant was considered by Y. Kurzweil [41] and R. E. Kalman [42]. It is easy to see that the substitution of *15* into *14* reduces the inverse problem to the first form just discussed, since the closed-loop system of *14* and *15* is asymptotically stable.

However, it is precisely such a formulation of the problem that may be of some practical interest. The point is that the control law of *15* is often constructed on the basis of various considerations which are entirely practical. In these cases it is very interesting to know in precisely what sense is the closed-loop system of *14* and *15* optimal.

In such a formulation, the inverse optimal control problem can easily be solved if optimality can be established on the basis of the sufficient Liapunov-Bellman conditions.

Indeed, we seek a function W in the form

17 $$W = U(y,t) + \phi(y,t) \cdot f(\zeta,t)$$

where ϕ and f are known, positive-valued functions.

The sufficient conditions for optimality have the form

18 $$-\frac{\partial \psi}{\partial t} = U + \phi \cdot f + (\text{grad } \psi)Y$$

19 $$0 = \phi \frac{\partial f}{\partial \zeta} + (\text{grad } \psi) \frac{\partial Y}{\partial \zeta}$$

If $\zeta(y,t)$, defined by *15*, is an optimal control, then there corresponds to it the function

20 $$\psi = \int_t^\infty W(y,\zeta(y,t),t)\, dt$$

which satisfies the partial differential equation

21 $$\left[\phi \frac{\partial f}{\partial \zeta} + \text{grad } \psi \cdot Y\right]_{\zeta=\zeta(y,t)} = 0$$

If we know at least one function *20* which satisfies *21*, we can find the function W from Eq. *18*, which establishes the sense in which the control of *15* is optimal. The function W must be positive-definite or positive-semidefinite.

Hence a consequence of a practical nature arises. Suppose an asymptotically stable system of *1* is given. We consider some positive-definite function $U(y,t,p)$, and we take the expression

22 $$\mathcal{E}(p) = \int_0^\infty U(y,t,p)\, dt$$

as an index of the quality of the transient process of *1*.

Then, using the given function $U(y,t,p)$, we find a Liapunov function from the Liapunov equation

23 $$\frac{\partial V}{\partial t} + (\text{grad } V) \cdot Z = -U$$

From the preceding, we have

24 $$\mathcal{E}(p) = V(z_0,t_0,p)$$

which thus defines the quality index for the transient process [43, 44].

The quality index depends greatly on z_0. We can cast it into a more convenient form which is invariant. With this in mind, we consider the hypersphere Γ, defined by $\|z_0\|^2 = 1$, and compute the integral

25 $$\tilde{\mathcal{E}}(p) = \int_\Gamma V(z_0,t_0,p)\, dz_0$$

This integral depends only on the parameter p. Thus we can either minimize $\tilde{\mathcal{E}}(p)$ over S as an integral quality indicator for the transient process, or else seek inf $\tilde{\mathcal{E}}(p)$ over S.

In [42] Kalman gives definite preference to considering the inverse optimal control problem rather than the basic problem. The main reason for such a preference is, apparently, the unjustified and subjective choice of the optimization functional, because of which the basic problem seems to make no practical sense.

It is not possible to agree with such a point of view. The fact is that the optimization functional need not be considered as a basic postulate. We simply need to know, as in any synthesis problem, which properties we want the system to have and then correspondingly choose an optimization functional. Since, so far, we have no such knowledge, the content of the basic problem is not reduced by it. Furthermore if the optimization functional has all these desired features (and we remain indifferent to its other features), we obtain an optimal control law which, in most cases of practical interest, happens to be unique.

In the inverse optimal control problem we are deprived of any alternative in the choice of an optimization functional, and we have to be content merely with the one which, as a natural consequence, is imposed upon us by the system of *1* whose index of perfection is expressed by the ready-made number of *4*. Hence, agreement with R. E. Kalman's point of view would mean an obvious rejection of possibilities which can always be effectively utilized whenever we are in a position to distinguish good from bad and the better from the good. Liapunov's direct method and Bellman's principle of optimality enable us to obtain the desired result.

REFERENCES

1 Liapunov, A. M.: "On the General Problem of Stability of Motion," *GITTL*, 1950.
2 Chetaev, N. G.: "Stability of Motion," Gostekhizdat, 1955.
3 Krassovskii, N. N.: "On Certain Problems of the Theory of Stability of Motion," Fizmatgiz, 1959.
4 Malkin, I. G.: "Theory of Stability of Motion," Gostekhizdat, 1952.
5 Duboshin, G. N.: "Fundamentals of the Theory of Stability of Motion," Moscow University Press, 1952.
6 Zubov, V. I.: "The Methods of Liapunov and Their Application," Leningrad University Press, 1957.

7 Bellman, R.: "Stability Theory of Differential Equations," McGraw-Hill, New York, 1953.
8 LaSalle, J. P., and S. Lefschetz: "Stability by Liapunov's Direct Method with Applications," Academic Press, New York, 1961.
9 von Hahn, W.: "Theory and Application of Liapunov's Direct Method," Prentice-Hall, Englewood Cliffs, N.J., 1963.
10 Kalman, R. E., and J. E. Bertram: Control System Analysis and Design via the Second Method of Liapunov, *ASME J. Basic Eng.*, June, 1960.
11 Lur'e, A. I., and V. N. Postnikov: On the Theory of Stability of Control Systems, *PMM*, vol. 13, no. 3, 1944.
12 Lur'e, A. I.: "Certain Nonlinear Problems in the Theory of Automatic Control," Gostekhizdat, 1951.
13 Letov, A. M.: "Stability in Nonlinear Control Systems," 2d ed., Fizmatgiz, 1961; also, Princeton University Press, Princeton, N.J., 1961.
14 Bass, R. W.: Zubov's Stability Criterion, *Reimpresso del Boletin de la Sociedad Mathematica Mexicana*, 1959.
15 Bass, R. W.: "Extensions of the Lur'e-Letov-Yakubovich Stability Criteria for Nonlinear Dynamical Systems," *Tech. Rept.*, Aeronca Corp., 1960.
16 Gibson, J. E.: "Nonlinear Automatic Control," McGraw-Hill, New York, 1963.
17 Rekasius, Z. V., and J. E. Gibson: Stability Analysis of Nonlinear Control Systems by the Second Method of Liapunov, *IRE Trans.*, vol. AC-7, no. 1, January, 1962.
18 Schultz, G. D., and J. E. Gibson: The Variable Gradient Method for Generating Liapunov Functions, *IEEE Trans. Appl. Industry*, September, 1962.
19 Szegö, G. P.: A Contribution to Liapunov's Second Method: Nonlinear Autonomous Systems, *ASME Trans., J. Basic Eng.*, paper no. 61-WA-192.
20 Szegö, G. P.: On the Applications of Zubov's Method of Constructing Liapunov Functions for Nonlinear Control Systems, *ASME Trans., J. Basic Eng.*, June, 1963.
21 Zubov, V. I.: "Mathematical Methods for Analyzing Automatic Control Systems," Sudpromgiz., 1959.
22 Mel'nikov, G. I.: Certain Problems of the Direct Method of Liapunov, *Dokl. A. N. SSSR*, vol. 110, no. 3, 1956.
23 Kalman, R. E.: On the General Theory of Control Systems, *Proc. 1st IFAC Congr., Moscow*, A.N. SSSR, 1961.
24 Krassovskii, N. N.: On the Stabilization of Unstable Motions by Means of Compensating Forces with Incomplete Feedback, *PMM*, issue 4, 1963.
25 Mufti, J. H.: On the Stability of Nonlinear Control Systems, *J. Math. Anal. Appl.*, no. 4, 1962.
26 Bell, J.: Stabilizing the "Queen Mary," *Control Eng.*, March, 1959.
27 Barbashin, E. A.: On the Construction of a Liapunov Function for Nonlinear Systems, *Proc. 1st IFAC Congr., Moscow*, A.N. SSSR, 1961.
28 Zubov, V. I.: Certain Sufficient Indications of the Stability of Nonlinear Systems of Differential Equations, *PMM*, vol. 17, issue 4, 1953.
29 Letov, A. M.: The Problem of Quality for Nonlinear Control Systems with Quadratic Metric, *IRE Trans.*, vol. CT-7, no. 4, December, 1960.
30 Pontriagin, L. S., V. G. Boltianskii, R. V. Gamkrelidze, and E. F. Mishchenko: "Mathematical Theory of Optimal Processes," Fizmatgiz, 1961; also, Interscience, New York, 1962.
31 Krassovskii, N. N.: On the Choice of Parameters for Stable Optimal Systems, *Proc. 1st IFAC Congr., Moscow*, vol. 2, no. M, pp. 482–489, A.N. SSSR, 1961.

32 Letov, A. M.: Analytic Construction of Regulators, Part 1, *Avtom. i Telemekh.*, vol. 21, nos. 4, 5, and 6, 1960.

33 Letov, A. M.: Analytic Construction of Regulators, Part 4, *Avtom. i Telemekh.*, vol. 22, no. 4, 1961.

34 Letov, A. M.: Analytic Construction of Regulators, Further Developments, *Avtom. i Telemekh.*, vol. 23, 1962.

35 Kalman, R. E.: Contributions to the Theory of Optimal Control, *Symposium International de Ecuasiones Differentiales Ordinaries, Mexico*, 1961.

36 Merriam, C. W.: A Class of Optimal Control Systems, *J. Franklin Inst.*, vol. 267, 1959.

37 Bellman, R.: "Dynamic Programming," Princeton University Press, Princeton, N.J., 1957.

38 Letov, A. M.: Problem of Optimal Control Synthesis, Survey of the Major Problems, *Proc. 2nd IFAC Congr., Basel*, 1963.

39 Repin, Yu. N., and V. E. Tretiakov: Solution of the Analytic Construction of Regulators by Means of Analog Computers, *Avtom. i Telemekh.*, no. 6, 1963.

40 Bolza, O.: Lectures on the Calculus of Variations, Chelsea, N.Y., 1947.

41 Kurzweil, Y.: On the Analytic Construction of Regulators, *Avtom. i Telemekh.*, vol. 22, no. 6, 1961.

42 Kalman, R. E.: When Is the Linear Control Optimal? 1963 *JACC, Univ. Minn.*, Minneapolis, Minn., June 19–24, 1963.

43 Krassovskii, N. N.: On the Degree of Stability of Linear Systems, in V. V. Solodovnikov (ed.), "Fundamentals of Automatic Control," Mashgiz., 1965.

44 Balchen, J. G.: Dynamic Optimization of Continuous Processes, *Inst. Regulungs Teknikk. Trondheim*, 1961.

45 Letov, A. M.: On the Theory of Nonlinear Control Systems, *Contributions to Differential Equations*, vol. II, no. 2, 1963.

46 Aiserman, M. A., and F. R. Gantmaker: Absolute Stability of Controlled Systems. Moscow, 1963.

Part Four

STOCHASTIC AND LEARNING SYSTEMS

10

Stochastic finite-state system theory

J. W. Carlyle[1]
College of Engineering
University of California, Los Angeles

1 *Introduction*

Stochastic (probabilistic, random) finite-state representations have been employed for such entities as digital systems with random faults, noisy communication channels, nerve nets and learning models in psychology. We shall not review such applications here, but we shall examine some basic system-theoretic concepts which contribute to a mathematical framework for applications. Attention is restricted to structural questions in which the objects of interest are not the actual observed (or desired) values of input, output, and state variables, but the probability laws connecting them; in this sense, definitions and results are interpreted as stochastic generalizations of those encountered in the theory of deterministic finite-state systems (switching circuits, sequential machines, automata). Two principal lines of generalization have appeared, based on machine equivalence [5] and events defined by automata [18], respectively. The former will be discussed in some detail, the latter will be summarized, and some interconnections and recent developments related to both areas will be mentioned. We shall not attempt to discuss current research in this rapidly developing field, but the chapter should prepare the reader for consultation of the

[1] The preparation of this chapter was supported in part by the Air Force Office of Scientific Research, Office of Aerospace Research, United States Air Force, under AFOSR Grant 700-65.

references; other important contributions not referenced here may be located through the bibliographies in [35], [47], and [48].

At this point, we mention a recurring notational matter. To avoid special symbols, the same letter p is used repeatedly to denote different probability distributions; the various functions p are to be distinguished by their arguments and by the context.

2 The basic model

A stochastic sequential machine is defined [5] through the specification of three finite sets, say X, Y, and S, and a conditional probability function

1 $$p(y,s'|s,x)$$

defined for all s and s' in S, x in X, and y in Y. The physical interpretation is that the numerical value of *1* is supposed to be the probability, when the internal state of the machine is s and the input is x, that the observed response will be y and the new state will be s'. An *autonomous* machine (a finite-state stochastic generator or source) is governed by *1* with x and X deleted, or with X a one-element set.

When the only values assumed by the probabilities of *1* are 0 and 1, we have a nonrandom or *deterministic* sequential machine, for which y and s' can be expressed explicitly in terms of s and x through a functional relation; the model governed by *1* is thus a direct stochastic generalization of conventional models for completely specified finite-state machines operating in discrete (synchronous) time. For such deterministic machines, the functional relationship between (s,x) and (y,s') is usually exhibited in an operation table or a state diagram; the probability law of *1* can be regarded as a natural generalization of these descriptions. In particular, a state diagram in the stochastic case is constructed as follows: whenever s, x, y, and s' are such that *1* is positive, an oriented branch is drawn from vertex s to vertex s', and the branch is labeled with the probability that it will be traversed (the numerical value of *1*) as well as with the pertinent input and output symbols x and y.

In some situations it may be desirable to convert the basic stochastic machine model into a form more closely identifiable with the operational behavior of the actual physical device being modeled; in Sec. *9* we compare various equivalent alternatives, but otherwise we generally adhere to the form based on *1* because of its notational convenience. We note that *1* was suggested by Shannon [19] as a mathematical description for discrete noisy communication channels, and the channel capacity for model *1* or its equivalent has been studied extensively [3, 20, 21, 23].

We make the following notational conventions. With superscripts or subscripts where needed, x and y are *sequences of length 1* (*input symbols* and *output symbols*, respectively), whereas u and v are, respectively, *input sequences* and *output sequences* of any finite length (including the *empty sequence* ϕ having zero length); that is, u and v denote finite sequences of elements of X and Y, respectively (X and Y are finite input and output sets or *alphabets*). As in automata theory, a finite sequence is also called a *tape*. If t is any tape, $|t|$ denotes its length. A string of tapes and/or symbols of the same alphabet is to be regarded as a concatenation; for example, uxu' is the tape consisting of u followed by the symbol x followed by u'. When both u- and v-sequences appear in the same expression, it is understood that for each pair with identical superscripts or subscripts, we have $|u| = |v|$.

If a stochastic sequential machine governed by *1* is initially in state s_1 and we apply input x_1 followed by x_2, then the quantity

$$\sum_{s_2 \text{ in } S} p(y_1,s_2|s_1,x_1)p(y_2,s_3|s_2,x_2)$$

is the probability $p(y_1y_2,s_3|s_1,x_1x_2)$ that the outputs will be y_1 followed by y_2 and the final (or terminal) state of the machine will be s_3. In this way we extend the domain of definition of function *1* to include tapes of any length; thus

2 $$p(v,s'|s,u)$$

is determined recursively from *1* and the relation

3 $$p(v_1v_2,s'|s,u_1u_2) = \sum_{\sigma \text{ in } S} p(v_1,\sigma|s,u_1)p(v_2,s'|\sigma,u_2)$$

and we set

$$p(\phi,s'|s,\phi) = 1 \qquad \text{for } s' = s$$

Relation *3* is, of course, not a conclusion, but an assumption; it is part of the machine model and contains implicitly the basic assumptions that (1) the state set is adequate (in the sense that when the state is known, preceding inputs and outputs provide no new information) and (2) the machine is time-invariant (that is, *1* depends upon the input x but not the time at which x is applied). By analogy with the nomenclature of deterministic system theory, *2* (and its generator, *1*) may be called a *stochastic input-output-state relation.*

In typical applications, the state transitions are not observable;

it is therefore necessary to consider such expressions as

4 $$p_s(v|u) = \sum_{s' \text{ in } S} p(v,s'|s,u)$$

the probability that output tape v is observed when input tape u is applied starting in initial state s, and

5 $$\frac{p(v,s'|s,u)}{p_s(v|u)}$$

the probability that the terminal state will be s' given that v is observed when u is applied with initial state s. For deterministic machines, the final state is uniquely determined by the initial state and the input sequence applied; however, *5* shows that for stochastic machines, an initial state, an input sequence, and an output sequence determine only a terminal probability distribution on states, and not the actual terminal state, unless *5* yields a degenerate distribution (i.e., has the value 1 for a single s' and 0 for all others). Evidently, the latter is a special case (studied in Sec. *8*) and in general the final state has the nontrivial distribution of *5*. Since final conditions after one operation become initial conditions for the next operation, the concept of initial condition is broadened in the following discussions to encompass probability distributions on the states (a fixed initial state is then identified with the degenerate distribution concentrated on that state).

A *stochastic finite-state system* (M,π) consists of a machine M and a probability distribution

6 $$\pi = \{\pi_s : s \text{ in } S\}$$

on the machine state set S; π is called an *initial distribution*. The *input-output relation for the system* (M,π) is

7 $$p_\pi(v|u) = \sum_s \pi_s p_s(v|u)$$

If we set

8 $$p(v,s'|\pi,u) = \sum_s \pi_s p(v,s'|s,u)$$

then *7* may be rewritten as

9 $$p_\pi(v|u) = \sum_{s'} p(v,s'|\pi,u)$$

To each initial distribution π, input sequence u, and output sequence v for which *7* is positive, there corresponds a *terminal distribution* [or *final* (-state) distribution]

10 $$\pi(u,v) = \{\pi_s(u,v) : s \text{ in } S\}$$

where $\pi_s(u,v)$, the probability that the final state is s, is given by

11 $$\pi_s(u,v) = \frac{p(v,s|\pi,u)}{p_\pi(v|u)}$$

With the aid of *3*, we obtain the identity

12 $$p_\pi(vv'|uu') = p_\pi(v|u)p_{\pi(u,v)}(v'|u')$$

This is a natural generalization of the fact that if M is a deterministic machine and

$$vv' = \text{response of } (M,s) \text{ to } uu'$$

then

$$v = \text{response of } (M,s) \text{ to } u$$
$$v' = \text{response of } (M,s') \text{ to } u'$$

where s' is the final state of (M,s) after input sequence u is applied.

Many of the items *1* through *11* are recast in a convenient matrix or vector form in Sec. *3*. When it is necessary to identify the machine M under consideration, superscripts M may be added to any of the probability laws in *1* through *11* or to their vector equivalents where defined.

In general, any function $p(v|u)$ [defined for all pairs (u,v) of input and output sequences], subject only to the obvious restrictions

13 $$\begin{aligned} p(v|u) &\geq 0 \\ p(\phi|\phi) &= 1 \\ p(v|u) &= \sum_y p(vy|ux) \end{aligned}$$

will be called a *stochastic input-output relation*. Such a function can be regarded as the input-output probability law of an arbitrary (not necessarily finite-state) nonanticipative stochastic black box with finite input and output alphabets, operating in discrete time (beginning at some initial or reference time). An input-output relation p is said to be *of finite-state type* if there exists a stochastic finite-state system (M,π) whose input-output relation coincides with p; then (M,π) is called a *finite-state representation* or realization for p. If a representation having c states can be found, we say that p *requires at most* c *states*.

3 *Equivalence*

We recall that in the theory of deterministic finite-state machines, two states s_1 and s_2 of a given machine M are said to be equivalent if they are experimentally indistinguishable as initial conditions, from the viewpoint of an external observer; that is, s_1 and s_2 are equivalent if the systems (M,s_1) and (M,s_2) have the same input-output relation. We also recall that equivalences are removable redundancies in the sense that there is a constructive procedure for identifying and deleting all redundant equivalent states in the deterministic machine description or state diagram. In the stochastic case, outputs are random variables, so that an "experimental" interpretation of indistinguishability is meaningful only in a statistical sense. Nevertheless, as a direct generalization of the deterministic definition, equality among (stochastic) input-output relations is still a natural criterion for state equivalences; such equivalences are again removable redundancies (Sec. *4*). This motivates the following definitions.

Let M be a stochastic sequential machine, and let π and λ be distributions on the state set for M; π and λ are *equivalent* as initial distributions for $M(\pi \sim \lambda)$ if

1 $$p_\pi(v|u) = p_\lambda(v|u)$$

for all (u,v). More generally, let π and λ be distributions on the state sets for machines M and N, respectively. If

2 $$p_\pi{}^M(v|u) = p_\lambda{}^N(v|u)$$

for all sequences we again say that π and λ are equivalent (with respect to M and N), or that (M,π) and (N,λ) are *equivalent systems;* thus

$$(M,\pi) \sim (N,\lambda)$$

Equivalences involving *states* are understood to be covered in the above definition by identifying states with degenerate distributions, and by replacing one with the other in the notation when convenient; for example, if π in *2* is concentrated on state s, we may write

$$(M,s) \sim (N,\lambda)$$

Two distributions or states are *distinguishable* if they are not equivalent; any (u,v) for which *2* does not hold is said to be a pair of *distinguishing sequences.* We speak of *k-equivalence* (where k is a nonnegative integer) when the input-output relations agree for all tapes u and v of length k, and of *k-distinguishability* when they disagree for some u and v of length k (note that from our conventions involving ϕ, every pair of distributions is 0-equivalent and none is 0-distinguishable). With the aid of *10.2.13* we conclude that k-distinguishability implies $(k + 1)$-distinguishability, and $(k + 1)$-equivalence implies k-equivalence.

If M is a stochastic sequential machine with state set S, let $\omega = \omega(M)$ be the partition of S into classes of equivalent states with respect to M, and for $k = 0, 1, 2, \ldots$, let ω_k be the k-equivalence partition of S. Let θ_k and θ be the k-equivalence and equivalence partitions of the set of all probability distributions on S. According to the preceding paragraph, for each k, ω_{k+1} and θ_{k+1} are refinements (not necessarily proper refinements) of ω_k and θ_k, respectively (of course ω and θ are refinements of all ω_k and θ_k, respectively). We recall for reference two fundamental results for deterministic machines: (1) if $\omega_k \neq \omega$, then ω_{k+1} is a proper refinement of ω_k, and (2) if M has c states, $(c-1)$-equivalence of any two states is a sufficient condition for their equivalence. For deterministic machines (2) follows from (1) since $\#\omega_0 = 1$ and $\#\omega \leq c$, where "#" means "number of classes of." For some stochastic machines, (1) does not hold (simple counterexamples have been reported to the author by T. Nieh); however, (2) does generalize to the stochastic case. First, we note (Theorem *3*) that the method of proof of (1) has its stochastic analog in the context of distribution partitions θ_k and θ (the remarks following *10.1.5* show that for stochastic machines we should anticipate the necessity of studying the hierarchy $\{\theta_k\}$ before $\{\omega_k\}$ can be examined).

3 **Theorem** Let M be any stochastic sequential machine, and suppose that π and λ are distinguishable as initial distributions for M. Let t be the integer for which π and λ are t-equivalent but $(t+1)$-distinguishable, and fix any integer $k \leq t$. Then there exists a pair of distributions possessing the properties of k-equivalence and $(k+1)$-distinguishability.

Proof Let (u'',v'') be distinguishing sequences for π and λ having the minimal length $t+1$, and write

$$u'' = uu' \qquad v'' = vv'$$

where u and v have length $t-k$. Using *10.2.12*, consider the identities

$$p_\pi(vv'|uu') = p_\pi(v|u)p_{\pi'}(v'|u')$$
$$p_\lambda(vv'|uu') = p_\lambda(v|u)p_{\lambda'}(v'|u')$$

where $\pi' = \pi(u,v)$ and $\lambda' = \lambda(u,v)$. The left-hand sides of these identities differ by assumption, whereas the first factors on the right are equal because of t-equivalence, and hence $(t-k)$-equivalence, of π and λ; thus (u',v') are distinguishing sequences of length $k+1$ for π' and λ'. [Note that $p_\pi(v|u)$ and $p_\lambda(v|u)$ are not only equal but also positive; for if they were both zero, v'' would also have probability zero given u'' under both π and λ, contradicting the assumption that (u'',v'') distinguishes π and λ. Therefore, π' and λ' are well-defined $(k+1)$-distinguishable terminal distributions.] To establish the k-equivalence of π' and λ', observe that if u and v are left fixed while u' and v' are replaced by arbitrary sequences of length k, the above identities still hold, the first factors on the right are still equal (and positive), and the left-hand sides are equal by assumption, so that the second factors on the right must be equal; i.e., there are no distinguishing sequences of length k for π' and λ'.

From Theorem *3*, we see that there is an integer n for which θ_{k+1} is a proper refinement of θ_k for all $k < n$, and $\theta_k = \theta$ for all $k \geq n$, or perhaps $n = \infty$ (that is, θ_{k+1} is a proper refinement of θ_k for all k). We wish to rule out the case $n = \infty$ and show that n is in fact not greater than $c - 1$, where c is the number of states in the stochastic machine under consideration, as in the deterministic result (1) quoted preceding Theorem *3*. A result along these lines is essential since it guarantees that equivalence questions can be answered after a *finite* number of calculations based on the given machine description (in other words, we wish to show that the phrase "for *all* sequences" in the definition of equivalence can be replaced by "for all sequences of predetermined length"). We cannot proceed to bound n directly by class-counting arguments since it is possible for some θ_k partitions to have infinitely many classes (this may occur in many ways, but for a rudimentary example, consider an autonomous two-state deterministic machine with two distinct outputs, one from either state; then any pair of distinct initial distributions is trivially 1-distinguishable, so each distribution is in a one-element equivalence class and θ therefore has a continuum of classes). We obtain the key result $n \leq c - 1$ by indirect methods, as an immediate corollary of Theorem *14* below. In the proof of Theorem *14* we study not the hierarchy $\{\theta_k\}$ of partitions but instead a related hierarchy of linear spaces; for this purpose, and for use in other proofs and examples, we first list convenient matrix and vector formulations for machine probability functions.

Let $M = (X,Y,S,\ p(y,s'|s,x))$ be a machine with c states; for notational convenience we identify S with the set of integers $1, 2, \ldots, c$. For each pair (x,y) of input and output symbols, let $M(y|x)$ be the matrix whose ij element is

$$m_{ij}(y|x) = p(y,j|i,x)$$

Then $\{M(y|x): x \text{ in } X,\ y \text{ in } Y\}$ is a family of $c \times c$ matrices with nonnegative elements such that for each x, the *state transition matrix*

4 $$M(x) = \sum_y M(y|x)$$

is a Markov matrix; any family $\{M(y|x)\}$ of matrices with these properties determines a c-state machine. Thus, as an alternate machine notation, we write $M = \{M(y|x)\}$; the input and output sets X and Y are not mentioned explicitly unless required by the context.

If $\{M(y|x)\}$ is a c-state machine, then the $c \times c$ matrices $M(v|u)$ are defined by

$$M(v|u) = M(y_1|x_1)M(y_2|x_2) \cdots M(y_n|x_n)$$

when $u = x_1x_2 \cdots x_n$ and $v = y_1y_2 \cdots y_n$, while $M(\phi|\phi)$ is the identity matrix. From *10.2.2*, $p(v,j|i,u)$ is the ij element of $M(v|u)$, and *10.2.3* is a typical element of the matrix equality

5 $$M(vv'|uu') = M(v|u)M(v'|u')$$

If $h(v|u)$ is the c-component column vector whose ith component is $p_i(v|u)$ and if e is the c-component column vector with all components equal to 1, then *10.2.4* becomes

6 $$h(v|u) = M(v|u)e$$

The probability distribution of *10.2.6* on the states is now viewed as a c-component row vector whose ith component is the probability assigned to state i. Then *10.2.7* and *10.2.9* become

7 $$p_\pi(v|u) = \pi h(v|u) = \pi M(v|u)e$$

8 $$p_\pi(v|u) = g_\pi(v|u)e$$

where $g_\pi(v|u)$ is a row vector with $p(v,i|\pi,u)$ as its ith component; *10.2.8* and *10.2.11* are typical elements of the vector equalities

9 $$g_\pi(v|u) = \pi M(v|u)$$

10 $$\pi(u,v) = \frac{1}{g_\pi(v|u)e}\, g_\pi(v|u)$$

Using *5*, we obtain the following recursive constructions for g-vectors and h-vectors and for p_π [note that $g_\pi(\phi|\phi) = \pi$ and $h(\phi|\phi) = e$]:

11 $$g_\pi(vy|ux) = g_\pi(v|u)M(y|x)$$

12 $$h(yv|xu) = M(y|x)h(v|u)$$

13 $$p_\pi(vv'|uu') = g_\pi(v|u)h(v'|u')$$

14 **Theorem** If M is a machine with c states and if π and λ are any two distributions on the states of M, then $(c - 1)$-equivalence of π and λ is a sufficient condition for their equivalence.

Proof If z is any c-component column vector, let $\psi(z) = (\pi - \lambda)z$; in particular, then, using *7*, we obtain

$$\psi(h(v|u)) = p_\pi(v|u) - p_\lambda(v|u)$$

so that π and λ are k-equivalent if and only if ψ vanishes on the linear subspace (of c-dimensional space) spanned by the vectors $h(v|u)$ for all u and v of length k. Let this subspace be $L_k(M)$; the theorem follows if it can be established that for sufficiently large k (that is, $k \geq c - 1$) all spaces $L_k(M)$ are identical. First, observe that for any k, L_k is a subset (in fact, a subspace) of L_{k+1} since

$$h(v|u) = \sum_y h(vy|ux)$$

On the other hand, if $L_k = L_{k+1}$, then $L_{k+1} = L_{k+2}$, since L_{k+2} is spanned by the vectors $h(yv|xu)$ for all x and y and for all u and v of length $k+1$, and since for such x, y, u, and v, we have

$$\begin{aligned} h(yv|xu) &= M(y|x)h(v|u) \\ &= M(y|x)(\text{vector in } L_{k+1}) = M(y|x)(\text{vector in } L_k) \\ &= M(y|x)\begin{Bmatrix}\text{linear combination of the vectors } h(v'|u')\text{: } |u'| = \\ |v'| = k\end{Bmatrix} \\ &= \{\text{linear combination of } h(yv'|xu')\} \text{ in } L_{k+1} \end{aligned}$$

Thus there is an integer $J = J(M)$ such that $L_k = L_j$ for all $k < J$ while the dimension of L_{k+1} is strictly greater than the dimension of L_k for all $k < J$. In particular,

$$\dim L_0 + J \leq \dim L_J \ (\leq c)$$

But $\dim L_0 = \dim \{\text{space spanned by } e\} = 1$ for any machine, so that $J \leq c - 1$, which completes the proof.

15 **Theorem** If M has c states, N has d states, and π and λ are distributions on the states of M and N, respectively, then $(c + d - 1)$-equivalence of (M,π) and (N,λ) is a sufficient condition for their equivalence.

Proof Let $M + N$ be the sum machine defined by

$$(M + N)(y|x) = \left[\begin{array}{c:c} M(y|x) & 0 \\ \hdashline 0 & N(y|x) \end{array}\right]$$

and apply Theorem *14* to the machine $M + N$ and the distributions

$$\begin{aligned} \pi' &= (\pi_1,\pi_2, \ldots ,\pi_c,0,0, \ldots ,0) \\ \lambda' &= (0,0, \ldots ,0,\lambda_1,\lambda_2, \ldots ,\lambda_d) \end{aligned}$$

The sufficient (and trivially necessary) conditions given in Theorems *14* and *15* are the best obtainable which depend only on the number of states, since there are situations in which the bounds $c - 1$ and $c + d - 1$ are actually attained; we may, for example, appeal to the well-known deterministic constructions where this is the case when π and λ are concentrated on single states.

Theorem *15*, with $M = N$, was established for functions of stationary Markov chains (see Example *10.9.1*) by Gilbert [13] and previously (with a bound $2c^2 + 1$ rather than $2c - 1$) by Blackwell and Koopmans [4]. It is the latter method of proof which has been modified [5] to yield the present Theorems *14* and *15* separately, as generalizations of the corresponding basic theorems regarding state equivalence in deterministic machine theory.

The next theorem (which follows directly from definitions) characterizes equivalences and equivalence classes in terms of the linear spaces L_k introduced above. The results can be viewed as (1) computational routines, based on a given machine description, for determining equivalences and (2) geometrical characterizations of distribution equivalence classes as convex polyhedra defined through systems of linear inequalities. Consequences of the latter characterizations will not be discussed here.

16 **Theorem** Let $M = \{M(y|x)\}$ be a stochastic machine with c states, let H be a $c \times (\dim L)$ matrix whose columns form a basis for the linear space $L(M)$ introduced in the proof of Theorem *14*, and let H_k be a matrix (a submatrix of H if desired) whose columns are a basis for $L_k(M)$. (We shall call H an *L-basis matrix for M*, and H_k an *L_k-basis matrix for M*.) Then:

1. Two states i and j are k-equivalent (or equivalent) if and only if rows i and j of H_k (or H) are identical; hence, the ω_k-partition can be obtained through a comparison of the rows of H_k.

2. Let π and λ be probability distributions on the states of M; π and λ are k-equivalent with respect to M if and only if

17 $$\pi H_k = \lambda H_k$$

and equivalent if and only if

18 $$\pi H = \lambda H$$

3. Let $C(\pi)$ be the equivalence class (with respect to M) containing the distribution π; then $C(\pi)$ can be obtained by solving *18* as a set of linear equations in the variables λ_i and retaining those solution vectors λ for which all λ_i are nonnegative. Thus

19 $$C(\pi) = \{\lambda: \pi H = \lambda H \text{ and all } \lambda_i \geq 0\}$$

Similarly if $C_k(\pi)$ is the k-equivalence class containing π, then

20 $$C_k(\pi) = \{\lambda: \pi H_k = \lambda H_k \text{ and all } \lambda_i \geq 0\}$$

4 Reduction

Given a stochastic machine description, the state set can always be partitioned into classes of equivalent states by a finite number of calculations as shown above (e.g., as in Theorem *16*). If equivalence classes containing two or more states are found, it should be possible (as in the deterministic case) to condense the machine description in such a way as to leave the family of distinct input-output relations *10.2.4* invariant; this is verified by Theorem *1*. The situation can be restated formally as follows.

If to each state of a stochastic machine M there corresponds an equivalent state of machine N and to each state of N there corresponds an equivalent state of M, we say that M and N are *state-equivalent machines.* Among the machines which are state-equivalent to a given machine M, those having the smallest number of states are called *reduced forms of* M. A machine for which any two states are distinguishable (i.e., there are no equivalent states) is said to be *in reduced form.* The terminology is consistent since the reduced forms of any machine M are precisely those machines which are state-equivalent to M and in reduced form; this follows from Theorem *1* below and from the transitivity of state equivalence.

1 **Theorem** Let M be a c-state stochastic machine with at least one pair of equivalent states. Then there exist $(c-1)$-state machines which are state-equivalent to M. In particular, if s and t are equivalent states of M, let $N(y|x)$ be the matrix formed from $M(y|x)$ by deleting row t and column t and replacing column s with the sum of columns s and t; then $N = \{N(y|x)\}$ is a $(c-1)$-state machine which is state-equivalent to M.

Proof For notational convenience, let the states of M be renumbered in such a way that $s = c - 1$ and $t = c$. Then

$$n_{ij}(y|x) = m_{ij}(y|x) \qquad i = 1, 2, \ldots, c-1; j = 1, 2, \ldots, c-2$$

$$n_{i,\, c-1}(y|x) = m_{i,\, c-1}(y|x) + m_{ic}(y|x) \qquad i = 1, 2, \ldots, c-1$$

It is clear that $\{N(y|x)\}$ is a machine. We wish to show that for all u and v

2 $$p_i^N(v|u) = p_i^M(v|u) \qquad i = 1, 2, \ldots, c-1$$

and

3 $$p_{c-1}^N(v|u) = p_c^M(v|u)$$

Observe that *3* follows from *2* with $i = c - 1$, since states c and $c - 1$ of machine M are assumed to be equivalent. The asserted equalities are evident (by construction of N) for $|u| = |v| = 1$, and if they hold for all sequences u and v of length k, then for such sequences and for any x and y

$$p_i{}^M(yv|xu) = \sum_{j=1}^{c} m_{ij}(y|x)p_j{}^M(v|u)$$
$$= \sum_{j=1}^{c-1} n_{ij}(y|x)p_j{}^N(v|u) = p_i{}^N(yv|xu)$$

for $i = 1, 2, \ldots, c-1$. Thus *2* holds for sequences of length $k+1$, which completes the proof by induction.

The rule for construction of machine N in Theorem *1*, called the *merging of equivalent states*, is a direct generalization of the manner in which deterministic state diagrams are simplified. If we merge the states in each equivalence class of a given machine M, we obtain a reduced form of M (containing one state for each equivalence class of states of M). If M is deterministic, it is well known that the reduced form of M is unique (apart from a relabeling of the states); however, if M is stochastic, it may possess a continuum of distinct reduced forms, as shown by Theorem *4* and the subsequent discussion and example.

4 **Theorem** Let M be a machine having c states, and let H be an L-basis matrix for M. Let $\{N(y|x)\}$ be any set of $c \times c$ matrices satisfying

5 $$N(y|x)H = M(y|x)H$$

6 $$n_{ij}(y|x) \geq 0 \qquad i, j = 1, 2, \ldots, c$$

Then $N = \{N(y|x)\}$ is a c-state machine which is state-equivalent to M; in fact,

7 $$(N,s) \sim (M,s) \qquad s = 1, 2, \ldots, c$$

Conversely, if a c-state machine satisfies *7*, then it must also satisfy *5* and *6*.

Proof The converse follows immediately from *10.3.12* and the fact that *7* can be rewritten in the form

8 $$h^N(v|u) = h^M(v|u) \qquad \text{for all } u, v$$

For the direct assertion, first observe that if $\{N(y|x)\}$ is a set of matrices satisfying *5* and *6*, then in particular (since e is a vector in L)

9 $$N(y|x)e = M(y|x)e$$

Summing over all y (for any fixed x), we obtain $N(x)e = M(x)e = e$, verifying (with *6*) that $N(x)$ is a Markov matrix; thus $\{N(y|x)\}$ is a machine. Assertion *7* (or *8*) follows by induction on v; it has been established for $|v| = 1$ in *9*, and if it holds for all sequences u and v of length k, then for such sequences and for any x and y,

$$\begin{aligned} h^N(yv|xu) &= N(y|x)h^N(v|u) = N(y|x)h^M(v|u) \\ &= M(y|x)h^M(v|u) = h^M(yv|xu) \end{aligned}$$

using *10.3.12* and *5*.

If M is a c-state machine with a input symbols and b output symbols, the set $\{N(y|x)\}$ of solutions of *5* depends upon $abc(c - \dim L)$ unrestricted real parameters. According to Theorem *4*, if one restricts the ranges of the parameters in such a way that *6* is always satisfied, this parametric family of sets $\{N(y|x)\}$ of matrices coincides (apart from permutations of the states) with the family of all c-state machines which are state-equivalent to M. Applying this result to a reduced form of M, say M' (which might be obtained by repeated application of Theorem *1* to M), we see that the family of all reduced forms of M may depend upon as many as $abc'(c' - \dim L)$ parameters, where c' is the number of states of M', that is, the number of equivalence classes of states of M [it is apparent from their definitions that $\dim L(M)$ cannot exceed c' and that $\dim L(M') = \dim L(M)$]. Thus, M has a unique reduced form if $\dim L = c'$, whereas M may possess a continuum of distinct reduced forms (as in the example below) when $\dim L < c'$. The condition $\dim L < c'$ can also occur when the reduced form is unique (see Example *10.7.17*).

10 *Example* Let $X = Y = \{0,1\}$, $S = \{1,2,3\}$, and

$$M(0|0) = \begin{bmatrix} 0.2 & 0.2 & 0.2 \\ 0.2 & 0.2 & 0.2 \\ 0.2 & 0.2 & 0.2 \end{bmatrix} \qquad M(1|0) = \begin{bmatrix} 0.4 & 0 & 0 \\ 0.1 & 0.3 & 0 \\ 0.2 & 0.1 & 0.1 \end{bmatrix}$$

$$M(0|1) = \begin{bmatrix} 1 & 0 & 0 \\ 0 & 0 & 0.6 \\ 0.6 & 0.1 & 0.1 \end{bmatrix} \qquad M(1|1) = \begin{bmatrix} 0 & 0 & 0 \\ 0.4 & 0 & 0 \\ 0.2 & 0 & 0 \end{bmatrix}$$

It is evident that M is already in reduced form; i.e., there are no equivalent states since (for example) the three components of

$$h(1|1) = M(1|1)e$$

are distinct. Calculation of the vectors $h(v|u)$ for $|v| = 1$ and 2 shows that $J = 1$ (that is, $L_1 = L$) and that $\dim L = 2$ ($<3 = c = c'$). A convenient choice for the matrix H of Theorem *4* is

$$H = \begin{bmatrix} 1 & 0 \\ 1 & 2 \\ 1 & 1 \end{bmatrix}$$

When Eqs. *5* are solved with the constraints of *6*, we obtain the following seven-parameter family of all distinct forms $\{N(y|x)\}$ for M:

$$N(0|0) = \begin{bmatrix} A & A & 0.6 - 2A \\ B & B & 0.6 - 2B \\ C & C & 0.6 - 2C \end{bmatrix} \qquad N(1|0) = \begin{bmatrix} 0.4 & 0 & 0 \\ D & D + 0.2 & 0.2 - 2D \\ E & E - 0.1 & 0.5 - 2E \end{bmatrix}$$

$$N(0|1) = \begin{bmatrix} 1 & 0 & 0 \\ F & F & 0.6 - 2F \\ G & G - 0.5 & 1.3 - 2G \end{bmatrix} \qquad N(1|1) = \begin{bmatrix} 0 & 0 & 0 \\ 0.4 & 0 & 0 \\ 0.2 & 0 & 0 \end{bmatrix}$$

$$0 \leq A,B,C,F \leq 0.3 \qquad 0 \leq D \leq 0.1 \qquad 0.1 \leq E \leq 0.25 \qquad 0.5 \leq G \leq 0.65$$

Selection of the minimum value for each parameter yields a machine whose state diagram has particularly simple connection properties. On the other hand, if maximum values are chosen for all parameters, it becomes apparent that the machine M, although in reduced form, can be "reduced" further in the following sense: the two-state machine M^*, defined by

$$M^*(0|0) = \begin{bmatrix} 0.3 & 0.3 \\ 0.3 & 0.3 \end{bmatrix} \qquad M^*(1|0) = \begin{bmatrix} 0.4 & 0 \\ 0.1 & 0.3 \end{bmatrix}$$

$$M^*(0|1) = \begin{bmatrix} 1 & 0 \\ 0.3 & 0.3 \end{bmatrix} \qquad M^*(1|1) = \begin{bmatrix} 0 & 0 \\ 0.4 & 0 \end{bmatrix}$$

is such that $(M,1) \sim (M^*,1)$, $(M,2) \sim (M^*,2)$, and $(M,3) \sim (M^*,\pi)$, where $\pi = (0.5,0.5)$.

5 *Minimization*

In Example *10.4.10*, M^* is not an admissible reduction of M from the "mechanical" viewpoint where it is tacitly assumed that machines commence operation with some fixed initial state, but the problem of finding all possible reductions is clearly of interest from a more general stochastic-systems viewpoint. Bacon [1] has solved the problem by showing that when states of one machine are permitted to correspond to distributions on the states of another, the only additional reductions possible (beyond the reduced form) are of the type illustrated in Example *10.4.10*. We summarize Bacon's solution in Theorems *1* and *7*; first, some definitions are needed.

If to each distribution on the states of a stochastic machine M there corresponds an equivalent distribution on the states of N and conversely, then we say that M and N are *distribution-equivalent machines.*

(Note that actually we need only require that to each state of M there corresponds a distribution of N, and conversely.) Evidently, if M and N are state-equivalent, they are distribution-equivalent, but the converse does not hold in general. Among the machines which are distribution-equivalent to a given machine M, those with the smallest number of states are called *minimal forms of M*. A machine is said to be *in minimal form* if no state is equivalent to a distribution assigning zero probability to that state. The terminology is consistent in the sense that a machine is in minimal form if and only if there is no distribution-equivalent machine with fewer states; this follows from a combination of Theorems *1* and *7*.

1 **Theorem** (Bacon [1]) Let $M = \{M(y|x)\}$ be a stochastic machine with c states, and suppose that a state of M is equivalent to a distribution concentrated on the remaining states. For notational convenience, say that state c is equivalent to distribution

$$(\pi 0) = (\pi_1, \pi_2, \ . \ . \ . \ , \pi_{c-1}, 0)$$

Then there exists a machine M^* with $c - 1$ states such that

2 $$(M,i) \sim (M^*,i)$$

for $i = 1, 2, \ldots, c - 1$, and

3 $$(M,c) \sim (M^*,\pi)$$

Specifically, $M^* = \{M^*(y|x)\}$ is constructed as follows: for i and $j = 1, 2, \ldots, c - 1$,

4 $$m^*_{ij}(y|x) = m_{ij}(y|x) + \pi_j m_{ic}(y|x)$$

Proof (First we note that *4* indeed defines a machine.) Let H and H^* be L-basis matrices for M and M^*, respectively. Let H' be obtained from H by deleting its last row. By hypothesis, from *10.3.18* $(\pi 0)H$ coincides with row c of H; that is,

5 $$\pi H' = c\text{th row of } H$$

Applying Theorem *10.4.4* to M, and using *5* with *10.4.5*, we see that M is state-equivalent to the c-state machine N defined by

6 $$N(y|x) = \left[\begin{array}{c:c} & 0 \\ & \cdot \\ M^*(y|x) & \cdot \\ & \cdot \\ & 0 \\ \hdashline 4 \text{ for } i = c \ \cdots & 0 \end{array}\right]$$

Multiplication of matrices of the form of *6* shows that $N(v|u)$ likewise has $M^*(v|u)$ in the upper left and a cth column of zeros; therefore, the first $c - 1$ components of $h^N(v|u)$ agree with $h^*(v|u)$ (where the h^* are h-vectors for machine M^*), and this fact together with *10.4.8* shows that we may choose H' to be identical with H^*. Substituting $H' = H^*$ in *5*, we obtain 3; 2 is also an immediate consequence of $H' = H^*$.

7 **Theorem** (Bacon [1]) Let M be in minimal form with c states, and let N be distribution-equivalent to M. Then N must have at least c states.

Proof For each state s of M, let $\lambda(s)$ be a distribution for N to which s is equivalent; likewise for each state t of N let $\pi(t)$ be a distribution for M to which t is equivalent. Then we have (directly from definitions of equivalence)

8 $$(M,s) \sim (N,\lambda(s)) \sim (M,\delta(s))$$

where the distribution $\delta(s)$ for M is given by

9 $$\delta(s) = \sum_t \lambda_t(s)\pi(t)$$

From the relations of *8* we see that

10 $$s \sim \lambda(s) \text{ with respect to } M$$

Let δ be any distribution for M which is equivalent to the state s; according to *10.3.18*

$$\delta H^M = s\text{th row of } H^M$$

so that if $\delta_s < 1$,

11 $$\delta' H^M = s\text{th row of } H^M$$

where δ' has its sth component zero and otherwise the components of δ' are those of δ divided by $1 - \delta_s$. From *11* and *10.3.18*, $s \sim \delta'$; since the sth component of δ' is zero, this violates the assumption that M is in minimal form. Therefore, we must have $\delta_s = 1$; that is, each state s of a machine M in minimal form is a one-element equivalence class (and in particular there are no equivalent states; that is, M is already in reduced form). Returning to the particular distribution of *9*, we now know that *10* means that $\delta(s)$ must be degenerate on state s. This can happen if and only if $\lambda_t(s) = 1$ for some t, which we denote by $t(s)$ [and $\pi(t)$ is degenerate on the state s]. Therefore, state s of M is equivalent to some state $t(s)$ of N; since this is true for every s, we conclude that to each state of M there corresponds an equivalent state of N. This result, together with the transitivity of equivalence and the fact that M has no equivalent states, shows that the number of states of N must be at least that of M.

To construct a minimal form of any given machine, we apply Theorem *10.4.4* repeatedly. This procedure requires that one be able to recognize or determine whether a state is equivalent to a distribution vanishing on that state, or alternatively, in view of *10.3.18*, whether one row of an L-basis matrix H is a convex combination of the remaining rows. The first row of H can always be taken to be $h(\phi|\phi) = e$ (and the remaining elements of H can be taken to lie between 0 and 1 if this is convenient), and if this choice is made, "convex combination" may be replaced by "linear combination with nonnegative coefficients"; thus, linear programming methods may be useful. We shall not discuss such computational problems here; we refer the reader to the work of Even [12], who calls rows which are not combinations of the rest *extremal*, mentions preliminary tests to detect certain extremal rows by inspection of H, describes a linear programming technique to test the remaining rows and in general to provide an algorithm for minimization, and gives illustrative numerical examples.

The machine M of Example *10.4.10* is in nonunique reduced form and is nonminimal; Example *12* below shows that machines in unique reduced form may also be nonminimal. The minimal forms in both examples are unique, but other simple examples [12] show that minimal forms may be nonunique. However, it is easy to see that for any deterministic machine, the minimal form coincides with the (unique) reduced form.

12 *Example* Let M be the autonomous machine defined by the following matrices. The machine is in unique reduced form (any two states are 1-distinguishable and $\dim L = c = 3$); state 3 is equivalent to the distribution assigning probabilities $\frac{1}{2}$ to states 1 and 2, so that the minimal form has two states.

$$M(y = 0) = \begin{bmatrix} 1 & 0 & 0 \\ 0 & 0 & 0 \\ \frac{1}{2} & 0 & 0 \end{bmatrix} \qquad M(y = 1) = \begin{bmatrix} 0 & 0 & 0 \\ 0 & 1 & 0 \\ 0 & \frac{1}{2} & 0 \end{bmatrix}$$

6 *Events*

If $M = \{M(y|x)\}$ is a stochastic machine, for each u let $M(u)$ be the sum of the matrices $M(v|u)$; thus

1 $$M(u) = \sum_{v} M(v|u)$$

(*10.3.4* is the special case $|u| = 1$). The ij element of $M(u)$ is the probability that j will be the terminal state if input tape u is applied when

i is the initial state. Evidently each $M(u)$ is a Markov matrix; from *10.3.5* we have

2 $$M(uu') = M(u)M(u')$$

This identity also determines state transition matrices $M(u)$ when we are given any family $\{M(x)\}$ of (one-step) state transition matrices (not necessarily arising from *10.3.4* but Markov matrices nevertheless).

A probabilistic automaton as defined by Rabin [18] consists of a family $\{M(x)\}$ of state transition matrices, an initial state s, and a set F of designated final states; the probability function of interest is $p(F|u)$, the probability that the terminal state will be a member of F if input tape u is applied when s is the initial state. Thus

3 $$p(F|u) = \sum_{s' \text{ in } F} m_{ss'}(u) = \pi M(u)o$$

where $\pi_s = 1$, and o is a column vector with $o_i = 1$ when i is a member of F and $o_i = 0$ otherwise. Let M be a machine, with binary output alphabet, such that $M(y|x)$ is obtained from $M(x)$ by replacing column j with zeros when $y = 0$ and j is a member of F, or when $y = 1$ and j is not in F, and let $p(y|u)$ be the probability that y is the final output of system (M,s) if u is applied. Then (for $|u| \geq 1$)

4 $$p(y = 1|u) = p(F|u)$$

and in this sense the automaton $(\{M(x)\},s,F)$ may be identified with the system (M,s). The special structure of this system is not an important part of the automaton concept, which relates to the choice of observables to be studied (final y vs. tape v) rather than to the internal structure; i.e., the essential feature is the attention given to the probability function $p(y|u)$. Therefore, we may use the term *stochastic automaton* as an alternate designation for any stochastic finite-state system (M,π), with the understanding that the probability law of interest is the *(automaton) final output distribution* $p(y|u)$ defined through

5 $$\begin{aligned} p(y|ux) &= \sum_v p(vy|ux) \\ &= \pi M(u)M(y|x)e = g(u)h(y|x) \end{aligned}$$

where $g(u)$ is the sum, over v, of the vectors of *10.3.9*. The particular structures governed by *3* and/or *4* will be called *Rabin automata*.

Let (M,π) be an automaton with final output distribution $p(y|u)$. For each real number ϵ $(0 \leq \epsilon < 1)$ and output symbol y, we define an *event*, or more precisely an *input event* (set of input sequences), $T(\epsilon,y)$

as follows:

6 $$T(\epsilon,y) = \{u: p(y|u) > \epsilon\}$$

The number ϵ is called a *cut point*, and we say that the event *6* is *defined by the automaton* (M,π) *with cut point* ϵ *(and output* y*).* In case there are only two output symbols, as in *4*, any $T(\epsilon,0)$ may be expressed in terms of the family $\{T(\epsilon,1)\}$ so that we may dispense with the input events for $y = 0$; that is, we then consider the events [18]

7 $$T(\epsilon) = \{u: p(F|u) > \epsilon\}$$

defined by Rabin automata.

The definition of *6* or *7* is a natural stochastic generalization of the concept of event in deterministic automata theory; for the case of a deterministic system (M,s) with binary output, *7* is independent of ϵ $(0 \leq \epsilon < 1)$ and is simply the set T of input tapes for which the final output is 1 (or the final state is in F). We recall that an event is said to be *regular* if it is definable by some deterministic automaton.

8 **Theorem** (Rabin [18]) There exist stochastic automata defining non-regular events. On the other hand, if R is a Rabin automaton and ϵ is a cut point such that for some $\delta > 0$

$$|p^R(F|u) - \epsilon| \geq \delta \qquad \text{for all } u$$

(such an ϵ is called an *isolated* cut point), then $T^R(\epsilon)$ is regular (coincides with the event T defined by some deterministic automaton). If in addition every transition probability for R is positive (such an R is called an *actual* automaton), $T^R(\epsilon)$ is a definite event (i.e., definable by a deterministic automaton which can be realized using combinational circuits and unit delays but no feedback loops); conversely, every definite event is definable by some actual automaton with isolated cut point. If R is actual and ϵ is isolated, then $T^R(\epsilon)$ is *stable* in the sense that there is a $\gamma > 0$ such that

$$T^{R'}(\epsilon) = T^R(\epsilon)$$

for all R' whose state transition probabilities differ from those of R by less than γ.

The statement of Theorem *8* is intended to be a partial summary of the important contributions of Rabin. The example below verifies the first assertion of the theorem; we shall not discuss the remaining proofs here. A summary of Rabin's work also appears in the textbook by Harrison [14]. Paz [16] has given further details and extensions, and additional recent results on the general subject of events may be found in [34], [36], [37], [38], [43], [46], [47], [48], [50].

9 *Example* (Rabin [18]) Consider the following two-state machine M with binary input and output alphabets:

$$M(0|0) = \begin{bmatrix} 1 & 0 \\ \frac{1}{2} & 0 \end{bmatrix} \qquad M(1|0) = \begin{bmatrix} 0 & 0 \\ 0 & \frac{1}{2} \end{bmatrix}$$

$$M(0|1) = \begin{bmatrix} \frac{1}{2} & 0 \\ 0 & 0 \end{bmatrix} \qquad M(1|1) = \begin{bmatrix} 0 & \frac{1}{2} \\ 0 & 1 \end{bmatrix}$$

It is easily verified that if $p(y|u)$ is the terminal output distribution for the system $(M,1)$, then

$$p(y = 1|x_1x_2 \cdot \cdot \cdot x_n) = 0.x_nx_{n-1} \cdot \cdot \cdot x_1 \text{ in binary notation}$$

Let $0 \leq \epsilon < r \leq \epsilon' < 1$, where ϵ and ϵ' are cut points and r is a rational number between them. If we express r in binary notation and reverse the symbol sequence, we obtain a tape u for which $p(y = 1|u)$ is equal to r; therefore, u is a member of $T(\epsilon)$, but not of $T(\epsilon')$. The conclusion is that the family of input events $T(\epsilon)$ for all real numbers ϵ $(0 \leq \epsilon < 1)$ is a continuum of distinct events, and since the number of distinct regular events is only countably infinite, there exist events $T(\epsilon)$ which are not regular.

We now examine some relationships between the event concept and the concept of system equivalence (equality of input-output relations). First, we observe that for an automaton, the final output distribution of *5* is calculated under the assumption that responses at intermediate times are unavailable; this means that either (1) such responses are physically unobservable (or at least ignored as observables), or (2) the calculation is imagined to be carried out before u is applied (so that the responses have not yet occurred) and only the final output is of interest. For a stochastic system, the entire response sequence is regarded as observable, and we must define the *(system) final output distribution* to be

10 $$p(y|ux,v) = \frac{p(vy|ux)}{p(v|u)}$$

Using *10*, we define *input-output events* $\tilde{T}(\epsilon,y)$ to be sets of pairs (ux,v) of tapes, as follows:

11 $$\tilde{T}(\epsilon,y) = \{(ux,v): p(y|ux,v) > \epsilon\}$$

We say that two systems are *input-output event equivalent* if their events, as given in *11*, agree (for each ϵ and y), and *input event equivalent* if their events, as given in *6* or *7*, agree.

12 **Theorem** Two finite-state systems are equivalent if and only if they are input-output event equivalent. If two systems are equivalent, they are input event equivalent. Deterministic systems are equivalent if

and only if they are input event equivalent. However, there are distinguishable stochastic systems which are input event equivalent.

The final assertion of Theorem *12* may be established by constructing a simple example such as the one below (the remainder of Theorem *12* consists of direct consequences of the pertinent definitions).

13 *Example* Let M be a two-state machine with binary input and output alphabets and input-output-state transitions as follows:

$$M(0|0) = \begin{bmatrix} \frac{1}{2} & 0 \\ \frac{1}{2} & 0 \end{bmatrix} \qquad M(1|0) = \begin{bmatrix} 0 & \frac{1}{2} \\ 0 & \frac{1}{2} \end{bmatrix}$$

$$M(0|1) = \begin{bmatrix} \frac{1}{2} & 0 \\ 0 & \frac{1}{2} \end{bmatrix} \qquad M(1|1) = \begin{bmatrix} 0 & \frac{1}{2} \\ \frac{1}{2} & 0 \end{bmatrix}$$

Let the machine N be defined by

$$N(0|0) = M(0|0) \qquad N(1|0) = M(1|0)$$

$$N(0|1) = \begin{bmatrix} 1 & 0 \\ 0 & 0 \end{bmatrix} \qquad N(1|1) = \begin{bmatrix} 0 & 0 \\ 0 & 1 \end{bmatrix}$$

If $\pi = \lambda = (\frac{1}{2},\frac{1}{2})$, then (M,π) and (N,λ) have identical automaton final output distributions $p(y|u)$ ($\equiv \frac{1}{2}$ for all y and u); therefore, (M,π) and (N,λ) are input event equivalent. However, the two systems are not equivalent; i.e., they have distinct input-output relations $p(v|u)$. For example, $p(01|11)$ has the value $\frac{1}{4}$ for (M,π) and 0 for (N,λ).

The above example shows that input event equivalence of stochastic systems does not, in general, suffice to establish system equivalence (see also Theorem *10.8.2*). In the deterministic case, the two concepts are evidently in agreement (as noted in Theorem *12*); this fact is recognized, at least implicitly, when regular expression techniques are used to design deterministic systems with presecribed input-output relations, because the relations may be restated in terms of (regular) input events. Since such a restatement is not generally possible in the stochastic case, there may be occasion to consider input-output events, in addition to the input events introduced by Rabin, in characterizing the "work" done by a stochastic system.

7 *Recursive structure of external probabilities*

Let $p(v|u)$ be any input-output relation (not necessarily of finite-state type); we define its *initial segment* of length n, denoted by $\{p\}_n$, to be the restriction of p to arguments of length no greater than n. Thus

$$\{p\}_n(v|u) = p(v|u)\text{: all } u \text{ and } v \text{ of length} \leq n$$

(note that from *10.2.13*, "length $\leq n$" can be replaced by "length $= n$"). Any input-output relation which has a specified initial segment is called a *completion* of that segment. It is clear that, in general, there may be many completions of a given segment; i.e., there may be many different input-output relations having identical characteristics for some initial time period. However, if p is known to be an input-output relation of finite-state type requiring at most c states, then $\{p\}_n$ has one and only one completion (that is, p itself), provided that

$$n \geq 2c - 1$$

This is an immediate consequence of Theorem *10.3.15*. This result implies that there exists a rule whereby, using only the information contained in an initial segment of appropriate length, one can calculate the entire input-output relation for a finite-state stochastic system (M,π). Note that, except for an upper bound on the number of states, no information is assumed to be available on the internal structure (M,π); the rule of calculation must determine probabilities $p(v|u)$ of "long" sequences solely from probabilities of certain "short" sequences, even though finite-state systems may in general exhibit infinite memory. Explicit constructions for such rules should therefore place in evidence some of the basic structural restrictions imposed on external behavior (i.e., on stochastic input-output relations) when only finitely many internal states are permitted; this information can be expected to be pertinent to problems of system identification, realization or design, etc. Here we review the development of a recursive rule of this type, obtained [6] by revising and extending Gilbert's work [13], cited previously. An application to random sequences is proposed in [40].

Let M be a stochastic machine having c states, let π be an initial distribution for M, and let $p(v|u)$ be the input-output relation for (M,π). If

$$(u_1,v_1),\ (u_2,v_2),\ \ldots,\ (u_n,v_n)$$
$$(u_1',v_1'),\ (u_2',v_2'),\ \ldots,\ (u_n',v_n')$$

is any collection of $2n$ pairs of sequences, we have from *10.3.13* that

1 $$P = GH$$

where P, G, and H are $n \times n$, $n \times c$, and $c \times n$ matrices, respectively, with

$$ij \text{ element of } P = p(v_iv_j'|u_iu_j')$$
$$i\text{th row of } G = g(v_i|u_i)$$
$$j\text{th column of } H = h(v_j'|u_j')$$

From *1*, we see that the rank of the $n \times n$ matrix P cannot exceed c, so that if n is sufficiently large (in particular, if $n > c$), the determinant of P vanishes, no matter what collection of pairs of sequences is considered; this establishes a relationship among the numbers $p(v_i v_j' | u_i u_j')$. Our objective is to show that in this way, probabilities of long sequences can be expressed in terms of probabilities of short sequences.

Given an arbitrary input-output relation p, one can construct square matrices of the form

2 $$P = (p(v_i v_j' | u_i u_j'))$$

(of course, in general P may not be decomposable into factors as in *10.2.3*). Such matrices will be called *compound sequence matrices;* their determinants will be called *compound sequence determinants.* The *rank* $r(p)$ of any input-output relation p is defined to be the maximum among the ranks of all compound sequence matrices which can be formed from p, or to be $+\infty$ if no such maximum exists. It is easily seen that the input-output relations of rank 1 coincide with those having zero memory, namely, those for which

$$p(vv'|uu') = p(v|u)p(v'|u')$$

for all sequences, and any such input-output relation has a trivial one-state machine representation. More generally, according to the remarks following *1*, the rank of any input-output relation p of finite-state type cannot exceed the smallest number c for which there is a c-state system representation for p.

Let p be any input-output relation having finite rank r. Then every compound sequence determinant of order $r + 1$ vanishes; in particular, for all (u,v) and (u',v'),

3 $$\left|\begin{array}{ccc|c} & & & p(v_1 v'|u_1 u') \\ & & & p(v_2 v'|u_2 u') \\ & P & & \vdots \\ & & & p(v_r v'|u_r u') \\ \hline p(vv_1'|uu_1') & \cdots & p(vv_r'|uu_r') & p(vv'|uu') \end{array}\right| = 0$$

where $P = (p(v_i v_j' | u_i u_j'))$ is any $r \times r$ compound sequence matrix. If P is chosen to be nonsingular, an expansion of *3* about the last column may be written in the form

4 $$p(vv'|uu') = \sum_{i=1}^{r} a_i(v|u)p(v_i v'|u_i u')$$

where the numerical coefficients $a_i(v|u)$ are uniquely determined as functions only of the elements of the matrix P and the probabilities $p(vv'_j|uu'_j)$.

To exhibit the recursive nature of *4* in convenient matrix form, we note that

$$p(v_ivv'v'_j|u_iuu'u'_j) = \sum_{k=1}^{r} a_k(v_iv|u_iu)p(v_kv'v'_j|u_ku'u'_j)$$

or

5 $$P(vv'|uu') = A(v|u)P(v'|u')$$

where $P(v|u)$ and $A(v|u)$ are the $r \times r$ matrices whose ij elements are $p(v_ivv'_j|u_iuu'_j)$ and $a_j(v_iv|u_iu)$, respectively, with $P(\phi|\phi) = P$ and $A(\phi|\phi) = I$ (the identity matrix). In particular,

6 $$P(v|u) = A(v|u)P$$

Using *6* on both sides of *5* and canceling the common (nonsingular) factor P in the result, we obtain

7 $$A(vv'|uu') = A(v|u)A(v'|u')$$

which shows that any matrix $A(v|u)$ can be formed by repeated multiplication of factors $A(y|x)$; the latter matrices are calculated from

8 $$A(y|x) = P(y|x)P^{-1}$$

If $P = (p(v_iv'_j|u_iu'_j))$ is constructed with

9 $$u_1 = v_1 = u'_1 = v'_1 = \phi$$

the probability $p(v|u)$ becomes the (1,1)-element of the matrix $P(v|u)$, and calculation of probabilities $p(v|u)$ of long sequences is then equivalent to calculation of the corresponding matrices $P(v|u)$, which can proceed in recursive fashion using *8*, *7*, and *6*. The choice of *9* is always possible; this can be verified by (for example) considering both last-row and last-column expansions of *3* with $u = v = u' = v' = \phi$.

The above recursive scheme for calculating long sequences $p(v|u)$ is of little significance unless it is known that a maximal-rank compound sequence matrix can be found among those defined by sequences of bounded length (short sequences). For input-output relations of finite-state type requiring no more than c states, the bound $c - 1$ is obtained as follows. Let (M,π) be a c-state representation for p, let H' be a matrix whose columns are a maximal linearly independent set of h-vectors (*10.3.6*), let G' be a matrix whose rows are a maximal linearly independent set of g-vectors (*10.3.9*), and let $P' = G'H'$. Then from *1* any compound sequence matrix P must be of the form $CP'D$, so that the rank of P' cannot be less than the maximal rank r for csm's; on the other hand, the rank of P' cannot exceed r since every square submatrix of P' is a csm. Therefore, the rank of P' is r. The defining sequences for P' can be chosen to have length $\leq c - 1$, since the proof of Theorem *10.3.14* shows that H' can be so defined, and an entirely analogous argument for g-vectors (using *10.3.11*) shows that the same is true for G'. Hence, there exists a maximal-rank csm (a submatrix of P') among those defined by sequences of length not exceeding $c - 1$. This observation, together with our recursive scheme above, establishes the following theorem.

10 **Theorem** If p is any input-output relation of finite-state type which is known to require no more than c states, and if its initial segment of length $2c - 1$ is given, then the remainder of p is determined uniquely; a specific rule of calculation can be described as follows:

1. Evaluate the compound sequence determinants of order $\leq c$ whose defining sequences are all of length $\leq c - 1$ [evidently this utilizes only information contained in the initial segment of length $2(c - 1)$].
2. From those csd's in (1) which are nonvanishing choose any one having maximal order and such that its defining sequences satisfy *9*; let its matrix be denoted by P.
3. Calculate the matrices $A(y|x)$, using *8* [note that the elements of the matrices $P(y|x)$ are provided by the initial segment of length $2(c - 1) + 1 = 2c - 1$].
4. For any (u,v), the probability $p(v|u)$ is the (1,1)-element of the matrix $P(v|u)$, and this matrix can be calculated, with the aid of *7* and *6*, using only the matrix P and the matrices $A(y|x)$ found in (3).

One might expect that a specific rule of calculation such as that given in Theorem *10* could be developed further to yield not merely a method for completing the initial segment of p, but in addition a procedure for determining finite-state system representations for p. This problem has not been solved in general, but the next theorem is relevant.

11 **Theorem** Let p be an arbitrary input-output relation of finite rank r, let P be an $r \times r$ nonsingular compound sequence matrix formed from p and satisfying *9*, and let the $r \times r$ matrices $A(y|x)$ be determined as in *8*. Let Q be any $r \times r$ nonsingular matrix such that (1) Qe coincides with the first column of P and (2) the first row of Q has nonnegative elements [and is therefore a probability distribution, from (1) and *9*]. Define

12 $$M'(y|x) = Q^{-1}A(y|x)Q$$

13 $$\pi' = \text{first row of } Q$$

Then (M',π) is an r-state *pseudo-finite-state system representation* for p, in the sense that (as in *10.3.7*)

14 $$p(v|u) = \pi' M'(v|u)e$$

where π' is a probability distribution on r points, but the matrix elements $m'_{ij}(y|x)$ need not be nonnegative and hence cannot be interpreted as probabilities, even though for each x, the "state transition" matrix

15 $$M'(x) = \sum_{y} M'(y|x)$$

has unity row sums as required in the specification of a finite-state machine. If p is known to be of finite-state type and *of full rank*, i.e., if p possesses an r-state true system representation, then all such representations can be obtained from the matrices Q for which *12* has nonnegative elements.

Proof First observe that nonsingular matrices Q satisfying requirements (1) and (2) are readily constructed; one need only choose a probability distribution for the first row and then adjoin $r - 1$ rows, with the prescribed row sums, in such a way that all r rows are linearly independent. From *12* we see that

16 $$M'(v|u) = Q^{-1}A(v|u)Q$$

Assertions *14* and *15* follow by direct calculation from (1), (2), *6*, *9*, and *16*; the final assertion is verified by noting that if (M,π) is an r-state system representation, then from *10.3.5* and *1*, $P(y|x) = GM(y|x)H$, so that $M(y|x)$ is obtained from *12* when Q coincides with G.

Suppose that p is of finite-state type, known to require no more than c states, but it is found that $r(p) < c$; one might suppose that such a situation could arise only because c-state representations (M,π) are such that M is not in reduced form or has submachines not reachable from the initial condition π, so that among the pseudorepresentations of Theorem *11*, there is at least one true r-state representation even when p is not full rank. This is not the case in general; even the very rudimentary deterministic Example *17* below shows that r may indeed be strictly less than the number of states in any true system representation. As noted in the paragraph following Example *10.6.13*, the solution to the representation problem is already available in the deterministic case. We conclude that the techniques of Theorem *11* alone cannot lead to a general solution in the stochastic case. Theorem *10.8.2* provides a particular solution by more direct methods applicable to a useful class of systems. Finally, we note that there exist finite-rank relations which *cannot* be realized by finite-state systems; an example in the autonomous case was proposed by Fox [28] and has been expanded upon by Dharmadhikari [9, 29].

17 *Example* Let M be the deterministic machine with four states, binary input and output alphabets, and transitions as follows:

s	x	y	s'
1, 2	0	0	2
3, 4	0	1	3
1, 3	1	0	1
2, 4	1	1	4

It is readily verified that $L_1 = L$ for this machine and dim $L = 3$ ($<c = 4$ which coincides with $\#\omega$ here since the machine is in reduced form by inspection). Therefore $r(p) \leq 3$ for any system containing M. In particular, the deterministic system $(M,1)$ has $r(p) = 3$, since it is easy to find a nonvanishing compound sequence determinant of order 3. However it is clear by inspection that $p_1{}^M$ cannot be obtained as the input-output relation for any three-state system. Note also that M is strongly connected and the terminal state is a function of x and y only.

8 *State-calculable systems*

We say that a stochastic sequential machine M is state-calculable if, given the present state s, an external observer of the operation of the black box containing the system (M,s) can calculate the next state s'. More precisely, a machine M governed by *10.2.1* is *observer-state-calculable* [7] if there is a function f such that

$$p(y,s'|s,x) = 0 \qquad \text{if } s' \neq f(s,x,y)$$

If the function f depends only on arguments s and y, M is *output-state-calculable;* if f depends only on s and x, M is *state-deterministic* or *input-state-calculable* [7, 20, 23, 25]. For those (s,x,y) such that $p_s(y|x)$ from *10.2.4* is zero, $f(s,x,y)$ can be assigned arbitrary values or left undefined if convenient; here, we shall use both choices interchangeably without comment. Note that if $\{M(y|x)\}$ is an observer-state-calculable machine, the matrices $M(y|x)$ have, at most, one nonzero element in each row.

It is clear that state-calculable criteria do not lead to unrealistic restrictions on machine structure; systems perturbed by random faults of various types can still be modeled. In fact, the permissible state-diagram complexity (in connection properties and in stochastic behavior) increases in the following manner as we pass from (1) the deterministic case to (2) the input-state-calculable case, to (3) the observer-state-calculable case, and finally to (4) the unrestricted model:

1. From each state in the diagram there emanates exactly one transition for each output symbol x; the output y accompanying a transition is deterministic.
2. Each transition in (1) may be split into a set of parallel branches having different outputs y; each branch has a probability assigned to it, and the probabilities in each set sum to 1.
3. Each set of parallel branches in (2) is allowed to diverge; i.e., the requirement that all members of a set terminate on the same state is dropped.
4. In the unrestricted case, any branch in (3) may divide and diverge (with an accompanying partitioning of its probability), so that for a given s, x, and y, there may be more than one candidate for the next state s', destroying state-calculability.

The machine M of Example *10.6.9* is observer-state-calculable; in fact it is *state-observable,* for there is a one-to-one correspondence between s' and y. In Example *10.6.9*, $(M,1)$ defines nonregular input events; this provides further verification that even under state-calculable restrictions, stochastic systems can possess complex behavior patterns.

The list of results contained in our next theorem [7] has been selected to show that many of the difficulties encountered in preceding sections are suppressed when attention is restricted to situations in which state-calculability is assumed. It is convenient to extend the deterministic notion of "derivative of an event" or "state of a sequential function" to the stochastic case by defining the generalized states of an input-output relation p to be functions of the form

1 $$q(v|u) = \frac{p(v'v|u'u)}{p(v'|u')}$$

It is easy to see that all such functions (conditional probability laws) are themselves input-output relations (satisfying *10.2.13*).

2 **Theorem**

1. Let M be an observer-state-calculable stochastic machine with c states, and let s be any state of M [systems (M,s) of this form are called

observer-state-calculable systems]. Then every terminal distribution *10.2.5* for (M,s) is degenerate; i.e., the input-output relation for (M,s) has no more than c distinct generalized states and each is identifiable with an actual state of M reachable from s.

2. Every observer-state-calculable stochastic machine has a unique (apart from relabelings of the states) observer/state-calculable reduced form. [However, as in the general case, reduced forms and minimal forms need not coincide (Example *10.5.12*).]

3. Let M and N be stochastic machines which are state-deterministic; if (M,π) and (N,λ) are input event equivalent, then they are equivalent (and conversely from Theorem *10.6.2*). [This need not hold if M and N are only observer-state-calculable (Example *10.6.13*).]

4. Let p be an input-output relation known to have at most c distinct generalized states [for example, p may be known to have some representation (M,s), where M is observer-state-calculable, but nothing else is known except that M need have no more than c states]. Then knowledge of the initial segment of p of length $2c - 1$ is sufficient to determine, constructively, a (unique) system representation (N,s) for p having the minimum necessary number of states and such that N is observer-state-calculable [and from (N,s) the completion of p can evidently be calculated recursively].

Proof Parts (1), (2), and (3) follow from definitions with no essential difficulty; we sketch the proof of part (4). Let q be a generalized state of p; for given (x,y), the "next" generalized state q' satisfies

$$q(yv|xu) = q(y|x)q'(v|u)$$

(see *1*), and we define

3
$$f(q,x,y) = q' \qquad p(y,q'|q,x) = q(y|x)$$

The specifications of *3* determine an observer-state-calculable machine N whose state set consists of labels identifying the various generalized states q. It is then readily verified that if s is the label for p, (N,s) is the desired realization. It remains only to establish that we can identify all distinct q's by restricting attention to $\{p\}_{2c-1}$; this follows from (1) Theorem *10.3.3* rephrased for generalized states (and a class-counting argument), showing that two generalized states are distinct only if their initial segments of length $c - 1$ are distinct, and from (2) the fact that every distinct generalized state of p is reachable through tapes of length not exceeding $c - 1$ (proved by an extension of the well-known argument for deterministic finite-state machines).

9 *Comparison of models*

We have consistently employed the stochastic machine model defined directly by *10.2.1*; we now list some obvious alternative sets of specifications. In each case, we state how *10.2.1* is obtained from the given data; all models are supposed to operate sequentially in the manner governed by *10.2.3*. As usual, the designations p and f are employed repeatedly for various functions, distinguished by their arguments.

Shannon model The probability law *10.2.1*, $p(y,s'|s,x)$, is supposed to be specified directly in that form.
Stochastic versions of the Mealy model Probabilities $p(y|s,x)$ and $p(s'|s,x)$ are given, and *10.2.1* is their product; thus, y and s' are conditionally independent (when s and x are fixed).
Stochastic versions of the Moore model Probabilities $p(y|s')$ and $p(s'|s,x)$ are given, and *10.2.1* is their product. Usually $p(y|s')$ is taken to be deterministic; that is, $y = f(s')$. The Rabin automaton of *10.6.4* is of this form, with binary output alphabet; for any output alphabet, the matrices $M(y|x)$ for a Moore model with $y = f(s')$ are obtained, as described by *10.6.4*, by partitioning the columns of $M(x)$ with respect to f.
Deterministic machine with random disturbances [24] To each symbol r in an alphabet R, there corresponds a deterministic state diagram, and r has a probability distribution; thus, we are given a function

$$(y,s') = f(s,x,r)$$

and a probability law $p(r)$, or $p(r|x)$ in some situations (the distribution of r is allowed to depend on x but not on s, y, or s'). The probability *10.2.1* is obtained through

$$p(y,s'|s,x) = \Sigma p(r) \qquad \text{or} \qquad \Sigma p(r|x)$$

where for fixed y, s', s, and x the sum extends over all r such that $(y,s') = f(s,x,r)$. The physical interpretation of the operation of the random-disturbance model is that a deterministic machine is subjected to a sequence of disturbances caused by the action of a sequence of independent random variables emitted from a memoryless stochastic black box (which may be either autonomous or controlled by the machine input). Similar models have been considered in a control-system context [39].

The descriptions given here view each model as a special case of the Shannon model. Actually, however, all models are of equal scope;

thus, the choice of model is relatively unimportant in theoretical discussions, but it may have considerable significance in applications. By "equal scope" we mean that (for fixed input and output alphabets) if M is in one of the forms listed and we wish to "convert" to another form, there is a machine N in the latter form such that M and N are state-equivalent. Two examples are sufficient to illustrate all cases; we shall sketch the straightforward conversion from Shannon to Moore models, and the less obvious conversion from Moore to random-disturbance models. Note that in general, attention may need to be directed to such matters as the exact time sequence of machine operations (this is basically a question of physical interpretation) and the possible presence of an observable initial output before inputs are applied. The latter may occur if M is a Moore model with deterministic output function $y = f(s')$ and the system (M,s) is such that $y_0 = f(s)$ is observable. We have tacitly assumed that the responses of any system (M,π) are consequences of the application of inputs, and any additional data, such as y_0, are absorbed by recalculating the initial distribution π. For further discussion of various models, see [32, 33, 47].

1 *Example* Let $M = (X,Y,S,p(y,s'|s,x))$ be a Shannon model. Define

$$\bar{S} = \{\bar{s} = (\bar{s}_1,\bar{s}_2): \bar{s}_1 \text{ in } Y,\ \bar{s}_2 \text{ in } S\}$$
$$\bar{p}(\bar{s}'|\bar{s},x) = p(\bar{s}_1',\bar{s}_2'|\bar{s}_2,x)$$
$$f(\bar{s}) = \bar{s}_2$$

Then $N = (X,Y,\bar{S},\bar{p},f)$ is a Moore model state-equivalent to M; in fact, (M,s) and $(N,\bar{s})$ are equivalent for $\bar{s}_2 = s$. This conversion shows that the sequence of output random variables for any autonomous stochastic finite-state system is a "function of a finite-state Markov chain" in the sense that the machine is (or can be converted to) a black box whose internal state transitions are governed by a Markov chain and whose output at any time is a function f of the state at that time. For stochastic finite-state systems with input, the sequence of output random variables is a "function of a controlled Markov chain" (the selection of the Markov transition matrix applicable at any time is controlled by the input at that time).

2 *Example* Let $M = (X,Y,S,p(s'|s,x),\ y = f(x))$ be a Moore model with c states. Identify S with the first c integers, and for each x display $p(s'|s,x)$ as a Markov matrix $M(x)$. Using Theorem *3* below, for some finite set R we have

$$M(x) = \sum_{r \text{ in } R} \bar{p}(r|x)D_r$$

where $\bar{p}(r|x)$ is a probability distribution on R for each fixed x, and the

D_r are deterministic Markov matrices. For fixed r, the matrix D_r and the function $y = f(x)$ define a deterministic (Moore) sequential machine M_r. The collection of all M_r may be written in the form

$$(y,s') = \bar{f}(s,x,r)$$

Then $N = (X,Y,S,\bar{f},\bar{p}(r|x))$ is a random-disturbance model such that (M,s) and (N,s) are equivalent for all s.

3 **Theorem** (A. S. Davis [8]) A $c \times c$ matrix is a Markov matrix if and only if it is a convex combination of $c \times c$ deterministic Markov matrices.

The proof of Theorem *3* consists of an easily described direct construction, but is omitted here; for further details, see the note by Davis [8], in which the theorem is established for rectangular stochastic matrices.

4 *Continuation of Example 2* In *2*, we have converted to a random-disturbance model in which the disturbance distribution depends on the input symbol applied. This dependence can always be eliminated, if desired, by a second application of the preceding theorem to the disturbance distributions arranged as a rectangular stochastic matrix [30]. In fact, it is easy to see that one can convert directly from the Shannon model to a model with input-free disturbances by applying the Davis theorem to a single partitioned rectangular stochastic matrix whose blocks are the individual matrices $M(y|x)$. In general, conversion to the random-disturbance form may provide a basis for assessing the essential internal complexity of a stochastic machine [31]. Finally, we note that the interesting special case of disturbances which are additive (in a finite field) has been studied [32].

10 *Remarks on additional topics*

1. Bacon [2] has studied *decompositions* of stochastic sequential machines into interconnections of concurrently operating component machines; he has obtained stochastic generalizations of corresponding results in deterministic decomposition theory.

2. Page [17] has defined *expectation-equivalence* for stochastic automata whose outputs are numerical; two automata are expectation-equivalent if, for each tape u, the two final-output distributions $p(y|u)$ have equal mean values. Page compares expectation-equivalence with other equivalence definitions, and studies conditions under which a stochastic automaton is expectation-equivalent to a suitable deterministic

automaton. Numerical inputs and outputs can be viewed as costs and returns, respectively, and the net expected payoff can then be studied as a machine performance criterion [45].

3. From Example *10.9.2*, with Theorem *10.9.3*, a general solution is obtained for the problem of realization of a stochastic machine in terms of deterministic machines and zero-memory random sources. Thus, through simulation of such sources, one may simulate the operation of the machine. Alternatively, the simulation problem may be combined with the realization problem to seek an integrated approach more compatible with practical details of real-time simulation by computers; schemes such as those cited by Tsertsvadze [22] may be of interest from this viewpoint if all required transition probabilities are expressible as ratios of small integers.

4. As noted earlier, proofs of Theorems *10.3.14*, *10.3.15*, *10.7.11*, and *10.8.2* were obtained by revising and extending methods used by Blackwell and Koopmans [4] and Gilbert [13] to study the identifiability problem for functions of stationary finite-state Markov chains; further work on this problem [9, 10, 11, 15] likewise has relevance to stochastic system theory. Heller's form [15] of necessary and sufficient conditions for a process to be a function of a finite-state Markov chain has recently been given a simple reinterpretation in the context of stochastic machine theory by Arbib [26], whose methods are related to some of those in Sec. 8 above. Additional work on realization theory can be found in [44, 49].

5. Machine N is said to *dominate* M ($N \geq M$) if to each distribution on the states of M there corresponds an equivalent distribution on the states of N; thus M and N are distribution-equivalent if, and only if, both $M \geq N$ and $N \geq M$. Dominance has been defined and studied by Ott [27], who notes that $N \geq M$ can hold when N has fewer states than M, even with M in minimal form. Hence in this sense the concept of dominance is of considerable interest as an alternative to equivalence when one is searching for state set reductions, in those cases where the application requires only that the modification N have at least the behavioral complexity of the original machine M (for example, additional behavioral patterns are permitted in N). For further developments in minimization theory and related topics, see [41], [42], and the survey paper [35].

REFERENCES

In the interest of brevity, references in *deterministic* system theory have not been cited, except for the textbook by Harrison [14] which contains all definitions needed here, with references to other texts and to the original literature.

Stochastic Finite-state System Theory

1 Bacon, G. C.: Minimal-state Stochastic Finite-state Systems, *IEEE Trans. Circuit Theory*, vol. CT-11, pp. 307–308, 1964.
2 Bacon, G. C.: The Decomposition of Stochastic Automata, *Inform. Control*, vol. 7, pp. 320–339, 1964.
3 Blackwell, D., L. Breiman, and A. J. Thomasian: Proof of Shannon's Transmission Theorem for Finite-state Indecomposable Channels, *Ann. Math. Statist.*, vol. 29, pp. 1209–1220, 1958.
4 Blackwell, D., and L. Koopmans: On the Identifiability Problem for Functions of Finite Markov Chains, *Ann. Math. Statist.*, vol. 28, pp. 1011–1015, 1957.
5 Carlyle, J. W.: Reduced Forms for Stochastic Sequential Machines, *Jour. Math. Anal. Appl.*, vol. 7, pp. 167–175, 1963.
6 Carlyle, J. W.: On the External Probability Structure of Finite-state Channels, *Inform. Control*, vol. 7, pp. 385–397, 1964.
7 Carlyle, J. W.: State-calculable Stochastic Sequential Machines, *Proc. IEEE Sixth Ann. Symp. Switching Circuit Theory*, 1965.
8 Davis, A. S.: Markov Chains as Random Input Automata, *Amer. Math. Monthly*, vol. 68, pp. 264–267, 1961.
9 Dharmadhikari, S. W.: Functions of Finite Markov Chains, *Ann. Math. Statist.*, vol. 34, pp. 1022–1032, 1963.
10 Dharmadhikari, S. W.: Sufficient Conditions for a Stationary Process to Be a Function of a Finite Markov Chain, *Ann. Math. Statist.*, vol. 34, pp. 1033–1041, 1963.
11 Dharmadhikari, S. W.: A Characterization of a Class of Functions of Finite Markov Chains, *Ann. Math. Statist.*, vol. 36, pp. 524–528, 1965.
12 Even, S.: Comments on the Minimization of Stochastic Machines, *IEEE Trans. Electron. Computers*, vol. 14, pp. 634–637, 1965.
13 Gilbert, E. J.: On the Identifiability Problem for Functions of Finite Markov Chains, *Ann. Math. Statist.*, vol. 30, pp. 688–697, 1959.
14 Harrison, M. A.: "Introduction to Switching and Automata Theory," McGraw-Hill, New York, 1965.
15 Heller, A.: On Stochastic Processes Derived from Markov Chains, *Ann. Math. Statist.*, vol. 36, pp. 1286–1291, 1965.
16 Paz, A.: Some Aspects of Probabilistic Automata, *Inform. Control*, vol. 9, pp. 26–59, 1966.
17 Page, C. V.: Equivalences between Probabilistic and Deterministic Machines, *Inform. Control*, vol. 9, pp. 469–520, 1966.
18 Rabin, M. O.: Probabilistic Automata, *Inform. Control*, vol. 6, pp. 230–245, 1963; also in E. F. Moore (ed.), "Sequential Machines: Selected Papers," Addison-Wesley, Reading, Mass., 1964.
19 Shannon, C. E.: The Mathematical Theory of Communication, *Bell System Tech. J.*, vol. 27, pp. 379–423 and 623–656, 1948.
20 Shannon, C. E.: Certain Results in Coding Theory for Noisy Channels, *Inform. Control*, vol. 1, pp. 6–25, 1957.
21 Thomasian, A. J.: A Finite Criterion for Indecomposable Channels, *Ann. Math. Statist.*, vol. 34, pp. 337–338, 1963.
22 Tsertsvadze, G. N.: Certain Properties of Stochastic Automata and Certain Methods for Synthesizing Them, *Automat. i Telemek.*, vol. 24, pp. 341–352, 1963.
23 Wolfowitz, J.: "Coding Theorems of Information Theory," Prentice-Hall, Englewood Cliffs, N.J., 1961.
24 Zadeh, L. A.: The General Identification Problem, *Proc. of the Princeton Uni-*

versity Conference on Identification Problems in Communication and Control Systems, Princeton, N.J., 1963.
25 Carlyle, J. W.: Identification of State-calculable Functions of Finite Markov Chains, *Ann. Math. Statist.*, vol. 38, pp. 201-205, 1967.
26 Arbib, M. A.: Realization of Stochastic Systems, *Ann. Math. Statist.*, vol. 38, pp. 927–933, 1967.
27 Ott, E. H.: Theory and Applications of Stochastic Sequential Machines, *Res. Rep., Sperry Rand Res. Center, Sudbury, Mass.*, May 1966.
28 Fox, M., and H. Rubin: Functions of Processes with Markovian States, *Ann. Math. Statist.*, vol. 39, pp. 938–946, 1968.
29 Dharmadhikari, S. W.: Some Non-regular Functions of Finite Markov Chains, *Rept. RM-202, SD-2, Dept. Statist. Probability, Mich. State Univ. East Lansing, Mich.*, November, 1967.
30 Nieh, T. T., and J. W. Carlyle: On the Deterministic Realization of Stochastic Finite-state Machines, *Proc. Second Ann. Conf. Inform. Sci. and Systems, Princeton Univ., Princeton, N.J.*, pp. 189–193, 1968.
31 Nieh, T. T., and J. W. Carlyle: On a Measure of Complexity for Stochastic Sequential Machines, *IEEE Conf. Record Ninth Ann. Symp. Switching and Automata Theory*, 1968.
32 Sousa, C. R., and R. J. Leake: Stochastic Finite-state Systems—Four Models and Their Relationships, *Proc. Fifth Allerton Conf. Circuit and System Theory*, 1967.
33 Bruce, G. D., and K. S. Fu: A Model for Finite State Probabilistic Systems, *Proc. First Allerton Conf. Circuit and System Theory*, 1963.
34 Paz, A.: Fuzzy Star Functions, Probabilistic Automata, and Their Approximation by Nonprobabilistic Automata, *J. Computer and System Sci.*, vol. 1, pp. 371–389, 1967.
35 Starke, P. H.: Die Reduktion von stochastischen Automaten, *Electronische Informationsverarbeitung und Kybernetik*, vol. 4, pp. 93–100, 1968.
36 Turakainen, P.: On Probabilistic Automata and Their Generalizations, *Ann. Acad. Sci. Fennicae, Ser. A. I.*, no. 429, 1968.
37 Salomaa, A.: On Events Represented by Probabilistic Automata of Different Types, *Can. J. Math.*, vol. 20, pp. 242–251, 1968.
38 Turakainen, P.: On Stochastic Languages, *Inform. Control*, vol. 12, pp. 304–313, 1968.
39 Kashyap, R. L.: Optimization of Stochastic Finite-State Systems, *IEEE Trans. Autom. Control*, vol. 11, pp. 685–692, 1966.
40 Booth, T. L.: Statistical Properties of Random Digital Sequences, *IEEE Conf. Record Seventh Ann. Symp. Switching and Automata Theory*, pp. 251–261, 1966.
41 Paz, A.: Minimization Theorems and Techniques for Sequential Stochastic Systems, *Inform. Control*, vol. 11, pp. 155–166, 1967.
42 Paz, A.: Homomorphisms between Stochastic Sequential Machines, *Math. System Theory*, vol. 2, 1968.
43 Nasu, M., and N. Honda: Fuzzy Events Realized by Finite Probabilistic Automata, *Inform. Control*, vol. 12, pp. 248–303, 1968.
44 Depeyrot, M.: "Operand Investigation of Stochastic Systems," doctoral dissertation, Stanford University, Stanford, Calif., 1968.
45 Nieh, T. T.: Stochastic Sequential Machines with Prescribed Performance Criteria, *Inform. Control*, to appear 1969.
46 Starke, P. H.: Stochastische Ereignisse und Wortmengen, *Z. Math. Logik Grundlagen Math.*, vol. 12, pp. 61–68, 1966.

47 Paz, A.: "Probabilistic Automata," Academic Press, New York, to appear 1970.
48 Bukharaev, P.: Probabilistic Automata Theory (in Russian), *Kibernetika*, vol. 4, no. 2, pp. 6-23, 1968.
49 Paz, A., and J. W. Carlyle: On Realization Problems for Stochastic Systems, *Tech. Rept., Dept. of Eng., Univ. Calif., Los Angeles*, 1969.
50 Paz, A.: Regular Events in Stochastic Sequential Machines, *Tech. Note, Dept. of Eng., Univ. Calif., Los Angeles*, 1968.

11

Learning system theory

K. S. Fu
School of Electrical Engineering
Purdue University

1 *Introduction*

In the fields of modern automatic control, communications, operational research, economics, pattern recognition, prediction, and reliability study, there is a strong demand for realistic methods to treat problems when a priori knowledge about the processes under study is incomplete. In general, an optimal design or decision rule can be achieved only under the assumption that the characteristics of the process are completely known. If such knowledge is not available, one approach to optimization is to acquire the pertinent data from the actual measurements of the process as a source of information for the design or the construction of a decision rule. This design or decision rule should eventually approach a desired optimal design or decision rule, and consequently the performance of the overall system is gradually improved. The process which acquires necessary information for decision during the system's operation and which improves the performance of the system is usually called "learning" [1–8].

The problems of learning may be viewed as the problems of estimation or successive approximation of the unknown quantities of a functional which is chosen by the designer or the learning system to represent the process under study. The parametric and nonparametric methods of estimation studied in mathematical statistics have been used as a framework for the processes of learning in an unknown environment

[9, 10]. In general, these methods can be considered as special cases of successive approximations of unknown quantities. The unknown quantities may be either the parameters or the form and parameters which describe a (deterministic or probabilistic) function. However, as can be seen later, both cases can be formulated as the problems of successive estimations of unknown parameters. An analytic method of approximating known functions is the expansion of a "complicated" function as a convergent infinite series of terms with simpler (or otherwise more appropriate) functional form. These expansions may be regarded as infinite approximation processes in which the error may be made arbitrarily small by taking progressively more terms into account [11]. In general, the theory of approximations is not concerned with just continuous functions defined over an arbitrary measure space Ω.

In this chapter, the basic ideas of measuring the accuracy of approximations will be related to the problem of learning in an unknown environment, i.e., where the function to be learned (approximated, estimated) is known only by its form over the observation (feature) space. Any further specification of such a functional form can be performed only on the basis of experiments which offer the values of the approximated function in the domain of its definition. This implies that any desired solution which needs the knowledge of the approximated function is reached gradually by methods relying on experimentation and observation. Since it is assumed that the form of the function to be approximated (estimated, learned) is known, the problem of its successive approximations can be observed as a "wide sense" experience problem [12]. If no assumption is made on the possible form of the function to be learned (without even specifying a probability measure over possible functional representations of the process under study), the problem of approximation can be observed as a "strict sense" experience problem [12]. However, in that case, for the solution to be found the existence of the estimated or approximated unknown quantities must be assumed. One can then argue that the problems of learning are always wide sense experience problems.

2 *A basic mathematical model of learning in an unknown random environment*

In this section the problem of learning in an unknown stationary environment is defined as a problem of successive approximations of unknown quantities (coefficients or parameters) belonging to a preselected set of quantities which have to be estimated (learned). Let

$\{\Omega_X,F,p\}$ be a probability space. Ω_X is a set of elementary events (observation or feature space). $p(X)$ is a probability measure defined over Ω_X but unknown a priori, and F is σ-algebra of subsets in Ω_X. All set functions defined over Ω_X are assumed to be real-valued, nonnegative, and integrable with respect to $p(X)$ over Ω_X. If Ω_X is a euclidean space, the functions are also assumed to be Lebesgue integrable over Ω_X.

Let $p(z|X,\omega)$ be the conditional probability density function of a random variable z for $X \in \Omega_X$ and $\omega \in \Omega_c$, which is not known a priori. Ω_c is a countable set of pattern classes or actions (or stochastic processes in general). The complement of a pattern class or action ω with respect to Ω_c is denoted by $\bar{\omega}$. It is assumed that for every $X \in \Omega_X$ and $\omega \in \Omega_c$

1 $$E[|z|\ |X,\omega] = \int_{-\infty}^{+\infty} |z|p(z|X,\omega)\,dz < \infty$$

2 $$E[z^2|X,\omega] = \int_{-\infty}^{+\infty} z^2p(z|X,\omega)\,dz < \infty$$

and that

3 $$f(X;\omega) = E[z|X,\omega] = \int_{-\infty}^{+\infty} zp(z|X,\omega)\,dz$$

is real, single-valued, nonnegative, and bounded over Ω_X for $\omega \in \Omega_c$.

An engineering interpretation is given in Figure *11.2.1* with the

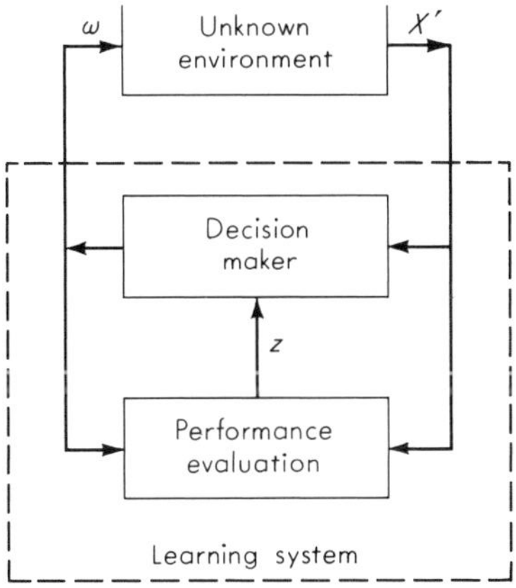

Fig. 11.2.1 A block diagram of a learning system.

reference to the randomly changing environment (plant, process) and a learning system (pattern classifier, detector, predictor, or controller) which is in general interacting with its environment. z is the performance evaluation of the classifications of $X \in \Omega_X$ into $\omega \in \Omega_c$ (or of a prediction that ω will occur, or of a decision to apply action or policy ω, after an $X \in \Omega_X$ was observed from the environment), and it is generally given by a prespecified positive-definite function, $z = \phi(X',\omega,X)$. X' is the observed current response of the environment due to the applied action $\omega \in \Omega_c$ following the occurrence of X; $X' \in \Omega_X$. $f(X;\omega)$ is in general the performance index function for the action, prediction, or classification $\omega \in \Omega_c$ defined over Ω_X.

The problem of learning can be stated as successively determining

4 $$\omega^*(X) \in \Omega_c \qquad \text{such that} \qquad f(X;\omega^*) = \max_{\omega} \{f(X;\omega);\omega \in \Omega_c\}$$

or finding a probability measure $P(\omega|X)$ over Ω_X such that

5 $$P(\omega|X) = P\{f(X;\omega) = \max_{\omega} \{f(X;\omega);\omega \in \Omega_c\}\}$$

Here, $P(\omega|X)$ should be interpreted (1) as the probability that the classification, prediction, or action $\omega \in \Omega_c$, following immediately after the occurrence of $X \in \Omega_X$, will be correct, optimal, favorable, or "rewarded," or (2) as the probability that the observed X belongs to the pattern class ω. If the probability $P(\omega)$, $\sum_{\omega \in \Omega_c} P(\omega) = 1$, is known, the equivalent problem of *5* is to find the conditional probability function $p(X|\omega)$ such that

6 $$\int_{\Omega_X} p(X|\omega)\, dX = 1$$

and

7 $$P(\omega|X) = \frac{P(\omega)p(X|\omega)}{p(X)}$$

Frequently the form of the function $p(X|\omega)$ will be known except for a certain parameter $\theta \in \Omega_\theta$. In that case the successive estimates of

8 $$\{p(X|\omega,\theta): \omega \in \Omega_c, \theta(\omega) \in \Omega_\theta\}$$

are obtained by successive approximations of the parameters $\{\theta(\omega): \theta(\omega) \in \Omega_\theta, \omega \in \Omega_c\}$.

The basic problem of learning in an unknown stationary environment is then reduced to that of successively establishing $f(X;\omega)$ or $p(X|\omega)$ on the basis of observations $\{z_n(X_n;\omega): n = 1,2, \ldots\}$ which are distributed according to $\{p(z|X_n,\omega): n = 1,2, \ldots\}$ where $\{X_n: n = 1,2, \ldots\}$ is a sequence of elementary events identically distributed over Ω_X by $p(X) = \sum_{\omega \in \Omega_c} P(\omega)p(X|\omega)$. The convergence of estimation assures us that the estimated value of the unknown quantity will approach to its true value. Consequently, the design or decision based on the estimated information will eventually approach a desired optimal design or decision rule.

The approaches of using Markov models or reinforcement learning algorithms [13–16] are actually based on *5*, where Ω_X is a countable set. A normalized measure of optimality is defined for *5* by

9 $$P(\omega|X) = \frac{f(X;\omega)g[f(X;\omega)]}{\sum_{\omega' \in \Omega_c} f(X;\omega')g[f(X;\omega')]}$$

where $g[\cdot]$ is a positive nondecreasing real-valued function defined on the real line. In those reinforcement models where a reward or "positive reinforcement" is associated with $z = +1$ in the case of a correct recognition, prediction, or action, and a "penalty" or "negative reinforcement" with $z = 0$ in the case of misrecognition of X, or wrong prediction or action,

10 $$f(X;\omega) = E[z|X,\omega] = P\{z = +1|X,\omega\}$$

and

11 $$P(\omega|X) = P\{z = +1|X,\omega\} = f(X;\omega)$$

such that for every $X \in \Omega_X$

12 $$\sum_{\omega \in \Omega_c} P(\omega|X) = 1$$

The learning automata using "linear tactic" models [14, 17, 18] can be described by *10, 11*, and *12* if a simple normalization of their states is performed at each step when a reward or penalty is obtained.

Point estimation of $\theta \in \Omega_\theta$ in $p(X|\omega,\theta)$ can be performed by successive applications of Bayes' formula; such a process is usually termed *bayesian learning* [9].

During the process of learning or successive estimation of unknown parameters, if the correct classifications ω of each observation are known or supplied by an external source, the process is called *supervised learning* or *learning with a teacher*. On the other hand, if the classifications of each observation are not available or known, the process is called *nonsupervised learning* or *learning without a teacher*. In the discussions following, unless otherwise specified, the learning process is always referred to as supervised learning.

3 *Stochastic approximation*

Stochastic approximation [19–29] is a scheme for successive approximations of a sought quantity when, because of the stochastic nature of the problem, the observations or measurements have certain errors. It has been applied to identification, adaptive and learning control, adaptive communication, and pattern recognition problems [30–38]. In the application to pattern recognition, the parameters of the optimal decision boundary or of probability density functions can be estimated by using a stochastic approximation procedure. In learning control systems, stochastic approximation procedures can be used both to estimate the system's performance index and to learn the optimal control action. Here, after a brief review of Dvoretzky's generalized stochastic approximation, a stochastic approximation procedure is proposed and its convergence and optimal properties are presented.

General stochastic approximation procedure

Dvoretzky considered a general stochastic approximation procedure and proved the following Theorem [19].

1 **Theorem** Let $\alpha_n(r_1, \ldots, r_n)$, $\beta_n(r_1, \ldots, r_n)$, and $\gamma_n(r_1, \ldots, r_n)$ be nonnegative measurable functions of real variables $r_1, r_2, r_3, \ldots, r_n$, satisfying the following conditions:

2 $\alpha_n(r_1, \ldots, r_n)$ are uniformly bounded and

$$\lim_{n \to \infty} \alpha_n(r_1, r_2, \ldots, r_n) = 0$$

uniformly for any sequence $r_1, r_2, \ldots$.

3 The sum of the series $\sum_{n=1}^{\infty} \beta_n(r_1, r_2, \ldots, r_n)$ is uniformly bounded and converges uniformly for any sequence $r_1, r_2, \ldots$.

4 The series $\sum_{n=1}^{\infty} \gamma_n(r_1, r_2, \ldots, r_n)$ uniformly diverges[1] for any sequence $r_1, r_2, \ldots$, bounded in absolute value, i.e., for any sequence $r_1, r_2, \ldots$, such that

$$\sup_{n=1,2,\ldots} |r_n| < C$$

C being an arbitrary finite number.

5 Let θ be a real number, and $T_1, T_2, \ldots$ be measurable transformations, satisfying the inequality

$$|T_n(r_1, r_2, \ldots, r_n) - \theta| \leq \max\,[\alpha_n, (1 + \beta_n)|r_n - \theta| - \gamma_n]$$

for any real sequence $r_1, r_2, \ldots$.

[1] The series $\Sigma\gamma_n(r_1, \ldots, r_n)$ diverges uniformly if for every $S > 0$ there is an N such that for $n \geq N$, $S_n > S$ for any sequence $r_1, r_2, \ldots$, where the S_n are the partial sums of the given series.

Further let X_1 and $Y_1, Y_2, \ldots$ be random variables, and for $n \geq 1$ let

6 $$X_{n+1} = T_n(X_1, \ldots, X_n) + Y_n + g_n(X_1, \ldots, X_n)$$

where $g_n(r_1, \ldots, r_n)$ are measurable functions such that

7 The series $\Sigma |g_n(r_1, r_2, \ldots, r_n)|$ uniformly converges and its sum is uniformly bounded for any $r_1, r_2, \ldots$.

8 $E[Y_n | X_1, X_2, \ldots, X_n] = 0$ with probability 1.

9 The series $\sum_{n=1}^{\infty} E[Y_n^2]$ converges; that is, $\sum_{n=1}^{\infty} E[Y_n^2] < \infty$, and $E[X_1^2] < \infty$. Then, as $n \to \infty$

10 $$P\{\lim_{n\to\infty} X_n = \theta\} = 1$$

and

11 $$\lim_{n\to\infty} E[(X_n - \theta)^2] = 0$$

Dvoretzky has shown that the special cases of his procedure are (1) the Robbins-Monro procedure [20] for finding the solution of the equation $E[Y(x)] = \int_{-\infty}^{+\infty} y\, dH(y|x) = \alpha$, $x \in R$, under the assumption that it has a unique root $x = \theta$ and that the functions $E[Y(x)]$ and $H(y|x)$ are unknown, and (2) the Kiefer-Wolfowitz procedure [21] for finding an extremal point of $E[Y(x)]$.

In a multidimensional case, X_n and Y_n assume the values in a normed linear space Ω with $\|r\|$ denoting the norm of r [19, 24–27]. If $\theta \in \Omega_\theta$ and $T_n(r_1, \ldots, r_n)$ is a measurable transformation from the nth cartesian power of Ω into Ω and $\|T_n(r_1, \ldots, r_n) - \theta\| \leq F_n \|r_n - \theta\|$ with $F_n > 0$ and $\prod_{n=1}^{\infty} F_n = 0$, then

12 $$X_{n+1} = T_n(X_1, X_2, \ldots, X_n) + Y_n$$

and

13 $$E[\|X_1\|^2] < \infty$$

14 $$\sum_{n=1}^{\infty} E[\|Y_n\|^2] < \infty$$

and

15 $$E\{\|\phi(x_1, \ldots, x_n) + Y_n\|^2\} \leq E\{\|\phi(x_1, \ldots, x_n)\|^2\} + E\{\|Y_n\|^2\}$$

for every measurable function $\phi(x_1, \ldots, x_n)$, which implies

16 $$\lim_{n\to\infty} E[\|X_n - \theta\|^2] = 0 \qquad \text{and} \qquad P\{\lim_{n\to\infty} \|X_n - \theta\| = 0\} = 1$$

Derman and Sacks [27] prove the convergence of X_n with probability 1 to θ if $g_n(X_1, \ldots, X_n) \equiv 0$ for every n in *6* and *7* is replaced by *13* and *14*.

Continuous stochastic approximation procedures have been discussed in Refs. 39 and 40. However, they will not be described here since our discussions are mainly based on the discrete case.

The transformation $T_n(r_1, \ldots, r_n)$ of *5* will be frequently such that

17 $$|T_n(r_1, \ldots, r_n) - \theta| \leq F_n|r_n - \theta|$$

where F_n, $n = 1, 2, \ldots$, is a sequence of positive numbers satisfying

18 $$\prod_{n=1}^{\infty} F_n = 0$$

If $g_n(X_1, \ldots, X_n) \equiv 0$ for every n in *6*, then

19 $$\begin{aligned}(X_{n+1} - \theta)^2 &= (T_n(X_1, \ldots, X_n) - \theta + Y_n)^2 \\ &= (T(X_1, \ldots, X_n) - \theta)^2 + Y_n^2 + 2Y_n(T_n(X_1, \ldots, X_n) - \theta)\end{aligned}$$

and the conditional expectation of $(X_{n+1} - \theta)^2$ is, by considering *19*, *9*, and *17*,

20 $$E[(X_{n+1} - \theta)^2|X_n] \leq F_n^2(X_n - \theta)^2 + E[Y_n^2|X_n]$$

The unconditional expectation is

21 $$E[(X_{n+1} - \theta)^2] \leq F_n^2 E[(X_n - \theta)^2] + \sigma_n^2$$

where

$$\sigma_n^2 = E[Y_n^2] \qquad \text{and} \qquad \sum_{n=1}^{\infty} E[Y_n^2] < \infty$$

Relation *21* gives an estimate of the expected squared error for the successive estimate X_n at each stage $n = 1, 2, \ldots$, and as such it will be used in comparing different stochastic approximation algorithms.

A proposed stochastic approximation algorithm

The successive approximations of the functions which were considered in Sec. *2* can always be described by successive approximations of the quantities or parameters which belong to a preselected set of possible solutions. The following stochastic approximation algorithm is proposed for estimation of a quantity $\theta \in (-\infty, +\infty)$ on the basis of observations $z_1, z_2, \ldots, z_n, \ldots$, where each $z_k \in R^*$, $k = 1, 2, \ldots, n, \ldots$ ($R^* \triangleq \{R, +\infty, -\infty\}$, the extended real line), the

$(n + 1)$st estimate of θ is

22 $$X_{n+1} = X_n + \gamma_{n+1}(\Theta_{n+1}(z_1,z_2, \ . \ . \ . \ ,z_{n+1}) - X_n)$$

where $\Theta_n(z_1,z_2, \ . \ . \ . \ ,z_n)$ are the real-valued functions defined over all possible sequences $z_1, z_2, \ . \ . \ . \ , z_n, \ . \ . \ . \ ,$ such that

23 $$E[\Theta_n] = \theta$$

and

24 $$E[(\Theta_n - \theta)^2] < \infty$$

with

25 $$\gamma_n > 0 \qquad \lim_{n \to \infty} \gamma_n = 0 \qquad \sum_{n=1}^{\infty} \gamma_n = \infty \qquad \sum_{n=1}^{\infty} \gamma_n{}^2 < \infty$$

and $E[(X_0 - \theta)^2] < \infty$; X_0 is an initial estimate of θ.

To prove that $\{X_n\}$ converges both in mean square and with probability 1 to θ, it is sufficient to write

26 $$(X_{n+1} - \theta) = (X_n - \theta) + \gamma_{n+1}(\xi_{n+1}(z_1,z_2, \ . \ . \ . \ ,z_{n+1}) + \theta - X_n)$$

where, by *23* and *24*,

27 $$E[\xi_n] = 0 \qquad \text{and} \qquad E[\xi_n{}^2] < \infty$$

for every n. Since $\prod_{n=1}^{\infty} (1 - \gamma_n) = 0$ (see Ref. 41), *26* becomes

28 $$(X_{n+1} - \theta) = (1 - \gamma_{n+1})(X_n - \theta) + \gamma_{n+1}\xi_{n+1}(z_1,z_2, \ . \ . \ . \ ,z_{n+1})$$

with

29 $$F_n = (1 - \gamma_n) > 0 \qquad Y_n = \gamma_{n+1}\xi_{n+1}(z_1,z_2, \ . \ . \ . \ ,z_{n+1})$$

and

30 $$T((X_1 - \theta), \ . \ . \ . \ ,(X_n - \theta)) = F_n(X_n - \theta)$$

as related to *6* and *19*. Then from *30*

$$|T((X_1 - \theta), \ . \ . \ . \ ,(X_n - \theta)) - \theta| = F_n|(X_n - \theta) - \theta|$$

satisfies the condition *5*, and in particular *17*. Hence, the proposed algorithm of *22* is a special case of Dvoretzky's stochastic approximation and *10* and *11* hold.

Optimization of the algorithm consists of minimizing $E[(X_n - \theta)^2]$ at every $n = 1, 2, \ . \ . \ .$ over all possible sequences $\{\gamma_n\}$ which satisfy *25* and over all possible real-valued functions $\{\Theta_n(z_1, \ . \ . \ . \ ,z_n)\}$ which satisfy *23* and *24*.

Let $V_n = E[(X_n - \theta)^2]$ in *22*. Then considering *28* and *29*, one obtains

31 $$V_{n+1}^2 = (1 - \gamma_{n+1})^2 V_n{}^2 + \gamma_{n+1}^2 E[\xi_n{}^2]$$

For a selected function $\Theta_n(z_1, \ldots, z_n)$, by differentiating *31* with respect to γ_{n+1}, one obtains

32 $$\gamma_{n+1} = \frac{V_n^2}{V_n^2 + E[\xi_n^2]} \qquad \text{and} \qquad V_{n+1}^2 = \frac{V_n^2 E[\xi_n^2]}{V_n^2 + E[\xi_n^2]}$$

If $E[\xi_n^2] = \sigma^2$ for every n, the optimal $\{\gamma_n\}$ sequence is defined by

33 $$\gamma_n = \frac{1}{n + \sigma^2/V_0^2}$$

Hence, the optimal solution would be to select the function

$$\{\Theta_n(z_1 \ldots, z_n)\}$$

which satisfies *23* and gives the smallest possible variance

$$E[(\Theta_n(z_1, z_2, \ldots, z_n) - \theta)^2]$$

at every step n, and then choose the weighting sequence $\{\gamma_n\}$ according to *32* and *25*. This method will be used in Sec. *6* for optimal point estimation of unknown parameters of certain probability density functions.

4 *Linear reinforcement learning algorithm*

The linear reinforcement learning algorithm, originated from the psychology of learning [7, 8], has been applied to pattern recognition and learning control problems [13–18, 42, 43]. The basic concept is to relate the two successive estimates of the sought quantity by a linear relationship. For illustrative purposes, assume that $P(\omega|X)$ is the quantity to be estimated. The relationship between $P_{n+1}(\omega|X)$ and $P_n(\omega|X)$ is defined as

1 $$\begin{aligned} P_{n+1}(\omega|X) &= \alpha_{n+1}P_n(\omega|X) + (1 - \alpha_{n+1})\frac{n(X;\omega)}{n(X)} \\ &= \alpha_{n+1}P_n(\omega|X) + (1 - \alpha_{n+1})\rho_n(X;\omega) \end{aligned}$$

for every $\omega \in \Omega_c$ where $0 \le \alpha_n < 1$ and $0 \le P_0(\omega|X) \le 1$. $P(\omega|X)$ may be considered as (1) the probability that the decision to classify X into ω would be rewarded, (2) the probability that the event ω would occur after the occurrence of X, or (3) the probability that the application of the policy or action ω after X was observed would be optimal or satisfactory in a specified sense.

Let $\alpha_n = \alpha$ for every n. According to the Borel strong law

2 $$P\left\{\lim_{n(X)\to\infty} \frac{n(X;\omega)}{n(X)} = P(\omega|X)\right\} = 1$$

For any $\epsilon > 0$, there is a sufficiently large $N(\epsilon) > 0$ such that for every $k > N(\epsilon)$

3 $$|\rho_k(X;\omega) - P(X;\omega)| \leq \frac{\epsilon}{2} \qquad \text{and} \qquad \alpha^{k+1} \leq \frac{\epsilon}{4}$$

Then

$$\begin{aligned} P_{n+1}(\omega|X) = \alpha^{n+1}P_0(\omega|X) + (1-\alpha)\alpha^{k+1} \sum_{\mu=0}^{n-k-1} \alpha^{\mu}\rho_{n-k-\mu}(X;n) \\ + (1-\alpha) \sum_{\nu=0}^{k} \alpha^{\nu}\rho_{n+1-\nu}(X;\omega) \\ \leq \alpha^{n+1} + \alpha^{k+1} + \max_{\nu=0,1,2,\ldots,k} \{\rho_{n+1-\nu}(X;\omega)\} \end{aligned}$$

or

4 $$|P_{n+1}(\omega|X) - P(\omega|X)| \leq \epsilon$$

Hence, $P\{\lim_{n\to\infty} P_n(\omega|X) = P(\omega|X)\} = 1$ for every $X \in \Omega_X$ and $\omega \in \Omega_c$.
Now let

5 $$0 \leq \alpha_n < 1 \qquad \prod_{n=1}^{\infty} \alpha_n = 0 \qquad \sum_{n=1}^{\infty} (1-\alpha_n)^2 < \infty$$

Relation *1* can be written

6 $$P_{n+1}(\omega|X) - P(\omega|X) = \alpha_{n+1}(P_n(\omega|X) - P(\omega|X)) + (1-\alpha_{n+1})\xi_n(X;\omega)$$

where $E[\xi_n(X;\omega)] = 0$ and $E[(\xi_n(X;\omega))^2] < 1$. Hence *6* is a stochastic approximation algorithm of Dvoretzky's type with

$$T_n(P_n(\omega|X) - P(\omega|X)) = \alpha_{n+1}(P_n(\omega|X) - P(\omega|X))$$

which satisfies *11.3.30*.

From *6* we can obtain

7 $$E[(P_{n+1}(\omega|X) - P(\omega|X))^2] = \alpha_{n+1}^2 E[(P_n(\omega|X) - P(\omega|X))^2] + (1-\alpha_{n+1})^2 E[\xi_n^2(X;\omega)]$$

and the optimal sequence of reinforcement coefficients $\{\alpha_n\}$ is defined by

8 $$\alpha_{n+1} = \frac{E[\xi_n^2(X;\omega)]}{E[\xi_n^2(X;\omega)] + E[(P_n(\omega|X) - P(\omega|X))^2]}$$

and

9 $$E[(P_{n+1}(\omega|X) - P(\omega|X))^2] = \frac{E[\xi_n{}^2(X;\omega)]E[(P_n(\omega|X) - P(\omega|X))^2]}{E[\xi_n{}^2(X;\omega)] + E[(P_n(\omega|X) - P(\omega|X))^2]}$$

Hence if $\alpha_n = \alpha$ for every n, the optimal property of *1* is lost. In many cases, linear reinforcement algorithms give only the convergence in probability to the desired value. However, the stochastic approximation procedure provides the property of convergence with probability 1.

5 Potential function method

The potential function method, introduced and studied extensively by Aizerman, Braverman, and Rozonoer [44–47] is suitable for successive approximations of unknown uniformly bounded continuous functions defined over a probability space (Ω_X, F, p); Ω_X is a k-dimensional euclidean space, F is a σ-field, and $p(X)$ is the probability density function defined (but unknown) over Ω_X. The method is briefly described here in an alternative form. The proof of convergence is based on Dvoretzky's theorem (Sec. *3*).

Consider a conditional probability density function of a random variable z related to $X \in \Omega_X$ and $\omega \in \Omega_c$, $p(z|X,\omega)$. It is assumed that for every $X \in \Omega_X$ and $\omega \in \Omega_c$

1 $$E[z|X,\omega] = \int_{-\infty}^{+\infty} zp(z|X,\omega)\,dz \triangleq f(X;\omega)$$

is such that $|f(X;\omega)| < C_1 < \infty$, and

2 $$E[z^2|X,\omega] = \int_{-\infty}^{+\infty} z^2p(z|X,\omega)\,dz < \infty$$

It is also assumed that for a class $\omega \in \Omega_c$ there is a finite set of linearly independent real-valued uniformly bounded continuous functions defined over Ω_X; thus

3 $$\Phi(\omega) \triangleq \{\varphi_i(X): |\varphi_i(X)| < C_2 < \infty,\ X \in \Omega_X,\ i = 1,2, \ldots, N(\omega);\ N(\omega) < \infty\}$$

The elements of $\Phi(\omega)$ are also such that for every $X \in \Omega_X$

4 $$\sum_{i=1}^{N(\omega)} \varphi_i{}^2(X) > 0$$

that is, there is at least one function $\varphi_i(X)$ in $\Phi(\omega)$ such that

$$\varphi_i(X) \neq 0 \qquad X \in \Omega_X$$

It can also be assumed that the functions in $\Phi(\omega)$ are mutually orthonormal; that is,

5 $$\int_{\Omega_X} \varphi_i(X)\varphi_j(X)\,dX = \begin{cases} 0 & \text{if } i \neq j \\ 1 & \text{if } i = j \end{cases}$$

but in many applications it is more a convenience than a necessity. $\Phi(\omega)$ defines the basis for the function $f(X;\omega)$, $\omega \in \Omega_c$, $X \in \Omega_X$; thus

6 $$f(X;\omega) \triangleq \sum_{i=1}^{N(\omega)} c(i;\omega)\varphi_i(X)$$

Let the nth approximation of $f(X;\omega)$ be designated by

7 $$f_n(X;\omega) = \sum_{i=1}^{N(\omega)} c_n(i;\omega)\varphi_i(X)$$

The problem is to obtain a sequence of successive approximations $\{f_n(X;\omega)\}$, which converge in a certain sense to $f(X;\omega)$, using a sequence of observations

8 $$z_1(X_1;\omega),\ z_2(X_2;\omega),\ \ldots,\ z_n(X_n;\omega)$$

where

$$X_1(\omega),\ X_2(\omega),\ \ldots,\ X_n(\omega)$$

are independent and identically distributed with continuous conditional probability density function $p(X|\omega)$ for the pattern class or action or prediction $\omega \in \Omega_c$.

The successive estimates of $f(X;\omega)$ are formed by [45, 47]

9 $$f_{n+1}(X;\omega) = f_n(X;\omega) + \gamma_{n+1}(z(X_{n+1};\omega) - f_n(X_{n+1};\omega)) \sum_{i=1}^{N(\omega)} \varphi_i(X_{n+1})\varphi_i(X)$$

where

10 $$\gamma_n > 0 \qquad \lim_{n\to\infty} \gamma_n = 0 \qquad \sum_{n=1}^{\infty} \gamma_n = \infty \qquad \sum_{n=1}^{\infty} \gamma_n^2 < \infty \qquad |c_0(i;\omega,)| < \infty$$

or, equivalently, in terms of $c_{n+1}(i;\omega)$ and $c_n(i;\omega)$,

11 $$c_{n+1}(i;\omega) = c_n(i;\omega) + \gamma_{n+1}\Big(z_{n+1}(X_{n+1};\omega) - \sum_{j=1}^{N(\omega)} c_n(j;\omega)\varphi_j(X_{n+1}(\omega))\Big)\,\varphi_i(X_{n+1}(\omega))$$

for every $i = 1, 2, \ldots, N(\omega)$ and $n = 1, 2, \ldots$. Let $Y = X_{n+1}(\omega) \in \Omega_X$; then *9* becomes

12 $$f_{n+1}(X;\omega) = f_n(X;\omega) + \gamma_{n+1}(z(Y;\omega) - f_n(Y;\omega)) \sum_{i=1}^{N(\omega)} \varphi_i(X)\varphi_i(Y)$$

where Y is distributed according to $p(Y|\omega)$, $\omega \in \Omega_c$. If $X = Y$ in *12*, a stochastic approximation algorithm is obtained for a point $Y \in \Omega_X$,

13 $$f_{n+1}(Y;\omega) = f_n(Y;\omega) + \gamma_{n+1}(z(Y;\omega) - f_n(Y;\omega)) \sum_{i=1}^{N(\omega)} \varphi_i^2(Y)$$

since

14 $$E[z(Y;\omega)] = f(Y;\omega) \qquad E[z^2(Y;\omega)] < \infty \qquad \sum_{i=1}^{N(\omega)} \varphi_i^2(Y) > 0$$

Let $g_n(Y;\omega) = f_n(Y;\omega) - f(Y;\omega)$; then *13* can be written as

15 $$g_{n+1}(Y;\omega) = \left(1 - \gamma_{n+1} \sum_{i=1}^{N(\omega)} \varphi_i^2(Y)\right) g_n(Y;\omega) + \gamma_{n+1}\xi(Y;\omega)$$

Since Y is distributed according to $p(Y|\omega)$, *15* can be written

16 $$\int_{\Omega_X} g_{n+1}(Y;\omega)p(Y|\omega)\,dY = \int_{\Omega_X} \left(1 - \gamma_{n+1} \sum_{i=1}^{N(\omega)} \varphi_i^2(Y)\right) g_n(Y;\omega)p(Y|\omega)\,dY + \gamma_{n+1} \int_{\Omega_X} \xi(Y;\omega)p(Y|\omega)\,dY$$

Let

17 $$T_n\left[\int_{\Omega_X} g_n(Y;\omega)p(Y|\omega)\,dY\right] = \int_{\Omega_X} \left(1 - \gamma_{n+1} \sum_{i=1}^{N(\omega)} \varphi_i^2(Y)\right) g_n(Y;\omega)p(Y|\omega)\,dY$$

then

18 $$\left| T_n\left[\int_{\Omega_X} g_n(Y;\omega)p(Y|\omega)\,dy\right]\right| \le \int_{\Omega_X} \left|1 - \gamma_{n+1} \sum_{i=1}^{N(\omega)} \varphi_i^2(Y)\right| |g_n(Y;\omega)|p(Y|\omega)\,dY$$

It will be assumed that

19 $$P\left\{\left|\int_{\Omega_X} g_n(Y;\omega)p(Y|\omega)\,dY\right| > 0\right\} = 1$$

for all finite n. In that case if $(1 - \gamma_n M) > 0$ for every n, where M is defined by

20 $$0 < \sum_{i=1}^{N(\omega)} \varphi_i^2(X) < M < \infty$$

then

21 $$(1 - \gamma_{n+1}m) \int_{\Omega_X} |g_n(Y;\omega)|p(Y|\omega)\, dY > \int_{\Omega_X} \left| 1 - \gamma_{n+1} \sum_{i=1}^{N(\omega)} \varphi_i^2(Y) \right| |g_n(Y;\omega)|p(Y|\omega)\, dY > 0$$

where $m = \min_{\Omega_Y} \left\{ \sum_{i=1}^{N(\omega)} \varphi_i^2(Y) \right\} > 0$. Since

22 $$0 < \left| \int_{\Omega_X} g_n(Y;\omega)p(Y|\omega)\, dY \right| \leq \int_{\Omega_X} |g_n(Y;\omega)|p(Y|\omega)\, dY$$

a constant $0 < m' \leq m$ can be found such that

23 $$(1 - m'\gamma_{n+1}) \left| \int_{\Omega_X} g_n(Y;\omega)p(Y|\omega)\, dY \right| \geq (1 - m\gamma_{n+1}) \int_{\Omega_X} |g_n(Y;\omega)|p(Y|\omega)\, dY > 0$$

Hence,

24 $$\left| T_n \left[\int_{\Omega_X} g_n(Y;\omega)p(Y|\omega)\, dY \right] \right| \leq (1 - m'\gamma_{n+1}) \left| \int_{\Omega_X} g_n(Y;\omega)p(Y|\omega)\, dY \right|$$

Now, if *16* is to satisfy the conditions of Dvoretzky's theorem, it is sufficient to require that

25 $$E\left[\int_{\Omega_X} \xi(Y;\omega)p(Y|\omega)\, dY \right] = 0$$

and

26 $$E\left[\left(\int_{\Omega_X} \xi(Y;\omega)p(Y|\omega)\, dY \right)^2 \right] < \infty$$

where the expectation is taken with respect to the probability density function $p\left[\int_{\Omega_X} \xi(Y;\omega)p(Y|\omega)\, dY \right]$.

If $|z(Y;\omega)| < \infty$ for every $Y \in \Omega_X$ and $\omega \in \Omega_c$, the condition of *26* is satisfied. Because $E[\xi|Y;\omega] = 0$, the condition of *25* is always satisfied. Then,

27 $$P\left\{ \lim_{n\to\infty} \int_{\Omega_X} g_n(Y;\omega)p(Y|\omega)\, dY = 0 \right\} = 1$$

and

28 $$\lim_{n\to\infty} E\left[\left(\int_{\Omega_X} g_n(Y;\omega)p(Y|\omega)\, dY \right)^2 \right] = 0$$

Hence the convergence in the mean-square sense toward zero is proved for stochastic sequence $\left\{ \int_{\Omega_X} g_n(Y;\omega)p(Y|\omega)\, dY \right\}$ strictly on the basis of Dvoretzky's theorem. Results also have been obtained by Tsypkin [48], Aizerman, Braverman, and Rozonoer [49], and Blaydon [50] by direct application of Robbins-Monro procedure to the mean-square error of approximation.

As an example, if the function to be estimated is the conditional density function $p(X|\omega)$, then

$$p(X|\omega) = \sum_{i=1}^{N(\omega)} c(i;\omega)\varphi_i(X)$$

The following algorithm for successive approximation of the coefficients $c(i;\omega)$ is suggested:

29 $$c_{n+1}(i;\omega) = c_n(i;\omega) + \gamma_{n+1}(\varphi_i(X_{n+1}) - c_n(i;\omega))$$

where $\{\gamma_n\}$ and $c_0(i;\omega)$ satisfy the same conditions in *10*. Therefore, in the limit, the estimated coefficients $c_n(i;\omega)$ will approach $c(i;\omega)$ in the mean-square sense and with probability 1.

6 *Bayesian learning techniques*

Bayesian learning for the parameters of a normal distribution

In the classical approach of bayesian inference, it is assumed that there exists an a priori density function $p_0(\theta)$ which reflects the knowledge about the unknown parameter (treated as a random variable) θ. Consider what happens to our knowledge of θ when the observations are made: $p_0(\theta)$ changes according to Bayes' theorem; the a posteriori probability density of θ, given the first observation X_1, is

1 $$p(\theta|X_1) = \frac{p(X_1|\theta)p_0(\theta)}{p(X_1)}$$

where $p(X_1)$ is a constant of proportionality. The central idea of bayesian learning is to extract information from the observations X_1, X_2, . . . , X_n for the unknown parameter θ through successive applications of the recursive Bayes' formula. It is well known that, on the average, an a posteriori density function becomes more concentrated and converges to the true value of the parameter, which reflects an average gain in knowledge about the unknown parameter θ.

In each of the learning processes to be discussed, the iterative application of Bayes' theorem is accomplished by a fixed computational algorithm. This is made possible by carefully selecting a reproducing a priori density for the parameter so that the a posteriori densities are members of the same family of the a priori density (i.e., the form of the density function is preserved). The learning processes are then reduced to the successive estimation of parameter values. Some important results concerning the necessary and sufficient conditions admitting a reproducing density can be found in Refs. 51 and 52.

Case 1 *Learning the mean vector* M, *with known covariance matrix* K.

In this case, the unknown parameter θ to be learned is M whose uncertainty can be reflected by assigning a proper reproducing a priori probability density function $p_0(\theta) = p_0(M)$.

Let $p(X|\theta) = p(X|M) \sim N(M,K)$, a multivariate normal density function, and assign $p_0(\theta) = p_0(M) \sim N(M_0,\Phi_0)$ where M_0 represents the initial estimate of the mean vector and Φ_0 is the initial covariance matrix which reflects the uncertainty about M_0. By reproducing property of normal density, it is known that the a posteriori density $p(M|X_1,X_2, \ldots ,X_n)$, given the learning observations $X_1, X_2, \ldots, X_n$, is again normal with M_0 and Φ_0 replaced by M_n and Φ_n, where

2 $$M_n = n^{-1}K(\Phi_0 + n^{-1}K)^{-1}M_0 + \Phi_0(\Phi_0 + n^{-1}K)^{-1}\langle X\rangle$$

3 $$\Phi_n = (n^{-1}K)(\Phi_0 + n^{-1}K)^{-1}\Phi_0$$

and

4 $$\langle X\rangle = \frac{1}{n}\sum_{i=1}^{n} X_i$$

Equation *2* shows that M_n can be interpreted as a weighted average of the a priori mean vector M_0 and the sample information $\langle X\rangle$, with the weights being $n^{-1}K(\Phi_0 + n^{-1}K)^{-1}$ and $\Phi_0(\Phi_0 + n^{-1}K)^{-1}$, respectively. The nature of this weighting device can be seen more easily in the special case in which

5 $$\Phi_0 = \alpha^{-1}K \qquad \alpha > 0$$

Then *2* and *3* become

6 $$M_n = \frac{\alpha}{n+\alpha} M_0 + \frac{n}{n+\alpha}\langle X\rangle$$

7 $$\Phi_n = \frac{1}{n+\alpha} K$$

From *2* and *3*, or *6* and *7*, as $n \to \infty$, $M_n \to \langle X\rangle$, and $\Phi_n \to 0$ which means, on the average, the estimate M_n will approach the true mean vector M of the normal density. The fact that $M_n \to \langle X\rangle$ is independent of the initial estimate M_0 leads to the evidence that the initial uncertainty is going to be wiped out eventually by the gathering of information from the learning samples. It will be shown in the following that, under the same assumptions, *2* or *6* has the same structure as the stochastic approximation algorithm and, as a consequence, the estimate M_n can be proved to converge to the true value of M in the mean square and with probability 1.

In terms of M_{n-1} and X_n, *2* can also be written

8 $$M_n = K(\Phi_{n-1} + K)^{-1}M_{n-1} + \Phi_{n-1}(\Phi_{n-1} + K)^{-1}X_n$$

By adding and subtracting M_{n-1}, we alter *8* to

9 $$\begin{aligned} M_n &= M_{n-1} - M_{n-1} + K(\Phi_{n-1} + K)^{-1}M_{n-1} + \Phi_{n-1}(\Phi_{n-1} + K)^{-1}X_n \\ &= M_{n-1} + \Phi_{n-1}(\Phi_{n-1} + K)^{-1}(X_n - M_{n-1}) \end{aligned}$$

that is, the successive estimate M_n in terms of M_{n-1} and X_n assumes a special algorithm of stochastic approximation. The nature of this estimation procedure can be easily seen from *6* and *7*, where

10 $$\Phi_n = \frac{1}{n + \alpha} K = \frac{\alpha}{n + \alpha} \Phi_0$$

Then $\Phi_{n-1} = \dfrac{\alpha}{(n - 1) + \alpha} \Phi_0$, and

11 $$\begin{aligned} \Phi_{n-1}(\Phi_{n-1} + K)^{-1} &= (I + K\Phi_{n-1}^{-1})^{-1} \\ &= \left(I + \frac{(n - 1) + \alpha}{\alpha} K\Phi_0^{-1}\right)^{-1} = (1 + (n - 1) + \alpha)^{-1} = \frac{1}{n + \alpha} \end{aligned}$$

Equation *9* becomes

12 $$M_n = M_{n-1} + \frac{1}{n + \alpha}(X_n - M_{n-1}) = M_{n-1} + \gamma_n(X_n - M_{n-1})$$

where

13 $$\gamma_n = \frac{1}{n + \alpha}$$

satisfying

14 $$\gamma_n > 0 \qquad \lim_{n \to \infty} \gamma_n = 0$$

and

15 $$\sum_{n=1}^{\infty} \gamma_n = \infty \qquad \sum_{n=1}^{\infty} \gamma_n^2 < \infty$$

To see that the successive estimate of M in *12* is really the stochastic approximation algorithm, we can construct an underlying probability space in which X_n and M_n are random variables with $X_n = M + H_n$, where H_n is the random vector with components $(\lambda_n^1, \lambda_n^2, \ldots, \lambda_n^k)$ associated with the noise measurements at nth observation satisfying $E[\lambda_n^i] = 0$ and $E[(\lambda_n^i)^2] < \infty$, $i = 1, 2, \ldots, k$, for all n. Then *12* becomes

16 $$M_n = (1 - \gamma_n)M_{n-1} + \gamma_n M + \gamma_n H_n$$

Let $T_n(M_1, M_2, \ldots, M_{n-1}) = (1 - \gamma_n)M_{n-1} + \gamma_n M$ be the measurable transformation representing the "deterministic" part of the approximation. To verify that Dvoretzky's conditions of *11.3.2* to *11.3.9* are satisfied by the learning process defined in *12*, let

17
$$\begin{aligned}\|T_n(M_1, M_2, \ldots, M_{n-1}) - M\| &= \|(1 - \gamma_n)M_{n-1} + \gamma_n M - M\| \\ &= \|(1 - \gamma_n)(M_{n-1} - M)\| \\ &= (1 - \gamma_n)\|M_{n-1} - M\| = F_n\|M_{n-1} - M\|\end{aligned}$$

where $F_n = 1 - \gamma_n = 1 - 1/(n + \alpha) = (n + \alpha - 1)/(n + \alpha)$, satisfying $F_n > 0$ and

$$\prod_{n=1}^{\infty} F_n = \lim_{n\to\infty} \prod_{k=1}^{k} F_n = \lim_{k\to\infty} \frac{\alpha}{k + \alpha} = 0$$

Since $\|M_0\| < \infty$ is always assumed and $E[\|H_n\|^2]$ is bounded above by B [that is, $E[\|H_n\|^2] = \sum_{i=1}^{k} E[(\lambda_n^i)^2] \leq B < \infty$], then

$$\begin{aligned}E\{\|M_0\|^2\} + \sum_{n=1}^{\infty} E\{\|\gamma_n H_n\|^2\} &= E\{\|M_0\|^2\} + \sum_{n=1}^{\infty} \gamma_n^2 E\{\|H_n\|^2\} \\ &\leq E\{\|M_0\|^2\} + B \sum_{n=1}^{\infty} \gamma_n^2 < \infty\end{aligned}$$

which verifies the conditions of *11.3.13* and *11.3.14*. The condition of *11.3.15* is automatically satisfied for any measurable function

$$\phi_n(M_1, \ldots, M_n)$$

Therefore, by Dvoretzky's theorem

18
$$\lim_{n\to\infty} E\{\|M_n - M\|^2\} = 0$$

and

19
$$P\{\lim_{n\to\infty} M_n = M\} = 1$$

which simply means that learning the mean vector of normal distribution using bayesian inference is a special case of stochastic approximation which, as a consequence of Dvoretzky's theorem, gives the convergence of the estimate to the true mean vector in mean square and with probability 1.

Case 2 Learning the covariance matrix K, with zero mean vector.

In this case, $\theta = K$ is the unknown parameter to be learned. Let $K^{-1} = Q$ and assign the a priori density for Q to be the Wishart probability density with parameters (K_0, ν_0), where K_0 is a positive-definite matrix which reflects the initial knowledge of K, and ν_0 is a constant which reflects the confidence about the initial estimate K_0.

It has been shown that the a posteriori density Q, $p(Q|X_1, \ldots, X_n)$, is again the Wishart density with parameters K_0 replaced by K_n and ν_0 by ν_n where [53]

20 $$K_n = \frac{\nu_0 K_0 + n\langle XX^T\rangle}{\nu_0 + n}$$

21 $$\nu_n = \nu_0 + n$$

where

22 $$\langle XX^T\rangle = \frac{1}{n}\sum_{i=1}^{n} X_i X_i^T$$

Equation *20* can be again interpreted as the weighted average of the a priori knowledge about K^{-1}, K_0, and the sample information contained in $\langle XX^T\rangle$. It can be shown that the expression of *20* fits the stochastic approximation algorithm. Rewrite *20* as

$$K_n = K_{n-1} - K_{n-1} + \frac{\nu_0 K_0 + \sum_{i=1}^{n-1} X_i X_i^T + X_n X_n^T}{\nu_0 + n - 1}\,\frac{\nu_0 + n - 1}{\nu_0 + n}$$

Since $K_{n-1} = \left(\nu_0 K_0 + \sum_{i=1}^{n-1} X_i X_i^T\right)/(\nu_0 + n - 1)$, then

23 $$\begin{aligned} K_n &= K_{n-1} - K_{n-1} + \frac{\nu_0 + n - 1}{\nu_0 + n} K_{n-1} + \frac{X_n X_n^T}{\nu_0 + n} \\ &= K_{n-1} + \frac{1}{n + \nu_0}(X_n X_n^T - K_{n-1}) \\ &= K_{n-1} + \gamma_n (X_n X_n^T - K_{n-1}) \end{aligned}$$

where $\gamma_n = 1/(n + \nu_0)$ has the properties that $\gamma_n > 0$, $\gamma_n \to 0$, $\sum_{n=1}^{\infty} \gamma_n = \infty$, and $\sum_{n=1}^{\infty} \gamma_n^2 < \infty$. Equation *23* depicts the standard algorithm of stochastic approximation in which the current estimate of the covariance matrix depends on the previous estimate and the sample correction which is controlled successively by the sequence γ_n. In order to verify that this learning algorithm also satisfies Dvoretzky's conditions for convergence, the elements of the covariance matrix can be treated individually and the same procedure as in case 1 can be carried out to show Dvoretzky's theorem (special case, real random variable) applies for each and every element in the covariance matrix. As a result, the estimates obtained in *20* are shown to converge to the true covariance matrix (for each and every element in the matrix) in mean square and with probability 1 [54, 55].

Case 3 Learning the mean vector M and the covariance matrix K.

In this case, $\theta = (M,Q)$ and $Q = K^{-1}$, where both M and K are unknown. An appropriate a priori density function for the unknown parameters is found to be normal-Wishart; i.e., the random mean M is taken from a normal probability law with mean M_0 and covariance matrix $\Phi_0 = \mu_0{}^{-1}K$, and Q is taken from a Wishart density with parameters ν_0 and K_0. It is shown that the a posteriori density

$$p(\theta|X_1,X_2, \ldots ,X_n) = p(M,Q|X_1,X_2, \ldots ,X_n)$$

is again normal-Wishart with parameters ν_n, μ_n, M_n, and K_n where [53]

24 $$\nu_n = \nu_0 + n$$

25 $$\mu_n = \mu_0 + n$$

26 $$M_n = \frac{\mu_0 M_0 + n\langle X\rangle}{\mu_0 + n}$$

27 $$K_n = \frac{(\nu_0 K_0 + \mu_0 M_0 M_0{}^T) + [(n-1)S + n\langle X\rangle \langle X\rangle^T] - \mu_n M_n M_n{}^T}{\nu_0 + n}$$

where $\langle X\rangle = (1/n) \sum_{i=1}^{n} X_i$ and

$$S = \frac{1}{n-1} \sum_{i=1}^{n} (X_i - \langle X\rangle)(X_i - \langle X\rangle)^T$$

Expression *27* for K_n can be interpreted as follows: the first two terms are weighted estimates of the noncentralized moments of the observation X; the term $\nu_0 K_0 + \mu_0 M_0 M_0{}^T$ represents the a priori knowledge, and $(n-1)S + n\langle X\rangle \langle X\rangle^T$ represents the sample information. The last term $\mu_n M_n M_n{}^T$ is generated from the new estimate of the mean of X. The sum of these terms yields the new estimate of the covariance matrix. As in cases 1 and 2 it can be shown that *26* and *27* fit the standard form of successive estimation using the algorithm of stochastic approximation. Hence, M_n and K_n converge to the true mean and the true covariance matrix, respectively, in mean square and with probability 1 [54].

In the case of learning the parameters of a normal distribution, the interpretation that the new estimate of a parameter consists of the weighted average of a priori knowledge and the sample information seems to be obvious and reasonable. Unfortunately, the interpretation will become much less obvious if we look closely at distributions other than the normal [1, 51]. An illustrative example based on a binomial distribution can be found in Ref. 55.

Optimum property and rate of convergence of bayesian learning procedure (minimized mean-square error)

Consider the simplified problem of learning the mean value m of a univariate normal distribution with known variance which is proved to be a special algorithm of stochastic approximation. Let m_n be the nth estimate of m. Then

28 $$m_n = m_{n-1} + \gamma_n(x_n - m_{n-1})$$

where $x_n = m + \lambda_n$ is the noisy observation at nth step. In terms of the mean-square error of the estimate we can write

29 $$E\{(m_n - m)^2\} = (1 - \gamma_n)^2 E\{(m_{n-1} - m)^2\} + \gamma_n{}^2 E(\lambda_n{}^2)$$

Denoting $E\{(m_n - m)^2\}$ by $V_n{}^2$ one obtains

30 $$V_n{}^2 = (1 - \gamma_n)^2 V_{n-1}^2 + V_n{}^2\sigma^2$$

where a stationary distribution for the process has been assumed so that $\sigma_n{}^2 = E(\lambda_n{}^2) = \sigma^2$ for all n. For a practical problem it would be of interest to select a particular sequence γ_n satisfying $\gamma_n > 0$,

$$\sum_{n=1}^{\infty} \gamma_n = \infty$$

$\gamma_n \to 0$, $\sum_{n=1}^{\infty} \gamma_n{}^2 < \infty$, and making the mean-square error $V_n{}^2$ as small as possible. This can be achieved by setting the first derivative of $V_n{}^2$ with respect to γ_n equal to zero and solving for γ_n. The result is

31 $$\gamma_n = \frac{V_{n-1}^2}{\sigma^2 + V_{n-1}^2}$$

Let the initial mean-square error be $V_0{}^2 = E\{(m_0 - m)^2\}$. Using *30* and *31*, we can iterate $V_n{}^2$ and γ_n alternately, obtaining the optimum sequence γ_n^* and the minimized mean-square error $V_n{}^{2*}$

32 $$\gamma_n^* = \frac{1}{n + \sigma^2/V_0{}^2} = \frac{1}{n + \alpha}$$

33 $$V_n{}^{2*} = \frac{\sigma^2}{n + \sigma^2/V_0{}^2} = \frac{\sigma^2}{n + \alpha}$$

where $\alpha = \sigma^2/V_0{}^2$ is a positive constant equal to the ratio of the variance of the distribution to the variance of initial estimate of the mean.

Note that the optimum sequence γ_n^* is exactly the same sequence obtained in case 1 (see Eqs. *6* and *13*). The minimized mean-square error $V_n{}^{2*}$ is also the variance attained in bayesian learning procedure (Eq. *7*). Thus, it can be concluded that the bayesian learning technique described by *6*, when considered as a special algorithm of stochastic approximation, is optimum in the sense of minimizing the mean-square error at each and every step.

In practice, it would be desirable to find algorithms for which the mean-square error not only would become as small as possible, but approach zero rapidly in the limit. Consider the algorithm for estimating the mean of a distribution in *28*. The mean-square error for the nth estimate $V_n{}^2 = E\{(m_n - m)^2\}$ is bounded by

34 $$V_n{}^2 \leq F_n{}^2 V_{n-1}^2 + \gamma_n{}^2 B$$

where B is the upper bound for the variance of observations and $F_n = 1 - \gamma_n$ satisfying $\prod_{n=1}^{\infty} F_n = 0$. Iterating *34* and letting $\gamma_n = 1/n$, we obtain the expression of $V_n{}^2$ which becomes

35 $$V_n{}^2 \leq B\left[\frac{1}{n^2} + \frac{1}{(n-1)^2}\left(\frac{n-1}{n}\right)^2 + \cdots + \frac{1}{n^2}\left(\frac{m}{n}\right)^2 + \cdots + \frac{1}{n^2}\right] = \frac{B}{n}$$

Therefore

$$E\{(m_n - m)^2\} \sim 0\left(\frac{1}{n}\right)$$

Two approaches have been proposed to accelerate the stochastic approximation algorithm. One approach is to accelerate the rate of convergence by taking more observations (for example, see Refs. 56 and 57). Intuitively speaking, more observations will provide more information about the process under study, and, in turn, will give a more effective estimate of the sought quantity. The second approach is to improve the rate of convergence by properly choosing a $\{\gamma_n\}$ sequence. A brief description of the accelerated algorithm proposed by Kesten [28] is given to illustrate the second approach. The basic idea of Kesten's algorithm is based on the fact that if the difference between the two successive estimates retains its sign, γ_n is not decreasing, and it remains constant until the sign changes. Mathematically, the algorithm can be written in the form of Dvoretzky's algorithm as

36 $$m_{n+1} = T_n(m_1, \ldots, m_n) + d_n y_n$$

with

37 $$d_1 = \gamma_1 \qquad d_2 = \gamma_2 \qquad d_n = \gamma_{s(n)}$$

and

38 $$s(n) = 2 + \sum_{i=1}^{n} J[(m_i - m_{i-1})(m_{i-1} - m_{i-2})]$$

where

$$J(u) = \begin{cases} 1 & u \leq 0 \\ 0 & u > 0 \end{cases}$$

This simply means that d_n is constant so long as $m_n - m_{n-1}$ and $m_{n-1} - m_{n-2}$ have the same sign. The convergence with probability 1 for the algorithm of *36* can be proved under rather complicated conditions [28].

7 *Bayesian learning without supervision*

Most of the approaches in bayesian learning without supervision can be summarized into three categories: (1) estimating the parameters of a known decision boundary, (2) estimating the unknown parameters in a mixed probability distribution (mixture), and (3) approximating the unknown probability densities by more easily computed functions. In this section, several unsupervised learning techniques, particularly of categories (1) and (2), are discussed.

Estimation of parameters of a known decision boundary [59]

Consider that there are n learning observations, denoted by $x_1, x_2, \ldots, x_n$, drawn from one of the two classes having univariate normal distributions differing only in their means. From these observations the decision boundary which would achieve minimum error for classifying the observations into one of the two classes is to be determined. In the case where the learning is supervised, the optimum decision boundary is known to be the mean of the two means which can be estimated from the classified learning observations. In the case that the classification of the learning observations is not available, the problem can then be viewed as one of estimating the mean of a mixture distribution whose components are the univariate normal distributions. In order to achieve a reasonable solution, the following assumptions are made:

1 The two component distributions are normally distributed, differing only in their means; that is,

$$p(x|\omega_j) \sim N(m_j,\sigma^2) \qquad j = 1, 2$$

2 The a priori probabilities for each component distribution to occur are equal; that is, $P_1 = P_2 = \frac{1}{2}$; then the overall distribution can be expressed as

3 $$p(x) = P_1N(m_1,\sigma^2) + P_2N(m_2,\sigma^2)$$
$$= \frac{1}{2}\frac{1}{\sigma\sqrt{2\pi}}e^{(-1/2\sigma^2)(x-m_1)^2} + \frac{1}{2}\frac{1}{\sigma\sqrt{2\pi}}e^{(-1/2\sigma^2)(x-m_2)^2}$$

From Eq. *3* it is easily seen that the decision boundary is simply the mean of the mixture distribution $p(x)$. In terms of the n learning observations $x_1, x_2, \ldots, x_n$, which are supposedly drawn from $p(x)$, the simplest estimate of the mean is the sample mean

4 $$m_n = \frac{1}{n}\sum_{i=1}^{n} x_i$$

and

5 $$\text{var}\,(m_n) = \frac{1}{n}(\sigma^2 + \alpha)$$

where

$$\alpha = \frac{m_2 - m_1}{2}$$

It should be remarked here that the solution provided by *4* is also one form of stochastic approximation algorithm, with γ_n being a harmonic sequence. By rewriting the sample mean m_n, we have

6 $$m_n = m_{n-1} + \frac{1}{n}(x_n - m_{n-1})$$
$$= m_{n-1} + \gamma_n(x_n - m_{n-1})$$

where

7 $$\gamma_n = \frac{1}{n} \qquad \text{satisfying } \gamma_n > 0,\ \gamma_n \to 0,\ \sum_{n=1}^{\infty}\gamma_n = \infty$$
$$\sum_{n=1}^{\infty}\gamma_n^2 < \infty \qquad \text{and} \qquad \prod_{n=1}^{\infty}(1-\gamma_n) = 0$$

If we consider the transformation in *6* to be

8 $$T_n(m_1, \ldots, m_{n-1}) = (1 - \gamma_n)m_{n-1} + \gamma_n m$$

where m is the true value of the mean, then

9 $$|T_n(m_1, \ldots, m_{n-1}) - m| = (1 - \gamma_n)|m_{n-1} - m|$$

which satisfies Dvoretzky's conditions for convergence, and hence

10 $$\lim_{n\to\infty} E\{(m_n - m)^2\} = 0 \qquad \text{and} \qquad P\{\lim_{n\to\infty} m_n = m\} = 1$$

Some generalizations [59] to this problem have been suggested as follows:

Generalization 1 (multivariate normal distribution) It is known that two spherically symmetric multivariate normal distributions differing only in mean are partitioned with a hyperplane which is the perpendicular bisector of the line connecting the two means. In the nonsupervised case in which the individual means cannot be directly estimated, the learning process becomes a successive estimation of the overall mean vector and the determination of principal axis of the mixture distribution. The latter is equivalent to determination of the eigenvector corresponding to the largest eigenvalue of the overall covariance matrix.

Generalization 2 (unequal a priori probabilities) If a priori probabilities for the component distributions are unequal, then the decision boundary is defined in terms of four distribution parameters, m_1, m_2, σ, and P, where P is one of the a priori probabilities. These parameters can be estimated in terms of the central moments of the mixture distribution from which the learning samples are supposedly drawn.

Bayesian learning with unbounded and bounded solution

The nonsupervised learning proposed in Refs. 60 and 61 essentially has the following formulation:

11 It is true that a set of unclassified learning observations is drawn from one of the two classes of distributions $f(X|\omega_1)$ and $f(X|\omega_2)$; ω_1 is the class of signal plus noise, and ω_2 is the class of noise.

12 Let the set of learning observations be denoted by

$$O^{n-1} = \{X_1, X_2, \ldots, X_{n-1}\}$$

where $X_l = Y_l\theta + N_l$, for $l = 1, 2, \ldots, n-1$, and

$$Y_l = \begin{cases} 1 & \text{if } X_l \text{ is from class } \omega_1 \\ 0 & \text{if } X_l \text{ is from class } \omega_2 \end{cases}$$

θ is some fixed unknown parameter of the signal, and N_l is the noise measurement with zero mean and finite covariance matrix.

13 A priori probabilities for the events $\{Y_l = 1\}$ and $\{Y_l = 0\}$ to occur are known; that is,

$$P(\omega_1) = P \qquad \text{and} \qquad P(\omega_2) = 1 - P$$

where P is fixed and known.

14 The distributions are assumed to be stationary; that is,

$$P(N_l) = p(N) \qquad \text{for all } l$$

and $p(X_l) = Pf(X_l - \theta) + (1 - P)f(X_l)$ implies

15 $$p(X) = Pf(X - \theta) + (1 - P)f(X)$$

where $p(X)$ is again a mixture density function comprising the component density functions $f(X|\omega_1) = f(X - \theta)$ and $f(X|\omega_2) = f(X)$.

The problem is to learn the fixed but unknown parameter θ of the signal through the set of learning observations O^{n-1}. The solution proposed is basically one of using bayesian inference where a posteriori densities $p(\theta|O^{n-1})$ are computed through the learning observations O^{n-1} and a priori density $p_0(\theta)$.

16 **Unbounded solution** [60] Let Z_i^{n-1} be the ith partition of

$$O^{n-1} = (X_1, \ldots, X_{n-1})$$

Then we have 2^{n-1} partitions for O^{n-1} since each sample may come from one of the two classes of distributions. The a posteriori probability density is obtained by computing

17 $$p(\theta|O^{n-1}) = \sum_{i=1}^{2^{n-1}} p(\theta|O^{n-1},Z_i^{n-1})P(Z_i^{n-1}|O^{n-1})$$

For each partition Z_i^{n-1}, it is known exactly which members of the partition contain the signal. Therefore one can use the above equation to build 2^{n-1} machines which learn with supervision. If the outputs of the 2^{n-1} machines are weighted by the appropriate probabilities of occurrence, $P(Z_i^{n-1}|O^{n-1})$, and then summed, the problem will be solved. However, as is easily seen, the number of computations will grow exponentially as the learning observations increase, and for this reason it does not seem to be practical for large numbers of observations.

18 **Bounded and recursive solution** [61] Following the above notations, define

19 $$\text{Likelihood ratio } L(X_n|\theta) = \frac{f(X_n|\omega_1,\theta)}{f(X_n|\omega_2)}$$

and

20 $$\text{Conditional likelihood ratio } L(X_n|O^{n-1}) = \frac{f(X_n|O^{n-1},\omega_1)}{f(X_n|O^{n-1},\omega_2)}$$

Since θ is the unknown parameter, we can write

21 $$L(X_n|O^{n-1}) = \int L(X_n|\theta)p(\theta|O^{n-1})\, d\theta$$

Again, the problem of interest involves the computation of a posteriori probability $p(\theta|O^{n-1})$. The following recursive formula for this computation is obtained from 17 and the iterative application of Bayes' theorem; thus

22 $$p(\theta|O^{n-1}) = \left\{\frac{L(X_{n-1}|\theta) + \beta}{L(X_{n-1}|O^{n-2}) + \beta}\right\} p(\theta|O^{n-2})$$

where $\beta = P(\omega_2)/P(\omega_1) = (1 - P)/P$. In obtaining 22, the following assumptions have to be made:

23 The a priori probabilities $P(\omega_2)$ and $P(\omega_1)$ are known.
24 It is possible to compute $L(X_n|\theta)$ and $p(\theta|O^{n-1})$ for all values of θ, which is unknown.

Note that assumption 24 has posed a difficult problem in practical situations. In order to circumvent this difficulty one has to assume that θ-space can be finitely quantized so that the learning system needs to compute $L(X_n|\theta)$ for only a finite number of values of θ. Of course, the quantization of θ-space poses a further problem if θ itself is unknown.

Equation 22 has been extended to the case in which m $(m > 2)$ possible distributions are involved in the learning observations. Basic assumptions include the following:

25 Each class of distribution is characterized by an unknown parameter θ_i, $i = 1, 2, \ldots, m$.
26 $P(\omega_i) = P_i$, $i = 1, 2, \ldots, m$, are known a priori.
27 θ_i's are independent, and X_l's are conditionally independent; that is,

$$p(\theta_1,\theta_2, \ldots ,\theta_m) = \prod_{i=1}^{m} p(\theta_i).$$

28 $$p(X_1,X_2, \ldots ,X_n|\theta_i,\omega_i) = \prod_{l=1}^{n} p(X_l|\theta_i,\omega_i)$$

The proposed solution is given by computing

29 $$p(X_n|\omega_i,O^{n-1}) =$$

$$\int p(X_n|\omega_i,\theta_i) \frac{p(X_{n-1}|\omega_i,\theta_i)P(\omega_i) + \sum_{j\neq i}^{m} p(X_{n-1}|\omega_j,O^{n-2})P(\omega_j)}{\sum_{j=1}^{m} p(X_{n-1}|\omega_j,O^{n-2})P(\omega_j)} p(\theta_i|O^{n-2})\, d\theta_i$$

or equivalently by computing the a posteriori probability density of the unknown parameter

30 $$p(\theta_i|O^{n-1}) = p(\theta_i|O^{n-2},X_{n-1}) = \frac{p(X_{n-1}|\theta_i,O^{n-2})}{p(X_{n-1})}\, p(\theta_i|O^{n-2})$$
$$= \frac{p(X_{n-1}|\theta_i,\omega_i)P(\omega_i) + \sum_{j\neq i}^{m} p(X_{n-1}|\omega_j,O^{n-2})P(\omega_j)}{\sum_{j=1}^{m} P(\omega_j)p(X_{n-1}|\omega_j,O^{n-2})}\, P(\theta_i|O^{n-2})$$

Since *29* or *30* computes only one of the m conditional probabilities, there will be $m - 1$ more machines that are identical except for initial distributions of the parameters $p_0(\theta_i)$ and the probabilities $P(\omega_i)$. Either $p_0(\theta_i)$ or $P(\omega_i)$ for $i = 1, \ldots, m$ must be different; otherwise all the machines will learn the same thing (since they compute the same quantities), and the system as a whole will learn nothing.

Learning in mixture distributions

Most of the approaches to the problem of nonsupervised learning can be considered as estimating the parameters in an overall distribution comprising the component distributions. As a generalization, the problem can be further formulated in terms of a class of mixture distributions (which includes the previous approaches as special cases), whose actual construction is determined by the physical assumptions of the learning process [62–66]. A significant aspect of the mixture approach to nonsupervised learning is that a sufficient amount of a priori knowledge for a unique solution to exist can be properly determined. This will become apparent after we have reviewed some of the mechanisms necessary for learning a mixture distribution.

31 **Mixture distributions** A mixture distribution results when the set of learning observations $O^n = (X_1, \ldots, X_n)$ can be partitioned in W ways, $Z_1^n, Z_2^n, \ldots, Z_W^n$. For example, if each of the X_i's is possibly generated by one of the two classes of distributions, then $W = 2^n$. The mixture distribution is defined as

32 $$P(X) = \sum_{i=1}^{W} P(X|Z_i^n)P(Z_i^n)$$

where $P(X|Z_i^n)$ is called the ith-partition conditional distribution, and $P(Z_i^n)$ is called the ith mixing parameter.

If the mixture distribution is considered to be characterized by sets of parameters, then the parameter-conditional mixture distribution $P(X|\theta,P)$ can be constructed by the family of the ith-partition, parameter-conditional distributions, $\{P(X|Z_i^n,\theta_i); i = 1,2, \ldots, W\}$, and two sets of parameters $\theta = \{\theta_i;\ i = 1,2, \ldots, W\}$ and

$$P\{P(Z_i^n);\ i = 1,2, \ldots, W\}$$

The basic mixture equation *32* becomes

33 $$P(X|\theta,P) = \sum_{i=1}^{W} P(X|Z_i^n,\theta_i)P(Z_i^n)$$

The problem of nonsupervised learning is then reduced to finding a unique solution for θ and P, given $P(X) = P(X|\theta,P)$. It is shown that the class of mixture distribution which may have a unique solution for θ and P is limited, and whether it admits a unique solution will depend on the identifiability of the mixture distribution [64].

34 **Identifiability of a mixture distribution** Let $\{P(X|Z_i^n,\theta_i)\}$,

$$P = \{P(Z_i^n)\}$$

and $\theta = \{\theta_i\}$ be defined as before. Then the parameter-conditional mixture distribution defined in *33* is the image under the above mapping, say φ, of the parameter sets θ and P. $P(X|\theta,P)$ is said to be identifiable [62–64] if φ is a one-to-one mapping of θ and P onto $P(X|\theta,P)$.

Note that the question of whether $P(X|\theta,P)$ is identifiable or not is one of unique characterizations; that is, for a particular family of the ith partition, the distribution $P(X|\theta,P)$ uniquely determines the sets of parameters $\{\theta_i\}$ and $\{P(Z_i^n)\}$. It is then clear that if the nonsupervised learning problem is such that the mixture distribution is not uniquely characterized by $\{\theta_i\}$ and $\{P(Z_i^n)\}$ (not identifiable), then there exists no unique solution to the underlying problem.

To show the type of constraints that have to be put on the parameters in order to assure identifiable mixture distribution, consider the mixture of two univariate normal distributions, $N_1(m_1,\sigma^2)$ and $N_2(m_2,\sigma^2)$. The mixture is characterized by $\theta = (m_1,m_2,\sigma^2)$ and $P = (P_1,\ 1 - P_1)$. Then, given $P(X|\theta,P) = P_1N_1(m_1,\sigma^2) + (1 - P_1)N_2(m_2,\sigma^2)$, there is a unique solution for θ and P if $m_1 < m_2$ when N_1 and N_2 are lexicographically ordered as $N_1 < N_2$. Note that this constraint is satisfied by the problems treated in this section in which a unique solution exists.

8 *Nonsupervised learning using stochastic approximation*

It has been noticed that most of the existing learning techniques, without supervision in particular, are made feasible by reducing the learning problem to the process of successively estimating some unknown parameters of the underlying functions. For instance, the parameter involved in Sec. 7 (see "Estimation of Parameters of a Known Decision Boundary") is a parameter of the decision boundary, the parameters discussed in Sec. 7 (see "Bayesian Learning with Unbounded and Bounded Solution") are the unknown parameters of the signal, and in Sec. 7 (see "Learning in Mixture Distributions") the parameters may be considered as those characterizing the mixture distribution comprising the component distributions to be learned. The method of estimating these parameters, however, seems to depend on the particular problem on hand. It is therefore desirable to seek a unified procedure for the successive estimation of parameters involved in a variety of learning processes. In the following proposed algorithm, the stochastic approximation procedure is used to provide a general access to the problem of nonsupervised learning. An example of learning the mixture of univariate normal distributions will be given to show under what conditions a solution can be unique.

Let the following assumptions be made for the underlying learning process:

1 There are m classes of probability distributions whose a priori probabilities are fixed but unknown. Let $\Omega_c = \{\omega_i: i = 1,2 \; . \; . \; . \; ,m\}$ be the set of m classes and $\{P(\omega_i) = P_i: i = 1,2, \; . \; . \; . \; ,m\}$ be the set of m a priori probabilities $\sum_{j=1}^{m} P_j = 1$.

2 Each distribution is characterized by a probability distribution function $P(X|\omega_i,\theta_i)$, or, equivalently, by a probability density function $p(X|\omega_i,\theta_i)$, where θ_i is the unknown parameter whose existence is assumed (that is, $\|\theta_i\| < \infty$ in a certain metric space of parameters Ω_θ).

3 Learning observations are assumed drawn from the mixture distribution constructed by the component distributions; that is,

4 $$P(X|\theta,P) = \sum_{i=1}^{m} P(X|\omega_i,\theta_i)P(\omega_i)$$

where $P(X|\theta,P)$ denotes the mixture distribution function conditioned by $\theta = \{\theta_i: i = 1,2, \; . \; . \; . \; ,m\}$ and $P = \{P_i: i = 1,2, \; . \; . \; . \; ,m\}$.

5 There exist unbiased estimates of certain statistics $\{\Theta(X)\}$ for the mixture (first moment, second moment, etc.).

The functional relation between the estimates $\{\Theta(X)\}$ and the sets of parameters, θ and P, is known; that is,

6 $$F(\{\Theta(X)\},\{P_i\},\{\theta_i\}) = 0$$

is known at each step of the learning process.

7 Additional equations $G_j(\{\theta_i\},\{P_i\}) = 0, j = 1, 2, \ldots$, are available to give unique solution to the unknown parameters $\{\theta_i\}$ and $\{P_i\}$.

If *3* to *7* are satisfied with probability 1, then the true parameters $\{\theta_i\}$ and $\{P_i\}$ are defined in the limit by

$$F(\{\Theta(X)\},\{P_i\},\{\theta_i\}) = 0$$

and $G_j(\{\theta_i\},\{P_i\}) = 0$. The learning problem is then to find the unique solution for $\{\theta_i\}$ and $\{P_i\}$ through the functions F and G, where F is obtained from the successive estimates of $\{\Theta(X)\}$ and G's are given a priori or sought by auxiliary estimation procedures. The following example will illustrate the application and the procedure used to achieve a unique solution by the algorithm of stochastic approximation.

Example Let $\Omega_c = (\omega_1,\omega_2)$, $P(\omega_1) = P_1 = P$, and $P(\omega_2) = 1 - P$. The component distributions are univariate normal; that is,

$$p(x|\omega_1) \sim N(m_1,\sigma_1^2),\ p(x|\omega_2) \sim N(m_2,\sigma_2^2)$$

The mixture density function conditioned by $\theta = (m_1,m_2,\sigma_1^2,\sigma_2^2)$ and $P = (P, 1 - P)$ is then given by

8 $$p(x|\theta,P) = PN(m_1,\sigma_1^2) + (1 - P)N(m_2,\sigma_2^2)$$

We wish to learn the unknown parameters θ and P through the unclassified samples $x_1, x_2, \ldots, x_n$ generated from $p(x|\theta,P)$.

Solution: Let the first, second, and third moment of x with respect to $p(x|\theta,P)$ be computed from *8*; thus

9 $$E(x) = Pm_1 + (1 - P)m_2 = m_2 + P(m_1 - m_2)$$

10 $$E(x^2) = P(m_1^2 + \sigma_1^2) + (1 - P)(m_2^2 + \sigma_2^2)$$

11 $$E(x^3) = P(m_1^3 + 3m_1\sigma_1^2) + (1 - P)(m_2^3 + 3m_2\sigma_2^2)$$

Case 1. Consider that $\sigma_1^2 = \sigma_2^2 = \sigma^2$ and P are fixed and known. $m_2 = 0$ and m_1 is to be learned. Using *9*, we can solve for m_1. Thus

12 $$m_1 = \frac{E(x)}{p}$$

It remains only to obtain the estimate of $E(x)$. A stochastic approximation algorithm can be used to give an asymptotically unbiased estimate of $E(x)$ which will in turn give an asymptotically unbiased estimate of m_1. Let $E_n(x)$ be the nth estimate of $E(x)$. Define

13 $$E_n(x) = E_{n-1}(x) + \gamma_n(x_n - E_{n-1}(x))$$

where

14 $$\gamma_n > 0 \qquad \gamma_n \to 0 \qquad \sum_{n=1}^{\infty} \gamma_n^2 < \infty \qquad \prod_{n=1}^{\infty} (1 - \gamma_n) = 0$$

Then by Dvoretzky's theorem we have

15 $$\lim_{n\to\infty} E\left\{\left(\frac{E_n(x)}{P} - m_1\right)^2\right\} = 0$$

and

16 $$P\left\{\lim_{n\to\infty} \frac{E_n(x)}{P} = m_1\right\} = 1$$

that is, the true value of m_1 is learned in mean-square sense and with probability 1.

Case 2. Let $\sigma_1^2 = \sigma_2^2 = \sigma^2$ be known and $m_2 = 0$. The problem is to find P and m_1. Equations *9* and *10* give

17 $$m_1 = \frac{E(x^2) - \sigma^2}{E(x)}$$

18 $$P = \frac{E(x)}{m_1}$$

The solution of m_1 and P can be obtained by successively estimating the first and second moment of the mixture distribution and alternately applying *17* and *18*. The stochastic approximation procedure will provide an asymptotically unbiased estimate for $E(x)$ and $E(x^2)$ which in turn gives the true values of m_1 and P.

Case 3. Let $m_2 = 0$ and let m_1, P, and $\sigma^2 = \sigma_1^2 = \sigma_2^2$ be the parameters to be learned through the first three moments. Equations *9*, *10*, and *11* become

19 $$E(x) = Pm_1$$

20 $$E(x^2) = Pm_1^2 + \sigma^2$$

21 $$E(x^3) = P(m_1^3 + 3m_1\sigma^2)$$

Solving *19*, *20*, and *21* simultaneously gives

22 $$m_1^2 + 3E(x)m_1 + 3E(x^2) - E(x^3)/E(x) = 0$$

The discriminant of *22* is

23 $$9E^2(x) - 12E(x^2) + 4E(x^3)/E(x)$$

Substituting the relations *19*, *20*, and *21* for the moments, we see that *23* becomes

24 $$m_1^2(3P - 2)^2$$

Since $m_1 \neq 0$, the condition for a unique solution is $P = \frac{2}{3}$. Thus, if $P = \frac{2}{3}$ for the mixture distribution, then the parameters P, σ^2, and m_1 can be learned uniquely through *19*, *20*, and *21* by defining stochastic approximation procedures to give asymptotically unbiased estimates of $E(x)$, $E(x^2)$, and $E(x^3)$. Otherwise, the problem will have multiple solutions.

It is noted that:

1. The assumptions in these cases are essentially the constraints that have to be put on the component distributions in order to achieve a unique solution for the unknown parameters using first-, second-, and third-order statistics. At each step of the learning process, the parameters can be successively estimated through the moment estimators of the mixture distribution.

2. If σ_1^2 and σ_2^2 are unknown and unequal, then higher moments of $p(X|\theta,P)$ would be needed to give sufficient functional relations for θ and P. Usually, as in case 3, multiple solutions are expected in solving simultaneous nonlinear equations. A unique solution is attainable only if more information about the parameters is available to assure that the solution obtained is the one characterizing the mixture distribution. These additional constraints may well be interpreted as the conditions for identifiability in learning the mixture with stochastic approximation.

9 *Further remarks*

Learning techniques based on (1) the stochastic approximation, (2) the linear reinforcement algorithm, (3) the potential function method, and (4) the bayesian estimation have been discussed. These learning techniques, in some cases, fall within the general framework of stochastic approximation and possess the same type of convergence properties. However, from an engineering viewpoint, the computational difficulties involved, as well as the a priori information required in each technique, are different. Learning processes, supervised or unsupervised, using parametric or nonparametric statistical estimation procedures, can be formulated in general as problems of successive approximation of unknown parameters. The unknown parameters can be estimated by applying any one of these four learning techniques. The performance of the estimation may be measured on the basis of mean-square error.

Additional topics of interest which have not been discussed in this chapter include:

1. Nonprobabilistic training techniques [67–75]. The main problem is concerned with training algorithms for successive adjustments of a

decision function which is used to separate the given samples from two disjoint classes. The potential function method can also be applied in this case.

2. Stochastic automata as models of learning systems [14–16, 76]. Because of the stochastic nature in state transitions, stochastic automata are suitable for modeling learning systems. Modifications or successive estimates of state transition probabilities or state probabilities are achieved by using reinforcement learning algorithms such that the performance of the automaton will be improved during its operation.

3. Inductive inference [77, 78]. Watanabe has related the information theory to inductive and deductive inference. The time rate of decrease of entropy, defined by the system's response probabilities, was proposed as a measure of the rate of learning.

4. Heuristic approaches [79–81]. In very complicated learning situations, such as games of checkers and chess, and programs for theorem-proving, it is hardly possible to formulate the corresponding mathematical models. Heuristic approaches have been applied to this type of learning problem. The nature of these approaches varies widely and depends upon the particular problem at hand.

The research in learning systems is still in its infant stage although results from initial study seem promising. Much effort will be needed in the future for the investigations of new and improved learning techniques.

REFERENCES

1 Bellman, R.: "Adaptive Control Processes, A Guided Tour," Princeton University Press, Princeton, N.J., 1961.
2 Tsypkin, Ya. Z.: Adaptation, Learning and Self-learning in Automatic Systems, *Avtomat. i Telemek.*, vol. 27, no. 1, pp. 23–61, 1966.
3 Fu, K. S.: Learning Control Systems, in J. T. Tou and R. H. Wilcox (eds.), "Computer and Information Sciences," Spartan Books, 1964.
4 Sklansky, J.: Learning Systems for Automatic Control, *IEEE Trans. Automatic Control*, vol. AC-11, no. 1, January, 1966.
5 Murphy, R. E.: "Adaptive Processes in Economic Systems," Academic, New York, 1965.
6 Ivakhnenko, A. G., and V. G. Lapa: "Cybernetic Predicting Devices," The Academy of Sciences of Ukr. SSR, Naukova Dumka, Kiev, 1965 (in Russian; translation to appear as *Tech. Rept.* TR-EE66-5, *School of Electrical Eng., Purdue Univ., Lafayette, Ind.*, April, 1966).
7 Bush, R. R., and F. Mosteller: "Stochastic Models for Learning," Wiley, New York, 1955.
8 Bush, R. R., and W. K. Estes (eds.): "Studies in Mathematical Learning Theory," Stanford University Press, Stanford, Calif., 1959.
9 Abramson, N., and D. Braverman: Learning to Recognize Patterns in a

Random Environment, *IRE Trans. Information Theory,* vol. IT-8, pp. 58–63, September, 1962.
10 Aizerman, M. A., E. M. Braverman, and L. I. Rozonoer, Probability Problem of Pattern Recognition, Learning and Potential Function Method, *Avtomat. i Telemek.,* vol. 25, no. 9, pp. 1307–1323, September, 1964.
11 Jackson, D.: "The Theory of Approximation," The American Mathematical Society, New York, 1930.
12 Driml, M., and O. Hans: On Experience Theory Problems, *Trans. Second Prague Conf. Information Theory, Statistical Decision Functions, and Random Processes,* 1959, Academic, New York, 1960.
13 Sklansky, J.: Two-mode Threshold Learning, *Aerospace Medical Res. Labs., Wright-Patterson Air Force Base, Ohio, Tech. Documentary Rept.* AMRL-TDR-64-39, May, 1964.
14 Varshavskij, V. I., and I. P. Vorontsova: On the Behavior of Stochastic Automata with Variable Structures, *Avtomat. i Telemek.,* vol. 24, no. 3, pp. 353–360, March, 1963; *Automation and Remote Control,* pp. 327–333.
15 Fu, K. S., and R. W. McLaren: An Application of Stochastic Automata to the Synthesis of Learning Systems, *Tech. Report* TR-EE65-17, *School of Electrical Eng., Purdue Univ., Lafayette, Ind.,* September, 1965.
16 McMurtry, G. J., and K. S. Fu: A Variable Structure Automaton Used as a Multi-model Searching Technique, *Proc. Natl. Electronic Conf.,* vol. 21, 1965.
17 McMurtry, G. J., and K. S. Fu: On the Learning Behavior of Finite State Systems in Random Environments, *Second Ann. Allerton Conf. Circuit and System Theory, Univ. of Illinois, Monticello, Illinois,* 1964.
18 Tsetlin, M. L.: On the Behavior of Finite Automata in Random Media, *Avtomat. i Telemek.,* vol. 22, no. 10, pp. 1345–1354, October, 1961; *Automation and Remote Control,* pp. 1210–1219.
19 Dvoretzky, A.: On Stochastic Approximation, *Proc. Third Berkeley Symp. Math. Stat. Prob.,* vol. 1, pp. 39–55, University of California Press, Los Angeles, 1956.
20 Robbins, H., and S. Monro: A Stochastic Approximation Method, *Ann. Math. Stat.,* vol. 22, pp. 400–407, 1951.
21 Kiefer, J., and J. Wolfowitz: Stochastic Estimation of the Maximum of a Regression Function, *Ann. Math. Stat.,* vol. 23, pp. 462–466, 1952.
22 Blum, J. R.: A Note on Stochastic Approximation, *Proc. Amer. Math. Soc.,* vol. 9, pp. 404–407, 1958.
23 Krasulina, T. P.: A Note on Some Stochastic Approximation Processes, *Theory of Probability and Its Applications,* vol. 7, no. 1, 1962 (English translation of *Teoria Veroyatnosti i ee Primeneniya* by SIAM).
24 Schmetterer, L.: Stochastic Approximation, *Proc. Fourth Berkeley Symp. Math. Stat.,* vol. 1, 1961.
25 Blum, J.: Multidimensional Stochastic Approximation Methods, *Ann. Math. Stat.,* vol. 35, pp. 737–744, 1954.
26 Sacks, J.: Asymptotic Distribution of Stochastic Approximation Procedures, *Ann. Math. Stat.,* pp. 373–407, 1958.
27 Derman, C., and J. Sacks: On Dvoretzky's Stochastic Approximation Theorem, *Ann. Math. Stat.,* vol. 30, pp. 601–606, 1959.
28 Kesten, H.: Accelerated Stochastic Approximation, *Ann. Math. Stat.,* vol. 29, pp. 41–59, 1958.
29 Dupac, V.: On the Kiefer-Wolfowitz Approximation Method, translated by M. D. Friedman, *MIT Lincoln Lab Report,* 22G-0008, 1960.
30 Ho, Y. C., and R. C. K. Lee: A Bayesian Approach to Problems in Stochastic

Estimation and Control, *IEEE Trans. Automatic Control,* vol. AC-9, pp. 333–338, 1964.

31 Kushner, H. J., A Simple Iterative Procedure for the Identification of the Unknown Parameters of a Linear Time-varying Discrete System, *ASME, J. Basic Eng.*, vol. 85, pp. 227–235, 1963.

32 Hill, J. D., and K. S. Fu: A Learning Control System Using Stochastic Approximation for Hill Climbing, preprint volume of the 1965 Joint Automatic Control Conference, pp. 334–340.

33 Sakrison, D. J.: Application of Stochastic Approximation to Optimum Filter Design, *1961-IRE Conv. Rec.*, pt. 4, pp. 127–135.

34 Kushner, H. J.: Adaptive Techniques for the Optimization of Binary Detection Systems, *1963-IEEE Intern. Conv. Rec.*, pt. 4, pp. 107–117.

35 Cooper, D. B.: Adaptive Pattern Recognition and Signal Detection Using Stochastic Approximation, *IEEE Trans. Electronic Computers,* vol. EC-13, pp. 306–307, 1964.

36 Wilde, D. J.: "Optimum Seeking Methods," Prentice-Hall, Englewood Cliffs, N.J., 1964.

37 Nikolic, Z. J., and K. S. Fu: A Mathematical Model of Learning in an Unknown Environment, *Proc., 1966 Nat. Electronics Conf.*, vol. 22, pp. 607–612.

38 Nikolic, Z. J., and K. S. Fu: An Algorithm for 'Learning Without External Supervision' and Its Application to Learning Control Systems, *JACC, Univ. Washington, Seattle, Washington,* 1966 (also *IEEE Trans. Automatic Control,* July, 1966).

39 Driml, M., and O. Hans: Continuous Stochastic Approximations, *Trans. Second Prague Conf. on Information Theory, Statistical Decision Functions, and Random Processes,* pp. 113–122, Czechoslovak Academy of Sciences, Prazn, 1959.

40 Sakrison, D. J.: A Continuous Kiefer-Wolfowitz Procedure for Random Processes, *Ann. Math. Stat.*, vol. 35, no. 2, pp. 591–599, 1964.

41 Knopp, K.: "Infinite Sequences and Series," pp. 96–97, Dover, New York, 1956.

42 McLaren, R. W.: A Markov Model for Learning Systems Operating in an Unknown Environment, *Proc. 1964, Nat. Electronics Conf.*, vol. 20.

43 Waltz, M. D., and K. S. Fu: A Heuristic Approach to Reinforcement Learning Control Systems, *IEEE Trans. Automatic Control,* vol. AC-10, pp. 390–398, 1965.

44 Aizerman, M. A., E. M. Braverman, and L. I. Rozonoer: Theoretical Foundations of Potential Function Method in Pattern Recognition, *Avtomat. i Telemek.*, vol. 25, no. 6, pp. 917–937, June, 1964.

45 Aizerman, M. A., E. M. Braverman, and L. I. Rozonoer: Method of Potential Functions in the Problem of Restoration of Functional Converter Characteristic by Means of Points Observed Randomly, *Avtomat. i Telemek.*, vol. 25, no. 12, pp. 1705–1714, December, 1964.

46 Braverman, E. M., and E. S. Pyatnitskii: Estimations of Algorithms Convergence Rate Based on the Method of Potential Functions, *Avtomat. i Telemek.*, no. 1, pp. 95–111, January, 1966.

47 Braverman, E. M.: On the Potential Function Method, *Avtomat. i Telemek.*, vol. 26, no. 12, pp. 2205–2213, December, 1965.

48 Tsypkin, Ya. Z.: On Restoration of Characteristics of a Functional Generator by Randomly Observed Points, *Avtomat. i Telemek.*, vol. 26, no. 11, pp. 1947–1950, November, 1965.

49 Aizerman, M. A., E. M. Braverman, and L. I. Rozonoer: The Robbins-Monro

Process and the Potential Functions Method, *Avtomat. i Telemek.*, vol. 26, no. 11, pp. 1951–1955, November, 1965.
50 Blaydon, C. C.: On a Pattern Classification Result of Aizerman, Braverman, and Rozonoer, *IEEE Trans. Inform. Theory*, vol. IT-12, no. 1, pp. 82–83, January, 1966.
51 Spragins, J. D., Jr.: Reproducing Distributions for Machine Learning, *TR* No. 6103-7, *Stanford Univ.*, Stanford, Calif., November, 1963.
52 Spragins, J. D., Jr.: A Note on the Iterative Application of Bayes Rule, *IEEE Trans. Inform. Theory*, vol. IT-11, no. 4, pp. 544–549, October, 1965.
53 Keehn, D. G.: A Note on Learning for Gaussian Properties, *IEEE Trans. Inform. Theory*, vol. IT-11, pp. 126–132, January, 1965.
54 Fu, K. S., Y. T. Chien, Z. J. Nikolic, and W. G. Wee: On the Stochastic Approximation and Related Learning Techniques, *Rept.* TR-EE66-6, *School of Electrical Eng., Purdue Univ.*, Lafayette, Ind., April, 1966.
55 Chien, Y. T., and K. S. Fu: On Bayesian Learning and Stochastic Approximation, *IEEE Trans. System Science and Cybernetics*, vol. SSC-3, no. 1, pp. 28–38, June, 1967.
56 Fabian, V.: Stochastic Approximation of Minima with Improved Asymptotic Speed, *Ann. Math. Stat.*, vol. 38, pp. 191–200, 1967.
57 Venter, J. H.: An Extension of the Robbins-Monro Procedure, *Ann. Math. Stat.*, vol. 38, pp. 181–190, 1967.
58 Fabian, V.: Stochastic Approximation Methods, *Czechoslovak Math. J.*, vol. 10, pp. 123–159, 1960.
59 Cooper, D. B., and P. W. Cooper: Nonsupervised Adaptive Signal Detection and Pattern Recognition, *Inform. and Control*, vol. 7, no. 3, pp. 416–444, September, 1964.
60 Daly, R. F.: The Adaptive Binary-Detection Problem on the Real Line, *Stanford Electronics Lab.*, Stanford, Calif., *TR* No. 2003-3, February, 1962.
61 Fralick, S. C.: The Synthesis of Machines Which Learn Without a Teacher, *TR* No. 6103-8, *Stanford Univ.*, Stanford, Calif., April, 1964.
62 Patrick, E. A.: "Learning Probability Spaces for Classification and Recognition of Patterns with or without Supervision," Ph.D. Thesis, Purdue University, Lafayette, Ind., January, 1966.
63 Teicher, H.: On the Mixture of Distributions, *Ann. Math. Stat.*, vol. 31, pp. 55–73, 1960.
64 Teicher, H.: Identifiability of Finite Mixtures, *Ann. Math. Stat.*, vol. 34, pp. 1265–1269, December, 1963.
65 Stanat, D. F.: Nonsupervised Pattern Recognition Through the Decomposition of Probability Functions, *Sensory Intelligence Lab., Tech. Rept.*, University of Michigan, April, 1966.
66 Sammon, J. W.: Adaptive Decomposition of Superposition of Probability Density Functions, *RADC Tech. Rept.* TDR66-40, 1966.
67 Mays, C. H.: Adaptive Threshold Logic, *Rept.* SEL-63-027 (*TR* No. 1557-1), *Stanford Electronics Lab.*, Stanford, Calif., April, 1963.
68 Widrow, B., and M. E. Hoff: Adaptive Switching Circuits, *Stanford Electronics Lab.*, Stanford, Calif., *Rept.* 1553-1, June 30, 1961.
69 Novikoff, A.: On Convergence Proofs for Perceptrons, *Symp. Math. Theory of Automata, Polytechnic Inst. of Brooklyn*, April, 1963.
70 Ho, Y. C., and R. L. Kashyap: An Algorithm for Linear Inequalities and Its Applications, *IEEE Trans. Electronic Computers*, vol. EC-14, no. 5, pp. 683–688, October, 1965.

71 Koford, J. S.: Adaptive Pattern Dichotomization, *TR* No. 6201-1, *Stanford Electronics Lab.*, Stanford, Calif., April, 1964.

72 Koford, J. S., and G. F. Groner: The Use of an Adaptive Threshold Element to Design a Linear Optimal Pattern Classifier, *IEEE Trans. Inform. Theory,* vol. IT-12, no. 1, pp. 42–50, January, 1966.

73 Blaydon, C. C., and Y. C. Ho: On the Abstraction Problem in Pattern Recognition, *Fifth Symp. on Discrete Adaptive Processes, Chicago,* October 3–5, 1966.

74 Agmon, S.: The Relaxation Method for Linear Inequalities, *Can. J. Math.*, vol. 6, pp. 382–392, 1954.

75 Nilsson, N. J.: "Learning Machines," McGraw-Hill, New York, 1965.

76 Fu, K. S.: Stochastic Automata as Models of Learning Systems, *Second COINS Symp., Columbus, Ohio,* August 22–24, 1966.

77 Watanabe, S.: Information Theoretical Aspects of Inductive and Deductive Inference, *IBM J. Res. Dev.*, vol. 4, pp. 208–231, 1960.

78 Watanabe, S.: Learning Processes and Inverse H-Theorem, *IRE Trans. Inform. Theory,* vol. IT-8, pp. 246–251, September, 1962.

79 Samuel, A. L.: Some Studies in Machine Learning Using the Game of Checkers, *IBM J. Res. Dev.*, vol. 3, pp. 211–229, July, 1959.

80 Feigenbaum, E. A., and J. Feldman (eds.): "Computers and Thought," McGraw-Hill, New York, 1963.

81 Newell, A., J. C. Shaw, and H. A. Simon: A Variety of Intelligent Learning in a General Problem Solver, in M. C. Yovits and S. Camerson (eds.), "Self-Organizing Systems," pp. 153–189, Pergamon, New York, 1960.

82 Sebestyen, G. S.: Pattern Recognition by an Adaptive Process of Sample Set Construction, *IRE Trans. Inform. Theory,* vol. IT-8, pp. 82–91, September, 1962.

83 Fu, K. S., and C. H. Chen: Sequential Decisions, Pattern Recognition and Machine Learning, TR-EE65-6, *School of Electrical Eng., Purdue Univ.*, Lafayette, Ind., April, 1965.

84 Block, H. D.: Estimates of Error for Two Modifications of the Robbins-Monro Stochastic Approximation Process, *Ann. Math. Stat.*, vol. 28, no. 4, pp. 1003–1010, 1957.

85 Dupac, V.: A Dynamic Stochastic Approximation Method, *Ann. Math. Stat.*, vol. 36, no. 6, pp. 1695–1703, 1966.

86 Yudin, D. B.: Methods of Quantitative Analysis of Complex Systems, I and II, *Tekhnicheskaia Kybernetika,* no. 1, 1965 and no. 1, 1966.

Part Five

OPTIMAL SYSTEMS

12

Decomposition of large-scale systems

P. P. Varaiya[1]
Department of Electrical Engineering and Computer Sciences
University of California, Berkeley

1 *Introduction*

Many problems in decision-making can be reformulated as problems in mathematical programming (MP) so that the methods of MP can be used to yield a practical solution to these problems. Now the usual (i.e., general-purpose) algorithms developed in MP are such that the amount of computational effort required for solving a problem grows much faster than the size of the problem. So if one wishes to find a solution to a large problem it may become impossible (too much computer storage space required) or uneconomical (too much computer time needed) to apply these methods.

To overcome this obstacle of "large size," considerable attention has recently been devoted [1–3][2] to devise algorithms which are particularly suited to these problems. The usual means of approach seems to be the following. It is assumed that the "large" problem consists of a number of "small" problems that are tied together, as it were, by some "coupling" constraints (including perhaps the objective function) or "coupling" variables, or both. One then supposes that these subsystems and their coupling relationships have a special form. For example, we may suppose that the subsystems give rise to convex programming problems and the coupling can be represented by linear equations.

[1] The research reported herein was supported in part by the United States Army Research Office, Durham, under Grant DA-ARO-D-31-124-G576.

[2] These references are representative and not exhaustive.

Advantage is then taken of this special structure to devise algorithms that produce the solution to the original large problem after solving a sequence (finite or infinite) of "smaller" problems. These methods therefore make possible the resolution of important classes of problems which were previously either impossible or impractical to tackle. Furthermore, they yield some important insight into aspects of multilevel decision-making [3, 4].

We shall present here a slight modification of the usual problem in convex programming and show how different specifications of this problem yield different classes of problems which are amenable to a solution by "decomposition." In each case we shall present "existence" results. By this we mean that we can demonstrate the existence of a sequence of derived problems simpler than the original one such that a solution to this sequence of problems yields a solution to the original problem. To arrive at such existence results is a relatively simple matter. What is more interesting in a practical situation is the determination of these derived problems. In most cases we shall give computational methods which achieve this goal. A large part of this material is based on a paper by the author [5]. For a presentation of some similar ideas see Ref. 6.

2 Statement of the problem and conditions for its solution

At this stage, it is convenient to introduce some notation and present some concepts which facilitate the exposition and comprehension of what follows.

Notation Let Ω_1 and Ω_2 be nonempty subsets of a linear space X. Then

$$\Omega_1 - \Omega_2 = \{x_1 - x_2 | x_1 \in \Omega_1,\ x_2 \in \Omega_2\}$$

If x is an arbitrary point of X,

$$\Omega_1 - x = \Omega_1 - \{x\}$$

Definition Let Ω be a *convex* set in R^n, and let $\hat{x}$ be an element of Ω.

1 By the *closed radial cone of Ω at $\hat{x}$* we mean the set

$$C(\hat{x},\Omega) = \overline{\{\alpha(x - \hat{x}) | \alpha \geq 0,\ x \in \Omega\}}$$

where the overbar denotes closure of the set under the bar.

2 By the *polar cone of Ω at $\hat{x}$* we mean the set

$$P(\hat{x},\Omega) = \{z \in R^n | \langle z,x \rangle \leq 0 \text{ for all } x \in C(\hat{x},\Omega)\}$$

It should be clear that $C(\hat{x},\Omega)$ and $P(\hat{x},\Omega)$ are closed convex cones with vertices at the origin and that

$$P(\hat{x},\Omega) = \{z \in R^n | \langle z,x \rangle \leq 0 \text{ for all } x \in \Omega - \hat{x}\}$$

Thus the set $C(\hat{x},\Omega)$ is a "linear" approximation to the set Ω at the point $\hat{x}$, and $P(\hat{x},\Omega)$ is the set of vectors which make obtuse angles with all the elements of $\Omega - \hat{x}$. See Fig. *12.2.1* for an illustration of these definitions.

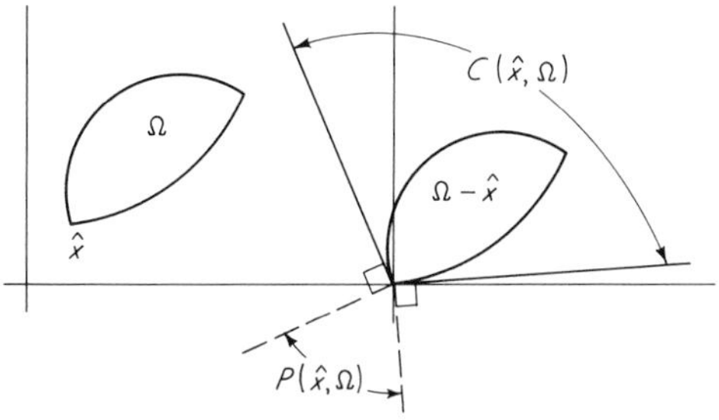

Fig. 12.2.1

As we shall soon see, the conditions for extremality are merely various relationships that hold among these sets, and assumptions are made (see Theorem *18*) in a given situation so that we can explicitly state these relationships. We shall now prove an extremely simple theorem that is basic to our subject and shows the relevance of the notions introduced above.

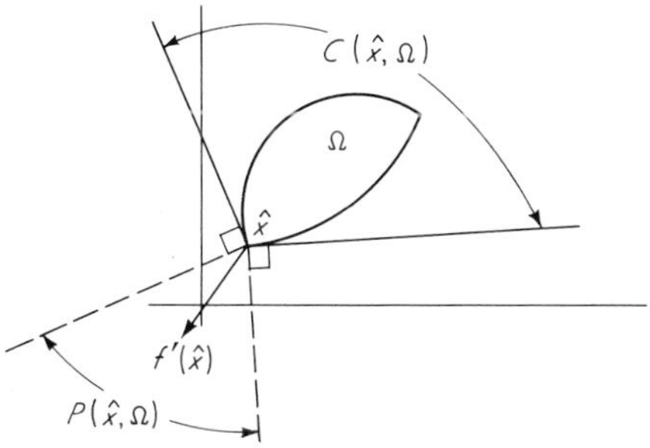

Fig. 12.2.2

3 **Theorem** (See Fig. *12.2.2.*) Let Ω be a *convex* set in R^n, and let f be a real-valued, *concave*, differentiable function defined on Ω. Then $\hat{x}$ in Ω

is a solution of

4 $$\max_x \{f(x) | x \in \Omega\}$$

if and only if

5 $$f'(\hat{x}) \equiv \frac{df}{dx}(\hat{x}) \in P(\hat{x},\Omega)$$

Proof Suppose $\hat{x}$ is a solution of *4*. Let $x \in \Omega$ and $0 < \epsilon < 1$. Since Ω is convex, $(\hat{x} + \epsilon(x - \hat{x})) \in \Omega$, and we have

$$\begin{aligned} f(\hat{x}) &\geq f(\hat{x} + \epsilon(x - \hat{x})) \\ &= f(\hat{x}) + \epsilon\langle f'(\hat{x}), x - \hat{x}\rangle + o(\epsilon) \end{aligned}$$

where $\frac{o(\epsilon)}{\epsilon} \to 0$ as $\epsilon \to 0$. Hence,

$$0 \geq \epsilon\langle f'(\hat{x}), x - \hat{x}\rangle + o(\epsilon)$$

or

$$0 \geq \langle f'(\hat{x}), x - \hat{x}\rangle + \frac{o(\epsilon)}{\epsilon}$$

Passing to the limit as $\epsilon \to 0$, we obtain

$$0 \geq \langle f'(\hat{x}), x - \hat{x}\rangle \qquad \text{for } x \in \Omega$$

so that by definition $f'(\hat{x}) \in P(\hat{x},\Omega)$. Conversely, suppose $f'(\hat{x})$ satisfies *5* so that

6 $$\langle f'(\hat{x}), x - \hat{x}\rangle \leq 0 \qquad \text{for } x \in \Omega$$

Since f is a concave function, we have

$$f(x) \leq f(\hat{x}) + \langle f'(\hat{x}), x - \hat{x}\rangle \leq f(\hat{x})$$

by *6*. Therefore $\hat{x}$ is a solution of *4*.

For any given constrained maximization problem, let us call the set of vectors which satisfy the constraints the *feasible set* of solutions. Then Theorem *3* says that at the optimal point, the gradient of the profit function must make an angle of more than 90° with every ray that starts at the optimal point and passes through the feasible set. In terms of the notation introduced earlier, Theorem *3* tells us that in order to determine whether a feasible solution $\hat{x}$ is optimal, we need to verify whether the gradient at the point $\hat{x}$ lies in the polar cone generated by the feasible set at $\hat{x}$.

In most cases of interest, the feasible set is not given explicitly. For our purposes we can restrict ourselves to the following situation:

7 $$\max_x \{f(x) | Ax \in \Omega_1, x \in \Omega_2\}$$

where $x \in R^n$, $\Omega_1 \subset R^m$, and $\Omega_2 \subset R^n$ are fixed closed convex sets, A is an $m \times n$ matrix with full rank, and f is a function satisfying the conditions of Theorem *3*. In this case, the feasible set is given by Ω where

$$\Omega = \Omega_1' \cap \Omega_2 \qquad \Omega_1' = \{x | Ax \in \Omega_1\}$$

Therefore, in order to obtain a useful optimality criterion we need to relate $P(\hat{x},\Omega)$ at a solution $\hat{x}$ with the sets Ω_1 and Ω_2 and the matrix A. The three assumptions given below are related to the constraint qualification of Kuhn and Tucker [6] and yield a valuable characterization of $P(\hat{x},\Omega)$.

Assumption 1 Let $\hat{x} \in \Omega$; that is, $A\hat{x} \in \Omega_1$, and $\hat{x} \in \Omega_2$. Suppose that there is a vector $\Delta x \in R^n$ such that

$$A\,\Delta x \in C(\hat{y},\Omega_1) \qquad \text{and} \qquad \Delta x \in C(\hat{x},\Omega_2)$$

where $\hat{y} = A\hat{x}$. Then we shall assume that there is a differentiable arc $x(\theta)$, $0 \leq \theta \leq 1$, such that $x(\theta) \in \Omega$ for all θ, and

8
$$x(0) = \hat{x}$$

9
$$\left.\frac{dx(\theta)}{d\theta}\right|_{\theta=0} = \Delta x$$

The proofs of Lemmas *10*, *16*, and *17* are given in the Appendix.

10 **Lemma** Under Assumption 1,

11
$$C(\hat{x},\Omega) = C(\hat{x},\Omega_1) \cap C(\hat{x},\Omega_2)$$

We now give two examples to illustrate Lemma *10*; the first satisfies Assumption 1 and hence Lemma *10*, but the second does not.

12 *Example* Let $R^n = R^2$ and $R^m = R^1$. Let A be the 1×2 matrix $(1,-1)$ and let

$$\Omega_2 = \{x = (x_1,x_2) | (x_1)^2 + (x_2)^2 \leq 1\}$$
$$\Omega_1 = \{x | x \geq 0\}$$

so that

$$\Omega_1' = \{x = (x_1,x_2) | x_1 - x_2 \geq 0\}$$

It can be easily verified that Assumption 1 is satisfied and that

$$C(\hat{x},\Omega) = C(\hat{x},\Omega_1') \cap C(\hat{x},\Omega_2)$$

See Fig. *12.2.3*.

13 *Example* Let Ω_2 be the same as above, let A be the identity matrix, and let $\Omega_1 = \Omega_1' = \{(x_1,x_2) | x_2 = 1\}$. Then $\Omega = \Omega_1' \cap \Omega_2 = \{(0,1)\}$. Let $\hat{x} = (0,1)$. Then $C(\hat{x},\Omega_2) = \{x = (x_1,x_2) | x_2 \leq 0\}$, and

$$C(\hat{x},\Omega_1') = \{x = (x_1,x_2) | x_2 = 0\}$$

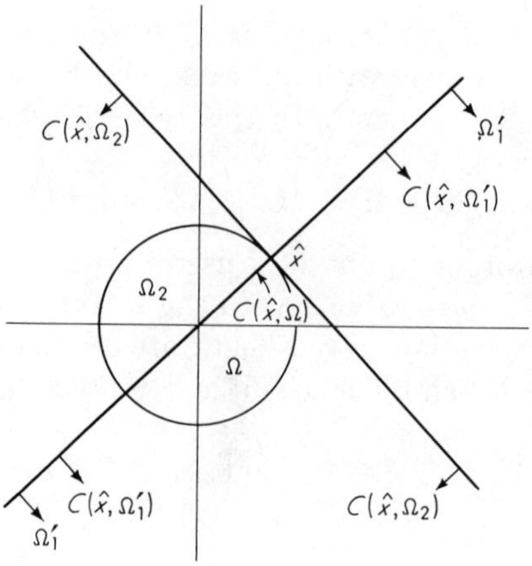

Fig. 12.2.3

so that $C(\hat{x},\Omega_2) \cap C(\hat{x},\Omega_1') = C(\hat{x},\Omega_1')$. However,

$$C(\hat{x},\Omega) = C(\hat{x},\{\hat{x}\}) = \{0\} \neq C(\hat{x},\Omega_1')$$

It can be verified that Assumption 1 is not satisfied at $\hat{x}$. See Fig. *12.2.4*.

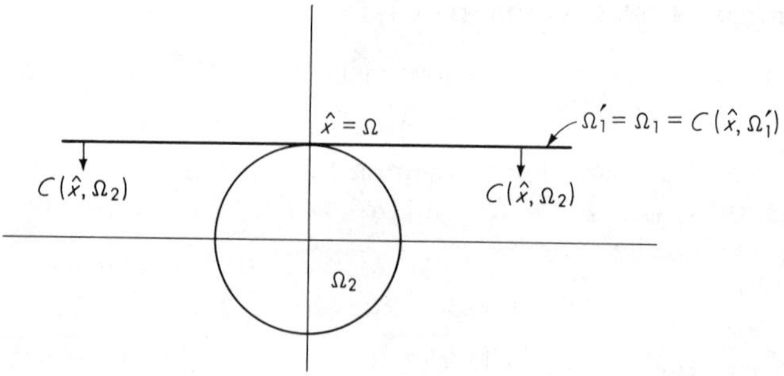

Fig. 12.2.4

Assumption 2 Let $\hat{x} \in \Omega_1'$; that is, $\hat{y} = A\hat{x} \in \Omega_1$, and suppose that there is a vector $\Delta x \in R^n$ such that

$$A\,\Delta x \in C(\hat{y},\Omega_1)$$

Then we shall assume that there is a differentiable arc $x(\theta)$, $0 \leq \theta \leq 1$, such that $x(\theta) \in \Omega_1'$ for each θ, and

14 $$x(0) = x$$

15
$$\left.\frac{dx}{d\theta}\right|_{\theta=0} = \Delta x$$

16 **Lemma** Under Assumption 2,

$$C(\hat{x},\Omega_1') = \{\Delta x | A\ \Delta x \in C(\hat{y},\Omega_1)\}$$

and

$$P(\hat{x},\Omega_1') = \overline{A^T[P(\hat{y},\Omega_1)]}$$

where

$$A^T[P(\hat{y},\Omega_1)] = \{A^T z | z \in P(\hat{y},\Omega_1)\}$$

We now give an example to illustrate Lemma *16*. Let $x \in R^n = R^2$ and $y \in R^m = R^1$. Let $\Omega_1 = \{y | y \geq 0\}$, and $A = (1,1)$ so that $\Omega_1' = \{x = (x_1,x_2) | A(x_1,x_2) \in \Omega_1\} = \{(x_1,x_2) | x_1 + x_2 \geq 0\}$. See Fig. *12.2.5*. If $\hat{x} = \hat{x}_1$, $C(\hat{x}_1,\Omega_1') = R^2$. Also $A\hat{x}_1 = \hat{y}_1 > 0$ so that

$$C(\hat{y}_1,\Omega_1) = R^1$$

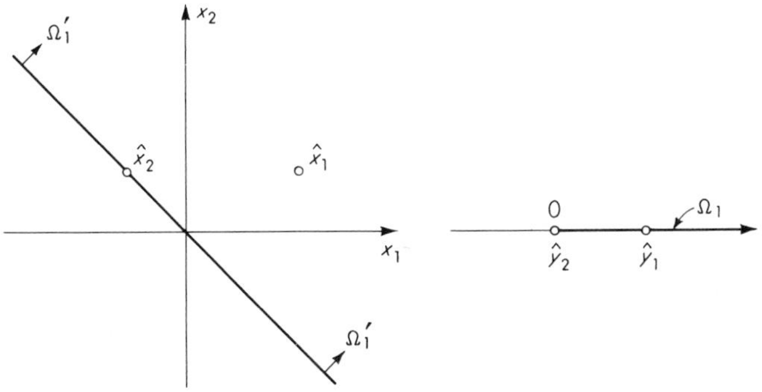

Fig. 12.2.5

It can be verified that

$$C(\hat{x}_1,\Omega_1') = \{\Delta x | A\ \Delta x \in C(\hat{y}_1,\Omega_1)\}$$

Since $C(\hat{x}_1,\Omega_1') = R^2$, $P(\hat{x}_1,\Omega_1') = (0,0)$. Also the fact that $C(\hat{y}_1,\Omega_1) = R^1$ implies $P(\hat{y}_1,\Omega_1) = \{0\}$. Hence

$$P(\hat{x}_1,\Omega_1') = A^T P(y_1,\Omega_1)$$

If $\hat{x} = \hat{x}_2$, then $C(\hat{x}_2,\Omega_1') = \Omega_1'$. Also $A\hat{x}_2 = \hat{y}_2 = 0$ so that $C(\hat{y}_2,\Omega_1) = \Omega_1$. Again Lemma *16* holds.

17 **Lemma** Under Assumptions 1 and 2,

$$P(\hat{x}, \Omega_1 \cap \Omega_2) = \overline{A^T[P(\hat{y},\Omega_1)] + P(\hat{x},\Omega_2)}\dagger$$

† If K_1 and K_2 are subsets of R^n, then $K_1 + K_2 = \{x_1 + x_2 | x_1 \in K_1, x_2 \in K_2\}$.

Assumption 3 The set $A^T[P(\hat{y},\Omega_1)] + P(\hat{x},\Omega_2)$ is closed.

It can be easily shown that if Ω_1 and Ω_2 are polyhedral convex sets, i.e., if they are formed by the intersection of a finite number of closed half spaces, then Assumption 3 is automatically satisfied.

18 **Theorem** Under Assumptions 1, 2, and 3, $\hat{x}$ is a solution of

19
$$\max_x \{f(x)|Ax \in \Omega_1, x \in \Omega_2\}$$

if and only if

$$f'(\hat{x}) \in A^T[P(\hat{y},\Omega_1)] + P(\hat{x},\Omega_2)$$

where $\hat{y} = A\hat{x}$. In other words, $\hat{x}$ is a solution of *19* if and only if there exist vectors $u_1 \in P(\hat{y},\Omega_1)$ and $u_2 \in P(\hat{x},\Omega_2)$ such that

$$f'(\hat{x}) = A^T u_1 + u_2$$

Proof By Theorem *3* $\hat{x}$ solves *19* if and only if

$$f'(\hat{x}) \in P(\hat{x},\Omega) = A^T[P(\hat{y},\Omega_1)] + P(\hat{x},\Omega_2)$$

by Lemma *17* and Assumption 3.

20 **Remark** The vector (u_1,u_2) in Theorem *18* is called a Lagrange multiplier (vector). Note that the Lagrange multiplier may not be unique. We shall return to this point later.

3 *Classes of decomposition problems and computational techniques*

In the following sections we shall consider the particular cases of *12.2.7* which yield a class of problems which can be resolved by "decomposition." We shall assume that the reader is familiar with the main results of linear programming [7]. At this point it is necessary to adopt certain notational conventions which prove extremely convenient. Since we shall need to consider submatrices $\tilde{A}$ of a matrix A, we shall assume throughout that the columns of A are labeled in such a way that A can be factored as $A = (\tilde{A}|B)$. Then any vector z has a corresponding factorization as $z = \begin{pmatrix} \tilde{z} \\ z' \end{pmatrix}$ which we write as $z = (\tilde{z},z')$ so that $Az = (\tilde{A}|B)\begin{pmatrix} \tilde{z} \\ z' \end{pmatrix} = \tilde{A}\tilde{z} + Bz'$.

4 *Case* 1

Consider the following special case of *12.2.7*:

1 $$\max_x \{\langle c,x\rangle | Ax \in \Omega\}$$

where A is an $m \times n$ matrix with $n > m$. Let $\hat{x}$ be a solution of *1*, and let $A\hat{x} = \hat{y}$. Then certainly $\hat{x}$ is a solution of *2*.

2 $$\max_x \{\langle c,x\rangle | Ax = \hat{y}\}$$

Since we have assumed that A has maximum rank (see *12.2.7*), there is a submatrix $\tilde{A}$ of A with $A = (\tilde{A}|B)$ such that $\hat{x} = (\tilde{x},0)$† where $\tilde{x} = (\tilde{A})^{-1}\hat{y}$. Also if $u = (\tilde{A}^T)^{-1}\tilde{c}$, then we must have $A^Tu = c$. By Theorem *12.1.18* $\hat{x} = (\tilde{x},0)$ is a solution of *1* if and only if

$$c \in A^T[P(\hat{y},\Omega)]$$

or

$$u \in P(\hat{y},\Omega)$$

Now consider *3*.

3 $$\max_y \{\langle u,y\rangle | y \in \Omega\}$$

Again by Theorem *12.1.18* we see that $\hat{y}$ solves *3* if and only if

$$u \in P(\hat{y},\Omega)$$

Combining these facts, we have the following theorem.

4 **Theorem** $\hat{x} = (\tilde{x},0)$ is a solution of *1* if and only if $\hat{x}$ and $\hat{y} = A\hat{x}$ are solutions of *2* and *3*, respectively.

We therefore propose the following algorithm.

Step 1 Select $\hat{y} \in \Omega$. Formulate and solve *2*. Obtain $\hat{x} = (\tilde{x},0)$ and u.
Step 2 Formulate and solve *3*, and obtain a solution $\hat{y}'$ to *3*.
Step 3 If $\langle u,\hat{y}\rangle = \langle u,\hat{y}'\rangle$, stop. If $\langle u,\hat{y}\rangle < \langle u,\hat{y}'\rangle$ go to step 1 with $\hat{y}$ replaced by $\hat{y}'$.

Remarks By an iteration we mean one pass through steps 1, 2, and 3. We shall show that only a finite number of iterations are necessary to obtain an optimal solution. Suppose that we do not stop at the $(k - 1)$th iteration. Then at the beginning of the kth iteration we have the vector $\hat{y}_k$ (obtained from step 3 of the previous iteration). At the

† Here and throughout whenever we consider optimum solutions to linear programming problems, we shall only consider basic optimal solutions.

end of step 1 of the kth iteration we obtain the vectors $\hat{x}_k = (\tilde{x}_k, 0)$, u_k, and $\tilde{c}_k$ corresponding to the submatrix $\tilde{A}_k$ of A. Let $\hat{y}_{k+1}$ be the vector obtained at the end of step 2 of the kth iteration. If

$$\langle u_k, \hat{y}_k \rangle = \langle u_k, \hat{y}_{k+1} \rangle$$

then we stop, and the algorithm ends. Hence suppose that $\langle u_k, \hat{y}_k \rangle < \langle u_k, \hat{y}_{k+1} \rangle$. On substituting for the u_k and recalling the definitions of $\hat{x}_k$ and $\tilde{c}_k$, we see that this inequality implies

$$\langle c, \hat{x}_k \rangle = \langle \tilde{c}_k, \tilde{x}_k \rangle = \langle u_k, \hat{y}_k \rangle < \langle u_k, \hat{y}_{k+1} \rangle$$

It follows that if we start the $(k + 1)$th iteration with the vector $\hat{y}_{k+1}$ and we obtain the vector $\hat{x}_{k+1}$ and the submatrix $\tilde{A}_{k+1}$, then we must have $\langle c, x_k \rangle < \langle c, x_{k+1} \rangle$; that is, we obtain an improved solution, and furthermore $\tilde{A}_{k+1}$ is a different A from $\tilde{A}_k$. Furthermore, $\tilde{A}_{k+1}$ is different from $\tilde{A}_j$ for all $j \leq k$. This is true because if $\tilde{A}_{k+1} = \tilde{A}_j$, then $\langle c, \hat{x}_{k+1} \rangle = \langle c, \hat{x}_j \rangle$, which contradicts the fact that we get improved solutions at each iteration. Since there are only finitely many submatrices of A, the algorithm must terminate after finitely many iterations.

We shall now formulate an amusing example which illustrates Theorem *4*.

Example

$$\max_{x_i} \left\{ \sum_{i=1}^{N} \langle c_i, x_i \rangle \,\middle|\, \sum_{i=1}^{N} \|A_i x_i - b_i\|^2 \leq \alpha \right\}$$

where c_i and x_i are n_i-dimensional vectors, A_i are $m_i \times n_i$ matrices with $n_i > m_i$, b_i are m_i-dimensional, and $\alpha > 0$ is a fixed number. We now apply the algorithm formulated above.

Step 1 Select vectors $\hat{y}_i$ with $\sum_{i=1}^{N} \|\hat{y}_i\|^2 \leq \alpha$, and solve

5 $$\max_{x_i} \left\{ \sum_{i=1}^{N} \langle c_i, x_i \rangle | A_i x_i = b_i + \hat{y}_i;\ i = 1, \ldots, N \right\}$$

$$\equiv \sum_{i=1}^{N} \max_{x_i} \{ \langle c_i, x_i \rangle | A_i x_i = b_i + \hat{y}_i \}$$

Thus we solve N smaller subproblems and obtain the individual $\hat{x}_i = (\tilde{x}_i, 0)$, $u_i = (\tilde{A}_i^T)^{-1} \hat{c}_i$.

Step 2 Now we have to solve

$$\max_{y_i} \left\{ \sum_{i=1}^{N} \langle u_i, b_i + y_i \rangle \,\middle|\, \sum_{i=1}^{N} \|y_i\|^2 \leq \alpha \right\}$$

However, the solutions $\hat{y}'_i$ to this problem can be written by inspection. It is easy to see that

$$\hat{y}'_i = \left(\frac{\alpha}{\sum_{i=1}^{N} \|u_i\|^2}\right)^{\frac{1}{2}} u_i \qquad i = 1, 2, \ldots, N$$

Step 3 If

$$\sum_{i=1}^{N} \langle \hat{y}_i, u_i \rangle = \sum_{i=1}^{N} \langle \hat{y}'_i, u_i \rangle = \alpha^{\frac{1}{2}} \left(\sum_{i=1}^{N} \|u_i\|^2\right)^{\frac{1}{2}}$$

we stop. If not, we substitute $\hat{y}'_i$ for $\hat{y}_i$ in *5* and continue.

5 *Case* 2

Consider the following special case of *12.2.7*.

1 $$\max_x \{\langle c,x \rangle | Ax \in \Omega, x \geq 0\}$$

where again $x \in R^n$, A is an $m \times n$ matrix with $n > m$, and Ω is a closed convex subset of R^m. Let $\hat{x}$ be a solution of *1*, and let $A\hat{x} = \hat{y}$. Certainly then $\hat{x}$ is a solution of *2*.

2 $$\max_x \{\langle c,x \rangle | Ax = \hat{y}, x \geq 0\}$$

For convenience, we shall assume that the solutions to problems of the form of *2* are nondegenerate[1] [7, p. 54]. We can suppose that $\hat{x}$ has the form $\hat{x} = (\tilde{x},0)$ with $\tilde{x} = (\tilde{A})^{-1}\hat{y} > 0$. Let $u = (\tilde{A}^T)^{-1}\tilde{c}$ be *the* Lagrange multiplier vector. Then

3 $$c = A^T u + v$$

with $v = (\tilde{v},v') \leq 0$ and $\tilde{v} = 0$. Moreover, since $\hat{x}$ is a solution of *1*, by Theorem *12.1.18* we have

4 $$c \in A^T[P(\hat{y},\Omega)] + P(\hat{x},R^{n+})$$

where R^{n+} is the nonnegative orthant of R^n. Comparing *3* and *4*, we see by the nondegeneracy assumption that

5 $$u \in P(\hat{y},\Omega)$$

Now consider *6* as follows:

6 $$\max_y \{\langle u,y \rangle | y \in \Omega, (\tilde{A})^{-1}y \geq 0\}$$

[1] By this we mean that every set of m columns of the augmented matrix $(A|\hat{y})$ is linearly independent. It then follows that the Lagrange multiplier vector associated with $\hat{x}$ is unique.

By Theorem *12.1.18* it is clear from *5* that $\hat{y}$ is a solution of *6*. Conversely, suppose that $\hat{x} = (\tilde{x},0)$ and $\hat{y} = A\hat{x}$ are solutions of *2* and *6*, respectively. Equation *3* is still valid with $v \leq 0$ and $\tilde{v} = 0$. Also, since $\hat{y}$ is a solution of *6*, we must have (by Theorem *12.1.18*) vectors $u_0 \in P(\hat{y},\Omega)$ and $v_0 \in P(\tilde{A}^{-1}\hat{y},R^{m+})$ such that

$$u = u_0 + (\tilde{A}^T)^{-1}v_0$$

By the nondegeneracy assumption, we have $x = \tilde{A}^{-1}\hat{y} > 0$ so that $v_0 = 0$. Therefore, $u = u_0$. From *3* we then obtain

$$c = A^T u + v$$

and $u = u_0 \in P(\hat{y},\Omega)$. By Theorem *12.1.18*, therefore, x is a solution of *1*. We have proved the following theorem.

7 **Theorem** Under the nondegeneracy assumption of *2*, $\hat{x}$ is a solution of *1* if and only if $\hat{x}$ and $\hat{y}$ are solutions of *2* and *6*, respectively.

Remarks

1. The algorithm suggested in the previous section is applicable to Theorem *7* if we replace *12.4.2* and *12.4.3* by *2* and *6*, respectively.

2. If we admit degenerate solutions, the "only if" part of Theorem *7* is still valid, but the "if" part is not. The reason is that in solving *2*, if we obtain a degenerate solution $x = (\tilde{x},0)$ (that is, some components of $\tilde{x}$ vanish), then we can have more than one Lagrange multiplier vector u which gives rise to more than one problem *6*. We therefore have to consider alternate multiplier vectors.

Example We modify the example of Theorem *12.4.4* as follows:

$$\max_{x_i} \left\{ \langle c_i,x_i \rangle \,\middle|\, \sum_{i=1}^{N} \|A_i x_i - b_i\|^2 \leq \alpha;\, x_i \geq 0;\, i = 1,2, \ldots ,N \right\}$$

where all vectors and matrices are defined as before.

Step 1 As before, we select vectors $\hat{y}_i$ with $\sum_{i=1}^{N} \|\hat{y}_i\|^2 \leq \alpha$, and we solve the N subproblems

8 $$\max_{x_i} \{ \langle c_i,x_i \rangle | A_i x_i = b_i + \hat{y}_i;\, x_i \geq 0 \} \qquad i = 1, \ldots , N$$

We obtain the solutions $\hat{x}_i = (\tilde{x}_i,0)$, the corresponding Lagrange multiplier u_i, and the basis matrices $\tilde{A}_i$.

Step 2 We formulate

9 $$\max_{y_i} \left\{ \sum_{i=1}^{N} \langle u_i,y_i \rangle \,\middle|\, \sum_{i=1}^{N} \|y_i\|^2 \leq \alpha;\, \tilde{A}_i^{-1}y_i \geq 0;\, i = 1, \ldots ,N \right\}$$

This problem can also be decomposed. Let z_i be a solution of

$$\max_{y_i} \{\langle u_i,y_i\rangle \,|\, \|y_i\|^2 \leq 1,\ \tilde{A}_i^{-1}y_i \geq 0\}$$

and suppose that $p_i = \langle u_i,z_i\rangle > 0$ for $i = 1, \ldots, k$ and $p_i = \langle u_i,z_i\rangle = 0$ for $i = k + 1, \ldots, N$. Then the solutions $\hat{y}'_i$ of *9* are given by

$$\hat{y}'_i = \left(\frac{\alpha}{\sum_{i=1}^{N} p_i^2}\right)^{\frac{1}{2}} p_i z_i \qquad i = 1, \ldots, N$$

We check to see whether

$$\sum_{i=1}^{N} \langle \hat{y}'_i,u_i\rangle = \sum_{i=1}^{N} \langle \hat{y}_i,u_i\rangle$$

If so, we stop. Otherwise, we substitute $\hat{y}'_i$ for $\hat{y}_i$ in *8* and continue the iteration.

Figure *12.5.1* is a block diagram of the various steps of our proposed solution.

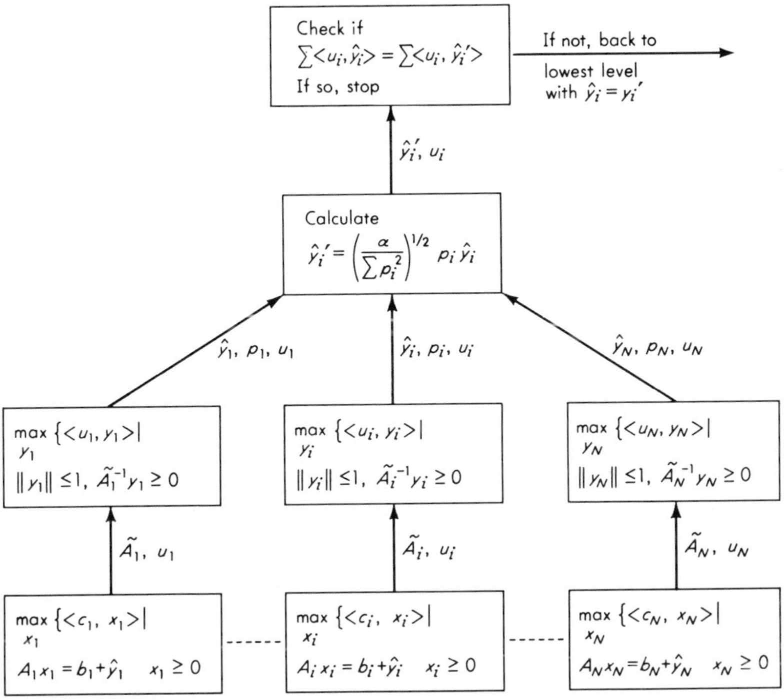

Fig. 12.5.1

6 *Case 3*

This time we consider a problem which is similar to Rosen's convex partition programming problem [2]. Thus,

1 $$\max_{x,y} \{\langle c,x\rangle | A^T x \geq y \text{ for some } y \in \Omega'\}$$

where A is an $m \times n$ matrix with $n > m$, and $\Omega' \subset R^n$ is a set such that the set

$$\Omega = \{w + y | w \geq 0,\ y \in \Omega'\}$$

is closed and convex. Thus, *1* can be reformulated as

2 $$\max_{x} \{\langle c,x\rangle | A^T x \in \Omega\}$$

so that by Theorem *12.1.18* $\hat{x}$ is a solution of *2* if and only if there is a vector u such that

3 $$c = Au, \qquad u \in P(A^T\hat{x},\Omega)$$

Suppose $\hat{x}$ is a solution of *1*, and let $y_0 \in \Omega'$ such that $A^T\hat{x} \geq y_0$. Certainly then $\hat{x}$ is a solution of *4*.

4 $$\max_{x} \{\langle c,x\rangle | A^T x \geq y_0\}$$

We can then assume that $\hat{x} = (\tilde{A}^T)^{-1}\tilde{y}_0$, where $A = [\tilde{A}|B]$, $y_0 = (\tilde{y}_0,y_0')$, and the vector $u = (\tilde{u},0) \leq 0$, where

5 $$\tilde{u} = (\tilde{A})^{-1}c$$

Let us define $Q = (\tilde{A})^{-1}B$ and $y = (\tilde{y},y')$ and consider *6*.

6 $$\max_{y} \{\langle u,y\rangle | Q^T\tilde{y} \geq y',\ y \in \Omega\}$$

7 **Lemma** If $\hat{x}$ is a solution of *1*, then $\hat{x}$ and y_0 are solutions of *4* and *6*, respectively.

Proof We only need to prove the second assertion. Let y be any vector satisfying the constraints of *6*, and let $x = (\tilde{A}^T)^{-1}\tilde{y}$. Then $A^Tx = (\tilde{y},Q^T\tilde{y}) \geq (\tilde{y},y') = y$, and $y \in \Omega$. Hence, x is a feasible solution of *2*. Therefore, we must have

$$\langle c,x\rangle \leq \langle c,\hat{x}\rangle$$

or

$$\langle \tilde{A}\tilde{u},x\rangle \leq \langle \tilde{A}\tilde{u},\hat{x}\rangle$$

by *5* or

$$\langle \tilde{u},\tilde{A}^Tx\rangle \leq \langle \tilde{u},\tilde{A}^T\hat{x}\rangle$$

or

$$\langle \tilde{u},\tilde{y} \rangle \leq \langle \tilde{u},\tilde{y}_0 \rangle$$

since $\tilde{u} \leq 0$ and $\tilde{A}^T\hat{x} \geq \tilde{y}_0$. However, $\langle u,y \rangle = \langle \tilde{u},\tilde{y} \rangle$, which proves the lemma.

We shall now prove the converse result. Suppose that $\hat{x}$ and $y_0 = (\tilde{y}_0,y_0')$ are solutions of *4* and *6*, respectively. By Theorem *12.1.18* the second postulate holds only if there are vectors v and u_1 such that

8 $$v \leq 0 \qquad \langle v, Q^T\tilde{y}_0 - y_0' \rangle = 0$$

9 $$u_1 \in P(y_0,\Omega)$$

and

10 $$u = (Qv,-v) + u_1$$

From *10* and *5*, we have

$$c = Au = \tilde{A}Qv - Bv + Au_1 = Au_1$$

Hence, in order to prove *3* we must show that $u_1 \in P(A^T\hat{x},\Omega)$. By *9* we have $u_1 \in P(y_0,\Omega)$, so it suffices to show that $\langle u_1,A^T\hat{x} \rangle = \langle u_1,y_0 \rangle$. However,

$$\langle u_1,y_0 \rangle = \langle \tilde{u}_1,\tilde{y}_0 \rangle + \langle u_1',y_0' \rangle$$

$$= \langle \tilde{u} - Qv, \tilde{y}_0 \rangle - \langle -v,y_0' \rangle$$

by *10*

$$= \langle \tilde{u},\tilde{y}_0 \rangle - \langle v, Q^T\tilde{y}_0' - y_0' \rangle$$

$$= \langle \tilde{u},\tilde{y}_0 \rangle$$

by *8*

$$= \langle \tilde{u},\tilde{A}^T\hat{x} \rangle = \langle Au,\hat{x} \rangle = \langle Au_1,\hat{x} \rangle$$

We therefore have the following theorem.

11 **Theorem** $(\hat{x},y_0)$ is a solution of *1* if and only if $\hat{x}$ and y_0 are solutions of *4* and *6*, respectively.

Remark It should be clear that the algorithms of the preceding sections may be modified for problem *7*.

7 *Case* 4

This time we shall briefly consider the Dantzig-Wolfe decomposition principle for linear programs [1]. Consider the following linear programming problem:

1 $$\max_x \{\langle c,x\rangle | Ax = b,\ Bx = d,\ x \geq 0\}$$

where A is an $m \times n$ matrix, B is an $l \times n$ matrix, and $n > (m + l)$. Let Ω be the set defined by

2 $$\Omega = \{x | Bx = d,\ x \geq 0\}$$

As we know from the theory of linear inequalities, Ω can be expressed as a sum of a convex polyhedral cone K and a convex polyhedral set S; thus

3 $$\Omega = \left\{\sum_{i=1}^{r} \mu_i k_i + \sum_{j=1}^{p} \lambda_j s_j \,\middle|\, \sum_{j=1}^{p} \lambda_j = 1,\ \lambda_j \geq 0,\ \mu_i \geq 0\right\}$$

Here the n-vectors k_i and s_j are the generators for the sets K and S; the vectors s_j are just the basic solutions of the set Ω, whereas k_i are vectors along rays emanating from some s_j and can be constructed as in the simplex algorithm. With this characterization of Ω *1* can be transformed into the following form:

4 $$\max_{\mu_i \lambda_j} \left\{\sum_{i=1}^{r} \alpha_i \mu_i + \sum_{j=1}^{p} \beta_j \lambda_j = 1, \,\middle|\, \sum_{i=1}^{p} \lambda_j = 1,\ \sum_{i=1}^{r} h_i \mu_i + \sum_{j=1}^{p} g_j \lambda_j = b,\ \lambda_j \geq 0,\ \mu_i \geq 0\right\}$$

where $\alpha_i = \langle c,k_i\rangle$, $\beta_j = \langle c,s_j\rangle$, $h_i = Ak_i$, and $g_j = As_j$.

Thus, if we have a characterization of Ω in the form of *3*, we can solve *4* to obtain an optimal solution of *1*. It is important to note that in *4* we have only $m + 1$ equality constraints, whereas in *1* we have $m + l$ equality constraints. More important, however, is the fact that if we use the simplex algorithm to solve *4* we do not need to precompute all the s_j and k_i beforehand but can generate them sequentially as new vectors enter the basis. Thus in practice one can follow the procedure roughly outlined as follows. We first compute an initial basis for *4* from *2*. Next we return to *4* and obtain the pricing variables. With these we go back to *2* and obtain a replacement for one of the basis vectors. We return to *4* and repeat the cycle.

This technique of decomposition will be very advantageous in the case in which the matrix B in *1* has a block-diagonal structure because then the basis vectors for *4* can be generated easily, whereas if the simplex algorithm is applied directly to *1*, then the structure of B cannot be used to advantage.

8 *Case 5*

The solution of the next class of problems is based upon the notion of what has been sometimes called the "penalty function." The main idea is the following. We can show fairly easily that in many cases we can neglect some of the constraint equations if we change the objective function appropriately. This change is called the *penalty function*. In general, the existence of a penalty function is easy to prove. The difficulty arises, of course, in finding it. In the case that we discuss below, we are able to suggest a method that enables us to determine the penalty function. We first guess at the penalty function and add it to the original objective function. Neglecting certain constraints, we solve the new simpler problem and check to see whether the solution satisfies the neglected constraints. If not, we calculate the error and appropriately modify our guess of the penalty function and repeat the process.

The problem dealt with here is a generalization of one due to Lasdon [3]. For an application of a similar idea to an optimal control problem see Pearson [8]. For the use of penalty functions to convert a constrained maximization problem to one without constraints see Fiacco and McCormick [9]. Arrow, Hurwicz, and Uzawa [10] have proposed a method similar to ours. See also Abadie [4].

Consider the following special case of Theorem *12.1.18*:

1 $$\max_x \{f(x) | Ax = b, x \in \Omega\}$$

where A is an $m \times n$ matrix with $n > m$, and Ω is a convex, compact subset of R^n. By Theorem *12.1.18* $\hat{x}$ is a solution of *1* if and only if there is a vector $\hat{u} \in R^m$ such that

2 $$f'(\hat{x}) + A^T\hat{u} \in P(\hat{x},\Omega)$$

Now consider *3* for a fixed vector u; thus

3 $$\max_x \{f(x) + \langle A^T u, x\rangle | x \in \Omega\}$$

Again $\hat{x}'$ is a solution of *3* if and only if

4 $$f'(\hat{x}') + A^T u \in P(\hat{x}',\Omega)$$

Comparing *2* and *4*, we see that if in *3* we have $u = \hat{u}$, then certainly $\hat{x}$ is also a solution of *3*. Conversely, if a solution $\hat{x}'$ to *3* also satisfies the constraint equation $Ax = b$, then $\hat{x}'$ is also a solution of *1*. We therefore have the following "existence" theorem.

5 **Theorem** (1) If x is a solution of *1* then it is a solution of *3* for $u = \hat{u}$; (2) There is a u and a solution of *3* for that u, which is also a solution of *1*. Moreover, this is the case if and only if this solution satisfies $Ax = b$.

However, this fact is not very useful because for every u we need to examine all the solutions of *3*. However, if for each u there is a unique solution to *3*, we can use Theorem *5* to obtain a computational method which solves *1* via a sequence of problems of the form of *3*.

Therefore, henceforth we assume that f is a *strictly* concave function to insure uniqueness of the solution of *3*. Let $p = A^T u$. Then *3* is equivalent to

6
$$\max_x \{f(x) + \langle p,x \rangle | x \in \Omega\}$$

We select an arbitrary penalty vector p. Let $x(p)$ be *the* solution of *6*. We next verify whether $x(p)$ satisfies the neglected constraints. Let $e(p) = Ax(p) - b$, and let $v(p) = \frac{1}{2}\|e(p)\|^2$. Then by Theorem *5*, $x(p)$ is a solution of *1* if and only if $v(p) = 0$. Suppose $v(p) > 0$. Since we want to reduce $v(p)$, we want $x(p)$ to move along the direction $(-\partial/\partial x)v(p)$. From *6*, therefore, we see intuitively that p should be changed to $p + \Delta p$, where

$$\begin{aligned}\Delta p &= -\frac{\partial}{\partial x} v(p)\, \Delta t \\ &= -\frac{\partial}{\partial x}\left[\frac{1}{2}\|Ax(p) - b\|^2\right] \Delta t \\ &= -A^T(Ax(p) - b)\, \Delta t \\ &= -A^T e(p)\, \Delta t\end{aligned}$$

where Δt is some positive number. If we convert this discrete adjustment of p to a continuous version, we obtain the rule

7
$$\frac{dp(t)}{dt} = -A^T e(p)$$

We can now prove the following theorem.

8 **Theorem** For any initial condition $p(0)$ which lies in the range of A^T, the solution $p(t)$ to *7* converges to a fixed vector $\hat{p}$, and the corresponding solution $x(t)$ of *3* with $p(t) = A^T u$ converges to a vector $\hat{x}$ which is a solution of *1*.

The proof of Theorem *8*, although intuitively clear, involves a lot of technicalities and is therefore omitted. The interested reader is referred to Varaiya [11] for a proof.

We now show how the procedure described above can lead to a decomposition of a class of large-scale systems. Suppose that *1* is of the form

9 $$\max_{x_i} \left\{ \sum_{i=1}^{N} f_i(x_i) | x_i \in \Omega_i, \ \sum_{i=1}^{N} A_i x_i = b; i = 1, \ldots, N \right\}$$

Then *3* becomes

$$\max_{x_i} \left\{ \sum_{i=1}^{N} f_i(x_i) + \sum_{i=1}^{N} \langle A_i^T u_i, x_i \rangle | x_i \in \Omega; i = 1, \ldots, N \right\}$$

which is equivalent to *10*;

10 $$\sum_{i=1}^{N} \max_{x_i} \{ f_i(x_i) + \langle p_i, x_i \rangle | x_i \in \Omega \}$$

where $p_i = A_i^T u_i$. The adjustment rule for the penalty function is

$$\frac{dp_i}{dt} = -A_i^T \left(\sum_{i=1}^{N} A_i x_i - b \right)$$

9 *Conclusion*

We have shown how a simple reformulation of the usual problem in convex programming enables us to obtain a class of results which are useful for solving large problems. It is also clear that the results are helpful mainly for problems which have a "natural" formulation as convex programming problems, that is, as a single-stage decision problem. A great amount of work needs to be done for large multistage decision problems and, as far as is known to the author, there are no results which take advantage of the dynamics of the problem.

APPENDIX

Proof of Lemmas 12.2.10, 12.2.16, and 12.2.17 Before we begin with the proof, it will be helpful to obtain an alternate characterization of $C(\hat{x}, \Omega)$.

1 *Fact* $\Delta x \in C(\hat{x}, \Omega)$ if and only if there is a sequence $\{\Delta x_n\}_{n=1}^{\infty}$ of vectors Δx_n in $\{\Omega - \hat{x}\}$ and a sequence of positive numbers $\{\lambda_n\}_{n=1}^{\infty}$ such that

2 $$\Delta x_n \to 0 \qquad \text{as } n \to \infty$$

and

3 $$\lambda_n(\Delta x_n) \to \Delta x \qquad \text{as } n \to \infty$$

Proof Suppose there is such a pair of sequences. Since $\Delta x_n \in \Omega - x$, $\Delta x_n \in C(\hat{x},\Omega)$. Also since $C(\hat{x},\Omega)$ is a cone, $\lambda_n(\Delta x_n) \in C(\hat{x},\Omega)$. Since $C(\hat{x},\Omega)$ is closed,

$$\Delta x = \lim_n \lambda_n(\Delta x_n) \in C(\hat{x},\Omega)$$

Conversely let $\Delta x \in C(\hat{x},\Omega)$. Now let $C = \{\alpha(x - \hat{x})|\alpha \geq 0,\ x \in \Omega\}$. Then certainly $C(\hat{x},\Omega)$ is the closure of C, so that

$$\Delta x = \lim_n z_n$$

where $z_n = \alpha_n(x_n - \hat{x})$ with $\alpha_n \geq 0$ and $x_n \in \Omega$. Since Ω is convex, $\lambda(x_n - \hat{x}) + (1 - \lambda)\hat{x}$ belongs to Ω for $0 \leq \lambda \leq 1$, so that we can suppose (by changing α_n appropriately) that

$$\|x_n - \hat{x}\| \leq \frac{1}{n} \qquad \text{for all } n$$

Letting $\lambda_n = \alpha_n$ and $\Delta x_n = x_n - \hat{x}$,the result follows. We now prove the Lemmas.

4 *Proof of Lemma 12.2.10* Since $\Omega = \Omega_1' \cap \Omega_2$ and $\hat{x} \in \Omega$, we must have $\Omega - \hat{x} \subset \Omega_1' - \hat{x}$ and $\Omega - \hat{x} \subset \Omega_2 - \hat{x}$. It follows that

5 $$C(\hat{x},\Omega) \subset C(\hat{x},\Omega_1') \cap C(\hat{x},\Omega_2)$$

Using the Assumption 1, we prove the reverse inclusion relation. Let $\Delta x \in C(\hat{x},\Omega_1') \cap C(\hat{x},\Omega_1')$. We first show that $A\ \Delta x \in C(\hat{y},\Omega_1)$. By *1*

$$\Delta x = \lim_n \lambda_n\ \Delta x_n$$

where $\lambda_n \geq 0$ and $\Delta x_n \in \Omega_1' - \hat{x}$. Therefore,

$$\begin{aligned} A\ \Delta x &= \lim_n A(\lambda_n\ \Delta x_n) \\ &= \lim_n \lambda_n(A\ \Delta x_n) \end{aligned}$$

Since $\Delta x_n \in \Omega_1' - \hat{x}$ we have $A\ \Delta x_n \in \Omega_1 - \hat{y}$, so that again from *1* we have

$$A\ \Delta x \in C(\hat{y},\Omega_1)$$

We also know that $\Delta x \in C(\hat{x},\Omega_2)$. By Assumption 1 then,

$$\Delta x = \left.\frac{dx(\theta)}{d\theta}\right|_{\theta=0}$$

where the arc $x(\theta)$ satisfies the conditions of Assumption 1 and specifically *12.2.8* and *12.2.9*. Let $\Delta x_n = x(1/n) - \hat{x}$. Then clearly $\Delta x_n \to 0$ and $n(\Delta x_n) \to \Delta x$, so that

$$\Delta x \in C(\hat{x},\Omega)$$

6 *Proof of Lemma 12.2.16* Let $Q = \{\Delta x|A\ \Delta x \in C(\hat{y},\Omega_1)\}$. We saw in the proof of Lemma *12.2.10* that if $\Delta x \in C(\hat{x},\Omega_1')$, then $A\ \Delta x \in C(\hat{y},\Omega_1)$; that is,

$$C(\hat{x},\Omega_1') \subset Q$$

To prove the converse assertion, we need Assumption 2, and the proof is parallel to that of Lemma *12.2.10*. We therefore omit it. We prove the second assertion of Lemma *12.2.16*, assuming that $C(\hat{x},\Omega_1') = Q$ has been shown. Let $z \in P(\hat{y},\Omega_1)$; that is,

$$\langle z,\Delta y\rangle \leq 0 \qquad \text{for all } \Delta y \in C(\hat{y},\Omega)$$

Let $\Delta x \in C(\hat{x},\Omega_1')$. Then $A\,\Delta x \in C(\hat{y},\Omega)$ so that

$$\langle z,A\,\Delta x\rangle \leq 0 \qquad \text{for all } \Delta x \text{ and } C(\hat{x},\Omega_1')$$

or

$$\langle A^T z,\Delta x\rangle \leq 0 \qquad \text{for all } \Delta x \text{ and } C(\hat{x},\Omega_1')$$

Hence, $A^T z \in P(\hat{x},\Omega_1')$. Since $P(\hat{x},\Omega_1')$ is closed, we have

$$P(\hat{x},\Omega_1') \supset \overline{A^T[P(\hat{y},\Omega_1)]}$$

Conversely, suppose $\hat{z} \in P(\hat{x},\Omega_1')$, and $\hat{z} \notin \overline{A^T[P(\hat{y},\Omega_1)]}$. Then by the separation theorem of convex sets, there is a $\Delta x \neq 0$ and real numbers $\alpha > 0$ and $\epsilon > 0$ such that

7 $$\langle \hat{z},\Delta x\rangle = \alpha > \alpha - \epsilon \geq \langle z,\Delta x\rangle$$

for all $z \in \overline{A^T[P(\hat{y},\Omega_1)]}$. Since $P(\hat{y},\Omega_1)$ is a cone, we must have

$$0 \geq \langle z,\Delta x\rangle \qquad z \in \overline{A^T[P(\hat{y},\Omega)]}$$

Hence,

$$0 \geq \langle A^T w,\Delta x\rangle \qquad w \in P(\hat{y},\Omega)$$

that is,

$$0 \geq \langle w,A\,\Delta x\rangle \qquad w \in P(\hat{y},\Omega_1)$$

However, then $A\,\Delta x \in C(\hat{y},\Omega_1)$ [11], so that $\Delta x \in C(\hat{x},\Omega_1')$ by the first assertion of this lemma. However, then

$$\langle \hat{z},\Delta x\rangle \leq 0 \qquad \text{since } \hat{z} \in P(\hat{x},\Omega_1')$$

which contradicts *7*.

8 *Proof of Lemma 12.2.17* We first show that if

$$C(\hat{x},\Omega) = C(\hat{x},\Omega_1') \cap C(\hat{x},\Omega_2)$$

then

9 $$P(\hat{x},\Omega) = \overline{P(\hat{x},\Omega_1') + P(\hat{x},\Omega_2)}$$

Since $\Omega - \hat{x}$ is contained in $\Omega_1' - \hat{x}$, we must have

$$P(\hat{x},\Omega) \supset P(\hat{x},\Omega_1')$$

Similarly, $P(\hat{x},\Omega) \supset P(\hat{x},\Omega_2)$.

Since $P(\hat{x},\Omega)$ is a closed convex cone, we get

$$P(\hat{x},\Omega) \supset \overline{P(\hat{x},\Omega_1') + P(\hat{x},\Omega_2)}$$

To prove the converse, let $\hat{z} \in P(\hat{x},\Omega)$, and suppose that $\hat{z}$ does not belong to the right-hand side of *9*. Then again there is a $\Delta x \neq 0$ and numbers $\alpha > 0$ and $\epsilon > 0$ such that

10 $$\langle \hat{z},\Delta x\rangle = \alpha > \alpha - \epsilon \geq \langle z_1 + z_2,\ \Delta x\rangle$$

for all $z_1 \in P(\hat{x},\Omega_1')$ and for all $z_2 \in P(\hat{x},\Omega_2)$. Then

$$0 \geq \langle z_1,\Delta x\rangle \qquad z_1 \in P(\hat{x},\Omega_1)$$

and

$$0 \geq \langle z_2,\Delta x\rangle \qquad z_2 \in P(\hat{x},\Omega_2)$$

However, then again these imply, respectively,

$$\Delta x \in C(\hat{x},\Omega_1')$$

and

$$\Delta x \in C(\hat{x},\Omega_2)$$

so that

$$\Delta x \in C(\hat{x},\Omega_1') \cap C(\hat{x},\Omega_2) = C(\hat{x},\Omega)$$

by hypothesis. However, $\hat{z} \in P(\hat{x},\Omega)$, so that

$$\langle \hat{z},\Delta x\rangle \leq 0$$

which contradicts *10*.

Lemma *12.2.17* now follows from *9* and Lemmas *12.2.10*, and *12.2.16*.

REFERENCES

1 Dantzig, G. B., and P. Wolfe: Decomposition Principle for Linear Programs, *Operations Research*, vol. 8, pp. 101–111, 1960. Also see The Decomposition Algorithm for Linear Programs, *Econometrics*, vol. 29, pp. 767–778.

2 Rosen, J. B.: Convex Partition Programming, in P. Wolfe and R. L. Graves (eds.), "Recent Advance in Mathematical Programming," pp. 159–176, McGraw-Hill, New York, 1963.

3 Lasdon, L. S.: A Multi-level Technique for Optimization, *Systems Res. Center, Case Inst. Technology, Cleveland, Ohio*, SRC 50-C-64-19, April, 1964.

4 Abadie, J.: Electricite de France, Direction des Etudes et Recherches, Service des Etudes de Reseaux et Calcul Automatique HR 6.290, HR 6.310, HR 6.341, HR 6.346/0.

5 Varaiya, P. P.: Decomposition of Large-scale Systems, *First Intern. Conf. on Programming and Control, Colorado Springs*, 1965; also *SIAM J. Control*, vol. 4, no. 1, pp. 173–178.

6 Dantzig, G. B.: "Linear Programming and Extensions," chap. 22, Princeton, Princeton, N.J., 1963.

7 Hadley, G.: "Linear Programming," Addison-Wesley, Reading, Mass., 1962.

8 Pearson, J. D.: Duality in Control Programming, *First Intern. Conf. on Programming and Control, Colorado Springs*, 1965, also *SIAM J. Control*, vol. 4, no. 1.

9 Fiacco, A. V., and C. D. McCormick: The Sequential Unconstrained Minimization Technique for Nonlinear Programming, A Primal-Dual Method, *Management Science*, vol. 10, no. 2, January, 1964.

10 Arrow, K., L. Hurwicz, and H. Uzawa: "Studies in Linear and Nonlinear Programming," Stanford University Press, Stanford, Calif., 1958.

11 Varaiya, P. P.: A Decomposition Technique for Nonlinear Programming, *IBM Res. Rept. RJ-345*, July 1, 1965.

13

Conditions for optimality

P. L. Falb[1]
Center for Dynamical Systems
Division of Applied Mathematics
Brown University

and

E. Polak[1]
Department of Electrical Engineering and Computer Sciences
University of California, Berkeley

1 *Introduction*

Control problems can be viewed as special cases of the general problem of determining minimal elements of a partially ordered set. Adopting this point of view, Neustadt [14, 15], Halkin [8], Canon, Cullum, and Polak [3], and Da Cunha and Polak [4] have developed very beautiful and very general necessary conditions for optimality which encompass such familiar and diverse results as the Pontryagin maximum principle of optimal control theory and the Kuhn-Tucker conditions of mathematical programming. Here we shall attempt, without undue emphasis on generality, to indicate the basic ideas behind their approach and to show how the Pontryagin maximum principle can be derived using these ideas. In the interest of completeness we shall also discuss some recent results of Boltyanskii [2] relating to the sufficiency of the maximum principle.

[1] This research was supported in part by the Air Force Office of Scientific Research, Office of Aerospace Research, United States Air Force, under AFOSR Grant No. 693-66, in part by the National Science Foundation, under Grant No. GK-967, and in part by the National Aeronautics and Space Administration under Grant NsG 354, Supp. 3.

We begin, in the next section, with a discussion of the notion of linearization as this is the key idea behind the development of the necessary conditions. We then examine a reasonably general optimization problem and derive a basic necessary condition lemma for this problem in Sec. *3*. In Sec. *4* we interpret the lemma in an optimal control context to obtain both discrete and continuous versions of the maximum principle. We next consider the Boltyanskii approach to the sufficiency of the maximum principle (Sec. *5*). Finally, we make some concluding remarks in Sec. *6*. Throughout, we rely heavily on the material in Refs. 2, 3, 4, 8, 14, and 15.

2 *Linearization*

Let us begin by examining the simple problem of determining necessary conditions for a local minimum of a continuous real-valued function $f(x,y)$ on the disc $\Omega = \{(x,y)\colon x^2 + y^2 \leqq 1\}$. Suppose that $(\hat{x},\hat{y})$ is such a local minimum (see Fig. *13.2.1*). Then we know that for (x,y)

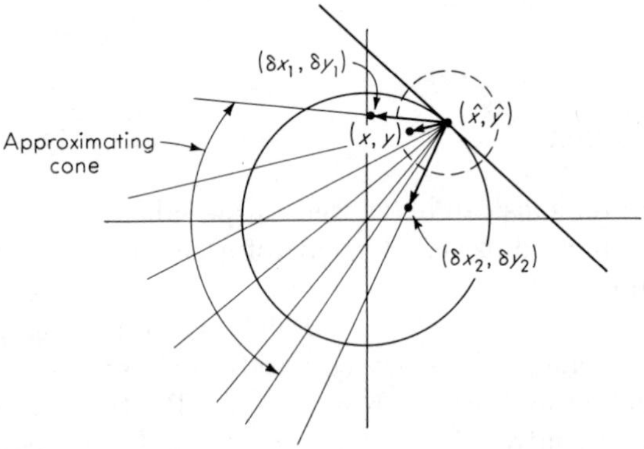

Fig. 13.2.1

in Ω and "near" $(\hat{x},\hat{y})$, $f(x,y) \geqq f(\hat{x},\hat{y})$. In other words, if we perturb $(\hat{x},\hat{y})$ along a direction pointing into Ω, then f will increase, provided that we do not go too far. We may represent the directions pointing into Ω by a cone with vertex $(\hat{x},\hat{y})$; this cone can be viewed as a way of approximating Ω at $(\hat{x},\hat{y})$. More explicitly, if we take directions $(\delta x_1,\delta y_1)$ and $(\delta x_2,\delta y_2)$ and consider the cone with vertex $(\hat{x},\hat{y})$ generated by them (see Fig. *13.2.1*), then we can reasonably call this cone an approximation to Ω at $(\hat{x},\hat{y})$ if for some small $\epsilon > 0$, the intersection of this cone with the (open) disc of radius ϵ about $(\hat{x},\hat{y})$ is contained in Ω.

Such an approximating cone gives us a way of choosing perturbations of $(\hat{x},\hat{y})$ for the purpose of obtaining necessary conditions. Now, knowing how to change $(\hat{x},\hat{y})$, we should like to analyze the effect of such a change on f. In other words, we want to find a way of expressing $f(\hat{x} + \epsilon\delta x,\ \hat{y} + \epsilon\delta y)$ in terms of $f(\hat{x},\hat{y})$ and $(\epsilon\delta x,\epsilon\delta y)$. If f has a continuous derivative (gradient) near $(\hat{x},\hat{y})$, then

$$f(\hat{x} + \epsilon\delta x,\ \hat{y} + \epsilon\delta y) = f(\hat{x},\hat{y}) + \epsilon \frac{\partial f}{\partial x}(\hat{x},\hat{y})\,\delta x + \epsilon \frac{\partial f}{\partial y}(\hat{x},\hat{y})\,\delta y + o(\epsilon)$$

and so the derivative of f can be viewed as an approximation to the change in f due to a change in $(\hat{x},\hat{y})$. Of course, this is a rather simple situation, and so, having bolstered our intuition, let us turn our attention to generalizing these ideas.

Suppose that X and Y are locally convex real topological vector spaces and that φ is a continuous map of X into Y. We then have the following definitions.

1 **Definition** The map φ is $o(x)$ if there is a family Q of seminorms defining the topology on Y,† such that given $\epsilon > 0$ and $q \in Q$, there is a continuous seminorm p and a $\delta > 0$ (δ may depend on ϵ, q, and p) for which $p(x) < \delta$ implies $q(\varphi(x)) < \epsilon p(x)$.

2 **Definition** Let Ω be a subset of X. A convex cone $C(\hat{x},\Omega) \subset X$ is a linearization of Ω at $\hat{x}$ if, given any finite collection $\{\delta x_1, \ldots, \delta x_k\}$ of linearly independent elements of $C(\hat{x},\Omega)$, there is an $\epsilon > 0$ and a continuous map ψ of co $\{\epsilon\delta x_1, \ldots, \epsilon\delta x_k\}$‡ into $\Omega - \{\hat{x}\}$ (where ψ may depend on ϵ and $\{\delta x_1, \ldots, \delta x_k\}$) such that $\psi(\delta x) = \delta x + o(\delta x)$ for all δx in co $\{\epsilon\delta x_1, \ldots, \epsilon\delta x_k\}$.

In the simple case of functions of several variables, we could take ψ to be the identity; however, as we shall see in Sec. *4*, the optimal control problem requires the more general definition of linearization given in definition *2*.

Now let f be a mapping of X into Y. We then have another definition.

3 **Definition** The mapping f is differentiable at $\hat{x}$ if there is a continuous linear transformation $f'(\hat{x})$ of X into Y such that

4 $$f(\hat{x} + \delta x) = f(\hat{x}) + f'(\hat{x})\delta x + o(\delta x)$$

for δx in X.§

In case $Y = R$(the reals), then $f'(x)$ is an element of the dual space X^* of X; that is, $f'(x)$ is a continuous linear functional on X.

† [11, 7].

‡ co $\{\cdot\}$ denotes the "convex hull of $\{\cdot\}$."

§ $f'(x)$ is often called the *Frechét derivative of f*.

Now in our later development we shall deal with the problem of minimizing a real-valued function f on a subset Ω of X subject to a finite-dimensional side constraint $g(x) = 0$. For such a problem, we incorporate both the notion of a linearization of Ω and the notion of a derivative into the single idea of an approximation [4]. More precisely, we have the following definition.

5 **Definition** Let f map X into R and let g map X into R_m. A convex cone $A(\hat{x},\Omega) \subset X$ is an approximation of Ω at $\hat{x}$ relative to f and g if there are (1) a continuous linear functional $f'(\hat{x})$ on X and (2) a continuous linear transformation $g'(x)$ from X into R_m such that, given any finite set $\{\delta x_1, \ldots, \delta x_k\}$ of linearly independent elements of $A(\hat{x},\Omega)$, there are (*a*) an $\epsilon_1 > 0$, (*b*) a continuous map ψ of

$$\text{co } \{\epsilon_1 \delta x_1, \ldots, \epsilon_1 \delta x_k\}$$

into $\Omega - \{\hat{x}\}$ (where ψ may depend on ϵ_1 and $\{\delta x_1, \ldots, \delta x_k\}$), and (*c*) continuous maps o_f and o_g of X into R and R_m, respectively, such that the following conditions are satisfied:

6 $$\lim_{\epsilon \to 0} \frac{|o_f(\epsilon \delta x)|}{\epsilon} = 0 \qquad \lim_{\epsilon \to 0} \frac{\|o_g(\epsilon \delta x)\|}{\epsilon} = 0$$

uniformly for δx in co $\{\delta x_1, \ldots, \delta x_k\}$;

7 $$\begin{aligned} f(\hat{x} + \psi(\epsilon \delta x)) &= f(\hat{x}) + \epsilon f'(\hat{x})\delta x + o_f(\epsilon \delta x) \\ g(\hat{x} + \psi(\epsilon \delta x)) &= g(\hat{x}) + \epsilon g'(\hat{x})\delta x + o_g(\epsilon \delta x) \end{aligned}$$

for all δx in co $\{\delta x_1, \ldots, \delta x_k\}$ and $0 < \epsilon \leqq \epsilon_1$.

We observe that if f and g are differentiable at $\hat{x}$ and if $C(\hat{x},\Omega)$ is a linearization of Ω at $\hat{x}$, then $C(\hat{x},\Omega)$ is also an approximation of Ω at $\hat{x}$ relative to f and g. We also note that if g is written in the form $g(x) = (g_1(x), \ldots, g_m(x))$, then some of the components $g_i'(\hat{x})$ can be replaced by convex functionals (rather than linear functionals), and the definition will still make sense [8, 14]. This generalization would lead to a somewhat stronger version of the necessary condition lemma of Sec. *3*; for details we refer the reader to Refs. 8 and 14. Another generalization would involve the replacement of R_m by any normed linear space E; however, in that case, we would also require that the cone $C(\hat{x}) = \{(f'(\hat{x})\delta x, g'(\hat{x})\delta x) : \delta x \in A(\hat{x},\Omega)\}$ in $R \oplus E$ (the direct sum of R and E) have (relative) interior points in the smallest closed subspace of $R \oplus E$ containing the cone $C(\hat{x})$. No essential change would be needed in the necessary condition lemma for this generalization of Definition *5*.

3 *A basic necessary condition lemma*

Having a satisfactory notion of approximation at hand, we are now ready to examine the question of necessary conditions. We consider the following problem.

Problem Let X be a locally convex topological vector space. Let f and g be mappings of X into R and R_m, respectively, and let Ω be a subset of X. Let X_g be the subset of X given by $X_g = \{x: g(x) = 0\}$. Then determine x^0 in $X_g \cap \Omega$ such that $f(x^0) \leqq f(x)$ for all x in $X_g \cap \Omega$. A solution x^0 of this problem shall be referred to as an *optimal element*. We then have the following lemma.

1 **Lemma** If x^0 is an optimal element and if $A(x^0,\Omega)$ is an approximation of Ω at x^0 relative to f and g, then there is a nonzero continuous linear functional p on $R \oplus R_m$ such that $p[(f'(x^0)\delta x, g'(x^0)\delta x)] \leqq 0$ for all δx in the closure $\overline{A(x^0,\Omega)}$ of $A(x^0,\Omega)$; that is, there is a nonzero vector $\mathbf{p} = (p_0,p_1, \ . \ . \ . \ ,p_m)$ in $R \oplus R_m$ such that $p_0 \leqq 0$ and

2 $$\langle \mathbf{p},(f'(x^0)\delta x, g'(x^0)\delta x)\rangle \leqq 0$$

for all δx in $\overline{A(x^0,\Omega)}$.

Proof [4] The proof, which we sketch here, is based on the separation theorem for convex sets [6] and the Brouwer fixed-point theorem [5].

Let x^0 be our optimal element and $C(x^0)$ be the cone

$$\{(f'(x^0)\delta x, g'(x^0)\delta x) : \delta x \in A(x^0,\Omega)\}$$

in $R \oplus R_m$. Since $A(x^0,\Omega)$ is a convex cone and the maps $f'(x^0)$ and $g'(x^0)$ are linear, $C(x^0)$ is also a convex cone. We let ρ be the open half ray in $R \oplus R_m$ given by

3 $$\rho = \{(y_0,0, \ . \ . \ . \ ,0) : y_0 < 0\}$$

and we note that ρ is a convex cone. We claim that $C(x^0)$ and ρ are separated in $R \oplus R_m$.

If our claim is valid, then there is a nonzero vector

$$\mathbf{p} = (p_0,p_1, \ . \ . \ . \ ,p_m)$$

in $R \oplus R_m$ such that

4 $$\langle \mathbf{p},(f'(x^0)\delta x, g'(x^0)\delta x)\rangle \leqq 0 \qquad \text{for all } \delta x \text{ in } A(x^0,\Omega)$$

5 $$\langle \mathbf{p},\mathbf{y}\rangle \geqq 0 \qquad \text{for all } \mathbf{y} \text{ in } \rho$$

which, in view of the continuity of $f'(x^0)$ and $g'(x^0)$, establishes the lemma.

So let us assume that $C(x^0)$ and ρ are not separated. Then $C(x^0) \cap \rho$ is not empty, and there is a δx_1 in $A(x^0,\Omega)$ such that

6 $$f'(x^0)\delta x_1 < 0 \qquad \text{and} \qquad g'(x^0)\delta x_1 = \mathbf{0}$$

Moreover, $g'(x^0)A(x^0,\Omega) = R_m$, that is, contains 0 as an interior point [otherwise there would be a vector of the form $(0,\mathbf{q})$, $\mathbf{q} \neq \mathbf{0}$, separating $C(x^0)$ and ρ]. It follows that there is a simplex $[z_1,z_2, \ldots ,z_{m+1}]$ in R_m containing $\mathbf{0}$ as an interior point such that

7 $$[z_1, \ldots ,z_{m+1}] \subset g'(x^0)A(x^0,\Omega); \text{ that is, } z_i = g'(x^0)\delta x_i$$

where $\delta x_i \in A(x^0,\Omega)$ for $i = 1, 2, \ldots , m + 1$;

8 $$\psi(\delta x) \in (\Omega - \{x^0\}) \qquad \text{for all } \delta x \text{ in co } \{\delta x_1, \ldots ,\delta x_{m+1}\}$$

where ψ is the map occurring in the definition of $A(x^0,\Omega)$;

9 $$f'(x^0)\delta x_i < 0 \qquad \text{for } i = 1, 2, \ldots , m + 1$$

and

10 $$\{z_2 - z_1, \ldots , z_{m+1} - z_1\} \text{ is a basis of } R_m$$

The existence of a simplex $[z_1, \ldots ,z_{m+1}]$ satisfying *7*, *8*, and *9* is not difficult to establish [4]. Condition *10* holds for any simplex. Since the $z_j - z_1$, $j = 2, \ldots , m + 1$, form a basis of R_m, we can define a linear mapping L of R_m into X by setting

11 $$L(z_j - z_1) = \delta x_j - \delta x_1 \qquad \text{for } j = 2, \ldots , m + 1$$

If $z = \Sigma r_j z_j + (1 - \Sigma r_j)z_1$ is an element of $[z_1, \ldots ,z_{m+1}]$, then we let

12 $$\varphi(z) = L(z - z_1) + \delta x_j = \Sigma r_j \delta x_1 + (1 - \Sigma r_j)\delta x_j$$

Clearly φ is a continuous map of the simplex into co $\{\delta x_1, \ldots ,\delta x_{m+1}\}$.

Now, for $0 < \alpha \leqq 1$, we define a continuous map h_α from

$$\alpha[z_1, \ldots ,z_{m+1}]$$

into R_m by

13 $$h_\alpha(\alpha z) = -g(x^0 + \psi(\alpha[L(z - z_1) + \delta x_1])) + \alpha z$$

In view of the properties of an approximation, we have

14 $$h_\alpha(\alpha z) = -o_g(\alpha L(z - z_1) + \alpha \delta x_1)$$

and

15 $$o_g(\alpha L(z - z_1) + \alpha \delta x_1) \in \alpha[z_1, \ldots ,z_{m+1}]$$

for all α with $0 < \alpha \leqq \alpha_0$ and some α_0. Moreover, since $f'(x^0)\delta x_i < 0$, $i = 1, \ldots , m + 1$, and since $A(x^0,\Omega)$ is an approximation, we also have

16 $$f(x^0 + \psi(\alpha L(z - z_1) + \alpha\delta x_1)) < f(x^0)$$

for all α with $0 < \alpha \leqq \alpha_1$ and some α_1.

Letting $\beta = \min\{\alpha_0,\alpha_1\}$, we deduce from the Brouwer fixed-point theorem [5] that there is an element z_β in $\beta[z_1, \ldots ,z_{m+1}]$ such that $h_\beta(\beta z_\beta) = \beta z_\beta$. It now follows from *13* that if

$$x = x^0 + \psi(L(z_\beta - \beta z_1) + \beta\delta x_1)$$

then $g(x) = 0$, $x \in \Omega$ (since $x - x^0 \in \psi(\text{co}\,\{\delta x_1, \ldots ,\delta x_{m+1}\}) \subset \Omega - \{x^0\}$), and $f(x) < f(x^0)$ (by *16*). This contradicts the optimality of x^0, and thus the lemma is established.

We shall use this basic lemma to obtain the maximum principle in the next section.

4 *The maximum principle*

We recall that the essential elements in an optimal control problem are

1. The system to be controlled
2. The class of admissible controls
3. The initial and terminal manifolds
4. The cost functional

With these essential elements in mind, we first consider the discrete optimal control problem (basically as formulated in Ref. 9). In other words, we examine a system described by the difference equation

1 $$x(i+1) - x(i) = f_i(x(i),u(i)) \qquad i = 0, 1, \ldots , k-1$$

where $x(i) \in R_n$ is the state of the system at time i, $u(i) \in R_m$ is the control vector, and f_i maps $R_n \times R_m$ into R_n. We assume that

2 $$u(i) \in U_i \subset R_m \text{ for all } i$$

and that

3 $$f_i(\cdot,u) \text{ is } C^1 \text{ for all } u \text{ in } U_i \text{ and all } i$$

We suppose that the initial and terminal manifolds are defined by C^1 functions h_0 and h_k from R_n into R_{l_0} and R_{l_k}, respectively, and that

4 $$\frac{\partial h_0}{\partial x}, \frac{\partial h_k}{\partial x} \text{ have maximum rank}$$

In other words, the initial and terminal manifolds S_0 and S_k are given by

5 $$S_0 = \{x\colon h_0(x) = 0\} \qquad S_k = \{x\colon h_k(x) = 0\}$$

and S_0 and S_k are smooth manifolds. We further require that the cost functional be defined by a family f_i^0 of maps from $R_n \times R_m$ into R such that

6 $$f_i^0(\cdot,u) \text{ is } C^1 \text{ for every } u \text{ in } U_i \qquad i = 0, \ldots, k-1$$

The cost of a control sequence $u(i)$ is then given by

7 $$J(x(0),\{u(i)\}) = \sum_{i=0}^{k-1} f_i^0(x(i),u(i))$$

if $u(i)$ transfers the state from S_0 to S_k. We make the additional assumption that the sets $\mathbf{f}_i(x,u_i)$ should be convex for every x in R_n and every i in $\{0, \ldots, k-1\}$ where $\mathbf{f}_i$ is the map of $R_n \times R_m$ into R_{n+1}, given by

8 $$\mathbf{f}_i(x,u) = (f_i^0(x,u),f_i(x,u))$$

With these assumptions, our problem becomes *determine a control sequence* $\{u(i):i = 0, \ldots, k-1\}$ *(with* $u(i) \in U_i$ *for all* i*) and a corresponding trajectory* $\{x(j):j = 0,1, \ldots, k\}$ *of 1 such that* $x(0) \in S_0$, $x(k) \in S_k$, *and* $J(x(0), \{u(i)\})$ *is minimized.*

Now let us see how this problem can be recast in such a way that the Lemma *13.3.1* will apply to it. To begin with, we let X be the space $R_{(k+1)n+k(n+1)}$ and we view a typical element $\mathbf{x}$ of X in the following way:

9 $$\mathbf{x} = (x(0), \ldots, x(k),\mathbf{y}(0), \ldots, \mathbf{y}(k-1))$$

where the $x(j)$ are in R_n and the $\mathbf{y}(l)$ are in R_{n+1}. We also write $\mathbf{y}(l)$ in the form

10 $$\mathbf{y}(l) = (y_0(l),y(l))$$

with $y_0(l)$ in R and $y(l)$ in R_n. We define the mappings f and g and the set Ω by

11 $$f(\mathbf{x}) = \sum_{l=0}^{k-1} y_0(l)$$

12 $$g(\mathbf{x}) = (x(1) - x(0) - y(0), \ldots, x(k) - x(k-1) - y(k-1), h_0(x(0)), h_k(x(k)))$$

13 $$\Omega = \{\mathbf{x}: \mathbf{y}(i) \in \mathbf{f}_i(x(i),U_i), i = 0, \ldots, k-1\}$$

where $\mathbf{f}_i$ is given by *8*.

We observe that Ω is convex and that the maps f and g are C^1. Now let us define a suitable approximation $A(\hat{\mathbf{x}},\Omega)$ of Ω at $\hat{\mathbf{x}}$ relative to f and g. We first note that

14 $$\hat{\mathbf{x}} = (\hat{x}(0), \ldots, \hat{x}(k),\mathbf{f}_0(\hat{x}(0),\hat{u}(0)), \ldots, \mathbf{f}_{k-1}(\hat{x}(k-1),\hat{u}(k-1)))$$

for some sequence $\{\hat{u}(j)\}$ with $\hat{u}(j) \in U_j$ for all j. Next suppose that $\delta x(i)$ is an element of R_n. Since $\mathbf{f}_i(\cdot,u(i))$ is C^1 in $x(i)$, we have

15 $$\mathbf{f}_i(\hat{x}(i) + \delta x(i),\, u(i)) = \mathbf{f}_i(\hat{x}(i),u(i)) + \frac{\partial \mathbf{f}_i}{\partial x}(\hat{x}(i),u(i))\,\delta x(i) + o(\delta x(i))$$

which can be interpreted as implying that

16 $$\frac{\partial \mathbf{f}_i}{\partial x}(\hat{x}(i),u(i))\,\delta x(i) \in \mathbf{f}_i(\hat{x}(i) + \delta x(i),\, U_i) - \mathbf{f}_i(\hat{x}(i),u(i))$$

to within $o(\delta x(i))$. This indicates that the elements of $A(\hat{\mathbf{x}},\Omega)$ should involve terms of the form $(\partial \mathbf{f}_i/\partial x)(\hat{x}(i),\hat{u}(i))\,\delta x(i)$. Although these terms alone would lead to an approximation, this approximation is not "rich enough" since it does not contain control perturbations. We introduce control perturbations by considering the radial cone of $\mathbf{f}_i(\hat{x}(i),U_i)$ at $\mathbf{f}_i(\hat{x}(i),U(i))$.† We denote the cone by $A_i(\hat{\mathbf{x}})$.

We are now ready to define $A(\hat{\mathbf{x}},\Omega)$. In particular, we have

17 $$A(\hat{\mathbf{x}},\Omega) = \left\{\delta\mathbf{x}\colon \delta\mathbf{y}(i) \in \left\{\frac{\partial \mathbf{f}_i}{\partial x}(\hat{x}(i),\hat{u}(i))\,\delta x(i)\right\} + A_i(\hat{\mathbf{x}}) \text{ for all } i\right\}$$

[where the $\delta x(i)$ are arbitrary elements of R_n]. The set $A(\hat{\mathbf{x}},\Omega)$ is clearly a convex cone. Let us show that $A(\hat{\mathbf{x}},\Omega)$ is indeed an approximation of Ω at $\hat{\mathbf{x}}$ relative to f and g. In view of the continuous differentiability of f and g, we need only exhibit a suitable mapping ψ. So we suppose that $\delta\mathbf{x}^\nu$, $\nu = 1, \ldots, N$, are linearly independent elements of $A(\hat{\mathbf{x}},\Omega)$. Then, by the definition of a radial cone, there is an $\epsilon > 0$ and there are elements $u^\nu(i)$ of U_i such that

18 $$\mathbf{f}_i(\hat{x}(i),u(i)) + \epsilon\,\delta\mathbf{y}^\nu(i) = \epsilon\,\frac{\partial \mathbf{f}_i}{\partial x}(\hat{x}(i),\hat{u}(i))\,\delta x(i) + \mathbf{f}_i(\hat{x}(i),u^\nu(i))$$

for $i = 0, \ldots, k-1$ and $\nu = 1, \ldots, N$ [where we recall that $\delta\mathbf{x} = (\delta x(0), \ldots, \delta x(k), \delta\mathbf{y}(0), \ldots, \delta\mathbf{y}(k-1))$ and that the $\delta x(i)$ are arbitrary elements of R_n]. Consider the set $\operatorname{co}\{\epsilon\delta\mathbf{x}^1, \ldots, \epsilon\delta\mathbf{x}^N\}$ [where $\delta\mathbf{x}^\nu = (\delta x^\nu(0), \ldots, \delta x^\nu(k), \delta\mathbf{y}^\nu(0), \ldots, \delta\mathbf{y}^\nu(k-1))$], and let $\delta\mathbf{x}$ be a typical element of this set. Then

19 $$\delta\mathbf{x} = \sum_{\nu=1}^{N} \alpha^\nu(\delta\mathbf{x}) \in \delta\mathbf{x}^\nu \qquad \alpha^\nu(\delta\mathbf{x}^\nu) \geqq 0 \qquad \beta(\delta\mathbf{x}) = \sum_{1}^{N} \alpha^\nu(\delta\mathbf{x}) \leqq 1$$

and

20 $$(\alpha^1(\delta\mathbf{x}), \ldots, \alpha^N(\delta\mathbf{x})) = \Gamma\delta\mathbf{x}$$

† If Φ is a convex set and if φ is an element of Φ, then the *radial cone of Φ at φ* is the set given by

$$\{\delta\varphi\colon \text{there is an } \epsilon_1 > 0 \text{ such that } \epsilon_1 < \varphi_1,\ \delta\varphi \gg 0 \text{ and } \varphi + \epsilon\delta\varphi \text{ is in } \Phi \text{ for } 0 \leqq \epsilon \leqq \epsilon_1\}$$

where Γ is an $N \times (2nk + n + k)$ matrix with rows Γ_ν such that

21 $$\langle \Gamma_{\nu}, \epsilon\delta\mathbf{x}^{\mu} \rangle = \delta_{\nu\mu} \qquad \text{(the Kronecker delta)}$$

We note that *20* implies that $\beta(\delta\mathbf{x})\delta\mathbf{x}$ is $o(\delta\mathbf{x})$. Now let us define the map ψ by setting

22 $$\psi(\delta\mathbf{x}) = (\delta x(0), \ldots, \delta x(k), \psi_0(\delta\mathbf{x}), \ldots, \psi_{k-1}(\delta\mathbf{x}))$$

where

23 $$\begin{aligned}\psi_i(\delta\mathbf{x}) &= \mathbf{f}_i(\hat{x}(i) + \delta x(i), \hat{u}(i)) - \mathbf{f}_i(\hat{x}(i), u(i)) \\ &= \sum_{\nu=1}^{N} \alpha^{\nu}(\delta\mathbf{x})[\mathbf{f}_i(\hat{x}(i) + \delta x(i), u^{\nu}(i)) - \mathbf{f}_i(\hat{x}(i) + \delta x(i), \hat{u}(i))]\end{aligned}$$

for $i = 0, 1, \ldots, k - 1$. Since Ω is convex, it is clear that ψ maps co $\{\epsilon\delta\mathbf{x}^1, \ldots, \epsilon\delta\mathbf{x}^N\}$ into $\Omega - \{\hat{\mathbf{x}}\}$. Moreover, *15, 18,* and *20* together imply that $\psi(\delta\mathbf{x}) = \delta\mathbf{x} + o(\delta\mathbf{x})$, and so $A(\hat{\mathbf{x}}, \Omega)$ is an approximation of Ω at $\hat{\mathbf{x}}$ relative to f and g.

Applying Lemma *13.3.1* and taking suitable elements of $A(\mathbf{x}^0, \Omega)$, we deduce the following result of Halkin [9].

24 **Theorem** (Discrete maximum principle) If $\{u^0(i)\}$ is an optimal control sequence with $\{x^0(j)\}$ as a corresponding optimal trajectory, then there are vectors $p(0), \ldots, p(k)$ in R_n, $\lambda(0)$ in R_{l_0}, $\lambda(k)$ in R_{l_k}, and a number $p \leqq 0$ such that the following conditions are satisfied:

1. $p, p(0), \ldots, p(k), \lambda(0)$, and $\lambda(k)$ are not all zero.
2. $x^0(0), \ldots, x^0(k)$ and $p, p(0), \ldots, p(k)$ satisfy the canonical system of difference equations; that is,

25 $$x^0(i + 1) - x^0(i) = f_i(x^0(i), u^0(i))$$

26 $$p(i + 1) - p(i) = -\frac{\partial f_i}{\partial x}(x^0(i), u^0(i))' p(i + 1) - \frac{\partial f_i^0}{\partial x}(x^0(i), u^0(i)) p$$

for $i = 0, \ldots, k - 1$.

3. $u^0(i)$ maximizes the hamiltonian over U_i at i; that is,

27 $$\begin{aligned} p f_i^0(\hat{x}(i), u) + \langle p(i + 1), f_i(\hat{x}(i), u)\rangle \leqq{} & p f_i^0(\hat{x}(i), \hat{u}(i)) \\ & + \langle p(i + 1), f_i(\hat{x}(i), \hat{u}(i))\rangle \end{aligned}$$

for all u in U_i and $i = 0, \ldots, k - 1$.

4. $p(0)$ and $p(k)$ are transversal to S_0 and S_k at $x^0(0)$ and $x^0(k)$, respectively; that is,

28 $$p(0) = -\frac{\partial h_0}{\partial x}(x^0(0))' \lambda(0)$$

29 $$p(k) = \frac{\partial h_k}{\partial x}(x^0(k))' \lambda(k)$$

A more general version of this theorem has been proven by Holtzman and Halkin [10] using the notion of directional convexity, but we shall not pursue this matter here.

We now turn our attention to the continuous optimal control problem and indicate how this problem can also be recast in such a way that the Lemma *13.3.1* will apply. In other words, we consider a system described by the differential equation

30 $$\dot{\mathbf{x}} = \mathbf{f}(\mathbf{x},\mathbf{u}) \qquad t \in [t_0,t_1]$$

where $\mathbf{x}(t) \in R_n$ is the state, $\mathbf{u}(t) \in R_m$ is the control vector, and $\mathbf{f}$ maps $R_n \times R_m$ into R_n. We assume that

31 $$\mathbf{u}(t) \in U \subset R_n \qquad \text{for (almost) all } t$$

32 $\mathbf{u}(\cdot)$ is measurable and essentially bounded

33 $\mathbf{f}(\mathbf{x},\mathbf{u})$ is continuous on $R_n \times \bar{U}$

34 $\mathbf{f}(\mathbf{x},\mathbf{u})$ is continuously differentiable in $\mathbf{x}$

We suppose that the initial manifold is a single point $\mathbf{x}_0$, that is, $\mathbf{x}(t_0) = \mathbf{x}_0$, and that the terminal manifold is defined by a C^1 function $\mathbf{h}$ from R_n into R_p such that

35 $$\frac{\partial \mathbf{h}}{\partial \mathbf{x}} \text{ has maximum rank}$$

In other words, the terminal manifold S_1 is given by

36 $$S_1 = \{\mathbf{x}: \mathbf{h}(\mathbf{x}) = \mathbf{0}\}$$

and S_1 is a smooth manifold. We further require that the cost functional be defined by a trajectory cost term $L(\mathbf{x},\mathbf{u})$, where L maps $R_n \times R_m$ into R and is continuous in $\mathbf{x}$ and $\mathbf{u}$ and continuously differentiable in $\mathbf{x}$. The cost of a control $\mathbf{u}(\cdot)$ is then given by

37 $$J(\mathbf{u}(\cdot)) = \int_{t_0}^{t_1} L(\mathbf{x}_\mathbf{u}(t),\mathbf{u}(t))\, dt$$

where $\mathbf{x}_\mathbf{u}(t)$ is the solution of *30* starting from $\mathbf{x}_0$ at t_0 generated by $\mathbf{u}(\cdot)$ and where it is assumed that $\mathbf{u}(\cdot)$ transfers $\mathbf{x}_0$ to S_1 (that is, $\mathbf{x}_\mathbf{u}(t_1) \in S_1$). With these assumptions, our problem becomes *determine a control* $\mathbf{u}(t)$ *[with* $\mathbf{u}(t) \in U$ *for all* t*] and a corresponding trajectory* $\mathbf{x}_\mathbf{u}(t)$ *of 30 such that* $\mathbf{x}_u(t_0) = \mathbf{x}_0$, $\mathbf{x}_\mathbf{u}(t_1) \in S_1$ *and* $J(\mathbf{u}(\cdot))$ *is minimized.*

Now let us see how this problem can be transcribed in such a way that the Lemma *13.3.1* will apply to it. We first embed the problem in an augmented state space R_{n+1}. In other words, denoting a typical element $\mathbf{y}$ of R_{n+1} by

38 $$\mathbf{y} = (x_0,\mathbf{x}) \qquad \mathbf{x} \in R_n$$

and letting $\mathbf{F}$ be the map of $R_{n+1} \times R_m$ into R_{n+1} given by

39 $$\mathbf{F}(\mathbf{y},\mathbf{u}) = (L(\mathbf{x},\mathbf{u}),\mathbf{f}(\mathbf{x},\mathbf{u}))$$

we consider the differential equation

40 $$\dot{\mathbf{y}} = \mathbf{F}(\mathbf{y},\mathbf{u})$$

with initial condition

41 $$\mathbf{y}(t_0) = \mathbf{y}_0 = (0,\mathbf{x}_0)$$

and with terminal manifold $R \times S_1$. We then seek a control $\mathbf{u}(t)$ [with $\mathbf{u}(t) \in U$ for all t] and a corresponding trajectory $\mathbf{y}_\mathbf{u}(t)$ of *40* such that $\mathbf{y}_\mathbf{u}(t_0) = \mathbf{y}_0$, $\mathbf{y}_\mathbf{u}(t_1) \in R \times S_1$ and $y_0(t_1)(= J(\mathbf{u}(\cdot)))$ is minimized. Clearly this problem is equivalent to our original problem.

We next observe that the solutions $\mathbf{y}_\mathbf{u}(\cdot)$ of *40* are absolutely continuous functions on $[t_0,t_1]$, and so we let Ω be the set of all absolutely continuous functions $\mathbf{y}_\mathbf{u}(\cdot)$ which satisfy *40* and *41* for some $\mathbf{u}(\cdot)$ satisfying *32*. Before defining the maps f and g, we shall introduce a locally convex linear topological space X containing Ω. To do this, we let $C[t_0,t_1]$ denote the normed linear space of continuous R_{n+1}-valued functions $\mathbf{y}(\cdot)$ on $[t_0,t_1]$ with $\|\mathbf{y}(\cdot)\| = \sup_{t \in [t_0,t_1]} \{\|\mathbf{y}(t)\|\}$ as norm. We let $\mathcal{U}$ denote the set of all R_{n+1}-valued functions $\mathbf{z}(\cdot)$ on $[t_0,t_1]$ for which there is a sequence $\mathbf{x}_j(\cdot)$ in $C[t_0,t_1]$ such that

42 $$\mathbf{x}_{j,i}(t) \leqq \mathbf{x}_{j+1,i}(t) \qquad \text{for all } t;\ i = 0, \ldots, n;\ j = 1, \ldots$$

where $\mathbf{x}_{j,i}$ is the ith component of $\mathbf{x}_j$, and

43 $$\lim_{j \to \infty} \mathbf{x}_j(t) = \mathbf{z}(t)$$

for all t in $[t_0,t_1]$. Note that $\mathcal{U} = \pi\mathcal{S}_i$ where $\mathcal{S}_i$ is the set of upper semicontinuous real-valued functions of t on $[t_0,t_1]$. Letting $X = \mathcal{U} - \mathcal{U}$, we observe that X is a linear space. We define a topology on X by choosing as subbase the family of sets

44 $$\{\mathbf{z}(\cdot) : z(t) \in \mathcal{O}\}$$

where t is an element of $[t_0,t_1]$ and $\mathcal{O}$ is an open set in R_{n+1}.† X is a locally convex topological vector space with respect to this topology, and $\Omega \subset X$. We now define the mappings f and g by setting

45 $$f(\mathbf{z}(\cdot)) = \mathbf{z}_0(t_1)$$

46 $$g(\mathbf{z}(\cdot)) = \mathbf{h}(\mathbf{z}_1(t_1), \ldots, \mathbf{z}_n(t_1))$$

† This is the so-called *pointwise* topology [13].

where $\mathbf{z}_i(\cdot)$, $i = 0, \ldots, n$, is the ith component of $\mathbf{z}(\cdot)$. The mappings f and g are clearly continuous.

Now let $\hat{\mathbf{y}}_{\hat{\mathbf{u}}}(\cdot)$ be an element of Ω, and let us construct an approximation $A(\hat{\mathbf{y}}_{\hat{\mathbf{u}}},\Omega)$ of Ω at $\hat{\mathbf{y}}_{\hat{\mathbf{u}}}$ relative to f and g. We let $I \subset [t_0,t_1]$ be the set of regular points of $\hat{\mathbf{u}}$; that is, $t \in I$ if and only if $t_0 < t < t_1$ and

47
$$\lim_{\mu(J)\to 0} \frac{\mu(\hat{\mathbf{u}}^{-1}(N) \cap J)}{\mu(J)} = 1$$

holds for every neighborhood N of $\hat{\mathbf{u}}^{-1}(t)$ and every subinterval J of I with $t \in J$ (where μ is the Lebesgue measure on I).[1] We note that $\mu(I) = t_1 - t_0 = \mu([t_0,t_1])$. We denote the fundamental matrix of the linear differential equation

48
$$\delta\dot{\mathbf{y}} = \frac{\partial F}{\partial \mathbf{y}} (\hat{\mathbf{y}}_{\hat{\mathbf{u}}},\hat{\mathbf{u}})\,\delta\mathbf{y}$$

by $\Phi(t,\tau)$. In other words, $\Phi(t,\tau)$ is the solution of the matrix differential equation

49
$$\frac{d}{dt}\,\Phi(t,\tau) = \frac{\partial \mathbf{F}(\hat{\mathbf{y}}_{\hat{\mathbf{u}}}(t),\hat{\mathbf{u}}(t))}{\partial \mathbf{y}}\,\Phi(t,\tau)$$

satisfying the condition

50
$$\Phi(\tau,\tau) = \mathbf{I}$$

where $\mathbf{I}$ is the $(n + 1) \times (n + 1)$ identity matrix. If $s \in I$ and $\mathbf{u} \in U$, then we let $\delta\mathbf{y}_{s,\mathbf{u}}$ be the solution of *48* satisfying the condition

51
$$\delta\mathbf{y}_{s,\mathbf{u}}(s) = \mathbf{F}(\hat{\mathbf{y}}_{\hat{\mathbf{u}}}(s),\mathbf{u}) - \mathbf{F}(\hat{\mathbf{y}}_{\hat{\mathbf{u}}}(s),\hat{\mathbf{u}}(s))$$

and we let $\delta\mathbf{z}_{s,\mathbf{u}}$ be the element of X given by

52
$$\delta\mathbf{z}_{s,\mathbf{u}}(t) = \begin{cases} 0 & t_0 \leqq t < s \\ \delta\mathbf{y}_{s,\mathbf{u}}(t) & s \leqq t \leqq t_1 \end{cases}$$

Finally, we let

53
$$A(\hat{\mathbf{y}}_{\hat{\mathbf{u}}},\Omega) = \{\delta\mathbf{z}\colon \delta\mathbf{z} = \Sigma\alpha_i\delta\mathbf{z}_{s_i,\mathbf{u}_i},\ s_i \in I,\ \mathbf{u}_i \in U,\ \alpha_i \geqq 0\}$$

and we define the linear maps $f'(\hat{\mathbf{y}}_{\hat{\mathbf{u}}})$ and $g'(\hat{\mathbf{y}}_{\mathbf{u}})$ by setting

54
$$f'(\hat{\mathbf{y}}_{\hat{\mathbf{u}}})\,\delta\mathbf{z} = \delta\mathbf{z}_0(t_1)$$

[1] The significance of a regular point lies in the following observation: if τ is a regular point of $\mathbf{u}(\cdot)$ and if $g(t,\mathbf{u})$ is continuous, then

$$\int_{\tau+a\epsilon}^{\tau+b\epsilon} g(t,\mathbf{u}(t))\,dt = \epsilon(b - a)g(\tau,\mathbf{u}(\tau)) + o(\epsilon)$$

where a and b are elements of R and ϵ is small.

55 $$g'(\hat{\mathbf{y}}_{\hat{\mathbf{u}}})\delta\mathbf{z} = \frac{\partial\mathbf{h}}{d\mathbf{x}}(\delta\mathbf{z}_1(t_1), \ldots, \delta\mathbf{z}_n(t_1))(\delta\mathbf{z}_1(t_1), \ldots, \delta\mathbf{z}_n(t_1))$$

where $\delta\mathbf{z}_0, \delta\mathbf{z}_1, \ldots, \delta\mathbf{z}_n$ are the components of $\delta\mathbf{z}$. The basic work of Pontryagin [16] includes a proof of the fact that the convex cone $A(\hat{\mathbf{y}}_{\hat{\mathbf{u}}},\Omega)$ is indeed an approximation of Ω at $\hat{\mathbf{y}}_{\hat{\mathbf{u}}}$ relative to f and g. To illustrate what is involved in the proof, we shall exhibit the map ψ for the case of two linearly independent vectors $\delta\mathbf{z}_1$ and $\delta\mathbf{z}_2$ of $A(\hat{\mathbf{y}}_{\hat{\mathbf{u}}},\Omega)$. We may assume (reordering and inserting zeros if necessary) that

56 $$\delta\mathbf{z}_i = \sum_{j=1}^{k} \alpha_j{}^i \delta\mathbf{z}_{s_j,\mathbf{u}_j}$$

for $i = 1, 2$ and that $s_1 \leqq s_2 \leqq \cdots \leqq s_k$. We then note that $\delta\mathbf{z} \in \text{co}\,\{\delta\mathbf{z}_1,\delta\mathbf{z}_2\}$ implies that

57 $$\delta\mathbf{z} = \lambda_1\delta\mathbf{z}_1 + \lambda_2\delta\mathbf{z}_2 = \sum_{j=1}^{k} \delta t_j(\lambda_1,\lambda_2)\,\delta\mathbf{z}_{s_j,\mathbf{u}_j}$$

where $\lambda_1 + \lambda_2 = 1$, $\lambda_i \geqq 0$ for $i = 1, 2$, and

58 $$\delta t_j(\lambda_1,\lambda_2) = \lambda_1\alpha_j{}^i + \lambda_2\alpha_j{}^2$$

for $j = 1, \ldots, k$. Clearly, $\text{co}\,\{\delta\mathbf{z}_1,\delta\mathbf{z}_2\}$ is homeomorphic to the set $\Lambda = \{(\lambda_1,\lambda_2)\colon \lambda_1 + \lambda_2 = 1,\ \lambda_i \geqq 0\}$. Let $\epsilon > 0$ be a small positive number and let

59 $$j = \begin{cases} -(\delta t_j + \cdots + \delta t_k) & \text{if } s_j = s_k \\ -(\delta t_j + \cdots + \delta t_r) & \text{if } s_j = \cdots = s_r < s_{r+1}\ (j < k) \end{cases}$$

We consider the half-open intervals I_j given by

60 $$I_j = \{t \in I\colon s_j + \epsilon\nu_j < t \leqq s_j + \epsilon(\nu_j + \delta t_j)\}$$

and we suppose that ϵ is small enough to insure that the I_j are disjoint. We define a perturbation $\mathbf{u}(t)$ of $\hat{\mathbf{u}}(t)$ by setting

61 $$\mathbf{u}(t) = \begin{cases} \hat{\mathbf{u}}(t) & t \notin \bigcup I_j \\ \mathbf{u}_j & t \in I_j \end{cases}$$

and we let $\mathbf{y}(t;\epsilon,\lambda_1,\lambda_2)$ be the solution of *40* satisfying the initial conditions of *41* for which the control is $\mathbf{u}(t)$. We note that $\mathbf{u}(t)$ is an admissible control and that $\mathbf{y}(t;\epsilon,\lambda_1,\lambda_2)$ depends on λ_1 and λ_2 since the δt_j depend on λ_1 and λ_2. Using the standard result on dependence of solutions of a differential equation on parameters (see, for example, Ref. 5), we can deduce that $\mathbf{y}(t;\epsilon,\lambda_1,\lambda_2)$ is a continuous function of ϵ,λ_1, and λ_2. It then follows that the mapping ψ of $\text{co}\,\{\epsilon\delta\mathbf{z}_1,\epsilon\delta\mathbf{z}_2\}$ into $\Omega - \{\hat{\mathbf{y}}_{\hat{\mathbf{u}}}\}$ defined by

62 $$\psi(\epsilon\delta\mathbf{z}) = \mathbf{y}(t;\epsilon,\lambda_1,\lambda_2) - \hat{\mathbf{y}}_{\hat{\mathbf{u}}}(t)$$

is continuous. The proof that ψ has the other requisite properties *13.2.7* is based upon the properties of regular points and some standard results on differential equations. The details are given in Ref. 16.

Applying Lemma *13.3.1*, we deduce the following theorem of Pontryagin [16].

63 **Theorem** (Continuous maximum principle) If $\mathbf{u}^0(\cdot)$ is an optimal control with $\mathbf{x}^0(\cdot)$ as corresponding optimal trajectory, then there are a vector-valued function $\mathbf{p}(\cdot)$, a vector $\boldsymbol{\lambda}(t_1)$ in R_p, and a number $p \leqq 0$ such that the following conditions are satisfied:

1. p, $p(t)$ is not identically zero.
2. $\mathbf{x}^0(\cdot)$ and p, $\mathbf{p}(\cdot)$ satisfy the canonical system of differential equations; that is,

64 $$\dot{\mathbf{x}}^0(t) = \mathbf{f}(\mathbf{x}^0(t),\mathbf{u}^0(t))$$

65 $$\dot{\mathbf{p}}(t) = -\frac{\partial L}{\partial x}(\mathbf{x}^0(t),\mathbf{u}^0(t))p - \frac{\partial f}{\partial x}(\mathbf{x}^\circ(t),\mathbf{u}^0(t))'\mathbf{p}(t)$$

3. $\mathbf{u}^0(t)$ maximizes the hamiltonian over U for almost all t; that is,

66 $$pL(\mathbf{x}^0(t),\mathbf{u}^0(t)) + \langle \mathbf{p}(t),\mathbf{f}(\mathbf{x}^0(\cdot),\mathbf{u}^0(t))\rangle \geqq pL(x^0(t),\mathbf{u}) + \langle \mathbf{p}(t),\mathbf{f}(\mathbf{x}^0(t),\mathbf{u})\rangle$$

for all u in U.

4. $\mathbf{p}(t_1)$ is transversal to S_1 at $x^0(t_1)$; that is,

67 $$\mathbf{p}(t_1) = \frac{\partial \mathbf{h}}{\partial \mathbf{x}}(\mathbf{x}^0(t_1))\boldsymbol{\lambda}(t_1)$$

A more general version of this theorem involving (for example) state space constraints has been proven by Neustadt [14], and the reader is advised to consult Ref. 14 for details. It is also possible to generalize these results to vector-valued cost functionals [4]; this generalization may allow the satisfactory treatment of problems involving "engineering trade-offs" between several quantities of interest. Although we have considered only a fixed terminal time problem for an autonomous system with an autonomous trajectory cost term, Theorem *63* can be used to obtain necessary conditions for other versions of the control problem by making suitable changes of variable. For example, if the system and cost involved t [that is, $\mathbf{f} = \mathbf{f}(\mathbf{x},\mathbf{u},t)$, and $L = L(\mathbf{x},\mathbf{u},t)$], then we would introduce a variable x_{n+1} with $\dot{x}_{n+1} = 1$, $x_{n+1}(t_0) = t_0$, and $x_{n+1}(t_1) = t_1$, and we would apply the theorem to our new problem with state space R_{n+1}. Full details relating to this and various other changes of variable can be found in Ref. 1.

5 A sufficiency condition

The maximum principle, being a set of necessary conditions for optimality, is most frequently used to isolate the possible candidates for a solution to a given optimal control problem. It is therefore natural to inquire about the sufficiency of the maximum principle. In other words, we would like to know under what circumstances an extremal control and trajectory are actually optimal. A basic approach to this sufficiency question is the Hamilton-Jacobi theory or, "equivalently," the dynamic programming method. We shall analyze this approach here.

Consider the continuous optimal control problem of Sec. 4, and let Y be a subset of X with $S \cap Y \neq \phi$ (where $S = S_1$ is our target set). Then we have the following definition.

1 **Definition** If $u(\cdot)$ is an admissible control, then we say that $u(\cdot)$ Y-transfers x_0 to S if the trajectory $x_u(\cdot)$ lies in Y for $t_0 \leqq t \leqq t_1$ and if $x_u(t_0) = x_0$ and $x_u(t_1) \in S$. An admissible control $u^0(\cdot)$ is called Y-optimal if (1) $u^0(\cdot)$ Y-transfers x_0 to S, and (2) if $u(\cdot)$ T-transfers x_0 to S, then $J(u^0(\cdot)) \leqq J(u(\cdot))$.

We note that a Y-optimal control need not be optimal. The following lemma of Caratheodory leads to a sufficiency theorem for Y-optimality [12].

2 **Lemma** Suppose that, for each x in Y, the function $L(x,u)$ has, as a function of u, zero as its absolute minimum with respect to U at $u^0(x)$; that is,

3 $$0 = L(x,u^0(x)) \leqq L(x,u)$$

for all u in U. Let $\hat{u}(\cdot)$ be an admissible control such that (1) $\hat{u}(\cdot)$ Y-transfers x_0 to S, and (2) $\hat{u}(t) = u^0(\hat{u}(t))$, where $\hat{u}(t) = x_{\hat{u}}(t)$ for convenience. Then $\hat{u}(\cdot)$ is Y-optimal.

Proof Simply note that

$$J(\hat{u}(\cdot)) = \int_{t_0}^{t_1} L(\hat{x}(t),u^0(\hat{x}(t)))\,dt = 0$$

and that

$$J(u(\cdot)) = \int_{t_0}^{t_2} L(x_u(t),u(t))\,dt \geqq \int_{t_0}^{t_2} L(x_u(t),u^0(x_u(t))\,dt = 0$$

where $u(\cdot)$ is any admissible control which Y-transfers x_0 to S.

In order to apply this lemma, we must introduce both the notion of regularity for the hamiltonian and also the Hamilton-Jacobi partial differential equation. Thus, we have the following definition.

4 **Definition** Let $H(x,p,u) = L(x,u) + \langle p,f(x,u)\rangle$ be the hamiltonian of our problem. If, for each x in Y and p in R_n, the function $H(x,p,u)$ has, as a function of u, an absolute minimum with respect to U at $u^0(x,p)$, that is,

5 $$H(x,p,u^0(x,p)) \leqq H(x,p,u)$$

for all u in U, then H is called regular relative to Y. If H is regular relative to Y, then the partial differential equation

6 $$H\left(x, \frac{\partial v}{\partial x}, u^0\left(x, \frac{\partial v}{\partial x}\right)\right) = 0$$

is called the *Hamilton-Jacobi equation relative to* Y.

With this definition, we can now prove the following theorem.

7 **Theorem** Suppose that H is regular relative to Y and that if $u(\cdot)$ Y-transfers x_0 to S then $\dot{x}_u(\cdot)$ is continuous.[1] Let $\hat{u}(\cdot)$ be an admissible control such that

8 $$\hat{u}(\cdot)\ Y\text{-transfers } x_0 \text{ to } S$$

and

9 $$\hat{u}(t) = u^0\left(\hat{u}(t), \frac{\partial v}{\partial x}(\hat{x}(t))\right)$$

where $v(x)$ is a C^1-solution of the Hamilton-Jacobi equation relative to Y which vanishes on $S \cap Y$. Then $\hat{u}(\cdot)$ is Y-optimal.

Proof The proof is a direct application of Lemma *13.5.2*. The function $M(x,u)$ given by

10 $$M(x,u) = H\left(x, \frac{\partial v}{\partial x}, u\right) = L(x,u) + \left\langle \frac{\partial v}{\partial x}, f(x,u)\right\rangle$$

satisfies all the hypotheses of the lemma. The theorem then follows from the lemma and the observation that

11 $$M(x_u(t),u(t)) = L(x_u(t),u(t)) + \frac{d}{dt}v(x_u(t))$$

if $u(\cdot)$ Y-transfers x_0 to S.

Now there are several weaknesses in this theorem. First of all, the theorem is essentially local in that everything is relative to Y. Secondly,

[1] This condition can be relaxed [12].

the requirement of regularity is considerably stronger than the maximization condition (for $-L(x,u)$) of the Pontryagin principle. Finally, even if the hamiltonian is globally regular, it may not be possible to obtain a global solution of *6*. In practice, these difficulties can sometimes be circumvented by "splitting" the space $X = R_n$ into suitable regions and "piecing together" a globally optimal solution. The conditions for the validity of these ideas are given by Boltyanskii's notion of "regular synthesis." Before delving into this more deeply, we shall examine a simple example.

Let us consider the time optimal control problem for the double-integral plant [1]. In other words, our system is

12 $$\dot{x}_1 = x_2 \qquad \dot{x}_2 = u$$

The control constraint set U is given by

13 $$U = \{u: |u| \leqq 1\}$$

The target set S is simply the origin (0,0), and the cost functional $J(u(\cdot))$ is given by

14 $$J(u(\cdot)) = \int_0^{t_1} 1\,dt$$

that is, $L(x,u) = 1$. It is well known that the time optimal control is given by

15 $$u^0(x_1,x_2) = \begin{cases} 1 & \text{if } (x_1,x_2) \in \gamma_+ \cup R_+ \\ -1 & \text{if } (x_1,x_2) \in \gamma_- \cup R_- \end{cases}$$

where

16 $$\gamma_+ = \{(x_1,x_2): x_1 = +\tfrac{1}{2}x_2^2,\ x_2 < 0\}$$

17 $$\gamma_- = \{(x_1,x_2): x_1 = -\tfrac{1}{2}x_2^2,\ x_2 > 0\}$$

18 $$R_+ = \{(x_1,x_2): x_1 < -\tfrac{1}{2}x_2|x_2|\}$$

19 $$R_- = \{(x_1,x_2): x_1 > -\tfrac{1}{2}x_2|x_2|\}$$

The curve $\gamma = \gamma_+ \cup \{(0,0)\} \cup \gamma_-$ is often called the *switching curve.* We note that the minimum time $t^0(x_1,x_2)$ required to go from (x_1,x_2) to (0,0) is given by

20 $$t^0(x_1,x_2) = \begin{cases} -x_2 + \sqrt{-4x_1 + 2x_2^2} & \text{if } (x_1,x_2) \in R_+ \\ |x_2| & \text{if } (x_1,x_2) \in \gamma \\ x_2 + \sqrt{4x_1 + 2x_2^2} & \text{if } (x_1,x_2) \in R_- \end{cases}$$

and that $t^0(x_1,x_2)$ satisfies (*6*) in $R_+ \cup R_-$. Now let us observe that the curve γ is a piecewise-smooth set of dimension 1, that the function $t^0(x_1,x_2)$ is continuous in R_2, that the function $t^0(x_1,x_2)$ is continuously differentiable in $R_+ \cup R_- = R_2 - \gamma$, and that

21 $$\frac{-\partial t^0}{\partial x_1}(x_1,x_2)x_2 - \frac{\partial t^0}{\partial x_2}(x_1,x_2)u \leqq 1\dagger$$

for all (x_1,x_2) in $R_2 - \gamma$ and u in U. Moreover,

22 $$\int_0^{t^0(x_1,x_2)} 1\, dt = -(-t^0(x_1,x_2))$$

is the cost associated with the control $u^0(x_1,x_2)$. Boltyanskii's Theorem 1 [2] asserts that $u^0(x_1,x_2)$ is indeed optimal.

Before stating the major results, let us recall the definition of a piecewise-smooth set.

23 **Definition** A compact set κ is called a smooth s-dimensional set if $\kappa = \phi(\sigma)$ where (1) σ is a compact, convex s-dimensional polyhedron in R_s, (2) $\phi(\cdot)$ is a continuous injection of σ into R_n, and (3) $\partial\phi(\mathbf{v})/\partial\mathbf{v}$ has rank s at every point of σ. A subset Γ of Y is called a piecewise-smooth set in Y if Γ is the countable (possibly finite) union of smooth sets κ_i; that is, $\Gamma = \bigcup \kappa_i$, such that only a finite number of κ_i meet any compact subset of Y. Γ is called s-dimensional if $s = \max\{d(\kappa_i)\}$ where $d(\kappa_i)$ is the dimension of κ_i.

For example, it is easy to see that the curve γ of the double-integral plant problem is the countable union of smooth sets κ_i which are all images of the closed interval $[0,1]$ and that only finitely many κ_i meet any sphere in R_2.

Let us now suppose that our target set S consists of a single point x_1. We then have the following theorem:

24 **Theorem** Let Γ be a piecewise-smooth set in Y of dimension s with $s \leqq n - 1$, and let $v(x)$ be a real-valued function on (a neighborhood of) Y such that

25 $$v(x) \text{ is continuous on } Y$$

26 $$v(x) \text{ is continuously differentiable on } Y - \Gamma$$

If $\hat{u}(\cdot)$ is an admissible control such that

27 $$\hat{u}(\cdot)\ Y\text{-transfers } x_0 \text{ to } x_1$$

28 $$J(\hat{u}(\cdot)) = \int_{t_0}^{t_1} L(\hat{x}(t),\hat{u}(t))\, dt = v(x_1) - v(x_0)$$

† This is an easy consequence of the fact that the u in U which minimizes $H(x_1,x_2,p_1,p_2,u)$ is $-sgn\{p_2\}$.

and if

29 $$H\left(x, \frac{\partial v}{\partial x}(x), u\right) = -L(x,u) + \left\langle \frac{\partial v}{\partial x}(x), f(x,u) \right\rangle \leqq 0$$

for all x in $Y - \Gamma$ and u in U, then $\hat{u}(\cdot)$ is Y-optimal. A proof of this theorem is given in Ref. 2.

We observe that the function $v(x)$ plays a role analogous to that played by the solution of the Hamilton-Jacobi equation in Theorem *7* and that condition *29* may be viewed as the analog of the requirement of regularity of the hamiltonian. In fact, we might speak of *29* as the regularity of H relative to Y and along $v(x)$. Theorem *24* is thus a considerable improvement over Theorem *7*, particularly in regard to the weakening of the requirement of regularity. However, Theorem *24* is still not a sufficient condition involving the maximum principle directly. We shall state such a sufficient condition shortly.

Let us now reexamine the double-integral plant problem. If we let $P^0 = (0,0)$, $P^1 = \gamma$, and $P^2 = R_2$, then the P^i, $i = 0, 1, 2$, are piecewise-smooth sets and $P^0 \subset P^1 \subset P^2$. Moreover, the components of $P^1 - P^0$ are $\gamma_+ - P^0$ and $\gamma_- - P^0$, and the components of $P^2 - P^1$ are R_+ and R_-; it is easy to see that $\gamma_+ - P^0$ and $\gamma_- - P^0$ are one-dimensional manifolds (i.e., are diffeomorphic with R) and that R_+ and R_- are two-dimensional manifolds (i.e., are diffeomorphic with R_2). The function $u^0(x_1,x_2)$ is continuous and (being a constant) is continuously differentiable on $\gamma_+ - P^0$, $\gamma_- - P^0$, R_+, and R_-. Also, through any point of R_+ (or R_-), there is a unique trajectory of the system

30 $$\dot{x}_1 = x_2 \qquad \dot{x}_2 = u^0(x_1,x_2)$$

and this trajectory intersects $\gamma_- - P^0$ (or $\gamma_+ - P^0$) at a nonzero angle and with nonzero $\dot{x}_1$ and $\dot{x}_2$ as is illustrated in Fig. *13.5.1*. Moreover, $\gamma_- - P^0$ and $\gamma_+ - P^0$ are trajectories of *30*, and if we consider the trajectories of *30* as being "marked," then these trajectories are extremal (i.e., satisfy the maximum principle). Under these conditions, we say

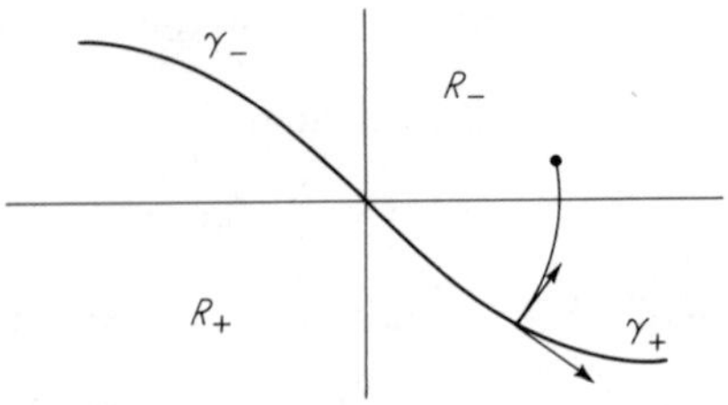

Fig. 13.5.1

that the sets P^0, P^1, and P^2, and the function $u^0(x_1,x_2)$, effect a "regular synthesis" for the time optimal control problem for *12*. The substance of the theorem to follow is that the marked trajectories are optimal.

Now let us examine the general optimal control problem. We assume that $S = \{x_1\}$ consists of a single point and that

31 $$\frac{\partial f}{\partial x} \text{ and } \frac{\partial f}{\partial u} \text{ are continuous}$$

and that

32 $$L(x,u) > 0$$

for all x and u in U. We now have the following definition.

33 **Definition** Let N be a piecewise-smooth set of dimension ν with $\nu \leqq n - 1$, let P^i, $i = 0, 1, \ldots, n$, be piecewise-smooth sets in Y with

34 $$\{x_1\} = P^0 \subset P^1 \subset \cdots \subset P^n = Y$$

and let $u(x)$ be a function from Y into U. The sets P^1 and N are a regular decomposition of Y if

35 every component of $P^i - (P^i \cup N)$ is an i-dimensional manifold for $i = 1, 2, \ldots, n$

In that case, the components of $P^i - (P^i \cup N)$ are called i-cells (or simply, cells). $\{P^i,N\}$ is a regular decomposition of Y relative to $u(x)$ if

36 $u(x)$ is continuous on each cell and can be extended to a continuously differentiable function on a neighborhood of each cell (where the extension may well depend on the cell).[1] A regular decomposition $\{P^i,N,u(x)\}$ of Y relative to $u(x)$ is called a regular synthesis for the given optimal control problem in Y if the following conditions are satisfied:

1. Each cell is either of type 1 or of type 2 where a cell μ is of type 1 if either

a. μ is n-dimensional.

b. μ is one-dimensional, and μ is a portion of a trajectory x_μ of the system

37 $$\dot{x} = f(x,u(x))$$

with the property that $x_\mu(t_\mu) = x_1$, and $\dot{x}_\mu(t_\mu) \neq 0$ for some t_μ.

c. μ is s-dimensional with $1 < s < n$ and has the following two properties: first, if ξ is an element of μ, then there is a unique trajectory $x^\xi(t)$ of *37* passing through ξ, and $x^\xi(t)$ is in μ for a finite time; and second,

[1] For example, in the case of the double-integral plant, $u^0(x_1,x_2) = 1$ on the cell $\gamma_+ - P^0$, and $u^e(x_1,x_2) = 1$ is an extension to all of R_2.

there is an $(s-1)$-dimensional cell $\delta(\mu)$ such that $x^\xi(t_\xi) \in \delta(\mu)$ and $x^\xi(t) \notin \mu$ for $t > t_\xi$ and $\dot{x}^\xi(t_\xi) \neq 0$, and $x^\xi(t)$ approaches $\delta(\mu)$ at a nonzero angle for all ξ in μ.

and where a cell μ is of type 2 if there is an $(s+1)$-dimensional cell of type 1, $\Sigma(\mu)$, (where s is the dimension of μ) with the following properties: first, if ξ is an element of μ, then there is a unique trajectory $x^\xi(t)$ of *37* passing through $\Sigma(\mu)$; and second, $u(x)$ is continuously differentiable on $\mu \cup \Sigma(\mu)$.

2. Every trajectory of *37* which passes through $Y - N$ meets only a finite number of cells and hence terminates at x_1.†
3. If η is an element of N, then there is a (possibly not unique) trajectory $x_\eta(t)$ of *13.5.37* which terminates at x_1;
4. If $x(\cdot)$ is a trajectory of *13.5.37* as in (2) *or* (3), then $x(\cdot)$ is an extremal trajectory (i.e., satisfies the maximum principle) and is called a marked trajectory;
5. $J(x_0, u(x))$ is a continuous function of x_0 along marked trajectories.

We have already exhibited a regular synthesis for the double-integral plant problem. In this synthesis, all cells are of type 1. If, on the other hand, we consider the time optimal control problem to the origin for the harmonic oscillator system

38 $$\dot{x}_1 = x_2 \qquad \dot{x}_2 = -x_1 + u \qquad |u| \leqq 1$$

then there will be cells of type 2. Recalling that the solution of the harmonic oscillator problem has the switch curve γ as illustrated in Fig. *13.5.2* [1], we can see that $N = \{(\pm 2n, 0): n = 1, 2, \ldots\}$ and that the curves (say) $\gamma_+{}^j - \{(2j,0),(2j+2,0)\}$ are cells of type 2.

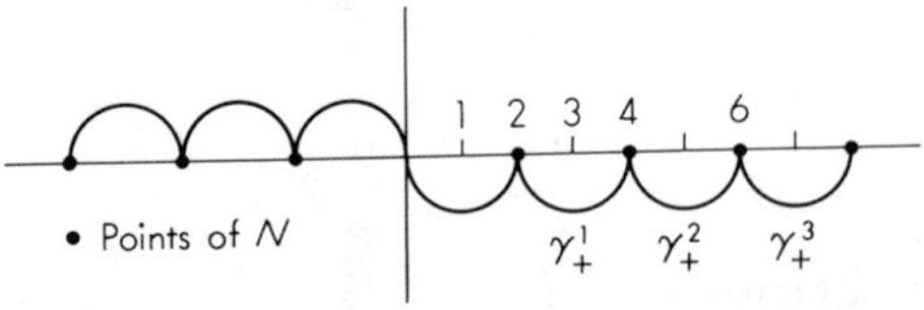

Fig. 13.5.2

After the lengthy definition *33*, we have the following short (but important) theorem of Boltyanskii [2]:

39 **Theorem** If *31* and *32* hold and if $\{P^i, N, u(x)\}$ is a regular synthesis in Y, then all marked trajectories are Y-optimal. A proof of this theorem can be found in Ref. 2.

† (1) insures that trajectories can be extended from cell to cell and that the trajectories in (2) are unique.

Since all the marked trajectories are extremal, Theorem *39* may be viewed as a sufficiency condition which involves the maximum principle directly. We also observe that the notion of regular synthesis is, in effect, the splitting and "piecing together" process to which we referred earlier in this section.

6 *Concluding remarks*

We have examined the question of determining conditions for optimality in this chapter. We derived a basic necessary condition lemma which applies to a broad class of optimization problems. The crucial idea behind this lemma was the notion of an approximation which, in effect, was an abstract representation of the familiar idea of perturbation. We used the lemma to obtain the maximum principle both for the discrete and the continuous optimal control problems. We note that the convexity of various sets played an important part in the development and that the choice of a suitable approximation was a vital aspect of the derivation of the maximum principle. In other words, we had to choose our perturbations wisely. Finally, we discussed several sufficiency conditions for the continuous optimal control problem and introduced the notion of regular synthesis. We note that the sufficiency conditions involved the "topology" of the problem as well as the value of the cost functional.

Here we have basically provided only an introduction to the problem of optimality conditions, and we suggest that the reader consult the various references for further details and generalizations.

REFERENCES

1 Athans, M., and P. Falb: "Optimal Control: An Introduction to the Theory and Its Applications," McGraw-Hill, New York, 1966.

2 Boltyanskii, V.: Sufficient Conditions for Optimality and the Justification of the Dynamic Programming Method, *SIAM J. Control,* vol. 4, pp. 326–361, 1966.

3 Canon, M., C. Cullum, and E. Polak: Constrained Minimization Problems in Finite-Dimensional Spaces, *SIAM J. Control,* vol. 4, pp. 528–547, 1966.

4 Da Cunha, N., and E. Polak: Constrained Minimization under Vector-valued Criteria in Linear Topological Spaces, *Univ. of California at Berkeley Electronics Res. Lab. Rept.*, ERL-M191, 1966.

5 Dieudonne, J.: "Foundations of Modern Analysis," Academic, New York, 1960.

6 Dunford, N., and J. Schwartz: "Linear Operators, Part I: General Theory," Interscience, New York, 1958.

7 Falb, P., and M. Jacobs: On Differentials in Locally Convex Spaces, *J. Diff. Eq.*, vol. 4, pp. 444–459, 1968.

8 Halkin, H.: An Abstract Framework for the Theory of Process Optimization, *Bull. Am. Math. Soc.* (to appear).

9 Halkin, H.: A Maximum Principle of the Pontryagin Type for Systems Described by Nonlinear Difference Equations, *SIAM J. Control,* vol. 4, pp. 90–111, 1966.

10 Halkin, H., and J. Holtzman: Directional Convexity and the Maximum Principle for Discrete Systems, *SIAM J. Control,* vol. 4, pp. 263–275, 1966.

11 Horvath, J.: "Topological Vector Spaces and Distributions, Volume I," Addison-Wesley, Reading, Mass., 1966.

12 Kalman, R., P. Falb, and M. Arbib: "Topics in Mathematical System Theory," McGraw-Hill, New York, 1969.

13 Kelley, J.: "General Topology," Van Nostrand, Princeton, N.J., 1955.

14 Neustadt, L.: An Abstract Variational Theory with Applications to a Broad Class of Optimization Problems I. General Theory, *SIAM J. Control,* vol. 4, pp. 505–528, 1966.

15 Neustadt, L.: An Abstract Variational Theory with Applications to a Broad Class of Optimization Problems II. Applications, *SIAM J. Control,* vol. 5, pp. 90–137, 1967.

16 Pontryagin, L., V. Boltyanskii, R. Gamkrelidze, and E. Mishchenko: "The Mathematical Theory of Optimal Processes," Interscience, New York, 1961.

Index

Index

Page references in boldface indicate definitions.

Abadie, J., 483
Abelian group, **181**
Abstract object, 7, **8**
Across variable, **287**
Adaptive experiment, **54**
Adaptive homing experiment, **62**
Adder, **186**
Additive group, **181**
Admissible control, **495,** 499, 504
Admissible set, **55**
Admissible states, **55**
Admittance, **288**
Admittance matrix, **289**
Aggregate, 22, **28**
Aizerman, M. A., 317, 436, 460–462, 522
Anselone, P. M., 327
Arrow, K. M., 483
Asymptotically periodic, **320**
Asymptotically stable, **350**
Athans, M., 42
Autonomous machine, **388**

Bacon, G., 401, 403, 421
Balakrishnan, A. V., 95
Barbashin, E. A., 348, 352, 366
Bass, R. W., 326
Bayesian learning, **429**
Bellman, R., 348, 376
Bertram, J. E., 317
Beurling, A., 331
Black box, **96**
Blackwell, D., 397, 420, 421
Blaydon, C. C., 439, 462
Boltyanskii, V., 489, 506, 507, 510
Bona, B. E., 42
Bongiorno, J. J., 321
Branch, **283**
Branch mesh matrix, **284**
Branin, F. H., 279, 296, 310
Braverman, E. M., 436, 460–462
Brockett, R. W., 322
Brouwer fixed-point theorem, **493,** 495
Bulgakov problem, **362**
Bundle, **23**

Canon, M., 489
Canonical momenta, **160**
Canonical transformation, **356**
Carlin, H. J., 332
Carlyle, J. W., 387, 421, 422
Cascade decomposition, **71**
Castriota, L. J., 332
Causality, 331, **332**
Cayley-Hamilton theorem, **237**
Characteristic function, **18**
Characteristic matrix, **186**
Characteristic polynomial, **184**
Characterizing functions, **45**
Characterizing matrices, **186**
Chetaev, N. G., 347, 374
Circle condition, **319,** 320
Closure under segmentation, **7**
Closure under truncation, **24**
Companding, **330**
Companion matrix, **185**
Compatible finite-state systems, **49**
Complete connectedness, **110**
Complete controllability, **110,** 244
Complete finite-state system, **44**
Complete observability, **249**
Compound sequence matrix, **410**
Condition of physical realizability, **102**
Cone:
  approximation, **492**
  linearization, **491**
  polar, **468**
  radial, **468**
Connected finite-state system, **50**
Constraint set, **138**
Containment, **15**
Content function, **131**
Continuation, **7,** 25

Continuity condition, **97**
Controllability:
  complete, **110,** 244
  conditions for, **247**
Controllability matrix, **247**
Convex partition programming, **480**
Convex programming problem, **470**
Cornwell, F. L., 310
Cost:
  functional, **495**
  vector-valued, **503**
Courant, R., 146, 176
Covering, **24**
Critical circle, **319,** 320
Cullum, C., 489
CUS, **7**
Cut point, **406**
Cycle, **195**
  set, **197**
  term, **197**

d transform, **214**
da Cunha, N. O., 489
Damping, **328**
Datum node, **283**
Davis, A. S., 419, 421
Dead zone, **354**
Decomposition, **468,** 474
  algorithm, **475**
  Dantzig-Wolfe, **481**
Delayer, **186**
Delta function, **102**
Dennis, J. B., 128, 175
Derivative of regular expression, **77**
Describing functions, **326**
Desoer, C. A., 41, 176, 322
Deterministic finite-state system, **44**
Deterministic sequential machine, **388**
Dharmadhikari, S. W., 413, 422
Diagnosing experiment, **55**
Dimension of vector space, **184**
Dirac notation, **234**
Direct control, **356,** 358
Disc condition, **316**
Discrete analog, **338**
Dissipation function, **131,** 132
Distinguishability:
  finite-state systems, **53**
  state, **51**
Distortion, **329,** 330
Distribution-equivalent machines, **401**
Division algorithm, **182**
Domain, **8**
Doyle, T. C., 279
Dual program, **141**
Duinker, S., 160, 176
Dvoretzky, A., 430, 443, 449, 457, 460
Dyad, **238**

Eigenvalues, **238,** 239–241
Eigenvectors, **238,** 239–241
Elementary block, **185**
Elementary divisor, **184**
Elementary operations, **260**
Empty sequence, **389**
Energy-type conditions, **332**
Equivalence, 15, **16,** 17, 392
  finite-state system, **52**
  state, **51,** 98
Equivalent representations, **252**
  minimal, **254,** 260
  reduced minimal, **258**
  zero-state, **257**
Euclidean algorithm, **182**
Euler-Lagrange equations, **156**
Exclusive set, **62**
Experiment, **54**
Extended characterizing functions, **50**
Extended regular expression, **82**
Extremal trajectory, **508,** 510

Falb, P. L., 42, 489
Feasible set, **470**
Feasible vector, **138**
Fel'dbaum, A. A., 42
Fiacco, A. V., 483
Field, **181**
Filter, **324**
Finite-memory systems, 10, **65**
Finite-recognition systems, **76**
Finite-state systems, 12, **43**

Fisher, G., 150
Flow graphs, **220**
Forced response, **193**
Frechet derivative, **491**
Free response, **193**
Friedland, B., 42
FRS, **76**
FSS, **43**
Fu, K. S., 425
Function:
  class A, **354**
  Liapunov, 348, 351, **353,** 360
  of a matrix, **234**
  positive-definite, **351**
  positive-semidefinite, **351**
  upper semicontinuous, **500**
Fundamental period, **202**

Galois field, **183**
Gantmacher, F. R., 317
Gauge transformation, **293**
General position condition, **112**
Gilbert, E. J., 397, 409, 420, 421
Gill, A., 43, 179
Goldwyn, R. M., 321
Gradient method, **140**
Graph, **283**
  connected, **283**
  oriented, **238**
Group, **180**
Gyrator, **158**

Hahn, W., 317
Halkin, H., 489, 499
Hamilton-Jacobi equation, **505,** 508
Hamilton-Jacobi theory, **504**
Hamiltonian, **161,** 503, 505
Hamilton's principle, 128, **157**
Harrison, B. K., 279
Harrison, M., 406, 421
Heller, A., 420, 421
Hermitian matrix, **327**
Ho, B. L., 42
Holtzman, J., 499
Homing experiment, **60**

Hurwicz, L., 483
Hurwitz criterion, **373**
Hurwitz inequalities, **368,** 370
Hybrid dissipation function, **131**
Hybrid incremental resistance matrix, **130**

Identification of finite-state system, **62**
Impedance, **288**
Impedance matrix, **289**
Impulsive response, **213**
Incidence matrix, **148,** 284
Incomplete finite-state system, **44**
Incremental conductance matrix, **130**
Incremental parameter matrix, **130**
Incremental resistance matrix, **130**
Indirect control, **357**
Indistinguishability, **17**
Initial distribution, **390**
Initial manifold, **495,** 499
Initial state, **389**
Input, **8**
  alphabet, **44**
  event, **405**
  sequence, **44**
  space, **186**
  symbol, **44**
Input-output analysis, **18**
Input-output pairs, **8,** 96
Input-output relation, **11,** 390, 391
Input-output-state relation, **29,** 389
Integral equations, **318**
Interpolation formula, **237**
Interpolation polynomial, **237**
Inverse optimal control problem, **378**
Isomorphic finite-state systems, **49**
Isomorphism of state graphs, **195**

Jordan form, **238**
Jump phenomena, **320**

k-distinguishability, **51,** 392
k-equivalence, **51,** 392
Kalman, R. E., 4, 41, 42, 317, 380, 382

Kantorovich, L. V., 325
Katzenelson, J., 331
Kelley, H. J., 146, 176
Kesten, H., 447, 460, 461
Kiefer-Wolfowitz procedure, **431**
Koopmans, L., 397, 420, 421
Krassovskii, N. N., 348, 352, 367
Krohn, K., 4, 41
Kron, G., 280, 282, 293, 295, 307, 309–311
Krylov, V. I., 325
Kudrevicz, J., 321
Kuhn, H. W., 139, 175
Kuhn-Tucker conditions, **489**
Kuhn-Tucker constraint qualification, **471**
Kurzweil, Y., 380

Lagrange multipliers, **139,** 161, 474, 477
Lagrangian network, **155**
Landau, H. J., 331
LaSalle, J. P., 152, 176, 316, 350
Lasdon, L. S., 483
LAT algorithm, **303**
Leading divisor, **184**
Learning system theory, **425**
Lefschetz, S., 152, 176, 316
Legendre transformation, **135**
Length:
  of experiment, **54**
  sequence of, **44**
Leondes, C., 42
Letov, A. M., 347
Liapunov, A. M., 151, 347
Liapunov-Bellman conditions, **381**
Liapunov-Bellman method, **376,** 379
Liapunov functions, 348, 351, **353**
Liapunov's direct method, 348, **350**
Liapunov's second method, **315,** 348
Linear combination, **184**
Linear independence, **184**
Linear modular systems, **179, 231**
Linear program, **138**
Linear reinforcement, **434**
Linear systems, **14,** 97
Linearization cone, **491**
Lipshitz condition, **318**
LMS, 179, **186**
Lur'e, A. I., 348

McCormick, C. D., 483
Malmberg, A. F., 310
Manley-Rowe equations, **316**
Marked trajectory, **508,** 510
Markov matrix, **419**
Mathematical programming, **467**
Mathematical programming problem, **493**
Matrix, **184**
  controllability, **247**
  differentiation of, **234**
  function of, **234**
  Hermitian, **327**
  integration of, **234**
  similar, **240**
  transfer function, 243, **268**
  weighting, **267**
Maximum principle:
  continuous, **503**
  discrete, **498**
Maxwell, J. C., **127,** 175
Mealy, G., 417
Memory, **65**
Mesarovic, M., 41
Mesh, **283**
Method of squares, **397**
Method of tearing, **295**
Miller, W., **127,** 175
Minimal finite-state system, **54**
Minimal form, **402**
Minimum polynomial, **185**
Minty, G. J., 327
Miranker, W. L., 331
Mixture distribution, **453**
Modes, **242**
Modulus polynomial, **183**
Monic polynomial, **182**
Moore, E. F., 417
Moser, J., 131, 175
Motion:
  perturbed, **349**
  unperturbed, **349,** 350

Multiple diagnosing experiment, **58**
Multiple experiment, **54**
Multiplicative group, **181**
Multiplicity, **54**

Narendra, K. S., 321
Naumov, B. N., 321
Nearly linear, **328**
Nerode, A., 4, 41
Network, **323**
  N-port, **321**
  passive, **326**
  periodically time-varying, **324**
Neustadt, L. W., 489, 503
Newcomb, R. W., 42
Next-state function, **44**
Nilpotent linear modular system, **206**
Node, **283**
Nondegeneracy assumption, **477,** 478
Nondeterministic finite-state system, **44**
Nonsingular linear modular system, **195**
Nonsupervised learning, **454**
Null sequence, **45**
Null vector, **184**
Nyquist locus, **316**

Objective function, **138**
Observability, **248**
  complete, **249**
  conditions for, **249**
Observation interval, **5**
Ogata, K., 42
Ohmic matrix, **291**
Optimal control problem:
  continuous, **499**
  discrete, **496**
Optimal element, **493**
Optimality conditions, 469, **493**
Output, **8**
  alphabet, **44**
  function, **44**
  sequence, **44**
  space, **186**
  symbol, **44**

Page, C. V., 419, 421
Pairwise diagnosing experiment, **55**
Parametrically excited system, **328**
Passivity, **531**
Paz, A., 406, 421, 422, 423
Pearson, J. D., 483
Penalty function, **483**
Period:
  matrix, **196**
  polynomial, **182**
  state, **196**
Periodically time-varying network, **324**
Perturbed-unperturbed motion, **348,** 349
Peschon, J., 42
Peterson, W. W., **183**
Pettis integral, **116**
Polak, E., 233, 489
Polar cone, **468,** 473, 485
Poles, **268,** 271
Pontryagin, L. S., 163, 176
Pontryagin maximum principle, 489, **503**
Popov, V. A., 321, 322
Postnikov, V. N., 348
Potential function method, **436**
Preset experiment, **54**
Preset homing experiment, **61**
Primal program, **141**
Prime factorization theorem, **182**
Primitive component, **186**
Primitive element, **183**
Principal case, **322**
Principle of optimality, **376**

Quadratic program, **139**
Quality of control, **373**

Rabin, M. D., 405, 421
Radial cone, **468,** 471, 473, 485
Range, **8**
Rational canonical form, **185**
Realizability of experiment, **55**
Realization:
  completely observable, **270**
  minimal, **268**
  of transfer function matrix, **268,** 271

Reciprocal, of polynomial, **183**
Reciprocal basis vectors, **238**
Reciprocal element, **130**
Reciprocal network, **128,** 135
Recognizable set, **76**
Reduced, **398**
Reduced form, **398**
Reduced minimal equivalent, **258**
Reduced state space, **98**
Reduction, **398**
  to state form, **259,** 263, 274
  of state space, **98**
Regular expression, **75**
Regular synthesis, **506**
Regulator systems, **354**
Relation, **9**
Resolving equations, **358**
  simplified variant, **364**
Response, **9,** 27
Response separation property, **36**
Return difference, **329**
Rhodes, J., 4, 41
Ring, **181**
Ring of polynomials, **183**
Robbins-Monro procedure, **431**
Rohrer, R. A., 42
Rosen, J. B., 480
Roth, J. P., 279, 307, 309, 310
Rozonoer, L. I., 163, 176, 436, 461, 462
Rubin, H., 146, 176

Saddle points, **137**
Salovaara, S., 42
Samuelson, P. A., 140, 175
Sandberg, I. W., 315
Scalar product, **238**
Scaler, **186**
Schwartz kernel theorem, **101**
Schwartz space, **96**
Schwarz, R. J., 42
Sector condition, **317**
Segment, **5**
Seitelman, L., 331
Separation of variables, **366**
Shannon, C., 388, 421
Shift register, **211**
Similar matrices, **185,** 240
  representations, **253**
Simple diagnosing experiment, **57**
Simple experiment, **54**
Simple identification experiment, **64**
Single experiment, **17**
Singular points, **137,** 146, 355
Spectral decomposition, **237,** 240, 241, 242
SSS, **35**
Stability, **151**
  absolute, 321, **355**
  asymptotic, **350,** 361
  bounded-input, bounded-output, **320,** 322
  conditions for, 319, **352,** 353
  eventual, **350**
  global, **317**
  in the Liapunov sense, **350**
State, **28,** 44, 96, 186
State-determined finite-state system, **72**
State diagram, **12**
State equation, **30,** 31
State equivalence, **33**
State separation property, **38**
State set, **44**
State space, **28,** 97–99, 186
  cardinality, **100**
  finite-dimensional, **105**
  reduced, **98,** 121, 124
State terminal, **389**
State transition matrix, **394**
Stern, T. E., 127
Stochastic approximation, **430**
Stochastic automaton, **397,** 405
Strong equivalence, 17, **34**
Strongly connected finite-state system, **50**
Successor partition, **70**
Superposition property, **213**
Sylvester inequalities, **368,** 372
Sylvester matrix, **368,** 369
System, **17**
  differential, **39**
  discrete-time, **5**
  finite-state, **12,** 43
  linear, **14,** 97

System:
  regular, **325**
  state-calculable, **414**
  state-deterministic, **414**
  state-observable, **415**
  stochastic, **390**
System representation:
  convolution form, **267**
  linear standard form, **234**
Szegö, G., 369, 370

Terminal distribution, **390**
Terminal manifold, **495,** 499
Thévenin relation, **323**
Through variable, **287**
Time function, **5**
Time invariant, **13**
Timothy, L. K., 42
Topology:
  output-induced, **117**
  pointwise, **500**
  for state space, **100**
Tou, J. T., 42
Traditor, **160**
Trajectory:
  extremal, **508,** 510
  marked, **508,** 510
Transfer function, **217**
Transfer function matrix, 243, **268**
Transition graph, **44**
Transition table, **45**
Transmission system, **328**
Tree, **195**
Tricomi, F. G., 318
Truncated system of equations, **325**
Tsertsvadze, G. N., 420, 421
Tsypkin, Ya. Z., 321, 439, 459, 461
Tucker, A. W., 139, 175

Ungar, P., 146, 176
Unit impulse, **213**
Uzawa, H., 141, 175, 483

Varaiya, P. P., 467, 484
Vector space, **184**
Vector-valued cost, **503**
Virtual linearization, **369**
Von Neumann, J., 279

Watanabe, S., 459, 463
Weak null connectedness, **110,** 111, 113
Weighting matrix, **267**
Whittaker, E. T., 132, 175
Windeknecht, T., 4, 41
Wymore, W., 41

Y-optimal, **504**
Yacubovich, V. A., 321
Yoshizawa, T., 350
Youla, D. C., 332

Zadeh, L. A., 3, 41, 42, 96, 99, 310
Zames, G., 321
Zeiger, P., 4, 42
Zero-input response, **98**
Zero memory, **151**
Zero-state equivalence, **257**
Zero-state response, **99**
Zubov, V. J., 369